REVELATION

A Shorter Commentary

REVELATION

A Shorter Commentary

G. K. Beale

with David H. Campbell

William B. Eerdmans Publishing Company
Grand Rapids, Michigan / Cambridge, U.K.

Published 2015 by
Wm. B. Eerdmans Publishing Co.
2140 Oak Industrial Drive N.E., Grand Rapids, Michigan 49505 /
P.O. Box 163, Cambridge CB3 9PU U.K.
www.eerdmans.com

Printed in the United States of America

21 20 19 18 17 16 15 7 6 5 4 3 2 1

Library of Congress Cataloging-in-Publication Data

Beale, G. K. (Gregory K.), 1949-
Revelation: a shorter commentary / G.K. Beale, with David H. Campbell.
pages cm
ISBN 978-0-8028-6621-9 (pbk.: alk. paper)
1. Bible. Revelation — Commentaries. I. Title.

BS2825.53.B43 2015
228'.07 — dc23

2014031223

Contents

Preface

In 1999 Eerdmans published my commentary titled *The Book of Revelation* in the New International Greek Testament Commentary series. Since the publication of the commentary I have heard continual requests that I write a shorter commentary on Revelation that would be more accessible for pastors, students, and Christians in general. So, after fourteen years I have decided to respond to these requests. The present "shorter" commentary on Revelation is the result. G. K. Chesterton once remarked, "Though St. John the Evangelist saw many strange monsters in his vision, he saw no creatures so wild as one of his own commentators" (*Orthodoxy* [New York: John Lane, 1908; repr. San Francisco: Ignatius, 1995], 21-22). It is my hope that Chesterton would not include my 1999 commentary nor this "shorter" one in this assessment.

When embarking on the task of commentary writing, one often asks oneself whether it is really necessary to write another commentary. In the case of Revelation, I believed back in the late 1980s there was still a need for a commentary which did the following things: (1) study the Old Testament allusions in a more trenchant manner than previously; (2) study how Jewish exegetical tradition interpreted these same Old Testament allusions and how such interpretation related to the use in Revelation; (3) trace more precisely the exegetical argument in Revelation, which some say is difficult to do because of the sometimes ambiguous nature of visionary literature; (4) interact with the vast amount of secondary literature published since the time of the monumental commentaries by Charles and Swete in the early part of the twentieth century. My intention in writing the commentary was to provide an exegesis of Revelation that would be especially helpful to scholars, teachers, pastors, students, and others seriously interested in interpreting Revelation for the benefit of the church. This was also a commentary on the Greek text of Revelation, though I usually provided English translation in parentheses after Greek words or phrases in order that those who were not proficient in Greek would nevertheless be able to benefit from reading the commentary.

However, in this shorter commentary I have for the most part eliminated references to Greek, references to secondary literature, and references to and discussion of Jewish interpretations of OT passages that are used in Revelation. Accordingly, there are ideas in this commentary for which there are no references to primary and secondary literature. Those references appear in the longer commentary, which can be consulted by those wanting more substantiation of what I say here. Ultimately, the longer commentary serves as one big footnote to this shorter commentary. Nevertheless, I have kept a focus on discussion of many of the OT allusions that were included in the original, though without most of the Greek verbal basis for the allusions. I have also preserved most of the important exegetical argument throughout Revelation

The most obvious difference is that this shorter commentary is much "shorter" than the original. The small font single-space excurses have been cut out from the original commentary and the essential content and argument from each chapter have been preserved in revised form. Some nuances of interpretation and options in the interpretation of problem texts have not been kept; the focus is now on the most probable interpretive alternatives.

I have not attempted to interact with secondary literature published since the appearance of my commentary in 1999, since my intent has been even to cut out most of the secondary literature references from the original. Indeed, this shorter commentary is "longer" than most shorter commentaries, and to have tried to engage much of the secondary literature published since 1999 would have only made it longer yet. Furthermore, while some of my interpretations of particular passages would be influenced by some of this subsequently published material, my overall argument and the essential substance of the commentary would not be significantly altered. Finally, engaging with subsequent secondary literature would not be suitable for the purpose of this shorter commentary: to make my first commentary more accessible to pastors, students, and Christians in general.

A special word to preachers and teachers: the full-sentence titles at the beginning of each major section or subsection of the commentary represent the exegetical conclusions of that section and can serve as the basis of homiletical ideas. And for all readers of this shorter commentary, in addition to my longer commentary in the New International Greek Testament Commentary series (1999), I recommend the following commentaries and other works on Revelation as particularly helpful. Some are serious works of scholarship and some are more popular works.

Richard J. Bauckham. *The Climax of Prophecy: Studies on the Book of Revelation.* Edinburgh: T. and T. Clark, 1993.

———. *The Theology of the Book of Revelation.* Cambridge: Cambridge University Press, 1993.

G. B. Caird. *A Commentary on the Revelation of St. John the Divine.* London: A. and C. Black; New York: Harper and Row, 1966.

Colin J. Hemer. *The Letters to the Seven Churches of Asia in Their Local Setting.* Sheffield: JSOT, 1986.

William Hendriksen. *More Than Conquerors: An Interpretation of the Book of Revelation.* Grand Rapids: Baker, 1962.

Alan F. Johnson. *Revelation.* Expositor's Bible Commentary 12; Grand Rapids: Zondervan, 1981, 397-603. Published separately, 1996.

Dennis E. Johnson. *Triumph of the Lamb: A Commentary on Revelation.* Phillipsburg: Presbyterian and Reformed, 2001.

Martin Kiddle, with M. K. Ross. *The Revelation of St. John.* Moffatt New Testament Commentary; London: Hodder and Stoughton, 1940.

R. H. Mounce. *The Book of Revelation.* New International Commentary on the New Testament; Grand Rapids: Eerdmans, 1977.

Grant R. Osborne. *Revelation.* Baker Exegetical Commentary on the New Testament; Grand Rapids: Baker, 2002.

Vern S. Poythress, *The Returning King: A Guide to the Book of Revelation.* Phillipsburg: Presbyterian and Reformed, 2000.

Stephen S. Smalley. *The Revelation of John: A Commentary on the Greek Text of the Apocalypse.* Downers Grove: InterVarsity, 1979.

J. P. M. Sweet. *Revelation.* Philadelphia: Westminster; London: SCM, 1979.

M. Wilcock. *I Saw Heaven Opened: The Message of Revelation.* Downers Grove: InterVarsity, 1975.

I am especially thankful to David Campbell in encouraging me and helping me to produce this shorter commentary. He aided me in deciding what to preserve from each chapter of the original and he put it into an initial revised form, which I then revised. This would have been a much longer project and may have never been finished if it were not for David's labors. Nevertheless, I am responsible for the final form of this shorter commentary.

A few comments about some stylistic aspects of the commentary are in order. The New American Standard Bible is the default translation; where there are differences, it is the result of my own translation. Pronouns for God and Christ are capitalized in keeping with the style of the NASB. In general references to the Septuagint I refer to the eclectic Greek text of the Rahlfs edition, and sometimes I have used a text dependent only on Codex B (= *The Septuagint Version of the Old Testament and Apocrypha with an English Translation* [Grand Rapids: Zondervan, 1972], published by special arrangement by Samuel Bagster and Sons, London). When the Rahlfs Greek edition differs in chapter or verse numbering from the Greek-English Bagster edition (codex B), I always place the Rahlfs reference first and then that of the Bagster edition in parentheses or brackets. For example, in Daniel 4 and parts of Exodus (especially chs. 35–40) and Job (especially chs. 40–41) versification is different between the different printed editions of the LXX, including the Rahlfs edition and the Bagster edition. Such a stylistic convention will enable those not knowing Greek to follow the Septuagint in a readily available English edition even in those places where it differs in versification from the standard Greek edition of Rahlfs. In addition, in Daniel I sometimes use "LXX" to refer to the Old Greek version (and sometimes I merely refer to "OG" or "Old Greek") and "Theod." to refer to Theodotion's translation, which is in accordance with Rahlfs's system. Now there is also available the *New English Translation of the Septuagint,* edited by Albert Pietersma and Benjamin G. Wright (Oxford: Oxford University Press, 2007), where dual translations of the Greek OT may be found (for example, Daniel's Old Greek and Daniel's Theodotion).

G. K. Beale

Preface

I would like to thank Professor G. K. Beale for the privilege of working with him in this effort, in the hope that it will make his original commentary accessible to a much wider audience. I would like to acknowledge the invaluable assistance of my former pastoral intern David S. Balmford, who meticulously checked for accuracy every one of the thousands of biblical references and offered many helpful suggestions toward improving the readability of the text. Thanks also to my friend Chris Homans for holding me to deadlines. I am grateful for the support of the elders and congregation of Trinity Christian Church for their willing release of the time needed to complete this project. I am thankful for the support of my children, Katie (Josh), Anna (Chris), Michael, John, Rachel, Sarah, Julia, and James. Finally and most of all, I give thanks for the gift of my wife Elaine, without whose support and encouragement for the last thirty years I would be utterly lost.

DAVID H. CAMPBELL

Abbreviations

1QH	Qumran Hymn Scroll
ASV	American Standard Version
BAGD	W. Bauer, W. F. Arndt, F. W. Gingrich and F. W. Danker, *A Greek-English Lexicon of the New Testament.* Chicago: University of Chicago, 1979.
BECNT	Baker's Exegetical Commentary on the New Testament
CD	Qumran Damascus Document
ESV	English Standard Version
HR	E. Hatch and H. A. Redpath, *A Concordance to the Septuagint and the Other Greek Versions of the Old Testament* I-III. Graz: Akademische, 1954.
JB	Jerusalem Bible
JETS	*Journal of the Evangelical Theological Society*
KJV	King James (Authorized) Version
LXX	Septuagint
mg.	marginal reading
MM	J. H. Moulton and G. Milligan, *The Vocabulary of the Greek New Testament Illustrated from the Papyri and Other Non-Literary Sources.* Grand Rapids: Eerdmans, 1930.
MNTC	The Moffatt New Testament Commentary
NASB	New American Standard Bible
NEB	New English Bible
NETB	New English Translation Bible
NIBC	New International Bible Commentary
NICNT	New International Commentary on the New Testament
NIGTC	New International Greek Testament Commentary

NIV	New International Version
NovT	*Novum Testamentum*
NT	New Testament
NTA	*New Testament Apocrypha* I-II, ed. W. Schneemelcher. Philadelphia: Westminster, 1991, 1992.
NTS	*New Testament Studies*
OG	Old Greek translation of the Hebrew Scriptures
OT	Old Testament
RSV	Revised Standard Version
Theod.	Theodotion's Greek translation of the Hebrew Scriptures

Introduction

1. General Introduction

One of the great tragedies in the church in our day is how Revelation has been so narrowly and incorrectly interpreted with an obsessive focus on the future end time, with the result that we have missed the fact that it contains many profound truths and encouragements concerning Christian life and discipleship. The prophetic visions of Revelation can easily disguise the point that it was written as a letter to the churches, and a letter which is pastoral in nature. The goal of Revelation is to bring encouragement to believers of all ages that God is working out His purposes even in the midst of tragedy, suffering, and apparent Satanic domination. It is the Bible's battle cry of victory, for in it, more than anywhere else in the NT, is revealed the final victory of God over all the forces of evil. As such, it is an encouragement to God's people to persevere in the assurance that their final reward is certain and to worship and glorify God despite trials and despite temptations to march to the world's drumbeat.

It is difficult to understand Revelation without understanding the OT. John identifies himself as a prophet (1:3) in the line of the OT prophets, speaking the word of the Lord in both judgment and promise. Scholars estimate that as many as 278 out of 404 verses in Revelation contain references to the OT and that over five hundred allusions to OT texts are made in total (compared with less than two hundred in all of Paul's letters). These are allusions (though quite recognizable) rather than direct quotations. For instance, what John sees in 1:12-18 is the same as what Daniel saw in his vision of the Son of man and what Isaiah spoke of in his prophecy concerning the Servant of the Lord whose mouth is like a sharpened sword (for references see below). These allusions show the unity of the OT and NT and in particular demonstrate that the promise of the Messiah and His suffering, salvation, and victory are the same from the beginning to the end of the Bible and of human history. A quick look at just some of the OT allusions in the first chapter will illustrate our point. In 1:5 John alludes to Ps. 89:27; in 1:6 to Exod. 19:6; in 1:7 to Zech. 12:10; in 1:13-15 to Dan. 7:13-14 and 10:5-6; in 1:15 to Ezek. 1:24; and in 1:16 to Isa. 49:2.

OT prophecy called the people to a renewal of commitment to God and His law and to turn away from the pagan practices tempting them to compromise. When Revelation is thus understood as both prophetic and pastoral in nature, it becomes immediately relevant to each of us as we walk through its pages in our daily pilgrimage through the desert place of the world, where God is protecting us until He delivers us into the Promised Land of the final new creation. Much of the book becomes a commentary on Paul's teaching on spiritual warfare in Eph. 6:10-17. Every day we are to put on the armor of God and stand against the schemes of the evil one until the day when, having done all, we will stand forever in the Lord's presence. Most of all, we can be encouraged by the promise John's great vision holds out that this story will end in the triumph of God and the Lamb and that we will find our place reigning with them and worshiping them for all eternity.

2. Authorship

Revelation is the record of a prophetic vision given to a man called John in exile on the island of Patmos. The author identifies himself as John, a servant of God who bears witness to Jesus Christ and who is exiled for his faith (1:1, 9). He was either the apostle John or another man of the same name. He was well known to all the churches of Asia and carried sufficient authority that he could write a letter of this nature to these churches and expect it to be heeded. He was a leader of enough prominence that he had been exiled by the authorities, who must have considered him a threat. The way in which he uses the OT and its Hebrew text demonstrates that he was originally a Jew from Palestine rather than a native Greek-speaker. Nevertheless, John also knew his Greek OT quite well and used it adeptly. It is highly unlikely that another John, originally a Jew from Palestine but otherwise unknown to us, lived and worked among the churches of Asia and carried such a level of authority. Thus, the apostle John was likely the author of this book. Added to this is the fact that many of the themes we particularly associate with John's Gospel and letters — Jesus as the Word, the Lamb and the Shepherd, manna, living water, life and light, conquering, keeping the word and the commands of God, and others — also appear in Revelation. Revelation was preserved and circulated in the early church, was considered authoritative, and was believed from the earliest times to have been written by the apostle John. Particularly significant is the testimony of Irenaeus. Though he wrote about 180, Irenaeus was a disciple of Polycarp, who was martyred in 156, having been a Christian for eighty-six years, and who personally knew John. We can presume with confidence that this letter is indeed a record of a vision given to the beloved disciple, now an old man, at the very close of the New Testament period.

3. Date of Writing

John wrote to churches that had experienced an occasional localized persecution (2:3, 13; 3:8-9), which does not fit with the severe persecution under Nero in A.D. 64-65. The church at Ephesus, founded around 52, had been around long enough to have lost its first love (2:4). The Laodicean church is called rich (3:17), but Laodicea was devastated by an earthquake in 60-61 and would have taken many years to recover. Early Christian writers, including Irenaeus, held that John received his vision during the reign of Domitian (81-96), and it was during that reign that a cult of emperor worship was established at Ephesus and some form of persecution broke out against the church. Our study will show that the Christians to whom John was writing were being forced to participate in this imperial cult (see on 2:9, 13-14; 13:15). From about 100, the usual basis for charges against Christians was their refusal to worship the emperor. Judaism enjoyed certain freedoms under Roman law, including the right to worship in synagogues and some degree of exemption from the imperial cult. However, as Christians became identified as a separate group from Jews, such privileges would not have been extended to them. It seems from Revelation that some Jewish Christians were tempted to flee persecution by returning to the synagogue and that Gentile Christians were tempted to avoid persecution by giving in to the demands of emperor worship. In Asia Minor, where the churches addressed in Revelation were located, the demands of emperor worship were particularly strong from about 90 onward. People were even required to participate in sacrifices as ritual processions passed their homes. The impetus for this cult seems to have come more from local and provincial officials seeking to ingratiate themselves with Rome than from the emperor himself. Their attempts to make themselves look good depended on their ability to force the local population to support the cult enthusiastically, and detractors had to be punished. In Revelation Rome, along with other kingdoms, is identified with Babylon, yet Jews never referred to Rome as Babylon until after the destruction of the temple in 70, comparing that destruction with the similar destruction carried out by the Babylonians many centuries before. The evidence, therefore, seems to indicate that Revelation was written sometime shortly after 90, when John the apostle would have been an old man.

4. The Nature of the Book

Revelation combines aspects of three different kinds of writing — apocalyptic, prophecy, and epistle. The word "apocalyptic" comes from the Greek word for "revelation" and can refer to literature concerned with detailing events of the end times. Many apocalyptic books were written before, during, and after the time of the NT, most coming from Jewish circles rather than from Christians. Some scholars dismiss Revelation as just another of these wild and fanciful portrayals of the last days.

Though there are many definitions of apocalyptic, it is best to understand apocalyptic as an intensification of prophecy. Too much distinction has typically been drawn between apocalyptic and prophetic kinds of works. Indeed, some OT books combined the two to one degree or another. "Apocalyptic" should not be seen as greatly different from "prophecy," but the former contains a heightening and more intense clustering of literary and thematic traits found in the latter. What is sometimes heightened in apocalyptic literature is the origin of the revelation (that is, visions of God's throne, descriptions of His glorious appearance, angels around the throne, descriptions of the heavenly temple in which the throne is located, etc.). That this is above all the case in Revelation is borne out by the further description of this book as a "prophecy" in 1:3, as well as in 22:6-7, 10, where verbatim parallels with 1:1, 3 are found (which is indicated further by observing reference to "prophets" in 22:6; see further on 1:1). In addition, "apocalypse" in 1:1 is a direct allusion to Daniel 2, where the word refers to the prophetic revelation communicated from God to the prophet Daniel (see on 1:1). In this sense, Revelation is best seen as fitting into the genre of OT prophetic-apocalyptic works, especially those of Ezekiel, Daniel, and Zechariah. Accordingly, throughout the book there are repeated visions of God's heavenly throne room and His appearance there.

John thus sees himself in the line of the OT prophets, albeit those prophets who, like Daniel, Ezekiel, and Zechariah, have a specific interest in the end times. The interests of these prophets was both in *forth-telling* exhortations to apply to people in the present and in *foretelling* the future. As noted above, Revelation as an apocalyptic-prophetic work focuses more on the source of revelation than does prophetic literature. The origin of revelation is the throne room of God in the heavenly temple. This is a feature that forms a part of prophetic genre (e.g., Isaiah 6, Ezekiel 1–2), but in Revelation it becomes the dominating focus in order to underscore the divine, heavenly source of the revelation sent to the seven churches. There is also emphasis on this heavenly perspective so that the churches will be reminded that real spiritual struggles are going on behind the scenes of what appear to be insignificant earthly appearances or events. Indeed, the reason for addressing churches through their representative angels is to remind them that they have already begun to participate in a heavenly dimension and that their real and eternal home is in that dimension of the new heavens and earth (see on 4:4; 21:1–22:5), inaugurated through Christ's death and resurrection (see on 3:14). Such a reminder should motivate them not to place their ultimate security in the old world, as do unbelieving, idolatrous "earth-dwellers" (see on 6:17 for discussion). The focus on the heavenly perspective also makes the churches aware that their victory over the threat of idolatrous compromise comes ultimately from the heavenly sphere, where the Lamb and God sitting on the throne are centrifugal forces exerting their power on earth through the Spirit. The "lamps" of the Spirit give power to the ecclesiastical "lampstands" to shine their light of witness throughout the earth (see on 1:4, 12-13; 4:5; 5:6). One of the ways the church is to remember this heavenly perspective is by modeling its worship on the heavenly liturgy communicated in the apocalyptic vision (see on 4:4).

The apocalyptic-prophetic nature of Revelation can be defined as God's revelatory interpretation (through visions and auditions) of His mysterious counsel about past, present, and future redemptive-eschatological history, and how the nature and operation of heaven relates to this. This revelation irrupts from the hidden, outer heavenly dimension into the earthly and is given to a prophet (John), who is to write it down in order that it be communicated to the churches. The heavenly revelation usually runs counter to the assessment of history and values from the human, earthly perspective and therefore demands that people change and realign their views with the heavenly view. In this respect, people in the churches are exhorted to submit to the demands of the book's message, or else face judgment. John's readers live in a worldly culture which makes sin seem normal and righteousness appear strange (with acknowledgment to David Wells for this definition of "worldliness"). In particular, John writes because he perceives there is a real danger that the churches will conform to what are considered the "normal" values of the world-system rather than to God's transcendent truth. In the light of the overall above discussion, the pressure of imminent persecution, which already had commenced on a small scale, was the probable specific occasion which caused the readers/hearers to entertain thoughts of compromise.

The focus of the revelation John received from God is how the church is to conduct itself in the midst of an ungodly world. The heavenly revelation gives an entirely different perspective from that offered by the world. Believers are faced with the choice of lining their lives and conduct up with one perspective or the other, and their eternal destiny depends on that choice. As our study progresses, we will see that the events of the book deal with the real-life situation of the church in every age, not just that of the end-time future. Believers are always facing the threat of compromise in one form or another. They must submit to the message as John has brought it, or face God's judgment. How sad it is when the study of Revelation in today's church regards it merely as futurology rather than setting in place a redemptive-historical mindset or worldview for the church! In fact, from the very beginning (1:3), Revelation describes itself as a prophecy. And, as in the OT and as noted earlier, prophecy in Revelation involves both *forth-telling* exhortations for the present and *foretelling* of the future.

Not only this, but Revelation is also written as an epistle, a letter to the seven churches, in which instruction on godly living is given to the believers who received it. It begins and ends as a typical letter would. Like the other NT letters, Revelation addresses the situation and problems of the believers who receive it. John appeals to them, on the basis of all they have in Christ and all they will yet inherit not to forsake the faith by compromising with the world. Not only the specific addresses of chs. 1–3 but also the visions of chs. 4–21 convey truth and direction from God as to the nature of the battle raging in the heavenlies and how believers are to respond to this battle, not at some undetermined date in the future but in their lives here and now, and to do so not simply by an intellectual belief that events will unfold in a particular way but by concrete moral choices on the basis of the issues God faces them with in the present.

5. The Four Ways of Interpreting Revelation

Over the course of church history, there have been four main schools of thought on how to interpret Revelation:

The Preterist View. The word "preterist" refers to the past. This view holds that Revelation is a prophecy of the fall of Jerusalem in 70 and that everything in the book has already been fulfilled — and hence is "past." But we have seen, it is unlikely that Revelation was even written until some years later than the fall of Jerusalem. On the preterist view, "Babylon" represents rebellious Israel, which persecutes the church. "Babylon," however, is never used in ancient Jewish or Christian literature to refer to unbelieving or disobedient Israel, but rather to Rome. The prophecies of Daniel 2 and 7, alluded to throughout Revelation, speak of an end-time judgment of the pagan nations (as does Rev. 1:7), not of Israel. Daniel also says that the end-time judgment is to be universal, not just involving one nation. Finally, the book becomes irrelevant for anyone who lives after those first days of the church. Why would God include it in the Bible at all? A variation of this view is that "Babylon" refers to the Roman Empire and that the prophecies in the book were completely fulfilled when that empire was destroyed in the fifth century. This deals with some of the objections yet leaves the question as to how the universal end-times judgment of all nations pictured in Revelation could possibly fit with the gradual decay and eventual collapse of destruction of the Roman Empire. Further, the book would have become less relevant to believers following that event.

The Historicist View. The historicist view suggests that the seals, trumpets, and bowls paint a picture of the successive ages of the church. It sees the symbolism of Revelation as referring to a series of specific historical events (always in the history of the western or European church), such as the collapse of the Roman Empire, the corruption of the papacy, the Reformation, and various events since. Christ's return is always seen as imminent by the person interpreting the book. The problem is that each historicist interpreter views the book differently, so as to make it fit the realities of his or her own age, which is always seen as the final one before the Lord's return. This view illustrates the danger of trying to make the symbols of Revelation refer to specific historical events, without any justification from the book itself for such an interpretation. Nowhere does

Revelation indicate, for example, that the order of seals, trumpets, and bowls represent the chronological order of western church history. Finally, this view appears to have no relevance for Christians outside the western church, nor would it have had much relevance for those to whom it was originally written. As we proceed, we will see that the seals, trumpets, and bowls portray not a chronological sequence of events but the same set of events unfolded from different perspectives.

The Futurist View. The futurist view holds that the entire book, apart from the letters to the churches in chs. 1–3, prophesies events surrounding the return of Christ at the end of history. This view takes two forms. Dispensational futurism (or classic dispensationalism) interprets the visions very literally and chronologically as referring to events of history. Generally the order of the visions in chs. 4–21 is seen as representing the actual historical order of events to happen in the yet-future latter days. Israel is restored to its own land immediately prior to 4:1. Then events unfold in the following order: the church is raptured into heaven, there is a seven-year tribulation, the reign of the antichrist begins, the nations gather together to make war against Jerusalem, Christ returns and defeats the nations, Christ rules during the millennium, Satan gathers together unbelievers at the end of the millennium to fight against Christ, and Christ defeats the devil and begins His eternal reign in heaven. But there is no mention in Revelation of the geographical restoration of Israel to its land, nor of any rapture of the church. Interpreters holding this view are constantly changing their interpretation of historical events to make what is happening currently fit into the pattern. In the twentieth century alone, for instance, numerous individuals, from Hitler to Saddam Hussein, with various popes and other politicians (as has been the case from the medieval period up to the present), have been identified as the antichrist, and then quietly discarded when they pass from the scene. The same is true with specific historical events or institutions (the Second World War, the European Common Market, the Gulf War, Y2K, Saddam Hussein's supposed rebuilding of Babylon). In short, the Bible is interpreted by modern events first, instead of by itself. This view makes Revelation of relevance or value only to Christians living in the last days. As it also generally promotes the view that the church will be raptured out of the world before any of these events happen, it is irrelevant even to these believers, in which case there seems little reason why God would have given John the vision in the first place. Remember, this book was written to the "seven churches," which represents the church universal throughout the ages (see on 1:4). Progressive dispensationalism holds similarly to the above unfolding of events but maintains a looser approach (e.g., the "latter days" began during the church age, and many of the visions are interpreted symbolically and not literally). Modified futurism takes various forms, some affirming that the church is true Israel and that there will be no "pretribulation rapture." Rather, Christians will pass through the final period of trial. Most if not all events recorded in chs. 4–22 refer to a final period of tribulation and to succeeding events (though some hold that 4:1–8:1 covers the period from Christ's resurrection up to the end of history). This still leaves other difficulties of interpretation, including the fact that the book would have had less relevance for Christians of most ages than for those believers living later in the purported future fulfillment of Revelation's visions.

The Redemptive-Historical Idealist View. The idealist view sees the entire book as a symbolic presentation of the battle between good and evil. The seals, bowls, and trumpets speak over and over again to the events of human history in every age and give believers of all ages an exhortation to remain faithful in the face of suffering (hence "redemptive-historical"). We believe this view is substantially correct but must be modified in light of the fact that parts of Revelation do definitely refer to future end-time events concerning the return of Christ, His final defeat of the enemy, and the establishment of His heavenly kingdom. Many of the events prophesied speak equally to the life of the church in all generations, excluding those particular events dealing with the very end of history and the return of Christ. Preterists and historicists are to some extent correct in understanding that various parts of John's vision find a measure of fulfillment in actual historical events. The fact is, however, that their meaning is not linked exclusively to those particular events, for Revelation finds fulfillment in countless events throughout the church age.

As such, the message of the letter is of relevance and value to all believers of all ages, which is why the vision was given to John. We might call this an *eclectic* redemptive-historical idealist view, since, while the focus is on a symbolic presentation of the battle between good and evil and on specific repeated historical events during the church age, aspects of the preterist, historicist, and futurist views are incorporated (hence "eclectic"). As we unfold the outline of the book, the reasons we adopt this view will hopefully become apparent.

6. Revelation — Symbolic or Literal?

One of the great arguments over the interpretation of Revelation is whether it is to be taken symbolically or literally. Those taking a futurist view too often tend to a literal interpretation, in which the various people or events portrayed are so different and even shocking they could not possibly refer to anything known thus far in human history. But is such an interpretation justified? One of the keys to a correct interpretation of Revelation lies in its very first verse, which introduces and sets the tone for the entire book.

The Greek verb *sēmainō* is used in Rev. 1:1 to indicate the manner of God's revelation to John: "the Revelation of Jesus Christ, which God gave Him to show to His bond-servants, the things which must shortly take place; and He sent and *communicated it (sēmainō)* by His angel to His bond-servant John." Various English translations render this Greek word as "communicated" (NASB), "made known" (RSV, NIV, JB, ESV, NEB), "signified" (KJV, ASV, Douay, NASB mg. reading), and "made clear" (NETB).

The word *sēmainō* elsewhere in the NT and in Hellenistic Greek can have any of these meanings. "Made clear" is unusual, but the notion of "symbolize, signify, communicate by symbols," is not untypical. For instance, in classical Greek the word could have the idea of giving signals, as in "giving the signal" for a military attack to begin. In this respect, it is significant to recall that the related noun is *sēmeion,* which means "sign" and which the NT uses for Jesus' miracles as "signs" or "symbols" of His divine power (e.g., healing the lame man in Mark 2 was symbolic of Jesus' ability to forgive sin; feeding the multitudes in John 6 was symbolic of His ability to give and nourish spiritual life).

The word in Rev. 1:1 could mean merely "make known" or "communicate," and thus refer to a general idea of communication, not a symbolic mode of communication, as it often does in the ancient world. The fact, however, that Rev. 1:1 is an allusion to Dan. 2:28-29, 45 confirms that here the word does mean "symbolize."

John speaks here of four critical elements:

(i) a revelation
(ii) God showed
(iii) concerning what will come to pass
(iv) and He signified it (Greek *sēmainō*)

The source of John's statement is to be found in Dan. 2:28-30, 45 (the account of Daniel's interpretation of the king's dream concerning the statue), the only other place in the Bible where these same four elements occur, the first three in vv. 28 and 29 and the fourth in v. 45 at the conclusion of the dream's interpretation:

(i) God reveals mysteries
(ii) which He has shown
(iii) concerning what will take place
(iv) and these He has signified (Greek *sēmainō* in the Septuagint [LXX = OG], the main Greek translation of the Hebrew OT)

We need to summarize the context of Daniel 2, since John likely had in mind that wider context. In Dan. 2:45 in the LXX (= OG), *sēmainō* is used to describe the symbolic vision which King Nebuchadnezzar had: "the Great God has *symbolized* to the king what will come to pass in the latter days" ("symbolized" is a rendering of an Aramaic verb which has the default meaning "know" and in the causative form "make known"). This refers to a dream-vision that the king had. He saw a huge statue composed of four sections of different metals: gold, silver, bronze, and iron. The statue is smashed by a rock which grows and fills the earth. Daniel tells the king that this vision was symbolic. The statue was to be divided into four metallic sections symbolizing four kingdoms (Babylon, Medo-Persia, Greece, and Rome). The stone that smashed the statue represented God's kingdom, which would defeat the evil kingdoms of the world and dominate the world. The interpretation of the dream shows that the dream is not to be taken literally in terms of a statue and its various parts, but rather that the statue signifies or symbolizes something else (i.e., the four sections of the statue symbolize four world kingdoms). In Rev. 1:1, John deliberately uses the language of "signify" from Dan. 2:45 in part to portray that what God has been showing him is likewise symbolic. Most of the things that are about to unfold are not to be taken literally (lions, lambs, beasts, women, etc.), but each refers symbolically to another reality or set of realities.

The symbolic use of *sēmainō* in Daniel 2 defines the use in Rev. 1:1 as referring to symbolic communication and not mere general conveyance of information. Therefore, John's choice of *sēmainō* ("signify") over *gnōrizō* ("make known") is not haphazard but intentional. This conclusion is based on the supposition that John uses OT references with significant degrees of awareness of OT context.

The nuance of "signify" or "symbolize" in Rev. 1:1b is also confirmed by its parallelism with "show" *(deiknymi)* in the first part of Rev. 1:1, since "show" throughout the book always introduces a divine communication by symbolic vision (4:1; 17:1; 21:9; 22:1, 6, 8). In fact, whatever generally synonymous word John could have chosen here instead of *sēmainō* (whether *gnōrizō* or other like terms) would still have the sense of "communicate by symbols," because that is the mode of communication in Daniel 2 and the mode of revelation conveyed by *deiknymi* elsewhere in the book.

In this light, the dictum of the popular approach to Revelation — "interpret literally unless you are forced to interpret symbolically" — should be turned on its head. Instead, the programmatic statement about the book's precise mode of communication in 1:1 is that the warp and woof of it is symbolic, so that the preceding dictum should be reversed to say "interpret symbolically unless you are forced to interpret literally." Better put, the reader is to expect that the main means of divine revelation in this book is symbolic.

Therefore, most of the things that are about to unfold are not to be taken literally (lions, lambs, beasts, women, etc.), but each refers symbolically to another reality or set of realities. In the very first verse of the book, therefore, John sets out the principle that the visions to be unfolded in the book have a predominantly symbolic meaning, which may have various historical references, rather than referring in a literal manner to a particular person, thing, or event. Many of the visions are impossible to take literally, as we note below and elsewhere in the commentary (see, for instance, on 9:19). We understand Revelation, therefore (at least, outside the letters to the seven churches in chs. 2 and 3), as a series of revelatory visions which are to be interpreted symbolically. Unless there is strong evidence in the text to the contrary, the visions (whether, for instance, those of the beast, the false prophet, the seven kings, the ten horns, the army of two hundred million, the twenty-four elders, or the millennium) are for the most part to be taken non-literally. This does not mean that they have no meaning or historical reference, but that the meaning is to be found symbolically — and almost always within the context of OT references which run through the visions God gave to John (on which see further the next section). There is always a literal meaning underlying the symbolic meaning, though this literal meaning is often about spiritual realities and sometimes about physical realities, both of which have to do with some kind of historical reality.

This means that we must distinguish between the vision given to John, what that vision symbolizes, and to what or whom the vision may refer. For instance, the woman on the beast in ch. 17 symbolizes the ungodly world system (that is, its economic, cultural, and religious aspects combined together). This worldly system's values are opposed to God's values for His people. The mistake is to bypass the visionary and symbolic and go straight to a literal interpretation, according to which a literal woman on a beast, or something very much like that, is referred to. In that case, the text portrays something so strange and different from anything which has happened hitherto (as with the beast of ch. 13) that it must represent something yet to come. This kind of interpretation could turn Revelation into some kind of science fiction fantasy along the lines of an alien invasion film, which is bizarre, but unfortunately often set forth in popular portrayals. However, admittedly, few literal interpreters try to understand the woman on the beast in some crassly literal fashion. Nevertheless, some commentators take the falling of one-hundred-pound hail (Rev. 16:21) as literal, as well as attempting to interpret literally the fire coming from the mouth of the two faithful witnesses and devouring their enemies, so that their mouths become supernatural flame-throwers. The fact that John bases the plagues of chs. 8, 9, and 16 on the plagues of Exodus does not mean that these plagues are to be taken literally as equivalent to the Exodus plagues (in which case they are yet to come), but rather that they symbolize the judgment of God in various ways, the exact historical reference or references of which must be drawn out by examination of the context and the way in which they are alluded to. When this is seen, we no longer have to conclude that none of the events referred to have yet occurred and must refer to some future cataclysm. This opens up a far broader sphere of interpretation.

John does, however, occasionally explicitly identify something he has seen in a vision, such as when he says that the lampstands are to be identified with the churches (1:20). In that case, we are fairly confident that wherever lampstands occur, they must refer to the churches. But otherwise, we must search the context and the OT (see again below) for the symbolic meaning referred to, and then proceed cautiously to identify any historical reference or references. The impossibility of interpreting literally most of the things seen in the various visions is shown by the fact they are often expressed in a way impossible to understand in a literal manner. For instance, John speaks not only of the lampstands being the churches (see 1:20), but identifies the two lampstands and two olive trees with the two witnesses (11:3-4, on which see for how this correlates with the original identification of the lampstands with the churches). His visions speak of horses with the heads of lions, out of whose mouths come fire, smoke, and brimstone, and whose tails are like serpents with heads (9:17-18). He speaks of locusts which look like horses, have crowns on their heads yet have the faces of men, the hair of women, the teeth of lions, and breastplates of iron (9:7-9). He speaks of the lamb, standing though slain, with seven horns and seven eyes (5:6), and of the mysterious living creatures full of eyes, with six wings, and having the appearance of a lion, a calf, a man, and an eagle (4:6-8). None of these can be interpreted literally, outside of (as noted above) an understanding of Revelation as a strange work of science fiction.

Finally, there is the symbolic significance of numbers in Revelation. Three numbers — four, seven, and twelve, along with their multiples — feature repeatedly in the visions, and each is best interpreted in light of its OT significance. In view of the repeated and systematic use of these numbers, the Scriptural significance attached to them, and the overwhelmingly symbolic nature of the pictorial images in the book (as noted above), it is clear that the numbers in Revelation are also to be interpreted symbolically. The first number in the book is clearly symbolic, and it sets the pattern for the others to be likewise interpreted symbolically. In Rev. 1:4 reference is made to "the seven Spirits who are before His [God's] throne." Some commentators try to take this literally and say that there were seven angels or spirit beings around God's throne. However, it is clear that the reference is to the Holy Spirit, since God has just been mentioned in the preceding wording ("Him who is and who was and who is to come"), and then Jesus is mentioned in the following verse (v. 5). Thus, the book is "from" God the Father, the Spirit, and Jesus. Why refer to the Spirit by the phrase "the seven Spirits"? It is to highlight the fact that the fullness of the Spirit is being emphasized, since "seven" in the OT and elsewhere in Revelation figuratively refers to completeness or fullness. The reason for this is that it is rooted in the seven days of creation. The OT uses seven often in this connection (for instance, Gen. 4:15, 24 and Ps. 79:12 refer to the sevenfold anger of God, expressing His full or complete anger which satisfies His justice). The tabernacle had seven lamps because Israel's earthly temple and its furniture were the microcosmic copy of the archetypal heavenly temple of God, and the number symbolized the fact that God's dwelling was intended to be extended throughout the earth.

The number four was also used in the OT and other Jewish literature to express completeness. The four rivers of Gen. 2:10-14 referred to the totality of creation. The tribes of Israel were divided into four groups in the wilderness, and each group was located at one of the four points of the compass. In Revelation, four is used with reference to the worldwide or universal scope of something, as in the earth's four corners (see Rev. 7:1; 20:8) or the four winds (7:1). The allusion to Exod. 19:16ff. ("lightnings, sounds and thunders"), appears at four critical points in Revelation (4:5; 8:5; 11:19; 16:18) to express the universality of the final judgment.

The number twelve also represents completion, most notably in the fact the one nation Israel was composed of twelve tribes. Finally, ten can represent completeness, as in the ten commandments.

Revelation features seven seals, seven trumpets, and seven bowls, which are so numbered in order to underscore the completeness of God's worldwide judgment. The four corners of the earth are the particular targets of the first four trumpets and the first four bowls, expressing God's judgment over His creation. Names used of God and Christ ("the One who lives for ever and ever," "the Lord God Almighty," "the One who sits on the throne," "the Alpha and the Omega") are repeated in Revelation in patterns of four and seven, expressing God's complete rulership over the whole earth. The name "Christ" appears seven times, "Jesus" and "Spirit" fourteen times, and "Lamb" twenty-eight times. The "seven spirits" are mentioned four times, thus linking complete sovereignty and worldwide dominion. The number twelve is the number not only of Israel, as represented in the twelve tribes, but of the new Israel, as represented in the twelve apostles. Significantly, the number twelve occurs twelve times in the description of the new Jerusalem (21:9–22:5). Interestingly, "Babylon" appears six times, possibly to associate it with the number of the beast (666).

The symbolic use of numbers serves to express the sovereignty of God over all history. The repeated series of sevens (whether of letters, seals, trumpets, or bowls) form the structure of the book. Each sevenfold segment (even the letters) deals with the struggle of the forces of good and evil and concludes with the triumph of good and the victory of God. This underlines the sovereignty of God and His purposeful hand on all the events of human history. The overall figurative effect of this repeated complex patterning is that the reader is left with the impression of God's all-encompassing will being like an elaborate spiderweb in which Satan and his forces are caught. Though they attempt to free themselves from divine sovereignty, they cannot escape ultimate defeat. The repetition of the numbers highlights the idea that nothing is haphazard or accidental. The analogy of a chess game is also appropriate. The sacrificial move of Christ at the cross puts the devil in checkmate (deals him a mortal wound);

the devil continues to play the game of rebellion, but his defeat is assured. This is an important theme of John's vision, which seeks to assure believers going through difficult circumstances that God is with them and will faithfully bring them through to final victory.

7. The Significance of the Use of Symbols in Revelation

Given that Revelation is full of symbolism, why did God use such a possibly confusing way to speak His message? The answer is that John's use of symbols is very similar to Jesus' use of parables, which itself is rooted in the language and signs of the OT prophets. When asked by His disciples why He spoke in parables, Jesus turned to Isa. 6:9-10 and answered, "To you it has been granted to know the mysteries of the kingdom of heaven, but to them it has not been granted. For whoever has, to him shall more be given . . . but whoever does not have, even what he has will be taken away from him. Therefore I speak to them in parables; because while seeing they do not see, and while hearing they do not hear, nor do they understand. And in their case the prophecy of Isaiah is being fulfilled, which says, 'You will keep on hearing, but will not understand . . .' " (Matt. 13:11-14). The parables of Jesus served the same purpose as the language and signs of the OT prophets: He used them to get the attention of His believing listeners who had grown spiritually sleepy and might not have paid attention otherwise. But for unbelievers (including pseudo-believers), parables made no sense, and rejection of the parabolic message was simply a further evidence of the hardening of the heart which refuses to listen to God. In fact, one can say that when the prophets used parables in Israel, they were indicating that judgment was coming on the anesthetized majority, though a remnant would be shocked out of their spiritual malaise. How much more was this true of Jesus' use of parables?

The symbols of John serve the same point as the words of the prophets and the parables of Jesus. In fact, the sevenfold admonition to the churches, "He who has an ear, let him hear" (2:7, etc.), is based on Isa. 6:9-10 and its use in Matt. 13:11ff., and especially Matt. 13:9, "He who has an ear, let him hear," as well as a similar saying in Ezek. 3:27 ("He who hears, let him hear"). The repeated use of this phrase in the seven letters, along with its repetition in Rev. 13:9, shows that the symbolism of the visions functions in the same way as Jesus' parables. By their powerful and often shocking imagery, they open the eyes of true believers while leaving hardened unbelievers in deeper darkness, though it is also true that some unbelievers are shocked into the faith for the first time through hearing the parabolic visions read. Many of the symbols reveal the Satanic power behind earthly institutions and practices with which they have become tempted to compromise. The symbols in Revelation immediately attract the attention of those who desire to follow Christ. We could almost say they have a kind of "shock value" because of their vividness and presentation of unusual and even extraordinary images. Unbelievers, however, will turn away in lack of comprehension in the same way they turned away from Jesus and His parables. It is interesting to note that the plagues in Exodus were signs understood by the Israelites as the judgment of God, yet only served to harden the Egyptians, who did not perceive their significance. It is no coincidence that these plagues form the heart of the trumpet and bowl visions. They harden the unbelievers while calling the believers to renewed faith. Jesus' comment about those who heard but did not understand His words is thus behind the seemingly strange saying of Jesus to John at the conclusion of his vision: John is the one who, like those listening to the parables, "heard and saw these things" (Rev. 22:8). Jesus tells him that the words of this prophecy are to remain open to all who will hear in times to come, but the same two responses will be made: "Let the one who does wrong, still do wrong . . . and let the one who is righteous, still practice righteousness" (v. 11). Jesus is not endorsing continuing in sin but merely prophesying the nature of the response to God's word.

If all this is true, it suggests further that the message of Revelation does not merely concern the unfolding of future events but uses present events, understood in a symbolic manner, to speak both a warning and an encouragement to believers to persevere in their commitment to Christ and to divorce themselves from any allegiance to the world system, which expresses the rule of the kingdom of darkness. The visions of chs. 4–21 are about the present, not just the future. We will illustrate this truth further in the commentary below.

8. Revelation and the Old Testament

Revelation has more allusions to the OT than all other books of the NT put together. It should be noted that these are allusions rather than direct quotations. Most, however, are either clear allusions, where the wording is almost identical to an OT text, or probable allusions, where the wording is not quite as close but the idea is still directly and uniquely traceable to a text in the OT.

Some larger OT passages seem to serve as a pattern for similarly substantial portions of Revelation. For instance, patterns from Daniel 2 and 7 are found repeatedly in Revelation 1, 4, and 5. Sections of Ezekiel influence Revelation 4 and 5, as well as other passages, including most of ch. 6 and part of ch. 18. The earlier trumpet and bowl plagues (Rev. 8:6-12; 16:1-14) follow the pattern of the Exodus plagues (Exodus 7–14). Revelation also develops certain OT themes in a general way, examples being end-time judgment and salvation, Daniel's concept of the abomination of desolation, and the OT concept of earthquake as a sign of the end.

By far the greater number of allusions are uses in Revelation of an idea or phrase referring to a person, place, or event from an OT text. These simple allusions may be condensed or expanded and are obviously applied to different historical situations, but almost always an essential focus of the OT text is carried over such that there is a clear continuity between the OT and Revelation. The following are some examples, grouped by the point common to both:

Common Point Is Judgment

books of judgment (Ezekiel 2, Daniel 7 and 12/Rev. 5:1-5; Ezekiel 2/Revelation 10)
the lion of Judah exercising judgment (Gen. 49:9/Rev. 5:5)
horsemen as agents of judgment (Zechariah 1 and 6/Rev. 6:1-8)
locusts as agents of judgment (Joel 1–2/Rev. 9:7-10)
Exodus plagues inflicting judgment (Exod. 7:14–12:33/Rev. 8:6-12; 16:1-14)

Common Point Is Tribulation

ten days of tribulation (Dan. 1:12/Rev. 2:10)
three and a half years of tribulation (Dan. 7:25; 12:7/Rev. 11:2; 12:14; 13:5)
Sodom, Egypt, and Jerusalem as OT places where God's people are persecuted (Rev. 11:8)
rulers who persecute pictured as beasts (Daniel 7/Revelation 11–13 and 17)
Babylon the Great, who deceives and persecutes (Dan. 4:30/Rev. 14:8; 16:19; 17:5-6; 18:2, 24; 19:2)

Common Point Is Idolatrous Teaching
Balaam (Numbers 25; 31:16/Rev. 2:14)
Jezebel (1 Kgs. 16:31; 2 Kgs. 9:22/Rev. 2:20-23)

Common Point Is Divine Protection
the tree of life (Gen. 2:9/Rev. 2:7; 22:2, 14, 19)
the "sealing" of the Israelites (Ezekiel 9/Rev. 7:2-8)
the wings of eagles protecting in the wilderness (Exod. 19:4; Deut. 32:11/Rev. 12:14)

Common Point Is the Victorious End-Time Battle
Armageddon (Zech. 12:11/Rev. 16:16)

Common Point Is Falling Away (Apostasy)
the harlot (Ezek. 16:15/Revelation 17)

Common Point Is the Spirit as the Empowering for God's People
Zech. 4:1-6/Rev. 1:12-20; 11:4

One final point to be made concerns the way in which John takes OT references and universalizes them. What in the OT is applied to Israel is given a much wider sense by John. For instance, God gave Israel the title "kingdom of priests" (Exod. 19:6), but John applies this to the church (Rev. 1:6; 5:10). Where Zech. 12:10 states that the tribes will mourn over the Messiah, the reference is to Israel, but John widens it to all the tribes of the earth (Rev. 1:7). The concept of the Exodus plagues is extended by John from the land of Egypt to the whole earth (Rev. 8:6-12; 16:1-14). The three-and-a-half years of Israel's tribulation (Dan. 7:25; 12:7) are extended to the tribulation of the church as the true Israel throughout the world. This tribulation is instigated not by Daniel's literal Babylon (Dan. 4:30), but by the end-time Babylon or world system (Rev. 17:1-6), which persecutes not just Daniel's Israelite fellow believers but the church throughout the world (Rev. 17:5-8; 18:24). When Babylon falls, the "cities of the nations" (Rev. 16:19) also fall. The benefits of the end-time temple of Ezekiel are no longer reserved for Jews only, but are for all believing peoples. The leaves which are for the healing of Israel (Ezek. 47:12) are now for the healing of the nations (Rev. 22:2). The lampstands of the ark now represent the churches (1:12-13, 20), and the physical manna given to Israel becomes spiritual manna for all believers (2:17). Tyre as harlot (Ezek. 26:17–28:19) becomes the world system as represented by Babylon (Rev. 17:1–18:24). Physical Jerusalem becomes the "new Jerusalem," which is equated with the entire new creation (21:2-27). The reason for such universalization is rooted in the NT understanding of the work of Christ and of how through Christ the promise given to Abraham has been extended to the nations. When these nations trust in Jesus, who is the true Israel, they identify with him and thus become part of true Israel, riding on the Israelite coattails of Jesus. John's use of the OT should not, therefore, be seen as abuse of its true meaning. John simply understands the OT as prophetically pointing forward to the events of the NT and to Christ, and he does so in the same way that Jesus Himself and all the other NT writers did. The true people of God are now seen to be those who trust in the Savior promised in the OT, and believers from every nation, Jew and Gentile alike, constitute God's new covenant people, the continuation of true Israel. It was likewise prophesied in the OT that such people would be those upon whom God would in the latter days pour out His Spirit and upon whose hearts He would write His law. History is united by the plan of a sovereign God. In this history, the latter part (the work of Christ) interprets what has gone before, yet cannot be understood properly without it.

The simple yet amazing fact is that God chose to convey these visions to John in the best way he could have understood them — by using the language of the Bible. Far from being a rejection of the OT, this is the strongest possible affirmation of its authority. Everything God has given in Christ can and must be understood against the backdrop of the OT revelation, which not only points to Christ but alone makes it possible for us to understand who He truly is. Jesus told His listeners that if they only listened to what Moses wrote, they would understand who He was. Their problem was not that Moses contradicted Christ but that they refused to believe what Moses said about Him (John 5:45-47). The same truth applies to interpreting Revelation. By far the most important key to understanding John's vision is understanding the OT. As we study the book, we will find this conclusion verified over and over again. Most people take Revelation as a springboard for looking forward. However, without first looking back to the OT and seeing what it meant in John's time, and then moving forward from there to the present, we will not properly understand what it has to say about the past, the present, or the future.

9. The Outline and Plan of Revelation

Outline

1:1-20	Prologue
2:1–3:22	The letters: the church imperfect in the world
4:1–5:14	God and Christ glorified through Christ's resurrection
6:1–8:5	The seven seals
8:6–11:19	The seven trumpets
12:1–15:4	Seven visions or "signs"/deeper conflict
15:5–16:21	The seven bowls
17:1–19:21	Final judgment of Babylon and the beast
20:1-15	The millennium
21:1–22:5	The new creation: the church perfect in glory
22:6-21	Epilogue

Plan

The Two Positions on How the Visions Relate to One Another

Before we come to a closer study of the book, it may be helpful to lay out some kind of broad understanding of how these sections relate to one another and how this may point us toward a sense of the overall meaning of John's vision. There are two main schools of thought as to how the various sections relate to each other, the futurist position and the recapitulation position.

Chronologically Linear Futurist Position. The futurist position generally holds that the order of the visions, from 4:1 to 22:5 (i.e., excluding the letters of chs. 2–3), represents the chronological order in which the events described in the visions are to unfold. The seals are preparatory events preceding the trumpets and the bowls. The trumpets, visions (the "signs" in 12:1–14:20), and bowls are seen as the contents of the seventh seal, in that the seventh seal is said to have no content of its own. Some also argue that because the seventh trumpet appears to have no content of its own, the signs and bowls represent the content of the seventh trumpet. There are variations of this view (the most radical of which holds that the seals, trumpets, and bowls are all future though they recapitulate one another and all refer to the same time). Nevertheless, generally the futurist view sees the events of history unfolding in a chronological order corresponding closely, or at least roughly, to the visions as listed.

The following arguments are among those used to support the futurist position:

- 1:19 divides the book into three parts, the *past* ("the things which you have seen," that is, John's initial vision of Christ in 1:9-18), the *present* ("the things which are," that is, the situation described in the letters to the churches in 2:1–3:22), and the *future* ("the things which shall take place after these things," that is, the events yet to come, in 4:1–22:5).
- 4:1 ("I will show you what must take place after these things") reaffirms this order.
- The progression of numbered series of visions seems to suggest that a chronological order is involved. Further, 9:12 and 11:14 announce the completion of the first and second woes before the third woe begins.
- The judgments seem to intensify as the book progresses.
- It is natural to assume that the order of the visions represents the chronological order of future history.
- A "literal" interpretation of Revelation supports the futurist view. That is, the bizarre visions, if taken in a physically literal way, have never happened before in history (for example, according to 16:21, the last bowl says that at the end of time there will be hail that weighs one hundred pounds). Therefore, if literally understood, these things must take place at a future time.

Recapitulation Position. This position holds that the various series of judgments are parallel descriptions of the same events. The pattern is identical within each series. Toward the end of each series, there is a description of judgment followed by a depiction of salvation (6:12-17 and 7:9-17; 11:18a and 11:18b; 14:14-20 and 15:2-4; 16:17–18:24 and 19:1-10; 20:7-15 and 21:1–22:5). The following arguments are advanced in support of this position:

- The first scene of judgment occurs in 6:12-17 after the breaking of the sixth seal. This speaks of the destruction of the earth and heavens and of the great day of the wrath of the Lamb. It is hard to imagine how this could refer to anything other than the final judgment, or how any other judgment could possibly come after it. This means that the events of tribulation portrayed in the trumpets (beginning at 8:2) must go back before the time of the very final judgment depicted in 6:12-17.

As clear a statement as possible of final judgment comes in 11:14-18 after the sounding of the seventh trumpet, where the kingdom of this world is said to have become the kingdom of God and of Christ, where the dead have been judged and the saints have received their reward. Note also that 20:12, a further clearly parallel final judgment scene, repeats the same words as 11:18 regarding the judgment of small and great. Again, as in the preceding point, this means that the depiction of the events of tribulation in chs. 12–13 must go back before the time of the last judgment pictured in 11:14-18.

These same verses (11:14-18) describe the content of the seventh trumpet as expressing the last judgment, which contradicts the claim of some futurists that the seventh trumpet has no content in itself and must therefore have everything recorded in the subsequent chapters as its content. Once we understand the content of the seventh trumpet to be the final judgment, the entire scheme of futurism collapses.

The description of the final punishment of the lost is just as clear and final in 14:14-20 (the final harvest) and in 16:17-21 (the seventh bowl) as in what many futurists typically seem to take to be the only mention of the final judgment, the one in 20:11-15.

The earthquake spoken of in 6:12-17 (the sixth seal) seems identical to that of 16:17-21 (the seventh bowl): both speak of a great earthquake after which the mountains and islands cannot be found. In 6:14, 16, the splitting apart of the sky and disappearance of the islands and mountains are traced to the presence of the One who sits on the throne of heaven, whereas in 20:11, which follows the judgment scene of 20:7-10, earth and heaven flee away and are no longer found again because of the presence of the One who sits on the throne. This demonstrates again that 6:12-17 portrays the last, definitive judgment, so that the trials that follow in the trumpet and bowl plagues must go back in time before that final judgment.

The same language of God's judgment through thunders and sounds and flashes of lightning as recorded in Exod. 19:16 is used in 8:5 (the conclusion of the seven seals); 11:19 (the conclusion of the seven trumpets); and 16:18 (the conclusion of the seven bowls).

Each of these texts in Revelation also mentions in context the heavenly temple or altar. Each text thus narrates the last judgment, so that the latter two recapitulate the first.

The situation of believers and unbelievers during the time immediately preceding the final judgment is described in very similar terms in 6:12-17 (the sixth seal); 9:13–11:13 (the sixth trumpet); and 16:12-16 (the sixth bowl).

The phrase "It is done" in 16:17 and 21:6 appears in both instances to refer to the completion of the same final judgment. On both occasions the words come from the throne of heaven.

The repetition of the phrase "gather together for war" in 16:14; 19:19; and 20:8 indicates that the same (final consummative) battle is being described three times.

The declarations concerning the fall of Babylon occurring in 14:8 and 16:19 and in various places in chs. 17-19 must also be describing the same thing, thus revealing again recapitulated description of judgment.

The trumpets and bowls are both modeled on the Exodus plagues, alluding to the same plagues and presenting them in roughly the same order.

Given the fact that each series of judgments does express at its conclusion the same reality of final punishment and reward, and given the great similarities between the series of judgments, the observation that each series of judgments seems to intensify in effect is more easily understood as expressing the heart of God to express the same realities in ever more forceful terms as the book reaches its climax.

Our conclusion, therefore, is that the recapitulation position best explains the structure of Revelation. The book consists of a series of parallel visions in which God expresses the same truths in different ways. How, then, are we to account for the fact that the contents of each series of seven are not absolutely identical, or that some are identical but expressed in a different order? The seals speak of four horses, while the trumpets and bowls speak of the Exodus plagues, but in different order.

We begin with the understanding that John is relating what he saw in a series of visions, and he is doing so in the order in which he saw them. *The order in which he saw things is not necessarily the historical chronological order in which those things will happen.* This is clear from the fact the text shows he is speaking of the same events in different visions, but sometimes either not relating them in exactly the same order, or telling of different visions (e.g., horses instead of plagues) to express the same reality. Part of the reason for this is that, in general, the plagues recur throughout history, rather than being one-time historical events, hence there is not an exact correspondence in every detail.

John's phrase "after these things" or "after this" is used to introduce a number of visions throughout Revelation. Some futurists think that the phrase indicates that what is about to be narrated, following the "after this," will chronologically follow what is portrayed in the preceding vision. But strictly speaking "after this" only narrates the chronological order of the visions themselves, that is, that one vision comes after another in the visionary sequence. The phrase does not indicate that the history within the visions comes after the history recorded in the previous vision. For a further explanation, see also under 10. below. This means that the scope of John's sets of parallel visions deals with the course of history from the birth of the church at Pentecost until the return of the Lord. Understanding this gives us an absolutely critical key to understanding the meaning of Revelation as a whole.

The Relation of the Letters to the Visions

Readers of Revelation often fail to see much connection between the letters to the churches and the series of visions which follow. It is clear, however, that various themes in the seven letters reappear in the visions:

True and false Israel. False Israel is spoken of in 2:9 and 3:9, whereas the church, as the true Israel, is described in 7:4-8.

Suffering and persecution. The Christians at Smyrna will endure persecution (2:10), as have those in the vision slain for their faith (6:11). The Christians at Philadelphia will receive spiritual protection in trial (3:10) and will have written upon them the name of God and Christ (3:12), while believers in the vision are likewise spiritually sealed (7:3) so that they will not be harmed by the troubles to come, and also have the names of God and Christ written upon them (14:1). The Christians at Philadelphia will become pillars in God's temple (3:12), and the sealed believers will serve God in His temple (7:15). Antipas in Pergamum is described as God's witness (2:13), as are the believers in 6:9 and the two witnesses in 11:3-13.

Demonic figures. In Pergamum, Satan is said to have his throne (2:13), and there appears to be a false prophet there called Balaam (2:14). Satan later appears as the dragon (12:9) who is thrown out of heaven and attempts to establish his rule (throne) on earth. He is accompanied by a second beast described later as a false prophet (13:13-17; 16:13; 19:20). A Jezebel appears at Thyatira in 2:20-23, and Jezebel is used as a model for the harlot of ch. 17.

Other promises to believers. Believers at Laodicea are offered clean garments and invited to eat with the Lord (3:18, 20), and likewise believers at the return of Christ will be given clean garments and invited to the supper of the Lamb (19:8-9). Behind the door of the Laodicean believers stands Christ, the "faithful and true Witness" (3:14), and inside the open door to heaven is found the One who is "called Faithful and True" (19:11).

Other themes. Other common themes are that of overcoming (2:7, 11 and 12:11; 15:2; 17:14), idolatry (2:14, 20 and 9:20; 13:4, 12-15), and the picture of Jesus bringing judgment by the sword coming out of His mouth (2:16 and 19:15).

The letters, describing the present state of the church, and the concluding section, describing the glorified church in heaven, are closely and deliberately linked by the theme of promise and fulfillment. Notice the parallels between the imperfect church of the present and the perfect church of the future:

false apostles (2:2)	true apostles (21:14)
false Jews (2:9; 3:9)	tribes of the true Israel (21:12)
Christians dwell where Satan's throne is (2:13)	Christians dwell where God's throne is (22:1)
some in the church are dead (3:1)	all in the perfected church are alive (21:27)
the church is an earthly lampstand (1:20; 2:5)	God and the Lamb are the lamps (21:23-24; 22:5)
the church contains idolaters (2:14-15, 20-23)	the perfected church has no idolatry or lying (21:8)
Christians are persecuted (2:8-10, 13)	Christians reign as conquerors (21:6-7)

Notice also how the promises made to those who overcome are completely fulfilled in the new creation:

They will eat of the tree of life (2:7).	The tree of life bears fruit in heaven for the believer (22:2).
They will be a pillar in the temple (3:12).	God and the Lamb are the temple in heaven where the believer dwells (21:22).
They will be part of the heavenly Jerusalem (3:12).	They are part of the heavenly Jerusalem (21:23-27).
They will have the name of their God (3:12).	The name of God is on their foreheads (22:4).
Their names will be written in the book of life (3:5).	Their names are written in the book of life (21:27).
They will be clothed in white (3:5).	They are the bride adorned for her husband (21:2).
They will have a white stone and receive the morning star (2:17, 28).	They are part of the city whose foundations are precious stones (21:11, 18-21), whose light is God and the Lamb (21:23; 22:5), and that lives with Jesus, the bright morning star (22:16).
They will rule the nations (2:26-27) and sit with Christ on His throne (3:21).	They reign forever and ever (22:5).
They will be saved from the second death (2:11).	They are saved from the second death (21:7-8).

This close relationship between the letters and the rest of the visions is significant, because it shows that Revelation, like the other letters of the NT, is a pastoral letter written to believers. As in the other letters, grace is spoken over believers at the beginning and the end of the letter (1:4; 22:21). Like the other letters, Revelation deals with pastoral issues facing the churches and carries an appeal to believers to live for Christ. Like the other letters, it offers the hope to believers that, if they persevere in faithfulness to Christ, they will receive an eternal reward. This means that the content of the visions must have real and present relevance to all believers who read the book, no matter what age they live in. We understand that the letters of Revelation, though they deal (like all the other NT letters) with the situation of churches of long ago, still speak to us in each of the topics they deal with — perseverance, idolatry, courage to witness, moral purity, doctrinal orthodoxy, and so on. Why then do we suppose that the visions should deal only with events of the future, and so hold little or no present relevance for us? Far more likely is the proposition that, at least in large part, the visions also deal with the events which have affected believers since the very foundation of the church. As our study proceeds, we will support this conclusion by examination of the text, understanding, of course, that there are parts of Revelation which do deal specifically with the future and events surrounding the return of Christ.

10. The Significance of 1:19 as a Key for the Interpretation of the Book

As stated in an earlier section, 1:19 is a significant interpretative key in Revelation for a proper understanding of the futurist understanding of the book: "Write therefore the things which you have seen, and the things which are, and the things which shall take place after these things." The approach we will take in the commentary below is that a different understanding of 1:19 comes from wrestling with a variety of issues in the immediate context and throughout the book.

Those understanding Revelation from a futurist perspective (i.e., all the events spoken of in the visions are yet to come and will unfold in chronological order) view 1:19 in the following way: the "things which you have seen" refer, on this view, to the initial vision of the *past* described in the immediately preceding verses. The "things which are" concern the *present* situation in the seven churches dealt with in the letters, and the "things which shall take place after these things" concern the events of the *future,* specifically the events immediately prior to the return of Christ and that return.

This view has deficiencies which need to be addressed. To begin with, the command to write "the things which you have seen" does not seem to be merely a reference to past time, or to what John has seen in the preceding verses. It seems rather to pick up on 1:11, where the angelic voice tells John to write "what you see." There is no reason to limit the scope of this to the first vision John has; it seems more naturally to refer to the contents of the entire book. But what of "the things which are" and the things which are yet to come? It could very well be that "the things which are" alludes entirely to events occurring during the present time of the seven churches. Since these seven represent the church universal, this phrase would thus refer to the "present" of the entire church age. In other words, these are as relevant for us today as are Paul's instructions to any of the churches he wrote to.

Furthermore, the correct understanding of the last phrase in v. 19, "the things which shall take place after these things" is crucial. We will attempt to show that this last clause is not to be limited to events of the far-off future, but rather encompasses all the events of the period between the resurrection and the return of Christ. Critical to a proper understanding of this verse is the fact that God is communicating with John in the words He inspired Daniel to speak six centuries earlier. If God speaks prophetically in the OT, the fact that He fulfills these prophetic words in the NT should be no surprise to us. More surprising would be the thought that God communicated such significant visions to John without any reference to how He had spoken in earlier days to His servants the prophets. This verse, along with three others (1:1; 4:1; 22:6), is heavily influenced by the words spoken through Daniel to Nebuchadnezzar in the interpretation of his first dream (Dan. 2:28, 29, 45). In section 6. above, we noted how John's statement in 1:1 ("The Revelation . . . which God gave Him to show to His bond-servants the things which must shortly take place") is taken from Dan. 2:28, 29, 45, where God shows Daniel what must take place *"in the latter days"* or *"after these things":*

"He has made known . . . what will take place in the latter days" (Dan. 2:28) ". . . what would take place after this" (Dan. 2:29) ". . . what will take place after this" (Dan. 2:45)	"to show . . . the things which must shortly [or quickly] take place" (Rev. 1:1)

If we compare Rev. 1:1 with the passages in Daniel, the thought is almost identical. The significant difference in what God speaks to John involves the replacement of "the latter days" or "after this" (years yet far off to Daniel) with "shortly" or "quickly," thus implying that Daniel's "latter days" (= "after this") are on the brink of unfolding, in fact beginning to unfold. What was far off to Daniel is staring John in the face. In 1:3, John says that the time is "near," using a word similar to that spoken by Jesus in Mark 1:15, "The time is fulfilled and the kingdom of God *at hand.*" It is likely that "the kingdom of God is at hand" is parallel with and a further explanation of "the time is fulfilled." If so, the idea of "near" is a close synonym of "fulfilled." The Greek verb for "nearness" has the sense of "about to arrive" or "beginning to arrive." It will not be happening far off in the future: it is beginning to happen now, and much more is around the corner.

In Luke 20:18 Jesus equates the "stone" of His ministry with the end-time rock of Daniel's last-days kingdom. To Jesus, the prophetic words of Daniel are on the verge of fulfillment. And John is no different from Jesus in his understanding. Note the other parallels in Revelation 1 to Daniel. There are references to the kingdom (vv. 6 and 9), as in Dan. 7:14, which John sees being inaugurated in fulfillment. This kingdom belongs to a "Son of man" (1:13), just as in Dan. 7:13, and this Son of man is described in a heavenly vision (1:13-16), just as in Dan. 7:13-14. Jesus has begun in John's own time to begin to fulfill Daniel 7's Son of man prophecy. Out of this we draw the conclusion that Daniel 2 and Revelation 1 are describing the same reality, and that what is prophesied in Daniel is beginning to be fulfilled in Revelation. The events prophesied are actually occurring or beginning to occur. The death and resurrection of Christ have brought about the inauguration or beginning of the kingdom of God prophesied in Daniel. Such an understanding will have profound importance for our interpretation of Revelation as a whole.

Now we look at 1:19, in the light of both 1:1 and the passages in Daniel:

"What will take place in the latter days/after this" (Dan. 2:28, 29, 45)	"The things which must shortly [or quickly] take place" (Rev. 1:1)	"The things which shall take place after these things" (Rev. 1:19)

It is clear that Daniel's phrases *"in the latter days"* (Dan. 2:28) and *"after this"* (in Theodotion's translation, "after these things," exactly as in Rev. 1:19) are identical in meaning. The phrase "after this" (in the Hebrew text) or "after these things" (Theodotion) refers in Dan. 2:29 to something lying far off in the future, to which the phrase "in the latter days" also refers. However, in Revelation they allude to something which is already beginning to happen: as we have already seen, Rev. 1:1 replaces "in the latter days" with "shortly," and v. 3 adds the nuance "near," meaning "at hand." The phrase "after these things" in 1:19, therefore, is not a reference to events only of the future but to events that are already unfolding in these last days, since "after these things" is to be identified with the "latter days" in Dan. 2:28-29, which have been inaugurated by the death and resurrection of Christ. Thus, each of the three phrases in Rev. 1:19 may very well refer to the same reality of the entire church age. The interpretation of Rev. 1:19 is complex, and there are a variety of interpretations; for that reason no *overall view* of Revelation should be based primarily on it, whether futurist or any other.

The other place where the phrase "after these things" appears is at 4:1 which, significantly, is the introduction to the vision section of the book. The angelic voice tells John, "Come up here, and I will show you what must take place after these things." Again, this is an allusion to Dan. 2:29. If "these things" is synonymous with "the latter days," as it is in Dan. 2:28-29, it refers to the events of the last days understood as being inaugurated by the cross and resurrection of Christ. This is clear from John's understanding throughout Revelation 1 that the Daniel 2 and 7 prophecies have begun fulfillment in Christ's first coming. Consequently, the visions unfolding in the rest of the book will tell us what is going to unfold throughout the time period of these last days — that is, throughout the entire history of the church between Christ's resurrection and His return. We should expect, therefore, that the visions will speak to the life and history of the church in every age, including that in which the recipients of the book lived, even though there may be aspects which speak specifically to the time period immediately before Christ's return. It is important to remind ourselves that such an understanding runs completely contrary to much popular literature on Revelation, which takes the entire visionary portion of the book to refer only to the future events immediately surrounding the return of Christ. The understanding we have adopted, we are persuaded, provides a more satisfactory view of Revelation in another way, for otherwise the vast majority of the book would not have as much relevance either for those to whom it was written (the churches under John's apostolic authority) or to any believer who has ever lived since. This majority portion of the book would then refer primarily or only to one group of people living through the last tribulation and then later during the millennium. Though futurists protest that the book is still relevant in various ways for readers throughout the church age, we think our point still stands. As we proceed with our study, we will see our view supported by the text in a variety of other ways.

The final reference to Daniel occurs at 22:6, where the heavenly voice says to John, "The Lord . . . sent His angel to show to His bond-servants the things which must shortly take place." Thus the concluding verses of the book repeat the same words as occurred at the very beginning (1:1). The things which have been unfolded to John are the things that are about to unfold before his eyes and that have been unfolding ever since. It is interesting to note that the four main sections of the book, the introduction (1:1-18), the letters (1:19–3:22), the visions (4:1–22:5), and the conclusion (22:6-21) are all introduced by allusions to Daniel 2:28-29, 45, which themselves form the introduction and conclusion of Daniel's interpretation of the king's dream. This is hardly an accident. Thus the content of the dream in Daniel 2 provides a framework by which to interpret Revelation as a portrayal of the end-time battle between good and evil and of the establishment of God's kingdom, all of which has begun with the death and resurrection of Christ and will be consummated at His final coming.

11. The Main Theological Messages of Revelation

In the commentary below, we will attempt to outline from the text some of the major themes of Revelation. We would suggest that the following themes in Revelation express the heart of God in giving this series of visions to John:

Willingness to Suffer for Christ Is the Path to Ultimate Victory. Even as the cross turned out to seal Christ's victory over Satan, so the present suffering of Christians seals their victory over the powers of darkness. Even while, like Christ, Christians suffering tribulation and hardship (1:9) also share in Christ's kingly reign (1:6). In this present age, believers may suffer physical hardship, but their spirits will be kept safe (11:1-12). The church's persecutors, on the other hand, will find themselves in the same position as Satan. Even as Satan's apparent victory triggered his ultimate defeat, so the present evil actions of unbelievers (11:10) are only laying the basis for their final judgment (11:13, 18). One of the main goals of the book, therefore, is to exhort believers to remain faithful to Christ in spite of present sufferings and in spite of the temptation to engage in idolatry represented by compromise with the world-system, because this faithfulness will eventually be rewarded in the heavenly kingdom. Notice that after the portrayal of the heavenly kingdom in 21:1–22:5, the final words of the book revert to the command to remain faithful. The heavenly visions serve as motivators for Christians now suffering in adversity to hold to the glorious promises of God and not to fall away. And so in the same way, Christians today should still read Revelation and allow its portrayal of the divine majesty to motivate us to continued faithfulness. Christians are to live according to the values of this new world, not those of the world in which they live. Churches should be reminded that the scenes of heavenly worship are to be the model for our earthly worship every Lord's Day — for remember, it was as John readied himself for worship on the Lord's Day that he was given this vision.

The Sovereignty of God in Human History. In chs. 4 and 5 John is given a vision of the throne room of God. The word "throne" appears seventeen times in these two chapters (out of thirty-four times in the book as a whole), and signifies the sovereignty of God. In the vision, the Lamb is given a place of equal honor to God Himself, and so the chapters as a whole portray the victory of God and the Lamb. Because this vision serves as the introduction to all the subsequent visions in the book, its significance is to demonstrate the authority of God and of Christ over all that is about to unfold in the remainder of the book. The trials of the believers, the apparent triumph of the forces of the enemy, the eventual destruction of the latter, and the victory of the church are all under the sovereign control of God. It is therefore true to say that, according to Revelation, the hand of God is directly behind the tribulations of believers as well as those of unbelievers. Such trials are sent by God to refine His people. Not only that, but the OT passages which influence the visions of the seals, trumpets, and bowls also picture God as the cause of the woes which befall believers and unbelievers alike (see Zech. 6:1-8; Ezek. 14:21; Lev. 26:14-33 and their use in the seals in Rev. 6:2-8, or the sending of the Exodus plagues as formative for the trumpet and bowl plagues). The mystery as to how God would allow believers also to suffer is answered throughout the book: God's strategy is to use the woes to refine their faith, while reserving unbelievers for ultimate punishment. As the heavenly vision leads into the picture in ch. 6 of the horsemen and the initial unleashing of the divine judgments, it is clear that the resurrected Lamb (6:1) is in control of what is happening. The cross has been transformed from tragedy into triumph, and so also will God transform the earthly woes of believers into heavenly and eternal victory. The people of God have no other destiny during the church age than that of the Lamb during His earthly ministry. This is why Rev. 14:4 says that they "follow the Lamb wherever He goes."

The New Creation as Fulfillment of Biblical Prophecy. The main prophetic themes of both OT and NT culminate in the new covenant, the new temple, the new Israel, and the new Jerusalem, all of which are summed up in the concept of the new creation. These themes appear in 21:1–22:5 at the climax of the book. In both Revelation and other parts of the NT, these realities are seen to have already *begun* to be fulfilled in Christ — believers as the new creation, the church as the new Israel, and so on. These prophetic realities are then *consummately* fulfilled, especially as envisioned in 21:1–22:5.

Commentary on the Text

Prologue: The revelation was given so that John would bear witness to what God has done in Christ and so that believers would be blessed by understanding God's perspective on history and obeying His commands (1:1-20)

The revelation is given for the purpose of witness, resulting in blessing (1:1-3)

[1] The Revelation of Jesus Christ, which God gave Him to show to His bond-
servants, the things which must soon take place; and He sent and communicated
it by His angel to His bond-servant John, [2] who testified to the word of God and
to the testimony of Jesus Christ, even to all that he saw. [3] Blessed is he who reads
and those who hear the words of the prophecy, and heed the things which are
written in it; for the time is near.

1 **The revelation of Jesus Christ** could mean "the revelation by (or from) Jesus Christ" or "the revelation about Jesus Christ," or both may be included. The word **revelation** (or "apocalypse," Greek *apokalypsis*) expresses the subject and nature of the book. The book is a heightened form of prophecy, which can be referred to as "apocalyptic," as apparent from the use of "revelation" and "prophecy" in vv. 1-3 and in 22:7. John begins by describing his vision as a revelation which God gave him to show His servants **things which must soon take place**. The roots of this verse are in Dan. 2:28-30, 45-47, where in the Greek translations of the OT the verb "revealed" appears five times, the verb "show" ("signify," "communicate," Greek *sēmainō* [only in OG]) twice and the phrase "what must come to

pass" three times. The key to the significance of these allusions to Daniel is that Daniel is speaking there of the kingdom of God which will come to pass in the latter days. But what Daniel explicitly states will come to pass "in the latter days" John rewords: these events will take place quickly or **soon**. These words do not connote the speedy manner in which the Daniel prophecy is to be fulfilled, nor the mere possibility that it could be fulfilled at any time, but the definite, imminent time of fulfillment, which likely has already begun in the present. What Daniel expected to occur in the last days, John is announcing as imminent, or beginning to occur now. The change of phraseology implies that the final tribulation, defeat of evil, and establishment of the kingdom, which Daniel expected to occur distantly in "the latter days," John expects to begin in his own generation — and, indeed, it has already started to happen (for the idea of tribulation preceding the divine kingdom see Daniel 7, which is a parallel prophecy to Daniel 2). The focus of "quickness" and "nearness" in vv. 1-3 is primarily on the inauguration of prophetic fulfillment and its ongoing aspect rather than nearness of consummate fulfillment (the return of the Lord), though the latter thought is secondarily present.

The following context shows that the beginning of fulfillment and not final future fulfillment is the focus. The references to the imminent eschatological period (v. 3b), the fact of Christ's present kingship over the world's kings (v. 5), the beginning form of the saints' kingdom (vv. 6, 9) and the following "Son of man" reference (v. 13) and vision (vv. 13-15), also indicating initial fulfillment of Daniel 7, point strongly to this focus and to the presence of a Danielic frame of reference (cf. discussion of these texts below). Similarly, the allusion to seven lampstands from Zechariah 4 in vv. 12, 20 and the reference to Isa. 49:2 and 11:4 (the sword in the Messiah's mouth) in v. 16 also indicate that the OT prophecies in those texts have begun to be fulfilled. In fact, only one verse in all of Revelation 1 clearly includes reference to Christ's last advent. And even that verse, 1:7, refers to the progressive nature of the fulfillment of Dan. 7:13 throughout the age, which will culminate in Christ's final coming. There is no doubt that John saw the resurrection of Christ as fulfilling the prophecy of Daniel regarding the inaugurating of the kingdom of God. This indicates that what is about to be written concerns not just the distant future, but what is before us here and now.

The chain of communication in v. 1 is from **God** to **Christ** to **His angel** to **John** and on to God's **bond-servants**. The latter phrase refers to the community of faith as a whole, which has a general prophetic calling, rather than to a limited group of prophets. Where later in the book it is sometimes difficult to determine whether God, Christ, or an angel is speaking, the reality is that the message comes from all three. Therefore, John's book is a prophetic work which concerns the imminent and inaugurated fulfillment of OT prophecies about the kingdom in Jesus Christ.

2 The subject of the revelation is now made more explicit. John's seeing of all the visions is none other than his witness of the revelation about God and Jesus Christ, and the revelation given by them. The wording **the witness of Jesus Christ** is parallel with the preceding phrase, **the word of God**, clarifying its precise content. The revelatory **word of God** concerns what He has carried out through Jesus Christ.

3 In v. 3, John declares that the one who takes to heart **the words of the prophecy** will be **blessed.** The message of Revelation, as it unfolds, is not designed to provide fodder for intellectual speculation about the end times but is rather a series of commands addressed to the present-day lives of all who read it. Prophecy in the OT generally had two time references: it was a forth-telling of God's word for His people in the present, and a foretelling of events to happen in the future. Revelation maintains these two features of prophecy. Those **who read** and those who **hear** and **obey** its message will be **blessed.** That the book has an ultimate ethical aim is borne out by the conclusion in 22:6-21, which is an intentional expansion of the prologue in 1:1-3, and especially of the ethical emphasis of 1:3. The prophecy of v. 3 is not a set of predictions but, in the biblical tradition, a word from God calling for obedient response in the lives of believers.

The reason those who hear the prophetic words must heed them is now given: **for the time is near**. Here John echoes the words of Jesus in Mark 1:15, "The time is fulfilled, and the kingdom of God at hand," where "at hand" has the meaning of "about to arrive" or "is now arriving." The two clauses are parallel: the time Jesus spoke of is now fulfilled and the kingdom has arrived. The connection between **for the time is near** and **quickly** in v. 1 indicates that in v. 3b John is developing further the "inaugurated" latter-day perspective on the OT (especially Daniel 2) which v. 1a conveys. The connection between the two clauses is highlighted by the conclusion of the book, where 1:3a is reiterated in 22:7b ("blessed is he who heeds the words of the prophecy of this book") and introduced by a repetition of 1:1a in 22:6 ("to show to His bond-servants the things which must shortly take place"). John views the death and resurrection of Christ as inaugurating the long-awaited kingdom of the end times that the OT books (such as Daniel) predicted and that will continue to exist throughout the church age. He sees the end-time kingdom of Daniel as having arrived in the person of Jesus Christ. His prophetic words will speak into the heart of the present, not simply the distant future. To claim to have benefited from Christ's past redemptive work entails an acknowledgement to submit to Him as Lord in the present.

Suggestions for Reflection on 1:1-3

On understanding the book of Revelation. The fact that God spoke to John in the way that is unfolded throughout Revelation is remarkable. It would seem that God puts a premium on His people being prepared to understand how the OT is referred to in Revelation. Have we viewed Revelation in this way or have we tended to shy away from it because we feel unable to understand it properly? One of the main keys for understanding Revelation is to understand how the OT is used in the book.

On understanding prophecy. There is a great deal of emphasis on "prophecy" today. How do we relate the prophetic word that God spoke to John, which has begun fulfillment, with the "prophetic" messages or interpretations so commonly offered today, which view John's Revelation only as pertaining to yet future latter-day events?

On understanding prophecy: further reflections. Much teaching on prophecy today suggests that God gives prophetic words simply to show His servants what is about to happen in the future latter days. But is there more to it? What does it mean to "heed" the prophetic word (v. 3)? Is there a response to prophecy which is more than the accumulation of knowledge about the future?

John greets the churches on behalf of the Father, Spirit, and Son, whose redemptive work results in the Christians' new status, all to the glory of God (1:4-6)

4 John to the seven churches that are in Asia: "Grace to you and peace, from Him
who is and who was and who is to come, and from the seven Spirits who are before His throne, 5 and from Jesus Christ, the faithful witness, the firstborn of the
dead, and the ruler of the kings of the earth. To Him who loves us and released us
from our sins by His blood — 6 and He has made us to be a kingdom, priests to His
God and Father — to Him be the glory and the dominion forever and ever. Amen."

4 John now addresses **the seven churches**. His choice of the number "seven" is no accident. "Seven" is the favorite number of Revelation. Biblically, it signifies completion or fullness and is originally derived from the seven days of creation. In Lev. 4:6, 17, the sevenfold sprinkling of the blood signified a completed action, as did the seven-day duration of the festivals, services of ordination, the march around Jericho, and the length of periods of cleansing from uncleanness. The significance of the number here is that the seven churches represent the fullness of the church. The universal nature of the seven churches will become clearer from the following context (e.g., 1:6; 5:9-10), especially the significance of the seven lampstands of the temple as representing the entire people of God during the inter-advent age (on which see 1:12; 11:3-4ff.). Likewise, Zech. 4:2, 10 and Rev. 5:6 also understand the "seven lamps" (= **the seven spirits** = the "Holy Spirit") of the temple as carrying out God's effective, universal work (5:6: in "all the earth") as they are mounted on the lampstand(s). Therefore, the lampstands also must be included in that universal work and have a universal identity. That the seven churches represent the whole church, at least in Asia Minor if not the world, is suggested further by noticing that each letter addressed to a particular church in chs. 2–3 is also said at its conclusion to be addressed to all the churches. It is no accident that after chs. 2 and 3 only the universal church is alluded to, and these seven churches disappear from sight. John's prophetic message is actually addressed to the entire body of Christ, the church in every age.

The typical elements of the epistolary greeting (**grace to you and peace**) are, as in other NT epistles, conditioned by the following contents of the letter and the historical situation of the readership. The Christian readers need grace to persevere in their faith in the midst of tribulation, especially pressures to compromise (cf. chs. 2–3). And in the midst of such external turmoil, they need the inner "peace" which only the eternal God who is sovereign over and above the vicissitudes of space-time history can give. The purpose of this revelation is to give the eternal, trans-historical perspective of **Him who is and who was and who is to come**, which can enable the readers to understand His commandments and so motivate them to obedience (cf. v. 3). The complete threefold clause is a reflection of Exod. 3:14 together with twofold and threefold temporal descriptions of God in Isaiah (cf. Isa. 41:4; 43:10; 44:6; 48:12), which themselves may be developed reflections on the divine name in Exod. 3:14. All these phrases are used in their respective OT contexts to describe God not merely as present at the beginning, middle, and end of history, but as the incomparable, sovereign Lord over history, who is therefore able to bring prophecy to fulfillment and deliver His people despite overwhelming odds, whether from Egypt, Babylon, or other nations. Similarly, the expression is used here to inspire confidence in God's sovereign guidance of all earthly affairs and to instill courage to stand strong in the face of difficulties which test faith.

The prophetic message is not only from God and Christ, but also from the **seven spirits** before the throne. The reference here is to the Holy Spirit, the number "seven" again representing fullness. The Holy Spirit is needed to bring to believers the grace and peace John greets them with here, and His work will be needed if believers are to respond obediently to the prophetic words shortly to come. The Christian readers need grace to persevere in their faith in the midst of tribulation, especially the pressure to compromise (cf. chs. 2–3). And in the midst of such external turmoil they need the inner peace which only the eternal God, who is sovereign over and above the trials and struggles of the day-to-day realities believers face, can give. John is alluding here to Zech. 4:2-9, where seven lamps represent one Spirit which brings grace for the building of the temple. Note again how Rev. 4:5-6 identifies the seven lamps before the throne with the seven spirits. The Holy Spirit empowers us to become the temple in which God dwells.

5 John's greeting comes from **Jesus Christ**, who is described as **the faithful witness, the firstborn from the dead and the ruler of the kings of the earth.** John is quoting Ps. 89:27, 37, where all three phrases are used. The Psalm speaks of the king who will rule over his enemies and whose seed will sit on his throne forever (vv. 19-29). "Firstborn" from the Psalm is defined clearly as **firstborn from the dead.** Christ has gained a sovereign position over the cosmos. This is not to be understood in the sense that He is recognized as the first created being of all creation nor even as the origin of creation, but rather that He is the inaugurator of the new creation by means of His resurrection, as 3:14 explains. John thinks of Jesus as the seed of David, whose resurrection has resulted in the establishment of His eternal kingdom. The kings of the earth, as generally elsewhere in Revelation (6:15; 17:2; 18:3, etc., though see on 21:24 for an exception), are not the loyal subjects of the kingdom but those earthly kings who oppose Christ's rule. This includes not only the kingdoms and peoples represented by them but also the satanic forces behind these kingdoms. That Christ now rules over these kings shows again that the events unfolded in the visions refer to present realities throughout the church age, not just to events of the

future immediately preceding the Lord's return. As a result of reflecting on Christ's fulfillment of Psalm 89, at the end of the verse John breaks out into an exclamatory Christological doxology **To Him who loves us and released us from our sins by His blood** that continues through to the end of v. 6, concluding with a doxology to God.

6 The Christological praise continues from v. 5: what Christ has done has **made** believers **a kingdom and priests** to serve **His God**. Their identification with His kingship (v. 5a) means that they too are considered to be resurrected and exercising rule with Him as a result of His exaltation. They have been constituted kings together with Christ and share His priestly office by virtue of their identification with His death and resurrection. The reference here is to Exod. 19:6: "You shall be to Me a kingdom of priests and a holy nation." Notice how significant is the change of tense. What was prophesied as Israel's role as in Exodus, and never fulfilled by Israel, is now stated as accomplished by John, for the verb (**has made**) is in the past tense. **Kingdom** here refers not just to a place but, in parallel with **priests**, to an action. "Kingdom" can also mean "kingship" or "royal power." Believers do not merely live within a kingdom; they exercise its kingly power (albeit under Christ). Believers have already entered into this role as priests and as kings, even though the manner of their performance is still incomplete. Christ exercised His role as priest through His sacrificial death ("released us from our sins by His blood") and "faithful witness" (v. 5), and exercised His role as king by spiritually defeating sin and death on the cross and subsequently being raised from the dead ("firstborn" and "ruler," v. 5). The church is identified also with Christ as a priest and now exercises its role as priests by maintaining a faithful witness to the world and willingness to suffer for Christ. It defeats the strategies of the enemy even while suffering apparent defeat, yet still ruling in a kingdom (as Christ did on the cross). We will find these themes often revisited as Revelation unfolds, though it first occurs only three verses later (v. 9).

The expression from Exodus is a summary of God's purpose for Israel. This primarily meant that they were to be a kingly and priestly nation mediating Yahweh's light of saving revelation by witnessing to the Gentiles (e.g., Isa. 43:10-13), a purpose which, the OT prophets repeatedly observed, Israel never fulfilled (e.g., Isaiah 40–55). Like OT priests, the entire people of God now have free, unmediated access to God's presence, because Christ has removed the obstacle of sin by His substitutionary blood. It is the light of God's presence that they are to reflect to the world. That John sees Exod. 19:6 as fulfilled in the church indicates that the church now continues the true Israel as the inheritor of God's promises and as His covenant people, while unbelieving Jews are described not as true Jews but as a synagogue of Satan (2:9). This accomplishment of God's redemptive plan will bring eternal **glory** and culminate in His eternal **dominion**.

The Son's kingship and the Father's sovereignty over history are the basis of the church's grace and peace and the Father's glory (1:7-8)

[7] Behold, He is coming with the clouds, and every eye will see Him, even those who pierced Him; and all the tribes of the earth will mourn over Him. So it is to be. Amen. [8] "I am the Alpha and the Omega," says the Lord God, "who is and who was and who is to come, the Almighty."

7 The conclusion of John's greetings comes in this and the next verse. This verse is made up of two OT quotations. The first is from Dan. 7:13, referring to the enthronement of the Son of man over the nations. John sees this verse as fulfilled in the enthronement of Christ at the right hand of the Father. The second is from Zech. 12:10, which refers to the end-time victory of Israel over the nations and the repentance of Israel before the Lord, whom the people of Israel have pierced. Zechariah also speaks of mourning for a firstborn son, which echoes the quotation from Psalm 89 in v. 5. But the Zechariah text has been universalized, for in the original it speaks only of the house of David mourning over Him as a result of the Spirit of grace poured out upon them, whereas John speaks of **all the peoples of the earth** doing so, and also adds the phrase **every eye will see Him**. What is applied in Zechariah 12 to Israel is now transferred in Revelation to all the peoples of the earth, specifically those peoples who, having received the Holy Spirit and His grace (see v. 4), that is, all true believers in Jesus, **mourn over** what they have done to Him. This continues the same trend of application seen with the use of Exod. 19:6 in v. 6.

Therefore, repentant Gentiles are viewed as part of true Israel in fulfilling the Zechariah prophecy at the second coming of Christ. However, the Daniel 7 reference may include the whole course of the church age during which Christ guides the events of history in judgment and blessing, since the Son of man allusion in 1:13 has present application. Daniel's reference is to the "coming" of the Son of man to receive an end-time kingdom and authority. John understands this kingdom to have been received at the resurrection, and in this sense Jesus' final coming is the end of a process whereby He continually "comes" to the churches as their Savior and even Judge throughout the course of the church age. In 2:5, 16 and 3:3, the coming of Jesus referred to is definitely not His final return but rather His coming in present judgment to the churches. It could thus be argued that the phrase "I am coming soon" in 3:11 also alludes to a soon coming in judgment. Therefore, Christ's **coming** in v. 7 and elsewhere in Revelation is understood better as a process occurring throughout history, so that His so-called "second coming" is actually a final coming concluding the whole process of comings. Consequently His "comings" in blessing and judgment throughout the course of time are but manifestations of His exercise of latter-day authority. The Zechariah quotation perhaps connotes the climax of the historical process expressed in the Daniel 7 allusion (that is, Christ's return). However, in John 19:37, the Zech. 12:10 quotation refers to the Gentile soldier near the cross who "pierced" Jesus and then apparently repented (cf. John 19:34-37 and Mark 15:39). A strikingly similar application of Zech. 12:10 is found here. Consequently, the Zechariah 12 reference could also include application to a period preceding the final coming (the church age) when Gentiles believe in the Messiah. **Amen** concludes the verse to show the trustworthiness and dependability of what has just been said in the preceding part of the verse.

8 The greetings section is concluded by the Lord's description of Himself using the first and last letters of the Greek alphabet, **the Alpha and the Omega**. This is a figure of speech that involves the stating of polar opposites to highlight everything between the opposites. Hence the statement that God is the beginning and end of history stresses His presence throughout and His rule over all events in between. God's sovereign rule is highlighted by referring to Him as the One **who is and who was and who is to come**, which means that God is **the Almighty**. With this threefold formula not only is the totality of polarity expressed (**who was and who is to come**) but a middle element is added (**who is**) to show that God is, indeed, ruling over events between the beginning and end of history. This middle element is actually put first, out of order, to highlight for the readers that God is present with them, ruling over all the circumstances in which they find themselves. This emphasis serves as a basis for v. 7, since it is only with the presupposition of an omnipotent God that such a confident assertion about the consummation of history can be made.

SUGGESTIONS FOR REFLECTION ON 1:4-8

On the number seven. Given John's use of the number "seven" and its significance here as representing the church as a whole or the universal church, how should we think of the church today? Is our understanding often limited to our local congregation, or perhaps to other congregations with which we are familiar? How can we adjust our vision to see the church more broadly as God sees it?

On the Holy Spirit as the builder of the temple. Zech. 4:2-7 refers to the seven lamps representing one Spirit bringing grace for the building of Israel's second temple. John represents this same Spirit as building the temple of the church. How do we learn to appreciate more profoundly what it means that the Holy Spirit is building the church into a temple? Is He often an ignored figure in the process? How could 1 Cor. 3:16-17 and 6:19 shed light on this?

On Christ's resurrection. That Christ is the firstborn from the dead means that He has inaugurated the new creation through His resurrection. Do we appreciate the significance of the resurrection as the greatest dividing line in history, or do we think of other events, past or future, as constituting greater dividing lines? How does this understanding of Christ's resurrection as the beginning of the new creation affect the view of many that the end times are still yet future?

On believers as a kingdom and priests. Christ has made us a kingdom and priests to serve God. In what practical ways do we as believers exercise our kingly and priestly roles today? How could Rev. 1:6 help us reflect on this question?

On Jesus' coming. How do we understand the concept of Jesus' "coming" to His church throughout the course of history (as opposed to His final coming)? How might the idea of Jesus continually coming affect the way in which we live as Christians and conduct our church life today?

John is commissioned as a prophet to write to the churches, because their confidence is based on Christ's position as heavenly judge, priest, and ruler of the church as a result of His victory over death (1:9-20)

[9] I, John, your brother and fellow partaker in the tribulation and kingdom and
perseverance *which are* in Jesus, was on the island called Patmos because of the

word of God and the testimony of Jesus. [10] I was in the Spirit on the Lord's day, and I heard behind me a loud voice like *the sound* of a trumpet, [11] saying, "Write in a book what you see, and send *it* to the seven churches: to Ephesus and to Smyrna and to Pergamum and to Thyatira and to Sardis and to Philadelphia and to Laodicea." [12] Then I turned to see the voice that was speaking with me. And having turned I saw seven golden lampstands; [13] and in the middle of the lampstands I saw one like a Son of man, clothed in a robe reaching to the feet, and girded across His chest with a golden sash. [14] His head and His hair were white like white wool, like snow; and His eyes were like a flame of fire. [15] His feet were like burnished bronze, when it has been made to glow in a furnace, and His voice was like the sound of many waters. [16] In His right hand He held seven stars, and out of His mouth came a sharp two-edged sword; and His face was like the sun shining in its strength. [17] When I saw Him, I fell at His feet like a dead man. And He placed His right hand on me, saying, "Do not be afraid; I am the first and the last, [18] and the living One; and I was dead, and behold, I am alive forevermore, and I have the keys of death and of Hades. [19] Therefore write the things which you have seen, and the things which are, and the things which will take place after these things. [20] As for the mystery of the seven stars which you saw in My right hand, and the seven golden lampstands: the seven stars are the angels of the seven churches, and the seven lampstands are the seven churches."

9 In vv. 9-11 John is commissioned to write a prophetic revelation. He identifies himself as one with his readers in the **tribulation, kingdom, and perseverance** that are ours **in Jesus**. He thus introduces himself in a manner which continues the theme of the kingdom from vv. 5-7, especially v. 6. Only one Greek article precedes these three words, which conveys the idea that all three are part of the same reality. One cannot exercise kingdom rule except through tribulation and endurance. But this is a kingdom unanticipated by the majority of Judaism. The exercise of rule in this kingdom begins and continues only as one faithfully endures tribulation. This is the formula for kingship: faithful endurance through tribulation is the means by which one reigns in the present with Jesus. Believers are not mere subjects in Christ's kingdom. That John uses the word **fellow-partaker** underscores the active involvement of saints, not only in enduring tribulation, but also in reigning in the midst of it. Their being identified with Christ is the basis for the trials which confront them, as well as for their ability to endure such trials and to participate in the **kingdom** as kings. This paradoxical form of rule mirrors the manner in which Jesus exercised His authority in His earthly ministry and even from the cross, and Christians are to follow in His path. This becomes a major theme as Revelation develops. Believers will conquer by refusing to compromise in the face of trials (2:9-11; 3:8-10), by suffering as John himself did (v. 9), and in general by pursuing Christlike character (chs. 2–3). Like Jesus' beginning kingship, Revelation reveals that the saints' reign consists in "overcoming" by not compromising their faithful witness in the face of trials (e.g., 2:9-11, 13; 3:8; 12:11), ruling over the powers of evil (e.g., see 6:8 in relation to 6:9-11), defeating sin in their lives (see chs. 2–3), as well as having begun to rule over death and Satan through their identification with Jesus (cf. 1:5-6, 18). Their endurance is part of the process of "overcoming" (see the concluding promise in each of the letters).

The **tribulation** is a present reality (so also 2:9) and will continue among the churches in the imminent future (2:10). John himself was enduring this tribulation on **Patmos**, where he had been exiled due to his witness to Christ: **because of the word of God and the testimony of Jesus.** To "testify" could connote to witness in a court of law, which was its primary setting in the Greek world and is the way it is used in John's Gospel. This would mean that rejection of the "testimony" of Jesus and of Christians by the world and its courts becomes the basis for their judgment in the heavenly court (see on 11:3 and 22:20).

10 John introduces his commissioning (**I was in the Spirit**) by using language similar to Ezekiel's (Ezek. 2:2; 3:12, 14, 24), thus placing himself on a level with the OT prophets. This is reinforced by his hearing a **loud voice like a trumpet** similar to that heard by Moses in Exod. 19:16-20. John has been entrusted with testifying to the revelation of the heavenly Jesus because he has been faithful in witnessing to the revelation of the earthly Jesus (this is the significance of the phrases "the word of God" and the "testimony of Jesus" in vv. 2a and 9b).

11 John's prophetic commissioning is further enforced by the command to **write what** he has **seen in a book** (or scroll), just as Moses was told in Exod. 17:14, Isaiah in Isa. 30:8 (LXX), or Jeremiah in Jer. 36:2. The reader steeped in the OT would perhaps discern that all such commissions in the prophets were commands to write testaments of judgment against Israel (so also Jer. 37:2; cf. also Exod. 34:27; Isa. 8:1; Jer. 36:2; Hab. 2:2). Therefore, at this early point in the book there is already a hint that one of its major concerns is judgment (as we shall see, judgment against both the world and those in the church who compromise with the world; see on chs. 2–3). Why John was commissioned to send his prophecy to these seven churches we do not know, other than that they may have been the leading churches of the region, but it is apparent that the biblical significance of the number seven indicates these churches stand for all churches both then and now.

12-20 The vision related in vv. 12-20 follows the typical pattern of Old Testament visions (Isa. 6:1-7; Jer. 1:11-12, 13-14; Ezek. 2:9–3:11; Dan. 8:3-27; 10:2–12:3; 12:5-13; Zech. 4:1-3; 5:1-11; 6:1-8). First, the vision is related (vv. 12-16); next, the response of the one receiving the vision is given (v. 17a); then the interpretation of the vision follows (vv. 17b-20). The vision develops the themes of suffering, kingdom, and priesthood already found in vv. 1-9 and introduces the new theme of Christ as judge. In vv. 12-16, Christ is portrayed as the eschatological heavenly priest and the end-time ruler and judge. The interpretative section reveals that it was His overcoming of death which placed Him into these offices (cf. vv. 17b-18) and that His kingship primarily concerns His rule over the church. This vision in vv. 12-20 discloses that the overall function of vv. 9-20 is to serve as a commission to John from the risen Christ to write the totality of the vision which he witnessed, as evidenced by the restatement of the commission in v. 19. How does Christ's function as judge relate to His kingly and priestly roles? If the churches do not maintain their role as priestly kings by faithfully witnessing to "the testimony of Jesus" in the face of suffering, then they will be judged by Christ. If they are faithful and are unjustly persecuted, they need not fear (v. 17), because they can be assured that ultimately they will overcome their defeat in the same way Christ did. The OT allusions in this vision are essential (as generally throughout Revelation) for an understanding of its meaning.

12 The first things John **sees** are the **seven golden lampstands**, which represent the church (cf. 1:20). In Zech. 4:2-6, the lampstand with its seven lamps is a figurative expression by which part of the temple furniture stands for the whole temple, which by extension also represents faithful Israel (cf. Zech. 4:6-9). In the tabernacle and temple the lampstand, with its seven lamps, stood in the Holy Place before the very presence of God in the Holy of Holies, along with the bread of the presence, and the Jews understood the light that came from its lamps to represent the presence of the Lord (Num. 8:1-4). In Zechariah's vision the seven lamps (4:2) seem to represent the power of the Spirit (4:6) which will give the people of Israel (the lampstand on which the lamps sit) the power by which to rebuild the temple. John sees seven lampstands, each representing one of the seven churches and all together representing the universal church. The church, as the continuation of true Israel, is likewise to draw its power from the seven lamps, which represent the Holy Spirit (Rev. 1:4; 4:5), as it seeks to build the new temple of God. Thus for John, the latter-day temple has already been inaugurated in the church, as has been suggested by the earlier reference to Zechariah (see v. 4 above) and implied by the use of Exod. 19:6 in v. 6 (the church as *priests* and kings). This is confirmed by Rev. 11:1-13, where the lampstands represent the church as the true temple during the time between the first and second comings of the Lord. In the light of vv. 5-6, Christ's death and resurrection have laid the foundation for the new temple, which He will build through the Spirit (the lamps on the lampstand). The shift from one lampstand in Zechariah to seven in Revelation stresses not only that this letter is intended for the church universal of the escalated end times, but also the idea that true Israel is no longer limited to a nation but encompasses all peoples.

13-16 John now relates his vision of the **Son of man**. The vision is drawn from Dan. 7:13-14 and 10:5-6. Even as the OT priests tended the lamps and **lampstands**, so Christ is pictured here as a heavenly priest who tends the lampstands by correcting and exhorting them, as chs. 2 and 3 will unfold. That Christ's eyes are like **a flame of fire** (v. 14) speaks of His role of judgment, as is clear from 19:12, where the same phrase is used to describe Christ in His role as judge. Jesus' constant presence with the churches means that He always knows their spiritual condition, which results either in blessing or judgment. This role of judgment is enforced by Daniel 10, since there the primary purpose of the heavenly man is to reveal the divine decree that Israel's persecutors would assuredly be judged (see 10:21–12:13). Dan. 10:6 even depicts the man as having "eyes . . . like flaming torches," and Dan. 10:16 (Theod.) identifies this person as one having the "likeness of a son of man."

That Christ's **feet** are like **burnished bronze, fired in a furnace** (v. 15) speaks of a foundation of moral purity in Christ which He wants also to build in the church (note how the similar phrase in 3:18 refers to moral purity). The description of the Son of man's **head and hair** is taken from the picture of the Ancient of Days in Dan. 7:9, showing how Christ and God can be thought of in the same terms. The description of His **voice like the sound of many waters** is also taken from a vision of the Almighty, though this time from Ezekiel (Ezek. 1:24; 43:2). That Christ (v. 16) holds in His hand the **seven stars** (identified in v. 20 as the angels of the churches) shows that His authority extends also to the heavenly realms. This may suggest that the stars, even if angelic, represent the church's heavenly existence and the lampstands its earthly existence. The **sharp two-edged**

sword coming out of Christ's mouth (see also 2:16 and 19:15) is based on the prophecies in Isa. 11:4 and 49:2, both speaking of Christ in His role as judge ("He will strike the earth with the rod of His mouth," Isa. 11:4). With this sword, Christ will judge both disobedience in the church (2:16) and the world (19:15). Christ's **face** being **like the sun shining in its strength** is an allusion to Judg. 5:31, where the same is said of the victorious Israelite warrior. Here the portrayal in Judges is viewed as pointing to Christ as the ideal end-time messianic warrior.

17-18 In v. 17a is found John's response to this vision. It follows the same pattern as that of Daniel's (see Dan. 8:16-19 and 10:7-12): the prophet receives a vision, falls on his face in fear, is strengthened by a heavenly being, and then receives further revelation. The vision is interpreted in vv. 17b-20. The Son of man describes Himself as the **first and the last**, using the same words God attributes to Himself in Isa. 41:4; 44:6; and 48:12 and also in Rev. 1:8. This phrase refers to the complete sovereignty of God over human history from beginning to end, and its use by the exalted Christ here shows that He too is Lord over history, thus removing any doubt that He too is divine. This transferral is enlarged on in 22:13 in such a way that Christ there (and here) must be understood as such. Christ is the force behind history, causing it to fulfill His purposes. John's audience, like Isaiah's, is meant to take confidence in God's sovereignty by allowing it to strengthen their prophetic witness.

It is in this respect that John and his readership should **not fear**. In v. 18, Jesus refers to Himself as the **Living One**, thus alluding to His triumph over the power of death. The threefold formula describing the resurrection in v. 18a (**living . . . dead . . . alive**) cannot be accidental, but is designed as a further support of the divine attribute ascribed to Christ in v. 17b. It does this by being modeled on the threefold temporal formula of 1:4 and 1:8 (referring to God), to which v. 17b itself is closely related. From this similarity of the threefold clauses, the careful reader should discern that Jesus' death and resurrection was an integral working out of the divine purposes in history and established that He Himself was guiding this history. He also is the One who **lives forever and ever**, the same phrase used of God the Father in the OT (Deut. 32:40; Dan. 12:7).

That Christ has the **keys of death and Hades** shows that He now rules even over death. The background is probably Isa. 22:22, where Eliakim, who was given the key to the house of David, was seen by Jews as a type of the kingly and priestly messianic "servant" who would reign (see further on 3:7). Whereas once Christ Himself was held by death's grip, now not only has He been set free from it but He also has the power to determine who else will be thus liberated. This verse assures believers that, regardless of what sufferings or trials they may now endure, if they persevere they will indeed reign forever with Christ.

19 The **therefore** of v. 19 is significant. John is commissioned anew to prophesy on the basis of who Christ is and His triumph over the powers of death, as set forth in the vision of vv. 12-18. As to the meaning of the threefold clause in this verse, on the basis of our discussion in the Introduction above (part 10.), we conclude the meaning to be as follows. The angel commands John to write down **the things which you have seen**. This is a simple reference to the series of visions John is about to receive from the Lord, all of which he is to record, thus giving us Revelation as we have it in our Bible. This series of visions deals with **the things which are, and the things which shall take place after these things**. The latter phrase alludes to Daniel's revelation of the end times, which even now, according to Rev. 1:1, are beginning to be fulfilled in Christ. Hence, as John stands at the beginning of the end times, he is to record both what is already happening around him and the things which will continue to unfold as the end times proceed. Thus the scope of Revelation deals with all the events of world history commencing with the death and resurrection of Christ and concluding with His final return. The events recorded in it will recur throughout human history and thus remain relevant to readers of all times, though they also point to a final climax at the time of the Lord's return.

20 Now John begins to unfold the **mystery**, another clear reference to Daniel (2:29). The **lampstands** are now clearly identified as the churches. The **angels** are heavenly beings (the word is used with this reference approximately sixty times in Revelation) closely identified with the churches they represent and help. (Thus the "angels" are not human leaders or representatives of the churches or personifications of the churches or human letter carriers, though this last option is the most viable among these alternatives.) The churches are addressed through their representative angels, apparently in order to remind the believers that already a dimension of their existence is heavenly and that their real home is not with the unbelieving "earth-dwellers" (3:10 and elsewhere in Revelation). And one of the purposes of the church meeting on earth in its weekly gatherings (e.g., as "he who reads and those who hear" in 1:3) is to be reminded of its heavenly existence and identity by modeling its worship on that of the angels' and heavenly church's worship of the exalted Lamb.

This is why scenes of heavenly worship are woven throughout Revelation. This initial vision has shown Christ standing in complete authority over human history, yet He does so standing amidst the churches (v. 13), which are undergoing all sorts of trials and even apparent defeats (as chs. 2 and 3 will unfold). Rev. 1:13-16, 20 shows the "Son of man" in a present position of sovereignty among the weak and suffering churches of His kingdom, bringing into sharper focus the unexpected form in which the expected Danielic kingdom has reached its initial fulfillment.

And the **mystery** has been utilized also from Daniel precisely at this point to emphasize the ironic nature of the fulfillment and its reversal of expectations. In Daniel 2, "mystery" has to do with the hidden meaning of a symbol whose interpretation has eschatological significance. **Mystery**, on the surface, refers to the hidden meaning of the stars and lampstands, which are about to be interpreted. But **mystery** also carries the connotation of unexpected, end-time fulfillment included in the meaning of the stars and lampstands in the present context. The **mystery** that Christ reveals here to John is the reality that His rule coexists with the suffering of the churches. This is in fact the mystery of the cross, the same mystery by which Christ Himself, though the Creator of the universe, had to submit to the power of death. This same mystery is referred to in Rom. 11:25; 1 Cor. 2:7; and Eph. 3:3-6. Jesus spoke of the mysteries of the kingdom (Matt. 13:11), by which He meant the beginning fulfillment of biblical prophecy, in a way surprising and contrary to what was commonly predicted, and, above all, the form which the kingdom of heaven took in His life and death, unlike the way in which the Jewish people expected it to come. This **mystery** is applied here to the church, in both its present and future situations.

Suggestions for Reflection on 1:9-20

On the idea of tribulation. If the kingdom as marked by tribulation and endurance was unexpected by Judaism, in what ways could we say it is also unanticipated by contemporary Christians? What happens when we wrongly understand Christianity by focusing on "conquering" or health and wealth in our lives without reference to Jesus' cross and our imitation of his suffering?

Further thoughts on tribulation. How does understanding end-time tribulation as a present reality rather than referring to a defined future period affect how we understand challenges we may expect to face as Christians?

On Christ's presence with the church. It seems that John is commissioned, like the OT prophets, to bring a message both of comfort and of judgment. How could these two themes coexist? The reality of Christ's presence in the church by His Spirit reminds us of His awareness of all that goes on within it. Are we as aware of His presence as He is aware of the state of our hearts? We know that Christ comes to judge the world, but how could it be said that He also comes to judge the church? Reflect on this in the light of Rev. 2:23 (and see the comments there).

On God's sovereign presence. God is the Alpha and Omega, and Christ is the first and the last, the force behind human history. How do the sovereignty of God and Christ and their continued presence with their people help believers to view the challenges and suffering that come into their lives?

On the significance of the end times. If Revelation teaches that the end times began with the cross and the resurrection, what then does this mean for us? Do we see this truth consistently witnessed to in other parts of the NT? Given the frequent understanding of the end times as only a future reality, how is it that we have misunderstood such a critical biblical truth?

The letters to the seven churches: Christ encourages the churches to witness, warns them against compromise, and exhorts them to hear and to overcome compromise in order to inherit eternal life (2:1–3:22)

In our comments on the outline and plan of Revelation, we discussed at length the interrelationship of the letters and the visions. The development of the Son of man vision (1:9-20) throughout the letters best explains the presence of phrases and concepts from the letters in the following visionary portion. The vision is primarily developed in the introductions of the letters (although it is developed also in the body of some of the letters and in subsequent parts of the book). The concluding promises of the letters overtly anticipate the end of the book and the final paradisal vision (cf. chs. 19–22). This accords with the fact that John places the visions within the framework of the traditional Christian letter form with an extended introduction (chs. 1–3), concluding admonitions (22:6-19) and benediction (22:20-21). It is clear that the introductions of the seven letters and the introductory Son of man vision pertain to the same general time period and mutually interpret one another, as primarily do also the conclusions of the seven messages and the book's final vision of bliss. This points to the likelihood that the same relationships cohere between the body of the letters and the visionary body of the book. This further underlines our point that the events being described in the visions were, in some measure at least, already occurring when John was writing, for the content of the visions mirrors that of the letters, which were addressed to the present situation of the seven churches. If the seven churches are also representative of the universal church, as we have further argued, then the contents of both the letters and the visions are also applicable to the church through the ages.

The flow of thought in each letter is similar: (i) Christ presents Himself with certain attributes particularly suitable to the situation of each church, faith in which provides the basis for overcoming the specific problem faced; (ii) the situation and the particular problem are reviewed; (iii) on the basis of the situation and problem, Christ issues either an encouragement to persevere in the face of conflict (for faithful churches) or to repent in order to avoid judgment (for unfaithful churches); (iv) this then forms the ground for Christ issuing a call for the churches to respond by heeding ("hearing") either the preceding encouragement or exhortation; (v) on the basis of a positive response (= "overcoming"), Christ promises the inheritance of eternal life with Him, an inheritance which uniquely corresponds to His attributes or to the churches' situation. Therefore, the logical flow of each letter climaxes with the promise of inheriting eternal life with Christ, which is the main point of each letter.

The seven churches fall into three groups. The first and last are in grave spiritual danger. They are exhorted to repent in order to prevent their judgment and to inherit the promises which genuine faith deserves. The three in the middle have, in varying degrees, some who have remained faithful and others who are compromising with pagan culture. Among these Pergamum is in the best condition and Sardis is in the worst. These churches are exhorted to purge the elements of compromise from their midst in order to avert judgment on the compromisers (and probably also the others), and to inherit the promises due those who overcome compromise. Only the second and sixth have proven themselves faithful, even in the face of persecution from both Jews and pagans. Even though they are poor and "have little power," they are encouraged to continue persevering as the true Israel, since more trials will confront them. They are to endure with the hope that they will inherit the promises of eternal salvation. The significance of this is that the Christian church *as a whole* is perceived as being in poor condition, since not only are the healthy churches in a minority, but also the literary pattern points to this emphasis, because the churches in the worst condition form the literary boundaries of the letters, and the churches with serious problems form the very core of the presentation. All of the letters deal with the theme of faithfulness to Christ in the midst of an often-threatening pagan culture.

Christ commends the Ephesian church for its orthodoxy, condemns it for its lack of witness, and exhorts it to overcome this lack in order to inherit eternal life (2:1-7)

1 To the angel of the church in Ephesus write: "The One who holds the seven stars
in His right hand, the One who walks among the seven golden lampstands, says
this: 2 'I know your deeds and your toil and perseverance, and that you cannot
endure evil men, and you put to the test those who call themselves apostles, and
they are not, and you found them to be false; 3 and you have perseverance and
have endured for My name's sake, and have not grown weary. 4 But I have this
against you, that you have left your first love. 5 Remember therefore from where
you have fallen, and repent and do the deeds you did at first; or else I am coming
to you, and will remove your lampstand out of its place — unless you repent. 6 Yet

this you do have, that you hate the deeds of the Nicolaitans, which I also hate.
7 He who has an ear, let him hear what the Spirit says to the churches. To him who
overcomes, I will grant to eat of the tree of life, which is in the Paradise of God.'"

1 Here, as in the other letters, the churches are addressed through their representative angel. The point of this seems to be to remind the churches that their primary existence is spiritual and that they have help ready for them in heaven. In this light it is implicit that the church on earth is to model its worship on that proceeding now in heaven (as is shown in chs. 4–5; 7:9-17, etc.). The parallels to Daniel are again noteworthy, in that there also angels are presented as helping those on earth (Dan. 10:20-21; 12:1). In each letter, Jesus introduces Himself with variations of the phrase "the words of Him" or (as here) **says this**, which draws us back to the OT language used only by God Himself, "These things says the Lord." The use of the formula "these things says the Lord Almighty" (occurring well over one hundred times in the OT prophetic writings) to introduce the sayings of Christ emphasizes that Christ assumes the role of Yahweh, and thus also the letters become prophetic messages rather than mere epistles.

2 Christ comes to the Ephesians as the One who walks **among the seven golden lampstands**, that is, as One intimately aware of all that is going on in the churches. The Ephesian church is first commended for testing and rejecting false apostles. Perhaps they still recalled the warning Paul gave in his last words to their elders (Acts 20:28-30). They had considerable discernment, for false teachers often appeared disguised as angels of light (2 Cor. 11:13-15). Ignatius, writing in the second century, also commended the Ephesian church for its vigilance against false teaching.

3-4 V. 3 emphasizes the point just made in v. 2 by repeating the observation concerning the church's **perseverance and endurance**. They have persevered in guarding the internal doctrinal purity of the church's faith, yet **have not grown weary** (v. 3). However, they have **lost** their **first love** (v. 4). This probably means they had lost their passion for the message of the gospel. Their focus was on maintaining the inward purity of the church, for which they are commended, so the rebuke must deal with their focus toward the outside world. This is why Christ chooses to introduce Himself in the way He does in v. 1. The mention that He **walks among the seven golden lampstands** is intended to remind the introverted readers that the primary role in relation to their Lord should be that of a light of witness to the outside world. A passionate love for Christ leads us to love those outside and seek to win them. This they have lost. That losing their

first love was tantamount to becoming unzealous witnesses is suggested further by seeing a link with Matt. 24:12-14, which shows such an end-time expectation: "Most people's love will grow cold. But the one who endures to the end, he shall be saved. And this gospel of the kingdom shall be preached in the whole world for a *witness* to all the nations, and then the end shall come." The Ephesians were to remember how far they had fallen in the loss of their **first love**, and to return to what they had done at first (v. 5) — a reference to those days in which the entire province of Asia heard the word of the Lord through Paul and the Ephesian church (Acts 19:10). Otherwise, their **lampstand** will be removed. Those who had contained and shed abroad so much light through their possession of truth might lose it entirely.

5 Israel had been a lampstand (Zech. 4:2, 11), but when they forsook their call to be a light to the nations (Isa. 42:6-7, 49:6), their lampstand was removed and the church in Christ continued the role of true Israel. The primary meaning of **lampstand** is that of witness, as is shown by Rev. 11:3-7, 10, where the lampstands refer to the prophetic witnesses. Jesus talked of the church as a lamp to be put on a lampstand (Mark 4:21; Luke 8:16), emphasizing the church's role as witness to the nations. The lampstands also generally represent the power of the Spirit, since this is how they are implicitly identified in Zech. 4:6, although we have seen more precisely that John views the "lamps" as the Spirit which burns on the lampstands (the churches), thus empowering them for witness (see on 1:4, 12-13). Therefore, it is possible that the Ephesians' leaving their **first love** refers to their lack of dependence on the Spirit, which was necessary for an effective witness. In fact, 11:3-7, 10 shows that witnessing is carried out through exercising a prophetic role.

If they do not respond, Jesus Himself will come in judgment and the church at Ephesus will be no more. It is interesting to note that a **coming** of Jesus is referred to here which is definitely not His final return. The actual wording **I will remove your lampstand from its place** indicates the removal of the church as a light of witness to the world, which points to the removal of it *before* Christ's final coming, since the churches' witness is a relevant activity only before the final advent, not afterward. If Jesus was ready to come in this way to the Ephesian church, He must have come repeatedly throughout history to various churches in similar judgment. The analysis likewise fits 2:21-22, where Jezebel's lack of repentance elicits from Christ a promise to send tribulation on her and her followers, a tribulation which precedes the end of history, and appears to be limited to that particular situation. Though the Lord will return in a final sense at the end of history, He comes regularly to visit His church in this present age, both to encourage and to judge(see also our comments on 2:16; 3:3, 20).

6 Despite their shortcoming, the church is commended for not tolerating the **Nicolaitans** (see further on 2:12-21), as they had not tolerated the false apostles (v. 2). The **Nicolaitans** probably taught that Christians could participate in the idolatrous culture of Ephesus. The city was dominated by the cult of the goddess Artemis, goddess of fertility, and her temple had thousands of priests and priestesses, with heavy involvement in prostitution. Part of the prosperous economy of the city was dependent on trade associated with the temple (Acts 19:23-41). The city had also been declared a "temple warden" of two temples dedicated to the imperial cult (worship of Caesar), which meant that this cult also played an essential part in the city's life. Therefore, the church's resistance to internal pressures to accommodate aspects of this idolatrous society was very commendable.

7 The conclusion of the letter, as in all the letters, is composed of a final exhortation: **He who has an ear, let him hear what the Spirit says to the churches.** This is an exhortation to heed what has been said throughout the letter so far and a promise of inheriting salvation. The letter concludes with a clause which occurs in all seven letters and was used by Jesus (Matt. 13:1-17), who Himself borrowed it from Isaiah (6:9-10), Jeremiah (5:21), and Ezekiel (3:27; 12:2): "he who has an ear, let him hear!" The significance of this exhortation in the prophets was its connection with their use of symbolic actions and parables. The primary function of the prophets who lived toward the end of Israel's history was to warn Israel of its impending doom and divine judgment. They delivered their warnings in a rational way, but these kind of prophetic messengers had little success because of Israel's idolatrous allegiances, spiritual lethargy, and stiff-necked attitude against changing the ways to which they had grown accustomed. Isaiah preaches straightforwardly in chs. 1–5 (with the primary exception of the parable in 5:1-7), then has an encounter with the Lord in which he is given the commission to render the ears of unbelievers dull so that they can no longer hear with them (6:9-10), following which his preaching becomes mixed with parables and symbolic actions. Ezekiel receives a similar commissioning to harden the hearts of unbelievers, in which God commands him to say, "He who hears, let him hear; and he who refuses, let him refuse; for they are a rebellious house" (Ezek. 3:27). Immediately following this, he is directed to perform his first symbolic action (4:1). When their straightforward preaching got no attention, the prophets resorted to more

dramatic means. But such a change in warning form is effective only with those who already have spiritual insight. Symbolic parables cause those who "have ears to hear and hear not" to misunderstand further. This is the point of Isa. 6:9-10, where the prophet is commissioned to tell Israel to "*keep on listening* but do not perceive . . . render the hearts of this people insensitive, *their ears dull* . . . lest they . . . *hear with their ears* . . . and repent and be healed."

These actions and parables had the effect of gaining the attention of true believers, shocking some unbelievers or backsliders into repentance and hardening the hearts of the rest, whose lack of spiritual wisdom prevented them from seeing the significance of the actions or parables. Jesus' use of parables, therefore, is very much in line with the prophetic pattern. Prior to Matthew 13, He taught straightforwardly but now, as He quotes Isaiah, He begins more emphatically to teach in parables. His teaching, like that of the prophets, is meant to enlighten believers while further hardening unbelievers.

The use of the hearing formula in the seven letters, therefore, is highly significant. As in Isaiah 6 and the Synoptic Gospels, the formula refers to the fact that Christ's message will enlighten some but blind others. Speaking through John, Jesus indicates by this phrase that what is about to unfold will be parabolic or symbolic in nature. However, now the formula is addressed to the church, which continues in the role of God's people as true Israel. But like Israel, the church has also become compromising and spiritually lethargic and has entertained idolatrous allegiances, so that the parabolic method of revelation is instituted. The parables throughout the book not only have a judicial effect on the unbelieving but are meant also to shock believers caught up in the church's compromising complacency by revealing to them the horrific, beastly nature of the idolatrous institutions they are being tempted to identify with and trust in. Use of the various pictures and images throughout Revelation — beasts, dragons, harlots, horsemen, strange creatures, plagues, and so on — is meant to shock believers out of their complacency and the danger of compromising with the idolatrous culture in which they live. Meanwhile, unbelievers will fail to understand what God is saying to them and will sink further into unbelief, though some, of course, may be reached and saved. There are also visions of comfort that are to assure true believers about their salvific condition (e.g., 21:1–22:5), though there is still probably some degree of shock value even in these visions.

The visions in chs. 4–21, therefore, are developments of the more "straightforward" teaching given in chs. 2 and 3, much as was the case with the prophets or with Jesus in the Gospels. This is confirmed when we consider that the trumpet and bowl visions are clearly modeled on the Exodus plagues, which likewise strengthened believers while hardening God's enemies.

To **overcome** or **conquer** is the condition in each of the seven letters for inheriting the promise of salvation. Believers must obey the exhortation to persevere and remain faithful if they wish to be heirs of the divine promise. Although the promises are phrased differently in each letter, they are all versions of the final promise of the book to the conquerors, which is generally stated in 21:7 as "he who overcomes shall inherit these things." The inheritance there is immediately explained to be the enjoyment of God's covenantal presence among His people (so also 21:3). This is precisely the force of the promise in 2:7. To **eat of the tree of life, which is in the paradise of God** is alluded to again at the conclusion of the book as a picture of forgiveness, where it is a clear reference to the restoration of mankind to its original unfallen state, the tree of life standing for the presence of God (22:1-3). Here in 2:7, it is not persecution and tribulation which must be overcome but the church's own sin of not testifying about Christ to the outside world. The overcoming is motivated by the model of Christ's own overcoming sinful temptations (see 3:21; 5:5).

Suggestions for Reflection on 2:1-7

On losing our first love. The Ephesians were zealous for doctrinal purity . . . but so were the Pharisees. Is it possible for us truly to preserve doctrinal purity and lose our first love for Christ? Is there something deficient in the way we look at doctrine? Is there a disconnect between doctrine understood as intellectual truth and doctrine understood as truth walked out in life? Paul told Timothy to watch his life and doctrine (1 Tim. 4:16), implying a close relationship between the two. How do we obey his admonition?

On spiritual introspection. How can churches who have experienced the grace of God and His power become as inward-looking as the Ephesians had? Why is there such a close relationship between lack of love and lack of evangelism? Do we define evangelism in such a way that it discourages many of us from stepping out in it? If we see love for Christ as the beginning and heart of evangelism, how might that affect our practice of it? Do those who profess faith in Christ really love Him and desire His presence? To the degree that we do, to that degree we will become an effective witness to Him. What does it mean to be a witness for Christ?

On the power of the Holy Spirit and evangelism. If the lampstand represents the power of the Holy Spirit, that power is an integral component of evangelism. Paul operated in the power of the Spirit in extraordinary ways during his ministry in Ephesus (Acts 19:1-20). We may not expect to experience exactly the same kinds of supernatural manifestations, but can it be said that the church in the west has suffered in its evangelism through a lack of conscious dependence on the Spirit's work in witnessing? Is it possible that we in the western world have relied too much on resources the world also has — techniques and technology — and lost sight of that greatest resource only believers in Christ have access to — the powerful work of the Holy Spirit? We must ever keep in mind the great promise of Acts 1:8!

On John's use of the prophetic parabolic form and the hardening of peoples' hearts. The use of the parabolic form from the OT prophets through Jesus to John shows that when people do not respond to instruction, God speaks through more indirect means which reach those seeking Him, but harden the hearts of the lost. What does this have to say to the "seeker-sensitive" approach so popular today in western churches? Are we removing stumbling blocks God set in place to reveal the heart? Are we seeking to fill our churches with people who are drawn to a reduced version of the gospel but without a true commitment to follow Christ in the way of the cross, which is the ultimate stumbling block (Matt. 16:21-28)? Is preaching the story of the cross in a hedonistic, postmodern society such as ours close to functioning like a parabolic declaration?

Christ commends the church at Smyrna for enduring tribulation and encourages it to continue to be faithful in anticipation of imminent, more severe persecution, in order to inherit eternal life and heavenly kingship (2:8-11)

8 And to the angel of the church in Smyrna write: "The first and the last, who was
dead, and has come to life, says this: 9 'I know your tribulation and your poverty
(but you are rich), and the blasphemy by those who say they are Jews and are not,
but are a synagogue of Satan. 10 Do not fear what you are about to suffer. Behold,
the devil is about to cast some of you into prison, that you may be tested, and you
will have tribulation ten days. Be faithful until death, and I will give you the crown

of life. [11] He who has an ear, let him hear what the Spirit says to the churches. He who overcomes shall not be hurt by the second death.'"

8 Again Christ introduces Himself with an element of the initial vision (1:17-18) which suits the situation of this church, members of which are facing persecution and possible death. He is the divine sovereign over history who alone possesses the attribute of eternity (**the first and the last**).

9 Christ's rule over history provides a basis of comfort to the church which is suffering economic hardship (their **tribulation and poverty**) because of Jewish slander. Nevertheless, their faithfulness in the face of such affliction demonstrates that they are spiritually **rich**.

The mention of Jewish **slander** or **blasphemy** suggests that Jews, jealous of the inroads Christianity was making, may have informed on the Christians to the Roman authorities. Until the latter part of the first century, Christianity enjoyed a degree of protection under the umbrella of Judaism, which was an acceptable religion to Rome. The Jews were not forced to worship Caesar as a god, but were allowed to offer sacrifices in honor of emperors as rulers and not as gods. But after the Neronian persecution Christianity was increasingly seen as distinct from Judaism and ceased to enjoy protection under its umbrella. It then came under suspicion, since new religions were not acceptable in the empire. And the Jews, who sometimes had no qualms in semi-revering other deities (especially the Roman emperor) along with their OT God, often were only too willing to make the Roman authorities aware that the Christians were not a Jewish sect. Jews would have viewed Christianity as a religion distorting the Jewish Law and offering a perversely easy way of salvation. They also considered the Christian worship of a crucified criminal as the divine Messiah a blasphemy (cf. Acts 26:9-10). The mention of Roman persecution in v. 10 directly following that of Jewish slander conforms to historical reports of Jews allying with and encouraging Romans and Gentiles to oppress Christians (e.g., Acts 13:45, 50; 14:2-7, 19; 17:5-9; 1 Thess. 2:14-16). The imperial cult permeated virtually every aspect of city and often even village life in Asia Minor, so that individuals could aspire to economic prosperity and greater social standing only by participating to some degree in the Roman cult. Citizens of both upper and lower classes were required by local law to sacrifice to the emperor on various special occasions, and sometimes even visitors and foreigners were invited to do so. In addition, the city's history reveals its particular loyalty to Rome, especially the fact that it had built more than one temple in honor of Roman religion.

That the Jewish community is identified as false Jews and a **synagogue of Satan** confirms again that the church is seen by Christ as the true people of God, true Israel (see also our comments above on 1:6-7, 12). This identification is confirmed not only by broad contextual indicators (e.g., Rev. 1:6, 9, 12; 2:17; 3:9, 12; 5:9-10; 7:4-9, 15-17; 11:1-4), but also by recognizing that in the immediate context the church is seen as fulfilling Isaiah's prophecy about Israel (see on 1:17; 2:10). The false accusations against the saints which induced oppression identifies the Jews with **Satan** (which means "false accuser"), since this is also a characteristic trait of the beast in persecuting God's people (cf. **blasphemy** in 13:1, 5-6; 17:3-6).

10a The church of Smyrna is exhorted not to **fear** such economic and political persecution, even if it takes the harsher forms of imprisonment and capital punishment, as it sometimes did. In fact, Christ tells them to brace for severer punishment. The reason that they are not to **fear** the imminent trial is that their lives and destiny are in the hands of the eternal Lord of history, who has already experienced persecution, even to death, and yet overcome it through resurrection. Jesus has defeated the devil (1:1, 18; 12:1-12), and even the devil's rebellious efforts can only fulfill Christ's sovereign plan for history (cf. 17:17). Therefore, the true saint should not be afraid of the devil's attempts to bring about compromise in the church through persecution. Indeed, Jesus employs the devil's efforts for the purpose (**that you may be tested**) of strengthening His people through these tests. The Greek word translated **that** or **in order that** expresses the overruling purpose of God. Even the work of the devil is used by God for the furtherance of His plan. As the devil's plans at the cross were used by God to bring salvation to the world, so the suffering of the Smyrneans will result in blessing and ultimate deliverance for them. The self-description of Christ as **the first and the last** is taken from God's own self-description in Isa. 41:4; 44:6; and 48:12. Interestingly, in the context of the first two texts in Isaiah (41:10; 44:2, 8), God commands the Israelites "Do not fear" — the same command He now gives the Smyrneans (v. 10). The implication once more is that the Christians at Smyrna are now the true Israel, for God addresses them as He did the faithful in Israel in the days of Isaiah.

Because Jesus is the ultimate disposer of history, He is able to reveal that their coming **tribulation** will be brief. This serves as a further impetus for them to remain faithful, knowing that the time of testing is ultimately in His hands and will soon be over. The identification of the Christians at Smyrna with Israel is enhanced by associating their tribulation with that of Daniel and his three friends, who likewise refused to participate in acts of idolatry ordered by the king (Dan. 1:2; 5:3-4), and who were likewise tested for **ten days** (Dan. 1:12-15). The **ten days** persecution does not have to refer to a literal period of ten days because it is an allusion to the ten days when Daniel and his friends were "tested." Daniel was tempted to compromise with idolatry, which was likely the main reason he abstained from eating at the king's table, where the food was probably dedicated to idols (see Dan. 1:2; 5:1-4). Likewise, whether or not the ten days is literal, the point is that the Christians at Smyrna were also, like Daniel of old, not to compromise with idolatry. The pagan rituals in Asia Minor also included meals dedicated to the local gods and to Caesar (understood as a god), so the Smyrneans would have understood the significance of Christ's comparing them to Daniel and his friends. The Smyrneans will undergo this brief but severe period of trial. The word for **trial** or **tribulation** *(thlipsis)* is one commonly used by Paul. In the period between the resurrection and the return of Christ, Christians can from time to time expect to undergo periods of tribulation, where tribulation refers to the beginning birth pangs of last-days events, which are a regular feature of church life — a fact verified throughout church history and today, when more Christians are dying for their faith than ever before.

10b-11 If they are faithful in responding to this **testing**, they will receive the **crown of life**. In the midst of their trials, the Smyrneans are promised the **crown of life** and victory over the **second death**. Yet their possible defeat in death by the authority of the Roman crown meant their victory of life and inheritance of a heavenly **crown**. This **crown** connotes participation in Christ's heavenly, victorious rule (so **crown** in 6:2; 14:14), for Christ alone, **the first and the last**, holds the keys of death and is alive forever (1:18). "Overcoming" here refers to an ironic victory wherein the earthly defeat of death is heavenly victory and life, which is patterned after the same use of "overcome" with respect to Christ in 5:5-6. Similarly, the saints' conquering is also based on the pattern introduced in 2:8, where Christ's death is said to lead to His resurrection life. The **crown** is a reward given at death (possibly in 2 Tim. 4:8 and Jas. 1:13; in 1 Pet. 5:4 the "crown" is a reward to be received at Christ's future coming), but already enjoyed in part, since in 3:11 the Philadelphians are commanded to "hold fast what you have" which is immediately explained to be their "crown" ("in order that no one take your crown"). The promise of vv. 10-11 is expanded in 20:4-6, where also believers who die because of their faith are rewarded with life, rule with Christ, and are protected from the second death. The devil is given power to cast them into a physical prison and to put them to **death**

(v. 10). However, his power is limited because he himself has already been cast into a spiritual prison, which prevents him from harming them with the ultimate **second death.** Christ's resurrection gave Him power over the entire sphere of death (He now has "the keys of death and Hades," 1:18b), which enabled Him both to bind the satanic prince of that realm and to protect His own people from its ultimate harmful effects.

Suggestions for Reflection on 2:8-11

On the limits of obedience to civil government. Paul commands us to honor civil authorities (Rom. 13:1-7). Daniel and his friends drew the line when such obedience violated God's law (Dan. 1:8-10; 3:12, 16-18). Under what circumstances could we be drawn into such a dilemma? Are we sufficiently aware of similar circumstances Christians around the world are facing today? How can we support them?

On the nature of religious persecution. It appears that the persecution the Christians at Smyrna experienced originated in Jewish religious circles. Jesus was put to death by religious leaders. Why is it that so often persecution seems to come from religious people, even apparently-professing Christians (in past times, for example, the Inquisition or established churches in Russia and China)?

On the sovereignty of God and the suffering of believers. Revelation pictures Christ as holding the keys of death and as triumphant over its power, yet here believers are warned of certain tribulation and possible death. In light of 3:11, what does it mean to have the crown of life yet still wait for it? Why is it in God's purpose that believers suffer? Should we pray against tribulation because it originates in the will of Satan, or should we welcome it because it originates in the will of God? Or is there a third approach which sees God as the ultimate originator and Satan as an agent under God's hand? And if so, what should our response be? How can God use the sufferings of His people?

Christ commends the church in Pergamum for its persevering witness in the midst of persecution, condemns it for its permissive spirit of idolatrous compromise, and exhorts it to overcome this in order not to be judged but to inherit end-time fellowship and identification with Christ (2:12-17)

12 And to the angel of the church in Pergamum write: "The one who has the sharp
two-edged sword says this: 13 'I know where you dwell, where Satan's throne
is; and you hold fast My name, and did not deny My faith, even in the days of
Antipas, My witness, My faithful one, who was killed among you, where Satan
dwells. 14 But I have a few things against you, because you have some there who
hold the teaching of Balaam, who kept teaching Balak to put a stumbling block
before the sons of Israel, to eat things sacrificed to idols, and to commit acts of
immorality. 15 Thus you also have some who in the same way hold the teaching
of the Nicolaitans. 16 Repent therefore; or else I am coming to you quickly, and I
will make war against them with the sword of My mouth. 17 He who has an ear, let
him hear what the Spirit says to the churches. To him who overcomes, I will give
some of the hidden manna, and I will give him a white stone, and a new name
written on the stone which no one knows but he who receives it.'"

12 Christ once more introduces Himself with an image from the initial ch. 1 vision appropriate to the situation of the church at Pergamum: He is the One who holds the **sharp double-edged sword** (v. 12), an image which is repeated in v. 16. This means that the idea of Christ standing over the church as a threatening judge because of their sin is the thought pervading the entire letter to Pergamum.

13 The Lord has a word of warning to bring to this church, but first He brings an encouragement — a good example of how to bring correction. But before confronting them with the sin that plagues them, He commends them for an area where they have been loyal. Much like the Christians of Smyrna, they also openly witnessed to their faith in Christ (**you hold fast My name**) and, even when severe persecution broke out, they did not deny their **faith** in Christ (so 3:8). As in Smyrna, Satan is identified as the real enemy of the believers. Indeed, this is the city where he has his **throne**. This is likely a reference to the fact that Pergamum was the first city in Asia Minor to build a temple for emperor worship, proudly referring to itself as "temple-warden" for such worship, and it became the leading center for this idolatrous practice in the province. Not only that, Pergamum was a center for the cult of Asclepius, the god of healing, whose symbol was a serpent (still notable in medical symbolism), which may also have contributed to Christ's view of the city as a center of satanic authority. Finally, a cone-shaped hill behind Pergamum was the site of various pagan temples, including one in the form of the throne of Zeus, father of the gods — yet another factor behind Christ's declaration. As Revelation proceeds, we will see how Satan (the dragon) gives the political system (the beast) the power to persecute God's people, as was undoubtedly occurring in this city. In most Greek cities, citizens were typically expected to sacrifice to the gods, who had long been honored in the area because of local religious tradition. Such veneration was likely expected even before paying homage to Caesar. Often when Christians were coerced to sacrifice to the emperor it was because they had already refused to recognize the pagan gods who were locally venerated and, consequently, they were being called to account by the Roman authorities.

14 The picture of Christ's **sword** in vv. 12 and 16 is not accidental, as an expression of His judicial authority not only over the church, but also over the kingdom of darkness. Yet Christ also comes to judge His church for, even though the believers at Pergamum have resisted the demonic power of the cults and the state, yet they have tolerated in their midst certain idolatrous practices. Christ compares such practices to those of **Balaam**, who encouraged Israel to sin through engaging in idolatry and immorality (Num. 25:1-3; 31:16). **Balaam**'s name became a biblical catchword for false teachers who for financial gain sought to influence God's people to engage in ungodly practices (Deut. 23:4; Neh. 13:2; 2 Pet. 2:15; Jude 11). The spiritual link between the OT story and the church at Pergamum is that of the condoning of such practices. The false teachers were arguing that believers could have closer relationships with pagan culture, institutions, and religion than John thought proper. This is the significance of the expression **to eat things sacrificed to idols and to commit acts of immorality**, which applies here not only to the Numbers account but also to the actual situation in Pergamum, as is evident from the application of the identical phrase to the situation in Thyatira (2:20), where it is not just a warning from Scripture but clearly identified as occurring in the church. Eating food **sacrificed to idols** refers to eating meals in idol temples, the same problem Paul confronted in Corinth (1 Cor. 10:1-22). The pagan feasts held in Asia Minor, honoring the emperor or other deities, featured indulgence in both idolatry and immorality, and citizens were expected to participate. In particular, what may be thought of here are trade guild festivals involving celebration of patron deities through feasts and sometimes immoral activities. Refusal to participate in such activities could result in economic and social ostracism (cf. 1 Pet. 3:13-17). Therefore, there was much pressure to compromise. And just as Israel was influenced to fornicate both sexually and spiritually, the same was true of Christians in Pergamum.

Perhaps a faction in the church had been worn down by the pressure (and the martyrdom of at least one of the church members, **Antipas**), and were pointing the church in the direction of compromise. The comparison to **Balaam** also suggests that false prophets were involved in this faction, and that financial gain (as in the case of **Balaam**) may have been the motivator. Christians would no doubt have suffered financially from sticking with their principles. The word "fornicate" (Greek *porneuō,* noun *porneia*), translated **sexual immorality** in NIV or **acts of immorality** in NASB, has both a spiritual and physical meaning here and elsewhere in Revelation (e.g., 2:20-23). If anything, the spiritual meaning is predominant, referring to illicit spiritual intercourse with false deities and the spiritual forces standing behind those idolatrous deities. However, it is interesting to note that spiritual fornication (idolatry) can lead to sexual misconduct now as much as it did in those days, and that pagan and "new age" religion, as well as cults, can degenerate into such immoral practices.

15-16 Because of such idolatrous influences, Christ now comes to the church to fight against such error in its midst. It is interesting to note that **Balaam** was originally threatened with the sword in the angel's hand if he continued to oppose Israel (Num. 22:23, 31) and was eventually killed by the sword for his evil-doing (Num. 31:8). The false teachers will face the same fate as **Balaam** unless they repent, and neither should the church think it is exempt from punishment if it continues to tolerate these evildoers — for toleration, contrary to popular thinking in our culture, is also a sin, as will become even clearer in the letter to the church at Thyatira. In the days of **Balaam**, the judgment fell on many in Israel (Num. 25:9, where twenty-four thousand died in the plague) for their failure to judge the idolaters. In fact, Paul explicitly links this very judgment of God upon the Israelites with his warning to the Corinthian church in the same matter of tolerating idolatry (1 Cor. 10:7-11). The **Nicolaitans** referred to here are probably similar to the **Balaam** group, being connected by the phrase **in the same way** as well as by the meaning of the two names (**Nicolaus** meaning "one who overcomes the people," and **Balaam** meaning "one who consumes or rules over the people").

17 Like Ephesus, Pergamum needs to **have an ear** and **hear what**

the Spirit says about their own sin that they need to **overcome**, and they are admonished now to do just that. If they can **overcome** their sin of toleration and execute discipline on both groups, Christ promises them an inheritance. The reward promised for those in Pergamum who are faithful is threefold: they will receive some of the **hidden manna**, and they will also receive a **white stone**, and this stone has a **new name** written on it. The **hidden manna** refers to the food (now not visible) to be consummately consumed at the marriage supper of the Lamb (19:9) and thus represents fellowship with Christ. The reference to the **manna** as **hidden** means that it will be revealed to God's people at the end of time, and possibly beginning at death. Though there is no tangible evidence of this promise which can be seen, overcomers must place their hope in the unseen word of God (cf. Hebrews 11). It is to be contrasted with the food sacrificed to idols, which may be consumed now but will exclude participation in the eternal feast later. Jesus warned the Jews not to look back to the manna given through Moses, but to look instead to Himself as the true bread from heaven (John 6:32-33). The idea of the manna may have arisen because of the preceding meditation on Israel's confrontation with Balaam in their wilderness journeying: Israel should have relied on God's heavenly food for their sustenance rather than partaking of idolatrous food, and the church will begin to partake of the heavenly manna in the present if it does not compromise in the same way.

The **white stone** is probably connected to the **manna**, as Num. 11:7 describes **manna** as looking like bdellium, a white stone. The **white stone** thus reinforces the idea of the **manna** as a heavenly reward. **White**, of course, also portrays righteousness (see 3:4; 6:2; and 19:14 for this image). The **white** color of the stone portrays the righteousness of the saints in not compromising and "soiling" themselves (cf. 3:4), for which righteous action they are acquitted. The **white stone**, in light of the Jewish use of stones as votes of acquittal or of white stones as a pass of admission to special occasions, probably refers to the reversal of the overcomer's guilty verdict issued by the world's institutions because of refusal to participate, which itself becomes the invitation pass to take part in Jesus' supper. The association of white with righteousness in direct connection with the admission to a banquet is expressed in 19:8-9, where the "fine linen, bright and clean" represents "the righteous acts of the saints," which is directly followed by the reference to being "*invited* to the marriage supper of the Lamb."

The **new name** is a shortened reference to the longer description in 3:12 of "the name of My God, and the name of the city of My God, the new Jerusalem, which comes down out of heaven from My God, and My

[Christ's] new name," which is written on the believer. In addition, 21:2 describes God's people as the "new Jerusalem, coming down out of heaven from God" so that the name written on "overcomers" from 3:12 becomes synonymous with their very identity. Therefore, the **new name written which no one knows except the one receiving** in 2:17 refers to receiving Jesus' victorious, kingly "name . . . no one knows except Himself" (19:12-16). Nevertheless, He *reveals and imparts it only to His people* in the present, in an escalated manner at the end of their life and fully at the conclusion of history (so 3:12). Rev. 2:17 and 19:12 seem to develop the similar thought from Luke 10:22: "all things have been handed over to me by my Father, and *no one knows who the Son is except* the Father, and who the Father is except the Son, and anyone to whom the Son wills to reveal Him" (cf. also Luke 10:17). The **new name** refers to being in the eternal presence of God, as Rev. 22:3-4 makes clear, "They shall see His face, and His name shall be on their foreheads." To know someone's name, especially that of God, in the ancient world and the OT often meant to enter into an intimate relationship with that person and to share in that person's character or power. To be given a **new name** was an indication of a new status. Therefore, the reception of this name by believers in 2:17 represents their final reward of being consummately identified and united with the intimate, end-time presence and power of Christ in His kingdom and under His sovereign authority. Identification with this name actually begins when Christ reveals Himself to people and they confess His name by faith. When this happens, they have a new spiritual status and are given "a little power" not to deny His name" and to persevere even in the final tribulation (3:8-10; likewise 2:13a).

It is interesting that the promise of a new name comes in the letters to Pergamum and Philadelphia, the two churches in which believers are said to have been loyal to Christ's name (2:13; 3:8). Note also the contrast between receiving Christ's **new name** in v. 17 and those who have received the mark of the beast's name in 14:11. Finally, receiving this **new name** fulfills the prophecy of Isaiah, in which the faithful in Israel would be called by a new name (Isa. 62:2; 65:15), thus showing again how Christ sees the church as the new Israel. The promised blessings of this prophecy will be fulfilled among those in the church, the latter-day Israel, who do not compromise. Isaiah's prophecy of Israel's restoration to God's latter-day presence lies as the basis also for all the other references in the book to the believer's "name" (3:12; 14:1; 22:4) and God's or Christ's "name" (3:12 and 22:4, as well as 19:12-13, 16). Jesus is the first one to receive a **new name** (3:12) and to begin to fulfill the Isaiah prophecy. This must mean that He represents latter-day Israel. Others come to be identified with His **new name** when they believe, as apparent from their identification with Christ's name in the present (2:13), so that they are identified as part of the beginning fulfillment of Isaiah's prophecy.

Suggestions for Reflection on 2:12-17

On administering pastoral correction. Christ comes to the church at Pergamum with a measure of correction, yet first He brings them encouragement for their faithfulness in general. How important is it to observe this order when we need to bring a shortcoming to someone's attention? Psychologists tell us that one word of correction outweighs many words of praise. Why do we fail to come to others the way Christ came to the Christians at Smyrna?

On the nature of Satan's throne. Pergamum is the only city said to contain Satan's throne. How could a city come to be described in such a way? What are the implications? Are we aware of the demonic strongholds which may exist in our own community? What is the appropriate response to them?

On toleration and the pressure to compromise. The church at Pergamum was in danger of judgment because it tolerated some within it who compromised their faith in Christ through participation in idolatrous practices, probably to avoid social and economic penalties. Is your local church or fellowship of churches threatened with some form of compromise with the world? What are the kinds of spiritual compromise which might bring us or our church under God's judgment?

On God judging churches. Christ comes to the church at Pergamum with a sword which He will use to make war against it if necessary. How could this be related to what we know of Christ's mercy and compassion? What does it mean for God to come in judgment against His own people? Do we as Christians live in a sufficient measure of holy fear that such a thing might happen to us? May we not be among those whom Christ addresses in Matt. 7:20-23: "So then, you will know them by their fruits. Not everyone who says to Me, 'Lord, Lord,' will enter the kingdom of heaven, but he who does the will of My Father who is in heaven will enter. Many will say to Me on that day, 'Lord, Lord, did we not prophesy in Your name, and in Your name cast out demons, and in Your name perform many miracles?' And then I will declare to them, 'I never knew you; depart from Me, you who practice lawlessness.' "

Christ commends the church of Thyatira for its Christian works of witness, condemns it for its permissive spirit of idolatrous compromise, and exhorts it to overcome this in order not to be judged but to inherit end-time rule together with Christ (2:18-29)

18 And to the angel of the church in Thyatira write: "The Son of God, who has eyes
like a flame of fire, and His feet are like burnished bronze, says this: 19 'I know your
deeds, and your love and faith and service and perseverance, and that your deeds
of late are greater than at first. 20 But I have this against you, that you tolerate
the woman Jezebel, who calls herself a prophetess, and she teaches and leads
My bond-servants astray, so that they commit acts of immorality and eat things
sacrificed to idols. 21 And I gave her time to repent; and she does not want to
repent of her immorality. 22 Behold, I will cast her upon a bed of sickness, and
those who commit adultery with her into great tribulation, unless they repent
of her deeds. 23 And I will kill her children with pestilence; and all the churches
will know that I am He who searches the minds and hearts, and I will give to
each one of you according to your deeds. 24 But I say to you, the rest who are in
Thyatira, who do not hold this teaching, who have not known the deep things of
Satan, as they call them — I place no other burden on you. 25 Nevertheless what
you have, hold fast until I come. 26 And he who overcomes, and he who keeps My
deeds until the end, to him will I give authority over the nations; 27 and he shall
rule them with a rod of iron, as the vessels of the potter are broken to pieces, as
I also have received authority from the Father; 28 and I will give him the morning
star. 29 He who has an ear, let him hear what the Spirit says to the churches.'"

18 The situation of this church being very similar to that of Pergamum, Christ introduces Himself with elements of the ch. 1 vision emphasizing His role as a judge. The **eyes like a flame of fire** and **feet . . . like burnished bronze** are also taken from the heavenly vision in Dan. 10:6, 16, where the man who appears unfolds the judgment of God against the pagan nations. The image of Christ with the eyes of fire appears also in His depiction in Rev. 19:12 as the rider on the horse who judges and makes war. The fact that Jesus refers to Himself here as the **Son of God** may be because the citizens of Thyatira had two deities they worshiped as sons of Zeus. It also anticipates the reference at the end of the letter to Psalm 2, where the authority and judgment spoken of is, in the context of the Psalm, executed by God's "Son" (see Ps. 2:7-9).

19 The Thyatirans are initially commended for their works of witness to Christ despite opposition. The reference to their **faith and service**

and perseverance probably indicates their readiness to witness faithfully to Christ in spite of persecution, because these terms are used similarly in other passages (Christ Himself as faithful witness in 1:15 and 3:14, the faithful witness Antipas in 2:13, the perseverance of the Philadelphians who have refused to deny Christ's name despite persecution in 3:8-10, the endurance and faithfulness of the saints persecuted by the beast in 13:7-10 and 14:12, and the faithful followers of the Lamb in the war against the ten kings in 17:12).

20 However, the Thyatirans, like those at Pergamum, have given space to a false teacher (probably a woman) described here as **Jezebel**. Their sin — toleration — is the very thing commended in our postmodern culture as the greatest virtue. This new Jezebel, like the Jezebel of old (1 Kgs. 16:31; 21:25-26), stood for compromise with idolatrous practices, and so the teaching was probably similar to that of the Balaam party and the Nicolaitans at Pergamum. In both cases (cf. vv. 14, 20) **acts of immorality** and eating of meat **sacrificed to idols** is mentioned. The Greek word for immorality is used elsewhere in Revelation to refer not so much to literal sexual immorality but to engaging in illicit intercourse with gods who stand behind idols that are worshiped. The Greek word for "immorality" (*porneia* and the related word group) typically has this metaphorical meaning elsewhere in Revelation (so 13× outside ch. 2, vs. the literal sense in 9:21; 21:8; 22:15). The metaphorical use is likely in mind here, since it is unlikely that all the forms of compromise in this church involved sexual immorality. This emphasis is borne out in this verse, where the verb form of "immorality" (literally "to fornicate") derives its meaning from the OT figure of Jezebel, who influenced Ahab and Israel to adopt Baal worship. Sexual immorality could be secondarily in mind since this was often part of Baal worship (indeed, such immorality was often involved in the worship of pagan gods in John's day). Likewise, "adultery" in v. 22 is to be understood in the same way, especially against the background of Israel being accused of adultery by God because of her idolatry. Thyatira was an economic center with a particularly large number of trade societies or guilds, each of which required members to participate in idolatrous practices to retain membership. Practically, it would be difficult to engage in commerce in the city without being a part of such an organization, and so the pressure on Christians living in the city to engage in such practices would have been substantial. The situation at Thyatira is more serious than at Pergamum, where Christ held only a "few things" (2:14) against the church. Here, a false prophetess has led the church astray and into serious sin.

21 Moreover, this prophetess has refused to **repent**, which suggests that there have been unsuccessful attempts at dealing with the situation. Paul warned Timothy against a woman being allowed to teach with authority over the church, partly on the grounds that it was Eve, not Adam, who was led astray (1 Tim. 2:12-14). Here, the same verb (Greek *planaō*) is used in the active sense of this woman teacher leading others astray, thus demonstrating that Paul's instructions had not been followed in Thyatira, with disastrous results. Later in Revelation, it is revealed that the false prophet (representing the religious system), like Jezebel, leads people astray (13:14; 19:20), as does the harlot Babylon in 18:23. This again shows the interconnection of the letters and the visions, as no doubt Christ intended the similar language in the picture of the false prophet to jolt the Thyatirans (and Christians of all ages tempted to compromise) into realizing the danger of what they were tolerating. Note also how the judgment on Jezebel foreshadows the judgment on the harlot Babylon in ch. 18. In both cases, people fornicate with a harlot (see 17:1, 2 and 18:3, 8-9), who deceives them (see 18:23), and sexual immorality is a picture of participation in shadowy forms of commerce (see 18:3, 11-22 and note that many of these forms of commerce, such as trade in linen, purple, bronze, and slaves, were present in Thyatira). In both cases God's people are commanded not to participate in her sins lest they be judged by being put to death (see 18:4, 8), and in both cases God judges everyone according to their deeds (see 18:6). The extraordinary similarities are not coincidental and show how to some degree the visions portray present realities in society and even in the church.

22-23 Christ's judgment is now about to come upon Jezebel and her followers for not repenting of their idolatrous teaching, a fact which should cause us both to live in holy fear of God's righteous anger, and also to be comforted by His care for the purity and survival of His church. Jezebel has led astray God's own servants (v. 20), and it may well be these same believers who, unless they repent, will suffer death due to their deception. This may shed some light on what Paul meant (in a similar context of dealing with idolatry and immorality) when he spoke of consigning a man to Satan for the destruction of the flesh so that his spirit might be saved (1 Cor. 5:5). This man was to be put out of the church (1 Cor. 5:2) and into the realm of the kingdom of darkness, the same strategy God was pursuing in His cleansing of the Thyatiran church by the removal of sin from its midst. Christians do suffer and even die because of disobedience, and others who profess to be Christians turn out in the end not to be so (on which see Matt. 7:20-23; 13:19-22). It would appear likely that Jezebel was of the later category, in light of her OT counterpart also called "Jezebel," who clearly was not a true believer. Jezebel's association with **the deep things of Satan** in the next verse enhances this identification of Jezebel. Finally, Jezebel's identity with the Babylonian harlot in ch. 17 contributes to viewing her as an unbelieving figure, despite appearing as a Christian teacher who is accepted as such by the church's leaders.

God will not compromise or tolerate such sinful teaching — and neither should we. The clause **He who searches the minds and hearts** explains the literal meaning of the prior picture of his **eyes like a flame of fire** (v. 18): Christ's knowledge pierces to the core of our beings and is the basis for the judgment or reward which He renders, further indication of His divine nature and functions: **I will give to each one of you according to your deeds.** Some in the church will at the end be found to be authentic followers of Christ and others pseudo-followers. Jer. 17:10 is uppermost in mind, since both the above expressions of **searching the minds and hearts** and **giving to each one of you according to your deeds** appear together only in that text. Furthermore, the statement in Jeremiah is especially suitable because it refers to God's judgment of those within the Israelite community who practice idolatry out of economic motives (cf. Jer. 17:3, 11; also 11:10-17, 20). As in Jeremiah, the false teachers who promote involvement in idolatry may be able to hide their evil motives from human eyes, but not from God's searching vision. They will be found not to be true believing Israelites.

24 But **the rest who are in Thyatira** have not known the **deep things of Satan** and have not been led astray by the false teachers. The latter is possibly Christ's description of what Jezebel and her followers may have called the "deep things of God." This expression implies the erroneous view that it was possible for Christians to participate worshipfully to some degree in idolatrous situations and thus to have experience with the demonic-satanic realm, and yet not be harmed spiritually by such participation. Jezebel's "revelation" was similar to that of the Israelites who created the golden calf (Exod. 32:1-6) or that of the Corinthians who frequented the idol temples (1 Cor. 10:14-24). Possibly the false teachers were misapplying Paul's statement in 1 Cor. 8:4 by saying that if, indeed, an idol has no real existence in the world, then participation at a feast honoring an idol could not harm one spiritually. This teaching may also have emphasized the spiritual dimension to such a degree that the physical world was considered unimportant, so that one's presence in an idolatrous temple or at an idol's

feast table had no effect on one's faith. Christians must always beware of those who lay claim to new revelations or deeper truths that have never before been discerned or widely practiced in the body of Christ.

Christ emphasizes to those who had not been persuaded by this line of thinking that their only real concern should be to continue holding fast their non-compromising stand until He comes (this is the importance of **I cast no other burden on you** at the end of v. 24). For discussion of whether the "coming" is a reference to the final parousia or a conditional, temporal coming see above on 1:7; 2:5. Christ is placing on them no other burden than that placed on Gentiles in general by the apostolic decree of Acts 15:28.

25-27 Despite the false teaching and in the face of it, those who remain faithful are commanded by Christ to **hold fast** to what they have **until I come**. Christ promises to those who "overcome" compromise and who discipline the compromising Jezebel party that they will reign with Him in His kingdom. Their perseverance until the end is the condition which must be met in order for them to receive the promise. He says that, if they so persevere, He will grant them a share in the messianic kingdom prophesied in Psalm 2, over which He has already received authority to rule: they will receive **authority as I [Christ] also have received authority**, and will rule **over the nations**. Here He quotes Ps. 2:8-9, which is significant because v. 7 of that Psalm refers to Christ as God's Son, the very phrase with which He introduced Himself to the Thyatiran church in v. 18.

28-29 Those who hear what the Spirit is saying will also receive the **morning star**. This is a reference to Christ Himself, who reveals Himself as the "bright morning star" in 22:16, and who is spoken of prophetically as a star and scepter (or rod) in Num. 24:17, and is said to break His enemies with a rod or scepter in Ps. 2:9 (the Psalm just quoted in v. 27), the latter of which develops the former passage. Therefore, the **morning star** is a symbol associated with the messianic reign which has commenced with Christ's resurrection. The application of this emblem to believers indicates that they will participate in this reign if they overcome. The fact that Roman emperors claimed to be descended from Venus, whom they considered the morning star, may suggest that here Christ reveals Himself as the true ruler of the world, over against all human pretenders — even those worshiped in cities like Thyatira.

It is significant to note that Christ's promises in vv. 26-28 are given to those who have begun to overcome *before* inheriting the eternal reward. Their overcoming occurs in this life, not the next. Likewise, in 12:11 believers are said to have overcome the devil because of their willingness to stand for Christ even if it meant death. Paul makes the same point in Rom. 8:37 when he says that we overcome in the midst of the trials he has listed in v. 35. This overcoming of the believer is modeled on that of Christ, who overcame by maintaining faithfulness to God throughout His life until His eventual death on the cross (John 16:33; see Rev. 5:5-6). The vision John sees of the overcoming Christ pictures Him as a Lamb that has been slain (5:5-6), whereas Paul pictures overcoming believers as sheep to be slaughtered (Rom. 8:36-37). All the churches are faced with the temptation to compromise, and some are succumbing to this temptation (Pergamum, Thyatira, Sardis, and Laodicea). Therefore, the exhortation to overcome is an encouragement either to continue standing strong against compromise or to stop compromising. In this regard, "overcome" (Greek *nikaō*) is probably an ironic play on words with "Nicolaitans."

The beast is said to overcome the believers by causing them to suffer (11:7; 13:7), but believers in turn overcome the beast by remaining faithful even while suffering (5:5-6; 12:11; 15:2). Those who overcome are not just those who die for their faith, for the promise is made to all the believers in, for instance, Smyrna, even though only some of them will suffer to the point of being imprisoned, let alone dying (2:10-11). In 2:26, overcoming is defined by the parallel phrase "keeps my deeds," which shows that overcoming spans the whole course of Christian obedience and faithfulness up to and including death. Christians overcome by their faithful living, not just their dying, and in particular, by their willingness to withstand the temptation to engage in compromise or idolatry of any sort. They refuse to put anything else ahead of the cause of Christ. All the promises made to overcomers in the letters are described in the final section of the book which speaks of the eternal kingdom — believers are protected from judgment (2:10; 3:5; 21:1-8), gain an inheritance in God's city (3:12; 21:7, 27), share in Christ's reign (2:26-28; 3:21; 22:5), and gain eternal life (2:7; 3:5; 21:27; 22:1-5).

Suggestions for Reflection on 2:18-29

On Jezebel's threat to the church. The church at Thyatira is initially commended for its faith, service, and perseverance, yet all this is in danger of being negated by the presence of a false teacher described as Jezebel. How can one person so affect the health of a church? Is it possible for Satan to send emissaries into churches to destroy them? Where were the elders of the church when this threat arose? Were they perhaps already tempted to compromise and so susceptible to Jezebel's message? Or were they negligent in exercising their governmental responsibilities? What can church leaders do to ensure their flocks are guarded against such attacks?

On the causes of compromise. At Thyatira compromise arose out of pressure to conform to idolatrous practices in the community involving perhaps immoral conduct and likely participation in observances in idol temples. Revelation teaches (see the discussion in the Introduction of the link between the letters and the visions) that the Jezebel at Thyatira will reappear throughout the church age in different forms. What practices or social norms exist in our culture that place churches under pressure to conform and compromise? Have you observed specific instances of compromise in your church or fellowship of churches? Are there false teachers today who lead churches astray under the guise of a need to make the gospel more palatable to the world or to help Christians get along better in dealing with the world in their own situations (e.g., in workplaces)?

On the results of compromise. Like the Thyatirans, we compromise because it seems to be the easiest route for us to acceptance by the wider community. Like them also, perhaps, we do not realize the dire consequences of our actions. At Thyatira, Christ is pictured as One who comes in judgment, and at least some of those involved in this deception will be judged temporally and at the final judgment. How do we reconcile this picture of Christ with what we know of His infinite grace and mercy? Have we lost sight of the holiness of God because of a preoccupation with the mercy of God? Do we focus on God's mercy because we are involved in compromise and would prefer to believe He will tolerate our behavior? Is it possible that Christ could come in such judgment of pseudo-believers to local churches today?

On overcoming. What is the significance of the fact that believers are pictured as overcoming in this life? And what does it mean that so often in Revelation this overcoming is expressed in suffering and even death? This makes the message of Revelation especially applicable and comforting in nations where Christians are persecuted, for in their faithful witness and suffering they are pictured as truly following in the footsteps of Christ. But how are those who do not live under threat of persecution to apply these truths to their own lives? How can we express overcoming through suffering? And how are we to understand teachings that appear to present believers unconditional offers of material blessing in this life for their faithfulness? Sometimes where persecution is not present there is the temptation to compromise in some way (sexually, theologically, financially, etc.), and not to give in to compromise is to "overcome."

Christ condemns the church in Sardis for its lack of witness and its compromise and exhorts it to overcome this in order to inherit the blessings of salvation (3:1-6)

1 And to the angel of the church in Sardis write: "He who has the seven Spirits
of God, and the seven stars, says this: 'I know your deeds, that you have a name
that you are alive, but you are dead. 2 Wake up, and strengthen the things that
remain, which were about to die, for I have not found your deeds completed in
the sight of My God. 3 Remember therefore what you have received and heard;
and keep it, and repent. If therefore you will not wake up, I will come like a thief,
and you will not know at what hour I will come upon you. 4 But you have a few
people in Sardis who have not soiled their garments; and they will walk with Me
in white; for they are worthy. 5 He who overcomes shall thus be clothed in white
garments; and I will not erase his name from the book of life, and I will confess
his name before My Father, and before His angels. 6 He who has an ear, let him
hear what the Spirit says to the churches.'"

1 Christ's introduction to the church at Sardis is almost identical to that in the letter to the church at Ephesus (2:1), and there are similarities between the two churches. Like the Ephesians, the Sardians have lost the power of their outward witness to Christ. Sardis was a city which had known fame in the past but whose glory had faded, and Christ now warns the church that they are in a similar predicament. The attitude of the city had infected the church. They retained a reputation (literally **name**) for being spiritually alive, but in fact were spiritually nearly **dead**.

2 In response to their almost dead condition, they are to **wake up** and **strengthen the things that remain** and which are **about to die.** The readers had become lethargic about the radical demands of their faith in the midst of a pagan culture. The mention of **things that remain** implies that the readers had begun a life of faithful service, but something had happened which impeded further progress. What is in question is their **name.** This is significant in light of the use of the word "name" in 2:17. Do they truly bear the name of Christ? This is what is now in doubt. Are they more like those who say they are (true) Jews but are not, who are alluded to in 2:9? There certainly had been life here, but the genuine **deeds** of the past (referring to a faithful witness to Christ; see on 2:2) had gone. Like the Ephesians (2:5), they are called to return to their former deeds. However, the fact that Christ appears to them (as to the Ephesians) holding the **seven stars**, representing angelic support, and also the **seven spirits**, representing the power of the Holy Spirit (see 1:4), means that He has supernatural strength available to enable them to have a renewed obedience. In 3:1, therefore, there is more emphasis on the supernatural source empowering the church's witness than in 2:1. This is particularly appropriate since the church of Sardis is the only one among the seven that is so lethargic in fulfilling their Christian role that they are on the verge of being considered spiritually dead. Consequently, in order to carry out their call from the risen Lord to proclaim the gospel they need the Spirit's life-giving power, which raised Jesus from the dead and will revive them from their spiritual torpor. Their spiritual lethargy likely included not actively witnessing to their faith before the unbelieving culture, which we argued was part of the problem in Ephesus, where likewise Christ presents Himself in connection with the seven lampstands. This was a form of compromise which we can only surmise was partially due to the pressures of pagan society already alluded to in the messages to Smyrna, Pergamum, and Thyatira. That is, the Sardian Christians feared that if they maintained too high a Christian profile in the city, they would encounter persecution of various sorts, perhaps not too different from that also mentioned in the preceding letters.

3 Because their deeds have not been found complete, they must **remember** what they **have received and heard; and keep it, and repent**. If they **will not wake up**, Jesus says, **I will come like a thief**, not in support but in judgment, where His "coming," because it is expressed in conditional terms, refers not to His final return but to a historical judgment upon the local church. Nevertheless, this coming is connected to the final one, in that both are part of the same inaugurated end-time process. The distinction between the two lies in the fact that the final coming is the conclusion of the process begun at the resurrection, and possibly even in Christ's earthly ministry. The repeated reference to the "coming" in the letters is ambiguous with respect to being able to discern the precise point along the continuum of the eschatological process in mind. This verse may well be an example of such an ambiguity. The reason for the ambiguity may be intentional in order to heighten the element of imminence so that the readers would sense the urgency to solve their problem.

The parallel to the Ephesian church continues, for the pattern is the same as in 2:5: they are to remember their former spiritual vitality and to repent. If they do not, Christ will come in judgment. Only a few of the Sardian Christians had not "soiled their garments" (v. 4), a phrase which refers to some kind of compromise with pagan or idolatrous practices. The word "soiled" occurs also in 14:4, where it refers to those "not defiled with women," which, in context (see 14:8 on the concept of idolatrous fornication with Babylon) refers not so much to literal sexual immorality (though that might be involved) as to involvement with pagan or idolatrous activity. The likelihood is that the Christians in Sardis had for the most part fallen into a stupor of compromise and fear of the consequences of a bold witness for Christ.

4 The **few** (literally, the "few names") who have been faithful, however, **will walk with Me in white; for they are worthy**. They are worthy because they **have not soiled their garments**, and these factors together become the basis for the future reward of walking with Christ in unsoiled clothes. That this concerns a reward for perseverance through suffering is further evident from 7:14, which refers to "the ones coming out of the great tribulation" and to those who "have washed their robes" and "made them white in the blood of the Lamb." That this is the significance of the overcomers receiving white garments is also evident from 6:9-11, where "those who had been slain because of the word of God and because of the testimony which they had maintained" were given a "white robe." Again the role of witness is echoed in the reward of the **white** garments.

5-6 These faithful saints are the ones who have overcome through a life of faithful witness, and (the promise is repeated) they will be dressed in white: **He who overcomes shall thus be clothed in white garments**. The repetition of the promise underlines its significance since here, as elsewhere in Revelation, white robes stand for a purity which, through the work of the One clothed in white, will result in an eternal reward in God's kingdom (see 3:18; 6:11; 7:13-14; 19:8). The reward probably begins in this life, because (i) v. 4 pictures the faithful already wearing pure garments; (ii) Christ exhorts the saints in 3:18 to buy white garments; and (iii) 16:15 refers to those who keep their garments in order not to be naked. This promise of white garments is only the first of three promises made to the faithful believer in v. 5.

The second promise is that Christ **will not erase** the faithful saint's **name from the book of life**. The **book of life** appears five other times in Revelation (13:8; 17:8; 20:12, 15; 21:27), and contains the names of believers written in it before the foundation of the world. This is in contrast to the "books" that record the sins of unbelievers, on the basis of which they will be judged (20:12-13). Note the "book" in Dan. 12:1 recording the names of the saved, and the "books" mentioned in Dan. 7:9-10 in the context of heavenly judgment. The promise **I will not erase his name** contains no inference that the names of the genuinely saved might for some reason be erased, but is rather an assurance that they will not. In both 13:8 and 17:8, the point is that the names have been in the book of life since the foundation of the world and thus cannot be erased, whereas those about to perish have not had their names thus written. Unbelievers are never associated with the book of life, but only with the books of judgment. It is significant that the word "name" or "names" appears four times in this letter. The point is that Christ has come to inspect the reality of each person's "name" or Christian identity, recalling that the OT notion of "name" represented the character of a person. Are they true believers, or are they not? In the early days of the church, the church corporately had a good name (its identity with Christ was strong), but over the years it had become very mixed, composed of true believers and those professing faith but not truly saved. The whole church, Christ warns, is now in danger of destruction.

The third promise made by Christ to the believer in v. 5 is that **I will confess his name before My Father, and before His angels**. The point is that those who confess Christ's name in spite of possible persecution will in turn have their names confessed by Christ. There is no doubt that Jesus is here repeating His declaration that those who confess Him (i.e., witness to him openly), He will confess before the Father (Matt. 10:32) and before the angels (Luke 12:8). The context of the Gospel saying is that of persecution ("Do not fear those who kill the body," Matt. 10:28 and Luke 12:4), the same situation facing the believers at Sardis. V. 5 again shows that the promise to those who overcome includes all believers, not just those martyred, for surely the names of all believers are written in the book of life.

The exhortation to have ears and to hear the Spirit's message expresses Christ's aim is to save this church from the brink of death. His words concerning garments and coming like a thief in vv. 3-4 are echoed in the bowl visions (16:15), which again shows the interrelationship of the letters and visions. The trials of the bowl visions are happening, in measure at least, to the church in Sardis even as it receives its letter, and the shocking imagery of the visions is meant to jolt them into realizing that what is being addressed to them in the letter is actually unfolding before their eyes (could they only but realize it), as the dragon, the beast, and the false prophet have already launched their attack — and sadly, are having some success. This verse shows that the promise to the overcomer cannot be limited to martyrs but includes all Christians, since it would be unthinkable that the names of all true believers would not be found in **the book of life**.

Suggestions for Reflection on 3:1-6

On how and why a church dies. These verses present a scenario in which a church is facing imminent death. How can a once-vital church (which Sardis was) find itself in such a place? As in Thyatira and Pergamum, it seems that compromise with the surrounding pagan culture (especially with idolatry) was at the heart of the problem. Yet Christ, because He loves His church and has so much invested in it, still comes with the promise of supernatural help to avert the looming disaster. Are we vigilant for early-warning signs that our church is losing its life? What are such signs? How might Christ speak to us in similar warning, and are we listening for His voice? And finally, how do we determine whether a church has actually died, even though some of its outward form may remain? Is it possible for God to restore it to life, or should any remaining believers move on to a church where Christ is still honored?

On the significance of our "name." The word "name" runs like a thread throughout this passage. The church had a name for being alive but was dead; there are a few "names" who were faithful; Christ will not erase the true believer's name from the book of life. If "name" represents our identity in Christ and our Christlike character (we are those who carry His "name"), what does this mean in terms of the nature of Christian commitment? Is the "name" of Christ — expressing at the deepest level who Christ truly is — reflected in who we are as men and women who profess to follow Him? Are we in danger of becoming dead like the Sardians if we begin to lose the reality of what bearing the "name" of Christ means?

Christ commends the church in Philadelphia for its persevering witness, in which He will empower its members further, and encourages them to persevere so as to inherit end-time fellowship and identification with Him (3:7-13)

7 And to the angel of the church in Philadelphia write: "He who is holy, who is
true, who has the key of David, who opens and no one will shut, and who shuts
and no one opens, says this: 8 'I know your deeds. Behold, I have put before you
an open door which no one can shut, because you have a little power, and have

kept My word, and have not denied My name. [9] Behold, I will cause those of the synagogue of Satan, who say that they are Jews, and are not, but lie – behold, I will make them to come and bow down at your feet, and to know that I have loved you. [10] Because you have kept the word of My perseverance, I also will keep you from the hour of testing, that hour which is about to come upon the whole world, to test those who dwell upon the earth. [11] I am coming quickly; hold fast what you have, in order that no one may take your crown. [12] He who overcomes, I will make him a pillar in the temple of My God, and he will not go out from it anymore; and I will write upon him the name of My God, and the name of the city of My God, the new Jerusalem, which comes down out of heaven from My God, and My new name. [13] He who has an ear, let him hear what the Spirit says to the churches.'"

7 The phrase **He who is holy, who is true** is a divine attribute elsewhere in Revelation (so 6:10), so that the use of it here suggests Jesus' deity. In fact, "holy" is used of Yahweh almost exclusively in Isaiah as part of the title "the Holy One of Israel" (ca. 20×). This background is probably present here in anticipation of the Isa. 22:22 quotation and of the Isaiah allusions in 3:9, where Jesus assumes the role of Yahweh and His followers represent the true Israel (see on 3:9; "the Holy One of God" is also a messianic title in contexts of fulfillment: Mark 1:24; Luke 4:34; John 6:69). The idea of **true** carries connotations of Jesus being the true Messiah, who has begun to fulfill messianic prophecy (see further on 3:14), though He is rejected by the Jews as a false messianic pretender.

Christ's self-introduction here is also based on His possession of the keys in 1:18, and the significance of this will shortly become evident. Here there is a slightly different nuance in that the keys in 1:18 were those of death and hell, whereas here Christ **has the key of David**. The reference is to Isa. 22:22, where Eliakim holds the key of David; where he opens no one shuts, and where he shuts no one opens. The picture in 1:18 is about to be amplified. There Christ's authority is over salvation and judgment, whereas here He also determines who will enter the kingdom. Eliakim is understood as a type of Christ, and Isaiah's declarations concerning him take on a prophetic form, as is evident from the following details about Eliakim, compared with the famous messianic prophecy of Isaiah 9:

The key (the government of the house of Judah) is set on Eliakim's shoulder (Isa. 22:22); compare "The government will rest upon His shoulders" (9:6).

Eliakim will become a father to those in Jerusalem and Judah (22:21); compare "His name will be called . . . 'Eternal Father' " (9:6).
Eliakim will become a throne of glory to his father's house (22:23); compare "There will be no end to the increase of His government . . . on the throne of David" (9:7).
Eliakim was appointed to his royal position by God (22:21), as would be the coming Messiah (9:6-7).

The point of this is that, whereas once Eliakim ruled over Israel, now Christ (of whom Eliakim is a prophetic type) rules over the church, the true Israel. Christ alone determines who will and will not enter God's kingdom.

8-9 Christ, who is "the faithful and true Witness" (see 3:14) and sovereign over the realms of life and death, exercises His power in this regard on behalf of the Philadelphian church: **Behold, I have put before you an open door which no one can shut**. This has particular significance for the Philadelphians, who were being persecuted by the local Jewish community (described as the **synagogue of Satan**), who claimed that they represented a part of true Israel. But this claim was a **lie**. Even latter Rabbinic authorities condemned the Jewish community in Philadelphia for its compromise with the pagan culture. Their wealth gave them added weight with which to attack the Christians. Christ reassures these believers that He has the key which alone provides entry into God's kingdom, described in v. 7 as David's house ("the key of the house of David," Isa. 22:22), or in v. 12 as God's temple or city. Christ gives them power to remain in His kingdom, in spite of their being persecuted, and in spite of the fact they have little strength in themselves (**a little power**). More than this, He has put before them **an open door**. The phrase **open door** in the NT refers to the opportunity to preach the gospel and witness for Christ (Acts 14:27; 1 Cor. 16:9: "wide door"; 2 Cor. 2:12; Col. 4:3). Christ understands they have little strength, probably owing to lack of numbers, yet He says of them that they have **kept My word** and **not denied My name**. That they **had not denied My** (Christ's) **name** underscores the focus on witnessing in this letter. But now an amazing thing is about to happen. These Jews — called a **synagogue of Satan** because they do not recognize Christ as the true Messiah or the church as His true people, the new Israel — are about to turn to Christ. This will be a sovereign visitation of God, a result of Christ **opening the door** of witness for the Philadelphians, who will **make** the unbelieving Jews come and **bow down at your feet**. This refers not to humiliation but to repentance. The allusion is to Isa. 45:14; 49:23; and 60:14, where Isaiah prophesies that the Gentiles will come and bow down before Israel in the last days and that this will represent a genuine turning to and worship of the true God (made clear by the whole context in Isa. 60:1-14).

Note the "reverse" form of the prophetic fulfillment. The "Gentiles" of Isaiah, referring to unbelievers, are now considered to be the ethnic unbelieving Jews, whereas Isaiah's "Israel," referring to God's faithful covenant people, is now the church. Whereas it was God who was said to bring all this about, now it is revealed that it is Christ — another indication of His divinity. The Jews will come to worship Christ — to **bow down** is the word for "worship." And this worship is to be voluntary, for nowhere in Revelation is worship anything other than a voluntary activity (whether worship of God [ten times] or of the beast or idols [eleven times]). Elsewhere in the NT, these and other OT prophecies allude to the nations turning to the Messiah, but this does not exclude Christ here from using the passage to show how unbelieving Israel can itself prophetically fulfill the role of a pagan nation that finally comes to repentance.

Likewise, the prophecy that God will demonstrate His love for persecuted Israel before the nations is also fulfilled in an apparent reverse manner: **I will make them . . . to know that I have loved you** is applied to the church instead of to ethnic Israel, as apparently in Isa. 43:4 (and the LXX of Isa. 41:8; 44:2; 60:10; 63:9; cf. 48:14). Therefore, Isaiah's prophecies that the end-time salvation of Israel would spark off the salvation of the Gentiles has been fulfilled in an ironic manner. This is likely true even if a remnant of Jewish Christians composed a part of the Philadelphian church, since the majority would have been Gentile. And, while the church assumes the role of Israel in these fulfilled prophecies, Christ performs the role that Isaiah foretold of Yahweh. Christ is the One causing the unbelieving Jewish community to recognize that the Gentile church composes His beloved people. These Isaiah prophecies are to be fulfilled imminently in the Philadelphia church's own experience, though not exclusively so, since the letter is also addressed to all the churches which exist in the first century and until the final coming of Christ. Therefore Jesus, who holds sway over the power of salvation and judgment, exerts this power through His followers (so Matt. 16:18).

10 Christ promises that His power, which made it possible for the church to become His people (vv. 7-8a) and to maintain their status as His people (vv. 8b-9), will continue to protect them spiritually from the tribulation which is about to come. Because of their faithfulness in trial, particularly in witnessing to Christ, Christ will keep the Philadelphians **from**

the hour of testing, that hour which is about to come upon the whole world. The phrase **the whole world** is not necessarily to be taken in a literal sense, but in the NT usually has a more localized sense. For instance, the same phrase refers in Luke 2:1 only to Palestine and in Acts 11:28 to a somewhat wider region (see also Acts 17:6; 19:27; 24:5, though in Rev. 12:9 and 16:14 it has a more universal sense). The **testing** could, therefore, refer to a localized trial either in Asia Minor or more generally in the Roman Empire, which would make sense of the fact the Philadelphians themselves would experience it and be kept through it. If the phrase **the whole world** is taken literally, the reference would be to the final period of testing or trial leading up to and including the Lord's return (depicted in 11:7-13 and 20:8-10), and the meaning would have to involve the Philadelphian Christians' salvation in the refining fire of the final judgment, which is possible but perhaps less natural (though in support of a notion of final judgment is the observation that the vast majority of the uses of **hour** in Revelation [11:13; 14:7, 15; 18:10, 17, 19] refer to the time of the last judgment).

Note that Christ is speaking here primarily of spiritual rather than physical protection, for nowhere in Revelation are believers promised immunity from physical suffering — indeed, as the letters already studied make clear, they are to expect it. Paul also frequently makes the same point (Rom. 8:35-39; 2 Cor. 4:16–5:10; Phil. 3:10; Col. 1:24, etc.). The words spoken by Christ here (that He will *keep* them *from* testing) are the same words He used in John 17:15, the only other place in the NT where the phrase *(tereō ek)* occurs. There Jesus prayed, "I do not ask Thee to take them out of the world, but to *keep* them *from* the evil one." In John 16:33, Jesus promises believers peace in the midst of certain tribulation. According to Jesus' words, therefore, believers will endure physical suffering, but will be kept spiritually safe in the midst of it. Therefore, this verse does not speak of a physical rapture before the beginning of a coming "Great Tribulation." Rather, it refers to Christ's protection through the end-time tribulation, which had already started in the first century and would become worse as the final end neared. That John has in mind a spiritual protection of Christians as they *go through tribulation* is evident also from the likely allusion in v. 10 to Dan. 12:1, 10 (LXX), where "that hour" is immediately described as "that day of tribulation" when "many are *tested* and sanctified and sinners sin." This suggests that the "testing" of Rev. 3:10 has the double effect of purifying and strengthening believers but of being at the same time a divine punishment. This assessment is confirmed from 7:14, where saints are depicted as coming "out of the great tribulation" and wearing white robes, in allusion respectively to Dan. 12:1 and 12:10. That the end-time tribulation has begun during the church age is also apparent because Jezebel and her followers will suffer "great tribulation" (2:22, the same phrase as in 7:14, except for the omission of the definite article), even in the first century, if they do not repent.

The purpose of God's action is to **test those who dwell upon the earth**. The purpose of this testing is a judgment on unbelievers, for the phrase **those who dwell on the earth** (or **earth-dwellers**) is a technical term which in Revelation refers exclusively to the unsaved, especially idol worshipers (6:10; 8:13; 11:10; 13:8, 12, 14; 14:6; 17:2, 8). Believers, however, though remaining in the world and exposed to its physical dangers, will be kept from the spiritual harm of testing, that is, from the negative effects of this judgment, in that they will be kept spiritually safe and even strengthened in their faith, while unbelievers will be further hardened against God by the very same trials. The truth of this interpretation will become clear as we see the effects of the various judgments of God as the visions unfold, hardening unbelievers while keeping believers spiritually safe by refining their faith.

11 If then our understanding is correct, it makes sense also of the next verse. Here Christ promises the Philadelphians that He is **coming quickly** and that they are to **hold fast to** what they have — in other words, they are to persevere in the midst of trial. His **coming quickly** does not likely refer to His final return, as almost two thousand years have passed since the promise was given. It must instead refer to the fact He will shortly come, by the power of the Spirit, to aid the Philadelphians in the trial that is about to come upon them (v. 10). The promise of that verse is not that they will escape this tribulation, but that Christ will strengthen them so that they will be kept spiritually safe through it. Christ's promise here thus becomes relevant for believers of any age going through trial — Christ will always come and strengthen them in it.

12 The four promises Christ now gives to the one who overcomes are really (as in 2:17) four aspects of the one promise. Writing upon him **the name of my God, the name of the city of My God**, and **My new name** are all expressions of eternal union with God and fellowship with His presence. Note that the name of the city of God in Ezek. 48:35 is "the Lord is there." It is the place of the presence of God and the location of His temple, which brings us to the fourth element in the promise, that Christ will make the overcomer **a pillar in the temple of My God**. In v. 7, Jesus has unlocked the doors of the kingdom to the Philadelphians, and here He holds before them the culmination of this promise — opening the door of **the temple** and entering into His temple forever. It is no accident that God's eternal temple is mentioned in the same letter as the synagogue of Satan in v. 9. The religious system — perhaps in our day even institutional churches — will always attack genuine believers who draw their strength from fellowship with Christ, not identification with an earthly system about to be unmasked in the visions in all its horrible reality as the servant of the beast and the dragon.

This line of thought in which Jesus' followers persevere through tribulation and are then rewarded with the presence of God and Christ in the temple is also found developed in 7:14-17. In fact, the believer's permanent identification with the temple in v. 12 is the consummation of the process which began with Christ unlocking the doors of the invisible sanctuary of salvation to them, as expressed in vv. 7b-8a: ". . . I have put before you an open door which no one can shut" (note the Aramaic Bible's interpretative paraphrase of Isa. 22:22: "I will place the key of the *sanctuary* and the authority of the house of David in his hand . . ."). This true sanctuary is placed in clear contrast with the false synagogue of the Jews, who now give ultimate allegiance to Satan. This linking of present tribulation and future reward is borne out further by noticing that the closest parallels to vv. 8 and 12 are found in ch. 21 (21:25 and 21:2, 10 respectively). Christ begins to open the doors of the heavenly Jerusalem for the faithful here on earth, which no one can shut (3:8), and this is consummated when His people enter through the gates of the new Jerusalem, which "shall never be closed" (21:25). The promise of v. 12 is fulfilled in the saints' participation in the new Jerusalem coming down from heaven (21:2, 10).

13 The saints are given the concluding exhortation **hear what the Spirit says** because they need spiritual discernment in the midst of the affliction which they are about to endure in order not to **deny** Christ's **name** (cf. 3:8b; cf. v. 10a) and thus inherit the final reward. If they are not heavenly-minded and focusing on their final reward, they will be tempted to conform themselves to earthly circumstances around them, which includes compromising their faith because of persecution.

Suggestions for Reflection on 3:7-13

On Israel and the church. These verses use passages from Isaiah to show that the church is the continuation of the true Israel in God's covenant purposes. Eliakim, the de facto ruler of Israel, becomes a type of Christ. The pagan Gentiles of Isaiah now depict the unbelieving Israel of John's day. And the local Jewish community in Philadelphia is depicted as a synagogue of Satan. Yet in the midst of this, God is about to do a saving work among the Jewish people there, with the result that they will acknowledge the church as the "true" synagogue. Examine these verses in light of Rom. 9:6, 24-26 and Gal. 3:16, 29: Do the Romans, Galatians, and Revelation 3 passages shed light on each other's meaning? As Revelation progresses, keep an eye out for how the theme of the church as fulfilling the promises of Israel is further developed.

On being kept safe from testing. These verses speak of testing as a form of God's judgment on the lost. This must refer to events which, however, necessarily affect believers and unbelievers alike: economic trials, warfare, climatic catastrophes, and so on. How then can it be said that God keeps believers safe from such events? Does this have something to do with having our treasure in heaven where no thief can break in and steal (Matt. 6:19)? Could it be said that believers are kept safe even if they die in such a calamitous time? Have you noticed a difference in how believers and unbelievers respond to the same difficult events such as natural disasters? How might this reveal the judgment of God on the one hand and, on the other, the refining work of God with respect to believers?

On no believer or church being insignificant to God. Like many churches today, the Christian community at Philadelphia was small. In its own eyes, as well as the eyes of others, it may have seemed insignificant, and perhaps some in it, facing persecution, wondered whether God had even forgotten them. Yet this church receives special commendation and promises from God. Does our Christian culture place too much significance on size? The church at Laodicea, which stood under threat of God's judgment, was apparently thriving. How can the church at Philadelphia be an encouragement to us when, either as individuals or as a church community, we feel insignificant or even forgotten by God?

Christ condemns the church in Laodicea for its ineffective witness and deplorable spiritual condition and exhorts its members to persevere by becoming faithful witnesses and renewing their fellowship with Him so as to reign with Him (3:14-22)

14 And to the angel of the church in Laodicea write: "The Amen, the faithful and true Witness, the Beginning of the creation of God, says this: 15 'I know your

deeds, that you are neither cold nor hot; I would that you were cold or hot. [16] So because you are lukewarm, and neither hot nor cold, I will spit you out of My mouth. [17] Because you say, "I am rich, and have become wealthy, and have need of nothing," and you do not know that you are wretched and miserable and poor and blind and naked, [18] I advise you to buy from Me gold refined by fire, that you may become rich, and white garments, that you may clothe yourself, and that the shame of your nakedness may not be revealed; and eyesalve to anoint your eyes, that you may see. [19] Those whom I love, I reprove and discipline; be zealous therefore, and repent. [20] Behold, I stand at the door and knock; if anyone hears My voice and opens the door, I will come in to him, and will dine with him, and he with Me. [21] He who overcomes, I will grant to him to sit down with Me on My throne, as I also overcame and sat down with My Father on His throne. [22] He who has an ear, let him hear what the Spirit says to the churches.'"

14 What does Christ mean by referring to himself as **the Beginning of the creation of God**? How does this self-ascription relate to the situation in Laodicea? How can Christ encourage the Laodiceans to be spiritually cold? What does it mean to buy from Christ gold, white garments, and eye salve?

Christ's self-introduction here as the **faithful and true Witness** and **Beginning of the creation of God** goes back to John's description of Christ in 1:5 as the faithful witness and firstborn of the dead and to the declaration of Christ in the vision that He was dead and is now alive forever (1:18). Christ as the beginning of God's creation refers here not to the events surrounding the world's creation and foundation but to the resurrection, the new creation expected in the latter days, in the same way as Paul describes Christ as "the beginning, the first-born from the dead" in Col. 1:18. Jesus is also described as the **Amen**, which is a Hebrew equivalent of **faithful and true**. The only other place in the Bible where "Amen" is used as a name is Isa. 65:16, "He who is blessed in the earth shall be blessed by the God of Amen" (translated as "God of truth" in NASB, NIV). And what is the blessing of this God of Amen? It is nothing other than the creation of a new heavens and a new earth (Isa. 65:17) — a new creation, of which Christ in His resurrection is the **Beginning.** Christ identifies Himself to the Laodiceans as the **Amen, the faithful and true Witness**, precisely because He is the beginning fulfillment of Isaiah's new creation prophecy (Isa. 65:16-17), and this quality of faithful witness is so woefully lacking in them. Not only that, they need His resurrection power as the firstborn of the new creation, for they are spiritually dead and need enlivening, which will no doubt lead to effective witness in the pagan culture. Even at

Sardis, a faithful remnant remained in a mostly dead church, but no such remnant is identified here, and there is no commendation of any sort for the Laodicean church.

15-16 The Laodiceans are **neither cold nor not**, but **lukewarm**. If some consider **hot** to be good, **lukewarm** to be mediocre and **cold** to be bad, why would Christ say He would prefer them **cold** to **lukewarm**? The answer reveals a different perspective on these levels of temperature. Laodicea had two neighbors, Hierapolis and Colossae. Hierapolis had hot waters which possessed medicinal effects, while Colossae had cold water, which was also thought to be healthy. Laodicea had no good water source, however, and had to pipe it in. By the time it arrived, it was lukewarm and dirty — fit only for spitting out. In fact, it was generally held to be true in the ancient world that cold and hot water or wine were beneficial for one's health, but not water which was lukewarm. Likewise, the Laodiceans' faith and witness did not have a healthy effect on the people who lived around them. We shall see that one of the main reasons for their ineffective faith was their compromise with idolatry. Christ now exposes the spiritual condition of the church to be no better than the city's water by asserting that **I will spit you out of my mouth**. If the Laodiceans will not identify faithfully with Christ in their culture, then neither will Christ identify them as faithful witnesses together with Him.

17 In contrast to Christ's assessment, the church of Laodicea considered itself to be in good condition because of its material prosperity. Revelation uses the words **rich** and **wealthy** to describe those who have prospered by association with the corrupt and ungodly world system (6:15; 13:16; 18:3, 15, 19), and the charge is that the Laodiceans have allied themselves with the local economic forces linked there (as in the other cities of Asia Minor) to idolatry and immorality. The Laodicean idolatry is pointed to by observing that not only are the words **rich** and **wealthy** in this verse applied elsewhere in the book to unbelieving merchants who have intercourse with idolatrous Babylon (so 18:3, 15, 19), but also overtly to those who make gains by involvement with idolatry (so 6:15, alluding to the idolaters of Isa. 2:10-21; and 13:16). It is a consistent theme of Scripture that wealth has to be handled carefully and stewarded to God's glory or it will consume its owner (Matt. 6:24; Luke 6:20-21, 25-26; 12:13-21; 16:1-15; Acts 5:1-10; 1 Cor. 4:8; 1 Tim. 6:5-10, 17-19; Jas. 2:1-9; 4:1-4; 5:1-6). Such an all-consuming pursuit of wealth leads to idolatry, as we will see is the case here. This is not an endorsement of poverty, for part of God's blessing on Israel was its prosperity. The question, however, is how we use what God has given us. A Christian's prosperity is measured by how much he gives rather than by how much he has. But the Laodiceans had fallen into the same trap the Israelites did, for the self-congratulatory words attributed to them here are quoted by Christ from Hosea's prophetic condemnation of the Israelites, "And Ephraim said, 'Surely I have become rich, I have found wealth for myself . . . they will find in me no iniquity' " (Hos. 12:8). Hosea exposes the fact that Israel has prospered through dishonesty (12:7) and engaged in idolatry (chs. 1–2), indeed assuming that it was the idols that brought this prosperity (2:5, 8). Hosea declares that God has in truth found them not rich but worthless (12:11).

The Laodiceans were likewise prospering, probably due to their participation in idolatrous and ungodly business practices, but Christ, like Hosea, exposes the truth. Whereas the Christians at Smyrna, though materially poor, were spiritually rich (2:9), the compromising Laodiceans are materially rich but spiritually bankrupt, especially due to their compromise with idolatrous economic institutions. They judged themselves to be in good condition, but Christ reveals the truth that they are **poor, blind, and naked** — probably ironic references respectively to Laodicea's well-known resources, in which they placed too much trust: its banking system, its school of ophthalmology, its famous eye salve, and its textile trade (representative of three areas of life in which the ancients placed too much trust: money, clothing, and health institutions, all of which were inextricably linked to idolatry).

18 The solution to their problems is now given. To combat their poverty they must **buy** from Christ **gold refined by fire** (a biblical expression for purity: cf. 3:4-5 and more generally 1 Pet. 1:7). To overcome their compromise with the world they must **buy . . . white garments** to cover their **nakedness** (on white as signifying purity see 3:4-5; 6:2; 19:8, especially by not becoming stained by idols). Uncovering **the shame of your nakedness** is language employed in God's accusation of Israel and other nations for participation in idolatry (so Isa. 47:3; Ezek. 16:36; 23:29; Nah. 3:5; probably also Isa. 20:4; cf. also Exod. 20:26). The prophetic idiom is repeated here also to highlight the idolatrous nature of Laodicea's sin. To combat their blindness (lack of spiritual discernment), they must buy **eyesalve**, especially so they are not deceived about the lethal danger that idol worship posed for their faith. Notice how in the initial vision Christ was attired with a golden girdle, His hair was white like wool, and His eyes were like flaming fire, which correspond strikingly to the three products mentioned in this verse. The **gold**, the **white garments**, and the **eyesalve**

all point to one thing — Christ. Their illness can be remedied only through a renewed relationship with Christ, by buying true spiritual resources from Him (cf. Isa. 55:1-3!). Only in Christ are true riches, clothing, and insight. Indeed, Jesus himself established the fount of all true wealth through His own faithful witness in the midst of the suffering of the cross. He is all the Laodiceans really need. Even if they lost all else, they would still have everything they really need, but without Him they have nothing.

19-20 In spite of all this, Christ responds to the Laodiceans' poor condition in a way that shows He has not given up on them. He **stands at the door** of their lives and knocks, inviting them to renew fellowship with Him. The tense of both verbs (**stand** and **knock**) points to a present, continuing action on the part of Christ. He is standing there reaching out to the Laodiceans, as He is always standing at the doors of the hearts of those believers who have become cold in their love and enmeshed in the pursuit of what this world has to offer. Christ's words here are probably based on the words spoken to the bride in Song of Solomon 5:2, "A voice! My beloved was knocking: 'Open to me . . .'" This is an invitation, not for the readers to be converted, but to renew themselves in a relationship with Christ which has already begun, as is apparent from v. 19 (**those whom I love, I reprove . . . be zealous . . . and repent**). The allusion to the Song of Solomon points to a focus on renewal of a relationship, since there the husband knocks on the door of the bedchamber to encourage his wife to continue to express her love to him and let him enter, but she at first hesitates to do so. Christ, the husband, is doing the same thing with His bride, the church. This is the cry of God's heart toward those whom He loves. He calls them to **dine with** Him, to return to the fellowship they knew in days gone by.

21-22 For those who do renew their zeal for Christ and return to Him, whatever they have lost in the scheme of this world will be more than compensated for by their share in rulership in the eternal kingdom. If they do not renew their zeal, of course, they may not experience the joy of that kingdom at all. The description of the church at Laodicea is probably uncomfortably close to the situation of the church in our own culture. We must adjust our priorities to place the kingdom first and be willing to give up what we cannot keep to gain what we cannot lose — our share in the kingdom of God. This reward of kingdom reign has actually already begun (cf. Rev. 1:5-6, 9).

The letter ends again with an exhortation to him **who has an ear** to **hear what the Spirit says** in order to discern Christ's message in this letter, so that the reward of reign with Christ will be consummated.

Suggestions for Reflection on 3:14-22

On prosperity as a sign of God's blessing. God promised the Israelites abundant material provision in place of the slavery and deprivation they had experienced in Egypt. Yet when God gave them that provision, it so often became a stumbling block and a snare that took them away from true worship. Why did they respond in this way to the gracious provision of God? Why did God "take the risk" of giving it to them? Would they have been better off remaining in relative poverty? In what sense can we say that prosperity is or could be a sign of God's blessing at all?

On Christians living in a wealthy society. Laodicea was a wealthy community, as reflected in its financial, manufacturing, and medical institutions. The materialism of the city had rubbed off on the church, with disastrous results. At least in the west, most Christians today live in relatively wealthy communities consumed by materialism. How do we resist the same thing happening to us as it did to the Laodiceans? What are the warning signs that we are heading for this kind of trouble? How do we respond to some who suggest we should endorse a very simple lifestyle, or perhaps even relative poverty? Think of this passage in light of Jesus' words, "How hard it is for those who are wealthy to enter the kingdom of God!" (Luke 18:24). Jesus was thinking of those who were very wealthy; how does this apply to living in a society in which we may not be considered wealthy but are relatively much wealthier than those in other nations?

On the pricelessness of fellowship with Christ. This passage pictures relationship with Christ as of infinitely greater value than all the material possessions the Laodiceans have. How do we value our relationship with Christ? Do we from time to time stop to take inventory of what we are placing value on in life? How does our use of time and money reflect our values? How do we practically express the value of our relationship with Christ? Here Christ is pictured as longing to enter into hearts that are insensitive to Him. How often have we turned Him away simply because we were preoccupied with other things? Though in this letter Christ "knocking on the door" refers to the door of the corporate church, it includes reference to individuals (cf. vv. 19-21). Have we even noticed that He is standing and knocking at the door of our hearts? What is the state of our prayer life? If we are not on speaking terms with the Lord, how is He to communicate with us what are the treasures He wants us to place greatest value on? Is it possible to slip into lukewarmness without even noticing it? And how can we apply all these lessons to the life of our local church to guard it against falling into a Laodicean stupor and eventual death? The Laodiceans' self-confidence about their wealth was really a self-sufficiency that arose from dependence on earthly security. In what ways do any of our earthly securities lead us to a self-sufficiency that excludes dependence on God? Does an excessive concern about the following things push God out of our lives: financial resources, clothing and the way we look, and health issues (whether that be over health problems or over trying to stay healthy and fit)? These were three areas on which the Laodiceans had too much reliance (recall their implied trust in gold, clothing, and health facilities). When self-sufficiency occurs, we do not see Christ as our security and we become spiritually anaesthetized and out of touch in our relationship with Christ. We judge ourselves spiritually healthy when we are really spiritually sick. We are content to feed on the putrid resources of the world, which we think are delicious, instead of feeding on the rich resources of Christ. And sometimes we do not come to Christ's Word, because it is a true lens evaluating us as we are and not as we think of ourselves. How can Christians overcome self-sufficiency and spiritual insensitivity? The same way the Laodiceans were to do it: by acknowledging their sin (repenting) and renewing their relationship with Christ (v. 19), which expresses itself by listening to and obeying His word ("He who has an ear, let him hear what the Spirit says to the churches," v. 22).

God and Christ are glorified because Christ's resurrection demonstrates that they are sovereign over creation to judge and to redeem (4:1–5:14)

John now has another vision (**after these things**, 4:1). The picture of Christ in 3:21 presently sitting on His Father's throne leads into the vision of chs. 4–5. In these chapters John wants to explain in more detail and with more imagery the past act of Christ's exaltation upon His throne as ruler over the church *and* the cosmos, which was accomplished by His death and resurrection. John is taken up to the throne room of God, where he sees Christ enthroned along with the Father. The vision shows how Christ's exhortation to each of the churches to overcome is based on the fact that Christ Himself has already overcome (5:5). The first time their overcoming is compared to Christ's is in 3:21, where His act serves as the basis for their overcoming and consequent reign. 5:5-6 explains that Christ also overcame by persevering in the midst of suffering and, as a result, was granted kingship (cf. 5:7-13). This kingship is not simply a future reality, but something which began at the resurrection. The fact that chs. 4–5 perceive His kingship as an inaugurated reality is most evident from 5:9-10, where His death and resurrection have resulted in the redemption of believers and their *present* participation in a priestly kingdom (note the allusion to Exod. 19:6, which also appears in 1:6 and is applied to the present church). This observation obviously necessitates the assumption that Christ also has begun to reign. The contents of this vision, therefore, are closely linked to what has gone before — both the introduction and the letters. Support for the concept of the present reign of believers and hence of Christ also comes from the descriptions of the saints' white clothing (3:5, 18; 4:4), the saints seated on thrones (3:21; 4:4), their crowns (2:10; 3:11; 4:4), and the image of an "open door" (3:8, 20; 4:1). Also significant is the fact that Christ is said in the letters (3:1) to have the "seven spirits of God" (representing the Holy Spirit), and in the visions His reign from the throne is closely linked to the same "seven spirits" (4:5; 5:6), which appear to be part of the means by which He rules. Believers are motivated to persevere by their present possession of part of their eternal reward, which assures them of their full possession at the last day. Part of the pastoral purpose of chs. 4–5 is that suffering Christians (cf., e.g., 2:8-11, 13) be assured that God and Jesus are sovereign and that the events which they are facing are part of a sovereign plan which will culminate in their redemption and the vindication of their faith through the punishment of their persecutors.

The vision John has is so closely related to that of Daniel's vision of the Ancient of Days and Son of man (Dan. 7:9-14) that we must conclude he saw much the same thing, was aware of it, and recorded it deliberately with that similarity in mind. Note the following points of comparison:

The prophet "looks" (Dan. 7:9; Rev. 4:1).
He sees a throne in heaven with God sitting on it (Dan. 7:9; Rev. 4:2).
God's appearance is described (Dan. 7:9; Rev. 4:3).
There is fire before the throne (Dan. 7:9-10; Rev. 4:5).
"Myriads of myriads" of heavenly beings surround the throne (Dan. 7:10; Rev. 5:11).
Book(s) are opened (Dan. 7:10; Rev. 5:1-5).
A divine figure approaches the throne and receives a kingdom which will last forever (Dan. 7:13-14; Rev. 5:5-13).
This kingdom consists of all peoples, nations, and tongues (Dan. 7:14; Rev. 5:9).
The prophet experiences distress on account of the vision (Dan. 7:15; Rev. 5:4).
The prophet receives wisdom concerning the vision from one of the heavenly beings (Dan. 7:16; Rev. 5:5).
The saints are given authority to reign over a kingdom (Dan. 7:18, 22, 27; Rev. 5:10).
The vision concludes with mention of God's eternal reign (Dan. 7:27; Rev. 5:13-14).

There are also significant similarities to things Ezekiel saw in his initial vision: four living creatures (Ezek. 1:5; Rev. 4:6), a sea of crystal (Ezek. 1:22; Rev. 4:6), and a throne surrounded by fire on which God is seated (Ezek. 1:26-28; Rev. 4:1-5). Some believe that Ezekiel 1 is the main model for Revelation 4–5. But on the whole these chapters should be interpreted primarily within the conceptual framework of Daniel 7, since the allusions to Ezekiel 1 become less dominant in the ch. 5 vision, but Daniel 7 continues to be present. This has significant interpretative implications, as we shall see.

Chapters 4–5 also reflect the scene of a throne room in a heavenly temple. A temple scene is discernible from several observations:

The heavenly temple vision of Isa. 6:1-4 is alluded to in Rev. 4:8.
Rev. 11:19 and 15:5ff. develop the picture in ch. 4 with explicit ref-

erence to a "sanctuary" or "temple" ("the ark of the covenant" also appears in 11:19). In particular, John's entry through a "door standing open in heaven" in 4:1 is probably linked to the same language about the opening of the heavenly temple in 11:19 and 15:5. For example, see 11:19, "the temple of God which is in heaven was *opened,*" and almost identically 15:5.

The link between 4:1 and 11:19 and 15:5ff. is confirmed further by the repetition of "flashes of lightning and sounds and peals of thunder" (4:5) three times later in the book, in 8:5; 11:19; and 16:18, the latter of which is introduced in 15:5, each time with additions intensifying the imagery.

The "seven lamps" in 4:5 allude to the lamps of the lampstand in the temple.

The golden altar of incense in 8:3; 9:13; and 16:7 appears in passages which allude to the altar of 6:9-10, which itself is rooted in the chs. 4–5 vision (see on 8:3).

Recalling that Revelation 4–5 is modeled on Daniel 7, a temple depiction would be enhanced if Dan. 7:9-14 can be understood as a vision of a *temple* throne room in heaven.

God is glorified because He is sovereign judge and redeemer over creation at its inception and throughout history (4:1-11)

1 After these things I looked, and behold, a door standing open in heaven, and
the first voice which I had heard, like the sound of a trumpet speaking with me,
said, "Come up here, and I will show you what must take place after these things."
2 Immediately I was in the Spirit; and behold, a throne was standing in heaven,
and One sitting on the throne. 3 And He who was sitting was like a jasper stone
and a sardius in appearance; and there was a rainbow around the throne, like an
emerald in appearance. 4 And around the throne were twenty-four thrones; and
upon the thrones I saw twenty-four elders sitting, clothed in white garments, and
golden crowns on their heads. 5 And from the throne proceed flashes of lightning
and sounds and peals of thunder. And there were seven lamps of fire burning before the throne, which are the seven Spirits of God; 6 and before the throne there
was, as it were, a sea of glass like crystal; and in the center and around the throne,
four living creatures full of eyes in front and behind. 7 And the first creature was
like a lion, and the second creature like a calf, and the third creature had a face
like that of a man, and the fourth creature was like a flying eagle. 8 And the four

living creatures, each one of them having six wings, are full of eyes around and within; and day and night they do not cease to say, "Holy, holy, holy is the Lord God, the Almighty, who was and who is and who is to come." [9] And when the living creatures give glory and honor and thanks to Him who sits on the throne, to Him who lives forever and ever, [10] the twenty-four elders will fall down before Him who sits on the throne, and will worship Him who lives forever and ever, and will cast their crowns before the throne, saying, [11] "Worthy art Thou, our Lord and our God, to receive glory and honor and power; for Thou didst create all things, and because of Thy will they existed, and were created."

1 Just as Daniel 7 and Ezekiel 1 commence with introductory vision phraseology, so Revelation 4 begins: **After these things I looked, and behold**. The first use of the phrase **after these things** in this verse does not refer to the events of the visions from ch. 4 to the end of the book as coming after the events narrated in chs. 1–3, but indicates only that a new vision is coming after the previous one in chs. 1–3. This is the *sequential* order in which John saw the visions, but not necessarily the *historical* order of the events they depict. This is the way the phrase is used in subsequent sections of the book (7:1, 9; 15:5; 18:1; 19:1). As we saw above, it is more than coincidence that v. 1a has its closest and almost exact verbal analogy in Daniel 7:6a, 7a. John's reference to the **first voice** he had heard, along with mention of the **sound of a trumpet** and the phrase **in the Spirit** (v. 2) all refer back to 1:10, where John was originally commissioned, which shows that he is continuing to obey Christ's call to proclaim His message (see 1:10-11).

The phrase **what must take place after these things** is a reference to the vision of Dan. 2:28ff., in which Daniel prophesies the latter-day coming of the kingdom of God, which John sees as beginning to be fulfilled in Christ (see also on 1:19, as well as on 1:5-6, 13-18). The second occurrence in this verse of the phrase **after these things**, therefore, does not refer to the distant future, as some argue, but to the events between the first and second comings of Christ, including the events unfolding at the very time John was writing. **I will show you what must come to pass after these things** is apparently used in the same way as in 1:1 and 1:19. We have already seen that the **after these things** allusion from Daniel in 1:19 and its equivalent "shortly/quickly" in 1:1 indicated that the fulfillment of the Daniel 2 prophecy concerning the establishment of God's kingdom has begun in Christ and the church. Rev. 4:1 introduces not only 4:1–5:14, but also the rest of the visions in the book (4:2–22:5). It becomes clear, therefore, that all the visions about to unfold concern events throughout the church age, past, present, and future. Some may have already unfolded, others await their fulfillment, and yet others have multiple fulfillments throughout the church age. In this connection, the NT is both consistent and clear in its view that the "last days" or "latter days" started already with the resurrection of Christ (Acts 2:17-21, citing Joel 2:28-32 as fulfilled; 1 Tim. 4:1; 1 Pet. 1:20; Heb. 1:2; Jas. 5:3; 1 John 2:18; Jude 18, etc.).

In these verses, John is ushered into the timeless presence of God and His heavenly court. This places John firmly in the company of OT prophets such as Isaiah (6:1-13) and Micaiah (1 Kgs. 22:19-22), as well as Ezekiel and Daniel. Being ushered into the spiritual, timeless dimension of God's heavenly council means that the time of the events which he sees in vision may be difficult to determine precisely. All the visions from Rev. 6:1 to 22:5 flow out of the vision in chs. 4 and 5. They are all visions which come from the sealed book of 5:1ff. This means that all these visions probably have a mixture of past, present, and future elements.

2 John's vision progresses to the point where he is caught up **in the Spirit** to the heavenly realm. The introductory section of vv. 1-2a concludes with a reflection of the prophet Ezekiel's repeated rapture in the Spirit. This scene is a reproduction of the angelic council visions involving God's throne which other OT prophets in addition to Ezekiel had witnessed (note the following allusions to such scenes as Isa. 6:1-13 and 1 Kgs. 22:19ff. in 4:2b, 8a, 8b, 9a, 10a). Like other OT prophets, John is being commissioned and called as a prophet by being summoned into the secret heavenly council of the Lord (see on 1:10-20 for the initial commissioning vision). In his prophetic role, he should go back and communicate God's hidden purpose to His people and what part they are to have in carrying it out. He has been ushered into the timeless dimension where truth and reality can clearly be discerned. Thus, in vv. 1-2a, John identifies himself again with the prophetic authority of the OT (cf. 1:1, 10, 12, 19-20). Therefore, there is little basis for seeing the phrase "come up here" in 4:1 and John's spiritual rapture in v. 2 as symbolic of the church's physical rapture before the tribulation as some commentators maintain.

The first mention of the **throne** in the Revelation 4–5 vision occurs here in v. 1. According to the similar order of images in Daniel 7 and Ezekiel 1, the image of a divine being sitting on a throne would be suited to either OT context, though further references are made to Ezekiel 1 in the following verses. The divine throne is mentioned seventeen times in chs. 4 and 5 (and a further twenty-one times in chs. 6–22), the purpose being to emphasize the sovereignty of God over all human history. All heavenly beings find their significance in their placement around the throne, and all the earth's inhabitants are judged on the basis of their attitude to God's claim to rule over them from this throne. Regardless of how rampantly evil seems to run and to cause God's people to suffer, they can know that His hand superintends everything for their good and His glory. This is demonstrated by the observation that all the judgments of chs. 6–16 issue from His throne (e.g., 6:1-8 [cf. 5:7], 16; 8:2-6; 16:17). This is of special significance to churches facing persecution, suffering, and the temptation to compromise their faith.

3 Now there is elaboration on particular features associated with the one on the throne. The three precious stones mentioned in v. 3, **jasper, sardius,** and **emerald,** collectively represent God's sovereign majesty and glory, as in 21:10-11, 18-23, and look forward to the fuller list of stones given in ch. 21, where God's new creation and eternal city are described. The background is found in Ezek. 1:26, 28. Of particular significance is the mention of **jasper,** the only stone mentioned later in the book in explicit connection with the glory of God (21:11). It is at the head of the list of the twelve foundation stones of the end-time city's wall in 21:19. The stones intensify the light around the throne by reflecting the unapproachable brightness, and hence glory, surrounding God himself (cf. 1 Tim. 6:16; Ps. 104:2). The **rainbow around the throne** speaks of God's mercy, as in the days of Noah, and suggests that, even as God's judgments unfold, He will be gracious to His true people. Above all else, the rainbow evokes thought of God's glory, since Ezek. 1:28 metaphorically equates a "rainbow" with "the appearance of the surrounding radiance . . . the appearance of the likeness of the glory of the Lord." The precious stones, together with the rainbow, are an incipient hint not only that this vision will eventually issue into that of a new creation, but it already portrays the beginning of the new creation in heaven. The precious stones in 21:10-11, 18-23 are part of a depiction of the new creation, and the rainbow is the first revelatory sign of the new creation which emerged after the Noachic flood. That the new creation is inaugurated with Christ's redemptive work is apparent from 3:14 (see the comments there) and from the use of "new" in 5:9 to describe that work (see "new heaven and earth" in 21:1).

4 The next thing John sees is **twenty-four thrones** upon which are sitting **twenty-four elders.** There have been a variety of identifications of these elders. The number **twenty-four** is significant. As the picture here is of the throne room in the heavenly temple, the elders may be based on David's twenty-four orders of priests (1 Chron. 24:3-19), twenty-four Levitical

gatekeepers (1 Chron. 26:17-19), and twenty-four Levitical worship leaders (1 Chron. 25:6-31), in which case they represent the church at worship. In light of Rev. 21:12-14 (where the apostles and patriarchs are mentioned together in relation to the new Jerusalem), it likely also refers to the sum of the twelve patriarchs and the twelve apostles who, taken together, represent the church in its character as a universal priesthood of believers. The elders cannot be classified as actual redeemed saints, however, for they are clearly distinguished from the multitude of the saved in 7:9-17 (see on 7:13-14). And the fact that they present the prayers of the saints in 5:8 and sing of the redeemed in the third person also distinguishes them from believers.

Remembering that in the letters the angels were identified as representatives of the seven churches and that in Daniel 10–12 angels represent nations, the elders here are to be identified as angelic beings representing the church as a whole, including the saints of the OT. If the four living creatures are heavenly representatives of all animate life throughout creation (as most interpreters think), then the elders are probably heavenly representatives of God's people. The four living beings represent general creation and the elders the elect of God's special creation. Also suggesting an angelic identification of the elders is the fact that the angel who reveals the visions of the book to John is referred to as "a fellow-servant of yours and of your brethren the prophets and of those who heed the words of this book," all of whom are to worship together (22:9).

Therefore, the reality being conveyed is that the church is represented in heaven by powerful heavenly beings who attend the throne of God, and who therefore hold great power (they have their own thrones and wear **golden crowns**), which they exercise on our behalf. The elders are angels who operate in a priestly capacity by presenting the prayers of the saints to God (compare 5:8 and 8:3) and by interpreting heavenly visions to people (compare 5:5; 7:13 and 10:4, 8; 19:9; 22:8). This further reflects their Levitical priestly identification noted above, especially since the throne room vision of chs. 4–5 is also to be understood as occurring in the heavenly temple (note that the visions of Ezekiel 1 and Isaiah 6, both alluded to throughout chs. 4–5, are set within the context of a heavenly temple).

In this light, v. 4 is a development of the ideas of the previous chapters concerning the saints' participation in a heavenly temple (1:13, 20; 2:12) and possession of crowns, white clothing, and dominion, which in their fullness will be granted them if they persevere (cf. 2:10, 26-27; 3:4-5, 11, 18, 21). As in chs. 1–3, the church is pictured in such angelic guise to remind its members that already a dimension of their existence is heavenly, that their real home is not with the unbelieving "earth-dwellers," and that they have heavenly help and protection in their struggle to obtain their reward and not be conformed to their pagan environment. One of the purposes of the church meeting on earth in its weekly gatherings (as in, e.g., 1:3) is to be reminded of its heavenly existence and identity, and this to occur in part apparently as it models its worship on the angels' and the heavenly church's worship of the exalted Lamb, as vividly portrayed in chs. 4–5.

5 John witnesses next **flashes of lightning and sounds and peals of thunder** coming from the throne — the same as Moses beheld in Exod. 19:16. This phrase is repeated in 8:5; 11:19; and 16:18, all of which have to do with God's judgments. This becomes significant in light of the way many of the plagues of Revelation are clearly modeled (as we shall see) on those of Exodus. This then may serve as assurance to suffering Christians that their God is sovereign and has not forgotten them, because He has not forgotten their persecutors, whom He will surely judge by fire (e.g., 19:20; 20:9-10; 21:8).

The structural order of Dan. 7:9ff. and Ezek. 1:26ff. lies in the background, since both use fire metaphors following the mention of a throne and its occupant. The **seven lamps of fire** is the vision seen by Zechariah, where there is a vision of seven lamps in a temple, followed by its interpretation (Zech. 4:2-3, 10; so Rev. 1:12, 20) and associated with the Spirit of Yahweh (Zech. 4:6). The significance of the seven temple lamps in relation to the work of the Spirit is developed in 5:6 (see the comments there).

6-8a The vision continues to unfold. The **sea of glass like crystal** may be the heavenly equivalent of the massive "bronze sea" in the courtyard of Solomon's temple (2 Kgs. 25:13; Jer. 52:17, 20), since chs. 4–5, as we have seen, portray a vision of the temple in heaven. More prominently in view, however, is that this **sea** is the heavenly version of the Red Sea, for we find the same "sea of glass" mentioned in 15:2, where the victorious saints are standing on it singing the song of Moses. The two passages are also linked by the application of the notion of "overcoming" to heavenly beings or to people who "stand" either on or by the sea. Perhaps the most prominent background for the image of the sea is that of Ezek. 1:22 (which is confirmed by the wording there, "something like an expanse, like the awesome gleam of crystal," and by the preceding Ezekiel 1 allusions already observed). The Red Sea represents the obstacle to freedom, and the OT presents it as the dwelling place of the dragon or sea monster (Isa. 51:9-11; Ps. 74:12-15; Ezek.

32:2). The concept of "sea" in Revelation represents the reality of evil (13:1; 15:2; 16:3; 21:1, on which see; as well as in the concept of the "abyss" in 11:7). This thought receives support from the model for these chapters in Daniel 7, since the sea as a picture of the beast's origin is a significant feature there. The beast comes out of the sea (Rev. 13:1), which is equated with the "abyss" in 11:7. 4:6 gives a picture of the stilling of the hellish waters *from the heavenly perspective,* though the devil wreaks his wrath even more furiously on earth because he has been decisively defeated in heaven (see further on 5:6b; 12:12; 13:3). This is the calming of cosmic "D-Day," wherein the saints' redemption from the devil is accomplished; the devil's final, complete defeat awaits "mopping-up" operations by the saints and Christ's final coming in judgment at the end of history, the final "V-Day." The Lamb's overcoming has also paved the way for the saints' overcoming of the beast at the same sea, as pictured in 15:2-4. In the new Jerusalem, there is no longer any sea (21:1). God has now stilled these demonic waters and established His throne over them. In contrast to the sea, stilled *like crystal,* the river of life, clear *as crystal,* now flows freely from His throne (22:1).

Before the throne John sees **four living creatures full of eyes in front and behind, each one of them having six wings**. There are both similarities and differences between John's vision and the related visions of Ezekiel and Isaiah. Ezekiel saw similar creatures (cherubim); each had four faces with many eyes but only four wings, which formed part of the base of the throne (Ezek. 1:1-28; 10:1-22). Isaiah saw six-winged creatures called seraphim which stood above the throne (Isa. 6:1-7). The living beings here are said to be **in the center and around the throne** or **in the midst of the throne**, which probably means that they stood near it. This is elucidated further by noticing that later in the book the living beings fall down in worship *before* the throne (5:8; 19:4). The cherubim/seraphim-like angels and the creatures here would seem to represent a similar high order of angelic beings.

Some have interpreted the four figures as symbolizing the fullness of life and power inherent in the divine nature, since each of the animals listed is the head of its species. It is likely that the four figures are designed to be representative of the whole created order of animate life. The multitude of eyes in the living beings signifies divine omniscience, signifying that they are God's agents. In the light of 5:6 and 5:8ff., the living beings must also be seen as servants of the Lamb. They are mentioned in ch. 4 not only because they form part of the eternal royal entourage around the heavenly throne, but also because they inaugurate the judgments upon mankind and continue to mediate those judgments until the final consummation (cf. 6:1-8; 15:7). Their knowing eyes search the earth, and they execute punishments only upon those who truly deserve them. For the discerning reader, these **living creatures** are an encouragement to keep persevering under persecution, knowing that God is acutely aware of their plight and is already in the process of taking action in their favor and against their persecutors (as chs. 6ff. reveal).

The **four living creatures** may be symbolic rather than literal descriptions of heavenly creatures, a supposition suggested by the various differences between the visions of John, Ezekiel, and Isaiah. If the "book," "seals," "lion," "lamb," "horns," and "seven eyes" are all symbolic, so likely also are the other features of the vision in chs. 4–5. The same symbolic assessment is probably true with respect to the **twenty-four elders.** This does not mean what John was seeing is unreflective of the heavenly reality, merely that the pictorial representation should not be taken literally.

8b The hymns of vv. 8b-11 interpret the preceding vision (vv. 2-8a). The vision of God on the throne surrounded by heavenly beings, fire, and a sea is interpreted to mean that He is holy (v. 8b) and sovereign over creation (vv. 8b, 11b), which demonstrates His "worthiness" (v. 11a) to be praised, worshiped, and glorified (vv. 9-11). *The hymns make explicit the main point of the vision and of the whole chapter: God is to be glorified because of His holiness and sovereignty.* Also in this section is found the reason that the four living beings represent the whole of animate life. They are performing the function which all of creation is meant to fulfill. That is, all things were created to praise God for His holiness and glorify Him for His work of creation. The twenty-four elders specifically represent redeemed humanity's purpose to praise and glorify God, which is actually carried out, not only by them in heaven, *but also by the true community of faith on earth.*

Like Isaiah's seraphim (Isa. 6:2-3), the elders speak out praises to the Lord God Almighty, never ceasing to say **Holy, holy, holy, is the Lord God, the Almighty, who was and who is and who is to come**. Isaiah 6 was drawn into the vision in vv. 8-9 because its scene of a theophany in the heavenly temple has such striking likenesses to that of Daniel 7 and Ezekiel 1. The threefold name for God, **the Lord God, the Almighty**, is based on its recurrent use in the LXX (Amos 3:13; 4:13; 5:14-16; 9:5-6, 15; Hos. 12:5; Nah. 3:5; Zech. 10:3; cf. Mal. 2:16). The second name for God, the One **who was and is and is to come**, expresses an idea of divine infinity and sovereignty over history. In the light of 11:17, the last clause of the formula, the One **who is to come**, expresses a future, once-occurring eschatological coming of God (see also on 1:4 for discussion of this threefold name). The point of this threefold temporal phrase is to inspire confidence in God's control of all the details of history and to instill courage to stand strong in the face of whatever particular difficulties test our faith.

9 The fact of God's sovereignty is expressed once more by the statement that the living creatures, again like Isaiah's seraphim (see Isa. 6:1), give their praise **to Him who sits on the throne**. This declaration of God's power is made in the heavenly court of the temple throne room, but this authority, which is far more than an abstract idea, will be rigorously enforced on earth. Thus suffering saints throughout history can be comforted by this heavenly vision.

10 This worship of the living creatures sets off a further round of worship by the elders. Both the creatures and the elders are said to worship **Him who lives forever and ever**, the same term ("Him who lives forever") by which both Nebuchadnezzar (Dan. 4:34) and the linen-clad angel (Dan. 12:7) refer to God. This expression of God's eternity further emphasizes the divine attribute mentioned in v. 8 in the threefold title "who was and who is and who is to come." In both Dan. 4:34 and 12:7, "Him who lives forever" is intended as a contrast with the temporary reigns of evil kings, whose rule is taken away because they have arrogated to themselves claims of deity (Dan. 4:30-33; 11:36-37) and have persecuted God's people (11:30-35; 12:7). Both passages in Daniel contrast this everlasting God with evil kings who rebel against God and persecute His people, but are eventually brought low (Dan. 4:33; 11:36), the same situation of persecution faced by suffering saints both in the seven churches and ever since. This is a warning to compromisers not to worship pagan gods or kings who take for themselves titles which belong only to the true God. Christians are now trampled underfoot by such evil powers, but eventually will be vindicated by God and so are now encouraged to persevere in the midst of adversity, even though they are presently no match for their oppressors.

11 That such a contrast between God's eternal kingship and that of temporal rulers is meant in v. 10 is apparent from the striking similarity of the divine title **our Lord and our God** to the title *dominus et deus noster,* which became a way of addressing the emperor Domitian, in whose reign John received his vision. This verse commences the elders' praise of God, which is closely parallel to 5:12-13. The basis for the exclamation in v. 11a is given in v. 11b, where God is said to be worthy of the **glory and honor and power** ascribed to Him because He is the Creator of all things. The basis of the praise is twofold: God's creation is based solely on His will and proceeds from it, and God's power is revealed through creation, as demonstrated by the praising recognition of His created beings. The elders' praise is concluded with the phrase **because of Thy will they existed** [were] **and were created.** It is best to view the first verb as referring to God's ongoing preservation of the created order and the second to the overall act of creating all things at the beginning of history: "they continually exist and have come into being."

The fact that the elders refer to God's ongoing preservation of the universe before His original creation of it is meant to remind believers pastorally that everything that happens to them throughout history is part of God's created purposes. God has not retired from His throne. He initiated history and is still very much in charge of it, in spite of what appearances sometimes suggest. His people must trust in this fact so that, even when they experience suffering, they can rest assured that it has a redemptive purpose and is according to His will. But how does God carry out His plan on behalf of His people? Ch. 5 explains how: through Christ's death and resurrection and ongoing rule over all things, and through the Spirit whom He gives to his followers. The chapter builds to a crescendo in the giving of glory to God, which is the main point of the chapter and the central focus of heaven and should thus become the central focus also of the church on earth. God's people should remember that God is orchestrating history not to make them great but to make His name great and glorified.

SUGGESTIONS FOR REFLECTION ON 4:1-11

On the significance of the throne of God. In this vision John is ushered into God's throne room. One of the ways Revelation emphasizes the sovereignty of God is through its frequent use of the word "throne." The great majority of NT references to the throne of God occur in Revelation. The entire universe is pictured as having its center in God's throne, with angelic and human creatures subject to the One who sits on it. All the judgments of the subsequent chapters issue from the throne. How do we express our understanding of God's sovereignty in our day-to-day lives? Does it do justice to the vision John saw? Do we in practice live with a weak view of God's sovereignty? Revelation also depicts the activities of the enemy and his agents. How do we distinguish between what God has decreed and what the enemy is doing? What is the nature of their "interrelationship"? (we shall address this explicitly in our comments on 6:1-8). How can a strong theology of God's sovereignty bring both comfort and biblical perspective to those who are suffering? How can a weak view lead us into confusion and despair?

On the reality of heavenly beings. John witnesses a scene of worship involving the elders and the living creatures. Although his depiction is symbolic rather than literal, it is nonetheless real, in that real beings are portrayed with real functions. As subsequent chapters reveal, in addition to their role in heavenly worship, the elders present our prayers and interpret heavenly visions to believers, while the living creatures administer judgment throughout the earth. How often have we taken seriously the existence of these beings? Have we relegated them to the realm of biblical allegory? What have we lost because of that? How does a western worldview affect our ability to understand and receive biblical truth of this nature?

On the nature of heavenly worship. The primary function of the heavenly beings is to worship God. Indeed, it seems that worship is one of the main activities of heaven. Why did God reveal this scene of worship to John (and hence to us)? If the elders represent the OT worship leaders, a strong connection is established between earthly and heavenly worship. How does the focus of heavenly worship as revealed here — the glorification of God — set a standard for our worship? Can we use what we see of heavenly worship here to help us in our understanding of what earthly worship should be? How does it affect the substance of what we say, pray, or sing? How do we work out the differences between outward forms of worship, which may be relative (styles or types of music, for instance), and the inward heart of worship (its focus on Christ and on God), which must never change? Do we argue in our church over outward forms of worship while missing its true nature and intent? And is it possible, if we sought to model our own worship, whether individual or corporate, on what is portrayed here, that, as we declared the same truths about God as the heavenly beings do, the same Holy Spirit who is pictured as being before the throne would deepen and transform our understanding of God and His glory in a way that touches our whole being, in its spiritual, intellectual, emotional, and even physical components?

God and the Lamb are glorified because they have begun to execute their sovereignty over creation through Christ's death and resurrection, resulting in inaugurated and eventually consummated judgment and redemption (5:1-14)

1 And I saw in the right hand of Him who sat on the throne a book written inside
and on the back, sealed up with seven seals. 2 And I saw a strong angel proclaim-

ing with a loud voice, "Who is worthy to open the book and to break its seals?"
3 And no one in heaven, or on the earth, or under the earth, was able to open
the book, or to look into it. 4 And I began to weep greatly, because no one was
found worthy to open the book, or to look into it. 5 And one of the elders said
to me, "Stop weeping; behold, the Lion that is from the tribe of Judah, the Root
of David, has overcome so as to open the book and its seven seals." 6 And I saw
between the throne (with the four living creatures) and the elders a Lamb standing, as if slain, having seven horns and seven eyes, which are the seven Spirits of
God, sent out into all the earth. 7 And He came, and He took it out of the right
hand of Him who sat on the throne. 8 And when He had taken the book, the four
living creatures and the twenty-four elders fell down before the Lamb, having
each one a harp, and golden bowls full of incense, which are the prayers of the
saints. 9 And they sang a new song, saying, "Worthy are You to take the book,
and to break its seals; for You were slain, and did purchase for God with Your
blood men from every tribe and tongue and people and nation. 10 And You have
made them to be a kingdom and priests to our God; and they will reign upon the
earth." 11 And I looked, and I heard the voice of many angels around the throne
and the living creatures and the elders; and the number of them was myriads
of myriads, and thousands of thousands, 12 saying with a loud voice, "Worthy is
the Lamb that was slain to receive power and riches and wisdom and might and
honor and glory and blessing." 13 And every created thing which is in heaven and
on the earth and under the earth and on the sea, and all things in them, I heard
saying, "To Him who sits on the throne, and to the Lamb, be blessing and honor
and glory and dominion forever and ever." 14 And the four living creatures kept
saying, "Amen." And the four living creatures kept saying, "Amen." And the elders
fell down and worshiped.

1 The heavenly scene of worship portrayed in ch. 4 continues uninterrupted. The One seated on the throne is now pictured with **a book written inside and on the back, sealed up with seven seals.** This book represents the judgment of God, as the following chapters reveal. The idea of judgment also comes from the allusion here to Ezek. 2:9b-10, where there is a book containing judgments against Israel. That this book is further described by the phrase **sealed up with seven seals** shows that it appears to be a merging of Dan. 12:4, 9 and Isa. 29:11, both of which refer to sealed books which conceal divine revelation and are associated with judgment. Perhaps the **book** should also be related to the opened books of judgment Daniel saw in God's heavenly court (Dan. 7:10), into which the Son of man comes to take up His eternal kingdom (Dan. 7:13-14). Indeed, the opening of the book comes into view in the next verse (v. 2). These OT "book" passages about judgment have been merged to highlight the idea of judgment. It should be recalled that 4:1–5:1 follows a structural outline identical to that of Dan. 7:9ff. and Ezekiel 1–2 (see above on ch. 4). The following analysis of 5:2-14 reveals that the outline of Daniel 7 continues to be followed, rather than that of Ezekiel 1–2. Further, while all allusive influence to Ezekiel 1–2 does not disappear in 5:2-14, more numerous allusions to Daniel 7 occur. The presence of all these OT backgrounds enhances further the notion of judgment with which this vision is saturated.

2 An angel now appears on the scene. The portrayal of the angelic questioner (**And I saw a strong angel proclaiming with a loud voice**) contains echoes of the angelic spokesman of Dan. 4:13-14, 23, who likewise came down from heaven and proclaimed aloud. He addresses the cosmos, asking for someone who is worthy or able or has the authority to step forward **to open the book and to break its seals.** Not only are the descriptions of the two angels verbally alike, but the angels also have the same kind of role. The Danielic angel is a divine spokesman for a heavenly council who proclaims a decree of judgment followed by restoration with respect to Nebuchadnezzar. The angel of Revelation 5 is also a spokesman of a heavenly council, who makes proclamation about a divine degree of judgment and redemption with respect to the cosmos. The implication of both proclamations in their contexts is that no created being except God possesses the worthiness and authority to be sovereign over history and to execute His cosmic plan. Daniel was ordered by the angel to "seal up the book" recording these divine judgments until the "end of time" (Dan. 12:4) or the "end time" (Dan. 12:9), phrases equivalent in Daniel to the "end of the days" or "latter days" (Dan. 2:28).

These latter days, as we have seen, are understood by John to have been inaugurated by the resurrection of Christ (see on 1:19). Thus we should also expect that Daniel's book has been unsealed by Christ. The mighty angel who comes forth here asks, **Who is worthy to open the book and to break its seals?** This continues the thought of the end-time unsealing of Daniel's book. It is important to note that Daniel 7 and 12 are the only places in the OT where the sealing and latter-day unsealing of books are mentioned, and John is clearly witnessing the fulfillment of Daniel's five-hundred-year-old prophetic vision.

Some have seen the book as the Lamb's "book of life" (cf. 3:5; 13:8; 20:12, 15; 21:27), but when the book's contents are revealed in the following chapters, they have to do not merely with events surrounding the elect but also and especially with judgments upon unbelievers. Furthermore, the books of Daniel 7, Daniel 12, and Ezekiel 2–3 have to do principally with events of judgment, which are then followed by the salvation of God's people. Others understand the book to represent the scroll of the OT. Christ alone is able to unlock (**open**) the true meaning of the OT, since its prophecies have found fulfillment in Him. However, against this view is the observation that the books of Daniel and Ezekiel do not symbolize the OT itself, but allude primarily to decretive events of judgment, as noted above. Still others view the book as containing the retributive events of a yet future tribulation leading up to the second coming of Christ, the consummate salvation of the saints, and the final judgment. However, this commentary has attempted to demonstrate that the events of the visions pertain not only to the eschatological future but also to the inaugurated latter-day period, including the past and present. We especially have seen this to be the case in our discussion of 1:1, 19 and 4:1.

The book is thus best understood as containing God's plan of judgment and redemption, which has been set in motion by Christ's death and resurrection but has yet to be completed. The question of the angelic spokesman concerns who in the created order has sovereign authority over this plan. That the book represents authority in executing the divine plan of judgment and redemption is clear from the parallelism of the hymns in 5:9-10 and 5:12. The former interprets Christ's worthiness to receive the book as indicating His authority to redeem His people and establish them as kings and priests. The latter hymn (5:12) interprets the Lamb's reception of the "book" mentioned in vv. 9-10 more generally as His reception of "power and riches and wisdom and might and honor and glory and blessing," thus showing that His receiving the book has given Him sovereign power. The first hymn points to the book being a testament or will which contains an inheritance to be received (see further below), which is then interpreted as sovereign power in the hymn of v. 12.

God promised Adam that he would reign over the earth. Although Adam forfeited this promise, Christ, the last Adam, was to inherit it. A man had to open the book, since the promise was made to humanity. Yet all are sinners and stand under the judgment contained in the book. Nevertheless, Christ is found worthy because He suffered the final judgment as an innocent sacrificial victim on behalf of His people, whom He represented and consequently redeemed (5:9). This legal picture breaks down in part because Jesus is both executor and inheritor of the promise. Nevertheless, this should not provide a great difficulty, since the book of Hebrews portrays him both as priest and sacrifice, and Revelation itself presents Him as both Lord and temple at the same time (cf. Rev. 21:22).

The book thus represents a covenantal promise. The extensive nature of the book primarily includes God's plan of redemption and judgment formulated throughout the OT, which encompasses the development of all sacred history, especially from the cross to the new creation. It concerns a predestined plan which is eschatological in nature, since the contents of the book are revealed in chs. 6–22 and are summarized in 4:1 as "what must take place after these things," a Danielic allusion to the end time. What is decreed concerning redemption and judgment is delineated in detail throughout the visionary section of Revelation: Christ's sovereignty over history, the reign of Christ and the saints throughout the course of the church age and in the new cosmos, Christ's protection of His people who suffer trial, His temporal and final judgments on the persecuting world, and so on. Once the seals are opened, the readers can understand the decretive nature of the book and therefore the purpose of history. Despite their present suffering amidst the chaos and confusion of the world, there is an ordered plan which cannot be thwarted and is, indeed, already being fulfilled.

Biblical scholars have debated whether the book represents a scroll or a codex (the forerunner of our modern book). If it is a codex, each seal could enclose a section of the book, with the contents revealed segment by segment as the seals are broken. Thus the seven seals could, taken together, as this commentary argues, unfold the whole course of history from Pentecost until Christ's return. But if it is a scroll, it is argued by some, only when all the seals are broken can the contents be identified. This argument is advanced by futurist commentators who see the sets of judgments operating in chronological sequence rather than in tandem. Hence, the seven trumpets of chs. 8–9 would represent the contents of the book (following the breaking of the seventh seal in 8:1) and would portray events following those depicted in the seal judgments, as opposed to the view we adopt, which sees the contents of the seals and the trumpets as different visions portraying the same events.

The codex appears to have been used more commonly at the end of the first century than the scroll, though the allusion to Ezek. 2:9-10 in v. 1 suggests that a scroll with writing on both sides is in mind (see also the allusion to the scroll of Isa. 34:4 in 6:14). But even if John did see a scroll, the contents of scrolls were often summarized on the outside by means of seals (representing witnesses), in which case, the breaking of each seal would release the fuller revelation of what is summarized on each. This may be in mind in 5:1-2 through the phraseology of "a book written on the back, sealed with seven seals," which a "worthy" person could "break," as our following comments will suggest further. Therefore, the unloosing of each seal could indicate the revelation of a detailed part of what was written in the document. Furthermore, it has been shown that the construction of some scrolls allows for part of the content to be revealed with the breaking of each seal. This would mean that the book's contents would begin to be revealed in chs. 6–7 instead of later in ch. 8. Thus the issue of whether the book is a scroll or codex is irrelevant for determining when the contents of the book are revealed, and thus the presence of a scroll no longer in itself supports the argument of the futurists.

But John may have seen a Roman will. Such wills were witnessed (sealed) by seven witnesses, and the content sometimes summarized in writing on the outside of the document. Only upon the death of the testator could the will be unsealed and the legal promise of the inheritance be executed. A trustworthy executor had to be found to put the will into effect. This picture fits the description of the book in 5:1 very well. Sometimes in the Roman world legal documents were doubly inscribed: the contents were written in summary form on the outside to protect against changing or falsifying the document. If this is what John is seeing, the abbreviated version on the outside may represent what God revealed in the OT (even Daniel had some knowledge of the contents of the sealed book: Dan. 10:21), while the breaking of the seals denotes not only a fuller revelation of prophetic fulfillment in Christ but also the execution of the contents. Therefore, the question posed by the angelic being and the response in vv. 2-4 concern who is able, not only to unveil the full contents of the document together with their meaning, but to put those contents into force. Although most futurist commentators disagree, the argument of this commentary so far is that ch. 5 portrays a vision of inaugurated fulfillment of OT prophecy. Whereas the divine response to Daniel's question about the consummation of history (how and when the prophecies would be fulfilled) was that the book was sealed up until the end time, now the answer finally comes and it is explained that the historically conclusive work of Christ's death and resurrection have begun to fulfill Daniel's prophecies, so that now the seals have been removed.

3 There is only silence in response to the angel's question. **No one in heaven, or on the earth, or under the earth, was able to open the book.** All are sinners and under the judgment of God. The image of the

opened book from Daniel 7 found in v. 2b continues to hover in the writer's thoughts in this verse.

4 As a consequence of the fact that **no one was found worthy to open the book, or to look into it**, John weeps. He is in despair because it appears to him that the book's seals cannot be broken and that God's glorious plan will not be carried out. Perhaps he feared momentarily that even the Lord Jesus has been found unworthy.

5 But his despair is short-lived, as a declaration comes from one of the elders that **the Lion that is from the tribe of Judah** (Gen. 49:8-12), **the Root of David** (Isa. 11:1-10), has overcome and can open the book. Both OT titles concern the prophecy of a Messiah who will conquer his enemies and judge them. Christ's overcoming of the enemy places Him in a sovereign position to effect the divine plan of redemption and judgment, as symbolized by the opening of the book and its seals. The fact that Christ **has overcome** is the basis for the exhortation to the believers in the seven churches to overcome, by His grace, in their daily lives.

6 V. 6 is crucial to understanding how the "Lion that is from the tribe of Judah, the root of David, has overcome." John sees a Lamb **as slain** (not "as if slain" as in NASB) standing (literally) **in the midst of the throne. In the midst of** is a figurative way of referring to the inner court area around the throne. **Slain** is an allusion both to the Passover lamb and also to Isaiah's prophecy of the lamb led to slaughter (Isa. 53:7), both pictures pointing to Christ's sacrifice which accomplishes redemption and victory for God's people. The sacrificial victim's prophesied sinlessness in Isa. 53:9 partly underlies the "worthiness" of Jesus in 5:9 ("Worthy art You . . . for You were slain"). The slain Lamb represents the image of a conqueror who was mortally wounded while defeating an enemy. The Lamb's **seven horns** signify its power (Deut. 33:17; Ps. 89:17). The picture here seems particularly to refer to Daniel 7, where the horn of the beast makes war against the saints (7:21). In John's vision, the Lamb makes a mockery of the prophesied apparent victory of the beast by showing that true power belongs to the One who was slain, the number seven indicating the fullness of that power.

This verse, with the slain Lamb elevated to the throne of God, describes Christ's death as not only redeeming humans, but also conquering the power of the enemy. His enthronement is a reference to His resurrection and ascension into heaven. The theme of this chapter is that Christ, as a Lion, overcame by being slaughtered as a Lamb. This is confirmed from 5:9, where the slaying of the Lamb, together with His redemption of people and establishing them as a "kingdom and priests," is a basis for

His worthiness and thus also for His overcoming. The phrase **standing as slain** is two Greek perfect participles, which express an ongoing reality or state. The Lamb continues to exist **as slain** to indicate the ongoing victorious effect of His *redemptive* death. Christ's death — as well as the ongoing sufferings of the church — have been and are continually being turned into victory. The reason John sees the Lion conquering as a slain Lamb is to emphasize the centrality of the cross. Christ's overcoming began even before the resurrection through His death. His overcoming is like that of His people: He conquers in the same way in which His people conquer (3:21). Whereas in chs. 1–3 a number of titles are applied more or less equally to Jesus, the predominant title for Him in chs. 4–22 is "Lamb" (27×). It was in an ironic manner that Jesus began to fulfill the OT prophecies of the Messiah's kingdom: strength coming through weakness. Through this vision, believers are reminded that their victory also will only come about as they follow the way of the cross. That is why saints are described as those who "follow the Lamb wherever He goes" (14:4) and have "washed their robes in the blood of the Lamb" (7:14). As an innocent victim, He became a representative penal substitute for the sins of His people. While He was suffering the defeat of death, He was also overcoming by creating a kingdom of redeemed subjects over whom He would reign and over whom the devil would no longer have power.

The **seven eyes** of the Lamb refer to the "seven eyes" on a stone set before Joshua the high priest, which are directly related to the removing of "the iniquity of that land in one day" (Zech. 3:8-9). In Zech. 4:2, 6, 10, the "seven lamps" and the "seven eyes" are associated with God's all-powerful Spirit. This conveys the notion not only of omniscience but also of sovereignty (as with "the eyes of the Lord" in 2 Chron. 16:9, where they "move to and fro throughout the earth that He may strongly support those whose heart is completely His"). The **seven Spirits of God** (= the seven burning lamps) are thus a figure of speech for the fullness of God's Spirit and have formerly been confined to the heavenly throne room (1:4, 12; 3:1; 4:5), implying that they are agents only of God as He operates throughout the earth (cf. Zech. 4:10, as well as Zech. 1:8-11; 6:5). But as a result of Christ's death and resurrection, these spirits also become Christ's agents in the world. The Spirit carries out the sovereign plan of the Lord (see further on 1:12; 11:4).

7 The Lamb now approaches the throne and takes the book from God (**He took it out of the right hand of Him who sat on the throne**), even as the Son of man came before God in Dan. 7:13-14 and received authority to rule over all the nations of the earth. The resurrected and

ascended Lamb takes His seat beside the Father (3:21) and begins to rule. More precisely, He exercises the Father's reign which has now been handed over to Him, as 6:1-8 shows (and as elsewhere in the NT, e.g., Acts 2:32-36; 1 Cor. 15:27; Eph. 1:20-22; Heb. 1:1-5).

8 Beginning with this verse, the effects of the Lamb's reception of authority are stated. Next unfolds a scene of heavenly worship, in which the living creatures and elders fall down before the Lamb as they have done before God Himself (4:9-11), thus clearly indicating the divinity of the Lamb. The phrase **having each one a harp**, refers grammatically only to the elders and not to the living creatures (incorrectly translated in NIV and NASB), which is appropriate in that the elders alone (being partly modeled on the twenty-four orders of Levites commissioned to give thanks and praise the Lord in 1 Chron. 25:6-31) have the priestly duty of presenting **the prayers of the saints** before God. The prayers of the saints, referred to again in 6:10 and 8:4, call for the judgment of God upon evildoers and His deliverance of the righteous. This picture brings assurance to the church that a powerful angelic ministry is operating in heaven on their behalf, even though the church is still suffering on earth.

9 Vv. 9b-10 express the content of the **new song** of the elders: **Worthy art Thou to take the book, and to break its seals; for Thou wast slain, and didst purchase for God with Thy blood men from every tribe and tongue and people and nation.** This song is, according to its OT roots, a "new song" of praise for God's victory and His judgment of the enemy (Pss. 33:3; 40:3; 96:1; 98:1; and especially Isa. 42:9-10, which speaks of the "new song" in relation to the prophetic purposes of God which will burst forth upon the earth).

The word **new** associates Christ's redemptive work with the beginning of a new creation for four reasons: (1) because this vision flows out of explicit mention of God's work of creation in 4:11, (2) because the following hymns in 5:12 and 13 about Christ and His redemptive work are explicitly paralleled with the hymn in 4:11 about God's work of creation, (3) because "new" describes the coming renovated creation three times in ch. 21 (vv. 1-2, 5), and (4) because "new" may be developing the hint of new creation already found in 4:3 (see the comments there).

The hymns in vv. 9-12 emphasize Jesus' deity since the Lamb is addressed there in the same way as God is in 4:11 and 5:13. The worship in general given the Lamb in vv. 9-13 demonstrates His deity since John implies elsewhere that worship is due only to God (22:9). The symbols of the "book" and "seals" in v. 9b connote the authority which the Lamb is worthy to receive. The sense of "worthy" is explained further in vv. 9c-10, where the basis ("for") for the Lamb's worthiness to receive authority is stated. This is first seen in **Thou wast slain**, which is a continuation of the Passover–Isaiah 53 lamb idea of v. 6. The Lamb's overcoming through death is a presupposition for His worthiness to receive sovereign authority. Although the following verb **purchase** could denote a result of the slaughtering of the Lamb, it is best seen as providing another basis for the reception of authority. The hymnic interpretation (vv. 9-14) of the vision (vv. 1-8) underscores Christ's death, not His resurrection, as the explanation of what it means in v. 5 that Christ conquered: by that death, He purchased and created a kingdom of priests. The fact that there is no explicit mention of the resurrection in the interpretative section of the hymns in vv. 9-14 is noteworthy and underscores the ironic nature of Christ's victorious death. The point of this is likely to emphasize the fact that it is through death — the way of the cross — that life comes, and that saints through the ages should take comfort in this truth even during their present sufferings. The redemption or purchase of **men from every tribe and tongue and people and nation** is a redemption which comes to people regardless of race. It is a redemption designed to save some **from** throughout the people groups of the world. It is a redemption without distinction, not a redemption without exception (people *from* all races), as 14:3-4, 6 will make clear.

10 These redeemed saints, people of every nation, have been made **a kingdom and priests**, and **they** (**will**: see below) **reign upon the earth**. This is just as Daniel (7:22, 27) prophesied when he likewise spoke of the saints being given a kingdom and rulership over the nations of the earth, but what the elders are singing goes back even farther, for it is the ultimate fulfillment of God's promise to Moses that if Israel obeyed His voice, He would make them a kingdom of priests and a holy nation (Exod. 19:6; see also on 1:5-6). This deliverance has come, even as did the deliverance through Moses, by the sacrifice of the Passover lamb. But whereas Israel was chosen instead of any other nation (Exod. 19:5) to become a kingdom and priests (Exod. 19:6), now God's people are chosen "from every tribe and tongue and people and nation" (v. 9). This means that the Exodus ideas of the kingdom and priesthood have been universalized and woven in with the concept of the Israelite saints' universal kingdom of Daniel 7. God's people have been delivered not from Egypt but from the rule of Satan, and they will enter not an old earthly Promised Land but one that covers the entire coming new earth. The slain lamb of the Israelite cult has become the end-time king of the cosmos.

The influence of Daniel 7 and of the Passover lamb from the preceding context continues in vv. 9b-10. Exodus 19 has been drawn in on account of its dual association with the Passover and the concept of the kingdom in Daniel. When Rev. 5:6-8 is seen together with vv. 9b-10, two more essential elements are added which correspond with the Dan. 7:9ff. model that chs. 4–5 have been following so far: Christ's sovereignty over all tribes, tongues, peoples and nations, and the reign of the saints over a kingdom. These saints have already been made a kingdom and even now have taken up their rule (**reign** could be present or future tense, depending on which Greek text is used, but the present is more likely). The kingdom of the new creation has broken into the present, fallen world through the death and resurrection of Christ. The new creation (3:14-15) has commenced in the present through Jesus' death and resurrection, which is witnessed to elsewhere in the NT (2 Cor. 5:15-17; Gal. 6:14-15; Eph. 2:15; Col. 1:18). This rule is exercised now in a real but limited way, triumphing through the way of the cross, but will be fulfilled triumphantly in the kingdom of the final new creation.

11-12 Like the song in vv. 9-10, this hymn further interprets the slain but risen Lamb's reception of the book to mean that His death and, implicitly, His resurrection made Him **worthy . . . to receive power and riches and wisdom and might and glory and honor and blessing.** John sees a great heavenly host — **myriads of myriads**, that is, millions, **and thousands of thousands**, exactly as in Dan. 7:10. The contents of this cry of praise before the heavenly temple, with its mentions of power, riches, might and glory, are strikingly similar to those of David's prayer at the dedication of the materials for the earthly temple (1 Chron. 29:11).

13 The hymn in vv. 13-14 underscores the point of the prior hymn in vv. 11-12 by further interpreting one more time the slain but risen Lamb's reception of the book to mean that His death and resurrection made Him worthy to receive praise and glory. Not only the heavenly host, but now **every created thing which is in heaven and on the earth and under the earth and on the sea** is giving glory to God and to the Lamb. God is mentioned as glorified together with Christ in order to highlight that Christ is in the same divine position as God and likewise is to be glorified. *The glory of God and the Lamb, which is grounded in their sovereignty, is the main point of the ch. 5 vision, and thus of chs. 4 and 5 together.* This appears to be a glimpse into the future, where even God's enemies will bow the knee before Him, and is strikingly similar to Paul's declaration (Phil. 2:10) that "at the name of Jesus every knee should bow, of those who are in heaven, and on earth and under the earth." Rev. 5:9-12 and 5:13 are good examples respectively of the "already" and "not yet" time reference of chs. 4–5 in particular and of Revelation in general. The evil rulers and earth-dwellers will be judged because they do not submit to and praise the sovereignty of Christ while they live on earth.

14 The vision ends with a final response of renewed worship by the **living creatures** and **elders**, the heavenly representatives of animate creation and of the church, confirming the hymnic praise ascending from the earth by respectively pronouncing a final "Amen" and worshiping. What is striking about this concluding section (vv. 9-14) in relation to Dan. 7:13-27 is that both present in the same order

> Christ's (the "Son of man's") reception of sovereignty (Rev. 5:9-14; Dan. 7:13-14), in association with
> a kingdom including "all peoples, nations, and tongues" (Rev. 5:9b; Dan. 7:14),
> the reign of the saints (Rev. 5:10; Dan. 7:18, 22, 27a LXX), and
> the reign of God (Rev. 5:13; Dan. 7:27b),

although the fourth element is not as emphatic in Daniel as in Revelation.

Suggestions for Reflection on 5:1-14

On the sovereignty of God in human history. This vision is shot through with allusions to various passages in Daniel. The angels of Daniel 4 and of this vision proclaim a message from the presence of God that ultimately He alone has power over history. Daniel's experiences show how God demonstrates His lordship over unjust governments and calls His servants to obey Him, even when it may cost them their lives. Christians today in many nations are faced with the same choice. What message does the angel of this chapter bring to them? How can God be said to be sovereign when His servants must sometimes suffer hardship and even death? What comfort does the vision of a heavenly council of God bring to us? How do we understand the care of God to be expressed to His people as the trials of chs. 6–22, pictured as part of the predestined plan of God, unfold?

On the meaning of an "as-slain" life. The commentary expresses the view that the perfect participle "as slain" (representing an ongoing reality or condition) in v. 6 expresses the fact that it is the slain Lamb who is presently ruling beside the Father in heaven. What is the significance of this? How does living a life shaped by the cross test our faith in the sovereignty of God? How does the concept of triumph or overcoming in Revelation overturn the normal meaning of those words? How important is it for Christians to model the "as-slain" lifestyle of the Lamb? What happens when we move away from this pattern? What implications does this have for the church's posture under hostile governments? What temptations are there for Christians in nations where the church is relatively influential? What is the balance between being salt and light in a society and desiring that our moral views be adopted by others in the culture? What are the implications of the "as-slain" model for Christians in politics?

On the present rule of the kingdom of God. If, as the commentary suggests, the saints have been made a kingdom (v. 10; see 1:6, 9), they have already entered into some form of kingdom authority. How is this authority exercised? How does its exercise relate to the "as-slain" life? What is the significance in this regard of the presenting before God of the prayers of the saints by powerful angelic forces (v. 8)? In what sense can it be said that the rule of Christ has broken into this present world?

On the glory of God and our corporate worship. If the main point of this vision, and also of the heavenly worship it portrays, is the glory of God and of the Lamb, how is this to be worked out not only in our personal lives but also in our corporate worship? What is the focus of our corporate worship? Why is it that worship in our churches today sometimes degenerates into the pursuit of experiences or into a mode of entertainment? How are we affected in our understanding of worship by the culture of the world around us rather than by the culture of the kingdom of God as portrayed in this vision? How can worship convey an experience of God and hold appeal for unbelievers without being diluted from its biblical norm? How do we recover the true meaning of worship in churches where it has clearly fallen far from God's standard?

On the glory of God and Christ. The main point of Revelation 4–5 is that the chief goal of God and Christ in everything is to glorify themselves. Does that not mean that God and Christ enjoy and desire being glorified? And, if so, does this not speak of what our chief goal in all things is? Should we not desire and enjoy God's glory? And, if we do not, does that mean we are worshiping something else or even ourselves? Is there a theological problem in understanding that God wants to be glorified and to have everything revolve around Him and His interests, since 1 Cor. 13:5 says that true "love seeks not its own"? See John Piper, *Desiring God* (Portland: Multnomah, 1986) for an elaboration of the theme of God glorifying Himself, our desire to honor Him, its implications, and the possible theological problems in connection to it (on the above-proposed particular theological problem, see *Desiring God,* 35-37).

Concluding thoughts on the vision in chapters 4–5

Dan. 7:9ff. has been seen to be the model which lies behind the vision of chs. 4–5 because of the same basic structure of common ideas and images, which is supplemented by numerous phrases having varying degrees of allusion to the text of Daniel. Of these various allusive references from Daniel (approximately 23), about half are from Daniel 7 and half from other chapters in Daniel. When the latter are studied, it becomes clear that they have parallels and themes associated with Daniel 7 and therefore may be present to supplement the interpretative significance of the scene of Daniel 7. The same supplementary approach was probably taken with respect to the allusions to the OT outside Daniel which were drawn into the portrayal (Ezekiel 1, Isaiah 6, Exodus 19). What better way to interpret the Daniel 7 scene than by drawing in parallel elements (themes, images, wording) from other theophanic (appearances of God), messianic, and eschatological sections of the OT? John may have turned his attention to Daniel 7 as a result of his attempt to describe a vision which was beyond description in human words but which corresponded in his mind to the theophanic visions of the OT, especially that of Daniel 7.

If this is the case, then we can say that John intends chs. 4–5 to depict the fulfillment of the Daniel 7 prophecy of the reign of the "Son of man" and of the saints, which has been inaugurated by Christ's death and resurrection, that is, His approach before the throne of God to receive authority. Further, the combination of such scenes as Isaiah 6 and Ezekiel 1–2 with the predominant one of Daniel 7 expresses a judgment nuance in the vision, since these scenes all serve as introductions to an announcement of judgment upon sinful Israel or the nations. The idea of judgment is also connoted by the image of the "book," which has been described in language from Ezekiel 2, Isaiah 29, Daniel 7, and Daniel 12. Each of these contexts has the central idea of judgment, but again together with ideas of salvation or blessing. Since Dan. 7:10 is the predominant influence for the "book," the nuance of judgment is probably more dominant, especially when seen in relation to the following chapters in Revelation, which announce judgment.

Even as the main point of ch. 4 was the giving of glory to God, so the main feature of ch. 5 is the same giving of glory to the Lamb, even by those who have rejected Him. The elders glorified God because He is the sovereign Creator of all things (4:11). This sovereign Creator is also, together with the Lamb, praised in 5:13 because of what He has done to redeem His creation. The parallels show that John intended to draw an integral interpretative relationship between God as Creator and God as Redeemer through His work in Christ. This suggests that the Lamb's redemption is a continuation of God's work of creation. Chs. 4 and 5 reveal that God's sovereignty in creation also makes Him sovereign over judgment and redemption, both of which He accomplished through the work of the Lamb. *The concluding hymns in 4:11 and 5:9-13 bear out that this idea is the main theme of the two chapters, since these hymns function as interpretative summaries of each chapter.* The work of Christ is a continuation of God's work in creation in that it causes all creation to return glory to its Creator, whether willingly or by force, as the following chapters reveal. The verbal links between the hymns in chs. 4 and 5 also mean that God's control of the whole creation mentioned in 4:11b is specifically accomplished by Christ through His death and resurrection and through the Spirit whom He imparts to His people in order to follow in His path and to convict the world of sin. In this sense, the vision given in these chapters already sets forth the truth of what is portrayed in chs. 21 and 22, where the purity of the Garden is restored in the new Jerusalem. This indicates further that chs. 4–5 portray a scene of the "already and not yet" new creation. This analysis shows that the goal of God in everything is to glorify Himself, to enjoy that glory, and to have His creation enjoy glorifying Him forever.

The seven seals (6:1–8:5)

The first four seals: Christ uses evil heavenly forces to inflict trials on people throughout the church age for either purification or punishment (6:1-8)

[1] And I saw when the Lamb broke one of the seven seals, and I heard one of the four living creatures saying as with a voice of thunder, "Come." [2] And I looked, and behold, a white horse, and he who sat on it had a bow; and a crown was given to him; and he went out conquering, and to conquer. [3] And when He broke the second seal, I heard the second living creature say, "Come." [4] And another, a red horse, went out; and to him who sat on it was granted to take peace from the earth, and that men should slay one another; and a great sword was given to him. [5] And when He broke the third seal, I heard the third living creature saying, "Come." And I looked, and behold, a black horse; and he who sat on it had a pair of scales in his hand. [6] And I heard as it were a voice in the center of the four living creatures saying, "A quart of wheat for a denarius, and three quarts of barley for a denarius; and do not harm the oil and the wine." [7] And when He broke the fourth seal, I heard the voice of the fourth living creature saying, "Come." [8] And I looked, and behold an ashen horse; and he who sat on it had the name Death; and Hades was following with him. And authority was given to them over a fourth of the earth, to kill with sword and with famine and with pestilence and by the wild beasts of the earth.

Christ has received all authority from the Father and taken up His rule over the kingdoms of the earth (1:5; 2:26-27; 5:1-14). The first four seals show how this authority extends even over situations of suffering sent from the hand of God to purify the saints and punish unbelievers. Examples of such suffering have been alluded to in the letters of chs. 2–3. Some Christians may have wondered if Christ really was sovereign over disastrous circumstances, such as Nero's mass persecution on so cruel a scale following the fire of Rome in AD 64. Rev. 6:1-8 is intended to show that Christ rules over such an apparently chaotic world and that suffering does not occur indiscriminately or by chance. This section reveals, in fact, that destructive events are brought about by Christ for both redemptive and judicial purposes. It is Christ sitting on His throne who controls all the trials and persecutions of the church.

The opening of the seals coincides with Christ's taking up His position at the right hand of God, so that the events depicted in the seals will begin to take place immediately and continue until the Lord's return. The opening of the seals begins the actual revelation and execution of the contents of the scroll of ch. 5. This makes sense of the exhortations in the seven letters to persevere in the face of suffering, for the suffering unleashed by the seals had already begun to take place even in the life of the seven churches to which John was writing. Christ opens each seal in the heavenly throne room and issues the command for the contents of each to be executed on the earth. The disasters that unfold are the same foreseen as the four judgments prophesied by Ezekiel (sword, famine, wild beasts, and plague, Ezek. 14:12-21, on which see below) and the judgments prophesied by Jesus (war, famine, and persecution, Matt. 24:6-28). In those cases, the calamities occur side by side, thus suggesting that the various disasters contained in the four seals also occur at the same time rather than in any particular order. In addition, the glorified saints in Rev. 6:9-11 appear to have suffered under all four trials portrayed in the seals, which points to their having taken place during the same general time period (see on vv. 9-11). Therefore, following on from ch. 5, Rev. 6:1-8 describes the operation of the destructive forces which were unleashed immediately upon the world as a result of Christ's victorious suffering at the cross, His resurrection, and His ascent to a position of rule at His Father's right hand.

This analysis is in line with the OT prophecies about the eschatological kingdom which are alluded to in chs. 1–3 as beginning to be fulfilled with Christ's death and resurrection (see 1:5-6, 9, 13-14, 16b; 2:18, 27; 3:7, 9, 14, 21). For example, 1:5, 1:13-14, 2:26-28 and 3:21 clearly refer to Christ as having begun His messianic kingship, a process which ch. 5 most naturally is seen as expanding upon in visionary form. As a result of Christ's exercise of kingship, He empowers each horseman through His angelic servants. The horsemen represent sufferings decreed to occur for all of Christ's followers. Yet, as will be seen, these same trials are also intended to be punishments for those who persecute Christians or reject the kingship of Christ. These tribulations will cease only at the time of Christ's final return, as the context of ch. 6 and the whole book demonstrates. The cry "How long?" of the fifth seal and the approach of the final judgment of the sixth seal demonstrate that the events of 6:1-8 precede the final judgment.

The most obvious background to this passage is Zech. 6:1-8. There, four groups of horses of different color (almost identical to the colors in Revelation) are commissioned by God to patrol the earth and to punish those nations on earth whom they find have oppressed His people (Zech. 6:5-8). These nations were raised up by God to be a rod of punishment to

His people, but they inflicted more retribution on Israel than they should have. As a consequence, God intended to punish the pagan nations for their transgression as a vindication of His jealous love for Israel (Zech. 1:8-15). Therefore, the horses in Rev. 6:1-8 signify that natural and political disasters throughout the world are caused by Christ in order to judge unbelievers who persecute Christians, and in order to vindicate His people. Such vindication demonstrates His love for them and His justice and may already be an anticipatory answer to the cry for vengeance in 6:9-11.

Ezek. 14:12-23 is also formative for this section. Ezek. 14:21 is explicitly quoted in Rev. 6:8b, where it functions as a general summary of the preceding trials, being conquered, the sword, and famine, the first two of which include death. The quotation has the same function as in Ezekiel, where it clearly sums up the four preceding statements about trials as "four evil judgments." These punishments come upon nations in general when they are unfaithful to God. The trials there are listed respectively as lack of bread and "famine" (14:13), "wild beasts" (14:15), "sword" (14:17), and "plague" or "death" (14:19). The point of Ezek. 14:21 is that *all* Israelites will suffer trials of persecution because of rampant idolatry (cf. 14:3-11). The purpose of the trials in Ezekiel is to punish the unbelieving majority in Israel while purifying the righteous remnant. The same dual purpose of the trials is likely in mind here in Revelation 6, except that now the church community is the focus rather than Israel. The faithful will be purified, but those who compromise through idolatry and become disloyal to Christ will be judged by the same tribulations. Yet the sphere of these calamities extends far beyond the borders of the church to the whole world, as the passages from Zechariah have shown, and they have the same universal reference in Ezek. 14:12-23. In addition, there is a universal frame of reference with respect to judgments in the following context (6:12-17) and subsequent chapters of Revelation. The Ezekiel passage itself is further developing the idea of four judgments from Lev. 26:18-28, which may be secondarily in John's mind. There God warned the Israelites in the desert how He would punish them for idolatry: four times He gave judgments, each consisting of seven punishments, each series of punishments being worse than the previous. All four of Revelation's punishments — war, famine, conquest, and death — are found there. Could the Leviticus passage be the model for the four series of seven punishments in Revelation? This is a viable consideration especially if the "seven thunders" in 10:3-4 are construed as one of these sets, even thought the content is unrevealed.

1 The vision opens with the Lamb's breaking of the first seal, following which **one of the four living creatures** calls out **as with a voice of thunder**. The presence of thunder shows that the command comes from God's throne (see 4:5).

2 In response to the command, a **white horse** comes forth with a rider: **and he who sat on it had a bow; and a crown was given to him; and he went out conquering, and to conquer**. The rider is thought by some to represent Christ, mainly because he is associated with white, a color used in Revelation fourteen times to signify purity. Also, in 19:11-16 Christ, who has diadems on His head, rides on a white horse and defeats His opponents. And the first horseman is different from the others in this chapter in a positive sense because there is no clear woe linked with him.

On the other hand, the following considerations point to the satanic character of the rider:

The horses in Zechariah, which form the prophetic foreshadowing of this vision, are clearly grouped together as one, and it is hard to see how the first horse here can be separated off from the next three, which are generally agreed to be evil in nature.

Chs. 12 and 13 portray Satan as deceiving people by imitating the appearance of Christ (see further on those chapters).

The first four trumpets and bowls of Revelation bring parallel judgments, and the same is likely with the horsemen.

In 9:7, as in 6:2, demonic agents are likened to horses with crowns on their heads.

The fact that "the four living creatures" who issue the commands in 6:1-8 are identical in nature points to the same parallelism among the riders.

The prophecy of "false Christs and false prophets" who will come in Christ's name and "mislead" is mentioned as the very first of the woes preceding Jesus' return in each of the Synoptic accounts of those events (Mark 13:5-6; Matt. 24:4-5; Luke 21:8). This may confirm the identification of the first rider as satanic, since it is generally acknowledged that John has partly patterned his four plagues here after the woes of these Synoptic accounts. War is also listed as the second woe in all three accounts, and the following two woes of famine and pestilence are found closely following in varying order, although pestilence appears only in Luke.

Therefore, our conclusion is that the first rider represents a satanic force attempting to defeat and oppress believers spiritually either through deception (the color white alluding to the attempt to deceive by imitating Christ and to appear as righteous, as in 2 Cor. 11:14), or persecution, or both (so 11:7; 13:7). This first destructive rider, however, is sent out by Christ, for he is commanded forth by the angelic living creature, and the crown **was given** to him (a phrase which in Revelation always implies God as the subject: 6:11; 7:2; 8:2-3; 9:1; 11:2-3, etc.). Since the first set of four judgments of the trumpets and bowls are divinely commissioned, so must be all four of the horsemen's woes. This is confirmed from Zech. 6:7, where an angel of the Lord commands the four groups of horses to "go" and to execute divine judgment. Thus believers can have confidence that, in spite of their present sufferings, God is in ultimate control, working out His purposes in all that is happening. Satan, of course, is intent on destroying the church (and the world), but God's plan includes Satan pursuing his wicked purposes, because only through them can God work out His higher strategy of refining the saints and punishing the wicked.

3 The description of the first rider can be taken as a summary statement explained in more detail by the following three horsemen in that he introduces war in a general sense and the other three bring conditions characteristic of war — not only literal warfare but spiritual warfare. And so vv. 3-8 describe how Satan attempts to conquer the saints through suffering so that they will lose their faith. Yet, it must be remembered that these trials also are ironically used by God ultimately as punishments for unbelievers.

4 Whereas the first horseman introduces the attempt of Satan to gain dominion over the world, the second horseman seeks **to take peace from the earth** by stirring up strife and warfare among the world's nations. This includes persecution of believers, as the allusion is to Jesus' warning to His disciples that His coming would bring not peace but a sword to the world (Matt. 10:34). The point of the Matthew text is that Jesus' followers should not be discouraged from confessing His name to the world when persecution comes, since such persecution is part of God's sovereign will. Their faithfulness amidst oppression may result in loss of their physical lives, but it will also result in the salvation of their spiritual lives (so Matt. 10:28-39). The gospel itself produces peace, but the attack of Satan upon its progress leads to war. The phrase **that men should slay one another** points to the persecution of believers, for the word **slay** is used otherwise in Revelation only to refer to the deaths of Christ and His followers (5:6,

9, 12; 6:9; 13:8; 18:24). Even the "slain" head of the beast in 13:3 is a mockery or false imitation of Christ's death. Those who are slaughtered in 6:4 are probably the believers pictured as slain in v. 9. The same connection between the woes of international strife and persecution is drawn in the Synoptic Gospels, where such strife is interpreted as a woe on unbelievers and testing for Jesus' followers (Mark 13:7-19; Matt. 24:6-21; Luke 21:9-19).

5 With the breaking of the third seal, the third living creature charges another horseman to carry out the decree contained behind the seal. The third rider again brings suffering, this time in the form of famine. In the ancient world, a **pair of scales** stood for a time of famine, as in such times food was rationed out by scales.

6 Immediately after hearing the angel's command, the seer hears another command issued to the horseman by someone else. The additional command does not likely come from one of the cherubim or another angelic being, but from Christ himself, since He is said to be "in the midst of the throne and of the four living beings" in 5:6 (cf. 7:17; 4:6) and since He is already present as the One opening the seals. This emphasizes further that the commands to the four horsemen come directly from the divine throne room.

This famine is to be serious but not utterly devastating, in that the **quart of wheat**, available for a denarius (or a day's pay), would be enough for a family, whereas the **three quarts of barley** would last three days. These prices were roughly eight to sixteen times the normal going price. **The oil and the wine**, representing more luxurious goods, would not be affected, but would not be available except for the very wealthy, as everyone else would be spending their entire income on the basics. Where Christians are a persecuted minority, they will be more severely affected. This develops the earlier theme of believers who are persecuted economically (2:9), a theme also found later (13:16-17). Famines affect everyone. But especially in such times of limited food supplies, Christians will be the first to be affected. They will be persecuted by not being allowed to have the same access as others to the basic commodities of life. Such persecution comes because Christians do not compromise. Those who suffer economic deprivation now because of their loyalty to Christ will be rewarded by Him at the consummation of all things when he will take away their hunger and thirst forever (7:16). To this very day, in places like India or many Muslim countries, when natural disasters occur, relief is often denied to Christians, who refuse to compromise with the worldly economic and social systems.

7-8 The breaking of the fourth seal causes a living creature to shout

out another command to yet another horseman. The last rider to be released has the name **Death**, with **Hades following with him**. **Death** and **Hades** are satanic forces under the ultimate governance of the throne room of God. The four riders all bring death in one way or another, and the more general term "death" here probably refers to disease or pestilence. In the Greek OT "death" *(thanatos)* translates the Hebrew word for "plague" thirty times, including twice in Ezek. 14:19-21 and once in Lev. 26:25, two contexts providing the model for Rev. 6:1-8, the former actually being directly alluded to here in v. 8. Hades is the abode of the dead. The satanic nature of death and Hades is evident from 20:13-14, where "death and Hades gave up the dead which were in them . . . and [they] were thrown into the lake of fire." The only other figures who are described with the same precise phrase as having been "thrown into the lake of fire" are the beast and false prophet (19:20) and the dragon (20:10). This verse indicates here that both death and Hades are under Christ's ultimate control, as was already made clear by 1:18 ("I have the keys of death and of Hades").

The judgments brought by the four horsemen are not independent or separate from one another but parallel — as parts of one overall judgment. This can be seen from the various OT texts which prophesy them, which frequently pronounce a fourfold judgment based often on idolatry (see Lev. 26:18-28; Deut. 32:24-26; Jer. 15:1-4; 16:4-5; Ezek. 5:12; 6:11-12; especially Ezekiel 14). This fourfold judgment, repeated in v. 8, signifies in the OT the whole range of God's judgments throughout history against people whenever they are disobedient to Him and is not to be literally interpreted as restricted to one particular famine, war, or plague. As in Ezekiel 14, these trials have the effect not only of punishing pagan nations but also of purifying the faithful within the covenant community, while punishing those even within the church who are not obedient to Christ. The fourth rider demonstrates that the previous afflictions have the potential to and sometimes do lead to death. This rider generally summarizes the previous three (of being conquered, the sword, and famine, all of which would include to some extent death), and adds one more (the plague of beasts). He uses the preceding three woes to bring death. But it is clear that they do not always result in death (see, for instance, the third horseman). Uppermost in mind are the antagonistic actions of Satan's forces, which are aimed at both the community of faith and unbelievers (as 6:9-10 reveals). Therefore, the fourfold OT formulas concerning the judgment of literal famine, plague, and warfare have been expanded by John to include woes of spiritual famine, plague, and warfare.

These four plagues have a partial effect, since the last horseman summarizes the previous three, and the disaster wrought by him is explicitly limited to a **fourth of the earth.** This means that the four woes do not harm every person without exception. Nevertheless, their destructive force is felt by many people throughout the world, since the four horses of Zechariah 1 and 6 also have a worldwide effect. The cosmic extent of the tribulations is emphasized by the fact that there are four horsemen, a figurative number for universality (as with the four living creatures in 4:6-8; cf. on 7:1-3). Therefore, just as the four living creatures represent the praise of the redeemed throughout the entire creation, so the plagues of the four horseman are symbolic of the suffering of many throughout the earth, which will continue until the final return of Christ. That the horsemen's plagues are representative of all kinds of woes is clear from observing that the fourfold covenant curse formula cited in the second half of v. 8 (**to kill with sword and with famine and with pestilence and by the wild beasts of the earth**) is used in the same figurative manner in the OT. In addition to the fact that the figurative meaning of "four" stands for completeness, Israel was threatened with many more curses than four in Leviticus and Deuteronomy. This is why no precise historical background can exhaust the meaning of these judgments in Revelation 6.

In summary, through His death and resurrection, Christ has made the world forces of evil His agents to execute His purposes of sanctification and judgment for the furtherance of His kingdom. This is most clearly seen in the reference here to Jesus' sovereignty over death and Hades, which is a further development of ch. 1. Through His death and resurrection, Christ has power over "death and Hades" (1:18), and now He uses them as His agents to carry out His will. God intended that the suffering of the cross should have both a redemptive and a judicial purpose (with respect to the latter, as a basis of judgment for those rejecting its saving significance). In like manner, the sufferings throughout the age following the cross have the same aim (indeed, one of the criminals crucified with Jesus was converted through his suffering, while the other was hardened by the same circumstance). And, as with Jesus, the apparent defeat of Christians is their spiritual victory, if they do not compromise their faith in the midst of suffering or persecution.

Notice that the very next verses (9-11) picture faithful believers who have been "killed" or "slain" (v. 11), the same verb used in vv. 4 and 8, and that "beasts" elsewhere in Revelation (34×) always refer to the agents of the enemy who persecute the church. It seems clear from vv. 1-8 that God and Christ are sovereign over these deadly horsemen. How can God be the author of such trials for the saints? The answer is that the trials come to judge the unbelievers, but to purify and refine the faith of believers, whose salvation is held secure in Christ (see 1 Pet. 1:3-9). Notice the relationship between chs. 4–5 and 6:1-8. In chs. 4 and 5, the prophetic vision of Daniel 7:9-14 concerning the Ancient of Days and the Son of man has been fulfilled in Christ's death and resurrection. But Daniel 7 also contains (in vv. 2-8) the vision of the four evil beasts who represent evil kingdoms that wage war on the saints. John's vision of the four horsemen fulfills the latter prophecy of Daniel, yet now we see that Christ's exalted place of rule gives Him authority even over these evil forces, such that He uses their evil intentions to accomplish a greater good — the judgment of unbelievers and the purifying of the saints. That is, 6:1-8 describes an effect of Christ's death and resurrection. He transformed the suffering of the cross into a triumph. Christ's sovereignty over the four horsemen shows this, so that the four horsemen are equivalent to the four evil kingdoms of Daniel 7. Specifically, the horsemen represent the evil heavenly counterparts of these kingdoms. This identification may also be understood through recognizing that both Daniel's four kingdoms and Zechariah's four sets of horses are directly associated with "the four winds of heaven" (Dan. 7:2; Zech. 6:5; see below on Rev. 7:1). Therefore, Christ has begun to fulfill Daniel's prophecy of the Son of man's exaltation over the evil, beastly kingdoms, which are explicitly alluded to in 12:3 and 13:1-2.

Suggestions for Reflection on 6:1-8

On the sovereignty of God in relation to the activities of the devil. This passage presents a picture of God sending trials on the earth through the workings of the satanic enemy. This could leave us with a need for discernment as to what around us represents the work of God and what represents the work of Satan. How can we say that a holy God can "use" the enemy as an agent? Is it that the enemy is busy wreaking destruction, but, unaware to him, God is using this destruction ultimately for His own purposes? Can God be said to include in His plan the reality of Satan's activity in a fallen world and turn it to His use? How can we say that God is behind the "slaying" of believers? What greater good would God bring out of that work of the enemy? How can God's role in the death of Christ serve as a model to help us toward answering these questions? How do we respond to a natural or economic calamity? Has God planned to send it and turn something the enemy does to His glory? Can you think of redemptive results of a tragic event in your nation, region, or community, whether it be persecution or some other calamity? How could Gen. 50:20; Rom. 8:28-30; and Rev. 2:10-11 give us a better perspective on such events? Can you also see how such events have hardened the hearts of unbelievers as they place blame upon God for the fallenness of the world we live in as the consequence of our own rebellion?

On the nature of the "white horseman." If Satan or his emissaries are pictured here as a white horseman, does this indeed reflect his ability to disguise himself as an angel of light? A new trend or ministry comes into our church and seems to be of God, but then has destructive consequences. Can you think of examples in your own life or experience?

On the defeat and victory of believers. How can it be said that the apparent defeat of believers (in their suffering or death) is in truth their victory? Do we find it hard to see into the ways of God because at least in the western world we see things too much from the perspective of this world only? How does that limit our ability to understand the purposes of God? Reflect again on the truth expressed in Hebrews 11 concerning those heroes of faith who suffered and died.

The fifth seal: the appeal to God by persecuted and glorified Christians to demonstrate His justice by judging their persecutors will be answered when all His people complete the suffering that He has determined for them (6:9-11)

[9] And when He broke the fifth seal, I saw underneath the altar the souls of those who had been slain because of the word of God, and because of the testimony which they had maintained; [10] and they cried out with a loud voice, saying, "How long, O Lord, holy and true, wilt Thou refrain from judging and avenging our blood on those who dwell on the earth?" [11] And there was given to each of them a white robe; and they were told that they should rest for a little while longer, until the number of their fellow servants and their brethren who were to be killed even as they had been, should be completed also.

Whereas the first four seals depict the world's sufferings from the perspective of the heavenly decree of God, the fifth seal describes the response of slain and glorified saints to these sufferings. Although the ordeals of 6:1-8 affect people generally throughout the earth, here the reaction is specifically to those trials of the four horsemen which afflict Christians in the form of persecution. This connection is pointed to from the observation that the primary verbs used in describing two of the woes of the horsemen reappear in describing the persecution of the saints in 6:9-11 ("slay" in vv. 4 and 9 and "kill" in vv. 8 and 11). The hymns of Revelation typically function to summarize the themes of preceding sections. Since 6:9-11 should be included in the category of these hymns, it is to be seen as a continuation of the thought of vv. 1-8, which focused on persecution. This further confirms that not only are the last three horsemen images of persecution, but so also is the first horseman. Such sufferings are not meaningless, but are part of God's providential plan that Christians should pattern their lives after the sacrificial model of Jesus. Seen from the heavenly perspective, such sufferings ironically advance the kingdom of God, as was the case for Christ himself (see on 5:5-6). If our understanding of the chronological relation of ch. 5 to ch. 6 is correct, then 6:9-11 reveals that persecution of Christians was already in full swing among some sectors of the church in John's time.

9 The loosing of the fifth seal does not reveal an angelic decree of suffering from the throne room but a human response to such suffering. John sees Christians who have been oppressed, having died and having received a heavenly reward (so v. 11a). These saints, then, are described as those **who had been slain**, as from the attacks of the second horseman (v. 4), and "killed" (v. 11), as from the attacks of the fourth horseman (v. 8). It is possible that only literal martyrs are in mind, but more likely those who are "slain" are metaphorical and represent the broader category of all saints who suffer for the sake of their faith (so 13:15-18 and perhaps 18:24; 20:4). These saints are all those believers who have suffered for their faith ("slain" likely figuratively including all forms of suffering and persecution), and are now before God in heaven (**underneath the altar** meaning in God's presence). As we have seen earlier (see on 2:26-29), those who "overcome" in chs. 2 and 3 are all those who remain faithful to Christ in the face of various kinds of suffering and temptations to sin and compromise, not only those who die for their faith. All genuine believers will experience suffering of one sort or another as a result of their faithfulness to Christ. As Jesus put it, "Whoever loses his life for My sake and the gospel's shall save it" (Mark 8:35). Whether or not they are literally put to death for their faith, they have so committed themselves to **the word of God** and to **the testimony** of Christ that they have come to be identified generally with the suffering destiny of the slain Lamb, a metaphor that becomes the identity of all Christians. This is also consistent with the figurative use of "sacrificial martyr" language with reference to all believers in the NT generally (e.g., Matt. 10:38-39; 16:24-26; Rom. 8:35-39; 12:1-2; Phil. 2:17). All Christians, therefore, must take up their cross and follow Christ and must find their lives by giving them up.

These people are described as **souls of those who had been slain** who are standing **underneath the altar**. They have been persecuted for bearing witness both in word and deed to Christ's redemptive work. The heavenly altar in Revelation is equated with the presence or throne of God (8:3-5; 9:13), which is why the saints are here described as being underneath it. The thought is not of the brazen altar of sacrifice (though there is the similarity that the sacrificial blood was poured out at the base of that altar: cf. Lev. 4:18, 30, 34) but of the altar of incense, also referred to in 8:3-5 and 9:13 (and 11:1; 14:18; and 16:7 being developments of these references), before which prayers were offered. On the literal altar, located in front of the Holy of Holies, incense was burned and the blood of the sacrifice on the Day of Atonement was poured out. The heavenly altar is that upon which the sacrifice of Christ was made, and this is where the glorified saints are appropriately found. The fact that they are **underneath the altar** emphasizes the divine protection which has held sway over their "souls" despite even their loss of physical life because of persecution. Indeed, these are persecutions God sends upon them in order to test their faith and to bring them forth purified. Those who persevere through persecution and temptations to compromise sacrifice themselves on God's heavenly altar, the counterpart to the cross of Jesus. This altar is, of course, in the midst of the invisible but real temple of God, where God's presence dwells. Therefore, this image in v. 9 connotes both the ideas of sacrifice and prayers as incense, which invoke God to vindicate those who have been persecuted for righteousness' sake. The comparison with Jesus' suffering is enhanced by the same description of the saints as having been "slain" (cf. "slay" in 5:6, 9, 12; 6:9). The purpose of the comparison is to emphasize that, as it was with Christ, those following Him will have their sacrificial suffering and apparent defeat turned into ultimate victory.

10 Now the response to the suffering of 6:1-8 is verbalized. The prayer of the saints in v. 10 is not a cry for revenge but a cry for the manifestation of God's justice (Paul expresses the same thought in Rom. 3:25-26 in relation to the work of Christ), for God will be considered unjust if He does not punish sinners and those who wrongfully persecute His people. The appeal is prefaced by the description of God as **holy and true** in order to emphasize that God is being requested to demonstrate His holiness and standard of truth by bringing wrongdoers to justice. This prayer is answered at later stages of the book, particularly in 19:2, where God's judgment on the harlot is announced along with His vindication of the saints (cf. also 16:7). The cry "How long?" echoes the psalmist (Pss. 6:3; 74:10; 79:5, etc.), but note also Zech. 1:12, where the same cry goes up, and is answered by the four horses of judgment going forth (Zech. 6:1-8), a clear prophetic foreshadowing of the four horsemen of Revelation 6. John's emphasis on God defending His own reputation by judging sinners who have persecuted the righteous is also evoked by **How long, O Lord, holy and true, wilt Thou refrain from judging and avenging our blood,** which is an allusion to Ps. 79:10, "Let there be known among the nations . . . vengeance for the blood of Thy servants." John intends that the judgments of the horsemen in vv. 2-8 should function as an anticipated answer to the cry of v. 10 (with respect to the horsemen representing partial punishments on unbelievers), and vv. 12-17 is then narrated as the conclusive answer.

11 A preliminary answer to the saints' prayer in v. 10, however, is given now as they are each given a **white robe** and told to rest until **the number of their fellow servants and their brethren** is completed. The metaphor of white robes connotes the idea of a purity which has resulted from persevering faith tested by the refining fire of tribulation (see on 3:4-5). Robes are given not only as a reward for purity of faith but as a heavenly declaration of the saints' purity or righteousness and an annulling of the guilty verdict rendered on them by the world. In this picture is an assurance to the saints still on earth that their vindication before God without doubt awaits them. But for the "earth-dwellers" (literally "those who dwell on the earth") of v. 10 (the standard expression in Revelation for unbelievers: 8:13; 11:10; 13:12, 14; 17:2), there remains the terrifying prospect of judgment. This assurance is verbalized in the last clause of the verse as a further response to the plea of v. 10 ("How long, O Lord"). The saints are told to **rest for a little while longer** until the sufferings of **their brethren who were to be killed even as they had been, should be completed also.** The expression "be killed," as with "slay" in v. 9, is to be taken figuratively rather than literally, although actual martyrdom is included (cf. the combined figurative uses of "put to death" and "slay" in Rom. 8:36).

The phrase **a little while longer** presents a theological problem, since it appears to allude to an imminent end of history. But from God's viewpoint what may be but a few moments could be a long period from the human perspective, as is evident from comparing the parallels of Rev.

12:12 ("short time") with 20:3 ("thousand years"; cf. also 2 Pet. 3:8-13 and see below on 12:12). Time in heaven, which is referred to in 6:11, may be reckoned differently than time on earth. This difference of reckoning is part of the tension inherent in the already-and-not-yet aspect of eschatology in Revelation and the NT in general (e.g., 1 Pet. 3:1-14). As we have repeatedly observed, the "latter days" span the entire period from Christ's resurrection to His final return. The exhortation to rest means that the saints in heaven are to be patient in their desire for God to answer their request. The assurance that God will unquestionably punish the evil world becomes a motivation for Christians to persevere in their witness through suffering on earth, knowing that they are key players in helping establish the kingdom in the same ironic fashion as their Lord (e.g., see on 1:6, 9; 5:5-10). That is, through faithful endurance in trial they begin already to reign with Christ (see, e.g., 1:9).

The portrayal of a group of apparently numerous martyrs presently petitioning God in vv. 9-11 is also problematic because chs. 1–3 do not picture a church which is yet undergoing full-scale martyrdom. However, this is not so difficult if our view so far is correct that the picture of martyrs here is figurative generally for those who are persecuted (see on v. 9 above). Therefore, although martyrdom was not yet widespread, persecution was affecting many of the churches, as was observed in chs. 1–3, and martyrdom certainly could have seemed to be on the horizon.

Suggestions for Reflection on 6:9-11

On suffering as a mark of the Christian life. If genuine believers are bound to face suffering for their faithfulness to Christ, how do we measure the fruitfulness of our Christian life? Do we look only for positive results (people favorably affected by our testimony)? Is a negative reaction to our suffering a godly reaction? Have we really understood that God calls us to suffering? Most of us presently in the western world are unlikely to be martyred, but in what other ways may we genuinely suffer? In what ways, even in our outward Christian witness, do we often suffer for our own disobedience or foolishness (1 Pet. 4:15)?

On justice versus revenge. What lessons can we learn from these deceased saints? In our anger against others, are our thoughts and even prayers motivated by a desire for their punishment or by a desire that God be glorified through the execution of His justice? In our anger, can we take the place of God in executing judgment (even in our thoughts) on those who have wronged us? What happens to us when we give our anger over to God and allow Him to be the judge? Do we come before God in the awful awareness that He might judge our own attitudes and actions? When we are holding bitterness against others, how can we pray for God's justice or His glory, when we are not reflecting His merciful character ourselves? Is our greatest desire that God's reputation and name be honored and not our reputation and name?

On waiting. The heavenly saints are pictured as patiently repeating the Psalmist's frequent cry, "How long?" Scripture says that God's ways are not our ways, and certainly His timing is often not our timing. How do we cope with the pressures of living in a society accustomed to instant gratification? What steps can we take to refashion our thinking along the lines of God's eternal gratification? How long are we prepared to wait for a return on our spiritual investment? Do our churches buy into programs designed to produce instant results? Do we give up witnessing after a few attempts? How many missionaries (such as those in China, Korea, or many other nations) spent a lifetime with little fruit only to see an enormous harvest after their death? What would have happened if they had given up? Do we express patience by resting in God's understanding, which surpasses ours?

The sixth seal: God will demonstrate His justice by executing final judgment on the unbelieving world (6:12-17)

12 And I looked when He broke the sixth seal, and there was a great earthquake;
and the sun became black as sackcloth made of hair, and the whole moon became like blood; 13 and the stars of the sky fell to the earth, as a fig tree casts its
unripe figs when shaken by a great wind. 14 And the sky was split apart like a scroll
when it is rolled up; and every mountain and island were moved out of their
places. 15 And the kings of the earth and the great men and the commanders
and the rich and the strong and every slave and free man, hid themselves in the
caves and among the rocks of the mountains; 16 and they said to the mountains
and to the rocks, "Fall on us and hide us from the presence of Him who sits on
the throne, and from the wrath of the Lamb; 17 for the great day of their wrath
has come; and who is able to stand?"

12-15 These verses express the explicit and final answer to the saints' plea in vv. 9-11. The time must be the last judgment, because we have just been told that the judgment pictured here will not be executed until the full number of the suffering saints has been completed (v. 11). The calamitous scene of vv. 12-17 assumes that the persecution of *all* Christians has finally run its course, and now all that remains is to execute final punishment on the persecutors, which strikes the very last note of world history. Consequently, this passage cannot deal with judgments of unbelievers before the return of Christ during an extended tribulation period, since they have not yet finished persecuting the saints at that point.

Not only that, but the **great earthquake** reappears in 16:18, which is undoubtedly about the final judgment (so also 11:13, on which see), and the reference to mountains and islands being removed recurs in 16:20. In 6:12-17, every mountain and island is removed in the presence of the One who sits on the throne, and in the description of the final judgment in 20:11 earth and heaven flee from the throne and Him who sits upon it. Many OT texts allude to judgment and the catastrophic events of the last days, all of which prophesy elements found in this text: the shaking of the earth (including mountains); the darkening and/or shaking of the moon, stars, sun, and heaven; and blood (e.g., Isa. 24:1-6; Ezek. 32:6-8; Joel 3:15-16; Hab. 3:6-11). Note in particular Isa. 34:4: "And all the host of heaven will wear away, and the sky will be rolled up like a scroll; all their hosts will also wither away as a leaf withers from the vine, or as one withers from the fig tree." Note also Joel 2:31: "The sun will be turned into darkness, and the moon into blood, before the great and awesome day of the Lord comes." In Isa. 34:3-4, "blood" is directly linked with the host of heaven wearing away or rotting, and 34:5-6 refers to God's sword being drunk or filled with blood "in heaven," which may be related to the moon becoming **like blood** in Rev. 6:12. Also included in Isaiah's depiction (34:12) is the statement that judgment will fall on "the rulers . . . the kings, and the great ones" (Greek OT; "nobles, kings and princes" in the Hebrew) which is nearly identical to the first three groups of people undergoing judgment in Rev. 6:15: **the kings of the earth and the great men and the commanders**. And likening the darkening of the sky to **sackcloth** was suggested by Isa. 50:3: "I clothe the heavens with blackness, and I make sackcloth their covering."

The cosmic phenomena of vv. 12-14 connote judgment as in the OT contexts, and various phrases from these verses are found later in the book as descriptions of the final judgment. In this respect, to highlight what was just mentioned above, note the earthquake in v. 12, and the same in 11:13 and 16:18. The mountains and islands are being removed in v. 14, and again in 16:20. In 20:11, the heaven and earth flee from the One sitting on the throne, even as the kings of the earth and their followers flee from the same in 6:16. Here the whole of the sun, moon, and stars are destroyed, whereas only a third of the same are in the affliction of 8:12, which clearly does not refer to the last judgment.

The judgment which comes upon **the kings of the earth and the great men and the commanders** means that they are forced to hide **in the caves and among the rocks of the mountains.** As in Isaiah 33:1–35:4, they are judged because of the persecution of God's people. They are also judged for idolatry, the reference being to Isa. 2:20, 18-21, where people must flee to the caves and rocks on account of their idolatry, which John applies typologically to the idolaters in this passage. The same groups are mentioned in Rev. 19:18-19 as giving allegiance to the beast. Yet even the poor are to be judged, for "the rich and the poor, and the free men and the slaves" alike bear "the mark of the beast" (13:16), which means that they have committed their lives to the worship of the beast (i.e., they "worship" the beast, 13:15). All unbelievers living on earth at the time of the final judgment are in mind.

There is debate about whether or not the description, especially in vv. 12-14, is literal or figurative. If it is literal, then the scene depicts the final dissolution of the cosmos, though some taking a literal view see the breakup of the earth as part of a long, drawn-out tribulation period. But if the scene is figurative, it could denote some temporal judgment or the last judgment. Our conclusion, in light of the explanation so far, is that regardless of whether the description is figurative or literal, it still depicts the last judgment and not prior trials in a final period of tribulation preceding the final judgment.

16 The idolaters now appeal to the mountains and rocks to fall upon them, the reference here being to the similar cry of the idolaters in Hos. 10:8. The original portrayal is that of Adam and Eve in the Garden hiding from God. John understands Genesis as a typological prophecy on the basis of his presupposition that God has determined that sinful history must end in the same way that it began — though with the provision of redemption for the saved.

17 Now the "wrath" mentioned in v. 16 is emphasized as the cause ("for") of the idolaters fleeing from God and the Lamb. Unbelievers or earth-dwellers will hide on account of the anger of God against sin, for the **great day** of the **wrath** of God and of the Lamb has come — surely a clear reference to the last judgment. This is indicated also by the portrait of the last punishment in 11:18, where occurs the parallel phrase "and Thy wrath came." The same phrase "great day" occurs in 16:14 in the description of the final war, and the same event is called the "great supper of God" in 19:17-18, where virtually the same classes of people listed in 6:15 are mentioned as being destroyed by Christ's final judgment. Behind this text lies Joel 2:11, which speaks of the great day of the Lord that no one can resist, and Nah. 1:5-6, which speaks of the mountains quaking at God's anger. These prophetic figurative descriptions of judgments on Israel or Nineveh, which were fulfilled in the past OT era, are taken here as foreshadowings of the last judgment.

The basic sin of men is still idolatry. Their idolatry is focused on the very things which are to be removed — the dimensions of the physical world in which they live. Those being judged in 6:15-17 are "those who dwell on the earth" in 6:10, who are the ungodly deserving judgment. Christians are only pilgrims on earth, whereas the earth-dwellers are at home in this world, with its material wealth, injustice, false religion, and moral pollution, some or all of which they have made their god. In contrast to pilgrim Christians, the ungodly earth-dwellers are at home in the present world order and trust in earthly security. The significance of these OT allusions is to emphasize not only the fact of judgment but also that the apparently secure home of the earth-dwellers will be destroyed. In the remainder of the book the phrase "earth-dwellers" or "ones who dwell upon the earth" continues to refer to those who rebel against God and are thus defined as idol worshipers because they fail to bow the knee before the one true God (8:13 [cf. 9:20]; 13:8, 12, 14; 14:6-11; 17:2, 8). Humanity has become perverted and worshiped the creation (cf. Rom. 1:21-25; Rev. 9:20) instead of the Creator.

The unbelievers' idolatrous refuge on earth must be removed because it has been made impermanent by the pollution of their sin. Therefore, creation itself — sun, moon, stars, trees, animals, etc. — has become an idol which must be removed. The heavenly bodies are repeatedly mentioned in the Bible as representing false deities whom Israel and the nations worshiped (e.g., Deut. 4:19; 17:1-4; 2 Kgs. 23:4-5; Jer. 8:2; Ezek. 8:16; Amos 5:25-27; Acts 7:41-43). However, the eternal home of believers with their God will remain (cf. Heb. 12:26-28). Six parts of the cosmos are described as destroyed in vv. 12-14: earth, sun, moon, stars, heaven, and "every mountain and island." Furthermore, six classes of humanity are likewise portrayed in vv. 15-17 as about to be judged: kings, great ones, rulers of thousands, the rich, the powerful, and "every slave and free man." These two lists point further to an intended identification of the idolaters — six being the number of fallen humanity — with the earth as their ultimate idol. If the most permanent and stable parts of the creation will be shaken to their roots (e.g., mountains and islands), so will the people living on the earth. Their earthly securities will be ripped away so that they will appear spiritually naked before God's judgment seat on the last day. The "earth-dwellers" have not trusted in the Lamb who was slain for the sins of the world (cf. 1:5; 5:9). Therefore, they will have to suffer His destructive wrath and will not be able to withstand it. The gentle Lamb who was slain on the cross is now in an exalted position over the whole cosmos (1:5; 3:21; 5:5-6) to pour out His wrath (for the judgment comes not only from God but also from the Lamb), because He is not only loving to His people but also a just judge of His enemies.

The OT allusions used throughout vv. 12-17 heighten the Lamb's position, since they all picture judgment as coming from God. Now the judgment is seen as coming not only from God on the throne but also from the Lamb, who must likewise be viewed as functioning in a judicial divine capacity. This is especially expressed in the Isa. 2:10 allusion (likewise Isa. 2:19, 21) in Rev. 6:16: compare Isaiah's "from the terror of the Lord and from the splendor of His majesty" with Rev. 6:16, where the One "who sits on the throne" corresponds to the "Lord" of Isaiah and the "Lamb" is substituted for "the splendor of His majesty." Likewise, the allusion to Joel 2:11 is another particular example underscoring the Lamb's deity: "The *day of the Lord is indeed great*" becomes in Rev. 6:17 "For the *great day of their* [God and the Lamb's] wrath has come."

Two results of Christ's resurrection in 1:5-6 are that He became "ruler of the kings of the earth," many of whom He judges (6:15; 16:12; 17:12-18; 19:18-21), and also a loving Redeemer of his people. The "kings of the earth" who undergo the last judgment in 6:15 are to be identified with the same group being finally judged in 19:18-21 and not with those who are redeemed in 21:24 (a comparison of 21:8, 27 with 21:24 [see the comments there] also shows that the latter verse does not imply an ultimate universal salvation).

Suggestions for Reflection on 6:12-17

On idolatry as the fundamental expression of human rebellion against God. Idolatry commenced in the garden with Adam's choice to find his security without God and his independence from God in the fruit of the forbidden tree. The commentary maintains that idolatry is still the fundamental sin of men and women, and that it is always expressed in attachment to created things rather than the Creator. Some forms of idolatry are obvious — worship of other gods, various forms of addiction, and so on. But others are not. Is it possible to practice idolatry without knowing it? Satan's most powerful deceptions are often his subtlest. Is it possible for something to be idolatrous to one person and not to another, depending on the attitude with which it is approached? For instance, a focus on staying healthy could be a good thing for one person yet idolatrous for another. Traveling on holiday could be an innocent way of recharging our batteries — or could be idolatrous. Even devotion to our family, greatly commended in the Bible, can become idolatrous. If anything comes between us and God, or becomes a greater object of affection than God, it will become idolatrous for us. See further G. K. Beale, *We Become What We Worship: A Biblical Theology of Idolatry* (Downers Grove: IVP Academic, 2008).

On a biblical understanding of ecology. How do we balance the fact that God created a world we are to be stewards of with the realization that ultimately it will be destroyed in the fire of His judgment? Is the tension resolved with the realization that God's intention is the creation of a new heavens and earth? Should our focus on ecology be motivated not by reverence for the environment in itself, but the consequences of environmental degradation for other people? Should we now act as good stewards of this creation in order to point toward and be a witness of our greater stewardship of a greater new creation that is coming? What is the dividing line which, if crossed, leads to environmentalism becoming idolatrous? Is environmentalism an example of how a seemingly good cause can itself become a source of idolatry? Is this because people define themselves as virtuous for their apparent care for the environment regardless of their attitude toward the One who is its Creator?

Angels prevent the evil forces from commencing their destructive activity on earth until believers are given spiritual protection against losing their faith (7:1-8)

1 After this I saw four angels standing at the four corners of the earth, holding
back the four winds of the earth, so that no wind should blow on the earth or on
the sea or on any tree. 2 And I saw another angel ascending from the rising of the
sun, having the seal of the living God; and he cried out with a loud voice to the
four angels to whom it was granted to harm the earth and the sea, 3 saying, "Do
not harm the earth or the sea or the trees until we have sealed the bond-servants
of our God on their foreheads." 4 And I heard the number of those who were

sealed, one hundred and forty-four thousand sealed from every tribe of the sons
of Israel: 5 From the tribe of Judah, twelve thousand were sealed, from the tribe
of Reuben twelve thousand, from the tribe of Gad twelve thousand, 6 from the
tribe of Asher twelve thousand, from the tribe of Naphtali twelve thousand, from
the tribe of Manasseh twelve thousand, 7 from the tribe of Simeon twelve thousand, from the tribe of Levi twelve thousand, from the tribe of Issachar twelve
thousand, 8 from the tribe of Zebulun twelve thousand, from the tribe of Joseph
twelve thousand, from the tribe of Benjamin, twelve thousand were sealed.

What is the meaning of the seal, and who are the 144,000 from every tribe of Israel who were sealed? Are they a group of literal ethnic Israelites living at some future time, or do they represent figuratively some other group of people? The mention of the "great multitude . . . *standing* before the throne" in v. 9 may be an explicit answer to the question of 6:17 as to who can stand in the day of wrath. Both passages also refer to people standing before the throne and the Lamb. The picture of the Lamb "standing" before the throne in 5:6 is likely associated to a significant degree with His resurrection existence, so that the "standing" before the throne in 7:9 of people later described as sheep (v. 17) plausibly also reflects the resurrection existence of the saints. The "standing" of the saints on the sea of glass also in direct conjunction with mention of the Lamb later in the book also reflects the Lamb's resurrection existence from 5:6 (see on 15:2).

1 Chapter 7 commences with a new vision, as indicated by the introductory phrase **after this I saw**. Although John experienced this vision subsequent to that of ch. 6, what it depicts comes before what ch. 6 depicts chronologically. The section stands as a kind of parenthesis explaining how God will keep believers safe during the tribulations of the church age. As a result, the believers will not be harmed spiritually when they go through the trials unleashed by the four seals of 6:1-8.

John sees **four angels standing at the four corners of the earth, holding back the four winds of the earth**. That they are **standing at the four corners of the earth** refers to their sovereignty over the *whole world* (so Isa. 11:12; Ezek. 7:2; Rev. 20:8). That **four winds** refers figuratively to the entire known world is clear from the use of the same phrase in this manner in Jer. 49:36; Dan. 8:8; 11:4; Matt. 24:31; and Mark 13:27. **The four winds of the earth** are best identified as the four horsemen of 6:1-8, which were clearly modeled on the horsemen of Zech. 6:1-8 because the latter are also identified in Zech. 6:5 as "the four winds [or spirits] of heaven" (the Hebrew can be translated "winds" or "spirits"; LXX "winds"). Godly angels are **holding back** the evil forces of destruction from the earth, a destruction which in 6:1-8 is described as having already come to pass. That the winds have to be held back to prevent their harmful activity is evidence of their rebellious and wicked nature. Whether or not the earth, sea, and trees to be affected by the winds are literal is not crucial, since together with the winds they form a picture representing the woes of 6:1-8 and are to be understood likewise in terms of general judgments. Probably these three objects represent (by metonymy, or more specifically synecdoche, the literary device by which the part represents the whole) the earth and its inhabitants, who are affected by the woes of the four horsemen. The delaying action which prevents the destructive effect of the winds is only temporary, as is evident from vv. 2-3.

2-3 The reason the four angels are preventing the horsemen from being unleashed is now given. This delay is only temporary, until the godly angels **have sealed the bond-servants of our God** at the command of an angel coming from God's presence (**having the seal of the living God**). In these verses, the earth and its inhabitants are not yet harmed, and, before they are, God's servants are to be given a seal of protection. Thus, this section does not present a new series of events in a yet further future part of a final tribulation period following the trials of ch. 6, but it concerns matters related to trials throughout the church age that precede the final judgment and reward. As such, it is an interlude in its placement after ch. 6.

What it means for God to "seal" His servants is debated. The main alternatives are: protection from physical harm, protection from demons, and protection against losing one's faith and hence salvation. The picture of the **seal** here is the same as what was seen by Ezekiel when the Lord commands the angel to put a mark on the foreheads of those who hate sin before He strikes the city in judgment (Ezek. 9:4-6). This mark protects them spiritually and likely also physically from the coming judgment. This is comparable to the mark of blood on the doors of the Israelites so that they would be protected from God's judgment on Egypt (Exod. 12:7, 13, 22-28). This becomes significant when we note that this mark protects believers during the period of the trumpet and bowl plagues, which, as we shall see, are closely modeled on the plagues of Egypt.

The demonic powers are forbidden to harm those with the seal of God on their forehead. Uppermost in John's mind is not physical security, but protection of the believers' faith and salvation from the various sufferings and persecutions that are inflicted upon them, whether by Satan or his demonic and earthly agents. The sealing enables God's people to respond in faith to the trials through which they pass so that these trials become the very instruments by which they are strengthened in their faith (see on 6:1-8). The protective function of the seal is obvious from 9:4, where the satanic powers are commanded not to "hurt the grass of the earth . . . nor any tree, but only the men who do not have the seal of God on their foreheads" (note the almost identical verbal parallel with 7:3; 16:2 implies the seal's protective aspect). That this protection is spiritual is apparent because believers and unbelievers suffer similar physical afflictions (see again on 6:1-8). But the trials that purify God's servants result in hardening the ungodly in their response to God (so 9:19-21).

Those who have the **seal**, the 144,000 noted in 7:4, are mentioned again in 14:1 as those who have the name of God and of the Lamb written on their foreheads. Believers who are under the **seal** with the name of God and the Lamb possess an inviolable salvation relationship with both, which protects them (14:3-4: they are redemptively "purchased"). The **seal** and the name of God, therefore, must be identical, both indicating that these people belong to God (see 2 Tim. 2:19 for the same thought). The opposite is true of the earth-dwellers, who have on their foreheads the mark of the beast, which is also his name (13:17; 14:9-11; see further below).

Seal can also have the sense of "authenticate" or "designate ownership of," both of which are included with the idea of protection here. As the saints are empowered to persevere through adversity, the genuineness of their profession is authenticated, and they are shown truly to belong to God. That those who are sealed are called **bond-servants** or slaves **of our God** highlights the idea of ownership, since it was a common practice in the ancient world to mark slaves on the forehead to indicate ownership and to whom they owed service. That the **seal** includes the idea of authentication and ownership is evident from recognizing that John equates it in 14:1 and 22:4 with the name of Christ and God, which has also been written **on their foreheads** (a phrase occurring in all three passages; in 2 Tim. 2:19 God's "seal" and "name" together identify those who belong to him).

The equation of the seal with the divine name is confirmed by the identification of the "mark" of the beast on the forehead of unbelievers (13:17) as "the name of the beast," and in 14:9-11 "a mark on his (the beast-worshiper's) . . . forehead" is also called "the mark of his (the beast's) name." Hence, the seal empowers the 144,000 to perform the role of witness intended for true Israel (e.g., Isa. 42:6-7; 49:6; 51:4-8). Therefore, the "new name" and the "seal" are marks of genuine membership in the community of the redeemed, without which entry into the eternal "city of God" is impossible. And, as we have seen in 2:17, identification with Christ's new name (see 3:12) actually begins when Christ reveals Himself to people and they confess His name. When this happens, they gain a new spiritual status and are given power not to deny His name (3:8) and to persevere through the final tribulation (cf. 2:13a; 3:8-10; John 17:6-26, where Christ's revelation of God's name to believers means that they *now* share in God's protective presence; cf. Luke 10:17-22).

The equation of the "name" of Christ and God written on the saints' foreheads" (14:1) and the "seal" as designations of membership in God's covenant community is also confirmed by the similar equation in Exodus (especially in the LXX). In Exod. 28:17-21, the twelve stones to be placed on the priest's breastpiece were to be engraved with the names of the twelve tribes, and these stones were to be like "the engravings of a seal" (28:21). The names of each of the twelve tribes is written on each stone to show who is a member of the Israelite covenant community. Significantly, there was also to be a gold plate placed "on Aaron's forehead" like "the engravings of a seal" (28:36, 38), and "Holy to the Lord" was inscribed on it (28:36). This seal indicated that he was consecrated to and belonged to the Lord and, since he was Israel's representative in the temple, the same notion of the nation's consecration to God carried over to them. Note also that most of the stones of Exodus 28 reappear in Rev. 21:19-20 in connection with the new Jerusalem.

Likewise in these verses God's seal identifies His people and sets them apart from sinful compromise with the world because of the efficacious effects of the Lamb's blood, which has been sprinkled by Him as the high priest in the heavenly temple (Heb. 8:1–10:22), and which has been applied to them (see on 7:14). Consequently, they will not suffer the divine wrath which the world of unbelief must endure. It will become evident in the following verses that believers must also be sealed in order to enter the heavenly tabernacle and minister before God as priests (see on 7:13-15). The background of Exodus provides the link between Rev. 21:12-20 and 7:3-8: the precious stones and the seal of Exodus signify a people made holy through the sacrifice of the Lamb to enter the new Jerusalem built on these precious stones as its foundation.

The community of the "redeemed" in 7:3-8 is the same as in 14:1-4 because of the verbal parallels and ideas observed above. In 14:3-4, the 144,000 are those "who had been purchased from the earth" and who "have been purchased from among men as first fruits to God." And there is a parallel between 14:4 and 5:9b which is so close that the groups mentioned as "purchased" in both are probably identical (5:9b: the lamb purchased "for God . . . men from every tribe and tongue and people and nation"). This would mean that the 144,000 in 14:1-3 are not some small remnant of ethnic Israelites but another way of speaking of the larger remnant of humanity living during the church age whom Christ has redeemed from throughout the world. If this identification is correct, then the 144,000 in 7:3-8 must also represent the same redeemed remnant from all over the earth. In this case, 7:9 would interpret the group of 7:3-8 as those who are "from every nation and all tribes and peoples and tongues" (see further on 7:9). This is virtually the same phrase as that in 5:9b, both being based on the formulas of Daniel 3–7. This group is numbered as 144,000 to emphasize figuratively that this is a picture of the church in its entirety, not in part, which has been redeemed, as the vision of the multitude in 7:9-17 bears out (on the identity of the 144,000 see further on vv. 4-8 below).

That this is the case is apparent from the following reasons, among other considerations:

> All redeemed believers are included when the word "bond-servant" *(doulos)* refers in the book elsewhere to God's servants (2:20; 19:5; 22:3),
>
> The OT background in Ezekiel 9 likewise points to the sealed group as representing all of God's true people, since that context knows of no distinction between major groups of the faithful, but distinguishes only true believers from unbelievers, and
>
> if Satan puts his seal, mark, or name on all his followers (13:16-17; 14:9-11), God presumably does likewise to all of His followers, and not just some of them.

The divine seal and name empower the saints to remain loyal to Christ and not to compromise in the midst of pressures to do so by identifying with the idolatrous world system. They resist the harlot of ch. 17 and refuse the mark of the beast (20:4). Although the saints may suffer and even lose their physical lives, the **seal** protects them from losing their spiritual lives with God. This is why the **seal** is said to be **of the living God**, who imparts to them the eternal life which He alone possesses (for the saints' obtaining this kind of "life" as a future inheritance cf. 2:7, 10-11; 3:5; 11:11; 20:4, 6; 21:6, 27; 22:12, 14, 17, and note the attribute of God's or Christ's eternal life in 1:18; 4:9-10; 10:6; 15:7). Therefore, the **seal** also includes protection from the final day of judgment, which has just been mentioned in 6:17. The **seal** guarantees protection from this wrath for those believing that the Lamb has been dealt the death blow on their behalf (1:5; 5:6-9, 12). Those without the **seal** and with the "mark of the beast" have no such safeguard, but suffer the eternal wrath of God (so 14:9-11). They are deceived into worshiping the forces of evil (13:8; 19:20). This is because they have been destined to be excluded from everlasting life with the Lamb (so 13:8; 17:8; 20:15).

The seal, in light of 2 Cor. 1:22 and Eph. 1:13; 4:30, is to be identified with the Holy Spirit, though this is not explicitly stated in Revelation. Therefore, uppermost in John's mind is certainly not physical security but protection of the believers' faith and salvation from the various sufferings and persecutions that are inflicted upon them, whether by Satan or by his demonic and earthly agents. Spiritual protection is the focus.

Consequently, the group being sealed cannot be a special group of martyrs who are protected against physical harm until they have opportunity to give their witness (for discussion of how John applies the language of martyrdom to Christians in general see on 6:4, 8, 9). Nor are they a last generation of believers living at the end of the age who are protected from the severe destruction coming on the earth at that time. Unlikely also is the speculation that they are an unconverted Jewish remnant who are physically protected through the tribulation, after which they are converted as they see Christ descending at His second coming (this view is often fueled by a similar interpretation of Rom. 11:25-29). One reason for rejecting this idea is that it would be hard to understand why they are physically protected from the tribulation, but the Gentile believers described in 7:9-17 are not so sheltered. Nowhere else in Revelation or the NT is there any thought of a preference or advantage granted Jews over Gentiles *during* the inter-advent age. This is consistent with the above observation that the word "servant" (Greek *doulos*) never refers exclusively to Jewish Christians anywhere else in the book, but only to believers in general or to all saints.

That the angels must seal the **bond-servants of our God** implies that those receiving the seal are already servants of God, and therefore already believers. If so, as seems likely, it refers to a divine decree to seal all those who will believe throughout the church age. The decree would be fulfilled as each person believes in Christ. This notion is also suggested by the fact that the Lamb's death and purchase of a select group of people out from the nations is presented as an indicative or actual, not potential, transaction, which was consummated on the Lamb's part at the cross (5:9; cf. 14:3-4). Furthermore, this elect group was determined from the foundation of the world to benefit from the protecting influence of Christ's death, whereas it was likewise determined that others would not so benefit (13:8; 17:8).

4-8 Now the identity of those sealed is explained further. Who are the **one hundred and forty-four thousand**? They are unlikely to be literal Israelites living at the very end of history during a severe tribulation, nor are they literal Israelites living during the desecration of Israel's second temple in the first century, for in either case God's protection would apply only to ethnic Jews — and a limited number of them — rather than to His people redeemed from every nation, including Jewish believers in Jesus. Such a suggestion would be alien to the teaching of the NT (read Galatians, for instance).

A better understanding comes from the context. In 5:9, the Lamb is said to have purchased with His blood "men from every tribe and tongue and people and nation." In 14:3-4, the 144,000 are said to have been purchased "from the earth" and purchased "from among men." The almost identical language suggests that the two are the same group — the church of all ages. This would explain why, immediately after the vision of the sealing, John sees a great multitude of people from every nation and tribe and people and tongue (7:9). As we will see, this is a picture interpreting the number which has been heard in 7:4-8, thus representing those who have been sealed. As noted above, all Satan's followers bear his mark or name, and all the Lamb's followers must bear the Lamb's mark or name — hence, all believers in Christ throughout the ages are sealed and must be included in the **one hundred and forty-four thousand**.

But why speak of a specific number? In 21:13-14, the twelve tribes and the twelve apostles together form the foundational structure of the new Jerusalem. Multiplying twelve by twelve equals one hundred and forty-four, representing the entire people of God through the ages. Multiplying that figure by one thousand reinforces the notion of completeness.

In the list of tribes recorded in these verses, it is striking that **Judah** is mentioned first. This emphasizes Christ's descent from Judah (see 5:5), as prophesied in Gen. 49:8-10 and elsewhere in the OT where a descendent of David (and thus of Judah) is prophesied to arise as Messiah in the latter days (Ezek. 34:23; 37:24-26; Ps. 16:8-11; together with Acts 2:25-28). Therefore, this is a continuation of 5:5, where Jesus is identified as the fulfillment of the promised leader from Judah. Furthermore, the priority of **Judah** is appropriate because Gen. 49:10 predicts that the coming leader of Judah will bring about "the obedience of the peoples." In this respect, the LXX of Gen. 49:10 reads, "he is the expectation of nations," and Paul alludes to

Gen. 49:10 in Rom. 1:5 by referring to "the obedience of faith among all the Gentiles," which has been accomplished by Christ, the "descendant of David according to the flesh" (Rom. 1:3; cf. 16:26). Therefore, **the tribe of Judah** is mentioned first because the Messiah from Judah is the king who represents Israel, and through its new king Judah has become the door of blessing to the nations (so 5:5, 9). Accordingly, a kingly descendant from David would be a natural choice to provide entry for the nations into the blessings of Israel.

It is clear that one of the names written on Gentile Christians, in addition to those of God and Christ, is "the name of the city of my God, the new Jerusalem" (3:12). Since the name of the "new Jerusalem" is equated with Christ's "new name" in Rev. 3:12, it is likely that Christians can be identified with the "new Jerusalem," since they are identified with Christ; they are thus the true Israel. In the same way, Isa. 49:3, in relation to Isa. 53:10 and Gal. 3:16, affirms the Messiah as the true Israel. Jesus as the messianic "seed" of Israel (Gal. 3:16) represents all believers, so that they are also part of the Israelite "seed" (Gal. 3:29). However, this name is not written on those "who say that they are Jews, and are not" true Jews (Rev. 3:9), since they reject Christ. The name of "the new Jerusalem" applied to the church of Philadelphia is closely linked conceptually to the 144,000 **from every tribe of the sons of Israel**.

Christians are thus here portrayed as the true Israel, as also in 1:6 and 5:10 (applying Exod. 19:6); 5:9 (applying Dan. 7:18, 22); 2:17 and 3:12 (applying Isa. 62:2 and 65:15); 3:9 (applying Isa. 49:23 and 60:14); and in the picture of the new Jerusalem in chs. 21–22 (applying Ezekiel 40–48). In fact, a series of prophecies about Israel's restoration is cited as fulfilled in those who believe "from every nation and all tribes and peoples and tongues" in 7:9, 15-17 (on which see below). This is consistent with the identification elsewhere in the NT of the church (composed of Jews and Gentiles) as fulfilling predictions of Israel's restoration (so Rom. 9:24-26; 10:12-13; 2 Cor. 5:17; 6:2, 16-18) and being called true "Jews" (Rom. 2:28-29), "Israel" (Rom. 9:6; Gal. 6:15-16), true "circumcision" (Phil. 3:3), "the twelve tribes" (cf. Jas. 1:1), or dispersed Israelites (1 Pet. 1:1; 2:9). In fact, including Gentiles as part of true end-time Israel was prophesied in the OT (so Psalm 87; Isa. 19:18-25, especially v. 18; 56:1-8; Ezek. 47:21-23; Zech. 2:11; 9:7).

The implausibility of viewing the twelve tribes **of the sons of Israel** literally in vv. 3-8 is increased by realizing that it would mean that allusions to OT enemies of God's people elsewhere in Revelation (Sodom and Egypt in 11:8, Babylon in chs. 14–18, and Gog and Magog in 20:8) must entail the bizarre belief on John's part that all these enemies will also be literally revived.

A refinement of the above view of the church as true Israel has been made by Richard Bauckham in *The Climax of Prophecy: Studies in the Book of Revelation* (Edinburgh: Clark, 1993), 217-29. Bauckham has argued convincingly that the numbering in vv. 4-8 suggests that those numbered are an army. The evidence for this view is manifold, but, above all, the language of **from the tribe of** recalls the repeated phrases "of the tribe of" in OT census lists (e.g., Num. 1:21, 23, etc.). The purpose of the census in Numbers was to organize a military force to conquer the Promised Land.

The church is thus depicted in military terms as a remnant called out of the world to do battle for God. This force is ready to fight, and v. 14 interprets the manner of their fighting. They conquer their enemy ironically in the same way in which the kingly Lamb from Judah ironically conquered at the cross: by maintaining their faith and witness through suffering, they overcome their foe, the devil and his hosts (see on v. 14 below; for identification of the group in vv. 4-8 with the group in vv. 9-17 see further the introductory comments to vv. 9-17). Consequently, they are those "who follow the Lamb wherever He goes" (14:4).

The language of **from the tribe of** in vv. 4-8 may have no connotation of the church as a remnant called out from a larger unbelieving community to fight a battle, but may simply be part of the census terminology carried over from the OT to portray the church as the new Israel. Nevertheless, the repeated formula may refer to the selecting out of a remnant from a larger unbelieving group (the people of every tribe and nation) because of:

- the added idea in the Revelation context of "sealing" and its redemptive meaning, with the implication that there were others who were not thus sealed,
- the idea of a remnant in the Qumran *War Scroll* (1QM 2-3, 5-6, 14) in relation to the community's holy army,
- the similarity of **from the tribe of** in 7:4-8 to **from every nation and [all] tribes** in v. 9 and in 5:9 ("from every tribe," both referring to people redeemed out of a larger mass of earth's inhabitants), and
- the parallel in 14:1-4, which speaks of the 144,000 as both "purchased from the earth" and "purchased from among people" and then further defines "the earth" and "people" in 14:6 as "every nation and tribe and tongue and people."

Therefore, the selective service language of the OT census lists may have served the additional purpose of fitting into the theology of the remnant found throughout Revelation, and so was accordingly enriched.

Suggestions for Reflection on 7:1-8

On sealing and the assurance of salvation. If the "sealing" means protection from losing one's saving relationship with God, how can Christians be assured that they really have been "sealed with the Spirit" and have such life? This question deals with the sometimes difficult issue of how a Christian can have assurance of salvation. The following questions, based on the context of Revelation itself, should help to focus further reflection on this issue of how a sense of assurance can be gained and increased:

- Have Christians truly believed that the Lamb has purchased them by the price of His blood (Rev. 5:9; 12:11)?
- Does one desire to keep God's commandments (2:26; 12:17; 14:12; 22:3)?
- Is one so convicted of sin that it leads to repentance and renewal of one's relationship with Christ (2:4-5; 3:17-19)?
- Is one willing to bear witness to the Lamb in the midst of pressures to compromise faith (6:9; 12:11, 17; 19:10)?

The responses to these four questions have a cumulative effective on one's perception of assurance.

On being slaves or servants of God. Rev. 7:3 says that those who have been "sealed" are "bond-servants/slaves of God." Faithful slaves in the ancient world were to please their masters with their whole being, since their whole body was owned by the master, and Christians likewise should want to please their divine Master (so Gal. 1:10; Eph. 6:6; cf. Rev. 22:3). Is there a part of our lives which we do not allow to be in subjugation to Christ (financial considerations, sexual issues, etc.)? Paul says that we are to present our entire beings and bodies to Christ as "slaves to righteousness" (Rom. 6:16-19), since Christ has "bought" us with a "price" (1 Cor. 6:20). The true slave of Christ becomes "obedient from the heart" (Rom. 6:17). Does God have our entire hearts? God's "slaves" are those "who walk before him with all their heart" (1 Kgs. 8:23; cf. vv. 48, 61). Is our obedience to God only a duty, or do we also desire from our hearts to please Him by being subject to Him? Negative answers to these questions reveal degrees of idolatry, which Revelation speaks much about (e.g., 2:12-23; 9:20-21).

On the church as the true Israel. What difference does it make for Christians when they realize that they are part of the continuation of true Israel from the OT? One very practical difference is that the OT becomes much more a book for Christians, since it contains so many prophecies about Israel, the fulfillment of which occur in the church throughout the ages. In particular, as seen in the commentary, the prophecies about Israel's restoration to its land began to be fulfilled in unbelieving Jews and Gentiles being restored to God through Christ and thus coming to represent the true Israel and new Jerusalem. It is enlightening, for example, to read the prophecies of Isaiah 40–66 with this in mind. What are other implications of the church being the true Israel? For example, how does this relate to what is going on in Israel in the Middle East today?

On the nature of Christian warfare. As we have seen, the listing of those sealed from various Israelite tribes in vv. 4-8 could well represent a mustering of soldiers to fight in a holy war. But if those called out and sealed represent the church as true Israel, then what kind of war is being fought? As we saw above, 7:14 interprets the manner of their fighting: they conquer in no other way than that of the Lamb: by persevering in the midst of suffering. What are the various ways that Christians today participate in this battle? The hymn "Onward Christian Soldiers" is uniquely suited to this passage in Revelation. Note, for instance, the stanza, "Crowns and thrones may perish, kingdoms rise and wane/But the church of Jesus constant will remain/Gates of hell can never 'gainst that church prevail/We have Christ's own promise, and that cannot fail."

God and the Lamb are praised for making manifest the redemption of multitudes by protecting them through a purifying tribulation (7:9-17)

9 After these things I looked, and behold, a great multitude, which no one could
count, from every nation and all tribes and peoples and tongues, standing before
the throne and before the Lamb, clothed in white robes, and palm branches were
in their hands; 10 and they cry out with a loud voice, saying, "Salvation to our God
who sits on the throne, and to the Lamb." 11 And all the angels were standing
around the throne and around the elders and the four living creatures; and they
fell on their faces before the throne and worshiped God, 12 saying, "Amen, blessing and glory and wisdom and thanksgiving and honor and power and might, be
to our God forever and ever. Amen." 13 And one of the elders answered, saying

to me, "These who are clothed in the white robes, who are they, and from where have they come?" [14] And I said to him, "My lord, you know." And he said to me, "These are the ones who come out of the great tribulation, and they have washed their robes and made them white in the blood of the Lamb. [15] For this reason they are before the throne of God; and they serve Him day and night in His temple; and He who sits on the throne shall spread His tabernacle over them. [16] They shall hunger no more, neither thirst anymore; neither shall the sun beat down on them, nor any heat; [17] for the Lamb at the center of the throne shall be their shepherd, and shall guide them to springs of the water of life; and God shall wipe every tear from their eyes."

Whereas vv. 1-8 have portrayed the church in its symbolic significance as the true Israel, in vv. 9-17 John receives a glimpse into its actual dimensions. The first passage pictures the church as a restored remnant of true Israel whose salvific security has been guaranteed. They are said to be a certain number of people because God has determined exactly who will receive His redemptive seal, and only He knows the precise number of His true servants (so 7:3; 2 Tim. 2:19). Because of this, the exalted saints who have suffered so far are told in 6:11 that they must wait for vindication a "little while longer, until the *number* of their fellow *servants* . . . who were to be killed . . . should be completed also." This second picture in vv. 9-17 understands the same host now from the viewpoint of their actual vast number. Although they are a saved remnant, they are also those who have been gathered from all over the face of the earth and have lived throughout the period of the church age. Therefore, they are a multitudinous throng. The identification of the people in vv. 3-8 and vv. 9-17 as both being true Israel (the church) is deducible from observing that the group in the latter segment is described as fulfilling Isaiah's and Ezekiel's restoration prophecies concerning *Israel* (see on vv. 16, 17) and as persevering through the time of tribulation foretold by Daniel (12:1) to come upon faithful *Israelites* (see on v. 14).

This view of the relationship of the two segments in ch. 7 is strengthened by the observation of the pattern elsewhere, in which what John sees is repeatedly interpreted by what he then immediately hears, or what he hears is interpreted by what he then sees. For the former pattern, compare 5:6 with 5:7-14; 14:1 with 14:2-5; 15:2 with 15:3-4; 17:1-6 with 17:7-18. For the latter pattern, compare 5:5 with 5:6; 9:13-16 with 9:17-21. Note also that the relation between the two segments is precisely parallel to the relationship between the Lion and the Lamb in 5:5-6. In ch. 5, John first *hears* about a Lion (5:5), then understands its meaning through *seeing* the Lamb who appears to him (5:6). Likewise, in ch. 7 John *hears* of the number of those sealed from the twelve tribes, then understands its meaning through *seeing* the innumerable multitude who appear to him. To the Lion of the tribe of Judah (5:5) corresponds the list of the sealed of the twelve tribes, headed by that of Judah (7:4-8). To the slain Lamb (5:6) corresponds the ransomed from every tribe and nation (5:9) and the multitude from every tribe and nation (7:9), who "have washed their robes and made them white in the blood of the Lamb" (7:14).

Therefore, the sealing of the saints explains further how Christ will keep them from "the hour of testing" which is "to test those who dwell upon the earth" (3:10), that is, those who have persecuted them (see on 3:10 for the negative identification of the "earth-dwellers"; cf. 6:10; see further on 3:10 and 7:14 for the Dan. 12:1 background concerning the tribulation). All these connections concern matters which precede the final judgment and reward, so ch. 7 must function as an interlude or parenthesis in its placement after ch. 6. Yet the chapter also has a future aspect, especially toward the end (vv. 15-17). From this perspective, the chapter is, among other things, an answer to the concluding question of 6:17, "Who is able to stand" before God and not suffer the wrath of the last judgment? This is the definitive answer to 6:17 and the main point toward which the visionary narrative of vv. 9-17 drives.

In this respect the mention of the "great multitude . . . *standing* before the throne" (7:9) may be an explicit answer to the question of 6:17. This is suggested by: the close contextual placement of 6:17 and 7:9 and the common use of "stand"; the reference in both to people standing before the throne and the Lamb; the picture of the Lamb "standing" before the throne in 5:6, likely associated to a significant degree with His resurrection existence, so that the "standing" before the throne in 7:9 of people later described as sheep (7:17) plausibly also reflects their resurrection existence; and the "standing" of the saints "on the sea of glass" in 15:2, also in direct conjunction with mention of the Lamb, likewise reflecting the Lamb's resurrection existence from 5:6 (see on 15:2), in which saints share. The word "stand" appears also to have this meaning elsewhere with regard respectively to Christ (10:5, 8, assuming the angel to be Christ; 14:1), saints (11:11, though there likely a figurative or spiritual resurrection), and all humanity (20:12), though this does not signify that all resurrected humanity will be saved.

Therefore, ch. 7 does not present a new series of future events during a final tribulation period which follow those of ch. 6. Rather, the chapter is a parenthesis explaining the vision of ch. 6 in more depth and providing a larger background against which to understand it better. The events of 7:1-8 immediately precede those of 6:1-8, and 7:9-17 focuses on the time after the final judgment, which has been portrayed in its initial phase in 6:12-17 (though the pre-final judgment age could be secondarily in mind in 7:9-17, especially in vv. 13-14, which portray the *overall process* of those who persevere and enter into and begin to participate in the enjoyment of God's presence and eternal blessings).

In this light, the following flow of thought is discernible in ch. 7: God and the Lamb are glorified (vv. 9-12) because of the heavenly reward of redemptive rest they have bestowed upon the entire people of God (vv. 15-17). This reward is a result of the people of God's perseverance through "the great tribulation" (v. 14) of the "four winds" (vv. 1-3; cf. 6:1-8) by means of the protective seal given them by God (vv. 3-8).

9 **After these things**, as in v. 1 (in the conceptually equivalent form "after this") and other places in Revelation, means that this is the next vision John saw, not that the events depicted therein will necessarily occur immediately after those of the previous vision in vv. 1-8. In fact, the vision records events following the depiction of the final judgment in 6:12-17. The group here pictured is the same as in 5:9, the end-time people of God from every tongue and nation prophesied in Dan. 7:14, 22, and 27. These saints are those of God's people already glorified, for this scene takes place in heaven, **before the throne** of God. Having earned their reward through faithful perseverance in tribulation, they are now enjoying the presence of the Lord in eternity. The **great multitude, which no one could count** is the promised seed of Abraham, the "multitude of nations" (Gen. 17:5), which were "too many to count" (Gen. 32:12 and 16:10). The descendants or "seed" who would become so numerous according to these Abrahamic promises refer not to the nations in general but specifically to the future multiplication of Israel in Egypt, and thereafter in the Promised Land. The **great multitude** in v. 9 is the fulfillment of the Abrahamic promise and thus yet another way in which Revelation refers to Christians throughout the world as the true Israel. The **palm branches** the throng is waving allude to the Feast of Tabernacles, in which palm branches were used to build the booths in which the Jews live during the feast (Lev. 23:40-43). The Feast celebrates God's protection of the Israelites during their wanderings in the desert, and in the same way God seals His faithful ones during the present age. The imagery originally applied to Israel is now applied by John to people from all nations, who rejoice in their latter-day exodus redemption, in their victory over their persecutors and in the fact that God has protected them subsequently during their wilderness pilgrimage (12:6, 14!) through the "great tribulation" (see on 7:13-14).

10-12 As true Israelites, they celebrate an eschatological Feast of Tabernacles in heaven in order to commemorate joyfully their end-time salvation, which is attributed to **God . . . who sits on the throne, and to the Lamb.** Their salvation lies in their victorious resistance to the forces of evil which have attempted to thwart their faith (so 12:10-11; 19:1-2). The overcomers acknowledge that their victory is really God's victory, since it has been obtained by His power (so 12:10-11). The preservation of the saints' faith is attributed to God's sovereignty, since the white robes (v. 9) symbolize a purity resulting from perseverance through testing (see below on vv. 13-17). God protects their faith in the midst of trials by means of the seal which He imparts to them (vv. 1-3). This saving victory is consummated by God's judgment of the sinful world (portrayed, e.g., in 6:12-17), which has attempted to seduce the faith of His people and has persecuted them. These glorified saints are now joined by the **angels**, the **elders**, and the **four living creatures** in their praise and worship of God and the Lamb. The heavenly host recognizes that this redemptive work demonstrates that only God possesses these sovereign attributes and is alone worthy of receiving for eternity **blessing and glory and wisdom and thanksgiving and honor and power and might. Amen** introduces and concludes the praise formula in order to confirm emphatically the certainty and factual truth of the redemption wrought by God.

13-14 One of the elders informs John of the identity of these people. This great multitude represents those who have **come out of the great tribulation**. The only other place in the NT outside Revelation where the phrase "the great tribulation" occurs is in Matt. 24:21, and both that verse and this are clear references to Dan. 12:1 (LXX): "there will be a time of tribulation, such tribulation as has not come about from when a nation was upon the earth until that time." Use of the definite article ***the* great tribulation** indicates that this is the latter-day tribulation prophesied by Daniel and also by Christ rather than just another general occasion of tribulation. In Daniel's tribulation, the latter-day opponent of God's people persecutes them because of their faithfulness to Him (Dan. 11:30-39, 44; 12:10). Some will fall away (Dan. 11:32, 34), even as some are doing so in five of the churches of Asia (all but Smyrna and Philadelphia). The tribulation consists in pressures from the religious system to compromise one's faith and pressures from the world, which may include economic deprivation (see "your tribulation and your poverty" in 2:9).

This **tribulation** is not confined to the days immediately preceding Christ's return, but commences with the birth of the church and continues throughout the church age. We can give at least five reasons for this:

John elsewhere sees the end-time prophecies of Daniel as beginning to be fulfilled from the time of Christ onward (see on 1:1, 13, 19).

Jesus sees Daniel's prophecy of resurrection (12:2) fulfilled first spiritually in His own ministry and then physically at His return (John 5:24-29). Hence the resurrection of the saints predicted in Dan. 12:2 is being inaugurated in Jesus' ministry (which has significance for our understanding of the "first resurrection"; see on 20:6).

In Rev. 1:9; 2:9-10, 22 (the latter referring to false believers), the tribulation is referred to as a present reality. The "hour of testing" in 3:10 also alludes to Dan. 12:1, 10, and it appears to include the entire inter-advent period. Thus, 3:10 probably develops the idea of the "hour of testing" and applies it to the same period. In particular, the article ("the") in v. 14 is an article of previous reference, referring back in part to a "great tribulation" (2:22) which was to occur imminently in the church of Thyatira in the first century.

Jesus sees tribulation as a present reality in John 16:33.

Twenty-one of twenty-three uses of "tribulation" in Paul refer to a present reality, so the idea of an inaugurated end-time tribulation in Rev. 7:14 is compatible with the way "tribulation" (Greek *thlipsis*) is used elsewhere in the NT.

The great tribulation, therefore, began with the sufferings of Jesus and is now shared in by all believers, who are, with John, fellow-partakers "in the tribulation and kingdom and perseverance which are in Jesus" (1:9).

The fact that they are those who have **come out of the great tribulation** accounts for the whiteness of their **robes**, which have been **washed . . . in the blood of the Lamb**, an OT metaphor which speaks of the forgiveness of sins (Isa. 1:18; Zech. 3:3-5). Jesus Himself is described in Rev. 19:13 as clothed with a robe dipped in blood, and so their robes express the fact that these saints have followed Jesus faithfully in the way of the cross. In 6:9-11, those who were slain were given a white robe because they had maintained their testimony to Christ. Despite resistance, they continued believing in and testifying to the Lamb's death on their behalf, which has taken their sin away and granted them salvation. Conversely, those in the church who compromise and do not witness to Christ because of trials have "soiled their garments" (3:4).

Tribulation has only served to refine and purify the faith and character of the saints (see Rom. 5:3-5; 1 Pet. 1:7). It is significant that the only places in the OT where the saints are spoken of as having white clothing are in Dan. 11:35 and 12:10, speaking of the saints of the end times, which, as we have seen, began with the resurrection of Christ. Dan. 11:35 affirms that oppression and suffering comes "in order to refine, purge and make them white [Hebrew *laben;* NASB "pure"] until the end time." The saved multitude of every nation pictured here are the prophesied latter-day Israelites of Daniel's vision. Thus, the picture of latter-day cleansed believers of every nation fulfills the prophecy of Daniel 11–12 concerning Israel, once again identifying the church as the continuation of true Israel.

The image of saints with cleansed, white robes in vv. 9 and 14 and elsewhere in Revelation connotes a purity which has been demonstrated by the people's persevering faith in Christ's redemptive death (= "blood"), having been tested by a purifying fire. 3:18 emphasizes the aspect of purification by nearly equating the exhortations "buy . . . gold refined by fire that you may become rich" with "[buy] white garments, that you may clothe yourself." The picture appears again in 22:14, where it is clearly used to describe all believers who enter the new Jerusalem, as contrasted with unbelievers, who do not. Those receiving white robes in 3:4-5 have their names written in the "book of life," an allusion to Dan. 12:1. This is not a select group, but the entire company of the redeemed, for only those whose robes are thus washed will enter into the new Jerusalem (Rev. 22:14). The metaphor of washing white robes in blood primarily connotes the objective reality that the saints have been cleansed from their sin by their persevering faith in Christ's death for them, which has been refined by trials. Since **the blood of the Lamb** refers to Christ's own blood and not that of the saints, the focus is on the cleansing effects of His death on their behalf. When John wants to refer to the saints' suffering, he uses phrases like "the blood of the saints" (17:6; likewise 6:10; 18:24; 19:2). Therefore, the picture does not primarily connote the idea of a select group of martyrs but encompasses the entire company of the redeemed.

15 The introductory phrase **for this reason** explains that the saints' perseverance in Christ and resulting purity (vv. 13-14) are the basis for their entrance into the presence of God and the Lamb (vv. 15-17). Sinful people must flee "from the presence of Him who sits on the throne" because He is holy and must pour out His wrath on sin (6:16-17). But those believing that the Lamb has appeased God's wrath on their behalf and consequently have been declared "clean" and "righteous" (cf. 19:8b) are allowed entrance before God **who sits on the throne**. They are able to enter God's tabernacling presence and serve Him, because the Lamb has reversed the effects of Adam's fall by suffering the painful curse of death in their place (so 21:3-4, 6; 22:1-4; cf. 1:18; 5:6, 9, 12). Their steadfast faith is a qualification for entrance and their entrance itself is a reward for maintaining their faith despite tribulation (so 22:14). The final reward of rest in the presence of God and the Lamb forms the basis for the saints' glorifying God and the Lamb in vv. 9-12.

These believers become a new priesthood, serving God in His eternal temple. They wear white robes, having been purified with blood, and **serve Him day and night in His temple** (see Lev. 8:30, where also the priests' garments are sprinkled with blood to signify consecration for serving God in the tabernacle). The connection with Rev. 1:5-6 and 5:9-10 shows that here all Christians are in mind and not merely martyrs or some other special class of saints. This verse thus develops the idea of a new priesthood introduced in 1:6 and 5:10, all three passages alluding to God's promise to Israel in Exod. 19:6 that they would all become a kingdom of priests and a holy nation. All believers in Christ fulfill this promise to ancient Israel. Also fulfilled is the prophecy to Israel in Ezek. 37:26-27 that God would place His sanctuary in the midst of them and that His **tabernacle** (dwelling place) would be **over them**. The reference to the multitudes **in His temple** where God spreads **His tabernacle over them** is a clear echo from this prophecy of Israel's restoration in Ezek. 37:26-28. There God says, "I . . . will set my *sanctuary* in their midst forever. My dwelling place [= *tabernacle*] also will be over them . . . when My *sanctuary* is in their midst forever."

According to Ezekiel, the result of God tabernacling with His people is that the nations will recognize that He is the Lord who sanctifies Israel (Ezek. 37:28), whereas clearly this promise is now applied to Christian believers. The application of the Ezek. 37:27 prophecy to the church is striking, because Ezekiel emphasizes that when this prophecy takes place, the immediate result will be that "the nations will know that I am the Lord who sanctifies *Israel,* when my sanctuary is in their midst forever" (37:28). Therefore, Ezekiel 37 was a prophecy uniquely applicable to ethnic Israel in contrast to the nations, yet now John understands it as fulfilled in the church (for the same kind of reversed applications of OT prophecies see on 3:9, where also the title of "Jews" is seen to be inappropriate for unbelieving ethnic Jews). The application of this Israelite prophecy to the church is highlighted by observing that Ezek. 37:27 refers to Israel as "My people," which is a title included in the fuller quotation of Ezek. 37:27 found in Rev. 21:3, where it is again applied to the church, the continuation of true Israel.

The picture in v. 15 is not a reference to a localized temple building in which the saints serve God (so also 21:22!). Rather, as the second part of the verse reveals, the temple now consists in the presence of the Lamb and **He who sits on the throne** and who **spreads His tabernacle over them** (so also 21:22). The mention of God "tabernacling" with His people also continues the theme of the OT "feast of tabernacles" from v. 9 (cf. the "feast of tabernacles" in Lev. 23:34-44; Deut. 16:13-17, etc.).

16-17 The saved multitudes who enjoy God's presence continue to be described as a fulfillment of Israel's prophesied restoration. They enjoy the comforts of the divine presence which were promised as a part of the restoration. John appeals to Isa. 49:10, which affirms one of the resulting conditions of Israel's restoration into the presence of God: "They will not hunger or thirst, neither will the scorching heat or sun strike them down . . . for he . . . will guide them to springs of waters" (cf. John 6:35). Consequently, the church fulfills the restoration prophecy of Isa. 49:10. Rev. 22:17 suggests that saints begin to partake of this water in the present age: "Let the one who is thirsty come; let the one who wishes take the water of life without cost." It is Christ's divine position **in the center of the throne** which is the basis for removing the saints' former affliction (represented by hunger, thirst, and extreme heat). He is able to provide divine comforts because He is in the position of God. Because He is their divine shepherd and they are His sheep, He will protect them, as a shepherd guards his sheep. Even the image of the **Lamb** who is **their shepherd** comes from Isa. 49:9-10, where the One who has compassion on them will feed them and pasture them. Isaiah 49 portrays God as the shepherd, so that Christ's shepherding role here enhances His position as a divine figure.

To the end of the Isa. 49:10 allusion is appended an additional reference to a restoration promise from Isa. 25:8: **God shall wipe away every tear from their eyes.** There will no longer be any mourning because God "will swallow up death for all time," which is the introductory phrase of Isa. 25:8. Although John omits the initial line about the ceasing of death, he probably assumes it as the basis for the promise that there will be no more tears. He does in fact include this part of Isa. 25:8 in 21:4: "there shall no longer be any death," directly after "He will wipe away every tear from their eyes." As with Isaiah 49, John sees the OT hope of Israel's joyous restoration fulfilled in the salvation of Christian multitudes who had so faithfully suffered for Christ.

The language of shepherding here may have been substituted in place of the almost synonymous "pasturing" found in Isaiah. This is suggested by the context of Ezek. 37:24-28, just alluded to in v. 15, which says that at the time when God establishes His tabernacle among them, "My servant David will be king over them, and they will all have one shepherd" (Ezek. 37:24). The association of the Lamb with David is natural because of the Lamb's prior identification as "the Lion that is from the tribe of Judah, the Root of David" in 5:5 and the emphasis on Judah by its position as first in the list of tribes in 7:4-8. The reason for the picture here is to emphasize the identity of the Lamb with His people. He is the corporate representative of His saints. Therefore, just as He first suffered and received His reward at the resurrection, so His flock follow the same pattern in their own lives (see on 1:5, 9; 7:14). Whereas He led them by the Spirit on earth, He will lead them in person in the future.

The focus of the second half of ch. 7 is in vv. 9-12 and 15-17, where all Christians appear to be pictured as enjoying their eternal reward. And now, not merely a portion receive this reward (as in 6:9-11), but the totality of the faithful who have lived throughout the ages. This is suggested by observing that the section follows a vision of the last judgment (6:12-17) and the sealing of God's servants (7:1-8). Therefore, the saints' eternal comfort is contrasted with the terror of punishment for the ungodly and is set forth as a reward for enduring the tribulation as a result of having been sealed. That this is a picture focusing most on the consummated, eternal reward of all the saints is borne out by the verbal parallels which vv. 15-17 have in common with the portrayal of the eternal state in 21:3-4, 6 and 22:3. Those pictured in vv. 13-17 are those who conquer throughout the church age and have been promised that, when they have finished their witness, they will receive white robes (3:4-5) and a secure place in God's eternal temple (3:12) and will be given nourishment so that they will never hunger again (2:7, 17). In this light, the pre-consummative age may be partly in mind in 7:9-17. Lastly, the conclusion that all Christians are included in this picture of bliss is confirmed by seeing that the group with white robes mentioned in v. 9 is the same group that came out of the tribulation wearing white robes and entered into God's presence in vv. 13-17. In v. 9, this group is innumerable and "from every nation and all tribes and peoples and tongues," a formula which there and in 5:9 refers to all the redeemed throughout the church age (see on 5:9-10).

Suggestions for Reflection on 7:9-17

On the meaning and implications of the "great tribulation." According to the commentary, these verses (in conjunction with other passages in the Bible) identify the entire church age as the time of the "great tribulation." Why would the church age be thus characterized? How do we relate this to a picture of the church as triumphant or victorious? What is the nature or dimensions of our victory in this present world? What are the probable limits? Can we expect to establish godly forms of government in this time of tribulation? Pressure for Christians to conform to ungodly political and economic systems linked with idolatrous practices or attitudes is suggested by the commentary as the most consistent form of tribulation. Is this what we would identify as the ultimate cause of tribulation? Is it possible for there to be lesser or greater periods of tribulation, and if so, why would that be the case?

On the prevalence of "apocalyptic" expectations Any analysis of human psychology shows that people have an interest in speculation concerning the end of the world. How does this carry over into understanding of biblical passages such as this? Why do we prefer to view the "great tribulation" as an event associated only with a time directly preceding the final return of Christ rather than as something that the church has been living through throughout the church age and that will intensify before Christ's final coming? If we believe the tribulation is yet to come, how does this distort our understanding of the tribulation we are in fact living through? Do we "sensationalize" apocalyptic events to the point that we fail to recognize the dangers of the present? If we believe we are not in a time of tribulation, could this lead us to minimize the perils of the very real present pressures we face to conform to the world?

On the fulfillment of OT prophecies by the church This passage is shot through with OT prophetic references to Israel now applied to the church. If, then, Christ and the church are the fulfillment of biblical prophecy, what place in the plan of God is left for the Jewish people? If we understand Romans 9–11 as speaking to that issue, how then are we to differentiate between the Jewish people and the (secular) state of Israel? Does God have a prophetic plan from the OT for the latter at all? Why is it that so often people view biblical prophecy of Israel's restoration as fulfilled only in events concerning the state of Israel? How should Christians properly view the state of Israel? And can a focus on the Jewish people and/or the state of Israel as the fulfillment of biblical prophecy be held along with a high view of the inheritance God has for

His church in this present age? How can Christians be compassionate toward Jews without making them the centerpiece of biblical prophecy?

The seventh seal as the conclusion of the seal series: the last judgment is reiterated as a formal response to the saints' petition in 6:10 that God punish the unbelieving world (8:1-5)

[1] And when He broke the seventh seal, there was silence in heaven for about half
an hour. [2] And I saw the seven angels who stand before God; and seven trumpets
were given to them. [3] And another angel came and stood at the altar, holding a
golden censer; and much incense was given to him, that he might add it to the
prayers of all the saints upon the golden altar which was before the throne. [4] And
the smoke of the incense, with the prayers of the saints, went up before God out
of the angel's hand. [5] And the angel took the censer; and he filled it with the fire
of the altar and threw it to the earth; and there followed peals of thunder and
sounds and flashes of lightning and an earthquake.

1 When the Lamb opens the seventh seal, there results **silence in heaven for about half an hour**. Some argue that this silence means that the seal has no content, thus allowing for the idea that the following trumpets and bowls make up its content and thus refer to events subsequent to those of the first six seal judgments. The silence does have content, however. The OT associates silence with divine judgment. In Hab. 2:20–3:15 and Zech. 2:13–3:2, God is pictured (as in Rev. 8:1) as being in His temple and about to bring judgment on the earth. That the temple is in heaven is to be assumed from texts such as Ezekiel 1. At the moment this judgment is to be delivered, God commands the earth to be silent. In Zeph. 1:7-18, silence is likewise commanded in connection with the "great day" of the Lord and of His judgment (Zeph. 1:14, 18 forming part of the OT background to the phrase "the great day of their wrath" in Rev. 6:17). These announcements of judgment from the Minor Prophets express cosmic end-time expectations (as implied by the pregnant word "all"), which is explicitly expressed in a universal sense in Rev. 8:1. The thought is that this final judgment of God is so awful that the whole world falls utterly silent in its presence. Thus the seventh seal is a continuation of the sixth. Whereas the first five seals deal with the entire period of the church age, the last two deal with the final judgment. As such, they are God's response to the prayer of the saints in 6:10, "How long, O Lord, will you refrain from judging and avenging our blood on those who dwell on the earth?" It is interesting that in Jewish writings silence is associated not only with divine judgment but also with the fact that the prayers of the faithful for that judgment are being heard. John does not give any further details here of the punishment of the wicked because he will do so repeatedly later on (11:18; 14:14-20; 16:17-21; 18:9-24; 19:19-21; 20:11-15). And of course, there is more description of the judgments in 8:3-5.

The duration of this silence is **about half an hour**. "Hour" in Revelation often refers to the suddenness of the time of judgment of the wicked (3:3; 11:13; 14:7; 18:10), whereas "half" is associated with "times" of crisis and judgment in Dan. 7:25; 9:27; and 12:7 (which lie behind the forty-two month period of Rev. 11:3, 9; 12:6; 13:5). **About half an hour** might not refer so much to the precise temporal duration of the silence (**about**) but figuratively emphasize the suddenness and unexpectedness of a decreed judgment. Note that the last occurrence of the expression "one hour" (18:19) is directly followed in 18:22-23 by a description of the aftermath of judgment, which is absolute silence.

2 The vision of the seven trumpet angels appears to be an interruption of the last judgment scenario of v. 1 continued in vv. 3-5. The verse seems out of place by introducing a new series of judgments which is not picked up again until v. 6. However, we see the apparent awkwardness as part of an interlocking literary transition together with vv. 3-5, which has parallels elsewhere in the book. The placement of v. 2 before vv. 3-5 allows the latter to act as a parenthetical transition, both concluding the seals and introducing the trumpets. The transition functions on both a literary and thematic level (see further comments on the transition below). The narration of the trumpet series resumes in v. 6. John sees seven angels holding seven trumpets. The seven angels could be identified with the seven guardian angels of the seven churches in chs. 2–3 (see on 1:20).

3 The primary thematic function of the parenthesis in vv. 3-5 is to pick up and conclude the description of final judgment begun in 6:12-17 and 8:1. As already suggested, the temple atmosphere of this section is part of the OT judgment imagery, which includes the element of silence. Therefore, this parenthesis continues the imagery of the last judgment from v. 1. **Another angel** appears and stands **at the altar**. This may be the "angel of His presence" (Isa. 63:9) or even Christ Himself (as in 10:1; 14:14). The altar in view is the same of 6:9, under which were the souls of the persecuted saints. That **much incense was given to him** is a "divine passive" meaning "given by God" and showing, as elsewhere in Revelation, that the angel is an agent of God whose actions merely indicate prior divine decision. This is consistent with the fact that in 6:10 the saints presented their prayer directly to God and not to an angel, which demonstrates their direct access to the divine throne as priests. That the altar of v. 3 is the same as that of 6:9 is confirmed by the repetition of "altar" three times in vv. 3-5, in connection with the following statement that he added "much incense . . . to the prayers of all the saints." This phrase is almost identical in wording to 5:8, which is then developed in 6:9, showing that the altar and temple theme originate in the temple vision of chs. 4–5. The response to their prayers is that punishment cannot be executed until the number of God's people destined for persecution is completed (6:11). This cannot happen until history comes to an end. This is why, if 6:12-17 and 8:1 are viewed as a response to this petition, they must be understood as depicting the last great judgment (see on 6:12-17). Vv. 3-5 make this connection between 6:9-11 and 6:12-17/8:1 explicit by formally alluding to 6:9-10. This observation alone provides significant evidence against the traditional futurist view of Revelation, which depends on the contention that the various series of plagues depicted in the book are entirely consecutive in nature.

4 The fact that **the smoke of the incense** goes up **with the prayers of the saints** shows that the petition of 6:9-10 is now being presented before God. In the Bible, incense is always associated with sacrifice, so that the sacrifice, accompanied by a pleasing aroma, will be acceptable to God. These verses echo Lev. 16:12-13, where the priest takes the censer full of coals off the altar before the Lord, fills his hands with incense, and puts the incense on the fire before the Lord. In Ps. 141:2 prayer is associated with incense and compared to a form of sacrifice: "May my prayer be counted as incense before Thee, the lifting up of my hands as the evening offering." The fact that incense is offered from the altar shows that the prayers of the saints who were slain for their testimony (6:9) represent the sacrifice of their lives in the cause of Christ, and so their petition for judgment in 6:10 has been found acceptable to God.

5 God's formal acknowledgement of the angel's presentation of the saints' prayers and His positive response is the unmentioned link between vv. 4 and 5. This is evident from recognizing v. 5 as a clear divine answer to the petition of 6:10. The verse formally interprets the scenes of woe in 6:12-17 and 8:1 as the answer to the prayer of 6:10 and demonstrates that God has heard and answered these prayers, for the angel throws fire from the altar down to the earth to signify that the last

judgment is taking place. The phrase **peals of thunder and sounds and flashes of lightning and an earthquake** is almost identical to the description of the last judgment in 11:19 and 16:18 (see also 4:5, which serves as an introductory note giving expectation of a final judgment), and is rooted in descriptions of divine judgment in the OT, particularly at Sinai (Exod. 19:16, 18; see also Ps. 77:18 and Isa. 29:6, "You will be punished with thunder and earthquake and loud noise"). Jesus used earthquake imagery to portray woes preliminary to the final cosmic destruction but not part of it (Matt. 24:7, Mark 13:8, Luke 21:11). Richard Bauckham has shown in "The Eschatological Earthquake in the Apocalypse of John," *Novum Testamentum* 19 (1977), 228, that 4:5; 8:5; 11:19; and 16:18-21 form a progressive sequence of allusions to Exod. 19:16, 18-19 that systematically build upon one another, commencing with lightnings, sound, and thunders in 4:5 and at each step adding other elements. The effect of these progressive, yet virtually identical repetitions is to underscore the final judgment and that each recapitulated portrayal of the judgment fills out in more detail how it will occur. Therefore, after the introductory note of 4:5 announcing the expectation of the final judgment, each of the remaining phrases is a formal notation that the last judgment has been narrated, but not exhaustively so.

Note that in Exod. 19:16, 19, the judgment is accompanied by loud blasts of a trumpet, which is particularly interesting as the trumpet judgments are about to be unfolded. That v. 5 is about the last judgment is confirmed from 14:18-19, where the judgment day is commenced apparently by the same angel, described in the same language here as in vv. 3-5. There, "another angel, the one who has power over fire, came out from the altar," and commanded a second angel to execute God's final act of wrath against the earth. The portrayal here is modeled to a great extent on Ezek. 10:1-7, where an angel standing in the temple of the Lord takes fire from between the cherubim and scatters it over the city, emphasizing the decree of God's judgment narrated in Ezekiel 9. This judgment comes on all the unfaithful, those upon whose foreheads God's angel did not give a protective mark, exactly as the saints have their foreheads sealed in Rev. 7:3 so that they will be protected in a similar way. The pattern of this passage follows broadly that of some OT depictions of divine judgment against sinners: prayer for help, divine response to prayer, which leads to fire proceeding from the heavenly temple to consume the persecutors (e.g., Ps. 18:6-15; Hab. 3:15). Those not bearing the seal suffer final judgment.

Suggestions for Reflection on 8:1-5

On the silence of God. Many of the believers to whom John was writing were suffering for their faith. Some may have been asking, "Where is God?" (cf. Psalm 79 and Rev. 6:10). This passage states that there will be a time when God will right the wrongs perpetrated against His people, thus showing that evil will not remain unpunished forever. There are times God appears to be silent in response to our suffering, particularly the suffering of believers experiencing persecution in various parts of the world. How does this passage give us and those who so suffer hope in this regard? Are we in the western world particularly affected by our dependence on material things and relative freedom from persecution? Do our materialism and the philosophy of the age we live in hinder us from a full appreciation of the fact that there awaits a yet unseen judgment at the end of history that will show God and His people to have been in the right all along?

On the effectiveness of prayer. These verses present us with the effects of the prayers of the deceased saints pictured in 6:9-11. The power of these prayers seems to be related to the sacrificial witness of their lives. Do our prayers come out of a sacrificial life, or do we come asking God only to throw us life-preservers to rescue us from our own foolishness? The prayers of the saints as pictured there focus on the holiness and truthfulness of God and a desire for that to be manifested in the execution of His justice. Are our prayers directed toward obtaining benefit for ourselves or glory for God?

The transition from the seals to the trumpets

The seventh and last seal has finally been opened. The sixth seal introduced the beginning of the last judgment by portraying the cosmic conflagration and the shrieking cries of terror by the ungodly in response to their imminent judgment (6:12-17). This is contrasted in ch. 7 by the portrayal of the sealed saints, whose faith is thereby protected (7:1-8) with the result that they are enabled to stand in God's presence forever as a reward for their faithful perseverance (7:9-17). The focus of the last half of ch. 7 is on the time after the final judgment, when the saints receive their eternal reward. Therefore, the seventh seal picks up where the sixth left off, in order to continue the picture of the final judgment. Like 6:12-17, it is a further answer to the saints' request for judgment to be rendered against the world which persecutes them (so 6:9-11). The final judgment is the chronological end point on which 6:1–8:1 is focused. God will demonstrate Himself to be just and righteous at the conclusion of history. Saints in heaven and especially on earth can be comforted with that fact.

At 5:2ff., it was concluded that removing the seals signified both that Christ has revealed the meaning of OT prophecy concerning redemption and judgment and that He has actually begun to fulfill these prophetic words, as then portrayed in the first five seals. The last two seals, though they also clarify OT prophecy, have not yet been set in motion in history, as they refer to the last judgment. Similarly, the first six trumpets are woes which anticipate the final judgment day (see below).

Therefore, vv. 3-5 continue the final judgment scene of v. 1, and are a continuation of the seventh seal. This means that v. 2 is a parenthetical introduction to the revelation of the seven trumpet trials in vv. 6ff. Such an understanding is indicated by v. 6, where the seven angels have not yet sounded their trumpets, so that the trumpet judgments have not been announced. Therefore, vv. 3-5 record an activity of judgment distinct from the following trumpet woes. Vv. 3-5 are also a development of 6:9-11, where the persecuted saints are depicted "under the altar" and are appealing to God to judge their persecutors. This is apparent above all from the mention three times in vv. 3-5 of the altar in direct connection with the prayers of the saints. An angel takes incense and combines it with the prayers of the saints, and the smoke from the incense, together with the saints' prayers, ascends before God's throne (vv. 3-4). This can be nothing other than the saints' prayer in 6:9-11 that God punish their persecutors, which is now given angelic approval and is formally presented before the divine throne for consideration. The divine response in v. 5 is to send judgmental fire against the earth by the hand of an angel. The response is to be interpreted as the final judgment, not as some trial preliminary to that judgment. This is borne out by the observation that the phrase "peals of thunder and sounds and flashes of lightning and an earthquake" occurs (though the words are in different order) as a description of the last judgment in 11:19 and 16:18 as a part (respectively) of the seventh trumpet and seventh bowl in conjunction with the mention of the heavenly temple.

Thus vv. 3-5 are an answer to the saints' prayer for vindication in relation to their persecutors and continues the final judgment scene of v. 1, which itself has resumed at the point where 6:17 stopped. The unity of vv. 3-5 with v. 1 is indicated by the observation that the silence of v. 1 probably refers, at least in part, to the ceasing of angelic praise in heaven so that either God will hear the prayers for judgment or the angels themselves will hear God's revelatory answer to those prayers (see on v. 1). Vv. 3-5 state the divine answer anticipated in v. 1. The fact that the introduction to the trumpet judgments comes in v. 2 means that vv. 3-5 serve both as a conclusion to the seals *and* as an introduction to the trumpets. A similar phenomenon is found in 15:2-4. It likewise is preceded by an introductory reference to the seven angels who will execute the following sevenfold judgments, which thought is not continued again until 15:5. 15:2-4 temporarily interrupts the beginning narration of the following plague series by continuing a description of the final judgment scene found in 14:14-20 (see further on 15:2-4).

This "parenthesis" in 8:2, in conjunction with vv. 3-5, thus points to the fact that the entire following series of trumpets is also a divine response to the saints' petition in 6:9-11. This suggests that God is beginning to answer the saints' prayer for retribution even as they are praying and before the climactic and fundamental answer of judgment day. Indeed, prayer is one of the important military tactics used by the soldiers of Christ (see further the introductory comments on 8:6–11:19). Whereas the focus of the first four seal woes is primarily on the trials which test the faith of God's people, the focus of the trumpet woes is primarily on the trials which punish the unbelieving persecutors during the same period of the entire church age when the faith of believers is tested. This is suggested by the model of the Exodus plagues, where the same elements which struck the Egyptians were transformed to protect the Israelites.

Both the seals and trumpets literarily are subdivided into units of four followed by two, with parenthetical sections between the sixth and seventh. And, as will be seen, the seventh trumpet is likewise parallel with the sixth and seventh seal. Within the series of seven trumpets the first four form a subordinate literary unity, as do the last three. The first set are judgments affecting the sources of human life, while the final three directly strike humans themselves.

The seven trumpets (8:6–11:19)

The Exodus plagues and the trumpets of Jericho as the background to the trumpet judgments

The first five trumpets are patterned after five of the plagues of Exodus. The first trumpet (hail, fire, and blood) corresponds to the plague of hail and fire (Exod. 9:22-25); the second and third (poisoning of the sea and waters) to the plague on the Nile (Exod. 7:20-25); the fourth (darkness) to the plague of darkness (Exod. 10:21-23); and the fifth (locusts) to the plague of locusts (Exod. 10:12-15). As with the Egyptian plagues, the plagues punish hardness of heart, idolatry (since each plague had a judgment suited to a particular Egyptian god), and persecution of God's people. God's overall intention was to harden Pharaoh's heart so that he would not release Israel (Exod. 4:21) and so that God would have opportunity to perform His plague signs (Exod. 7:3; 10:1-2). Therefore, these signs were not intended to coerce Pharaoh into releasing Israel, but functioned primarily to demonstrate Yahweh's incomparable omnipotence to the Egyptians (Exod. 7:5, 17; 8:10, 22; 9:16, 29; 10:1-2). In this light, they are also judgments executed against the Egyptians because of their hardness of heart. The ultimate purpose of the plague signs was that Yahweh should be glorified. Even when God grants Pharaoh a change of heart so that He releases Israel, He hardens his heart again. The result of this last act of hardening leads to the defeat of the Egyptians in the Red Sea, which results in God's glory (Exod. 14:4, 8, 17). Although the plagues are warnings for which Pharaoh will be held accountable if he does not heed them, they are ultimately intended, at least for the majority of Egyptians, as judgments. For not only has God foreknown and predicted Pharaoh's obdurate response (Exod. 3:19; 4:21; 7:3), He has also caused it (Exod. 4:21; 7:3).

These plagues are now shown to be typological or prophetic foreshadowings of God's judgments against unbelievers throughout the church age and culminating in the last judgment, which initiates the final exodus of God's people from this world of captivity into eternal freedom. While the trumpet plagues bring warning and may cause repentance in some (as indicated by the limitation of the judgments in 8:7–9:21, which implies that God is restraining His wrath to allow for repentance), their primary purpose is the judgment of unbelievers. These plagues also function to demonstrate their hardness of heart and the fact that they are being punished because of such hardness, which is expressed by their persistence in idolatry (so 9:20-21) and their persecution of the saints (cf. 6:9-11).

In the OT, trumpets had a number of connotations, including judgment, warning, victory, and eschatological judgment. Against the background of the Exodus plagues, the emphasis in Revelation with the trumpets must be on the theme of judgment, a judgment unleashed by the resurrection and enthronement of Christ (5:5-14), which have given Him sovereignty over history. In the OT, trumpets also sounded an alarm that a battle against God's enemies was imminent (Judg. 7:16-22; Jer. 4:5-21; Ezek. 7:14). Undoubtedly, the main OT passage in view here is the story of the fall of Jericho in Joshua 6, where trumpets announced the impending victory of a holy war. Seven trumpets were blown by seven priests, and here the trumpets are blown by seven angels who are priestly figures (see 15:6). The ark was present at Jericho (Josh. 6:11-13) and, in its heavenly form, is also present in the heavenly temple (Rev. 11:19). Interestingly, at the Jericho episode (Josh. 6:10-20), there was verbal silence directly linked to a climactic trumpet judgment, which is a pattern found in Revelation 8. The trumpets blown at Jericho by the priests, like the plagues on Egypt, are not warnings at all, but only indicate judgment. This shows further that the trumpets in Revelation primarily connote the idea of judgment rather than warnings designed to induce repentance.

At Jericho, likewise, the first six trumpets precede, but are a necessary preparation for the climactic judgment of the seventh. Likewise, the first six trumpets of Revelation are necessary primary woes leading up to the decisive judgment of the seventh trumpet at the end of history (see on 11:15-19), when the "great city" (11:8), of which Jericho is a prophetic type, will be decisively destroyed (see on 11:13). This reminds us again that the contents of the seven trumpets do not occur subsequent to those of the seven seals, for the content of the seventh trumpet and the (sixth and) seventh seal is identical: the last judgment. But whereas the first five seals focus not only on the judgment of unbelievers but also on the purifying of believers through suffering, the content of the trumpets focuses only on the effect of the various judgments on unbelievers. In light of the Jericho background, it is suitable that the trumpet judgments are placed immediately after ch. 7, where God's people have been portrayed as a fighting army (7:3-8), which conducts victorious holy war ironically by remaining faithful despite earthly suffering (e.g., 7:14). The trumpet inflictions coming on the heels of ch. 7 should be seen as another of the ways the saints carry on holy war: they pray that God's judicial decree will be carried out against their persecutors. The saints wage ironic warfare by means of sacrificial suffering, which makes their prayer of vindication acceptable to God.

And finally, it is beyond coincidence that "a very loud trumpet sound" summons Israel to Mount Sinai to acknowledge God's kingship and presence among them after the plagues of Egypt have been executed (Exod. 19:16). This OT pattern of destructive plagues followed by the peace of kingship has been partially formative for John's introduction of the end-time kingship of God in 11:15-19 by the seventh trumpet following the plagues of the preceding trumpets. It is appropriate that likewise a trumpet sound marked a transition between the defeat of Egypt and the imminent defeat of Jericho, all of which was conducted under God's military leadership.

The first six trumpets: God responds to the saints' prayer by using angels to execute judgments on the persecuting world, leading up to the last judgment (8:6–9:21)

The first four trumpets: God deprives the ungodly of earthly security because of their persecution and idolatry in order to indicate their separation from Him (8:6-12)

6 And the seven angels who had the seven trumpets prepared themselves to
sound them. 7 And the first sounded, and there came hail and fire, mixed with
blood, and they were thrown to the earth; and a third of the earth was burned
up, and all the green grass was burned up. 8 And the second angel sounded, and
something like a great mountain burning with fire was thrown into the sea; and
a third of the sea became blood; 9 and a third of the creatures, which were in the
sea and had life, died; and a third of the ships were destroyed. 10 And the third
angel sounded, and a great star fell from heaven, burning like a torch, and it fell
on a third of the rivers and on the springs of waters; 11 and the name of the star
is called Wormwood; and a third of the waters became Wormwood; and many
men died from the waters, because they were made bitter. 12 And the fourth
angel sounded, and a third of the sun and a third of the moon and a third of the
stars were smitten, so that a third of them might be darkened and the day might
not shine for a third of it, and the night in the same way.

6 Now the description of the seven trumpet angels introduced in v. 2 but abruptly interrupted is continued. The trumpets do not follow the seventh seal chronologically but only in the order of the visions that John saw: he saw the trumpet visions after the seal visions. The trumpets are a temporal recapitulation of the same time periods pictured in the seals. But whereas the primary perspective of the first five seals was on the trials through which believers must pass, now the focus in the first six trumpets is on judgments which unbelievers, both inside and outside the visible church, must endure. The trumpets resemble some of the trials which were pictured in the seals, but their primary purpose is to punish.

7 The first angel sounds his trumpet and the first of the new series of judgments is sent forth. The first trumpet of **hail and fire, mixed with blood**, is patterned after the Egyptian plague of hail and fire (Exod. 9:22-25). The scope of the plague is widened throughout the earth (affecting parts of the whole world rather than simply Egypt): only **a third of the earth was burned up, and a third of the trees**. The fire is not literal, but figurative (as elsewhere in Revelation, most clearly in 4:5, but also in 1:14; 2:18; 10:1; 19:12). This is consistent with 1:1, where the visions are said to be a communication by symbols (see the comments there). Here it speaks of God's holy judgment. The fire burns before God's throne (4:5), and likewise the trumpet judgments have their origin "before God" (8:2). The parts of the earth affected by the first trumpet are those dealing with food supplies, as in Exod. 9:25, 31-32 (where likewise only a part of the food supply is destroyed); this is similar to the famine of the third seal in 6:6, where only some food supplies were affected. Another background to this trumpet is in Ezekiel's prophecy that the coming judgment on disobedient Israel would be characterized by famine (Ezek. 4:9-17; 5:1-17). Israel would (significantly) be divided into thirds, the judgment of one third being described in relation to a burning with fire "at the center of the city" (Ezek. 5:2). Ezek. 5:12 confirms the suggestion that the fire burning in 5:2 is a metaphorical portrayal of judgment by famine, since it summarizes the fire as plague and famine. As in v. 7 and in Exodus, Ezekiel's famine does not result in death for all (Ezek. 4:16-17; 5:10, 12, 16-17). Fire and famine are linked also in Rev. 18:8.

8-9 The second trumpet, continuing the judgment theme of the first, sees **a great mountain burning with fire . . . thrown into the sea**, following which **a third of the sea became blood**. Fire, in Revelation and elsewhere, is a well-known image of judgment. In Revelation, mountains speak of kingdoms, both good and bad, earthly and heavenly (14:1; 17:9; 21:10), but in the OT, mountains as representing nations are often used to portray the objects of God's judgment (Isa. 41:15; 42:15; Ezekiel 35; Zech.

4:7). Hence this picture speaks of judgment against an evil kingdom. Jeremiah speaks of Babylon as a destroying mountain which will be burned by fire (Jer. 51:25), and later in the same chapter (vv. 63-64) speaks of Babylon sinking into the waters, never to rise again. Clearly Jeremiah's vision lies behind the trumpet judgment here. Babylon is also described as a stone being thrown into the sea in Rev. 18:21. Jeremiah's prophetic pronouncements thus lie behind both of John's visions. This **mountain burning with fire** represents God's judgment on Babylon, the great city holding sway over the whole evil world system. As in v. 7, fire may again represent famine. The **third of the sea** turning to blood is a direct allusion to Exod. 7:20-21; just as the fish in the Nile died, so also now a third of the creatures in the sea die. That the death of **a third of the creatures in the sea which had life** includes not only non-human creatures but also humans is directly implied by the following clause, **and a third of the ships were destroyed.** This fits a picture of famine in which food sources are affected, while the partial destruction of marine commerce likewise represents partial economic deprivation throughout the world and anticipates the destruction of Babylon as the source of maritime commerce in 18:11-19.

10-11 With the third trumpet, the judgment of famine appears to be continued. A burning star falls from heaven and pollutes **a third of the rivers** and **the springs of waters.** The presence of fire continues the previous idea of famine, while the theme of undrinkable water also reinforces the judgment of the second trumpet. Note Ps. 78:44: God "turned their rivers to blood, and their streams, they could not drink." This time the fireball is in the form of not a mountain but **a great star . . . burning like a torch**. The star, as elsewhere in Revelation (1:20; 2:1, etc.), is an angelic being often representative of an earthly person or kingdom. The picture thus appears to indicate the judgment of an angel who represents sinful people. These kinds of judgments continue throughout history and culminate in the final judgment at the return of Christ. The picture here goes back first to Isa. 14:12-15, where Babylon's guardian angel is pictured as a star cast down from heaven into a pit. The star is called **Wormwood,** which is based on Jer. 9:15 and 23:15, where God judges His disobedient people by giving them wormwood and poisoned water to drink. The uses in Jeremiah are not literal but metaphorical for the bitterness of suffering resulting from judgment. In fact, the image of polluting "wormwood" was chosen to show that the judgment was well-suited to the crime: because Israel's religious leaders figuratively "polluted" Israel with idolatry, so God is pictured as polluting them with bad water, that is, with the bitterness of suffering. Wormwood is a bitter herb which contaminates water, and is mentioned in Jeremiah and other parts of the OT figuratively to refer to the bitterness of suffering resulting from divine judgment (Deut. 29:17-18; Prov. 5:4; Amos 5:6-7). The polluting of the fresh waters, along with the mention of fire, continues the thought of famine in the previous two plagues. The first three trumpets have been pictured as judgments of fire which affect parts of the earth, sea, and rivers, and of humanity.

12 The fourth trumpet continues the theme of woe from the preceding ones, but does not refer to famine. It brings a limited measure of darkness, a **third of the sun and a third of the moon and a third of the stars** being affected. It is similar to, but more limited in scope, than the description of the last judgment in 6:12-13, where the sun turns black and the moon is covered. The earlier passage refers to God's final judgment against idolaters and those who persecute His people, so something similar is in view here, though only in a partial sense. The allusion is to the plague of darkness in Exod. 10:21-29. The Jews interpreted the Exodus plague in a symbolic sense, as a spiritual, cultural, or mental darkness. The darkness here may refer to a series of divine judgments which plunge men into despair as it causes them to realize the futility of their idolatry and that disaster is rapidly coming upon them. Fear, terror, hopelessness, and depression may be their response.

That the interruption of light sources in v. 12 is figurative is pointed to by the fact that the vast majority of such imagery in the OT is clearly not literal but metaphorical. When Jeremiah speaks of the judgment which came against Israel because of Manasseh, he alludes to the sun setting while it is yet day (Jer. 15:9). Amos likewise speaks of Israel's historical judgment, part of it being that God will make the sun go down at noon (Amos 8:9). These were not climactic end-of-the-world events but figurative references to the depth of the effects of God's judgment which actually came upon the nation and were compared to the decisive destruction of the cosmos at the very end of history. Joel (2:1-10), in phrases similar to Revelation, refers to a trumpet blowing, a fire burning, the sun and moon growing dark, and the stars losing their brightness, all referring to events that actually occurred in Israel's history rather than to some strange final cosmic cataclysm. Actual historical events occurring from time to time throughout the church age are being referred to here in the same way actual historical events were referred to by Joel, Amos, and Jeremiah, and so the meaning of these events in the sky must be taken in the same figurative manner. Note Eccl. 12:1-2, where the "evil days" leading to death (so Eccl. 12:6-7) are a time when "the sun, the light, the moon and the stars are darkened, and clouds return after the rain" (cf. similarly Job 3:3-10). Zeph. 1:15-16 alludes to similar cosmic disturbances (darkness, gloom, and clouds) as symbolic of God's historical judgment against idolatrous Israel, in the context of the sounding of the trumpet and battle cry! See also Isa. 13:10 and Ezek. 32:7-8 for similar references. That these events occur throughout the church age is indicated, on the one hand, by the fact that, like the seals, they are unleashed by the resurrection and ascension of Christ to His heavenly throne and, on the other, by the fact that they are all clearly differentiated from the final judgment, as apparent from the OT allusions and parallels cited above.

The fourth trumpet is the logical climax and point of emphasis of the first set of four trumpets, since it expresses the underlying thought of the first three. It is an emblem of the hardened unbeliever's spiritual separation from God. The darkness is figurative and refers to all those divinely-ordained events intended to remind the church's idolatrous persecutors, and those within the church aligning with the idolatrous culture, that their idolatry is vain, that they are separated from the living God, and that they are already undergoing an initial form of judgment. All four trumpets are concerned with sufferings imposed on the ungodly. This conclusion is confirmed by 7:1-3, where genuine believers have their faith protected by being sealed from the harm directed at the earth, sea, and trees. Vv. 7-11 show that the unsealed are being affected by the trumpet woes, because now the same three objects of earth, sea, and trees are portrayed as harmed. With this in mind, it can be no coincidence that 7:3 is based on Ezek. 9:4-6 and that 8:3-5 is modeled on Ezek. 10:1-7 (see on v. 5). Just as the pouring out of punitive coals on Jerusalem (Ezekiel 10) occurs after the righteous remnant in the covenant community have been given a protective mark on their foreheads (Ezekiel 9), so the same pattern is intentionally followed here and combined with the recollection that the Israelites also received a mark on their doors to protect them from the Exodus death plague. The Exodus–Ezekiel background suggests further that the trumpet trials plague the unsealed both within and outside the visible boundaries of the covenant society.

The tribulations of vv. 6-12 are executed throughout various parts of the earth at all times during the church age, but they do not affect the entire earth or all people. The partial nature of the judgments signifies figuratively that these are not descriptions of the last judgment. It is possible that these are trials which affect all intractible unbelievers until the complete punishment of the judgment day. The command to John in 10:11

preceding the sounding of the seventh trumpet ("You must prophesy again concerning many peoples and nations and tongues and kings") refers to prophecy against ungodly peoples living throughout the world and shows the widespread effect of the trumpet judgments (reinforced by the fact that the woe comes to all "earth-dwellers"; cf. 8:13). The people John is commanded to prophesy against in 10:11 are the same people he prophesies against in 8:7–9:21.

The parallelism of the first four bowls with the first four trumpets confirms that the judgments in both series come because of idolatry (16:2), but adds the element that these woes also occur because of persecution of the saints (16:5-7). In particular, the second and third bowl portray water becoming blood. The description of the third bowl explains that this punishment was fitting because those judged had "poured out the blood of saints and prophets," and that God was therefore just when He gave them blood to drink, because they deserved it (16:6). Likewise, the two trumpet judgments where water becomes blood must be related to the same concern that persecutors get their just deserts.

As already argued, the first three trumpets evoke conditions of famine. Whether these are literal famine conditions or figurative portrayals of suffering is hard to determine. They may be figurative, whereby the famine conditions are nevertheless literal parts of a much broader suffering (the figure of speech is known as "synecdoche," whereby a part is named to indicate the whole of which it is a part).

The figurative nature of the first four trumpets is pointed to by at least two observations. First, the use of different Greek words for "like" throughout the narration of the trumpets indicates an intended lack of precision in describing what was seen in vision and in particular suggests a metaphorical portrayal (8:8, 10; 9:2, 3, 5, 7-10, 17, 19). This figurative emphasis is underscored by the use of the Greek word *sēmainō* ("communicate by symbols") in 1:1 and its background in Daniel, where it connoted a figurative depiction (see on 1:1). Second, the exegesis of various images throughout the trumpets has shown a probable figurative bent (e.g., the mountain and the star; see likewise on the speaking eagle in 8:13; see also on 9:1-19). For example, it is hard to imagine a literal situation in which one meteor could fall on a third of the world's fresh water at the same time.

The Exodus plagues are understood in Revelation 8–9 as a typological foreshadowing of the trumpet plagues, whose effect is escalated to the whole world. The images of famine themselves, as noted above, would not merely be literal references to actual situations of famine, but could generally connote sufferings of all kinds. The sufferings throughout vv. 7-12 are continual reminders of how transient the idolatrous object of the earth-dwellers' trust is. The sufferings result from deficiencies in the world's resources, which the ungodly depend on to meet their needs. These trials, coupled with actual death, remind them that they are ultimately insecure. The reason for their predicament is that they place their trust in what is unstable. The climax of these temporal judgments and sufferings is the final destruction of the entire world and its wicked system. The destruction occurs in order to demonstrate the world's ultimate insufficiency as an object of spiritual trust.

The fourth trumpet also serves as an appropriate transition to the demonic judgments of the fifth trumpet, both dealing with the theme of darkness. Those who abide in spiritual darkness must be plagued by the forces of darkness, whose work it is to draw the dark curtain of unbelief permanently over the spiritual eyes of the ungodly, who are intractable in their unbelief. The use of the word "plagues" (9:20) to describe the trumpet woes suggests that they occur throughout the church age, for in 22:18 "plagues" refers to a curse which can strike anyone throughout the entire church age (including the disobedient within the visible church) who is unfaithful to the message of John's vision. This telling observation strongly suggests that some if not most of the trumpet judgments happen during the entire period between Christ's first and second comings, and not merely at a tribulation period immediately preceding and including the second coming. The four trumpets affect three parts of the created order (earth, air, and water), suggesting that the basic content of creation in Genesis 1 is being systematically undone, though not in the same order; the elements affected are light, air, vegetation, sun, moon, stars, sea creatures, and humans. The notion of a "de-creation" in the first four trumpet judgments is supported by observing that the book climaxes in new creation (21:1ff.).

SUGGESTIONS FOR REFLECTION ON 8:6-12

On the purpose of disastrous events within the plan of God. These verses about the first four trumpets present the plagues of Egypt and God's hardening of Pharaoh's heart as a typological model for His judgments of unbelievers throughout the church age. How does this relate to the view we often take of cataclysmic events that happen throughout the course of history in this age? Do we think of such events primarily as warnings designed to wake unbelievers up so as to change direction? Do we think of them as beginning judgments on hardened unbelievers? Do we also see such destructive events, at the same time, as trials through which believers are refined and through which they draw closer to God (as with the purpose of the sufferings in the first five seals)? Many Christians think the events that happen in history are theologically or spiritually neutral, but in fact, Revelation says that they have divine purposes attached to them which are relevant for unbelievers and believers. How one responds to such events is one indication of whether or not a person has a genuine saving relationship to God: Do Christians accept disastrous events as sent from God to refine their faith and to cause them to draw even closer to Him, or do they blame God and become hardened to Him? Does a characteristic negative reaction to devastating events indicate the spiritual darkness that one is in, whether as a pseudo-believer or as an unbeliever outside the borders of the visible covenant community?

The fifth and sixth trumpets: demons are commissioned to punish hardened unbelievers (8:13–9:21)

Introduction to the fifth and sixth trumpets (8:13)

13 And I looked, and I heard an eagle flying in mid-heaven, saying with a loud voice, "Woe, woe, woe, to those who dwell on the earth, because of the remaining blasts of the trumpet of the three angels who are about to sound!"

13 The last three trumpets are introduced by a phrase indicating a new vision: **and I looked, and I heard.** These trumpets are marked off from the first four literarily by the introductory vision formula together with the eagle proclaiming a threefold "woe" to come upon the ungodly through the remaining three trumpet blasts. The purpose of the literary division is to highlight the harsher aspect of the remaining trumpets.

What John sees is **an eagle flying in mid-heaven.** The Exodus model is still in mind, since there also the plagues became increasingly severe and more specific in their application. The presence of the eagle points to more serious trials, as the phrase **flying in mid-heaven** refers elsewhere only to flying creatures which appear in anticipation of the last judgment (14:6; 19:17; cf. 18:2). The first two woes are also associated with the third, which alludes to the final judgment, by laying the basis for it in the lives of unbelievers and tormenting them in a way which foreshadows their eternal torment. The woes are also worse than the initial four trumpets in that they directly strike the wicked. The reason the wicked are directly affected is that they did not repent from the first four judgments against the environment which supported their lives and lifestyle. The spiritual heightening of the last three trumpets is indicated by the direct involvement of demons. The greater severity of these trumpets is also expressed by their being called "woes," whereas no name is given the first four trumpets. Vv. 7-12 have emphasized that the regular patterns of nature's cycles on earth and of the luminaries in the heavens will be interrupted. The implicit theological reason for this is to connote judgment on sinners who have broken God's established ethical and covenantal patterns (so above on v. 12). 8:13ff. makes this implicit theology explicit. This judgment is primarily spiritual in nature, as ch. 9 reveals.

Eagles often signal coming destruction in the Old Testament (Deut. 28:49; Jer. 4:13; 48:40; Lam. 4:19; Ezek. 17:3). Particularly relevant are Hos. 8:1 ("Put the trumpet to your lips! Like an eagle the enemy comes against the house of the Lord") and Jer. 4:13, where the destructive image of an eagle is followed by "woe to us" together with the threefold mention of the sounding of a trumpet as an announcement of judgment in Jer. 4:5, 19, 21. The figure here could be one of the living beings of Rev. 4:7, who is described as like a flying eagle. The metaphorical association of the eagle with judgment is not inconsistent with the probability that it also represents an angelic being, as pointed to by the parallel with 14:6, where the angel flies in mid-heaven to pronounce God's judgment (14:7). In Exod. 19:4, God compares himself to an eagle who protects His people, after having plagued the Egyptians: "You yourselves have seen what I did to the Egyptians, and how I bore you on eagles' wings, and brought you to Myself." Now an eagle announces new plagues on the idolaters and earth-dwellers.

The fifth trumpet: demons are commissioned to torment hardened unbelievers by further impoverishing their souls and reminding them of their hopeless spiritual plight (9:1-12)

1 And the fifth angel sounded, and I saw a star from heaven which had fallen to
the earth, and the key of the bottomless pit was given to him. 2 And he opened
the bottomless pit; and smoke went up out of the pit, like the smoke of a great
furnace; and the sun and the air were darkened by the smoke of the pit. 3 And out
of the smoke came forth locusts upon the earth; and power was given them, as
the scorpions of the earth have power. 4 And they were told that they should not
hurt the grass of the earth, nor any green thing, nor any tree, but only the men

who do not have the seal of God upon their foreheads. [5] And they were not permitted to kill anyone, but to torment for five months; and their torment was like the torment of a scorpion when it stings a man. [6] And in those days, men will seek death and will not find it; and they will long to die and death flees from them. [7] And the appearance of the locusts was like horses prepared for battle; and on their heads, as it were, crowns like gold, and their faces were like the faces of men. [8] And they had hair like the hair of women, and their teeth were like the teeth of lions. [9] And they had breastplates like breastplates of iron; and the sound of their wings was like the sound of chariots, of many horses rushing into battle. [10] And they have tails like scorpions, and stings; and in their tails is their power to hurt men for five months. [11] They have as king over them, the angel of the abyss; his name in Hebrew is Abaddon, and in the Greek he has the name Apollyon. [12] The first woe is past; behold, two woes are still coming after these things.

1 The fifth angel sounds the trumpet, and John sees another vision of judgment. He sees **a star from heaven which had fallen to the earth.** This star is probably the same or at least similar to the star of 8:10, an angel representing sinful people and undergoing judgment along with them. The OT background is Isa. 14:12-15. Jesus uses virtually the same expression to describe Satan's judgment in Luke 10:18: "I was watching Satan fall from heaven like lightning." The expression here may be another way of saying that "Satan . . . was thrown down to the earth, and his angels were thrown down with him" (Rev. 12:9; cf. 12:13). The conclusion that this is a fallen angel is also suggested by v. 11. There the "angel of the abyss" is called "king over" the demonic locusts and is referred to as "Abaddon" ("Destruction") and "Apollyon" ("Destroyer"). The heavenly being who is sovereign over the abyss and locusts in vv. 1-3 is probably the same figure as the one in v. 11, who is said to be "king" over them (for the Satanic nature of this angel see on v. 11).

This fallen angel is given the role of inflicting punishment on sinful humanity. He is given **the key of the bottomless pit**, the realm where Satan dwells, but this key or authority is ultimately given by Christ, who alone holds the keys of death and Hades (1:18). Neither Satan nor his evil servants can any longer unleash the forces of hell on earth unless they are given power to do so by the resurrected Christ (see further on 20:1-3). As the visions of ch. 9 and following are unveiled, the readers are given an ever-expanding definition of the extent of God and the Lamb's sovereignty. They are in ultimate control of Satan's realm. And the saints are to remember this when the forces of evil direct their wrath against them or self-destructively against their own allies, the followers of the antichrist. There is a grand purpose which God is working through it all, which is a basis for hope and encouragement for beleaguered Christians (for discussion of the problem of how a good God can be sovereign over evil see on 6:1-8).

2 Dense smoke arises from the abyss when the angel opens it: **The sun and the air were darkened by the smoke of the pit**. The image of darkening of the sun and other parts of the cosmos has already been seen to connote judgment (see on 6:12ff.; 8:12). The image is an allusion to the repeated references to the darkening of the sun in Joel 2:10, 31; 3:15 (cf. Isa. 13:10), where it is a sign of judgment. Joel's imagery itself is probably a development of the plague of locusts in Exod. 10:1-15 (see on v. 7 below). This was a judgment because of the Egyptians' hardness of heart in rejecting God's word through Moses. There is no reason to think that the connotation of judgment has changed here. This is confirmed by the clear meaning of judgment which "smoke" carries later in this chapter (vv. 17-20) and later in the book (14:11; 18:9, 18; 19:3). Consequently, the picture in v. 2 indicates that the judgment formerly limited to the demonic realm is being extended to the earthly realm. As a result of Christ's death and resurrection, the devil and his legions have begun to be judged, and now the effect of their judgment is about to be unleashed upon unbelieving humanity, who give their ultimate allegiance to him. An essentially identical pattern of widening judgment occurs in 12:7-12; 13:3-8; 16:10; and 17:8 (although in 12:12ff. the saints are also affected by the extension of judgment in the form of persecution and attempted deception). As will be seen below in vv. 3-6, the judgment partly involves deception, which is metaphorically anticipated by the darkening smoke. Darkness throughout the NT symbolizes spiritual blindness (Luke 11:36; John 1:5; 3:19-21; 8:12; 11:10; 12:35-36; Rom. 13:12; 2 Cor. 4:4; 1 Pet. 2:9; 1 John 1:5).

3 Demonic-like beings portrayed as locusts arise from the smoking abyss and go out to the earth. As in the original plague of locusts, it is God Himself who sends locusts upon the earth (the phrase **power was given them** implies God or Christ as the subject; for God as the subject in similar clauses see 6:2-8; 8:2, etc.). The model of the Exodus plagues here confirms that God is the one who has absolute sovereignty over the instruments of the plagues, as is indicated by the clause introducing the locust plague against Egypt: "Stretch out your hand . . . for the locusts, that they may come up on the land of Egypt" (Exod. 10:12).

4 But whereas the Exodus locusts harmed the vegetation, these locusts do not harm **the grass of the earth, nor any green thing, nor any tree**, but only those **who do not have the seal of God upon their fore-**

heads. The seal is given only to genuine believers. The seal is a sign of God's sovereign authority and ownership over those destined ultimately to be part of His kingdom and not of Satan's domain. This means that the faith of Christians is safeguarded by God's protective presence (see further on 2:17; 7:2-3). Of course, there are unbelievers who become believers throughout this time, but they are those who have been "sealed" beforehand by God's decree and will believe at some point during their lives. In fact, they become Christians as a result of the sealing activity directed toward them. Part of the harm inflicted has to do with keeping unsealed unbelievers in spiritual darkness (see on 8:12). At the same time, this link with 8:12 implies that these devilish beings cause events which remind the ungodly that they are separated from the living God. Such reminders induce fear and despair as people are forced to reflect on their hopeless situation. That this kind of torment is in mind is made explicit by vv. 5-6. Just as the plagues did not harm the Israelites but only the Egyptians (Exod. 8:22-24; 9:4-7, 26; 10:21-23), so true Christians are likewise protected from the fifth plague.

5 The locusts, however, **were not permitted to kill anyone**, but only **to torment** them, and only **for five months**. The five-month period could refer by analogy to the dry season or to the life-cycle of locusts, but it is probably symbolic (referring to a limited period of time), as are other numbers in Revelation. That the limitations are divinely imposed is clear from the fact that God determined the temporal limitations of the Egyptian plagues, which are in mind here. The **torment** is primarily spiritual and psychological suffering, since this is the connotation of the word elsewhere in the book with reference to the nature of trials both preceding and including the final judgment (cf. 11:10; 14:10-11; 18:7, 10, 15 [in ch. 18 synonymous with the emotional pain of "weeping" and "mourning"]; 20:10).

The theme of spiritual and psychological suffering explains why sealed believers are not affected, for they have confidence in their destiny in Christ. Deuteronomy 28 also predicts that "in the latter days" (so 4:30) Israel will suffer the plagues of Egypt (vv. 27, 60), including that of locusts (vv. 38-39, 42), because of their idolatry (e.g., v. 14; 29:22-27; 30:17; 31:16-20). This latter-day affliction includes "plagues" (Deut. 28:61) of "madness" (v. 28), darkness (v. 29), "trembling heart," "failing eyes" (darkness?), and "despair of soul" (v. 65). To whatever degree this Deuteronomy passage is in mind, the notion is applied to those in the visible community of the new Israel who are not part of the invisible community of faith. But this plague likely extends beyond the boundary of the covenant community, since the Egyptian plagues likewise struck those outside the believing community.

In fact, the plague predicted by Deuteronomy 28 to come on Israel in the latter days was to be constituted by the very plagues that God had sent on Egypt (Deut. 28:60), because those in the visible community of faith would become as unbelieving as the Egyptians.

6 John now gives a partial interpretative comment on the vision he has just seen. The spiritual and psychological nature of the torment is emphasized by the fact that **men will seek death and will not find it** — that is, they will want to die, yet be so afraid of death they will not find it within their power to kill themselves. The effect of the locusts is to remind the church's ungodly persecutors that their idolatry is vain and that they are separated from the living God, and consequently have no hope. In them the prophecy of Moses that the disobedient will be driven mad by what they suffer will be fulfilled (Deut. 28:28, 34). The Exodus plagues caused the Egyptians confusion and despair through the realization that Yahweh was the only true God and that they could not prevail against Him. This realization included an anxious conviction of sin yet unaccompanied by repentance (cf. Pharaoh's response in Exod. 9:27-28; 10:16-17). So now sinners will live in terror as they realize the idolatrous values on which they have built their lives are but foundations of sand in the face of Satan's attacks. And, as with the Egyptians, so now the fifth trumpet plague also hardens the victims against turning to God from their despair. Such hardening is actually a deceptive influence of the demons. Believers, by contrast, will fear no evil because they know that, whether they live or die, they are with Christ and that behind the apparent catastrophes and reversals of life a loving and sovereign God is working out His eternal will for their good (Rom. 8:28). In contrast to the ungodly, they take ultimate pleasure in the torments, even death, which the world imposes on them in order that they may give testimony to Jesus and the word of God: "because of the blood of the Lamb and because of the word of their testimony, and they did not love their life even to death" (12:11; cf. 1:9; 2:10; 6:9; 20:4).

7 John's detailed description of the **locusts** here contains three uses of the word **like**, as well as the phrase **as it were**, indicating his struggle to describe what he is seeing. The vision sparks in his mind similar scenes from the OT, as the following verses reveal. So he utilizes the prophetic language which most resembles what he sees. His vision of **locusts** like **horses prepared for battle** is clearly related to Joel's portrayal of the plague of locusts attacking Israel (itself modeled on the plague of locusts in Exodus 10), which likewise begins with the blowing of a trumpet (Joel 2:1). As God used locusts to judge Egypt, so in Joel God is portrayed as

using locusts to judge unrepentant Israel, out of which only a remnant will be saved (Joel 2:31-32). Joel mirrors the thought of Exodus that the primary purpose of the locust plague is to harden the hearts of unbelievers. Joel's locusts (whether literal or representing enemy armies) brought famine (1:5-12, 16-20; 2:25) and anguish (2:6). Here the locusts are pictured (v. 4) as not harming the earth's vegetation, so the damage now envisioned is that of a famine of the soul (the prophets sometimes spiritualize famine, e.g., Amos 8:11-14). This suggests that actual famine conditions observed in the first three trumpets ultimately point to punishments coming upon sinners because of the spiritual famine and barrenness of their souls. The description of John's locusts represents an exaggeration of their actual physiology: their head is shaped like horses' heads; their antennae become hair; the destructive effect of their mouth becomes ferocious teeth; their sound becomes the sound of chariots; their armor becomes breastplates of iron. In general, the locusts are translated into human terms and compared to an army. The comparison of the locusts' faces to **the faces of men** with **crowns like gold** on their heads evokes their demonic nature. Joel 2:4-7 also compares the locusts to horses and to men prepared for battle.

To attempt to find the *dominant* model for the locusts first in the realm of modern warfare (for instance, helicopters, as one popular writer suggests) instead of OT imagery is not the best approach. Rather than first going forward from John's time into our present or future, the commentator should first go back from John's time to the OT, since this is the first clear source from which Revelation derives its images and determines their meaning.

8 The phrase **their teeth were like the teeth of lions** is based on Joel 1:6, where the locusts were like "a nation" whose "teeth are the teeth of a lion."

9 The phrase **breastplates like breastplates of iron** is a general description of part of the armor of a soldier (or battle horse; cf. Job 39:19-20, where battle horses are compared to locusts). **The sound of their wings was like the sound of chariots, of many horses rushing into battle** is an allusion to Joel 2:4-5: "Their appearance is like the appearance of horses; and like war horses, so they run. With a noise as of chariots they leap on the tops of the mountains . . . like a mighty people arranged for battle." Also see Jer. 51:27, which speaks of the judgment of historical Babylon, is introduced with "a trumpet among the nations," and compares horses to "bristly locusts," and Jer. 51:14, which describes enemy armies as "a population like locusts." The locusts, like so much else in Revelation, must be understood figuratively, and so it would be a mistake to view them as actual physical locusts (note accordingly "likeness" in v. 7 and the repeated "like" in vv. 7-10).

10 The picture of the locusts concludes as it began in vv. 3-5 by comparing their authority to the power which scorpions have over their prey and by limiting their authority over people to **five months**. The combination of an army of horses who devour the land and serpents who bite occurs in Jer. 8:16-17, where the picture is similar to John's combination of horse-like locusts and scorpions who sting. In both passages, the judgment comes on idolaters (Jer. 8:2; cf. Rev. 9:20).

11 The angel who controls these demonic beings is called **Abaddon** or **Apollyon** (Hebrew and Greek respectively for "destroyer"). Abaddon is closely linked to Sheol or the place of death in the OT (Job 26:6; 28:22; Ps. 88:11; Prov. 15:11; 27:20). These names, together with the statement that the angel is "king over" the demons, suggest that this is either Satan himself or one of his most powerful representatives. Rev. 12:3-4 and 13:1ff. are compatible with this conclusion, since there the devil and the beast are pictured, respectively, with kingly diadems on their heads and as leaders of evil forces. This is in line with the same conclusion already reached about the angel's identification in 9:1. The two names for Satan express his function in utilizing demons to work among the impious so that they will eventually be destroyed by death of body and spirit. The demonic activity lasting only five months is but a part of the process leading to this final, macabre goal. The sixth trumpet pictures the completion of this process.

12 This verse is a transition, summarizing the preceding trumpet and introducing the next two. Does the transition indicate that the last three trumpets follow one another in the chronology of history or merely in the chronological sequence of the visions? The first hint that the second meaning is intended is found in the opening expression **the first woe is past**. This does not mean that the events have already transpired in history, but only indicates that the *vision* containing the events is now over. The introductory word **behold** shows an emphasis on the woes as visions instead of events. This is implied also by the concluding phrase **after these things**, which elsewhere in the book refers not to the order of historical events but to the order of visions coming one after another (see on 4:1). Consequently, the sense of v. 12 is, "The presentation of the first vision of woe has passed. See, two more visions of woe will be presented after this first one." Thus, the primary concern is with the order of visions and not the order of history represented in the three visions.

Suggestions for Reflection on 9:1-12

On God using Satan as His agent of judgment. These verses present a picture of a horrible judgment ultimately directed by God, who uses Satan and his agents to inflict it. Would our first reaction to this be that this is unworthy of a holy God? Why would we react this way? What does it say about our limited view of the seriousness of sin? From another perspective, these verses show that the enemy is not an independent agent, but operates only under God's authority. Do we tend practically to view spiritual warfare as a struggle between two equals (God and Satan) even though the Bible, as here, suggests otherwise?

On the significance of understanding the use of figurative language in the Bible. These verses show us how John uses the picture of horse-like locusts similar to scorpions to refer to the psychological and spiritual torment that Satan and his agents inflict at the command of God. John in turn borrows the picture from Joel, who likely uses the actual locusts of Exodus likewise figuratively to speak of enemy armies. Regardless of whether the locusts in Joel are literal, in Revelation they are figurative. John, like Jesus, uses pictures and parables which shock the believer into repentance while further hardening the heart of those intractable in unbelief. How best can we explore the true meaning of biblical passages like this? How often do we trace back the true meaning of such passages by discovering their roots in other passages of Scripture?

On the severity of the judgment of darkness. These verses present a view of the unbelievers' torment as the forceful reminder that their idolatry is vain, that they are separated from the living God, and that they are without hope. Why, when their situation is so desperate, do people not turn to Christ? Why did only one of the other men on the cross cry out for help? It is said of the atheist Voltaire that his dying words consisted of calling out the name of Christ, alternately as a prayer and as a curse. Is this a measure of the darkness God's judgment sends on the lost? And yet, at the cross, the one criminal who did cry out was answered and received God's mercy.

The sixth trumpet: demons are commissioned to judge hardened unbelievers by ensuring the final punishment of some through deception until death, leaving the deceived remainder unrepentant (9:13-21)

13 And the sixth angel sounded, and I heard a voice from the four horns of the
golden altar which is before God, 14 one saying to the sixth angel who had the

trumpet, "Release the four angels who are bound at the great river Euphrates."
[15] And the four angels, who had been prepared for the hour and day and month
and year, were released, so that they might kill a third of mankind. [16] And the
number of the armies of the horsemen was two hundred million; I heard the
number of them. [17] And this is how I saw in the vision the horses and those who
sat on them: the riders had breastplates the color of fire and of hyacinth and of
brimstone; and the heads of the horses are like the heads of lions; and out of
their mouths proceed fire and smoke and brimstone. [18] A third of mankind was
killed by these three plagues, by the fire and the smoke and the brimstone, which
proceeded out of their mouths. [19] For the power of the horses is in their mouths
and in their tails; for their tails are like serpents and have heads; and with them
they do harm. [20] And the rest of mankind, who were not killed by these plagues,
did not repent of the works of their hands, so as not to worship demons, and
the idols of gold and of silver and of brass and of stone and of wood, which can
neither see nor hear nor walk; [21] and they did not repent of their murders nor of
their sorceries nor or their immorality nor of their thefts.

13 The voice coming **from the four horns of the golden altar which is before God** may be Christ's (cf. 6:6) or an angel's (cf. 16:7). Mention of the **golden altar** draws us back to the cry to God for justice from the glorified saints from below the same altar (6:10), and also connects the sixth trumpet with the transitional segment of 8:3-5, which showed that both the seventh seal and the seven trumpets were God's response to the saints' petitions. **Four** stands for completeness in the Bible (on which see the discussion on numerology in the Introduction [6.] and also on 7:1) and **horns** stand for power, so the vision refers to the completeness of God's power coming from His presence (**the golden altar**), a power He is beginning to exercise in response to the prayers of the saints. In 14:18, the altar is directly linked to power over judgment: "Another angel, the one who has power over fire, came out from the altar." **Before** (or literally "in the presence of") appears six times elsewhere in Revelation in connection with explicit reference to some aspect of God's presence in the heavenly *temple* (4:5; 5:8; 7:15; 8:3-4; 11:4). All these texts have some connotation of judgment or protection from judgment. These links also point to 9:13 as an allusion to God's power of judging in response to the saints' prayers.

14 The voice from the altar issues a command to the sixth trumpet angel to release **the four angels who are bound at the great river Euphrates.** That they had been bound implies they had been restrained against their will, like the demons confined to the abyss in 9:1-3. They are probably also wicked angels. The **Euphrates** does not refer to the literal place the angels were bound and will raise their armies. Rather, the *regions around* the Euphrates (Isa. 7:20; 8:7-8), the "land of the north by the river Euphrates" (Jer. 46:10), or simply the "north," meaning the region of the Euphrates (Jer. 1:14-15; 6:1, 22; 10:22; Ezek. 38:6, etc.), are mentioned in the OT as the area from which armies of destruction come, sometimes against Israel, sometimes against other nations. The strongest OT echo comes from Jeremiah 46, which portrays the coming judgment on Egypt, the army of horsemen from the north being like serpents, innumerable locusts, having breastplates (cf. 46:4, 22-23), and being "by the Euphrates River" (46:2; likewise 46:6, 10). The **angels** had been **bound** by God and are now released by Him, since the command to **release** them emanates from the divine altar in heaven.

Mention of the **Euphrates** anticipates the battle of the sixth bowl, where the Euphrates is also mentioned. Indeed, the sixth trumpet and sixth bowl describe the same event, but from different perspectives; on the link with the sixth bowl see further on 9:19. As in the OT parallels of the northern invader, so here it is God who ultimately unleashes the corrupt angelic invaders. These angels could be identified as the angelic counterparts to the wicked nations, who dwelled at or north of this boundary (e.g., Dan. 10:13, 20-21). Looking back at 7:1 enables us to identify "the four winds of the earth" being held back with the four beings bound at the Euphrates (and see on 7:1 for the identification of these winds with malevolent angels). The destructive winds "at the four corners of the earth" may now be unleashed against the unsealed (as in 9:4), since the sealing of God's people has been completed (7:3-8), and they cannot be harmed by the effect of the angelic winds. John's vision thus understands the Euphrates as a biblical reference for the place (spiritual rather than geographical) where Satan will marshal his forces against God's people. The fact that the four angels of 9:14 are at the particular locality of the Euphrates and not the four corners of the earth is a mixing of metaphors, whereby the river sums up the end-time expectations concerning the direction from which will come the final onslaught of the Satanic enemy, which will affect the whole world (see on 16:12-16).

15 That the four angels had been "bound" means that they had not been allowed to carry out the function for which they had been waiting. But now, having been **prepared for the hour and day and month and year, they were released, so that they might kill a third of mankind**. The specific listing of time periods indicates that these angels are released according to God's sovereign timetable. The point of specifying down to the hour the time of releasing these hordes is to emphasize that all events of history, whatever Satan's involvement, are under the ultimate authority of God.

16 The four angels have power over ungodly spiritual forces, which are pictured as a multitude of armies on horses. The size of the demonic army is **two hundred million** (literally "double myriad of myriads" or "twice ten thousands of ten thousands"). The number is symbolic, as with other numbers in Revelation. The word *myrias* ("ten thousand") is used in Greek to refer to an innumerable multitude. In the plural, it is used in the OT in the same way (Gen. 24:60; Lev. 26:8; Deut. 32:30; 2 Chron. 25:11-12; Mic. 6:7; and especially Dan. 7:10). Never in the Bible does it refer to a specific number unless prefixed by a numerical adjective (as in "three myriads" or 30,000 in Esth. 1:7 LXX). Use of the double plural ("ten thousands of ten thousands"), prefaced by the further intensifier "twice," makes it almost impossible to calculate accurately and shows that a symbolic reference is indicated here. Note that in Jer. 46:2, 4, 6, 10, 22-23, one of the backgrounds to this text, the conquering armies ride on horses (v. 4), wear armor (v. 4), are compared to a serpent (v. 22) and locusts (cf. v. 23), and are (significantly) of innumerable number.

17 What John has heard in vv. 13-16 is explained further in visionary form in vv. 17-21. The riders have **breastplates the color of fire and hyacinth and brimstone**, the horses are described as having **heads of lions** (emphasizing their destructive power), and **out of their mouths proceed fire and smoke and brimstone**. As with the description of the locusts in the fifth trumpet, the piling up of hideous descriptions underscores the demons as ferocious and dreadful beings. Fire and brimstone in the OT (sometimes linked with smoke) indicate a fatal judgment (as here) within the course of history (Gen. 19:24, 28; Deut. 29:23; 2 Sam. 22:9; Isa. 34:9-10; Ezek. 38:22). The idea of God's judgment of His enemies is figuratively expressed in 2 Sam. 22:9 (= Ps. 18:8) by the similar phrase "smoke . . . and fire from his mouth." In Rev. 11:5, the expression "fire proceeds out of their mouth" refers to the punishment the two faithful witnesses execute against their persecutors. The fire is a figurative reference to their prophesying and testimony (11:6-7). There, the rejection of their testimony commences a spiritual judgment of the persecutors and lays the basis for their future final judgment (see further on 11:5-6). That the image of fire "proceeding from a mouth" is figurative is apparent from other parallels in the book. For instance, 1:16 (cf. 2:12, 16) and 19:15, 21 portray Christ judging His enemies by means of a sharp sword "proceeding from His mouth." 2:16 alludes to some form of temporal punishment, whereas 19:15, 21 has to do with the defeat of Christ's enemies at His return. Like the fire in 11:5, the sword in Christ's mouth is figurative and probably refers to the condemnation of sinners through His word (as implied from 19:11-13).

18 The destructive nature of the judgment executed by the demonic horses is reemphasized by repetition from v. 17 of **the fire and the smoke and the brimstone, which proceeded out of their mouths.** The overthrow of Sodom and Gomorrah from Gen. 19:24, 28 is uppermost in thought among other possible parallels, since the precise combination of **fire, smoke,** and **brimstone** occurs in the OT only there. As in v. 17 above, Genesis 19; Isa. 34:9-10; and Ezek. 38:22 describe the same kind of fatal judgment John foresees here. **The fire and the smoke and the brimstone** are now called **three plagues** from which **a third of mankind was killed.** This continues the description in v. 15, which means that these fiendish horses are the agents through whom the four angels of v. 15 conduct their dreadful work. They kill the whole person, both physically and spiritually. They carry out, not the final judgment, but a judgment that is linked to the final judgment and that prepares for it. They cause the physical death of idolaters, compromisers, and persecutors of the church, who are already spiritually dead. The plague of "killing" includes all kinds of death which the ungodly undergo (from illness, tragedy, etc.). *The death stroke against their bodies makes certain their spiritual death for eternity.* In this sense, it can be said that death here includes both the spiritual and physical dimensions. Thus fire and brimstone, referred to three times in vv. 17-18, refer exclusively elsewhere in John's writing to the final and eternal judgment of ungodly idolaters (14:10; 21:8), the devil, the beast, and the false prophet (19:20; 20:10). This connection with final judgment in other passages of the book implies that the execution of death by the demonic horses is the beginning of the divine action which eventually secures unbelievers for their final judgment in 14:10 and 21:8, for which they must wait.

19 The horses' **tails are like serpents and have heads,** and **with them they do harm,** like the scorpion-like locusts of 9:10, whose tails have "power to hurt men." This particular harm, then, may refer not to death, but may be similar to the spiritual torment (preceding death) of the fifth trumpet, although the sixth trumpet in general brings widespread death, intensifying the woe of the fifth. The smoke of the fifth trumpet is now joined by fire in the sixth trumpet. The smoke and resulting darkness are metaphorical for a punishment of deception (see 8:12; 9:2-3), and the fire is metaphorical for lethal judgment (see v. 18).

That **the power of the horses is in their mouths** points to demonic deception resulting in judgment. Part of the deception manifests itself through false teachers affirming the legitimacy of some form of idolatry for Christians (e.g., cf. 2:6, 14-15, 20-21). The harm of deception (usually leading to idolatry) is also seen as a judgment in the OT and NT generally (e.g., Isa. 6:10-12; 29:9-14; 63:17; Pss. 115:8; 135:18; Rom. 1:18-32; 2 Thess. 2:9-12; the hardening of Pharaoh's heart in Exodus 4–14 is a well-known example of the activity of Satan referred to in this text). The deceptive facet of the sixth trumpet is implied by its unique parallels with the sixth bowl, especially with respect to a judgment of deception "coming out of the mouth" of Satanic beings (16:13, where three evil spirits come out of the mouths of the dragon, the beast, and the false prophet). In like manner, the dragon's attempted deception of the church is depicted by the metaphorical statement, "the serpent poured water like a river out of his mouth after the woman" (12:15). The authority given by the dragon to the beast by which he deceives men is explained as "a mouth speaking arrogant words and blasphemies . . . against God, to blaspheme His Name and His tabernacle, that is, those who dwell in heaven" (13:5-6). Therefore, part of the effect of the demons' mouths in 9:17-19 is to intensify the deception of unbelievers.

The power of the horses lies not only in their mouths but also **in their tails; for their tails are like serpents and have heads; and with them they do harm**. This does not mean that the horses literally have serpents as their tails, for as the first part of the verse comments generally and implicitly on the *similarity* of the tails of the demonic horses to serpents, the second part continues the metaphor by saying that the harm inflicted by the heads of the serpent-like tails is as lethal *as* serpents who bite. The piling up of metaphors not completely consistent with one another is not for the purpose of portraying a nicely systematic or logical picture (of a literal but bizarre creature at home in a science fiction novel) but to *bring an emphasis* (in the same way, it is not in line with the intention of 5:8 to ask how each elder is able to play a harp and hold a bowl of incense at the same time). The metaphor of the serpent enforces further the connotation of the mouth of the demonically-inspired false teachers as that which harms through deception. Through the serpent simile, the idea of promoting falsehood is heightened. This reinforces the link of the horses to Satan himself, who is known in Revelation as "the serpent" (12:9, 14-15; 20:2). John understood that the sufferings he was narrating were already occurring, and were not to be limited to a period only immediately preceding the Lord's return. This is also hinted at by another conspicuous parallel in Luke 10:17-19, where "the demons" (v. 17) are called "serpents and scorpions and . . . the power of the enemy" over which Christians presently have power but which can still "injure" unbelievers (v. 19). Jesus called the Pharisees serpents and vipers because they were blind guides leading others astray (Matt. 23:16, 33), and Prov. 23:32-35 speaks of wine as a serpent whose sting leads to delusion. The sting of the serpent, as represented by the smoke of 9:2-3, comes first in the form of deception. This deception leads unbelievers on to the final effect of the sting — God's final judgment.

Our conclusion from the above is that the images of vv. 17-19 are not figurative for the destruction wrought by modern warfare, but connote the destruction of deception leading to spiritual and physical death. This conclusion has been arrived at by a contextual comparison of the images within the Apocalypse, rather than by comparing the images with similar ones in the world of modern warfare, or even of past warfare (for instance, some have attempted to identify the scene with the Islamic invasions of the fifteenth century).

Although a detailed analysis of ancient Jewish literature is beyond the scope of this shorter commentary, it may be helpful to note here that the combination of serpents and scorpions in Rev. 9:3-19 reflects the broader linkage in biblical and ancient Jewish thought, where the combination was metaphorical for judgment in general and deception or delusion in particular (e.g., Deut. 8:15; Sirach 39:30; CD VIII.9-11 ["vipers" and "snakes"]; Luke 10:19; Mishnah *Aboth* 2.10; Midrash Rabba Num. 10.2). In Num. 21:6 and Deut. 8:15 the reference is to "fiery serpents," which is similar to the threefold repetition of fire in connection with the serpents in 9:17-19. In the Numbers passage their bite, as here, kills a significant portion of the people because of unbelief. Sirach 39:27-31 provides a striking parallel with Rev. 9:3-4, 15-19, which reflects Jewish and biblical tradition standing in the background of John's train of thought: "All these things are for good to the godly; so to the sinners they are turned into evil. There be spirits that are created for vengeance, which in their fury lay on sore strokes; in the time of destruction they pour out their force, and appease the wrath of him that made them. *Fire* and . . . *death* . . . all these were created for vengeance . . . *scorpions [and] serpents* . . . punishing the wicked to destruction . . . *they shall be prepared on earth, when need is; and when their time is come, they shall not go beyond his word.*" According to Sirach, these afflictions occur generally throughout all ages.

Likewise, John understood that the sufferings he was narrating were already occurring and not to be limited to a period only immediately preceding Christ's return. This is also hinted at by another conspicuous parallel in Luke 10:17-19, where the demons are called "serpents and scorpions and . . . the power of the enemy," over which Christians presently have power, but which can still harm unbelievers. The harm associated with the two repellent creatures is sometimes metaphorically expressed as deception, which is undoubtedly implicit in the passage from Luke. Ps. 58:3-6 refers to the "wicked" who "speak lies," have "venom like the venom of a serpent," and are further compared to a "deaf cobra." The teeth of the wicked liars are compared to the "fangs of the young lions" (cf. Rev. 9:8-10, 17; Sirach 21:2). Similarly an early Dead Sea Scrolls document compares the High Priest in Jerusalem and the Roman authorities with "the poison of serpents and the head of asps." This metaphor explains the harm of false teaching and deception, which the High Priest has caused (CD VIII.9-13); in the same document, those participating in the same false teaching are compared to "kindlers of fire and lighters of brands" and to spiders and adders (V.14-15). The text of Deut. 32:33 in the Aramaic Bible (the Palestinian Targum) refers to the "evil counsels . . . [and] wicked thoughts" of idolatrous Israelites as being "as serpents' heads." Likewise, Aramaic Jerusalem Targum of Deut. 32:33 speaks of "their malice like the head of asps." In addition, in Targum Onkelos Deut. 32:32-33 affirms that upon Israelite idolaters "plagues will be evil as the heads of serpents, and the retribution of their works like their venom," and then compares their punishment to that of Sodom and Gomorrah, as does Rev. 9:18 (on which see above).

Prov. 23:32-33 states that strong wine "bites like a serpent, and stings like a viper" resulting in the eyes seeing "strange things" and the mind uttering "perverse things." The serpent-scorpion metaphor is thus used to describe a "woe" of delusion (Prov. 23:29-33). This may show that the rationale for using serpents and scorpions to signify doctrinal deception is that part of the literal suffering of their bites can be that of mental delusion, which precedes and then culminates in death.

In another Dead Sea Scrolls document, the "pit" and "abyss" open and spit out billows, arrows, and "the spirits of the Asp" against hardened hypocrites, "leaving [them with] no hope" (1QH III.16-18, 25-27; V.27). This affliction arising from the pit is interpreted as deceptive influences (especially false teaching) affecting the ungodly, but not those truly loyal to God (II.12-34; IV.5-22). In Mishnah *Aboth* 2.10, the words of the wise exponents of Torah do harm to those who do not obey them. In apparent contrast to the imagery in Revelation 9, it describes the effect of the *words of the wise* on the disobedient as "the sting of a scorpion . . . the hiss of a serpent . . . coals of fire." Yet this is actually similar to Rev. 11:5 (the judgment issuing from the mouths of the witnesses), and overlaps generally with some of the above imagery in its emphasis on judgment through the infliction of harm. Indeed, it associates closely the metaphors of scorpions and serpents with judgment, though in this case the focus is on the effects of true teaching on those responding wrongly to it.

These OT and Jewish parallels show that in John's time, scorpions and serpents, far from referring to instruments of modern warfare like destructive helicopters or jets, were metaphorical images for false teaching. If so, it is likely that the way the demons in Revelation work their deception is through human false teachers, which is a problem in the churches of Revelation (e.g., 2:14-15, 20-24; 22:18-19).

20a For **the rest of mankind who were not killed by these plagues**, the plagues served as warnings and were not intended to have a redeeming but a damning effect. In fact, they **did not repent of the works of their hands**, but continued to **worship demons** and **the idols of gold and of silver and of brass and of stone and of wood**. The torment of the tails did not kill all the wicked, but those remaining were nevertheless still affected in that they did not repent and continued to remain hardened toward God. Indeed, they worshiped demons (who continued to deceive them) and idols and continued headlong into their sinful lifestyle (on which see vv. 20b-21). This shows again that the sixth trumpet is an escalation of the fifth by its introduction of death, though the sixth still continues to unleash the affliction of the fifth against all the surviving non-elect. These plagues will have a redeeming effect only on a remnant of compromisers inside the church and idolaters outside the church who have been sealed beforehand and finally benefit from the seal's protective function. The pattern of the Exodus plagues is still apparent. Just as the death of the firstborn led to the decisive judgment at the Red Sea, so here the death of others as a warning sign does not induce repentance, but prepares for the final judgment of the intractably impenitent at the seventh trumpet (11:18). The theological purpose of the warning is that God, by providing sufficient opportunities for spiritual reform, should demonstrate His sovereignty and especially His justice in finally judging the entire host of "unsealed" people at the seventh trumpet. The pastoral purpose is to remind the readers that antagonism to their faithful witness will continue to the end of history and that they should not be disheartened because it is part of God's plan in which they can trust.

20b-21 The remainder of v. 20, together with v. 21, explains from what the ungodly did not repent. They **did not repent of the works of their hands**, but continued to **worship demons** and **idols**. The typical OT list of idolatrous practices according to their material substance (so Pss. 115:4-7; 135:15-17; Dan. 5:4, 23; Deut. 4:28; the list here most closely echoes Dan. 5:4, 23) is prefaced by a summary of the spiritual essence behind the idols (Ps. 106:36-37; 1 Cor. 10:20). Idols are one of the main instruments used by the forces of darkness to keep people in that darkness. Part of the OT judgment of idolaters is that they ironically reflect the unspiritual image of the idols, so that they likewise are spiritually not able to see, hear, or walk (Pss. 115:5-8; 135:18; cf. Isa. 6:9-10). This may be the precise manner in which the demons anesthetize the idolaters of Rev. 9:20-21 with spiritual ignorance and insensitivity. Hence, idolaters are punished by means of their own sin.

The vices listed here — **murders**, **sorceries**, **immorality**, and **thefts** — are associated with idol worship in both the OT and the NT (e.g., Jer. 7:5-11 [cited by Jesus in Matt. 21:13]; Hos. 3:1–4:2; 2 Kgs. 9:22; Isa. 47:9-10, 48:5; Mic. 5:12–6:8; Nah. 1:14; 3:1-4; Acts 15:20; Rom. 1:18-32; Gal. 5:20; Eph. 5:5; Col. 3:5), as in Revelation (see on Rev. 2:14, 20-22 with respect to "immorality" [*porneia*]; see also 21:8; 22:15). Indeed, idolatry is the root sin responsible for these other vices. The repetition of "repent" in 9:20-21 could be linked with the theme of repentance in the letters, especially 2:21-23, where the word occurs three times as a challenge to repent from idolatry, which is there synonymous with spiritual fornication *(porneia)*. This would mean that there are many in the churches who will not repent, and so the gruesome description of the demons here is intended also to shock some among the true people of God out of their complacent condition, as well as to bring others to true repentance.

Suggestions for Reflection on 9:13-21

On the seriousness of deception. These verses present a picture of ferocious creatures representing demonic spirits who bring torment on unbelievers. A careful examination of the picture shows that the actual form in which these creatures confront people is often that of human false teachers (inside and outside the visible church), who promote worship of anything other than the true God. Is it possible that by a literalistic interpretation of Revelation, whereby we expect to be confronted by supernatural horses with tails of serpents or by some modern military lethal force, we could miss the very present spiritual reality of these beings in our midst? How seriously do we take the threat of false teaching? Do we see it as a disagreeable but merely human phenomenon, or as something empowered by powerful demonic spirits? How do we respond to such threats? Do we always unswervingly go to God's Word for protection, since it is the only source of truth against such threats? Elsewhere John says, "You are strong, and the word of God abides in you, and you have overcome the evil one" (1 John 2:14); that is, strength to overcome the false teachings from the devil (in the context) comes only from "the word of God."

On the nature of idolatry. These verses present a picture of idolatry largely in line with that of the OT: the worship of idols of gold, silver, and other materials. The larger context of Revelation, which speaks of the destruction of all created things, shows that these human materials stand for anything that is not God, that is, worship of the creation rather than the Creator. What forms of idolatry exist in our society? Gold is not evil in itself, but is if it is worshiped. What about sports, careers, leisure activities, or the acquiring of money and material possessions? What of things clearly evil, such as pornography? How extensive is idolatry in our experience? Is part of the deception that we have restricted "idolatry" to the worship of literal idols? Whatever we are committed to more than God is an idol, including worship of ourselves.

On the perniciousness of idolatry. John links idolatry here with murders, sorceries, immorality, and thefts. If the OT observation is to be taken seriously, idolaters become as blind and dumb as what they worship. They thus become anesthetized, in the words of the commentary, to all that is good and of God, even as they fall deeper and deeper into the clutches of the forces of darkness, as John portrays so vividly. Is this how idolatry leads to these awful forms of sin and rebellion? How has Satan used idolatry to lead people into further darkness? Is there a point beyond which repentance is impossible? How can we guard ourselves against even the beginnings of idolatrous practices, since we know where these practices inevitably lead?

John is recommissioned to prophesy about judgment, concerning which he paradoxically rejoices and mourns (10:1-11)

[1] And I saw another strong angel coming down out of heaven, clothed with a
cloud; and the rainbow was upon his head, and his face was like the sun, and
his feet like pillars of fire; [2] and he had in his hand a little book which was open.
And he placed his right foot on the sea and his left on the land; and he cried out

with a loud voice, as when a lion roars; [3] and when he had cried out, the seven peals of thunder uttered their voices. [4] And when the seven peals of thunder had spoken, I was about to write; and I heard a voice from heaven saying. "Seal up the things which the seven peals of thunder have spoken, and do not write them." [5] And the angel whom I saw standing on the sea and on the land lifted up his right hand to heaven, [6] and swore by Him who lives forever and ever, who created heaven and the things in it, and the earth and the things in it, and the sea and the things in it, that there shall be delay no longer, [7] but in the days of the voice of the seventh angel, when he is about to sound, then the mystery of God is finished, as He preached to His servants the prophets. [8] And the voice which I heard from heaven, I heard again speaking with me, and saying, "Go, take the book which is open in the hand of the angel who stands on the sea and on the land." [9] And I went to the angel, telling him to give me the little book. And he said to me, "Take it, and eat it; and it will make your stomach bitter, but in your mouth it will be sweet as honey." [10] And I took the little book out of the angel's hand and ate it, and it was in my mouth sweet as honey; and when I had eaten it, my stomach was made bitter. [11] And they said to me, "You must prophesy again concerning many peoples and nations and tongues and kings."

Just as there was an interpretative parenthesis between the sixth and seventh seals, so again there is a similar parenthesis between the sixth and seventh trumpets. Here the parenthesis extends from 10:1 to 11:13. Ch. 10 is the introduction to the main content of the parenthesis in 11:1-13.

In this new vision, John is recommissioned to prophesy. His task is twofold. He is to prophesy about the persevering witness of Christians which brings them suffering, and about the destiny of those who react antagonistically to their witness. The prophecy he is given concerns the relationship between believers and unbelievers during the church age, culminating in the final judgment, at which point he resumes and concludes the relating of the trumpet vision, in which that judgment is set forth. Chs. 10–11 are put within the cycle of trumpets to connect the two halves of Revelation together. This is a literary device of interlocking, which functions to introduce the second part of the book while also linking it to the first part. The parenthesis does not chronologically intervene between the sixth and seventh trumpets but offers a further interpretation of the same period of the church age covered by the first six trumpets.

Even as ch. 7 shows that Christians are sealed against the spiritually destructive harm of the six trumpet judgments, so 11:1-13 reveals that they are sealed so as to bear an enduring and loyal witness to the gospel, which begins to lay a basis for the final judgment of those rejecting their testimony. This vision thus explains the theological basis for the judgment on the wicked in the first six trumpets. Non-Christians are punished by the trumpet judgments throughout the church age because they have persecuted believers. This expresses more explicitly the hint of the preceding chapters that the trumpets are God's answer to the saints' petition for their vindication and punishment of their oppressors (so 6:9-11; 8:3-5; 9:13-21). 10:6b-7, together with 11:14, announce that there will be no delay to God bringing an end to history (11:11-13, 18) when the full number of suffering believers has reached the predetermined number (6:10; 11:7a) and impenitence has reached its intractable height (9:21; 11:7-10).

1 John sees **another strong angel coming down out of heaven**. The first **strong angel** appeared in 5:2 and likewise proclaimed "with a loud voice." This is the first among a number of references which deliberately link this chapter in a significant manner with ch. 5. These links indicate that the revelation to this angel will be similar to the revelation given by the angel in ch. 5. This angel is not an ordinary angel, but is given divine attributes applicable in Revelation only to God or to Christ. He is **clothed with a cloud**. In the OT, it is God alone who is said to come in the clouds, except in Dan. 7:13, where the subject is the Son of man, but note that in Rev. 1:7 the one "coming with the clouds" in v. 7 is identified further in 1:13 as "like a Son of man," who in Daniel is given the attributes of the divine Ancient of Days. Another reference to clouds in Revelation occurs in 14:14, where John sees "a white cloud, and sitting on the cloud was one like a Son of man" (cf. continued references to this cloud in 14:15-16). In this light, the figure in 10:1 is probably equivalent to the "angel of Yahweh" in the OT, who is referred to as Yahweh Himself (e.g., Gen. 16:10; 22:11-18; 24:7; 31:11-13; Exod. 3:2-12; 14:19; Judg. 2:1; 6:22; 13:20-22; cf. Zech. 3:1-3 with Jude 9; see also Dan. 3:25; Acts 7:30, 35, 38). The angel has a **rainbow . . . upon his head**, as did the appearance of God in Ezek. 1:26-28. The Ezekiel reference has already been drawn on in the portrait of the Danielic Son of man in Rev. 1:13ff. The pattern of the Ezekiel 1–3 vision is followed again later in Rev. 10:2, 8-10, where the heavenly being like that in Ezekiel holds a book, and the book is taken and eaten by a prophet. Note also that the rainbow is around God's throne in Rev. 4:3. The angel's **face was like the sun**, just like that of Christ in Rev. 1:16, and this is an exact reproduction of the phrase describing Christ's transfigured appearance in Matt. 17:2. His **feet** are **like pillars of fire**, similar to the description of Christ's feet as "burnished bronze, when it has been caused to glow in a furnace" (Rev. 1:15).

The fact that the feet of the angelic figure are called **pillars of fire** evokes the presence of Yahweh with Israel in the wilderness, where He appeared as a pillar of cloud and a pillar of fire to protect and guide the Israelites (Exod. 13:20-22; 14:24; Num. 14:14; Neh. 9:12, 19). In Exod. 19:9-19, God's descent on Sinai "in a thick cloud" and "in fire" is announced by "thunder" and "the sound of a trumpet," which reflects the pattern of Revelation 10, where God's presence by His angel in vv. 1-3 is followed by thunder and the imminent trumpet sound in vv. 3-4, 7. The point of the reference here to God's presence with Israel in the wilderness is that the same divine presence protects and guides the faithful witnesses of the new Israel in the wilderness of the world, as the following chapters reveal (so 11:3-12; 12:6, 13-17). Therefore, the angel is the divine Angel of the Lord, as in the OT, who is to be identified with Yahweh or with Christ Himself. Enhancing this identification is the observation that Christ is compared to a lion in 5:5, and so is the angel in 10:3.

2 The divine angelic figure (Christ) **had in his hand a little book which was open**. What is the content of this little book, which John eats (vv. 9-10), and out of which he then prophesies (v. 11)? We know at least from the conclusion of ch. 10 (v. 11) that John's prophecy is to be against "many peoples and nations and tongues and kings," as in the universal formula used in subsequent chapters for multitudes who undergo forms of judgment (11:9; 13:7-8; 14:6ff.; 17:15). "Kings" is inserted into the formula to anticipate the "kings" in the later visions who will be judged (so 16:12, 14; 17:1-2, 10-12, 16, 18; 18:3, 9; 19:18-19). Furthermore, while it is true that Rev. 11:1-13 elaborates on ch. 10, chs. 12ff. continue the elaboration. Therefore, the **little book** includes reference, at least, to the contents of chs. 11–16, since another prophetic commission may be indicated in 17:1-3, which unleashes a new series of prophetic visions. The ch. 10 scroll may also include chs. 17–22, if the prophetic commission of 17:1ff. is merely a renewal of the previous one.

The **little book which was open** in the hand of the angel here and in the following verses is difficult to identify unless it is linked with the scroll that the Lamb was to open in ch. 5. Though there are some differences (the book is smaller; John takes the book instead of the Lamb), the similarities are far more significant:

> not only are both "books opened," but
> they are held by Christ (in 10:1ff.),
> who is compared to a lion;

both are allusions to the scroll of Ezekiel,
are associated with a "strong angel" who cries out
and with God who "lives forever and ever";
both books are directly related to the end-time prophecy of Daniel 12;
in both visions someone approaches a heavenly being and takes a book out of the being's hand;
part of the prophetic commission of John in both visions is stated in near identical language ("I heard a voice from heaven speaking"; cf. 10:4 and especially 10:8); and
both scrolls concern the destiny of "peoples and nations and tongues and tribes [kings]."

Therefore, a reasonable assumption is that the meaning of the scroll of ch. 10 is generally the same as that of ch. 5. In ch. 5, the scroll was symbolic of God's plan of judgment and redemption, which has been inaugurated by Christ's death and resurrection. The interpretation of 5:9-10 by the hymn of 5:12 also pointed to the book of ch. 5 being a testament or will which contained an inheritance to be received. God promised to Adam that he would reign over the earth. Although Adam forfeited this promise, Christ, the last Adam, was destined to inherit it. The reception of the scroll from God on the throne and the opening of it in ch. 5 connoted Christ's taking of authority over His Father's plan and beginning the execution of it. On the basis of His death and resurrection, by which He redeemed His people, He was worthy to take the book, assume authority over the plan in it, and establish His kingdom over the redeemed (see on 5:2-5, 9-10, 12). The plan of the book encompasses history from the cross to the consummation of the new creation, since a summary of the scroll's contents is revealed in chs. 6–22. It outlines Christ's sovereignty over history, the reign of Christ and the saints throughout the course of the church age and in the new cosmos, Christ's protection of His people who suffer trial, His temporal and final judgments on the persecuting world, and the final judgment. Ch. 5 revealed, though, that perseverance through suffering is the ironic means Christ used to overcome and take sovereignty over the book as His inheritance. The book of ch. 10 is also associated with the same ironic pattern, to be explained in the following verses (see further on v. 7).

The possession of the scroll-like testament means that now Christ has dominion over the entire cosmos, symbolized by the angel standing on both sea and land (placing one's foot on something indicates sovereignty over that thing, as in Josh. 10:24-26). This is the basis for the command to John to prophesy about Christ's sovereignty to "many peoples and nations and tongues and kings" in v. 11. The heavenly being's sovereignty over **sea** and **land** shows that God is also ultimately in control over the dragon, who stands on the "sand of the sea" to conjure up the beast "coming out of the sea" (13:1) and the "beast coming up out of the earth" (13:11).

3-4 The angelic figure **cried out with a loud voice, as when a lion roars**, thus further identifying the angel with Christ, the "Lion that is from the tribe of Judah" (5:5). Following this, **the seven peals of thunder uttered their voices**. The seven thunders are probably to be identified with the voice of a heavenly being, like the living creature of 6:1 who cries out with a voice of thunder, or like the heavenly host of 19:6, whose voice is as the sound of thunder (see also John 12:28-29 for the voice from heaven like thunder), or it could be the voice of God or Christ. As John was about to write down what the seven thunders had said, he **heard a voice from heaven saying, "Seal up the things which the seven peals of thunder have spoken, and do not write them."**

In the OT thunder often indicates judgment (five times in Exod. 9:23-34; 1 Sam. 7:10; Ps. 29:3; Isa. 29:6; and many other occurrences), as it does in Rev. 6:1, where it introduces the seven seals. References in Revelation (with slight variations) to thunders, sounds, lightnings, and an earthquake mark the last judgment (see on 8:5; 11:19; 16:18). The source of the thunders may be Psalm 29, where God's thunders of punishment are equated with "the voice of the Lord," an expression which is repeated seven times in the Psalm. The Psalm's thunders are now employed to underscore the newly obtained sovereignty of Christ (v. 2), which has been handed over to Him by the eternal God ("Him who lives forever and ever," v. 6a). Christ's sovereign authority is expressed by His (or His angel's) voice, which unleashes the revelation of the seven thunders. The use of the definite article (***the* seven peals of thunder**) could point to the fact that this was something known (presumably from Scripture) to John (and likely to his readers). On the basis of the use in the OT and elsewhere in the book, the image of "thunders" here could designate some judgment *preceding* the final judgment. On the same basis, they might be *premonitions* of divine wrath, as in John 12:28-31. The latter is indicated here by the use of the word by itself, apart from the fuller expressions of chs. 8, 11, and 16, and by the fact that the seventh trumpet, introducing the final judgment, has not yet been sounded.

The seven peals of thunder probably represent another sevenfold series of judgments parallel to the sets of seven seals, trumpets, and bowls, but not to be revealed. They would give yet another perspective on the same events as the seals, trumpets, and bowls, which would make sense in light of the four sets of seven judgments in Leviticus 26 that God says He will send against His people if they disobey Him. The thunder judgments are not revealed here perhaps because they are so repetitive of the previous two synchronous sevenfold cycles of seals and trumpets that they reveal nothing radically new. Enough has been said about the various punishments unleashed against the unrepentant throughout the church age. The focus is now on the relationship between the unrepentant and the faithful witnesses during the same time when the seals and trumpets occur. The *reason* for the punishments is the focus. The wicked suffer because they reject the message of the witnesses and persecute them, as 11:1-13 makes clear.

The command of v. 4b reflects the similar command given to Daniel by the angel, who is the model for the angel here and in vv. 5-6. The "sealing" in Daniel 12 referred partly to keeping hidden from Daniel and others how a prophecy was to be fulfilled. John, like Daniel, receives revelation, but, unlike Daniel, he understands it. The definite article with "thunders" may imply that the thunders are known to him (perhaps from an understanding of Psalm 29), and the fact that he is about to record the revelation of the thunders also suggests that he understands their significance to some degree. Nevertheless, like Daniel, he is still not to make it known to his readers. Also in line with Daniel 12 is the possibility that the sealing could allude to the seven thunders as judgments that, in contrast to the majority of the other sevenfold series, were events yet to occur in the distant future.

5-6 The angelic figure John **saw standing on the sea and on the land lifted up his right hand to heaven and swore by Him who lives forever and ever.** In contrast to the preceding command to seal up the revelation of the thunders, the angel makes an oath to God which is a revelation about the way redemptive history culminates. The description here is a direct allusion to the angel in Dan. 12:7, who stood above the waters, raised his hands to heaven, and swore by Him who lives forever. These words in turn mirror the prophetic words of God to Moses in Deut. 32:40-43, where God swears that He will judge the ungodly. In Deut. 32:32-35, God's judgment is described as "the wrath of serpents and . . . of asps," and one Aramaic version of Deut. 32:33 (the Palestinian Targum) compares the plans of the wicked to "serpents' heads" and "the head of asps," which was a significant image in the preceding context (Rev. 9:19). And in the same passage (Deut.

32:34-35), God says that His judgments are "sealed up" (cf. v. 4) and will be released in due time, as they were in Israel's subsequent history.

This Deuteronomy background is a further indication that the seven thunders which are to be "sealed up" in Rev. 10:4-5 are another series of seven judgments, whose contents are not revealed but whose execution is ever imminent and even has begun, in that they are parallel with the seals and trumpets and that the first six woes of each series are inaugurated. The Christ who describes Himself here in the same words as His Father did to Moses in Deut. 32:40 orders the judgments of the seven thunders to be sealed in Revelation 10, just as His Father told Moses that His judgments were sealed. God is described as **Him who . . . created heaven and the things in it, and the earth and the things in it, and the sea and the things in it.** The reference to heaven, earth, and sea, followed in each case by the phrase **and the things in it**, serves to underscore the absolute sovereignty of God in creating *all things.* This connects God's sovereignty over the beginning of creation to Christ's rule over creation in the latter days of the church age and into eternity, as symbolized by the angel's posture in vv. 2 and 5. The same connection between God's sovereignty and that of Christ was made between chs. 4 and 5, in reference to the book of ch. 5 coming from God but opened by Christ (see on chs. 4–5). The oath the angelic figure utters is that **there shall be delay no longer** (or literally "that time shall be no longer") but that, as in Dan. 12:7 (see above), everything will be "completed" or "finished."

7 The more precise meaning of the preceding phrase concerning delay (or time) is now given: **In the days of the voice of the seventh angel, when he is about to sound, then the mystery of God is finished.** The continuation of the oath explains further how the meaning of the oath from Daniel is altered. The prophecy in Dan. 11:29–12:13 concerned the end-time suffering of God's people, God's destruction of the enemy, the establishment of the kingdom, and the reign of the saints. The prophetic events were to lead up to and result in the consummation of history. Dan. 12:7 says that these prophetic events will occur during "a time, times, and half a time," after which God's prophetic plan will "be completed." John views the "times, time, and half a time" of Daniel as the church age leading up to the final judgment (see further on 11:3; 12:6, 14; 13:5).

The identification of this time formula from Daniel is evident in Rev. 12:4-6, where the period begins at the time of Christ's ascension and is the church's time of suffering (so also 12:14; see on 12:4-6, 14). In the context of the book, this period must cover the church age and be concluded by

Christ's final coming. Therefore, vv. 6-7 are speaking of the end of this period, which is the end of time or of history. The angel told Daniel that the meaning of the prophecy was sealed up until the end time, when it would be revealed. In contrast to Daniel 12, the angel's oath in Revelation 10 begins an emphasis on *when* and *how* the prophecy will be completed, which is amplified in ch. 11. When the seventh angel sounds his trumpet, the prophecy of Dan. 11:29–12:13 will be fulfilled and history (Daniel's "end of the age," 12:13) will come to an end (i.e., historical "time shall be no longer").

A strong verbal parallel between 10:6b-7 and 6:11 shows that the content of the mystery in ch. 10 concerns God's decree that the saints suffer, which leads directly to the judgment of their persecutors. At this time, the mystery of God will be finished. When in 6:10 the saints cry out as to when the judgment of God will come on those who have persecuted the church, the answer is that there is (literally) "yet a little time" (6:11) until the full number of those who are to be killed is completed. Now God says that there will (literally) "no longer be time" (v. 6b), but the mystery is to be fulfilled or finished. The prayer of the saints in 6:10 is thus answered by the events to be precipitated by the sounding of the seventh trumpet. V. 6 has alluded to Dan. 12:7 and Deut. 32:40, both of which speak of God's vindication of His people after their suffering. In Dan. 12:7, the angel says that "as soon as they finish shattering the power of the holy people, all these events will be completed." The days of the voice of the seventh angel probably refers to the definitive time when the decisive blow of the last judgment is struck, for there is to be no further delay. The **mystery of God** (= God's mystery) is, **as He preached to His servants the prophets**, an allusion to Amos 3:7, where God "reveals His secret counsel to His servants the prophets" (though the actual word "mystery" is not used, Amos 3:4-8 also pictures God as a lion roaring and has a trumpet blowing).

The gospel of Christ, including both salvation and judgment, was prophetically announced by God to His prophets in the OT (**preached** here is literally "preached the gospel" [*euēngelisen*]), and its inaugurated fulfillment has been announced to the prophets of the new age. The fulfillment of the prophesied gospel is occurring, and will continue to occur, in a mysterious and unexpected manner from the human perspective. The suffering of the saints will give way to their eventual vindication. Only those to whom God reveals the mystery can understand the meaning of this history. The reason the revelation can be made is that the death, resurrection, and exaltation of Christ have inaugurated the "latter days" and the fulfillment of the prophecies from Daniel which were to occur in the "latter days." In fact, the prophecy of the "latter days" in Dan. 2:28-45 is repeatedly called a "mystery" (Greek *mystērion*) there (vv. 27-30). Christ's removing of the seals from the scroll in ch. 5 connoted precisely the same idea of new revelation due to the inauguration of the difficult-to-understand latter day prophecies from Daniel 12 (see on 5:1-5, 9; and see Dan. 12:4, 8-9), which have been combined here with the "mysterious" prophecies of Daniel 2.

Note the striking parallel to Rom. 16:25-26, where Paul speaks of the mystery of God revealed according to God's eternal command by the Scriptures of the prophets and made known to the nations. This mystery is that of the cross. Where the word "mystery" occurs elsewhere in the NT, it often refers to fulfillment of OT prophecy in a way different than would have been expected in Judaism or was not so clear in the OT (e.g., Matt. 13:11; Mark 4:11; Luke 8:10; 2 Thess. 2:7 [cf. Dan. 8:23-25; 11:29-45]; Rom. 11:25; Eph. 3:3-4, 9). The angel is beginning to explain to John the "when" and "how," which Daniel did not understand about his own prophecy: John is told that the "latter days" prophesied to Daniel have *now* begun, and that this has been set in motion *through* the "mysterious" manner of Christ's death and resurrection. That is, the prophecy of God's defeat of the evil kingdom is being ironically fulfilled by this evil kingdom's apparent physical victory over Christ and the saints. The mysterious nature of the saints' victory is to be understood through the ironic way in which Christ obtained victory through His apparent defeat by the same evil kingdom.

The legitimacy of this comparison is based on the prior observation that ch. 10 is parallel to ch. 5 and to be interpreted in its light. In ch. 5, Christ's death was already a beginning victory, because He was a "faithful witness" resisting the spiritual defeat of compromise (1:5) and because He was accomplishing the redemption of His people by paying the penalty of their sin (so 5:9-10; 1:5-6). Jesus' death was also a victory because it was an initial step leading to the resurrection (1:5; 5:5-8). Likewise, ch. 10 is saying that those who believe in Christ will follow in His footsteps. Their defeat is also an initial victory, because they are faithful witnesses withstanding the spiritual defeat of compromise, and even their death is a spiritual resurrection, for they will receive a crown of victory (2:10-11). The same pattern will be shown in the following context of 11:1-13, where the persecution and defeat of the witnessing church is the means leading to their resurrection and their enemies' defeat.

Thus, just as Christ, so Christians have their "book," which is also symbolic of their purpose: they are to reign ironically as Christ did by being imitators on a small scale of the great cosmic model of Christ on the cross. And this may be why Christ is portrayed as a large, cosmic figure overshadowing the earth. Therefore, the little book is a new version of those same purposes symbolized by the book of ch. 5 insofar as they are to be accomplished by the people of God.

8 Now the heavenly voice of v. 4 commands John to **take the book which is open in the hand of the angel who stands on the sea and on the land.** This command continues the contrast of vv. 5-7 with v. 4, where the angel began to reveal truth about the climax of redemptive history in antithesis to the prohibition in v. 4 to seal up the revelation. In vv. 8-10, more revelation issues from the hand of the same angel in the form of the book. John's approach and taking of the book has similar significance to the Lamb's approach and taking of the book in 5:7-8. The Lamb's taking and opening of the scroll was symbolic of His newly gained authority, and John's similar action shows that he participates in and identifies with Jesus' authority in executing judgment and redemption, even though only Jesus has redeemed humanity and is sovereign over history. Ch. 11 will reveal that what is true of John as a prophet and of his reigning through suffering is true of all Christians in general. This is clear in that both John and the "two witnesses" of ch. 11 (representing the church: see on 11:3) are referred to as prophets (11:6, 10; cf. similarly 16:6; 18:20, 24; 22:6, 9). This close identification with Christ's reigning through suffering is another instance of the notion found elsewhere in the book that believers "follow the Lamb wherever He goes" (14:4). We will also see that in 11:3-12, the two witnesses' career of testimony is patterned after that of Christ.

9-10 John's reception of the book symbolically connotes his prophetic call. The command and the carrying out of the command to take the book and consume it is a picture portraying his formal recommissioning as a prophet. His call has already been stated in terms of Ezekiel's commissioning in 1:10 and 4:1-2, and the parallel here continues with specific reference to Ezek. 2:8–3:3, where, as part of his commissioning, the prophet eats the scroll, which is sweet but followed by a bitter response (3:14) because of the people's rebellion. The angelic figure, giving the little book to John, tells him to **take it, and eat it; and it will make your stomach bitter, but in your mouth it will be sweet as honey**. The eating of the scroll indicates the prophet's complete identification with its message (cf. Ezek. 3:10). The effect of "eating" or identifying with the book is that it is sweet because it contains God's own life-giving words (Deut. 8:3; Pss. 19:10; 119:103; Prov. 16:21-24; 24:13-14), in which the prophet will briefly delight. The bitterness comes from the scroll's purpose, which is to announce judgment and its effect in terms of the rebellious response of the people. Ezekiel was warned in advance that, except for a remnant who will respond and repent (9:4-6; 14:21-23), those who would listen were a rebellious people and would not respond. Therefore, his message is primarily one of judgment. This is explicitly emphasized by the description of the scroll: "it was written on the front and back; and written on it were lamentations, mourning, and woe" (Ezek. 2:10).

Note also the close parallel to Jer. 15:15-18. First, the prophet finds joy in his commission: "Thy words were found and I ate them, and Thy words became for me a joy and the delight of my heart" (v. 16). Yet, as his words are rejected, his joy turns to bitterness: *"I did not sit in the circle of merrymakers . . . for Thou didst fill me with indignation. Why has my pain been perpetual . . . ?"* (vv. 17-18; Jer. 15:19-21 further shows that vv. 15-18 are part of a prophetic commission). Likewise, John found joy and bitterness in his prophetic commission. In contrast to Ezekiel and Jeremiah, John is warning not Israel of old, but the church, the visible new Israel, against unbelief and compromise with the idolatrous world, as well as warning the world of unbelievers (see on v. 11 and 11:1ff. below).

John, along with the angelic creatures and the deceased saints in heaven, actually takes pleasure in God's pronouncement of judgment, because God's word represents His will, which works all things for His glory (11:17-18; 14:7; 15:3-4; 19:1-2). It does so in at least three ways:

because God's righteousness is demonstrated when He punishes sin,
because such punishment vindicates Christians in their suffering (cf. 6:9-11; 18:4-7), and
because part of the message about judgment is an encouragement to remain true to God's word (as in 11:1-13).

Nevertheless Christians, like God, do not take sardonic, emotional pleasure in the pain of punishment considered as an end in and of itself separately from its broader framework of justice.

The sweetness of the scroll likely includes reference to God's redemptive grace in the gospel to those believing, and its bitterness to the fact that this grace must be experienced in the crucible of suffering (cf. 2 Cor. 2:15-16). This is evident from recalling that the little scroll connotes the Christian's purposes on a small scale in imitation of the large-scale purposes of Christ signified by the larger book of ch. 5. Certainly, part of these purposes is the experience of divine grace through suffering. Part of the gospel's sweetness is that Christians already begin to be vindicated because of their persevering testimony when they reach heaven (6:9-11), and this process is completed when God vindicates them before all eyes at the end of history (e.g., 11:11-13, 18).

Yet it is the bitterness which will linger, for John's actual experience is revealed in the next verse: **it was in my mouth sweet as honey; and when I had eaten it, my stomach was made bitter.** The reality of the non-repentant response to his message by others in the church and the world is a "bitter" or mournful thing for John to contemplate, as it was for the OT prophets and for Jesus Himself (Luke 19:41). The only other time "bitter" appears in Revelation is in the third trumpet plague (8:11), where many die because of the bitter waters, thus showing that the period of bitterness (the world's rejection of the church's message) extends throughout the church age (during which the third trumpet plague occurs) and cannot be confined to the period immediately before the return of Christ.

The emphasis on judgment in relation to the scroll is paramount, as seen against the Ezekiel background and the following chapters of Revelation, which focus more on judgment than on reward, especially ch. 11. This is confirmed if we recall that the scroll of ch. 5 highlighted judgment, because it was modeled on Ezekiel 2–3; Dan. 7:10; 12:4, 9; and other OT theophanies introducing messages of judgment. The seven seals showed further that the ch. 5 scroll was primarily a scroll of woe.

11 This verse, containing John's further recommissioning, is directly linked by **and** (having the sense of "therefore" or "and so") to the sweetness, and even more to the bitterness, of the scroll in v. 10. John is to announce the bittersweet judgment of the scroll against the ungodly peoples of the earth because that is the message which he has been commissioned to deliver. Having digested the contents of the scroll, he must now make its contents known to others. The symbolic version of John's recommissioning portrayed in vv. 8-10 is interpreted to mean that he is to **prophesy again.** The use of **again** indicates that this is a *re*commissioning. He has been commissioned on at least two previous occasions (1:10-20 and 4:1-2), although the first includes the whole book as well and the second probably includes also the remainder of the book. These two previous commissionings directly resulted in the prophetic tracts of chs. 2–3 and chs. 4–9. The inclusion of **again** here indicates a continuation of the same kind of prophesying about the same people as in chs. 6–9. The commissioning here results in the prophetic tract of 11:1-13, and, as we saw on v. 2

above, this commissioning likely extends at least from ch. 11 to ch. 16, and perhaps even all the way to ch. 22.

Therefore, in 10:11, John's previous prophetic commissionings are renewed and deepened, as was the case with Jeremiah (Jer. 15:15-21). He is told to **prophesy again concerning many peoples and nations and tongues and kings**. He is addressed by a plurality of heavenly beings: **And they said to me.** John is commanded to **prophesy again concerning** or, more accurately, "prophesy against" (where "against" represents the Greek preposition *epi*). The usual meaning of the phrase in the LXX is one of judgment, and is often used that way in Ezekiel, which is the primary OT background to this passage. Use of the scroll image from Ezekiel 2–3 in the immediately preceding context of 10:8-10 also points to the theme of judgment. Finally, note the negative manner in which John uses variations of the fourfold phrase "peoples and nations and tongues and tribes" in the remainder of the book (11:9; 13:7; 14:6; cf. 17:15).

The verb "prophesy" does not refer just to predicting of future events but also to providing God's revealed perspective on what is happening in the present. Note how John exhorts his readers to "hear" and "keep" the words of prophecy in this book (1:3; 22:7, 9). The prophetic message of Revelation is designed not only for the future, but also for the present — for those who are currently hearing and reading its message and who are constantly being called to put it into practice in their lives now. This understanding of prophecy is consistent with the OT idea, which emphasizes a revealed interpretation of the present together with the future (forth-telling as well as foretelling), demanding ethical response from those addressed, who are primarily God's people. Therefore, John's prophesying is not only against the ungodly who reside outside the covenant community of the church but also against compromisers within the visible new Israel, who are from all "peoples and nations and tongues and tribes," and who ally themselves with the world from which they have purportedly been redeemed. Just as Ezekiel directed his message against old Israel, so John also directs his partly against unrepentant, compromising elements of the visible church, new Israel.

Suggestions for Reflection on 10:1-11

On the divinity of Christ. As presented here (10:1-6) and in many other places in the book, the divinity of Christ is a major and consistent theme in Revelation. The divine angel of the Lord, identified often in the OT with Yahweh, is here also identified with Christ, for which idea the commentary provides much support. Has a shallow reading of Revelation, with a focus on misguided eschatology, drawn us away from its presentation of the exalted Christ? What has drawn us to focus on (often poorly understood) eschatological timelines and miss the heart of the book, which is the glory of God and of Christ?

On the authority of Christ expressed through the church. John draws a strong parallel between the book of ch. 5, presented to Christ by God, and the little book of ch. 10, presented by Christ to John and, by extension, to the church. This shows that all authority comes from Christ, but that He chooses to invest His church with a measure of that same authority. If the book, as the commentary suggests, represents the inheritance of Christ in terms of His rulership over the cosmos, then the little book represents the inheritance of the church. What does this say about the authority that God's people exercise? The nature of our authority is linked here with the proclamation of the gospel message and the judgment of God. It is also linked with the sweetness of God's word to his people *and* with the bitterness that comes from the inevitable widespread rejection of that message and the consequent suffering of the church. Consider Jesus' words: "I lay down my life that I may take it again. . . . I have authority to lay it down, and I have authority to take it up again. This commandment I received from my Father" (John 10:17-18). How is our authority linked with that of Jesus? Have the times of the church's greatest temporal authority been the times of its weakest spiritual authority? How do we measure the true dimensions of the authority (as defined by John) of the church we are part of or that of the wider church in our own nation?

On the mystery of God. John states that the mystery of God will be finished or completed at the last judgment (the sounding of the seventh trumpet). The commentary contends that "mystery" in the NT involves the fulfillment of OT prophecy in ways that would not have been expected in Judaism or were not completely clear in the OT. The mystery is expressed above all in the cross. If the mystery is to be "finished" at the last judgment, when did it begin? How is this mystery worked out in the life of the church? How does it relate to Daniel's comment about the shattering of the power of the holy people (Dan. 12:7)? In the third century AD, Tertullian stated that "the blood of the martyrs is the seed of the church" (*Apology* 50). Was he speaking of this same mystery? How do we find rest in God when the forces of evil seem to be triumphant? Is the mystery John spoke of adequately reflected in the preaching of the church today?

God's decree ensures His presence with His people and their effective witness, which leads to their apparent defeat and culminates in judgment of their oppressors (11:1-13)

[1] And there was given me a measuring rod like a staff, and someone said, "Rise and measure the temple of God, and the altar, and those who worship in it. [2] And leave out the court which is outside the temple, and do not measure it, for it has been given to the nations; and they will tread under foot the holy city for forty-two months. [3] And I will grant authority to my two witnesses, and they will prophesy for twelve hundred and sixty days, clothed in sackcloth." [4] These are the two olive trees and the two lampstands that stand before the Lord of the earth. [5] And if anyone desires to harm them, fire proceeds out of their mouth, and devours their enemies; and if anyone would desire to harm them, in this manner he must be killed. [6] These have the power to shut up the sky, in order that rain may not fall during the days of their prophesying; and they have power over the waters to turn them into blood, and to smite the earth with every plague, as often as they desire. [7] And when they have finished their testimony, the beast that comes up out of the abyss will make war with them, and overcome them and kill them. [8] And their dead bodies will lie in the street of the great city which spiritually is called Sodom and Egypt, where also their Lord was crucified. [9] And those from the peoples and tribes and tongues and nations will look at their dead bodies for three and a half days, and will not permit their dead bodies to be laid in a tomb. [10] And those who dwell on the earth will rejoice over them and make merry; and they will send gifts to one another, because these two prophets tormented those who dwell on the earth. [11] And after the three and a half days the breath of life from God came into them, and they stood on their feet; and great fear fell upon those who were beholding them. [12] And they heard a loud voice from heaven saying to them, "Come up here." And they went up into heaven in the cloud, and their enemies beheld them. [13] And in that hour there was a great earthquake, and a tenth of the city fell; and seven thousand people were killed in the earthquake, and the rest were terrified and gave glory to the God of heaven.

Rev. 11:1-13 shows that the church is sealed for bearing an enduring and loyal witness to the gospel, which begins to lay a basis for the final judgment of those rejecting their testimony. The emphasis of ch. 10 on recommissioning John for his prophetic calling now shifts to a focus on the prophetic message he was commissioned to deliver. The message is that of judgment upon those who reject the persevering witness of Christians and who persecute them. This message, secondarily included in the introduction of ch. 10, now becomes the focus. The judgment is the first explicit answer to the saints' prayer for vindication and retribution against their antagonists (in development of 6:9-11 and 8:3-5). This explicitly expresses what the trumpets imply. The events portrayed in 11:1-13 occur during the same time as the first six trumpets.

1-2 The beginning of the prophetic message is an acted-out parable of measuring a temple. John is given a reed and commanded to **measure the temple of God, and the altar, and those who worship in it**. However, he is not to measure **the court which is outside the temple . . . for it has been given to the nations; and they will tread under foot the holy city for forty-two months**. Though this is not explicit, it is the commissioning angel of ch. 10 who continues to speak to John in 11:1ff. These verses are complex, and require careful comment on several points.

Differing interpretations of this passage

There are at least five broad interpretations of this passage:

The dispensational futurist, along with some modified futurist views, projects this into the time of tribulation immediately preceding Christ's final parousia. Typically, the temple and altar refer to a literal restored temple in the literal "holy city" of Jerusalem. **Those who worship in it** are a remnant of believing ethnic Jews. Unbelieving Jews are in **the court which is outside the temple** (henceforth referred to as the "outer court") and thus unprotected. The "measuring" of the temple, altar, and remnant indicates that they will be physically protected by God. Gentiles will enter the outer court, persecute the remnant, and overrun a literal Jerusalem during a literal forty-two month period.

The preterist view is virtually identical in its literal approach by also viewing the temple, altar, and outer court as the actual cultic complex in Jerusalem. However, according to this view, the portrayal depicts events occurring before and during the literal destruction of the temple and Jerusalem in 70 AD.

A modified futurist view understands the descriptions figuratively. The images of the sanctuary, the altar, and the worshipers refer figuratively to those within ethnic Israel whose salvation is secured at the end of history by the "measuring." The outer court and holy city refer to Jewish unbelievers whose salvation will not be secured.

Another position is similar but does not relegate the scenario to the future and understands the outer court as the professing but apostate church throughout history, which will be deceived and align itself with unbelieving persecutors of the true, spiritual Israel.

A final view, which we think is best, also understands the text figuratively but interprets the outer court as the physical expression of the true, spiritual Israel, which is susceptible to harm. This view is linguistically allowable because the language of "casting outside" (the text of v. 2 reading literally "the court outside the temple, cast it out [Greek *ekbale*] and do not measure it") can also refer to God's true people who are rejected and persecuted by the unbelieving world (cf. Matt. 21:39; Mark 12:8; Luke 4:29; 20:15; John 9:34-35; Acts 7:58). The significance of the measuring means that their salvation is secured, despite physical harm. This is a further development of the "sealing" of 7:2-8. In the OT generally, "measuring" was metaphorical for a decree of protection (e.g., 2 Sam. 8:2; Isa. 28:16-17; Jer. 31:38-40; Zech. 1:16) or of judgment (e.g., 2 Sam. 8:2; 2 Kgs. 21:13; Lam. 2:8; Amos 7:7-9).

The "measuring" is best understood against the background of the prophecy of the temple in Ezekiel 40–48. There, the sure establishment and subsequent protection of the temple are metaphorically pictured by an angel measuring various features of the temple complex (in the Greek text of Ezekiel, virtually identical Greek words for "measure" are used: the verb occurs about 30 times and the noun about 30 times). In Rev. 21:15-17 an angel, in dependence on the same Ezekiel text, uses a "measuring rod" (as in 11:1) to measure the city, its gates and its wall. There, the measuring of the city and its parts portrays the security of its inhabitants against the harm and contamination of unclean and deceptive people (so 21:27). Jewish and Gentile Christians will compose this temple community (as is evident from 3:12; 21:12-14 [the apostles representing the church from every nation]; 21:24-26; 22:2). What is figuratively established by the measuring in Ezekiel and Revelation 21 is the infallible promise of God's future presence, which will dwell forever in the midst of a purified community.

In Revelation 11, the "measuring" connotes God's presence, which is guaranteed to be with the temple community living on earth before the Lord's return. This means that the faith of God's people will be upheld by

His presence, since without His living presence there can be no living faith. In ch. 11, this means that the promise of God's eschatological presence begins with the establishment of the Christian community. Even before the church age began, God made a decree which secured the salvation of all people who would become genuine members of the church (see further on the meaning of the sealing in 7:3).

If the literal view of the temple, altar, and city were correct (the first two views described above), then John would be distinguishing believing Jews (in the sanctuary) from the nation of unbelieving Jews (the outer court). But one difficulty with this is that no distinction between believing ethnic Jews and unbelieving ethnic Jews clearly occurs anywhere else in the book. With regard to the fourth view, it is unlikely that the outer court would represent pseudo-believers (either Jews or the apostate church), because the following context of ch. 11 yields no hint of apostates or compromisers but only contrasts true witnesses with those who persecute them. Another theological objection to the futuristic literalist view is that a future literal temple with an altar would mean the revival of the OT sacrificial system, whereas Heb. 10:1-12 affirms that Christ's sacrifice typologically fulfilled and abolished that system forever. The response that such future sacrifices will be mere memorials of Christ's sacrifice is unconvincing. The fact that the temple prophesied in Ezekiel 40–48 includes a sacrificial system must be reinterpreted in the light of Heb. 10:1-12.

Consequently, some form of the last view described above is most plausible. The outer court of the Jerusalem temple did not have a completely negative function. This outermost portion of the Herodian temple was designed for "God-fearing" Gentiles. But, as noted above, it is the eschatological temple of Ezekiel 40–48 which is the focus here. In this case, the contrast would be between the innermost sanctuary and the outer court, which was intended for the Israelite worshipers. If John has the context of Ezekiel in mind, then it is unlikely that he is now affirming that, contrary to Ezekiel's expectation, part of the real end-time temple will be inhabited by unbelievers and idolaters. Rather, the bodies of those whose souls are a part of the invisible temple will undergo degrees of suffering. However, their souls will not be contaminated with idolatrous influences, so that they remain believers. Christ's work is now the dominant interpretative lens through which to understand OT expectations. In Rev. 11:1-2, the temple of the church is being patterned after the cross of Christ, who is the true temple. Just as Christ suffered, so the church will suffer and appear defeated. Nevertheless, through it all, God's tabernacling presence will abide with believers and protect them from any contamination leading to eternal death. God's abiding presence also guarantees them ultimate victory.

In 11:1, the focus is now on the whole covenant community dwelling in a spiritual temple in which God's presence dwells (so also 1 Cor. 3:16-17; 6:19; 2 Cor. 6:16; Eph. 2:21-22; 1 Pet. 2:5). What Ezekiel prophesied has begun to find its real, true fulfillment on a spiritual level, which will be consummated in fuller form physically and spiritually in a new creation (see on Rev. 21:1–22:5). Christians, who are identified with Christ, are also presently identified with the temple. Without exception, "temple" (Greek *naos*) elsewhere in Revelation refers not to a literal or historical temple, but either to the heavenly temple of the present (7:15; 11:19; 14:15, 17; 15:5-6, 8; 16:1, 17) or to the temple of God's presence dominating the new age of the future (3:12; 21:22). This usage points to the same identification in 11:1-2: the people of God who are members of God's temple in heaven are referred to in their existence on earth as being in "the temple of God." Already in John 2:19-22, Christ identified His resurrection body as the true temple, and this is developed in Rev. 21:22 (likewise Mark 12:10-11 and parallels). There John says he "saw no temple" in the new Jerusalem "for the Lord God . . . and the Lamb are its temple." There is no reason to limit this identification to the new, future Jerusalem, since the identification began to be made when Christ was resurrected, and the resurrected Christ is the central feature of the heavenly temple scene in 1:12-20.

The "altar" refers to the way God's people now worship in the community. In line with 6:9-10, the altar connotes the sacrificial calling, which entails suffering for their faithful witness (as affirmed by 6:3-9; see on 6:9-10). In fact, the Greek word here for "altar" *(thysiastērion)* can be translated as "the place of sacrifice." The picture of Christians portrayed as worshiping in a spiritual temple as priests at an altar is similar to 1 Pet. 2:5 (believers as "living stones, are being built up as a spiritual house for a holy priesthood, to offer up spiritual sacrifices"). Indeed, Rev. 1:6 and 5:10 (on which see) allude to the same OT text (Exod. 19:6) as 1 Pet. 2:5 in identifying Christians as priests (cf. Heb. 13:9-16, where believers have an altar, i.e., Christ, through which they offer up sacrifices to God).

If the temple signifies the church dwelling in the midst of Christ's and God's presence, the outer court (which is part of the temple) must therefore represent the church in its exposure and vulnerability to the world system in which it lives. The "holy city," which is to be trodden underfoot (v. 2), is equated with the outer court. In Revelation, the "holy city" refers either to the future heavenly city (3:12; 21:2, 10) or to its earthly manifestation in the form of the church (20:9: "they . . . surrounded the camp of the saints and the beloved city"). As Revelation develops, we shall see how the world system is ruled by demonic forces. Yet believers must live within it and remain physically unprotected in the midst of persecution. They will suffer as they maintain faithful witness to Christ in the midst of a pagan society, but they will be kept spiritually safe. Note that both parts of the temple (inner and outer court) belong to God, and the period of trampling down of the outer court (and the holy city) will cease, at which point all creation will be restored under the rulership of Christ.

What, then, is the significance of the **forty-two months**? If the picture here of the "temple" and the "altar" is symbolic, then so is the time period. The reference is to the time of tribulation prophesied by Daniel (7:25; 12:7, 11-12) either as a "time, times and half a time" (three and a half years or forty-two months) or as one thousand, three hundred and thirty-five days (the equivalent). For Daniel, this lay far off in the future, but for John it has begun, starting with the resurrection of Christ and continuing until His return (see on Rev. 1:1, 7). The reason for the exact number of "forty-two" here and in 13:5 is likely to recall the same time of Elijah's ministry of judgment (Luke 4:25; Jas. 5:17; see on 11:6) and Israel's entire time of wilderness wandering after the Exodus, which encompassed a total of forty-two encampments (so Num. 33:5-49). This is reinforced by possibly reckoning forty-two years for the Israelites' total sojourn in the wilderness, since it appears they were in the wilderness for two years before incurring the penalty of remaining there for forty years until the death of the first generation. Remember that the trumpet plagues take us back to God's judgments on Egypt, by which His people were released into the wilderness. In 11:6-8; 12:6, 14, the community of faith is pictured as battling against a spiritual Egypt, or as being protected in the wilderness. The uses in 12:6 and 12:14 confirm that 11:1-2 alludes to an attack on the community of faith throughout the church age. In 12:6, the messianic community (= the "woman") is protected from the dragon's onslaught during the three and a half years by taking refuge in "the wilderness where she had a *place* prepared by God." The picture of 12:14 is virtually identical. This "place" in which Christians are kept safe from the devil is likely none other than the invisible sanctuary of God (see 12:6, 14), since that is to be the object of attack during the three and a half years in Daniel, and since that is the idea in Rev. 11:1-2 and 12:5-6.

Rev. 12:5-6 shows that the three and a half year period was inaugurated at Christ's resurrection, since the "woman" (the covenant community") flees directly on the heels of the resurrection, and that time of fleeing commences the three and a half years (there is no hidden long time gap between v. 5 and v. 6, as contended by some futurists). This three and one half year time will be consummated at Christ's final coming (see on 12:5-6; cf. 14:14-20). 11:2 indicates that the period is the time of the treading under foot of the holy city. V. 8 implies that this treading under foot and, therefore, the three and a half years, was set in motion when "the Lord was crucified" in Jerusalem, especially since the ultimate basis for the trampling — the persecution of the church — is Christ's death. This period was inaugurated at Christ's resurrection, and will be consummated at His final coming. Another reason that a three and a half year period is chosen to represent the church's witness is that it is the approximate duration of Christ's ministry. *The pattern of the narration of the witnesses' career in 11:3-12 is intended as a replica of Christ's: proclamation and signs resulting in Satanic opposition, persecution (John 15:20) and violent death in the city where Christ was crucified, followed by the world looking on their victim (Rev. 1:7), the world's rejoicing (cf. John 16:20), and then resurrection and vindication by ascension in a cloud.* The prophetic precedents of Moses and Elijah point to this pattern and are alluded to in vv. 3-13 in order to fill out the pattern in more detail.

The last clause of 11:2, **and they will tread under foot the holy city for forty-two months**, further explains the preceding clause (the significance of the **and**) concerning the casting out of the outer court. In confirmation of our above analysis of the outer court, this further explanation of v. 2b means that the outer court should similarly be identified in a positive manner as the holy city. Therefore, the outer court is a part of the temple (the community of faith in which God dwells). As such it is the earthly expression of it. That the outer court is considered an essential part of the temple complex is suggested by the assumption in v. 2 that it was formerly under the protection of the temple walls but is now to be cast outside that protection. The "nations" who "trample" are persecutors who are not part of the true covenant community, as is clear from the way this text alludes to Isa. 63:18 ("Thy holy people possessed Thy sanctuary for a little while, our adversaries have trodden it down") and Dan. 8:13 ("while the transgression causes horror, so as to allow both the holy place and the host to be trampled"). That the "city" is measured in 21:15-17 shows its close identification with the prophesied Ezekiel 40–48 temple and, therefore, its identification with the temple in 11:1-2. Believers on earth are members and representatives of the heavenly Jerusalem. This identification of the holy city is confirmed from observing that the dragon and beast persecute the woman (= the earliest NT covenant community) and the saints throughout the church age for precisely the same time period of "three and a half years" (see on 11:3; 12:6, 14; 13:5). This background for the understanding of "trampling" and of the "city" shows that those metaphorically trampled are not being deceived or becoming apostates but represent the true community of faith undergoing persecution. In Revelation, the persecutors include both unbelieving Gentiles and Jews.

That all five descriptions ("measuring," "temple," "altar," "outer court," and "holy city") in 11:1-2 are likely figurative and applicable to the believing community has precedent in 3:12, where five similar images are figuratively applied to overcomers: pillar, temple, God's name, the name of the city of Jerusalem, and Christ's new name. The names of God and of Christ on the believer indicate that believers dwell in the tabernacling presence of God and Christ, who are the true temple (see again 21:22), with which believers are also identified (as "pillars").

3 Vv. 3-6 explain the primary purpose of the "measuring" of vv. 1-2. That is, God's establishment of His tabernacling presence among His end-time community is aimed at ensuring the effectiveness of the community's prophetic witness. The believers are to be prophets like the great prophets of the OT (like Moses and Elijah, so vv. 4-6). Though God's people will suffer, He will **grant authority** to stand against the enemy. The future tenses (**I will grant authority**, **they will prophesy**) probably highlight divine determination instead of future time, context being the ultimate determiner of the meaning. The **two witnesses** mentioned here who prophesy are not individuals, but rather represent the corporate church in its capacity as faithful prophetic witness to Christ. We can give a number of reasons for this:

They are referred to as "two lampstands" in v. 4, which should be identified as the churches (see 1:12–2:5). The OT had prophesied that the entire eschatological community of God's people would receive the Spirit's gift of prophecy (Joel 2:28-32), and the early Christian community understood that this prophecy had begun fulfillment in their midst (Acts 2:17-21).

In v. 7, it states that the beast will make war on the two witnesses. This alludes to Dan. 7:21, where not an individual but the nation as the covenant community is attacked.

In vv. 9-13, it states that the whole world will see the apparent defeat of these witnesses — a statement only understandable if they are understood as the corporate worldwide church (it is unlikely that the technologies of worldwide communication, by which two individual people could be seen by all throughout the world, were in mind).

The witnesses prophesy for three and a half years (v. 3), the same amount of time that the holy city (the church) is trampled underfoot (v. 2) and the woman of 12:6 (also representing the church) and those dwelling in heaven (13:6) are oppressed.

Often elsewhere in the book, the entire community of believers is stated as the source of the testifying when "testimony" is given to Jesus (6:9; 12:11, 17; 19:10; 20:4).

The powers of both Moses and Elijah are attributed to *both* witnesses equally and not divided between them. They are identical prophetic twins.

But why two witnesses? The OT required two witnesses to establish an offense against the law (Num. 35:30; Deut. 17:6; 19:15). Jesus also used the same principle (Matt. 18:16; Luke 10:1-24, where there are thirty-five — or thirty-six in some manuscripts — groups of two witnesses; John 8:17). So also did Paul (2 Cor. 13:1; 1 Tim. 5:19). God sent two angels to testify to the truth of the resurrection (Luke 24:4) and to the fact that Jesus would return (Acts 1:10-11). Above all, only two of the seven churches in chs. 2–3 escaped Christ's accusations of unfaithfulness (Smyrna and Philadelphia). That these two churches as representative of the faithful church are in mind is apparent from the identification of the "prophetic witnesses" here as "lampstands." Thus there is pictured here the faithful remnant church who witnesses.

Further, the words "witness" (Greek *martys*) in v. 3 and "testimony" (Greek *martyria*) in v. 7 are legal terms. At least six of the nine uses of "testimony" in Revelation refer to a witness rejected by the world, which results in legal consequences for those rejecting it (1:9; 6:9; 12:11, 17; 20:4). Like Elijah and his NT counterpart John the Baptist (2 Kgs. 1:8; Mark 1:6), the witnesses are clothed in sackcloth, emphasizing their mourning over the world's sins, which are about to be legally judged. The OT legal background of "two witnesses" noted above and the evidence of the following verses bear out the emphasis on mourning because of judgment. The stress on judgment is apparent from the witnesses' judicial relationship to their persecutors (especially vv. 5-6), and from the observation that their prophetic task is not to be viewed as a hopeful evangelistic campaign, as 11:13 bears out (on which see further).

4 Vv. 5-6 show that judgment is inaugurated through the witnesses themselves. But the identification of the witnesses is defined in more detail in v. 4 before the inaugurated verdict is portrayed in vv. 5-6. Even as the lampstands stood in God's presence in the tabernacle and the temple, so the witnesses **stand before the Lord of the earth**, emphasizing that, in spite of their position on earth, they stand spiritually in God's presence and in His heavenly courtroom. Though the prophetic witnesses live in a world of danger, they are never far from their Lord's sovereign presence, and nothing can separate them from their secure relationship with Him. The lamps on the lampstand in Zech. 4:2-6 are interpreted as representing God's presence or Spirit, which was to empower Israel (= the "lampstand") to finish rebuilding the temple, despite resistance (cf. Zech. 4:6-9). Just as lampstands were a part of Solomon's temple, so the church is part of God's new temple. Accordingly, new Israel, the church, as a "lampstand," is part of God's spiritual temple on earth, and is to draw its power from the Spirit, the divine presence, before God's throne in its drive to stand against the resistance of the world. Indeed, the "seven lamps of fire" in 4:5 "burn" in the heavenly temple, and they are most likely set on the lampstands. Thus, the Spirit empowers the lampstands, the church. This continues the theme from vv. 1-3 of God's establishment of His presence among His end-time community as His sanctuary, which is aimed at ensuring the effectiveness of its prophetic witness.

That the witnesses are called olive trees as well as lampstands comes from the vision of Zechariah, who saw two witnesses like olive trees standing before the lampstand (Zech. 4:12-14). The olive trees provided the oil to light the lamps. As in Revelation, Zechariah's two witnesses (in context representing Joshua the high priest and Zerubbabel the king) are described as standing in the presence of the Lord of the earth (Zech. 4:14). God would provide His fruitful Spirit (the oil) and cause it to issue forth from the priest and king (the olive trees) to lead the process of successfully completing the temple.

The establishment and preservation of the true temple despite opposition has been introduced in Rev. 11:1-2, and Zech. 4:14 is a climax to a section concerning the very same topic. Just as the priest and king are in Zechariah the key vessels used by the Spirit for the establishment of the temple against opposition, so here the two witnesses are likewise empowered by the Spirit to perform the same role in relation to 11:1-2. Zechariah speaks of the two witnesses, the king and the priest, who reestablish a literal temple, whereas John sees two witnesses helping to build the heavenly temple. In contrast with Zechariah, the two witnesses are not individuals but represent the church universal. Indeed the dual kingly-priestly role of the corporate church has already been explicitly affirmed (1:6; 5:10) and will be again (20:6). The broader context of Zechariah 4 shows the richness of the connection to the present context. First, in Zech. 1:16-17 and 2:1-5, an angel "measures" Jerusalem to signify that it will surely be re-established in order that God's house "will be built in it" (1:16), and that God "will be the glory in her midst" (2:5; cf. the measuring of the temple in Rev. 11:1-2). But, second, Satan, together with the world powers, opposed the reestablishment of God's temple in Jerusalem (Zech. 3:1-2; 4:7), as the beast and the world oppose the witnesses (Rev. 11:5-10).

5 The purpose and effects of the "measuring" are explained further. The souls of the witnesses cannot be harmed, because they are protected by the invisible sanctuary within which they dwell: **And if anyone desires to harm them, fire proceeds out of their mouth, and devours their enemies; and if anyone would desire to harm them, in this manner he must be killed**. Therefore, the powers given to them in vv. 5-6 do not so much demonstrate outwardly their prophetic legitimation as indicate God's spiritual protection of them. They may undergo bodily, economic, political, or social harm, but their eternal covenantal status with God will not be affected. Though they may suffer and even die, they will invincibly and successfully carry out the spiritual mission for which they have been "measured" and commissioned. The fire that **proceeds out of their mouth** is not to be taken literally but signifies the pronouncing of God's judgment on the world's sins, even as Christ's similar judgment is pictured symbolically as a sword "proceeding out of His mouth" (1:16; 19:15 [cf. likewise 2:12, 16], which allude to Isa. 11:4 and 49:2, according to which the Messiah's mouth will be like a sword in judgment). Note God's words to Jeremiah: "I am making My words in your mouth fire and this people wood, and it will consume them" (Jer. 5:14). The prophecy of Jeremiah concerning the need for repentance became a tool of judgment when the nation rejected the exhortation, and so it will be with the witnesses. Our interpretation of 9:17-18 (on which see) supports and is consistent with a figurative interpretation of the fire metaphor in 11:5. 9:17-18 also provides precedent for this fire metaphor being applied to an inaugurated, non-consummative judgment, which is likely the case here also.

Elijah called down fire on his enemies (2 Kgs. 1:10-12). The subtle allusion to Elijah here anticipates the explicit reference to him in the next verse. Moses' prophetic office was also demonstrated by his ability to call down fire from heaven to judge the ungodly. The manner of judgment is now further explained: **if anyone would desire to harm them, in this manner he must be killed**. This is a continued allusion to Deut. 19:15-19, first referred to in v. 3 as establishing the need for two witnesses in relation to the violation of God's law. Not only were two witnesses required in order for a just verdict, but the punishment often was to be patterned after the crime itself: "then you shall do to him just as he intended to do to his brother" (Deut. 19:19). Those who sin are to punished by the same means they used against the victim, thus practicing the OT principle of "an eye for an eye," which recurs throughout Revelation (11:18; 13:10; 16:6; 18:5-7).

6 The penal effect of the witnesses' prophetic announcement of judgment is inaugurated during the period of their testimony. Not all the witnesses die from persecution, though they suffer. They inflict spiritual punishments by means of their continuing witness during persecution. Their authority is patterned after the same prophetic authority by which Elijah and Moses carried out their punitive tasks against their antagonists. The witnesses are the fulfillment of the OT-Jewish expectation that the prophets Moses and Elijah were to come again before the end of history to restore Israel and to judge the ungodly. Indeed, in Mark 9:4-7 Moses and Elijah, as the two witnesses legally needed, appear on the mountain to bear witness that Jesus is the Son of God. The allusion to the two prophets may imply that the witnesses testify to that toward which the law (represented by Moses) and the prophets (represented by Elijah) ultimately pointed. The comparison to them here, especially in light of their connection to Israel's restoration, indicates that the church is the fulfillment of the latter-day restoration of Israel prophesied throughout the OT.

The specific reference here is first to Elijah's power to withhold rain from the earth (1 Kings 17–18): **These have the power to shut up the sky, in order that rain may not fall during the days of their prophesying.** The second reference is to Moses' ability to turn water into blood (Exod. 7:17-25): **and they have power over the waters to turn them into blood**. The same kind of power is carried over into this verse, except the focus is no longer on either individual prophets or kings, and the power is not expressed in literal drought or in literal water turning into blood. Now the whole prophetic community of the church executes afflictions against the antagonistic idolaters and reprobates who persecute them.

The first five verses of ch. 11 have been rich in symbolism — angels measuring, the temple, olive trees, lampstands, and fire coming out of mouths. Likewise v. 6 is symbolic; the ceasing of the regular order of the course of nature in the heavens is likely not literal but refers to all those divinely-ordained events intended to remind the persecutors that their idolatry is folly, that they are separated from the living God and that they are already experiencing an initial form of judgment.

The three and a half year period of the witnesses' ministry corresponds to the same time period of Elijah's ministry of judgment by drought (1 Kgs. 18:1; Luke 4:25; Jas. 5:17). It is interesting to note that in Luke 9:51-56 the disciples want to copy Elijah by calling down fire upon some Samaritan villagers. Jesus rebukes them, but in the next chapter sends out thirty-five (thirty-six in some manuscripts) groups of two (legal) witnesses to declare the judgment of God as well as His mercy through the proclamation of the gospel. Likewise, the two witnesses in John's vision here declare the judgment of God not by calling down literal fire, a practice no longer suitable in the gospel age, but by declaring the gospel and the consequences of disobeying it. The church's prophetic declaration of God's truth concerning the gospel, including the message of final judgment, unleashes torments toward those ultimately impenitent (just as were the kings whom Moses and Elijah confronted). The torments anticipate the last judgment and harden the reprobate in their sinful stance, making them ever more ripe for the punishment of the great day. These are torments which primarily affect the spiritual realm of a person, especially plaguing their conscience. This is evident from 11:10, where the earth-dwellers rejoice because of the death of the prophets who "tormented" them. This means the earlier effect of their ministry caused the hardened ungodly to be dismayed over their desperate plight. Perhaps Felix is an example of the kind of torment suffered by the unrighteous when they reject the gospel message: Paul "was discussing righteousness, self-control and the judgment to come," and Felix sent Paul away because of fear and resentment of the truth (Acts 24:25).

The plagues the witnesses bring are closely related to the trumpet plagues, which in turn are rooted in the plagues of Exodus. In both cases, the judgments are described as "plagues" (compare 8:12 ["smitten" is literally "struck by plague"]; 9:20; and 11:6). These judgments are directed against "earth-dwellers" (8:13 and 11:10) by those whose mouths are authorized or given power to pronounce judgment (9:13 and 11:6). Both include famine (8:7 [on our interpretation of that verse] and 11:6), killing (9:15

and 11:5), and harming (9:10 and 11:5). Fire comes from the mouths of executioners (9:17-18 and 11:5), water becomes blood (8:8 and 11:6), there are effects from heaven (8:10 and 11:6), and unbelievers are "tormented" (9:5-6 and 11:10). Each section — the narratives of the first six trumpets and of the witnesses — concludes with a final effect in which a specific percentage of unbelievers are killed and those remaining continue unmoved in their unrepentant stance (so 9:20 and 11:13, in both of which the phrase "the rest" occurs).

That the ungodly suffering judgment here are the same group as those suffering under the trumpet woes is evident from 10:11, where John is told to "prophesy *again*" to people throughout the world. The parallel wording of "the witness they had maintained" in 6:9 and "they should finish the testimony" in 11:7 suggests that both passages have in view the same idea of believers who persevere in their testimony to the end and are persecuted for it. The saints in heaven requesting judgment against persecutors (so 6:10-11) are told now that the "witness that they had maintained" (6:9) and for which they suffered is itself the instrument of the initial judgment of the oppressors. The judgment of vv. 5-6, therefore, is the first *explicit* answer to the saints' prayer of 6:9-11 and 8:3-5 for vindication and retribution against their antagonists, which the trumpet judgments imply. We concluded previously that the trumpet and seal judgments represent two visions describing the same set of events. Now it becomes clear that this section, placed as a "parenthesis" or interlude between the sixth and seventh trumpets, retells the story of the trumpet and seal judgments from yet another perspective, in this case one emphasizing what happens to the church during the period between Christ's resurrection and His return.

7 The introductory phrase **and when they have finished their testimony** shows that what follows in vv. 7b-13 is to occur at the end of history. At this time, the church will have completed its role of bearing witness to Christ before the world, and will appear defeated (so Matt. 24:9-22). V. 7 shows that the "measuring" of vv. 1-2 is for the purpose of and guarantees the successful completion of the church's witnessing task. In 6:9, 11, during the seals vision, John was shown that a time will come when the full number of the saints to be killed on account of their testimony is completed, and this verse describes the same series of events, thus reinforcing the fact that the two witnesses represent the corporate church. Both texts portray saints being killed by an antagonistic world because of their witness-bearing. The role of witness is to be completed at an appointed time in redemptive history. This is a further connection tying the witnesses of ch.

11 with the witnesses' prayer for vindication in 6:9-11. When their witness is completed, the faithful believers will be killed. Though they are about to be defeated in the eyes of the world (vv. 7-10), their demise will lead to the world's final defeat (vv. 11-13). This consummate judgment of earthly persecutors is the full answer to the saints' petition in 6:9-11.

Christ speaks to John in the same words (**the beast that comes out of the abyss will make war with them, and overcome them and kill them**) as the angel did to Daniel when he told him that the fourth and final beast ascending from the abyss would make war on God's people and overcome them. Since Dan. 7:21 thus refers to an attack on the Israelite saints, here also the beast makes war, not on two individuals, but on the community of the new faithful Israel, the church. The same event will be described again in 20:7-10, where the beast makes final war against the saints and the beloved city (both phrases representing the church as a whole).

The phrase **the beast that comes up out of the abyss** does not mean that the beast is active only at the end of the age, but rather that at the end of the age his activity will come out manifestly into the open. That is, his spirit has stood behind the earthly persecutors during the course of history, but at the end he manifests himself openly in order finally to defeat the church (which is the precise thought of 1 John 2:18 and 4:3, also based on the same Danielic expectation). The beast in Daniel 7 represents an evil king and kingdom which persecute the saints, and so likewise the persecuting activity in Rev. 11:7 begins to take place through antagonistic earthly authorities. The same series of events (the final onslaught of the beast followed by his own demise) is described in 17:8, where the beast comes out of the abyss only to go to his destruction, and again in 20:7: "when the thousand years are completed, Satan will be released from his prison."

8 This introduces the aftermath of the witnesses' death. The picture here (**their dead bodies will lie in the street of the great city**) probably indicates not a literal and complete extermination but that the true church will seem defeated in its role of witness, will appear small and insignificant, and will be treated with indignity. Though parts of the church's voice throughout history may be temporarily silenced (as in parts of the world even today), a universal silence will fall on the church at the very end of history. And just as small groups of believers continued to exist through earlier local and temporary silencings, so a small remnant of witnesses remain in the future scenario of vv. 8ff. The continued existence of a small church is pointed to by other parallels in the book which refer to a small community of believers undergoing persecution in the period immediately preceding the final judgment (so 20:7ff.; 17:8; so also Matt. 24:15-22, 37-39). In fact, the parallels in Revelation and the Gospels indicate that if God did not defeat the church's persecutors at this point, the church would actually be wiped out entirely. **The great city** where the bodies lie is best identified as the ungodly world, not the earthly city of Jerusalem (see further below). Without exception, the remaining uses of "the great city" in Revelation are identified with Babylon, not Jerusalem (16:19; 17:18; 18:10, 16, 18, 19, 21). In the OT prophets, Babylon was associated typically with the region in which God's people lived as aliens in exile under ungodly regimes.

The **great city** is compared here to **Sodom** (because of its wickedness) and to **Egypt** (because it persecuted the saints). The city is to be understood **spiritually**, as these references indicate. This means that the city is not located in any one geographical place but is to be understood as any ungodly spiritual realm existing on earth. The last clause, **where also their Lord was crucified**, continues the spiritual description of the city begun by the identification with Sodom and Egypt. This non-literal interpretation is borne out by observing that the word "where" (Greek *hopou*) elsewhere in Revelation never introduces literal but always symbolic, spiritual geography (e.g., the "wilderness" in 12:6, 14, "heads" and "mountains" in 17:9, and the "lake of fire and brimstone" in 20:10). In this light, the world-city is also spiritually like Jerusalem, which had become like other ungodly nations, and even worse, by killing Christ. In John's time, the reference to "the great city" would be primarily to Rome and any of its allies, since it was the center of the ungodly empire which persecuted God's people at that time.

9 The universal, negative identification of the city argued for in v. 8 is indicated further by the worldwide reference to unbelievers once in v. 9a and twice in v. 10. These are the citizens of the ungodly city, those who walk its global street. The universal formula (**the peoples and tribes and tongues and nations**) shows that the sardonic onlookers are those who live throughout the earth. The picture of those who **look at their dead bodies** continues the hyperbole of v. 8a that the church will seem defeated in its role of witness, appearing small and insignificant. The word "body" is actually in the singular in both v. 8 and v. 9a, though it is plural in v. 9b (the earth-dwellers **will not permit their dead bodies to be laid in a tomb**). The likely reason for the singular is to connote the corporate nature of the witnesses. They are one "body" of Christ who witness, but they are also many witnesses scattered throughout the earth, as is evident elsewhere in the book. A similar phenomenon occurs in 12:4-5, 13, 17, where the Christ child and those who "hold to the testimony of Jesus" are both identified as the offspring of the woman (see further on those verses). The three and a half day period during which they observe the bodies evokes the period Christ was in the tomb (though He lay in His tomb for only three days). Therefore, just as the three and a half year duration of Jesus' ministry is the same as the course of the witnesses' ministry (11:2-3), so also the time of His apparent defeat at the end of His ministry is similar to the conclusion of the witnesses' period of testimony. The short half week of **three and a half days** is also a contrast to the long yearly half week of three and a half years (11:3; 12:14; 13:5). The contrast is meant to emphasize that the antichrist's victory is brief and insignificant in comparison to the victorious testimony of the witnesses.

10 The beginning and end of v. 10 refer to those throughout the world who look on the witnesses' corpses as **those who dwell on the earth.** This is a technical phrase repeated throughout the book for unbelievers who suffer under incipient divine judgment because they persecute God's people (3:10; 6:10; 8:13, etc.). The phrase refers exclusively to idolaters in chs. 13–17 (so 13:8, 12, 14; 14:6-9; 17:2, 8; cf. also 8:13 with 9:20). Idolaters are called "earth-dwellers" because they are people who ultimately trust in some aspect of the world and not in God (see discussion of the phrase in 6:17). The earth-dwellers **rejoice . . . and make merry; and . . . send gifts to one another** when the witnesses are defeated, because part of the witnesses' message is that rejection of Christ amounts to idolatry and will be punished by judgment (Acts 17:30-31; 1 Thess. 1:8-10), a message that **tormented those who dwell on the earth.**

11 God restores the witnesses to Himself after their apparent defeat at the end of the church age: **And after the three and a half days the breath of life from God came into them, and they stood on their feet.** The wording here is taken directly from Ezek. 37:5, 10, where the breath represents God's Spirit and where the picture of physical resurrection signifies spiritual resurrection (especially in the light of Ezek. 36:26-27). Probably the spiritual resurrection of Israel comes to represent here the spiritual resurrection of the church (Ezekiel himself likely would have thought implicitly that spiritual resurrection inevitably leads to a final physical resurrection). This resurrection vindicates the authenticity of the witnesses' testimony. God now also vindicates the remaining community of believers by destroying their oppressors (so 20:7-10, which not coincidentally is based on Ezekiel 38). At the least, the ascent of the witnesses affirms a final, decisive deliverance and vindication of God's people at the end of time. Indeed, if the two witnesses symbolize persons and their actions are symbolic (e.g., sending fire from their mouth, shutting up the sky, etc.), then both their martyrdom and their ascent into heaven are probably symbolic. Ezek. 37:10-13 refers to restored Israel as "an exceedingly great army . . . the whole house of Israel . . . My people." Since Ezekiel prophesies the restoration of a *faithful nation* back to God, John sees the fulfillment in *all the faithful of the church,* and not merely in two faithful individuals. As a result, **great fear fell upon those who were beholding them**. This is not a genuine fear of God but is like the Egyptians' fear when they beheld the unexpected plagues and the Israelites' deliverance through the afflictions (Exod. 15:16; Ps. 105:38). Such a strong echo of the exodus would not be out of place here, since the plagues performed through Moses have been alluded to in 11:6, and the Exodus plague background stands behind much of the narration of the trumpets in chs. 9–10.

12 The description of the witnesses' deliverance continues: **And they heard a loud voice from heaven saying to them, "Come up here." And they went up into heaven in the cloud.** *If* this verse indicates a literal physical "rapture" (a taking of the witnesses out of the world), such an event would occur immediately before the final judgment (with no "tribulation" or "millennium" to follow), because the very next event (see v. 15) is the sounding of the seventh trumpet and the end of history. In this case, the vision would simply reveal that God's last act before consummating the destruction of the world and bringing about the return of His Son would be the taking up of the church. However, the wording is so closely parallel to 4:1 (where John beholds a door standing open in heaven and hears a voice saying, "Come up here"), that this similarity points to a different meaning than a physical rapture. There, the angelic voice commands John to come up to heaven. Both this verse (representing John's recommissioning) and John's original commissioning in 1:9-11 (as well as John's additional experiences as recorded in 17:1-3 and 21:9-10) are based on Ezekiel's repeated "raptures" in the Spirit (Ezek. 1:28–2:2; 3:12-14, 23-24; 11:1-5; 43:5), where the Spirit lifted the prophet up and carried him away in a spiritual, not physical sense (though 11:1-5 could be debated, but it likely refers to the invisible spiritual dimension). Ezekiel was not physically raptured, but received visionary experiences, much as Paul did when, according to 2 Cor. 12:1-4, he ascended to the third heaven. One further parallel between chs. 4 and 11 is the preceding description in 11:11, the "breath [i.e. Spirit] of life from God came into them," which is comparable with the end of 4:2a,

"I was in the Spirit," which refers to the Spirit conducting John into the invisible spiritual realm (the Spirit functions the same way in relation to John in 1:9; 17:3; and 21:10!). The heaven which the witnesses enter in 11:12, therefore, is an invisible dimension of reality not seen with the eyes of this world. This is a spiritual, not physical, transport, since all the other uses of the Spirit coming on people in Revelation (see just above) refer to a spiritual transport into an unseen dimension.

The reason for identifying John's rapture with that of the witnesses is partly also that the third, repeated prophetic commission in ch. 10 is applied generally to the witnesses in ch. 11. The cloud in which they ascend and from which **they heard a loud voice from heaven** speaking in 11:12 is to be identified with the cloud of 10:1, in which the angelic Christ descended from heaven and appeared to John and from which "he cried out with a loud voice" (10:3). Both John (10:11) and the witnesses (11:3, 10, 18) exercise a prophetic commission in announcing judgment to "many peoples and nations and tongues and kings" (10:11).

The "cloud" in the Bible refers to the presence of God (or Christ) with His people (Exod. 13:21-22; Num. 14:14; Deut. 1:33; Ps. 78:14; Isa. 4:5; Ezek. 1:4; Dan. 7:13; Matt. 17:5; 24:30; Mark 9:7; Luke 9:34-35; Acts 1:9). The significance of the church going up to heaven in a cloud, therefore, is primarily the church's vindication and acceptance by God. The world has rejected the witnesses' message of prophetic judgment and salvation (vv. 4-10). But at this time, just as Christ was vindicated by resurrection and ascending on a cloud (Acts 1:9-11), Christ will finally vindicate His people similarly to demonstrate to all that they were true prophets (that the voice is Christ's is implied by the parallel with 1:10-11 and 4:1-2). The persecutors perceive this divine seal of prophetic approval and are plagued by fear, because they have now realized that the prophets' announcement of judgment was not empty but will come to pass. Exactly in what way God vindicates the witnesses before the world is not clear in the text itself (though we have argued that the text is focusing on the spiritual facet of resurrection). But the point of the narrative is not the precise form of vindication, but the revelation that the witnesses are God's true representatives, who speak on His behalf.

13 The judgment of which the witnesses spoke commences immediately after the wicked see the vindication of those they had misjudged. The judgment is described in the form of **a great earthquake**. This phrase is virtually identical to those in 6:12 and 16:18, which are the only other occurrences of the word combination and which both describe the last judgment. If we have been correct in saying that the events of 11:11-13 transpire at the conclusion of world history, then the parallels with chs. 6 and 16 confirm this. Just as the "great earthquake" in 6:12 marked the beginning of the last judgment, which was consummated by the following seventh seal, so the **great earthquake** of 11:13 indicates the initial phase of the same final judgment, which is consummated by the following seventh trumpet. The wording comes from Ezek. 38:19, where the "great earthquake" refers to the final judgment of Gog at the end of history when it attempts to exterminate restored Israel. The reference to Ezekiel 38 is natural, since it comes directly after Ezekiel 37, which explains Israel's restoration through the picture of resurrection. There is a direct parallel to the restoration of the two witnesses representing the church, which is restored Israel (Rev. 11:11-12), and the subsequent earthquake destroying the latter-day persecutors of the church. The allusion to Ezek. 38:19 associates v. 13 with the final denouement, since that appears to be the obvious interpretation of Ezek. 38:19-23 and how John uses Ezekiel 38–39 in 19:17 and 20:8-9.

The partial effect of the earthquake indicates that this is but the beginning of the last judgment: **a tenth of the city fell; and seven thousand people were killed in the earthquake**. Both numbers are likely figurative; if the two witnesses are identified with the seven thousand faithful associated with Elijah, an "eye for an eye" retribution may be symbolically signified. As to the rest, they were **terrified and gave glory** to God. This could mean a mass repentance, for "giving glory to God" elsewhere in Revelation always refers to sincere worship. Yet the word **terrified** (Greek *emphobos*) is never used in Scripture of fear of the Lord, but simply refers to the human emotion of fear. The ministry of the witnesses (the church) is patterned after Christ's own ministry. At Christ's resurrection, there was an earthquake, an angel descended from heaven and the guards shook like dead men. Here, at the vindication of the righteous, there is also an earthquake, an angelic voice speaks from heaven, and those who observe it are terrified. "Giving glory to God" in the OT sometimes describes the response of unbelievers who, like the guards at the empty tomb, are forced to acknowledge God's reality rather than willingly submitting to it (Josh. 7:19; 1 Sam. 6:5). The phrase may go back to Nebuchadnezzar's giving praise and honor to God in Dan. 2:46-47 and 4:37 since he represents Babylon, the forerunner of the end-time Babylon of v. 13. Yet at the same time that Nebuchadnezzar honored God (Dan. 2:46-47), he carried on worshiping idols (Dan. 3:1). While Rev. 11:13 could be taken to refer to repentance or non-repentance, the fact is there is no indication elsewhere in Revelation, and particularly in the parallel visions of seals, bowls, and trumpets, of a last-minute mass conversion of the lost, so on balance it is better to see a reference here to a fear-induced acknowledgment of God's reality, rather than to an expression of saving faith.

The **tenth of the city** which fell and the **seven thousand** killed suggest that God was beginning to judge a significant portion of ungodly humanity, and the rest were soon to follow suit. In this respect, the judgment of the **seven thousand** so terrified the survivors that their only possible response was to accept their own imminent judgment and to acknowledge God as true sovereign in that judgment, as in 6:16-17 (as implied in Phil. 2:10-11; cf. Isa. 45:23-24). The context of judgment beginning at 8:6 up through 11:12, together with the OT background, favors an identification of the survivors as unbelievers suffering judgment. In fact, any sort of conversion would seem to be ruled out because v. 13a portrays the beginning of the last judgment rather than the repentance of the majority of "earth-dwellers." Furthermore, the fact that vv. 11 and 12 emphasize God's vindication of the whole church at the end of the age implies that those not vindicated in vv. 11-13 are not part of God's people. In addition, the primary purpose of the prophets' witness in vv. 3-6 appears to be not to induce repentance but to "torment" (so v. 10). They are God's agents executing the beginning of His judgment on recalcitrant humanity (see on 11:5-6). This is not to deny, of course, that some will respond in repentance.

The earthquake imagery of v. 13a, therefore, marks the beginning of the final punishment, which is consummated by the earthquake imagery of the last judgment in 11:19. The fact that the seventh trumpet, which includes a description of the last judgment (11:18), follows on the heels of 11:13 confirms this conclusion, especially since the earthquake imagery of 11:19 is the climax of the seventh trumpet itself.

Suggestions for Reflection on 11:1-13

On the implications of divergent interpretations of Revelation. Vastly different interpretations exist regarding the identity of the temple and the outer court in vv. 1-2. These divergences illustrate how dramatically opposite conclusions can be drawn from a text in Revelation, depending on one's interpretive framework. In thinking through these differences, what implications emerge for understanding God's plan for the church in history and for Israel in history? What are the implications for our understanding of the historical timeframe Revelation refers to?

On the temple as a unifying theme in Scripture. The concept of the temple (representing God's presence) is one of the central themes of the Bible (see G. K. Beale, *The Temple and the Church's Mission: A Biblical Theology of the Dwelling Place of God* [Downers Grove: InterVarsity, 2004] for a fuller perspective on this subject). On the basis of the interpretation of the unifying theme of the temple as given in the commentary, how do you see the interrelationship of Ezekiel 40–48; Rev. 11:1-2; and Revelation 21–22?

On the church's suffering and hope. Consider this statement from the commentary: "The pattern of the narration of the witnesses' career in 11:3-12 is intended as a replica of Christ's: proclamation and signs resulting in Satanic opposition, persecution (John 15:20) and violent death in the city where Christ was crucified, followed by the world looking on their victim (Rev. 1:7), the world's rejoicing (cf. John 16:20), and then resurrection and vindication by ascension in a cloud." In what way do vv. 3-12 give us a basis for a theology of suffering? In doing so, how do they give us also a basis for hope in the midst of suffering?

On dependence on the Holy Spirit. The commentary presents the two witnesses (representing the church) as standing in God's presence even while suffering. They draw their strength from the Spirit. The oil from the olive trees and the light from the lamp flow through them, empowering their witness to the unbelieving world. This paints a picture of the church's need for utter dependence on the Holy Spirit. To what degree are we personally dependent on the Spirit? In what measure are our churches dependent? How do we express this dependence? What is the role of personal and corporate prayer? One thing is for sure: when the time of testing or opposition comes, the degree of our dependence will be revealed.

On the wickedness of the nations and the judgment of God. According to the commentary, this chapter paints a picture of a severely persecuted church apparently falling prey to the attacks of its enemies especially in the time immediately before the return of Christ. This seems a discouraging message, but is there a silver lining to it when seen from God's perspective? Revelation compares the church to Israel making its way through the wilderness on its way to the promised heavenly land. According to Gen. 15:16, Israel could not possess the Promised Land until the "iniquity of the Amorite" was complete. Is there a parallel to this thought here? That is, the very hour when wickedness is complete releases both the judgment of God upon the lost and the entrance of the church into its eternal inheritance.

The seventh trumpet: God establishes the consummated kingdom and executes the consummated judgment (11:14-19)

14 The second woe is past; behold, the third woe is coming quickly. 15 And the seventh angel sounded; and there arose loud voices in heaven, saying, "The kingdom
of the world has become the kingdom of our Lord, and of His Christ; and He will
reign forever and ever." 16 And the twenty-four elders, who sit on their thrones before God, fell on their faces and worshiped God, 17 saying, "We give Thee thanks,
O Lord God, the Almighty, who are and who wast, because Thou hast taken Thy
great power and hast begun to reign. 18 And the nations were enraged, and Thy
wrath came, and the time came for the dead to be judged, and the time to give
their reward to Thy bond-servants the prophets and to the saints and to those
who fear Thy name, the small and the great, and to destroy those who destroy
the earth." 19 And the temple of God which is in heaven was opened; and the ark
of His covenant appeared in His temple, and there were flashes of lightning and
sounds and peals of thunder and an earthquake and a great hailstorm.

14 The literary and theological parenthesis of 10:1–11:13 has ended. Therefore, v. 14 begins where 9:21 ended: **The second woe is past** (9:13-21); **behold, the third woe is coming quickly**. As in 9:12, the chronological language does not concern the *order of history* represented in the three woe visions, but refers only to the *order of visions* (see further on 9:12; 4:1). This means that the second vision of woe has been completed and the third is imminent. The nature of this visionary chronology explains why a description of the last judgment both in the conclusion of the parenthesis in 11:11-13 and again in the conclusion of the seventh seal in 11:18-19 is not inconsistent.

It is sometimes thought that vv. 15-19 do not make up the seventh trumpet (or third woe), but introduce it and are anticipations of it. No action is portrayed by the blowing of the seventh trumpet, but only songs declaring a series of actions that are not specifically described. Some think that chs. 12–14 lead up to the seven bowls of ch. 16, which constitute the third woe. Some think chs. 12–14 themselves describe the third woe, and still others view all of chs. 12–21 as the content. In contrast to the above views, we see 11:15-19 as an explanation of the consummation of history, since 10:7 has announced that when the seventh trumpet sounds, God's accomplishment of His plan for history "is finished" (see on 10:7). It is reasonable to assume that 11:15-19 is the third woe, since the announcement has been made in 8:13 that the following three woes will all be equivalent respectively to the last three trumpets. If 11:15-19 is the seventh trumpet, then 8:13 has clearly said that it is also the third woe. The songs of the section depict actions of judgment and redemption and are not merely an anticipation of such actions. The descriptions are not detailed because they began in 6:12-17, and John knows that more descriptions of the same events will come later. A song can depict the content of a woe or trumpet as well as a vision can (e.g., 5:8-10 is a hymn narrating past events). Still, some think that vv. 15-19 cannot be the woe of the seventh trumpet because there is so much emphasis on the establishment of the kingdom instead of the severity of judgment. But the emphasis of this section lies not only on the kingdom but also on the woe of the final judgment (vv. 18-19), which demonstrates that the consummated, eternal kingdom of God has finally appeared on earth.

15 The third woe is the seventh trumpet, both of which are described in vv. 15-19. The proclamation here is that **the kingdom of the world has become the kingdom of our Lord, and of His Christ**. This can be said because the enemies of God's kingdom have all been defeated and judged (so 11:18). God now takes for Himself the rule which formerly He permitted Satan to have over the world. The seventh trumpet of 11:15-19, like the seventh seal and seventh bowl, narrates the very end of history. The consummated fulfillment of the long-awaited messianic kingdom prophesied in the OT has finally come to pass (12:10 makes the same point). The past tenses in this verse appear to be a projection into the future, when the kingdom has been established and the heavenly host offers praise in response. In this case, the past tenses are actual descriptions of past actions, but from the perspective of the future.

It is not clear whether it is the Lord or Christ who **will reign forever and ever**. It may well be that the singular includes both God and Christ together. The picture here is the same as that shown to Daniel, where the evil kingdoms of the world are defeated and handed over by the Ancient of Days to the authority of the Son of man, who then reigns forever. That the eventual transference of power (from the rule of evil to the rule of God) pictured in Daniel 7 is in mind is already indirectly apparent from v. 7. There allusion was made to Dan. 7:3, 21 concerning the antagonistic world kingdom which will persecute the saints, which Dan. 7:13-14, 18, 22, 27 says will be replaced by the reign of the Son of man and the saints.

16-17 **The twenty-four elders** around God's throne **fell on their faces and worshiped God** in response to the heavenly proclamation of v. 15 (see on 4:4 for identification of the elders). That they are praising

Him for the completed form of His kingdom is apparent from v. 18, where all the enemies of God have suffered their final defeat and judgment. The praise of the elders is similar to that of the heavenly multitude in 19:6, and refers to the same period at the end of time. God has been addressed three times in Revelation as the One who is and who was and who is to come (1:4, 8; 4:8), but in v. 17 there is a significant variation of this: God is still addressed as the One who is and who was, but instead of referring to Him as the One who is to come, He is now addressed as the One who has taken up His **great power** and **begun to reign**. Though this final consummation of the kingdom had not yet occurred when John received the vision, it had happened from the perspective of those offering the heavenly praise. This change in time perspective enforces the thought that this section is narrating the actual establishment of the future kingdom and the final judgment as the content of the seventh trumpet. This is a rule in which God not merely controls events of the world, but has defeated the spiritual and physical powers which held "the kingdom of the world" in its sway (so v. 15). The consummate nature of the kingdom is also discerned from the emphasis on God's reign more than on Christ's. This suggests a parallel with 1 Cor. 15:25-28, where God's rule is emphasized over Christ's because the consummation of the latter's rule has been reached.

18 It is best to see this verse as taking the reader back a step in the eschatological program to the time immediately preceding the establishment of the eternal kingdom mentioned in vv. 15-17. Nevertheless, it describes the first expression of God's beginning end-time reign. The wicked nations are pictured as **enraged** against God and His people. God judges them wrathfully in response to their sinful outrage. The final judgment is expressed by the clause **Thy wrath came.** This is apparent from noticing that every other use of "wrath" (Greek *orgē*) in the book concerns the time of the final, great outpouring of wrath at the end of history (see 6:16, 17; 14:10-11; 16:19; 19:15). The following phrase **and the time came for the dead to be judged** confirms without doubt that this passage is a description of the last judgment. The end of v. 18 expands on the nature of the judgment. This is the same judgment of the dead as is referred to in 20:12-13, only here the reason that the dead unbelievers are to be judged is given: God will **destroy** the oppressors because they are **those who destroy the earth** (i.e., His people). The use of the same verb in describing both God's judgment and the oppression of the godless is to emphasize once again the OT principle of the punishment fitting the crime.

The judgment on unbelievers here is patterned on the judgment of

Babylon as prophesied by Jeremiah: "Behold, I am against you, O destroying mountain, who destroy the whole earth" (Jer. 51:25). Babylon is a type of the eschatological world community, which will be judged at the end. This ties v. 18 in with Babylon, the great city, which is destroyed in 11:13. God's people are referred to here as being **bond-servants . . . and . . . the saints and . . . those who fear** [God], **the small and the great**. That this is a fulfillment of the saints' petition in 6:9-11 is evident from the parallel of 18:24–19:5, where, in an undeniable reference to the final judgment, God is to be praised by His *bond-servants, those who fear him, and the small and the great* (19:5) because He "judged the great harlot [Babylon] who *was corrupting the earth* . . . and He . . . *avenged the blood of His bond-servants* on her" (19:2, which develops both 6:10 and 11:18). All this shows again how the visions of Revelation describe the same set of events from different perspectives, rather than presenting a chronological listing of events.

The reward of the faithful is sandwiched literarily between the statements about judgment in order to indicate that part of their reward is the satisfaction arising from the knowledge that God has vindicated them by judging their persecutors. Again, this is linked to the prayer for retribution by the witnesses in 6:9-11. Whereas the trumpet woes and the parenthesis of 10:1–11:13 have shown how God has begun to answer that prayer in the midst of history, now He gives the climactic answer to it. The **reward** is given **to Thy bond-servants the prophets and to the saints and to those who fear Thy name**. These are probably three ways of describing the same group, because the entire church is identified in 11:3 with the two prophetic witnesses (which is consistent with Joel 2:28-32 in Acts 2:16-21). Compare also 19:10, where the angel forbids John to worship him and identifies himself simply as a fellow servant of all those who hold to the testimony of Jesus, for "the testimony of Jesus is the spirit of prophecy" — to testify or be a witness to Jesus is in some way to be a prophet. The **reward** is the saints' deliverance, their reception of a position of reign with Christ and the accompanying blessings (cf. 22:12).

19 Another note of the final judgment is struck, commencing with the phrase, **And the temple of God which is in heaven was opened**. The portrayal of the seventh trumpet closes in v. 19 with the mention of **flashes of lightning and sounds and peals of thunder and an earthquake**, which in Revelation are always indicators of the final judgment (4:5; 8:5; 16:18). Recall that the trumpet plagues are modeled on the plagues of Exodus. The seventh trumpet may be built around a segment from the Song of Moses in Exod. 15:13-18. There God is praised for redeeming His people by guiding them *to His holy habitation* (corresponding here to His **temple . . . in heaven**). When the "nations" heard about this deliverance, they became "enraged" (Exod. 15:14 LXX), but, in spite of this, God brought His people into His "dwelling" and "sanctuary" (15:17). After this, the declaration is made that "the Lord shall reign forever and ever" (15:18; see the verbatim parallel in Rev. 11:15). Such an allusive reference would be an appropriate way to conclude the series of trumpets, since the first six have been modeled on the Exodus plagues leading up to Exodus 15.

It is fitting that the trumpets should be concluded with a reminder of the pattern displayed in both the entrance of the Israelites into the Promised Land at Jericho and the entrance of the saints into the eternal kingdom. The seven trumpet plagues are followed by an earthquake and the victory of God's people. Likewise at Jericho, trumpets were blown on six successive days, and then on the seventh and last day the trumpet blasts brought the wall down. The appearance of **the ark of His covenant** along with the trumpet also points back to Jericho, where the ark followed the trumpets, declaring both God's judgment and His victory. The ark represents not just God's judgment, but is also the place of forgiveness and of God's presence with His people. The OT did not expect a literal reappearance of the ark, but rather looked forward to a reappearance of God's presence in Israel's midst (as clarified by Jer. 3:14-17), which was what the ark originally represented. This is the idea in Rev. 11:19, which is expanded on in 21:3, 22, where the establishment of the end-time temple is interpreted as God's special revelatory presence in the midst of His people. At the consummation, God dwells with His people in a more complete and intense manner than previously, as indicated by the observation that the curtain separating the ark from the rest of the temple and people in the OT is now gone in 11:19, the heavenly ark being in full view. Therefore, the ark in 11:19, in the light of its multiple OT backgrounds, is a suitable symbol to indicate the simultaneous judgment and reward of the Last Day. And so the full answer to the saints' petition for vindication in 6:9-11 is revealed in 11:15-19.

Suggestions for Reflection on 11:14-19

The nature of our reward. The commentary speaks about the reward of the faithful in relation to v. 18. How often do we as Christains think about eternal life and heaven in terms of reward? What is the nature of our reward? Is the downfall of our perscutors the greatest reward we can look for? Should we look for that downfall as an end in itself? Does it not merely serve another purpose in terms of the revelation of God's glory in the manifestation of His fulfilled rule over all creation?

Forgiveness and justice. Consider the following statement in the commentary: "The ark represents not just God's judgment, but is also the place of forgiveness and of God's presence with His people." We live in a culture which too often emphasizes forgiveness at the expense of justice, but in doing so have we lost a true understanding of both? Would you agree that the question of how God can be both forgiving and just is only truly understood through the cross? Why is this true?

Deeper conflict (12:1–15:4)

Revelation 12 has often been identified as the key to the whole Apocalypse. It starts off a new series of visions in the book, which ends at 15:4. 11:19 not only concludes the seven trumpets but also introduces the following vision *from a literary perspective.* The language of 11:19 serves elsewhere both as a thematic conclusion to the seven seals and as a literary introduction to the seven trumpets (see on 8:3-5; note "lightning and sounds and thunders" in 11:19, which also forms part of the introduction to the ch. 4 vision). Further, the mention of the opening of heaven or a temple in heaven introduces major visions in 4:1; 15:5; and 19:11.

Though the section from 12:1 to 15:4 can be divided in various ways, the best way objectively to discern its divisions is to trace the repeated introductory vision formulas such as "and I saw" or "and behold." When this is done, seven sections or "signs" are revealed (though we subdivide these for purposes of discussion):

> the conflict of the serpent with the woman and her seed (ch. 12),
> the persecution by the beast from the sea (13:1-10),
> persecution by the beast from the land (13:11-18),
> the Lamb and the 144,000 standing on Mount Zion (14:1-5),
> the proclamation of the gospel and of judgment by three angels (14:6-13),
> the Son of man's harvest of the earth (14:14-20), and
> the saints' victory over the sea beast and their victory song (15:2-4).

That seven sections can be discerned by objective means is not coincidental since other parts of the book are also divided into seven sections (seals, trumpets, and bowls), individually introduced by clear introductory formulas.

Despite the fact that ch. 12 starts a new vision, it does continue to develop the themes of the previous sections of the book. It goes into the deeper dimension of the spiritual conflict between the church and the world, which has been developed progressively in chs. 1–11. The letters speak of the pressures on Christians to compromise coming from inside and outside the church. The seals reveal that the spiritual forces of evil are unleashed against believer and unbeliever alike, in accordance with the command of the resurrected Christ. The trumpets demonstrate God's judgment on hardened humanity. Yet in all this, sections are interspersed to show how God's people will be protected spiritually throughout the woes.

Chs. 12–22 tell the same story as chs. 1–11, but explain in greater detail what the first chapters only introduce and imply. Ch. 12 now reveals that the devil himself is the deeper source of evil. Brief references to him have come already in 2:13; 6:8; and 9:11. The devil is the grand initiator of the trials and persecutions of the saints. He unleashes the beast and the false prophet. The harlot Babylon is also his servant. John pictures the four figures (the devil, the beast, the false prophet, and the harlot) rising in this order and then meeting their demise in the reverse order in chs. 12–20 in order to highlight the devil as the initiator, from first to last, of all resistance to God and His people. In this respect, ch. 12 can be seen as introducing the second half of the book.

But the devil is not autonomous. He and his agents can only persecute within divinely-prescribed time periods (12:6, 14; 13:5). In fact, the devil is enraged and attacks Christians, because his decisive defeat has already been set in motion by Christ's resurrection, and his time of rage is limited by God (12:7-17). When Christians understand that behind their earthly persecutors stands the devil and his agents, they should be motivated to persevere all the more (cf. Eph. 6:12). Christ has already defeated the devil and his host through His death and resurrection (12:5, 7-12; cf. Eph. 1:19-21 with Eph. 6:10-13). In fact, the troubles of the persecuted saints occur now not because Satan is too powerful for them but because he has been decisively overthrown. The devil does all the damage he can, but he cannot prevail over the church in any ultimate way. The readers must know now that, if they compromise, they are not compromising merely with the world, but with the devil himself. This realization should shock them out of any degree of spiritual complacency.

The majority of the portrait in ch. 12 pictures the destiny of believers during the church age. In characteristic style, the story is told through repeated allusion to the OT. As will be seen, the three sections of the chapter, vv. 1-6, 7-12, and 13-17, are temporally and thematically parallel in order to tell the story over again from different perspectives. Vv. 6, 13-16, and 17 are essentially the same in that they all narrate the protection of God's people through trial. The three segments in vv. 5, 7-9, and 10-12 describe the same victory over the devil. The first and third section form a frame around the middle, while the middle provides the central interpretation and theological underpinning of the first and third. Therefore, the main point of ch. 12 is the protection of God's people against Satan because of Christ's decisive victory over Satan through His death and resurrection. The purpose is to encourage the readers to persevere in their witness despite persecution.

As a result of Christ's victory over the devil, God protects the messianic community against the devil's wrathful harm (12:1-17)

God protects Christ and the messianic community against Satanic harm (12:1-6)

[1] And a great sign appeared in heaven: a woman clothed with the sun, and the moon under her feet, and on her head a crown of twelve stars; [2] and she was with child; and she cried out, being in labor and in pain to give birth. [3] And another sign appeared in heaven: and behold, a great red dragon having seven heads and ten horns, and on his heads were seven diadems. [4] And his tail swept away a third of the stars of heaven, and threw them to the earth. And the dragon stood before the woman who was about to give birth, so that when she gave birth he might devour her child. [5] And she gave birth to a son, a male child, who is to rule all the nations with a rod of iron; and her child was caught up to God and to His throne. [6] And the woman fled into the wilderness, where she had a place prepared by God, so that there she might be nourished for one thousand two hundred sixty days.

1 After the temple scene of 11:19, John sees a **great sign** which **appeared in heaven.** He first sees **a woman clothed with the sun, and the moon under her feet, and on her head a crown of twelve stars.** Vv. 2-6 reveal that this woman is a picture of the faithful community, which existed both before and after the coming of Christ. This identification is based on the OT precedent, where sun, moon, and eleven stars metaphorically represent Jacob, his wife, and eleven of the tribes of Israel (Gen. 37:9), who bow down to Joseph, representing the twelfth tribe. Song of Solomon 6:10 was used in later Jewish literature to describe Israel in terms of the sun, the moon, and the stars, and restored Israel (which in Revelation is identified as the church) is described similarly in Isa. 60:19-20. In fact, in Isaiah a woman often represents the picture of restored Israel (e.g., 52:2; 54:1-6; 61:10; 62:1-5), and Isa. 62:3, 5 prophesies that restored Israel will be like a bride wearing a crown. The brightness of the woman's appearance (**clothed with the sun**) reflects the same brightness in the face of Christ (1:16). Her glory is the reflected glory of Christ. Just as the sun, moon, and stars appear far from earth and immune from destruction by any earthly force, so also true Israel of the OT and NT epochs is ultimately indestructible on earth because ultimate identity is in heaven (mention of Michael, Israel's heavenly representative and protector [Dan. 12:1], in vv. 7-8 points further to this).

That the woman represents both the old and new covenant communities becomes even clearer in vv. 11-17, where her seed or offspring is not only Christ but also the entire community of His followers.

The **crown** on her head is best defined from within Revelation itself. It represents the saints' share in Christ's kingship and the reward which the true people of God throughout the ages receive for their victory over opposition to their faith (i.e., over persecution, temptations to compromise, and deception; so 2:10; 3:11; 4:4, 10; cf. 14:14). The stellar brightness of her appearance reflects the powerful and pure sunlight arising from God's and Christ's glorious image (as in 1:16; 10:1; 21:23; 22:5).

2 The woman is **in labor and in pain to give birth**. Catholic commentators have written an immense amount of literature arguing that the heavenly woman symbolizes Mary, the mother of Jesus. Though the mother of Jesus may be secondarily in mind, the primary focus is not on an individual but on the community of faith, within which the messianic line ultimately yielded a kingly offspring. This is evident, not only from the discussion of v. 1, but also from observing in the remainder of the chapter that the woman is persecuted, flees into the desert, and has other offspring than just the Messiah, offspring who are described as faithful Christians. The woman's birth-pangs refer to the persecution of the covenant community and the messianic line during OT times and especially the intertestamental period leading up to Christ's birth. The idea of persecution is expressed in the phrase **in pain** (literally "being tormented"), since the verb (Greek *basanizō*) is used in the NT of the suffering of punishment, trial, and persecution (Matt. 8:29; Mark 5:7; 6:48; Luke 8:28; 2 Pet. 2:8). The suggestion is that the woman is being tormented and suffering as she attempts to give birth, which fits with a picture of the faithful Jewish community being persecuted in the period leading up to the birth of Christ. It was a trial to continue to wait for the great deliverance which the Messiah would finally bring at His coming (cf. Luke 2:25-38). In John 16:19-22, Christ compares the grief of His disciples over His impending death to a woman about to give birth who "has sorrow" and is about to bear a child. There, in line with our view of Rev. 12:2, the disciples represent the mother, the messianic community, in the midst of which the Christ was born in resurrection, and which would later present the resurrected Christ to the world. In Rev. 12:2 it is, however, Christ's first birth that is in mind and not this later resurrection birth.

Since the harlot of ch. 17 is symbolic of the unbelieving community, so here the contrasting figure of the righteous woman must represent the believing community. The ultimate source of John's vision here is the prophetic word given in Gen. 3:14-16 that after Eve's pain in childbirth, her seed would bruise the head of the serpent (see on 12:17 for an explicit allusion). The woman, representing God's covenant people, gives birth to the One who will take back what was lost in the Garden. That the woman represents the faithful covenant community is shown also by the numerous parallels to Isaiah's prophecies concerning Israel. According to Isa. 7:10-14, a sign will be seen as high as heaven, the virgin will be with child and bear a son. In Rev. 12:1-2, a sign appears in heaven: a woman is with child and gives birth to a son. In Isa. 26:17–27:1, Israel is likewise in labor, but fails to give birth, but the day will come when things will change (it being assumed that in that day Israel will safely give birth), and God will punish the dragon who lives in the sea (Rev. 12:1-2, 7-10). In Isa. 51:2-11, Sarah is said to have given birth to Israel in pain, and it is stated that God will one day restore Israel and in that day will pierce the dragon (Rev. 12:1-2, 7-10). See also Isa. 66:7-10 for the picture of Israel giving birth to a boy. The last three Isaiah passages relate the birth to Israel's end-time restoration.

It is too limiting to view the woman (as do some writers) as representing only a remnant of Israelites living in trial at the last stage of history, since the following verses show that the woman symbolizes a believing community extending from before the time of Christ's birth to at least the latter part of the first century AD (see on vv. 6, 13-17). Furthermore, in the following verses the persecution is not directed against a nation of believers *and unbelievers* but a pure community of faith.

3 **Another sign appeared in the heaven**, which was **a great red dragon**. The dragon is described as **having seven heads and ten horns, and on his heads were seven diadems**. Without exception, the imagery of the dragon is used throughout the OT to represent evil kingdoms who persecute God's people. "Dragon" is in the OT another word for the evil sea monster which is symbolic of evil kingdoms who oppress Israel. Often, the wicked kingdom of Egypt is portrayed by this emblem. God is spoken of as defeating Pharaoh as a sea dragon at the exodus deliverance and at later points in Egypt's history (Pss. 74:13-14; 89:10; Isa. 30:7; 51:9; Ezek. 29:3; 32:2-3; Hab. 3:8-15). At the conclusion of history, God will again defeat the Egyptian dragon (Isa. 27:1). John sees in ch. 12 a replay of the exodus pattern. That the evil spirit of Egypt resides in the dragon is also evident from the widespread influence of exodus themes elsewhere in the book, especially the plagues of trumpets and bowls and the reference to the Red Sea deliverance (15:2-4; cf. also 11:6, 8). In the typological replay of

the Red Sea deliverance in 15:2-4, the beast in the sea is clearly a latter-day Egyptian foe (for the relationship of the beast to the dragon see on 12:13-17 and 13:1ff.). The dragon of 12:3 also has his home in the sea (13:1; 15:2). This is confirmed by the attribution to him of the ten horns of the fourth beast of Dan. 7:7, 24, who likewise had its origin in the sea. As is the case with the OT identifications of the dragon, the dragon of Revelation is to be identified with an evil kingdom (at least in part, first-century Rome). Yet the dragon is more than a mere metaphor for an evil kingdom. It also stands for the devil himself as the representative head of evil kingdoms, as 12:9 and 20:2, 10 will make explicit. The devil is the force behind wicked kingdoms which persecute God's people.

As with the Lamb's seven horns, so the number of ***seven*** **heads** and ***ten*** **horns** emphasizes completeness, but in this case, the completeness of oppressive power and its worldwide effect. The ten horns are those of Daniel's fourth beast (Dan. 7:7, 24), and will reappear on the beast of ch. 13, showing that the devil performs his oppressive will against the church and world through his kingly representatives on earth. The red color connotes the oppressive character of the dragon, since in 17:3-6 the scarlet color of the harlot and the beast is linked directly with "the woman drunk with the blood of the saints." Likewise, the second horse in 6:4 was red and had a sword with which people would slay one another, which included the shedding of the blood of the faithful (6:9-10). The concluding description of v. 3 is that **seven diadems** were on the heads of the dragon. The crowns represent the devil's false claims of sovereign, universal authority, which is in opposition to the true "King of kings and Lord of Lords," who also wears "many diadems" in 19:12, 19-21. The similarity between the two descriptions in Revelation 12 and 19 reveals a conscious intention to contrast them.

4 The picture of the dragon's tail sweeping away **a third of the stars of heaven** is an allusion to the prophecy of Dan. 8:10, according to which the end-time enemy of God will throw some of the stars down to the earth. The stars are identified in Dan. 12:3 with God's people, and those being oppressed in the vision of Dan. 8:10 are identified as the "holy people" in 8:24. However, in Daniel, angels represent peoples in the heavenly realm (Dan. 10:20-21; 12:1). That stars can represent Israelite saints and not only angels is apparent from Dan. 12:3, where the righteous are compared to "the brightness of the expanse of heaven . . . like the stars forever and ever" (for this application of Dan. 12:3 see Matt. 13:43; cf. Gen. 15:5; 22:17). Dan. 8:11 (according to Theodotion and the Old Greek, two versions of the Greek OT) interprets the falling "to the earth [of] some of the host of heaven and

of the stars" and their being "trampled" in 8:10 to represent "the captivity" of Israel which will be "delivered" in the future. Hence, we can understand the meaning as follows: Israelite saints have their true identity in heaven before the divine throne, so that when they are persecuted, the angels and God Himself are also seen as being attacked.

Though Dan. 8:10 first had application with respect to Israel's persecutor in the second century BC, Antiochus Epiphanes, it comes now to be applied by John in an escalated way to the devilish power behind Antiochus. The primary focus is on persecution of the godly community immediately before the birth of the Messiah, though in the telescoping style of the writer this could still include aspects of the OT age and the intertestamental period leading up to the time of Christ (e.g., Herod's massacre of the infants in Bethlehem, as well as the early persecution of Christ in Luke 4:28-30). The oppression takes the form of persecution as well as attempts to deceive (as in Dan. 8:10, 22-25; 11:30-35). The portrayal of the stars in v. 4 must have a close relationship with the "twelve stars" only three verses earlier in v. 1. The falling stars must symbolize an attack on Israel, the faithful covenant community, since the twelve stars in v. 1 represent the heavenly identification of the true Israel. But **the dragon stood before the woman who was about to give birth, so that when she gave birth he might devour her child**. The intention of the dragon, the second part of the verse reveals, is not only to attack God's people but to destroy the Messiah Himself, once the woman gives birth. Here we find a reference to all the ways in which the devil tried to tempt Jesus and to destroy Him during the time of His earthly ministry, as Jesus' earthly lifetime is telescoped into a single phrase. At the cross it appeared that the devil finally had succeeded, but the resurrection snatched Jesus out from under the power of death wielded by the serpent.

5 That temporal telescoping is involved in v. 4 is suggested by the following verse. Now a snapshot of Christ's entire life is given in one line — His birth, His destiny of kingship, and His incipient fulfillment of that destiny by ascending to God's throne in heaven after the post-resurrection ministry. The NT elsewhere condenses Jesus' life in a nearly identical way (John 13:3; 16:28; Rom. 1:3-4; 1 Tim. 3:16). The same kind of abbreviation occurs in Rev. 1:5, 17-18 and 2:8, though with a focus on Christ's death and resurrection. Jesus is the firstborn from the dead (1:5; 2:8; Col. 1:18), and the church is His body and kin, the "rest of the seed" of the woman (cf. Rom. 8:29; Gal. 3:16, 29; cf. Heb. 2:17; 12:22-23; and see further on 12:17). The **male child** who is born (**who is to rule all the nations with a rod of**

iron) is the One prophesied in Ps. 2:7-9 to "rule all the nations with a rod of iron." The context in the Psalm shows this to be a clear reference to Christ.

The destructive efforts of the dragon culminated in the cross, the very point where it appeared that he had succeeded in his evil plans. Yet something surprising happened next. Rather than being destroyed by the dragon's attack, the **child was caught up to God and to His throne**. This is certainly a reference to Christ's ascension, and probably alludes also to His resurrection. According to Rev. 2:27, it is the resurrected and ascended Christ who has received the "rod of iron" prophesied in Psalm 2. In fact, Christ is referred to as a "male son" to show that He is the fulfillment of the Psalm. The last clause about Christ's ascent implies that the prophecy about God's messianic Son has begun to be fulfilled. The period between Christ's birth and ascension is skipped because He began to rule at the ascension in a more formal sense than before, which is the purpose for which He was born. Rev. 19:15 affirms that the Ps. 2:7-9 prophecy will find consummated fulfillment in Christ at the end of the age. This inaugurated fulfillment is confirmed from Rev. 2:26-28, where Christ affirms that He already has received from the Father the prophetic authority spoken of in the Psalm. The NT sees this prophecy of Christ's kingly birth fulfilled in His resurrection and ascension (Acts 13:33; Heb. 1:2-6; 5:5). In context, this initial fulfillment means that, as in ancient times at the Red Sea, so once more the dragon has been defeated. This time, the defeat has occurred through the resurrection and ascension of Christ.

6 The woman flees from the dragon (**And the woman fled into the wilderness**) after the deliverance of her son. Consistent with the above identification in vv. 1-2, the woman represents the community of faith, though now it is not that of the OT epoch, but the messianic community, living in the post-resurrection age. She is now on earth, and not pictured in heaven because she represents the true people of God on earth.

The fleeing into the wilderness alludes to the time when Israel fled from Egypt into the wilderness and was protected and nourished by Yahweh (Exod. 16:32; Deut. 2:7). The same pattern of fleeing into the wilderness is observable in the case of Elijah (1 Kings 17; 19:3-8) and Moses (Exod. 2:15), who symbolize the church in 11:5-6. The parallel of v. 14 with v. 6 makes the Exodus background explicit, where the "two wings of the eagle" on which the woman is borne into the wilderness allude to God's care of Israel after the exodus during the wilderness sojourn (see on v. 14). The woman's fleeing to the wilderness refers to the end-time exodus or restoration, when true Israel will return in faith to the Lord and again be protected and nourished by Him in the wilderness (cf. Isa. 32:15; 35:1-10; 40:3-8; 41:17-20; 43:19-20; 51:3; Jer. 31:2; Ezek. 34:25-31). Hos. 2:15 explicitly compares the end-time wilderness expectation to "the day when she [Israel] came up from the land of Egypt." Jesus Himself began to fulfill these end-time expectations, since He was an ideal and true Israel figure who before and during His ministry lived under the protection of the Spirit "in the wilderness" (Matt. 4:1; Mark 1:12; Luke 1:80; 4:1). He withstood the temptations of the wilderness to which Israel of old succumbed (Matt. 4:1-11 = Mark 1:12-13 = Luke 4:1-13; for other wilderness experiences of Jesus see Mark 1:35; Luke 4:42; 5:16). In 12:6, the messianic community is pictured as beginning to experience the end-time protection of God in the wilderness following the ascension of the Messiah. Though the community's members experience tribulation in relation to the world, at the same time their covenant relationship with God is spiritually protected and nourished, as they continue to fulfill the OT promises of Israel's restoration.

The wilderness itself does not protect, but is the invisible place where divine protection occurs. Even in the wilderness, the dragon's oppressive efforts threaten the community of saints, but God protects them there. The nature of the protection is not physical, but God guards them from spiritual deception (see on 12:15-17). The wilderness is another image essentially identical to the sanctuary of 11:1 and the tabernacle of 13:6, since all three are attacked during the same period of **one thousand two hundred and sixty days** (or three and a half years), and since all three are metaphors of spiritual protection. Consequently, the woman is an equivalent picture to the two witnesses of ch. 11, since both suffer in body but are protected in spirit, by the wilderness and the sanctuary respectively. Yet even in the wilderness, the place of God's protection, perils remain. This dual nature of the wilderness is suggested also by the OT and Revelation 17. In the OT, the desert was not only where Israel was protected from the pursuing Egyptians, but also an uninhabitable place of sin, evil, or judgment, where only fierce animals and evil spirits dwelt (e.g., Lev. 16:10; Isa. 13:20-22; 34:10-15; Jer. 9:10-12). The harlot of 17:1-9 also dwells in the wilderness (17:3). She deceives earth-dwellers (17:8) and persecutes the saints who, however, are not ultimately susceptible to her temptation. Therefore, the wilderness is the saints' place of protection, but in the midst of a hostile world. Deut. 8:15-16 sums up the dual nature of Israel's wilderness experience: "He led you through the great and terrible *wilderness*, with its fiery [red?] serpents . . . in the *wilderness* He fed you *manna*

. . . that He might humble you and that He might test you, to do good for you at your end [your latter days?]." This text would have been highly charged with typological significance for John and probably lies behind his dual conception of the wilderness.

The **one thousand two hundred and sixty days** have been established as the time of tribulation predicted by Dan. 7:25 and 12:7, which commences at Christ's ascension and continues until His return. Among all of John's "three and a half years" formulas, v. 6 is the clearest in identifying the formulas' temporal boundaries (cf. 11:2-3; 13:5). Undoubtedly here the limited age extends from the resurrection of Christ (v. 5) until His final appearance (14:14-20). We argued previously (see on 11:2-3) that the church's three and a half years of witness during the inter-advent age was modeled after the approximate three and a half years of Christ's earthly ministry. The forty-two months also echoes the time of Israel's wandering in the wilderness and Elijah's ministry of judgment (see on 11:1-3 for fuller analysis of this time period as the church age).

The word "place" (**where she had a place prepared by God**; cf. also v. 14), Greek *topos,* is synonymous elsewhere in the NT with "temple" (e.g., Matt. 24:15) and was often used in the LXX (about forty times) for the "sanctuary." The **place prepared by God** is an invisible geographical area of cultic security like the temple of 11:1-2. The church at Ephesus is warned that an unrepentant spirit in the future will result in Christ removing their lampstand "out of its place *(topos)*" in His heavenly temple (2:5). This means that they will not have the benefit of spiritual protection provided by that temple.

The use of **where** (Greek *hopou*) to introduce the last half of v. 6 further highlights the unseen aspect of the cultic **place**, since that word elsewhere in Revelation always introduces symbolic realms of divine protection (see 12:14 and 14:4) or Satanic danger or presence (2:13; 11:8, 20:10; cf. 17:3 with 17:9, literally "where the woman sits"). Note the parallel between this verse, where God prepares a "place" of protection in the wilderness for believers following the death and resurrection of Christ, and John 14:2-3, where Jesus prepares a "place" (the place being His Father's "house") for believers, where He will again be with them following His death and resurrection (John 14:16-24; 15:26-27; 16:7, 13-16). Traditionally, we have understood this latter "place" to be heaven, but in the light of the parallel to Revelation, could it be that the "place" God prepares is simply the place of His presence, whether on earth or in heaven? Or it may be that the temple in heaven extends to earth, where believers participate in it. It is by being in the place where the Spirit is that believers are enabled to persevere and overcome temptations to compromise because of persecution (John 15:25-27; 16:1-16; 16:32-33). In this place, they are kept spiritually safe regardless of what other troubles they may suffer. Though they experience tribulation in relation to the world, at the same time their covenant relationship with God is spiritually protected and nourished.

Unlikely is the idea of some that, after v. 5 speaks of Christ's resurrection, v. 6 skips the age of the church and jumps all the way to the time of ethnic Israel's revival and a "Great Tribulation" directly preceding the second coming. This would mean that it is ethnic Israel and not the church that finds refuge from the dragon in the wilderness. But there is no evidence for such a time gap. Such a temporal hiatus can be read into the text only by a prior end-time scheme which an interpreter brings to the text. The natural reading is to see v. 6 following immediately in time from v. 5. The relation of the parallel sections of 12:10 to 12:11-17 bears out this reading, as does the relation of 1:5 and 1:6 (cf. also v. 9), 1:12-20 and chs. 2–3, 5:5-14 and 6:1-11, and 7:10-11 and 7:13-14. All of these parallel sections deal with aspects of the work of Christ and its *immediate* consequences in the life of the church, and the same is true of the relation of 12:5 to 12:6.

SUGGESTIONS FOR REFLECTION ON 12:1-6

On the implications of the interrelationship of faithful Israel and the church. John here presents a picture of the woman giving birth to the male child, then fleeing into the wilderness. Reflect on how many parallels the commentary presents between faithful Israel and the church. Neither can be fully understood without the other. What are the implications of this interrelationship? In drawing lines of division between Israel and the church in the new covenant age do we fail to understand how the church is the heir to faithful Israel, and prophetically fulfills its role? Do we understand the corresponding lack of connection between the faithful Israel represented here, and those "who say they are Jews and are not" (Rev. 2:9; 3:9)?

On the complex nature of the wilderness. These verses speak of the wilderness, in both its OT and NT forms, as a place of complexity: it is where God protects His people, yet also a place of danger. How do we find the place of God's presence in the midst of a hostile world? What is the nature of the safety or security He provides? What can we legitimately ask for in that respect?

Christ's death and resurrection result in the victory of Christ and the saints over the Satanic accuser and in the inaugurated messianic kingdom (12:7-12)

7 And there was war in heaven, Michael and his angels waging war with the
dragon. And the dragon and his angels waged war, 8 and they were not strong
enough, and there was no longer a place for them in heaven. 9 And the great
dragon was thrown down, the serpent of old who is called the devil and Satan,
who deceives the whole world; he was thrown down to the earth, and his angels
were thrown down with him. 10 And I heard a loud voice in heaven, saying, "Now
the salvation, and the power, and the kingdom of our God and the authority of
His Christ have come, for the accuser of our brethren has been thrown down,
who accuses them before our God day and night. 11 And they overcame him because of the blood of the Lamb and because of the word of their testimony, and
they did not love their life even to death. 12 For this reason, rejoice, O heavens
and you who dwell in them. Woe to the earth and sea, because the devil has
come down to you, having great wrath, knowing that he has only a short time."

7 John does not make the connection between vv. 1-6 and vv. 7-12 explicit, but a connection is demanded (apart from their adjacent placement) because the wording of v. 3 ("another sign appeared in heaven") and here (**and there was war in heaven**) suggests that vv. 7-12 is a continuation of the vision of vv. 1-6. Vv. 7-12 explain how **Michael and his angels** defeated the devil (**waging war with the dragon**) and his angels in heavenly combat, and record actions which are the heavenly counterpart of earthly events recorded in vv. 1-6.

From John's perspective, angels can be viewed as mediators for the church (cf. the angels in chs. 1–3 and the elders in chs. 4–5 as heavenly representatives of the church), primarily in the light of the following considerations of their representative nature as understood from Daniel. According to Daniel's vision, Michael is the great angel appointed to represent God's people (Dan. 10:13, 21; 12:1). Michael is closely associated with the Son of man (as a subordinate helper), since both are set forth as heavenly representatives of Israel (Dan. 12:1 and 7:13-27 respectively). This is why they are identified as fighting together for Israel against the demonic rulers over Persia and Greece (nations oppressing God's people) in Dan. 10:20-21 (cf. Dan. 10:5-21, where "one like a Son of man" is joined by Michael to fight these evil heavenly forces). John now sees Michael, representing God's covenant community and the messianic leader of that community, fighting in heaven, even as Christ fought on earth. Michael thus stands in John's vision beside the Son of man to fight for Him, even as he did in Daniel's vision. As in Daniel, so in Rev. 12:7, Michael is a representative of Israel and has the same relation to the "Son of man," Christ, as in Daniel 10. Rev. 12:1-5 has explained primarily what has occurred on earth in the person of Jesus, whereas Michael reflects Jesus' earthly victory as His representative in the heavenly sphere.

Consequently, v. 7 explains the heavenly counterpart to Christ's victory at the cross and resurrection. That is, Christ's resurrection and the beginning of His rule are immediately reflected in heaven by the defeat of the devil and his hosts by Michael and his angels. Michael's engagement in heaven was a direct, inexorable reflex action put into gear by Christ's redemptive work on earth. It is also appropriate that Michael reflects Jesus' earthly actions in heaven, since Jesus represents ideal Israel in His own person and Michael is Israel's representative angel (Dan. 12:1). Michael's actions on behalf of true Israel (which in Revelation 12 is Jesus) must be linked to Dan. 12:1, in which he is prophesied to "stand guard" in the latter-day tribulation as Israel's heavenly representative to defend faithful Israel from the ultimate harm of the final tribulation. Michael's prophesied representative work begins with his representation of Jesus' victory in heaven. Michael's later representative work on behalf of Jesus' followers, the corporate true Israel, also merely reflects in heaven the subsequent effects of the victory that Jesus achieved for them.

Dan. 7:21 refers to the horn "making war" with the saints and being too powerful for them. An allusion to this text has already been made in 11:7 and appears again in 13:7, both referring to the attacks of the beast against the saints. The language of Dan. 7:21 is now applied to the defeat of the dragon. The "rulers" of Persia and of Greece, whom Michael fights according to Dan. 10:20, are now revealed to be Satan himself or one of his demonic angels. What better language to use to portray the devil's defeat than that which the book of Daniel had used to speak of the devil's victory over the saints? The reversed application of the wording "waging war" may connote a literary parody whereby the devil is mocked by having his defeat described in the same way in which his defeat of God's people was described. Since the woman, the dragon, the serpent, the wilderness, the wings of the eagle, and other descriptions throughout ch. 12 are clearly symbolic, so also is the war of angels here. The remainder of ch. 12 elucidates the manner in which the devil was defeated by Christ's resurrection and the meaning of the symbolism in v. 7.

8 Just as the beginning of v. 8 completes a description from Daniel of the demise of Satan begun in v. 7, the remainder of the verse adds a further sketch, again based on Daniel. An immediate consequence of the defeat of the devil and his hosts is that **there was no longer a place found for them in heaven.** This is based on the nearly identical wording of Dan. 2:35 (OG; "not a trace of them was found" in the Hebrew Bible), which also prophetically describes the immediate consequence of the destruction of the hostile world kingdoms in the latter days. In Daniel 2, a stone strikes a statue representing the last four kingdoms of world history. The stone is equated with the force of God's kingdom (Dan. 2:44). Many commentators have equated the stone with the Son of man in Daniel 7, who overcomes and replaces the former oppressive regimes in the end times. Jesus saw the prophecy beginning its fulfillment in His own ministry (Luke 20:17-18). The Jews who rejected Him were identified with the ungodly nations who would be judged by Him. He was the stone of Daniel 2. Christ's resurrection immediately unleashes the effect of Michael's representative victory in heaven, and the Daniel 2 imagery shows this to be an absolute and universal judgment. The point of Dan. 2:35 and the allusion to it in Rev. 12:8b is that opposition to God's kingdom and His people is decisively thwarted. Jesus' defeat of the nations in fulfillment of Psalm 2 (cf. Rev. 12:5) is reflected in heaven by Michael's defeat of the heavenly representatives of those nations in fulfillment of Daniel 2 (cf. Rev. 12:7). Whereas v. 8b shows that the decisive defeat has begun, the same allusion to Dan. 2:35 is repeated in 20:11 to indicate complete fulfillment of the prophecy at the end of the age and the final judgment. But if this prophesied judgment is only inaugurated, how can it be absolute and universal? The following verses will explain how this is so.

9 A further explanation is now given about what it means that "there was no longer a place found for them in heaven": **he was thrown down to the earth, and his angels were thrown down with him**. Even as he unjustly threw the stars onto the earth (v. 4), so now the devil suffers the same punishment (again illustrating the biblical principle of the punishment befitting the crime). The dragon is now described as **the serpent of old**, that is, the serpent of Gen. 3:1, 14. The ancient foe of God's people is also **called the devil and Satan**, which respectively mean "slanderer" and "adversary." According to Genesis 3, the serpent is both slanderer and deceiver. He slanders God by questioning His motives in giving His command (Gen. 3:5), and he deceives Adam and Eve by suggesting that their disobedience will have a positive consequence (Gen. 3:4-5). The remainder of ch. 12 and of the book reveals that Christ's death and resurrection have resulted in drastically curtailing the devil's role of deception and nullifying his role of slanderer. This curtailment and nullification is what is meant by the depiction of Michael and his angels throwing the devil and his angels out of heaven. The "place" which the devil lost was his hitherto privileged place of accusation, formerly granted him by God as a temporary privilege (see further on v. 10b).

10 John hears **a loud voice in heaven** making proclamation. Often in Revelation, a hymn interprets or summarizes a vision (see 4:1-7 and 4:8-10; 5:5 and 5:6-14; 14:1 and 14:2-5; 15:2 and 15:3-4). Sometimes what is seen interprets what has been heard in a preceding section (cf. 7:1-8 and 7:9-17). Therefore, the hymn of vv. 10-12 interprets vv. 7-9 to show clearly that what Michael does is a heavenly reflection of what Christ does on earth. The first three lines of the hymn are especially parallel with that in 11:15, where also the multitude of saints extol God for the establishment of the kingdom. Therefore, it would appear that the multitude of saints in heaven are those from whom the voice comes. This is confirmed from the fact that they refer, not only to **our God**, but also to **our brethren**. Normally in Revelation, angels give expressions of judgment or salvation, whereas humans offer declarations of praise.

The meaning of Christ's ascension and the devil's expulsion from heaven (vv. 5-9) is now explained to be the long-awaited inauguration of the prophesied messianic kingdom (not the consummation, as in 11:15): **Now the salvation, and the power, and the kingdom of our God and the authority of His Christ have come.** The similar ascriptions of power to God and the Lamb in 4:11 and 5:11-12 confirm that here, as in those chapters, the focus is on Christ's resurrection, which has launched the initial stage of the kingdom. The introductory word **now** emphasizes the beginning aspect of fulfillment. Therefore, v. 10 is not a mere anticipation of the future kingdom, but celebrates the fact that the kingdom has begun immediately following Christ's death and resurrection. This is the direct fulfillment of the prophecy of the beginning of the Messiah's rule in Ps. 2:7-9 (alluded to in v. 5); the combination of **God** or "Lord" and **His Christ**, as in this verse, occurs in the OT only in Ps. 2:2. The resurrection is the turning point of all human history. It represents the moment at which the power of the enemy in heaven was crushed and his kingdom came crashing down to earth.

How in particular this happened can be seen from the declaration of the redeemed saints in v. 10b that **the accuser of our brethren has been**

thrown down. Christ's death and resurrection have resulted in Satan's excommunication from heaven. Just as Satan and his hosts fell at the beginning of the first creation (Isa. 14:11-16; Ezek. 28:12-19 [possibly]; 2 Pet. 2:4; Jude 6), so he had to fall at the start of what Scripture tells us is the second, new creation (see 1:5 and 3:14; cf. 2 Cor. 5:14-17; Gal. 6:15). Satan's job had always been to accuse the saints (Job 1:6-11; 2:1-6; Zech. 3:1-2), and from these texts it can be concluded that the devil was permitted by God to accuse His people of sin. Implicit also in the accusations was the charge that God's own character was corrupt. For example, Satan says to God in Job 1 that Job would not have been so faithful if God had not prospered or bribed him so much. The devil's accusation is based on the correct presupposition that the penalty of sin necessitates a judgment of spiritual death. Until the death of Christ, it could appear that the devil had a good case, since God ushered all deceased OT saints into His saving presence without exacting the penalty of their sin, God having delayed executing just punishment for our sin (Rom. 3:25). However, the devil's case was unjust even then, since the sins about which he was accusing and for which he wanted to punish people were instigated by his deceptions. This is why he is called both deceiver and accuser in vv. 9-10. Therefore, because of Satan's unjust accusations and because of the Messiah's anticipated redemptive death for His people (cf. Isaiah 53), OT saints were protected by God from the damning danger of these accusations.

Yet when Christ came, His death satisfied the anger of God against the sins of all the faithful, both those before Christ and after. He was the spotless, substitutionary Lamb who was slain and who purchased for our God by means of His blood a redeemed people from throughout the earth (so 5:6-9). The fact that the just judgment of God on human sin was visited on the sinless Christ has had the result that "there is therefore now no condemnation for those who are in Christ Jesus" (Rom. 8:1), and that no one can "bring a charge against God's elect," not even "angels, nor principalities . . . nor powers" (Rom. 8:33-34, 38). Now the devil has no basis for his accusations, and he is evicted from the heavenly courtroom and counsel of God. Jesus links the fall of Satan from heaven (Luke 10:18) with the empowering of the disciples over the work of the enemy (Luke 10:17, 19-20), and most of all with the fact that the disciples' names are recorded in heaven (Luke 10:20). Jesus prophesied that when He was lifted up, the ruler of this world would be cast out (John 12:31). The decisive and legal defeat of Satan occurs as the kingdom of God is inaugurated on earth; the final and complete destruction of the enemy will occur when the Lord returns to establish His kingdom in its completed or fulfilled state (Rev. 19:20-21; 20:10-15).

11 Now the decisive victory of Christ on earth (vv. 5, 10) and of Michael in heaven (vv. 7-9) is identified as the basis of the victory which suffering Christians on earth win over the serpent throughout history: **And they overcame him because of the blood of the Lamb**. Specifically, the initial **and** may point to v. 10 as the basis for v. 11 or may denote similarly that v. 11 is a result of v. 10. V. 11 summarizes the purpose of the whole chapter and especially of vv. 7-12, which is is to assure believers who encounter Satanic evil on earth that evil has been defeated, even though it seems otherwise. Christians can be assured that the serpent begins to battle against their bodies only after he has lost the battle over their souls. This expresses one of the major themes of the book: the suffering of Christians is a sign, not of Satan's victory, but of the saints' victory over him because of their belief in the triumph of the cross, with which their suffering identifies them. The saints' status in heaven has been legitimized finally by Christ's suffering on the cross. All believers, past, present, and future, have overcome the devil and thus "follow the Lamb wherever He goes" (14:4).

They have also overcome the enemy **because of the word of their testimony**. Here the focus is not on OT saints but on followers of Jesus, as is apparent from the parallel phrases in the book which refer to the persecuted faithful of the NT church (so 1:9; 6:9; 19:10; 20:4). Just as both Satan's and the world's guilty verdict on Christ was overturned through His resurrection, so His followers have their verdict reversed in the same manner through their identification with that resurrection. The phrase **they did not love their life even to death** refers to any suffering for Christ up until the point of (**even to**) actual martyrdom. That not only martyrs are referred to is shown by the fact that the devil's accusation comes against all believers, not just those who have laid down their lives for Christ. The parallel of 2:10 includes death, but does not necessitate that all who are imprisoned will die: "the devil is about to cast some of you into prison, that you may be tested, and you will have tribulation ten days. Be faithful until [literally 'up to the point of'] death." All believers are participants in suffering and tribulation (1:9), and the "overcomers" of chs. 2–3 are all faithful members of the churches. Believers must be faithful "up until" the point of death — to death if necessary, but certainly to any trial of a lesser nature.

12 Apparently it is the saints who dwell in heaven who command all heavenly beings to rejoice: **For this reason, rejoice, O heavens and you who dwell in them**. They are to rejoice because (**for this reason**, alluding to the events recorded in vv. 7-11) Christ's kingdom has been established, the enemy has lost his place in heaven as their accuser, and the saints can overcome his accusations. The command is rhetorically directed mainly to the saints themselves (those who dwell or tabernacle in the heavens; cf. 7:15; 21:3) because of the salvation which they now enjoy, though the address includes reference to all heavenly beings. While the heavens may rejoice because of the devil's expulsion, woe is coming to the earth, for the devil's power, though curtailed in the heavenlies, is still real in the earthly realm: **Woe to the earth and sea, because the devil has come down to you, having great wrath**. The devil's fury is expressed against Christians, as vv. 13-17 make clear. His destructive work on earth is also fueled by his **great wrath** over losing his position in heaven. But above all, his anger is sparked by his **knowing that he has only a short time** to work his destruction on earth. The expression **a short time** indicates an expectation of the imminent consummation of the kingdom and final defeat of Satan. First-century Christians hoped in the imminent coming of Christ, but acknowledged that only the Father knew the "day and hour" (Matt. 24:36; cf. Acts 1:7). The woe at the end of v. 12 shows that John understood that Satan had the same imminent perspective. Just as the imminent hope should motivate Christians to good works, it motivates Satan to do evil works, so that he can cause as much destruction as possible before the end comes. The **short time** is the same as the three and a half years of vv. 6, 14 and 11:2-3 and 13:5 and the time of the "delay" in 10:6. This identification fits well, since the three and a half years in Dan. 7:25; 12:7; Rev. 11:2; 13:5 is the period of the end-time enemy's persecution of God's people (see on 11:1-2), from which vv. 6 and 14 affirm that they are ultimately protected.

Hence, the **short time** is figurative, like the three and a half years. It probably also overlaps with or is equivalent to the "little time" of 6:11, during which deceased saints wait for the rest of the redeemed to join them in glory. The period in v. 12 is also synonymous with the "thousand years" of 20:3. That is, the deceased saints in heaven of 6:9-11 also reign triumphantly there (20:4-6) until the remainder of their brothers and sisters suffer and die and join them in their heavenly rule. This is the same time when the devil is locked in the abyss, where he cannot harm the souls of sealed saints, though he can harm their bodies through persecution (see on 20:1-6 for further discussion). Indeed, ch. 12 shows that, though the devil is "on the loose" against the church, he cannot ultimately thwart its spiritual, heavenly destiny and identification.

Because Christ's kingdom is not yet present in its fulfilled or completed state, God's people may physically suffer or even be killed, but because it is genuinely present in its initial or inaugurated state, their ultimate victory is assured, as much as was Christ's when He was dying on the cross. And in the midst of our battle on earth, we now have all the resources of heaven open to us, the same resources that hurled the enemy down to earth in the first place. The resurrection is thus the decisive event which decisively won the battle in the unseen world and released the power of the kingdom into the seen world.

Suggestions for Reflection on 12:7-12

On the battle in the unseen world. In vv. 7-12, John presents an astounding insight into the unseen world. What light does this shed on Paul's comment, "For our struggle is not against flesh and blood . . . but against the spiritual forces of wickedness in the heavenly places" (Eph. 6:12)? Christians can commit two errors, either being oblivious to the spiritual battle or being fixated on or fearful of demonic powers. How do these verses give us a balanced perspective?

On confronting the attack of the enemy by understanding God's sovereignty. How is it true that Satan's rampaging on earth is actually a reflection of his defeat in heaven and a portent of his ultimate doom? How can it be true that at the same time as the authority of Christ has been established in heaven, the devil is free to attack God's people on earth with great wrath? These verses present a view of the utter sovereignty of God in all things. Even the work of the devil occurs only on terms determined by God. How critical is it that we hold to a biblical view of the sovereignty of God, given that God's people will surely suffer during their earthly lifetimes? How do we find comfort in the fact of the establishment of God's rule in heaven even as we face trials on earth?

As a result of Christ's victory over the devil, God protects the messianic community against the devil's wrathful harm (12:13-17)

[13] And when the dragon saw that he was thrown down to the earth, he persecuted the woman who gave birth to the male child. [14] And the two wings of
the great eagle were given to the woman, in order that she might fly into the
wilderness to her place, where she was nourished for a time and times and half
a time, from the presence of the serpent. [15] And the serpent poured water like a
river out of his mouth after the woman, so that he might cause her to be swept
away with the flood. [16] And the earth helped the woman, and the earth opened

its mouth and drank up the river which the dragon poured out of his mouth.
[17] And the dragon was enraged with the woman, and went off to make war with the rest of her offspring, who keep the commandments of God and hold to the testimony of Jesus.

13 V. 13 picks up the story left off at v. 6, where the woman (representing the covenant community of Jesus' followers) had fled into the wilderness, and at v. 12, where the devil had come down to the earth in great wrath. The devil, seeing his defeat (**and when the dragon saw that he was thrown down to the earth**), and enraged over losing his heavenly office as a result of his inability to thwart the birth of Christ and especially His ultimate enthronement, expresses his anger by persecuting **the woman who gave birth to the male child**. It is clear that the woman (the church) is persecuted because of her association with the male child (Christ), who threw the devil down. Therefore, the dragon and his representatives also attack her (e.g., Matt. 5:11; 10:22; 24:9; John 15:18-21; Acts 9:4-5; 1 Pet. 4:14; Rev. 1:9; 14:13, assuming the latter verse includes reference to persecution).

14 V. 14 restates the content of v. 6 and interprets it further: **And the two wings of the great eagle were given to the woman, in order that she might fly into the wilderness to her place, where she was nourished for a time and times and half a time**. The latter phrase is equivalent to the three and a half years or forty-two months of 11:2-3 and 13:5 or the one thousand two hundred and sixty days of 12:6, that is, the time of the church's earthly existence. The purpose for her pilgrimage is to find protection from the threatening **presence of the serpent**. The image of **the two wings of the great eagle** has as its background Exod. 19:4 and Deut. 32:10-12, where God speaks of carrying Israel as an eagle in the wilderness, and it is undoubtedly this picture which is repeated here. The church is once again portrayed as latter-day Israel taking over the role of the old Israel, and with the spiritual wilderness representing God's protective presence substituted for the physical wilderness of Sinai. David likewise speaks of being given the wings of a dove to flee into the wilderness and await God's protection from his enemies (Ps. 55:1-8). But perhaps most significant as background for this verse is the prophecy of Isaiah that in the wilderness God's people will receive wings like eagles when He comes to deliver them in the last days (Isa. 40:27-31; cf. vv. 3-11 for context). So God will strengthen and nourish the church in its exodus wanderings through the wilderness of the world. He does this by providing manna, even as He did in the wilderness of Sinai (Exod. 16:32; Deut. 8:16). John 6:31-58 affirms that the presence of Christ Himself was the beginning of fulfillment of the latter-day, promised manna (and see Rev. 2:17 for God's promise of manna to those who overcome). V. 14 should thus be seen as portraying the escalated fulfillment of the manna expectation and of the restoration prophecies in the church, since the Isaiah restoration prophecies concerning Israel were never completely fulfilled. His presence nourishes, assures, and strengthens them in the midst of persecution and suffering in the **place** of His protection in the wilderness, thus causing the church to remain faithful in their testimony to Christ.

15 The devil's persecution of the church is pictured as **the serpent** pouring **water like a river out of his mouth after the woman, so that he might cause her to be swept away with the flood**. The picture is figurative, as are John's other metaphors of weapons coming out of someone's mouth. These figurative weapons represent words by which Christ and His agents judge sinners (1:16; 2:16; 11:5; 19:15, 21; cf. 3:16) or by which the devil and his agents deceive people (9:17-18; 16:13). V. 9 traces the first expression of this deceiving trait to the Garden of Eden by calling the devil "the serpent of old . . . who deceives the whole world." This is picked up again in vv. 14-15 by the repeated references to the devil as **the serpent**. In the OT, "flood" speaks of an army spreading out to conquer (Dan. 11:10, 22, 26, 40), and of persecution of God's people by enemies from whom the Lord delivers them (2 Sam. 22:5; Pss. 18:4, 16; 66:12; 69:1-2, 14-15; 124:4-5; 144:7-8; Isa. 43:2), which is the idea in mind here. In Ps. 18:4, David describes Saul's pursuit of him explicitly as "the torrents of Belial" which assailed him. Ps. 144:7-8, 11 is noteworthy because it is a prayer that God would deliver David "out of great waters," which is a picture of those who speak "deceit and . . . falsehood." Likewise, "a flood of great waters" in Ps. 32:6 refers to a threat of persecution by the ungodly.

The devil attempts to destroy the church from within (using deception) and without (using persecution). Just as the serpent deceived the first woman with words, so he attempts to deceive the latter-day woman with a flood of words (cf. 2 Cor. 11:3). Satanic agents in the form of false teachers, compromisers, and demons infiltrate the church in order to deceive her and to contribute to her demise (2:14-16, 20-22; 3:15-17; Rom. 16:17-20; 2 Cor. 11:3-4, 13-15; 1 Tim. 4:1; 5:15; 2 Tim. 2:23-26). Chs. 2–3 reveal that the churches to which John was writing had already begun to experience the devil's flood of deception (2:2, 14, 20), false accusations (2:9; 3:9), temptations, and persecution (2:10, 13). It is beyond coincidence that wherever chs. 2–3 mention these problems, the devil's "synagogue" (2:9; 3:9), "throne" (2:13), or "deep things" (2:24) is mentioned.

The waters of v. 15 allude to at least three OT backgrounds: the Red Sea, which was a barrier to the safety of the children of Israel, the waters standing in the way of His people's return to Zion which Isaiah prophesies in the last days God will again dry up or cause to be blocked (Isa. 42:15; 43:2; 44:27), and the flood associated with the end-time attack on God's people in Dan. 9:26. John's allusion to both the exodus and to Dan. 9:26 would be in line with his preceding allusions, which have combined the same two backgrounds (see on 11:2, 6, especially on the "forty-two months" and its background in the exodus and Daniel).

16 The swallowing of the flood by the earth is a further allusion to the Exodus and Israel's wilderness experience. The earth swallows the flood (**the earth opened its mouth and drank up the river which the dragon poured out of his mouth**). The flood swallowed Pharaoh and his armies (Exod. 15:12; the Aramaic Bible [Palestinian Targum] expands on the Hebrew of this verse and repeats that "the earth opened her mouth and consumed them"). And later the earth swallowed the families of Korah, Dathan, and Abiram, who were in rebellion against Moses (Num. 16:31-32). In both OT instances, God caused the earth to open and swallow that which opposed the establishment and welfare of His people. Interestingly, both Isaiah and the Psalms say that God defeated the evil dragon when He divided the Red Sea to allow Israel through, but closed it again over Egypt (Ps. 74:13-14 [where Leviathan represents Pharaoh]; Isa. 51:9-10), and Ezek. 29:3 and 32:2-3 identify Pharaoh with the sea-dragon. And so here, the allusion to the exodus deliverance once again connotes God's preservation and deliverance of His people and defeat of the serpent. The barrier of the sea had to be removed so that Israel could be guided to the "place" God had made in the wilderness for His dwelling (Exod. 15:17). The purpose of the protection in v. 16, as in Exodus, is to guide the church in the wilderness to the "place" prepared by God for her (12:6, 14), which is a sanctuary of protection.

17 The dragon becomes **enraged with the woman** because his efforts to destroy the church have been thwarted, but he does not cease his efforts to exterminate God's people. Thus, he goes off **to make war with the rest of her offspring, who keep the commandments of God and hold to the testimony of Jesus**. The relation of v. 17 to the preceding verses is one of the most challenging interpretive problems in the book. The difficulty focuses on the nature of the difference, if any, between the woman and her offspring, and how they are respectively depicted. The most plausible view is that the woman in vv. 6, 13-16 depicts the church (and the suffering she undergoes) as she is seen from the ideal, eternal, or heavenly perspective, and her offspring in v. 17 depict the multitude of individual believers (and the suffering they experience) as seen from an earthly or historical perspective. The woman is presented in v. 1 as "in heaven" and in heavenly attire, and the same woman is also presented as suffering on earth (vv. 6, 13-16). She continues to be viewed from a heavenly, ideal perspective even in the consideration of her sufferings on earth. In v. 17, however, the same suffering is portrayed from an earthly perspective as the suffering of individual believers. This simply represents two different ways of viewing the church: as a corporate or "ideal" body, the way God sees it from His perspective, and as a community of individuals, which is the way we experience it on earth. Likewise, in the OT the one female figure of Zion is always explained as the many people of Israel (Isa. 49:14-26; 50:1; 51:1-3, 16; Ezekiel 16; Hos. 4:4-5; and see on 12:2). The antithesis to the woman, the harlot of chs. 17–18, also represents a community composed of individuals. Perhaps specifically still hovering in the background is Isa. 66:7-10, 22, where Zion is referred to as a mother who, "before she travailed, brought forth . . . *a boy*" (66:7), which has already been alluded to in v. 2 (on which see). Strikingly, in the very next verse, Isaiah speaks of the same thing in referring to Zion: "as soon as (she) travailed, she also brought forth her *sons*." This is virtually the same as the woman of ch. 12, who bears a male and who also has other children.

If correct, this view of v. 17 is best taken as a contrast between the whole heavenly and the whole earthly church. Consequently, the point of vv. 13-17, taken together, would be that the *one* heavenly church being persecuted *on earth* cannot be destroyed (God's perspective) because it is heavenly and ultimately inviolable spiritually, but the *many* who individually compose the church can suffer physically from earthly dangers (our perspective), but not be destroyed spiritually. In relation to Revelation 11, this would mean that the woman would be equivalent to those dwelling in the spiritually invincible inner court of the temple and her offspring equivalent to those living in the outer court, which is susceptible to physical harm (see on 11:1-2). It amounts to two ways of viewing the same phenomenon. Understanding it from God's perspective, as John unfolds it to us, helps us in the very real battle we face in our earthly lives.

A viable (though somewhat less likely) view of the phrase **the rest of her offspring** is that four temporal stages are revealed as the narrative of ch. 12 progresses:

the messianic community before Christ (vv. 1-4),
the appearance of Christ in the covenant community (v. 5),
the persecuted messianic community immediately following Christ's ascension (vv. 6, 13-16), and
the later stages of the persecuted community (v. 17).

It is possible to view the third stage as the church age in general (parallel to 11:1-6), and the fourth as an era at the very end of history (parallel to 11:7-13). This temporal scheme is based on the possibility that v. 17 may affirm a distinction between the woman, as she implicitly represents *part* of her offspring as a group of believers in vv. 6, 13-16, and then the *remainder* of her offspring in v. 17. This would mean that the group pictured in vv. 6, 13-16 *is distinct* from that in v. 17. Even if this interpretation is correct, however, the heavenly, invincible nature of the church prominent in vv. 6, 13-16 is not lost sight of in v. 17, since the group there is called **the rest of** the offspring of the (heavenly) woman. This phrase shows a continuity between the groups of vv. 6, 13-16 and v. 17, since both are related to the heavenly woman.

The church keeps **the commandments of God** and holds to **the testimony of Jesus**. The latter phrase is intentionally ambiguous, as in 1:2, including both the "testimony from Jesus" given to the church and "the testimony to Jesus" given by the church. The focus of the phrase may be on Jesus' testimony to God, which the church is to reproduce. God's beneficent care and nourishment of the church consists in enabling it to continue to be faithful to Him and to Jesus. This is the "perseverance of the saints" (14:12). When this happens, the king of the abyss suffers a setback, since he loses subjects over whom to rule in his own murky kingdom. This is another escalated element of the original exodus pattern, in which Israel's obedience to God's commandments, contained in the earthly tabernacle, was seen as the very thing preserving them through the sea and the wilderness. Jesus now sums up in Himself the OT commandments of God (**the commandments of God = the testimony of Jesus**), as represented by the contents of the heavenly tabernacle of testimony (see further on 15:5).

V. 17 is also a partial fulfillment of the promise of Gen. 3:15, where God prophesies that the individual (messianic) and corporate seed of the woman will fatally bruise the head of the serpent (note the Aramaic Bible's corporate interpretation of the woman's "seed" in Gen. 3:15: "when the sons of the woman keep the commandments of the law . . . they will smite you [the Serpent] on the head; when they abandon the commandments you will wound them in the heel . . . in the days of King Messiah"). In Rev. 13:3 one of the heads of the beast is depicted as "slain," not only because of Christ's work, but also because of His followers' faithfulness (so 12:11, 17). Whenever persecution, deception, and compromise are resisted, the devil is seen as continuing to be defeated (as in 12:11; Rom. 16:17-20). On the other hand, the allusion to Genesis also shows that the church's persecution is prophetically determined by God's hand, since Gen. 3:15 is a prophecy that the serpent "will bruise" the woman's "seed." The Genesis 3 background also confirms our conclusion that in vv. 15-16 the serpent opposes the woman once again not only through persecution but also by deception, as in the Garden of Eden. This is but another instance of the end being modeled on the beginning (see on v. 9, where "serpent" is derived primarily from Genesis 3).

Suggestions for Reflection on 12:13-17

On the ebb and flow of spiritual battle. In vv. 13-17, we see portrayed both the violence of the enemy's attack and the magnificence of God's protection. The wings of the great eagle are given to the woman even while the serpent pours out water like a flood to destroy her. When there is a victory for the woman, the enemy becomes enraged and takes the battle elsewhere. How does this portray the ebb and flow of spiritual battle both through the ages and in our own personal experience? How can we take comfort in the midst of the storm that at some point God will deliver us? And how do we avoid the delusion in times of peace that times of testing will never come — which sometimes thus find us unprepared?

On the importance of spiritual nourishment. John tells us that the woman, representing the church, will be nourished in her time in the wilderness. What does it mean to be nourished by God? How is the church corporately nourished? How are we individually nourished? How in particular do we find nourishment in times of great testing? How could passages such as Rev. 1:3; 3:8, 10; and 22:7 contribute toward answering these questions (cf. also 1 John 2:14b)? If a malnourished church is ill-prepared for such a time, how vital it is to maintain nourishment even during the times of peace.

Believers are exhorted to be discerning about falsehood and not to participate in false worship propagated by the devil and his worldly allies in order to hold on to their faith (12:18–13:18)

12:18–13:18 explains in further detail the nature of Satan's persecution of the church and is temporally parallel with 12:13-17. Though the devil has been defeated, he still has ability to oppress the saints. The segment also delineates the agents through whom the devil executes his persecuting will. These agents are none other than the governing political and economic powers of the earth. In ch. 13, John draws predominantly from Daniel, especially Daniel 7. There has been debate since the earliest church fathers about the identification of the antichrist figure of ch. 13: Is he a personal figure or an evil spirit? The two interpretations are not incompatible. The context of Revelation and of the NT (especially 1 and 2 John) indicates that the antichrist has manifested himself as a corporate spirit inspiring false teaching and persecution since the first century, yet at a future time before the end will manifest himself individually in the flesh as the leader of opposition to God's people.

The devil authorizes the state as his agent to persecute the church and to deceive the ungodly (12:18[= 13:1a in NASB]–13:8)

18 And he stood on the sand of the seashore. 1 And I saw a beast coming up out of
the sea, having ten horns and seven heads, and on his horns were ten diadems,
and on his heads were blasphemous names. 2 And the beast which I saw was like
a leopard, and his feet were like those of a bear, and his mouth like the mouth of a
lion. And the dragon gave him his power and his throne and great authority. 3 And
I saw one of his heads as if it had been slain, and his fatal wound was healed. And
the whole earth was amazed and followed after the beast; 4 and they worshiped
the dragon, because he gave his authority to the beast, and they worshiped the
beast, saying, "Who is like the beast, and who is able to wage war with him?"
5 And there was given to him a mouth speaking arrogant words and blasphemies,
and authority to act for forty-two months was given to him. 6 And he opened his
mouth in blasphemies against God, to blaspheme His name and His tabernacle,
that is, those who dwell in heaven. 7 And it was given to him to make war with
the saints and to overcome them; and authority over every tribe and people
and tongue and nation was given to him. 8 And all who dwell on the earth will
worship him, everyone whose name has not been written from the foundation
of the world in the book of life of the Lamb who has been slain.

18 (= **13:1a** in NASB) The dragon positions himself **on the sand of the seashore** to call up his helpers who will carry out his will on earth. He summons them from the same hellish waters from which presumably he himself came. What the dragon was described as doing in ch. 12, he actually does through his servants portrayed in ch. 13. Some English translations include 12:18 as part of 13:1.

13:1 V. 1 (marked by **And I saw**) begins the second section of the major vision segment which commenced at 12:1. The first agent of the devil is a **beast coming up out of the sea.** Vv. 1-2 are a creative reworking of Dan. 7:1-7. The beast with **ten horns and seven heads** is based on Dan. 7:2-7, 19-24. This beast is like a leopard, a bear, and a lion. The seven heads are a composite of the heads of the four beasts Daniel saw, one like a leopard, one like a bear, one like a lion, and a fourth with ten horns. Other features of the Danielic beasts are also applied to the one beast in v. 2. In addition, the **ten diadems** on the **ten horns** are a reference to Daniel's fourth beast, whose "ten horns" are interpreted as "ten kings" (Dan. 7:24). Likewise, the **blasphemous names** on his heads are connected with the blaspheming figure of Dan. 7:8, 11, who is also associated with the fourth Danielic kingdom (see on vv. 5-6 below). That the monster in vv. 1-7 is modeled primarily on Daniel 7 is supported by the above analysis of the similar portrayal of the dragon in 12:3-4 (on which see), which was predominantly taken from Daniel 7–8.

Without exception, the imagery of the sea monster is used throughout the OT to represent evil kingdoms which persecute God's people (see on 12:3 for references). The same Daniel imagery of horns and heads (Dan. 7:7, 24; cf. 7:3-6) applied to the dragon in 12:3-4 is applied here to another sea beast to depict the dragon's earthly minion. As with the dragon's horns and heads, so here the number of *seven* heads and *ten* horns emphasizes the completeness of oppressive power and its worldwide effect, even as the crowned heads of demons in 9:7, 17-19 denote oppressive power and as the seven horns of the Lamb in 5:6 express His worldwide dominion. Because of the primary figurative force of the numbers **seven** and **ten**, the **heads** and **horns** are not to be identified only with a specific series of rulers of either the first century or later (on this transtemporal aspect, see further on v. 2 below). That the dragon had diadems on his heads and the beast has them on his horns shows that the dragon has the ultimate rule and mandates his will through the beast, who arises from the watery, dark home of the dragon (see 12:3). The dragon stations himself by the sea, spewing out floods after the church (12:15), the beast comes out of the sea, and the harlot "sits on many waters" (17:1), thus indicating that the sea is pictured symbolically as the dwelling place of evil. The dark realm of evil encompasses unbelieving people, so that the beast may also be seen as having its earthly origin from the mass of unregenerate humanity (for which idea see also 17:1, 15).

The **diadems** symbolize the beast's false claims of sovereign, universal authority which are in opposition to the true "King of kings and Lord of lords," who also wears "many diadems" (19:12, 16). The **blasphemous names** written on the beast's heads represent blasphemous claims to earthly, divine kingship by the beast in feeble imitation of Christ's true kingship (contrast 13:1 to 17:3 and 13:7-13 to 1:5; 17:14; 19:12-16).

2 Whereas in Dan. 7:3-8 the images of the lion, bear, leopard, and "terrifying" beast respectively represent four successive world empires, here these four images are all applied to the one beast: **And the beast which I saw was like a leopard, and his feet were like those of a bear, and his mouth like the mouth of a lion.** The combination of the four oppressive kingdoms of Daniel into one here does not merely signify the extreme power of first-century Rome but appears to symbolize also the temporal transcendency of the oppressive beast portrayed in v. 2. Just as the four beastly kingdoms in Daniel 7 spanned hundreds of years, so the empire dominant in the first century has latent within itself manifestations of other oppressive kingdoms that may be manifested in the future, as 17:10-11 shows. In the light of Daniel 7, the Roman Empire transcends many centuries and represents all world powers who oppress God's people until the culmination of history. The evil spirit behind Rome will also dominate other world powers which follow it, in the same way that in the OT, the sea beast symbolized not merely oppressing nations but the system of spiritual evil standing behind the nations and manifesting itself in successive world empires spanning hundreds of years (see on 12:3). Dan. 7:12 notes that when each of the first three world empires are defeated, their evil spiritual life will continue to exist in the next kingdom: "as for the rest of the beasts [the first three], their dominion was taken away, but an extension of life was granted to them." That the beast is described in v. 1 in exactly the same terms as the dragon (12:3), as **having ten horns and seven heads, and on his horns were ten diadems**, shows that its activity spans the same time period as that of the dragon, from OT history through to the return of Christ. The multifaceted character of the antichrist figure is confirmed by the Johannine epistles, where purely religious manifestations of its activity are present (1 John 2:18, 22; 4:4; 2 John 7).

The beast's ability (and more particularly that of the false prophet; see on vv. 11-18 below) to use religious institutions is evident from Rev. 2:9, where the persecution of the church by unbelieving Jews is called "blasphemy," the same word used elsewhere only of the beast and his followers (13:1, 5, 6; 16:9, 11, 21; 17:3). And, like the beast, the Jews there have Satan as their ultimate inspirer (they are "a synagogue of Satan," 2:9). The beast can express himself through subsequent religious institutions, whether or not they profess to be Christian institutions. The dragon authorizes this empire to act with his very own power: **And the dragon gave him his power and his throne and great authority**. This is a power which denies the true God and therefore perverts the original divine intention for the state (as in Rom. 13:1-7). Such rulers are described as beastly because they have fallen below the human standard of rule which God has ordained for them (cf. the examples of Nebuchadnezzar in Daniel 4 and Belshazzar in Daniel 5).

3 John now sees the beast with a wound on one of his heads: **And I saw one of his heads as if it had been slain, and his fatal wound was healed.** The wound comes from God, because the Greek word for "wound" *(plēgē)* is the word translated "plague" eleven times elsewhere in Revelation, always signifying something of divine origin. This wound on the beast's head is none other than that inflicted by Christ at His resurrection and is the fulfillment of Gen. 3:15: "He shall crush [or bruise] you on the head." Mention of the sword that struck the beast's head in Rev. 13:14 recalls the end-time prophecy of Isa. 27:1: "In that day the Lord will punish Leviathan [or sea monster] the fleeing serpent, with His fierce and great and mighty sword, even Leviathan [or sea monster] the twisted serpent; and He will kill the dragon who lives in the sea." The fact that Isa. 27:1 is also echoed in Rev. 12:3, 9 points to the conclusion that the death blow administered to the beast came through Christ's death and resurrection in initial fulfillment of the prophet's words. That one of the heads of the beast is depicted as **slain** because of Christ's death and resurrection is borne out by 12:5, 10-12, together with 1:5 and 5:9 (see on 12:10-12, where also other NT parallels are cited affirming that Christ's death and resurrection defeated the devil). The effects of this defeat are carried on by the faithfulness of Christ's followers (so 12:11, 17; Rom. 16:17-20).

One of the heads of the beast appeared **as slain** (not "as if it had been slain" as in the NASB text quoted above), but **his fatal wound was healed.** The use of **as** (Greek *hōs*), as elsewhere throughout the book, is part of John's visionary style in introducing something he has seen (cf. 4:6; 8:8; 9:7; 15:2; 19:6). It is his attempt to give an approximate description in earthly terms of what he saw in the heavenly vision. The wound was real and fatal, and yet it seems to have been healed, because the enemy is able to continue his activity. It is fatal because, from the resurrection on, Satan's power was fatally restricted and his days numbered. The temporary healing represents the fact that God allows the enemy to continue to use his agents through the three and a half year period until Christ's return, all the while safeguarding the spiritual security of His people. The phrase **as slain** is almost identical to that referring to the Lamb in 5:6, where Christ is described as "standing as slain" (not "standing as if slain," as in NASB). This alerts us to the fact that the beast is being set up as a Satanic counterfeit of Christ.

In 13:14, the beast's recovery is even referred to as a resurrection — though 17:8 will reveal that this is a "resurrection" which will end in eternal destruction. There is a difference between the Lamb's recovery and that of the beast. Whereas the Lamb really did overcome the defeat of death by resurrection, the beast's continued existence is not a reversal of his actual defeat, even though he continues to exist after being vanquished along with the dragon. He loses his authority to accuse the saints and has no authority except that allowed him by God. Nevertheless, the dragon and the beast deceptively cover up the fact that their authority has been removed. 17:8 likewise notes that the beast's apparent rising from death ("coming up out of the abyss") is only for the ultimate purpose that he should "go to destruction." Christ's defeat of the devil was like D-Day in the Second World War, and the subsequent existence of the devil (and his servant the beast) like the subsequent resistance of the German forces to the inevitable advance of the Allies. Like the turning point of D-day, the decisive outcome is now assured, even though the battle still rages.

Most commentators favor identifying the beast primarily with the Roman emperor Nero. However, the problem of narrowing the interpretation of v. 3 primarily to the fate and legend of Nero, who committed suicide in AD 68, is that the legend of Nero's death and resurrection does not fit precisely with either the historical facts or the descriptions in Revelation 13 and 17. Rumors spread after his death that Nero had not died and would stage a return. But the wound of Rev. 13:3, 12, 14 is inflicted by God or Christ, rather than self-inflicted. And Nero's death was not a blow to Rome — quite the opposite, as when he died he was an enemy to Rome and a fugitive. Furthermore, v. 4 says that the beast's revival resulted in his universal worship and authority, but the opposite would have been true with Nero, because he was considered a threat to the empire.

The key to a correct understanding of the beast's identity is in the fact there are so many parallels between the description of the beast in ch. 13 and that of Christ elsewhere in Revelation. Note the parallels between Christ and the beast:

both were slain and rise to new life (5:6 and 13:3),
both have followers with their names written on their foreheads (13:16 and 14:1),
both have horns (5:6 and 13:1),
both have authority over every "tribe, tongue, people, and nation" (5:9; 7:9 and 13:7; 17:12, 15),
both receive worldwide worship (5:8-14 and 13:4, 8), and
both have a final coming or manifestation, though one is to destruction and the other to eternal victory (17:7-18).

The beast's career is thus a kind of parody of Christ's death and resurrection, employed to show how the evil spirit behind the beast continues to operate (though within divinely imposed limits) in the period from Christ's resurrection until His return. The parallels show that the transtemporal beast is set up as the supreme enemy of Christ and His people. The figure behind this is the devil himself, as he repeatedly works through his chosen agents throughout history.

The significance of the parallels is that the chief opponent of Christ cannot be limited to one historical person or epoch. That is, just as the rule of Christ spans the whole church age, so the evil activities of His ultimate counterpart, the devil and his servants, span the same time. This analysis leaves open the possibility of an antichrist figure who comes at the very end of history and incarnates the devil in a greater way than ever before. Whether this consummate expression of evil will be manifested in an individual or an institution is hard to say. Probably, as throughout history, so at the end the individual tyrant is not to be distinguished from the kingdom or institution he represents (as in Dan. 7:17, 23).

Regarding the end of history, Rev. 17:7-18 also portrays the beast's career as a parody of Christ's, but this time the parody focuses on the final destinies of the two: whereas Christ's final coming results in the establishment of His kingdom, the final coming of the beast results in his decisive destruction (see on 17:8, 10-11). The healing of the beast's wound recorded here is thus a different event from the beast's re-emergence from the abyss and consequent destruction. In ch. 13, the beast's activity, together with that of its allied "ten kings," occurs during the time period of the church age ("forty-two months," 13:5; see on 11:2-3; 12:6), whereas in ch. 17 the activity of the beast lasts only "one hour" (probably equivalent to the "three and a half days" of 11:11).

The dragon is so convincing at camouflaging his defeat as apparent victory that **the whole earth was amazed and followed after the beast.** Those not protected by God's seal (7:1-4) give him allegiance.

4 The allegiance of the ungodly multitudes mentioned in v. 3 now expresses itself in worship of the dragon: **and they worshiped the dragon, because he gave his authority to the beast.** The phrase denoting this transferral of authority is based on Dan. 7:6, where authority is given to the third beast to rule over the earth and to persecute. The multitudes likewise worship the beast because of his purported incomparability. They proclaim in their worship, **"Who is like the beast, and who is able to wage war with him?"** Their words are a mockery and ironic use of similar words rightly used toward God in the OT (Exod. 8:10; 15:11; Pss. 35:10; 71:19; 86:8; 89:8; 113:5; Isa. 40:18; Mic. 7:18). In all of these OT texts, Yahweh's incomparability is contrasted polemically with false gods and idols.

5 The Danielic references to the beast and his reception of authority in vv. 1-4 are developed further in vv. 5-8. The point of the repeated Daniel allusions is to show that the fulfillment of the prophecy of Israel's oppression at the hands of a fiendish divine opponent commenced at Christ's death and resurrection and is continuing to be fulfilled in the persecution of the church. The reference to the beast expressing his authority through speech for a three and a half year period in v. 5 is a collective allusion to Dan. 7:6, 8, 11, 20, and 25. Much of the allusion is taken word for word from these texts in Daniel:

a blaspheming mouth: **And there was given to him a mouth speaking arrogant words and blasphemies** (cf. Dan. 7:6, 8, and 11 of OG and Theodotion),

an authorization clause: **it was given to him** twice in 13:5, and again in 13:7, and the similar phrase in Dan. 7:25, and

a decreed period of time during the end days (**forty-two months**), as in Dan. 7:25.

In fact, these three elements, taken together, are unique in the OT to Daniel. The Danielic time period has been clearly alluded to in the preceding context at 12:6, 14b, and earlier in 11:2-3. As shown in our examination of those verses (see also on vv. 2-3 above), this covers the period of time between Christ's death and resurrection and the end of history.

That God is the ultimate source of the beast's authority in these verses is implied by the *decreed time limit* of v. 5 and the *predestined number* of those who worship the beast in v. 8. Only God, not the devil, sets times and seasons. The devil would never want to limit his work against God's kingdom to a mere three and a half years, even if that is construed figuratively.

The beast's speech refers to three aspects of his activity. It alludes:

to his pride in exalting himself above God (cf. 13:3-4; Dan. 7:25; 8:10-11; 11:36),
to his deceptive powers (suggesting he is greater than God), and
to his blasphemy in defaming God's name.

His activity includes carrying out the dragon's will to "flood" even the church with deception.

6 Dan. 7:25 is referred to again here to describe the effect of the beast's authorization. Both texts speak of an eschatological fiend who speaks out against God: **And he opened his mouth in blasphemies against God, to blaspheme His name and His tabernacle, that is, those who dwell in heaven**. He equates himself with God (implicitly in vv. 4 and 6), and persecutes the saints, which is likewise the case in Dan. 8:10, 25; 11:36 (the time of "indignation" there includes persecution). Also included in his blaspheming are accusations or actions against Christians who have **His name** written upon them (3:12; 14:1; 22:4; cf. 7:3). The mention of **His tabernacle**, followed by the words **that is, those who dwell** (tabernacle) **in heaven** alludes respectively to the "holy place" in Dan. 8:11 and the heavenly "host" in Dan. 8:10, where the end-time tyrant causes some of the heavenly host and stars to fall to the earth and throws down the place of the prince's sanctuary (all this representing the suffering of God's people). The equation of the saints with the heavenly tabernacle is virtually the same as the equation already in 11:1-2 of true believers living on earth and dwelling in the invisible, indestructible sanctuary of God. Paul similarly views the whole church as seated in heaven (Eph. 2:6; Col. 3:1). The saints are oppressed because loyalty to their heavenly citizenship demands disobedience to their earthly citizenship. Yet the picture in 7:15 of the saints "tabernacling" in heaven, where the reference is to deceased believers, indicates that those who have died and are with the Lord are included in the number of **those who dwell in heaven**.

7a In v. 7a, the focus shifts back again to the prophecy of Daniel 7 (cf. Dan. 7:8, 11, 21) and the persecuting activities of the "horn" in order to show that the same activity of the beast is beginning its fulfillment. The phrase **to make war with the saints and to overcome them** is virtually identical to what is found in 11:7, both of which are based on Dan. 7:21. Daniel 7 predicts a final kingdom on earth which will persecute and defeat Israel. Afterward, the persecutors themselves will be judged, and the saints will inherit the kingdom of the world (so Dan. 7:22-27). John sees that the Daniel prophecy about Israel will be fulfilled in the world's persecution of the church in the latter days, which for him began with Christ's death and resurrection.

7b-8a The antagonistic activity of the beast affects all classes of people throughout the earth: **and authority over every tribe and people and tongue and nation was given to him.** In Daniel, the same language is thus used to describe both false (Dan. 3:7) and true (Dan. 7:14) worship. John may have noticed this and drawn an ironic implication from it. It may have been such a recognition which led him to apply the wording of Dan. 7:14 to the beast in order to show that the beast's conquering efforts are but an ironic parody of the "Son of man's" final triumph. Note similar ironic features comparing the beast and the Lamb in vv. 3 and 4 (on which see), as well as reference to the second beast as a "lamb with horns" (v. 11). The authority by which the beast overcomes the saints and wins universal worship, however, comes from the same source (ultimately God, as the authorization clause **was given** indicates) from which ultimately the Lamb will triumph over the beast, receive authority, and obtain universal adoration. Drawing the readers' attention to the context in Daniel 7 is intended to encourage them about the ultimate outcome of history and their own destiny. Though they suffer from oppression by the state, they will be the ultimate conquerors and will rule eternally with the Son of man. The fourfold formula for humanity in 13:7 has universal reference to all unredeemed people throughout the created earth, since it has such all-inclusive scope in Dan. 7:14. This universal geographical and temporal meaning is confirmed from the second part of v. 8, which says that these unbelieving multitudes were ordained not to have eternal life from before the creation of the whole world. The whole mass of unbelieving humanity living throughout the entire interadvent age is likely in mind here and not merely a part of it from one brief period of that age. This suggests further the trans-historical applicability of ch. 13.

8b All earth-dwellers will worship the beast, that is, **everyone**

whose name has not been written from the foundation of the world in the book of life of the Lamb who has been slain. Since the context of Daniel 7 has been in mind, it is not surprising that now the "book" or "books" of Dan. 7:10 and 12:1 (see also Ps. 69:28) should come into focus. The phrase "book of life" appears five times in Revelation outside 13:8 (3:5; 17:8; 20:12, 15; 21:27). The notion of predetermination is expressed by the phrase **from the foundation of the world** here and in 17:8. That saints were written in the book before history began is implied by the fact that the beast-worshipers are said not to have been so written. This implication that the names of saints have been written in **the book of life** occurs explicitly in 3:5 and 21:27 (cf. also 20:12, 15). This book stands in contrast to "the books" which record the sins of the ungodly (20:12-13). The notion of "a book of life" for the righteous and "books" of judgment for the wicked is based on the same dual idea in Daniel, respectively Dan. 12:1-2 (a book of redemption) and Dan. 7:10 (books in which sinful deeds of the ungodly are recorded). The phrase **of the Lamb who has been slain** may indicate that it is the Lamb who possesses the book or that the Lamb is the source of life associated with the book. Either way, He has sovereignty over who has life and who does not. This phrase, **the Lamb who has been slain**, is also a contrast with the similar description of the beast and the second beast in vv. 3 and 11. People reject Christ, the true **Lamb who has been slain**, because they follow the beast "having been slain" and the beast-like lamb of 13:11-17. Genuine believers have assurance that their souls can weather any Satanic storm because of the safety accorded by the Lamb's book. Because the book of life is unreservedly ascribed to Christ, the salvation of all, implicitly including OT saints, is represented as depending on the one redemptive act of Christ, **who has been slain** for the sins of His people.

Suggestions for Reflection on 12:18–13:8

On the beast as a parody of Christ and our response to civil government. These verses present the beast as a demonic counterpart to Christ. He draws his authority from the dragon, even as Christ draws His authority from the Father. He has been slain, as was Christ, and experienced an apparent resurrection. He exercises power on earth through human governments, opposing the rule of the ascended Christ and corrupting God's order for civil government as expressed in Rom. 13:1-7. How then are we to honor the command to obey civil government as laid out by Paul in those verses? Are governments universally corrupted by the beast, or is this an occasional phenomenon? Should

Christians seek to be involved in civil government or to affect it positively? How could the relation of Daniel and his three friends to the state in Daniel 1–6 help answer this question?

On God's granting authority to the beast. If, as the commentary suggests, God is the source of even the beast's authority, should this, as the commentary suggests, augment rather than diminish our concept of God's sovereignty? How do these verses bring comfort and assurance to the suffering church today? Have believers in the western world lost an understanding of what is expressed here because they have not had to endure persecution? Has this caused some western believers to see Revelation as having applicability only to the times immediately preceding Christ's return, when they do believe Christians will experience persecution?

Genuine believers are exhorted to discern true from false worship in order to persevere in their faith (13:9-10)

9 If anyone has an ear, let him hear. 10 If anyone is destined for captivity, to captivity he goes; if anyone kills with the sword, with the sword he must be killed. Here is the perseverance and the faith of the saints.

9 The scenario of vv. 1-8 is not something to occur only at some future time, but is happening in the midst of the seven churches. In the light of what has been narrated in vv. 1-8, John addresses the readers with the same exhortation with which he addressed them at the conclusion of each of the letters: **If anyone has an ear, let him hear**. As in Isaiah 6, the Synoptic Gospels (Matthew, Mark, and Luke) and the conclusions to the seven letters, the exhortation alludes to the fact that John's parabolic message will enlighten some while blinding others within the covenant community. Those not having ears will be further hardened by the parable (which in this context occurs in 13:1-8). But the command to "let him hear" is intended to jolt true believers caught up in the compromising complacency of the majority. Those shaken back into spiritual reality will perceive God's parabolic revelation in the book and discern the dangerous reality of the Satanic nature of the pagan institutions to which they may be tempted to accommodate.

10 The exhortation of v. 9 refers not only to the preceding verses, but also to the following decree: **If anyone is destined for captivity, to captivity he goes; if anyone kills with the sword** (or, better, **if anyone is**

to be killed with the sword), with the sword he must be killed. This is a paraphrase combining Jer. 15:2 and 43:11, which both say the same thing. Jeremiah prophesies to Israel that God has destined its people to go into "captivity" and suffer from the "sword." In Israel's case, this was a penalty for their unbelief and sin. But many texts from the major prophets affirm that a faithful remnant will also suffer the penalty of captivity, as Ezek. 14:12-23 especially makes clear. The text from Ezekiel has been used in 6:2-8 (on which see), with its original dual idea of punishing unbelievers and refining believers through suffering. The emphasis here, as in 6:2-8, 9-11, is more on the suffering of God's people than on the punishment of the wicked.

The exhortation in v. 9 was used repeatedly in the letters to encourage the readers not to compromise, and to bear up under the consequences of suffering for their faith (cf. 1:9; 2:10; 6:9; 11:7; 12:11; 17:6; 19:2; 20:4). Their spiritual insight should motivate them to "suffer according to the will of God" and to "entrust their souls to a faithful Creator in doing what is right" (1 Pet. 4:19). The concluding phrase, **Here is the perseverance and the faith of the saints**, confirms this interpretation. It links v. 10 with v. 7, where the last mention of "saints" occurred, and gives the proper response of believers to the warfare conducted against them by the beast, who makes war on them and overcomes them (see v. 7). Just as such perseverance meant that John was reigning in a "kingdom," yet in the midst of "tribulation" (1:9), so it meant the same for his readers. These things must happen, but believers must persevere in their faith and not give in. This conclusion is confirmed by noting that every use of "faith" or "faithful" in Revelation refers to the faith of Christ or the saints in the face of persecution (1:5; 2:10, 13, 19; 3:14; 14:12; 17:14).

Suggestions for Reflection on 13:9-10

On the perseverance of the saints. We think of the concept of the saints' perseverance as a theological truth related to the security of the believer's position in Christ. Yet this verse shows us that perseverance is walked out through times of testing, hardship, and even persecution. Do we sometimes fall into the trap of thinking of biblical doctrines as theoretical without realizing that every biblical truth must be made real in our lives? Some believers may ask God to spare them from testing, yet it is often testing that proves the genuineness of our faith and results in God being glorified: "that the proof of your faith, being more precious than gold which is perishable, even when tested by fire, may be found to result in praise and glory and honor at the revelation of Jesus Christ" (1 Pet. 1:7).

The state authorizes its political, religious, and economic allies as its agents to persecute the church and to deceive the ungodly (13:11-17)

11 And I saw another beast coming up out of the earth; and he had two horns
like a lamb, and he spoke as a dragon. 12 And he exercises all the authority of the
first beast in his presence. And he makes the earth and those who dwell in it to
worship the first beast, whose fatal wound was healed. 13 And he performs great
signs, so that he even makes fire come down out of heaven to the earth in the
presence of men. 14 And he deceives those who dwell on the earth because of
the signs which it was given him to perform in the presence of the beast, telling
those who dwell on the earth to make an image to the beast who had the wound
of the sword and has come to life. 15 And there was given to him to give breath to
the image of the beast, that the image of the beast might even speak and cause
as many as do not worship the image of the beast to be killed. 16 And he causes
all, the small and the great, and the rich and the poor, and the free men and the
slaves, to be given a mark on their right hand, or on their forehead, 17 and he
provides that no one should be able to buy or to sell, except the one who has the
mark, either the name of the beast, or the number of his name.

11 A new section begins, the third of seven in the larger vision series commencing at 12:1, marked by the phrase **And I saw.** Here John has another vision of a further beast: **And I saw another beast coming up out of the earth; and he had two horns like a lamb, and he spoke as a dragon.** Vv. 11-17 concern the same situation as vv. 1-8, but from the perspective of the state's ally, the second beast. As in v. 1, this vision also begins with the image of an ascending beast, which is a collective recollection of the beasts of Daniel 7, especially 7:17: "These great beasts . . . are four kings who will arise from the earth." As is generally accepted, this image is also a parody of the resurrected messianic Lamb of 5:6 and has an ironic relation with it. It, too, is a lamb with horns. But why two horns instead of the seven of the messianic Lamb in ch. 5? Perhaps one reason is to mimic the two witnesses, two lampstands, and two olive trees of 11:3-4. Yet the two horns also reflect the evil ruler of Daniel 8. Just as the first beast was described with attributes from the beasts of Daniel 7, so the description of the second beast as having **two horns like a lamb** is taken from Dan. 8:3: "a ram which had two horns" (similarly the opposing figure of Dan. 7:7 also "had ten horns").

Like the first beast, this beast speaks with the full authority of the devil: he was speaking **as a dragon.** This beast is later called "the false prophet" (16:13; 19:20; 20:10), suggesting that its role is primarily religious. A true prophet leads people to worship God, but the false prophet leads them to worship the state (and, by extension, the devil). False prophets and teachers have already infiltrated the churches (2:2, 6, 14-15, 20-24), even as Jesus prophesied (Matt. 7:15; 24:5, 11) and Paul warned (Acts 20:28-29). That manifestations of the beastly prophet occur within the church is also suggested by the OT, where false prophecy almost always takes place within the covenant community. The image of a wolf in lamb's clothing suggests a traitor within the fold of the church. Though the beast professes to represent the truth and appears harmless as a lamb, his inner Satanic nature is revealed through his speaking with the authority of the dragon. His speaking **as a dragon** reflects the alluring, deceptive speech of Satan, the dragon, which led to the sin of Adam and Eve (cf. 12:9). Therefore, this imagery and background suggest deception within the covenant community itself. Whereas the first beast speaks loudly and defiantly against God, the second beast makes the first beast's claims sound plausible and persuasive. False teachers within the church are encouraging compromise with the culture's idolatrous institutions.

12 The second beast is identified with and exercises the authority of the first beast, which is emphasized by saying that **he exercises all the authority of the first beast in his presence**. The second beast uses the first beast's authority for the purpose of making **the earth and those who dwell in it to worship the first beast, whose fatal wound was healed.**

13 The idea of counterfeit imitation is carried on in v. 13. The religious character of the second beast becomes clearer here. First, it is said that **he performs great signs.** This makes him a Satanic counterfeit of the true prophet Moses, who also performed signs (Exod. 4:17, 30; 10:2). Then it is said that **he even makes fire come down out of heaven to the earth in the presence of men**, making him a counterfeit of the true prophet Elijah, who did likewise (1 Kgs. 18:38-39; 2 Kgs. 1:10-14). The allusions to Moses and Elijah cannot be accidental, given the similar allusion to them in regard to the two witnesses in 11:3-12, who, taken together, represent the church (cf. Luke 9:54). 11:5 portrays "fire proceeding out of the mouth" of the two witnesses. There the fire indicates the speaking of God's word that convicts and judges sinners (cf. also fire consuming the saints' enemies in 20:9b). Therefore the fire represents the speaking of God's true word which judges sinners, and here the beast poses as a spokesman for truth but is a false prophet and false teacher. This is part of what Christ prophesied in Matt. 24:24: "False Christs and false prophets will arise and will show great signs and wonders, so as to mislead, if possible, even the elect" (so likewise Matt. 7:15; 24:5, 11; 2 Thess. 2:9; 2 Pet. 2:1-3). The second beast is a counterfeit of the church and the Spirit who empowers and indwells it. That an inside threat by a "false apostle" is alluded to (perhaps developing the "false apostles" of 2:2) is apparent from noticing that the second beast's authority is modeled on the authoritative credentials of Christ's apostles:

> he is a successor to his master in both ministry and authority (Acts 1:1-11; Rev. 13:12a),
> the attempt to persuade others to worship the master is inextricably linked to his resurrection (Acts 2:22-41; Rev. 13:12b, 14b), and
> miraculous "signs" are performed as concrete manifestations of authority (Acts 2:43; 5:12; 15:12; Rev. 13:13).

Daniel warns (11:30-39) that a latter-day deceiver will infiltrate the church and turn people away from God. When purported Christian teachers take their primary cues from the surrounding culture instead of from God's word, they corrupt the covenant community spiritually by encouraging it to live by norms and a faith that ultimately oppose the reign of God and Christ.

14 Why are the two beasts described with so many traits borrowed from those of OT prophets and of God and in terms strikingly similar to the descriptions of God, the Lamb, and Christians elsewhere in the Apocalypse? The reason is that they attempt to validate their divine authority in a similar manner to true prophets (see the description in 2 Cor. 11:13-15). This is explicitly expressed by the phrase: **And he deceives those who dwell on the earth because of the signs which it was given him to perform in the presence of the beast.** True prophets receive their inspiration and commissions as they stand before the presence of the Lord (11:4, on which see). Likewise, the false prophet receives his inspiration and commission as he acts **in the presence of the beast.** God's true agents, by the power of the Spirit, perform signs to bring glory to God, whereas these demonic signs convince the "earth-dwellers" of the authority not of God but of the beast.

The deception causes them to acquiesce to his command **to make an image to the beast.** This command anticipates the explicit reference to the image of Daniel 3 in v. 15. The command to perform idolatry alludes partly to the pressure placed on the populace and the churches in Asia Minor to give homage to the image of Caesar as a divine being. By the end of the first century all the cities addressed in the letters had temples dedicated to the deity of Caesar. In the light of the influence from Daniel throughout this chapter, the beast who deceives here may be an echo of the end-time king of Daniel who "causes deceit to succeed by his influence" (Dan. 8:25), and "by smooth words [turns] to godlessness those who act wickedly" (Dan. 11:32). The concluding description of the beast as he **who had the wound of the sword and has come to life** is an expanded repetition of the similar preceding descriptions of the beast as having been healed from his fatal wound (13:3, 12).

15 Again, the oft-repeated "authorization" concept of Dan. 7:6 appears ("and dominion was given to it," which is interpreted in the Greek OT as "speech was given to him"): **And there was given to him to give breath to the image of the beast, that the image of the beast might even speak.** This may include reference to magical tricks and similar phenomena attested among the superstitious, and even at the courts of Roman emperors, but the "signs" may include actual demonic activity, since demons were behind the idols. The expression is a metaphorical way of affirming that the second beast was persuasive in demonstrating that the image of the first beast (which in the first century context could apply to Caesar) represented the true deity, who really stands behind the image and makes decrees. This again points to the identity of the second beast as a counterfeit of the church and especially of the Spirit who empowers it ("breath" being a biblical metaphor for the Spirit; cf. Ezek. 37:9-14). Because of the trans-temporal nature of ch. 13 seen so far, the **image** transcends narrow reference only to an idol of Caesar and includes any substitute for the truth of God in any age. The description of the beast, who causes **as many as do not worship the image of the beast to be killed**, is inspired by Nebuchadnezzar's command in Daniel 3 that all should worship his image or be killed. The reference to the classes of people under the beast's control in v. 16 is also an echo of the diverse groups required to worship Nebuchadnezzar's image in Dan. 3:2-7. In the light of the exhortation in 13:9-10, the implication is that Christians were to persevere as did Daniel's friends in the fire; and, as in Daniel 3 but on an escalated scale, the reward for endurance will be deliverance from the eternal torment of fire and exaltation with Christ.

The background to this verse may lie in the establishment of an emperor cult at Ephesus, marked by the erection of a colossal statue to Emperor Domitian. Citizens of towns in Asia Minor were even pressured to offer sacrifices on altars outside their own houses as festive processions passed by. Such a major event at Ephesus, and others like it elsewhere on varying scales, may explain also why John himself alludes in this chapter to the narrative in Daniel 3 about Shadrach, Meshach, and Abednego's refusal to bow down to the huge statue, which was an image representing Nebuchadnezzar (especially according to the OG of Dan. 3:12, 18). Possibly this event in Ephesus and the persecution it aroused inspired the early church to view Daniel's three friends as the model for martyrs and for persecuted Christians and to see the Babylonian king's image as prototypical of the Roman emperor's image. In fact, there is early-second-century evidence for this in the catacombs of Rome, as well as evidence from the third and fourth centuries.

Popular pressure on Christians to show allegiance to Rome at various festive occasions would be understandable in this context. And when Christians would not participate, it is also understandable that this aroused animosity on the part of the general populace. It is not necessarily the case that all those refusing to worship the image will be killed, as John does not assert this unequivocally. Many (presumably Jews) refused to worship Nebuchadnezzar's image, but only the three young men were thrown into the furnace. Degrees of persecution varied from city to city. Surely much persecution in John's day was due to local enthusiasm for the imperial cult, which was probably not felt in every town of Asia Minor. Nevertheless, suffering would definitely be involved, and death for some, as had already happened with Antipas (2:13) and doubtless others as well (as implied in 6:9, 11; 12:11; 20:4, though the idea of death is figurative in these texts). The situation in the Asia Minor churches is generally relevant for all churches until the return of Christ, just as in the letters the historical situation of one church was generally relevant for the other six (the Spirit speaks to the "churches" in each case). The trans-historical nature of ch. 13 is a basis for universalizing the application of vv. 15-17 to all times.

16-17 The demand that everyone, **the small and the great, and the rich and the poor, and the free men and the slaves**, receive **a mark on their right hand, or on their forehead** could be an allusion to the ancient practice of branding or tattooing disobedient slaves, soldiers, and loyal devotees to gods of various religions. If the association with slaves is in mind, then the beast's worshipers are seen as his property; if soldiers or religious devotees are in view, the worshipers are seen as the beast's faithful followers. Here, the mark is clearly figurative for the way in which the state keeps check on whether people are submitting to compulsory idol worship. Those not submitting to receiving the mark are unable **to buy or to sell**. This is a reference back to 2:9 and 6:5-6 (on which see), where economic measures are directed against Christians. The **mark** (Greek *charagma*) was used for the emperor's seal on business contracts and for the impress of the Roman ruler's head on coins. If this background is in mind, then it enforces the metaphorical idea that the mark in Revelation 13 alludes to the state's political and economic "stamp of approval," given only to those who go along with its religious demands. The mark **on their forehead**, which is **the name of the beast, or the number of his name**, is the parody of and the opposite to the "seal" in 7:3-8, which is the divine name written on the foreheads of true believers (14:1; so likewise 22:4; cf. 3:12). Since the seal or name on the true believer is invisible, so is the mark on the unbeliever. That the two are of a parallel spiritual nature and intended to be compared is evident from the immediately following mention of the names of God and Christ written on the foreheads of the saints (14:1). Believers are protected by the power of Christ's name, which is His presence with them. They may suffer and even die, yet they will receive the ultimate reward of eternal life (20:4, on which see). Unbelievers may receive temporary prosperity, but will be punished ultimately with eternal death (see on 14:9-11). The mark may also connote that the followers of Christ and the beast both are stamped with the "image" (= character) of their respective leader.

That the mark of the name is figurative and not literal is also evident from the picture of the beast, who has written on his heads "blasphemous names," which figuratively connote false claims to earthly, divine kingship (see on 13:1). Likewise, the point of saying that the worshipers of the beast have his name written on their heads is to underscore the fact that they pay homage to his blasphemous claims to divine kingship. In the OT, God told Israel that the Torah was to "serve as a sign to you on your hand, and as a reminder on your forehead" in order to remind them continually of their commitment and loyalty to God (Exod. 13:9). The NT equivalent is the invisible seal or name of God (see on 7:2-3). The "forehead" represents ideological commitment and the "hand" the practical outworking of that commitment. Likewise, as a travesty of the signs of membership in the OT community of faith, the beast's marks on the foreheads and the hands of the worshipers refer to their loyal, consistent, and wholehearted commitment to him.

The second beast, though generally to be identified with the first, is not identical. Vv. 11-17 show that the expression of the beast in John's time included the political, religious, and economic institutions of the culture, all of which were connected with emperor worship, thus giving the second beast a primarily religious focus and identifying him as a counterfeit to the church and especially the Spirit who empowers it. Even the patron deities of the trade guilds were worshiped in association with the imperial cult (see on 2:9-21). There were few facets of social interaction in which Christians could escape pressures of idolatry.

Suggestions for Reflection on 13:11-17

On guarding against false teachers. According to the commentary, these verses express an assumption that false teachers will infiltrate the church. How can such a thing happen? What are the ways we can guard against it? In an age where truth is presented to us via the internet from teachers we rarely know personally, are we sufficiently cautious and discerning in how we receive this teaching? How do we apply Paul's exhortation to Timothy: "You, however, continue in the things you have learned and become convinced of, knowing from whom you have learned them" (2 Tim. 3:14)?

Genuine believers are exhorted to discern true from false worship in order to persevere in the faith (13:18)

18 Here is wisdom. Let him who has understanding calculate the number of the beast, for the number is that of a man; and his number is six hundred and sixty-six.

18 V. 18 is one of the most debated verses in the entire book because of widespread disagreement over the identification and meaning of the number 666. The most common line of interpretation is that of gematria. In the ancient world, letters of the alphabet substituted for numerals (our numerical system derives from later Arabic mathematicians). Hence, each letter stood for a number. The problem is that no clear identification can be made linking 666 with any particular name. Attempts have been made to alter spellings and incorporate titles to try to make a multitude of names fit, but nothing conclusive has emerged from this. Most commonly, the number has been identified with Nero, on the basis of a Hebrew transliteration of the title "Nero Caesar." However, this flounders on confusion concerning the exact Hebrew spelling of "Caesar" and does not fit the fact that John's readers were largely Greek-speaking, and Nero had many titles other than "Caesar." Additionally, if John were using gematria, he would have alerted his readers by saying something like "the number in Hebrew (or Greek) is . . . ," as he uses the phrases "in Hebrew" or "in Greek" in 9:11 and 16:16 when he wants to draw the readers' attention to the significance of the language. Attempts have been made unsuccessfully to identify the number with other Roman emperors or combinations of emperors. According to one study, over one hundred names were proposed in Britain between 1560 and 1830. In the past century the names of Kaiser and Hitler, among others, were also calculated to equal 666.

Through any interpreter's creative ingenuity, the number can be worked out on the basis of Greek, Hebrew, or Latin to identify hundreds of possible ancient and modern candidates. There are so many proposals because it is easy to turn a name into a number, but complicated to deduce the right name from a number. Salmon formulated three "rules" which commentators have used for making any desired name equal 666: "First, if the proper name by itself will not yield it, add a title; secondly, if the sum cannot be found in Greek, try Hebrew, or even Latin; thirdly, do not be too particular about the spelling. . . . We cannot infer much from the fact that a key fits the lock if it is a lock in which almost any key will turn" (G. Salmon, *An Historical Introduction to the Study of the Books of the New Testament* [London: Murray, 1904], 230-31).

All attempts to identify the number with the literal calculation of some individual's name encounter difficulty because of the metaphorical manner in which language and numbers are used in the book. If the number were intended to be identified with some ruler by means of such calculation, it would be a rare exception from the way numbers are employed elsewhere in the book (e.g., the twenty-four elders, the seven seals, the 144,000, three and a half years, the two witnesses, seven heads, and ten horns). There is no evidence of any other number in the book being used in such a way. All the numbers have figurative significance and symbolize some spiritual reality. None involve any kind of literal gematria calculation. This position is supported from the immediately following vision in 14:1 of saints with Christ's and God's name "written on their foreheads." The direct placement of this verse shows a parallel contrast is meant between the beast's name (= *his number*) and the Lord's name. If the Lord's name refers to a purely spiritual reality, which it does, then so does the former! This is true also of the beast's number, since it is synonymous with his name.

In addition, the word **number** (Greek *arithmos*) is always used figuratively in Revelation to connote an uncountable multitude (5:11; 7:4 [144,000 standing symbolically for all the saved], 9 [in verbal form]; 9:16

[2×]; 20:8). Neither is the number meant to be calculated here. The number seven refers to completeness and is repeated throughout the book. However, 666 appears only here. This suggests that the triple sixes are intended as a contrast with the divine sevens throughout the book and signify incompleteness and imperfection. The sixth seal, the sixth trumpet, and the sixth bowl depict God's judgment on the followers of the beast. The seventh trumpet, by contrast, portrays the eternal kingdom of Christ, though it also includes the final judgment. The seventh seal and bowl still depict a judgment, but one which, by implication and in the broader contexts of these two passages, eventuates in the establishment of the kingdom.

Furthermore, if the number of 144,000 saints in the following verse has the figurative force of signifying the complete number of God's people (see on 14:1), then the intentional contrast with the number 666 in the preceding verse would refer to the beast and his people as inherently incomplete. The number three in the Bible signifies completeness as, for example, is expressed by the completeness of the Godhead in 1:4-5, which is parodied by the dragon, beast, and false prophet here in ch. 13 and in 16:13. Therefore, 666, the repetition of six three times, indicates what might be called the "completeness of sinful incompleteness" found in the beast. The beast epitomizes imperfection, while appearing to achieve divine perfection. Three sixes are a parody of the divine Trinity of three sevens. Sometimes the number seven is appropriate to apply to the devil or beast in order to emphasize their thoroughgoing evil nature, severe persecution, and universal reign of oppression (e.g., 12:3; 13:1; 17:3, 9-11). The reason for using sixes instead of seven to describe the beast here is the repeated emphasis in vv. 3-14 on the beast as a counterfeit Christ and the second beast as a counterfeit prophet. When believers successfully resist the beast's deception, they avoid being identified with the essence of his name, which is imperfection personified, because to be identified with someone's name is equivalent to partaking of that person's character (see on 2:17).

V. 18 begins with an exhortation to believers not to be taken in by falsehood because Christ has given them ability to withstand it. This response is the main point of vv. 11-18: saints are exhorted to have spiritual **wisdom** and **understanding** to see through the deceptive and imperfect nature of the beast as narrated in vv. 11-17. The concluding exhortation is parallel to the exhortation concluding vv. 1-9. The exhortation of v. 18 has the identical meaning, except that the metaphor of an intellect able to calculate is used instead of the ear metaphor. If the exhortation to exercise intellect by calculating is taken literally, then the exhortation to "have ears to hear" must absurdly be taken in literal fashion to refer to hearing with physical ears.

This discussion so far points to understanding the number of the beast collectively, rather than only as a reference to an individual antichrist figure. This is suggested further by the phrase **for the number is that of a man**, which could be translated individually as, "for it is a number of a specific person" or better generically as "for it is a number of humanity." The word "man" (Greek *anthrōpos*) is often generic when it occurs without an article as here and in 21:17, where the "measurement of a man" (the literal Greek phrase) means a "human measurement." Likewise, the omission of the definite article ("a man," as opposed to "the man") in 13:18 suggests the general idea of humanity, not some special individual who can be discerned only through an esoteric manner of calculation. It is a number common to fallen humanity. This generic notion is consistent with 13:1, which affirms that the beast has its earthly origin in the sea of fallen humanity (for the latter idea see also on 17:15). The beast is the supreme representative of unregenerate humanity, separated from God and unable to achieve divine likeness, but always trying. Humanity was created on the sixth day, but without the seventh day of God's own rest, which Adam and Eve were designed to fulfill, they would have been imperfect and incomplete. The triple six emphasizes that the beast and his followers fall short of God's creative purposes for humanity.

The admonition **here is wisdom** teaches that believers are to beware of compromise, not just with a historical individual such as Nero but with all the facets of the state throughout the course of history, insofar as it colludes with the religious, economic, and social aspects of the idolatrous culture, all of which epitomize fallen humanity. **Wisdom** is best seen in the light of the words "wise insight" and "understanding" used in Dan. 11:33 and 12:10. Here, as there, the saints are to have spiritual perception to comprehend the latter-day tribulation brought about by an evil kingly figure who deceives others into acknowledging his sovereignty. The similar admonition in 17:9 ("Here is the mind which has wisdom. The seven heads are seven mountains on which the woman sits") also involves interpretation of a number figuratively (see on 17:9). John is exhorting saints to spiritual and moral discernment, not intellectual ability to solve a complex mathematical problem, which unbelievers as well as spiritual Christians are mentally capable of solving. Christians must be aware that the spirit of the antichrist can express itself in the most unexpected places, even in the church (so 1 John 2:18, 22; 4:1-3; 2 John 7). The prophecy of Dan. 11:30-39 already warned that apostates from the covenant community would be allies of the ungodly state and infiltrate the believing community. If John's readers have spiritual perception, then they will remain faithful and "come off victorious from the beast and from his image and from the number of his name" (15:2).

Suggestions for Reflection on 13:18

On discerning the identity and activity of the enemy. The commentary suggests that wisdom and understanding be directed not toward calculating literal numbers in order to identify a particular person, but instead toward developing discernment in relation to all the ways the enemy, as a demonic parody of the Trinity, opposes and infiltrates the church throughout its history. How is this related to one's interpretation of "666"? Is it possible, in the midst of a fixation on identifying demonic personalities in our own day, that we might miss the actual, subtler work the enemy is engaged in even within the church? Would you agree with the commentary's view that Revelation gives warnings against the activity of the enemy in every generation, not just his activity in the time immediately preceding Christ's return? If that is the case, what implications does this have for the way we understand and apply this aspect of Revelation in our lives?

Concluding comments on chapter 13

Revelation 13 has been influenced by a recurring pattern in Daniel 7:

> an agent steps forward,
> power is given over to the agent (he is "authorized"), and
> this giving over of power has an effect.

For example, the "Son of man"

> steps forward to God's throne (Dan. 7:13) and
> is given authority (v. 14a),
> the effect of which is seen in the serving of "all the peoples, nations and men of every language" (v. 14b) and his possession of an eternal kingdom (v. 14c).

The same threefold pattern is found in the vision of the beasts in Dan. 7:3-6. The first element of the pattern, the stepping forward, is to be seen in the rising from the sea of all the beasts (7:4a, 5a, 6). Secondly, in each case, something is given over to the beasts. The authorization of the beasts in Dan. 7:4b, 6c is designated with the same terminology employed for the Son of man's authorization. The third part of the threefold pattern is not clearly expressed in the case of the first three beasts, but it is implied that they make use of the authority which they receive. However, the effect of the fourth beast's reception of authority is explained in detail. While there are differences between the portrayal of the beasts and that of the Son of man, the authorization schemes of both are essentially the same. This points to an intention of parody or irony in the book of Daniel itself. That the threefold authorization scheme of Daniel 7 prevails throughout Revelation 13 supports our previous conclusion that ch. 13 has been shaped primarily according to Daniel 7. In the light of this, the combination of an authorization clause with the idea of the beast's universal worship in vv. 12, 14, and 15 may be a development of the ironic use (apparently contrary to the original meaning) of Dan. 7:14 in Rev. 13:7b-8a. In view of this, the combined concepts of Satanic authorization and the universal worship of Satanic figures is best seen through this ironic understanding of Daniel.

As past commentators have also observed, the dragon, the sea-beast, and the land-beast in Revelation 13 form a trinity competing with the Father, Son, and Holy Spirit. As the Son receives authority from the Father (2:27; 3:21), so the beast receives authority from the dragon (13:4). The beast has crowns (13:1), as does Christ (19:12), and appears as slain and is resurrected (13:3, 14), as does Christ (1:18; 5:6). As the Son of man steps forward and receives authority from God by which all peoples and nations serve Him (Dan. 7:13-14), so the beast steps forward, is given authority from the dragon, by which the whole world serves him (13:1-3). As the Spirit represents the breath of God (the meaning of the Hebrew word *ruaḥ*, Ezek. 37:9-14), so the false prophet gives breath to the statue of the beast (Rev. 13:15). As the Spirit glorifies the Son (John 16:14), so the false prophet glorifies the beast (Rev. 13:12-15). The parody of the Trinity is also hinted at by the triple six in imitation of but short of 777 for the divine Trinity. The point of the parody in Daniel and especially in Revelation is that, though the Satanic beasts appear successfully to feign the truth in their attempts to deceive, they remain ever evil and never achieve the divine character they are mimicking.

John views the apostasy, deception, and persecution prophesied by

Daniel 7–12 as beginning to occur in his own day. As he informs Christians of this, they should be all the more watchful of deception. They should understand that God is the One who ultimately sends the beasts of deception in order to test the genuineness of their faith and to purify it (as we have argued in regard to 6:2, 8). Likewise, in the history of Israel God "tested" Israel's love for him by sending false prophets to give "a sign or a wonder . . . saying, 'Let us go after other gods' " (Deut. 13:1-3; cf. Deut. 13:6-8; Rev. 13:13-14).

God accomplishes His glory through rewarding believers and punishing the beast and his followers at the end of history (14:1–15:4)

Ch. 14 marks the end of another cycle of visions. This cycle began in ch. 12 with the anticipation of Christ's birth, and ends here with the final judgment. As we have seen, the section is best divided by tracing the repeated introductory vision formulas "and I saw" or "and behold." When this is done, seven sections, visions, or "signs" can be observed, as listed in the introductory comments to ch. 12.

The majority of chs. 12–13 concerned the persecution of believers by the forces of unbelief led by Satan and his two beastly allies. These allies deceive multitudes into following them. Now ch. 14, together with 15:2-4, show the final reward of the persecuted faithful and the final punishment of the beast and those who follow him. The segment ends with the saints' victory over the beast and the praise of God's glory (15:2-4). God is glorified because He is the One who has judged the beast and enabled the saints to defeat him. Therefore, everything narrated in the segment of chs. 12:1–15:4 is to be seen as moving toward the end result of the glory of God. The same design has been observed in chs. 4–5, the seal judgments, and the trumpet judgments. It is best to view 14:1–15:4 as another prophetic narration of the actual, future final judgment and reward (as in 6:12-17 and 11:15-19).

God and Christ's presence with believers secures their ultimate identification with the Lamb, their redemption, and their persevering righteousness (14:1-5)

1 And I looked, and behold, the Lamb was standing on Mount Zion, and with
Him one hundred and forty-four thousand, having His name and the name of
His Father written on their foreheads. 2 And I heard a voice from heaven, like the

sound of many waters and like the sound of loud thunder, and the voice which I heard was like the sound of harpists playing on their harps. [3] And they sang a new song before the throne and before the four living creatures and the elders; and no one could learn the song except the one hundred and forty-four thousand who had been purchased from the earth. [4] These are the ones who have not been defiled with women, for they have kept themselves chaste. These are the ones who follow the Lamb wherever He goes. These have been purchased from among men as first fruits to God and to the Lamb. [5] And no lie was found in their mouth; they are blameless.

1 **And I looked** marks the beginning of the fourth visionary segment of the major vision section commencing at 12:1. The immediate juxtaposition of the Lamb in 14:1 to the beasts of ch. 13 serves as a contrast. The point of the contrast is to emphasize that Jesus is the true Lamb to whom allegiance is to be given in contrast to the pseudo-lamb of 13:11 and the first beast. He is seen **standing on Mount Zion. Zion**, the word used one hundred and fifty-five times in the OT to refer to the true city of God, can refer to God's dwelling in the temple or be a symbol for His people, but usually refers to the eternal city God will rule over at the end of history. In the last days God will install His Messiah or king on this hill: "But as for me, I have installed My King upon Zion, My holy mountain. I will surely tell of the decree of the Lord: He said to Me, 'Thou art my Son, today I have begotten Thee'" (Ps. 2:6-7). The fuller name **Mount Zion**, in distinction to "Zion" by itself, occurs only nineteen times in the OT, at least nine of which allude to a remnant being saved, in connection with either God's name or God's sovereign rule and sometimes both (2 Kgs. 19:31; Isa. 4:5; 10:12; 37:30-32; Joel 2:32, etc.).

Against this OT background, **Mount Zion** in Rev. 14:1 is to be seen as the end-time city where God dwells with and provides security for the remnant who have been bought out from the earth. Interestingly, elsewhere in the NT, OT prophecies of Yahweh's salvation of Israel at Mount Zion are viewed as having begun fulfillment during the church age (Acts 2:16-21; 13:33; Heb. 1:1-5; Rev. 2:26-27; 12:5). According to Acts 13:33, this promise has already been fulfilled in Christ, so that in one sense Christ is already installed on Mount Zion and reigning over His people. That the same notion of latter-day inaugurated fulfillment is conveyed in Rev. 14:1 is supported by the observation that vv. 1-5 present a contrast to the beast and his worshipers in ch. 13, who dwell on earth during the same period of the church age. Accordingly, Zion could be the ideal heavenly city to which saints aspire during the course of the church age (Gal. 4:25-27; Heb. 12:22-23). In this respect, deceased and glorified saints who have attained standing in that city may be included in the vision. This is supported by the fact that the only other times in the book when the Lamb is seen, he is always in heaven (7:9-14 portrays the Lamb in heaven with the redeemed multitudes). "Zion" thus can speak of God's presence in the church age, though its ultimate fulfillment is yet to come. This is consistent with 7:9-17, since that vision blends past, present, and future (see on 7:16-17).

It is beyond coincidence that a "new name" is repeatedly associated with eschatological Zion. The city is to be given various new names (Isa. 62:2; 65:15 LXX; cf. 56:5), all of which express the new nature of the restored city, for example, "My delight is in her" (62:4), "a city not forsaken" (v. 12), "throne of the Lord" (Jer. 3:17), "The Lord is our righteousness" (Jer. 33:16), and "The Lord is there" (Ezek. 48:35). This OT background suggests that the divine name written on believers (**having His name and the name of His Father written on their foreheads**) is a figurative way of speaking of God's presence with His people, which protects them. This is confirmed by the same conclusion reached earlier with regard to the new name (see on 2:17) and the seal (7:2-3). This is clarified further by 22:4: "they shall see His face, and His name shall be on their foreheads" (cf. 21:3). Likewise, in 3:12 Christ emphasizes the nuance of security by saying that He will write upon the overcomer "the name of My God, and the name of the city of My God . . . and My new name," and metaphorically equates this with making the "overcomer" an immovable "pillar in the temple of My God."

Since Zion was also where God sat enthroned in the temple of Israel, the Lamb's position on Zion shows that He is the only true claimant to the throne of the cosmos. The mention of **His Father**, together with mention of the Lamb only a few phrases later, further confirms Christ as the only legitimate heir to the throne at Zion in an "already and not yet" fulfillment of Ps. 2:6-9. Acts 13:32-35; Heb. 1:2-5; and Rev. 2:26-28 and 12:5 apply the Psalm 2 text to Christ's resurrection and subsequent reign.

The **one hundred and forty-four thousand** pictured with Christ here on Mount Zion are the same as those sealed in 7:4 — the saints of all ages. The name of Christ and of the Father are placed in opposition to the "name of the beast," which is written on the foreheads of unbelievers (13:16-17). The number — the twelve tribes and the twelve apostles, representing the church, multiplied by one thousand as symbolic of completeness — connotes the full number of God's true people throughout the ages who are viewed as true Israelites and is in antithesis to the beast's followers with

666 on their foreheads, which connotes their incompleteness in achieving the divine design for humanity. 22:3-4 suggests that those having His name "on their foreheads" represent the entire community of the redeemed from throughout history (the "bondservants" of 22:3). The name of Christ and God inscribed on Christians' foreheads is equivalent to the seal placed on the foreheads of the 144,000 in 7:1-8. The equation of the seal with the divine name is confirmed by recognizing that the "mark" (= the seal) of the beast on the forehead of unbelievers in 13:17 is identified as "the name of the beast," and in 14:9-11 "a mark on his [the beast-worshiper's] forehead" is also called "the mark of his [the beast's] name." And as we have seen in 2:17, identification with the divine name actually begins when Christ reveals Himself to people and they confess His name. When this occurs, it means that they have a new spiritual status and have been imparted with power not to deny His name (3:8-10), and thus to persevere through the latter-day tribulation (cf. 3:8-10; 2:13a). Hence, the seal empowers the 144,000 to perform the role of witness intended for true Israel (e.g., Isa. 42:6-7; 49:6; 51:4-8). Therefore, the divine name and the seal are marks of genuine membership in the community of the redeemed, without which entry into the eternal Zion is impossible. Therefore, the entire community of the redeemed, not part, is pictured here.

2-3 The 144,000 praise God with a voice **like the sound of harpists playing on their harps** and sing **a new song**. The images of harpists and a heavenly host singing a new song occur elsewhere in the book only in 5:8-10 and 15:2-4, which both emphasize the praise of the saints because of their victory, ch. 5 stressing victory over sin and ch. 15 underscoring victory over the beast. The imagery of 14:2-3, therefore, portrays redeemed saints praising God for this victory. Therefore, what John now hears in v. 2 interprets what he saw in v. 1 (for the pattern of sayings interpreting visions and vice-versa see on 5:5ff.; 12:10). What was seen in the OT and Jewish background of the latter-day Mount Zion in v. 1 is now expressed. Mount Zion, as in Ps. 2:6-12, is where the redeemed remnant from throughout the world have found divine refuge and final victory. In the OT the "new song" was always an expression of praise for God's victory over the enemy, which sometimes included thanksgiving for God's work of creation (cf. Pss. 33:3; 40:3; 96:1; 98:1; 144:9; 149:1; Isa. 42:10). Now the "new song" is sung again, but on an escalated scale and for the last time, "last" understood as carrying on into eternity. This means that vv. 1-5 focus not only on an ideal description of the church throughout the ages but also on the end of the age, when at last the church has been fully redeemed.

The loud sound of the singing is compared to **the sound of many waters** and **the sound of loud thunder**. The nearly identical expression occurs in 19:6, where it refers to the victorious reign of God as a result of judging the "great harlot" (19:2). The chorus is so loud because it originates from the "great multitude which no one could count, from every nation and all tribes and peoples and tongues" (7:9). These are the same ones whom Christ purchased (see 5:9). The voices are so loud because they come from such a multitudinous host, not a mere literal 144,000 but the full number of the redeemed of all ages. Just as only those redeemed by Christ can know the "new name" of God which they possess (2:17), so **no one could learn the song except the one hundred and forty-four thousand who had been purchased from the earth**. The reference to the **voice from heaven** speaks of the dimension from which revelation comes and could also be another reference to Mount Zion (v. 1) or to the heavenly Jerusalem in its pre-consummate as well as its consummated form (as in 21:2, 10ff.). Thus, there is a blurring of these two temporal stages of the heavenly Zion or Jerusalem.

4a In vv. 4-5, a description of the redeemed is given. First, they are **the ones who have not been defiled with women, for they have kept themselves chaste** (literally "male virgins"). The symbolism of v. 4 could well be based on the background of Israelite soldiers being required to preserve ceremonial purity before battle (e.g., Deut. 23:9-10; 1 Sam. 21:5; 2 Sam. 11:8-11; 1QM VII.3-6). Richard Bauckham develops this idea, seeing a figurative presentation of a remnant of saints fighting an ironic holy war, "ironic" in that the power inherent in Christian warfare lies in self-sacrifice in imitation of the Lamb (*The Climax of Prophecy: Studies in the Book of Revelation* [Edinburgh: Clark, 1993], 229-32). While possible, this does not account for the dominating metaphor of virginity, which is an essential part of the symbolism. This view also unnecessarily limits the 144,000 to a remnant of the true church. Nevertheless, the link via the number between 14:1 and 7:4-8 bears out to some degree the idea of a holy war, since the concept of holy warriors is present in ch. 7. The holy war theme receives further confirmation from the parallel of 14:4 (those "who follow the Lamb wherever He goes") and 19:14, the latter portraying Christians as an army following their military, messianic leader: "And the armies which are in heaven, clothed in fine linen, white and clean, were following Him [Christ] on white horses."

Some think **chaste** (or virgin in some translations) refers to a select group of Christians who are especially righteous in comparison to other saints who are married, thus suggesting that the latter are more tainted with sin. However, that **chaste** is to be taken symbolically is apparent since nowhere else does Scripture view sexual relations within the bond of marriage as sinful. Furthermore, if the 144,000 are symbolic for the entire people of God, then it would mean that John required celibacy for the whole church, which is highly improbable. It is preferable, on our view, to understand the **chaste** as a metaphor of *all true saints* (not just a remnant), who have not compromised in various ways with the world but have remained loyal as a pure bride to her betrothed (as in 19:7-9; 21:2; 2 Cor. 11:2). Of course, this must be the case if the conclusion already reached above is correct that the number represents all true believers. The only other times when saints surround Christ (7:9, 17; so apparently also in 19:8-9), it is always the whole redeemed community that does so. Additionally, if the 144,000 is figurative for completeness, why should not "virgins" also be figurative in like manner? This figurative interpretation is reinforced from the fact that not only is Jerusalem as a bride based on the OT (see 21:2), but "virgin" is a repeated name applied to the nation of Israel in the OT (see "virgin of Israel" and other similar variant phrases in 2 Kgs. 19:21; Isa. 37:22; Jer. 14:17; 18:13; 31:4, 13, 21; Lam. 1:15; 2:13; Amos 5:2). That at least the broad background of Israel as "virgin" may well be in mind is further suggested by the fact that behind the notion of "defilement" in Rev. 14:4 is "virgin" Israel's defilement with idolatry, and the same notion is ready at hand in 14:8 (on which see).

Chaste (Greek *parthenos,* which can also be translated "virgin") could be in the masculine simply because it is a picture of men who have kept themselves undefiled from women. They have not had illegitimate intercourse with "the great harlot" (17:1). Preventing defilement was mentioned earlier in the book in reference to Christians who have not identified with the idolatrous institutions such as emperor worship or trade guild idolatry (on defilement or non-defilement of professing Christians see on 2:9, 13-15, 20; 3:4-5). This is the same kind of portrayal as in 2:14, 20-22, where the idea of committing "acts of immorality" is a metaphor primarily referring to believers tempted to engage in spiritual intercourse with pagan gods. Likewise, Paul wants believers to be presented as a "pure virgin" to Christ by warning them to avoid the serpent's deception and perverted gospel (2 Cor. 11:2-4, 13-15).

4b Another characteristic of the truly redeemed is that, instead of identifying with the idolatrous world, they identify with Christ: **These are the ones who follow the Lamb wherever He goes.** Like the sacrificial

Lamb, they offer their lives up in sacrifice to God (cf. Rom. 12:1). The saints **have been purchased from among men as first fruits to God and to the Lamb.** In v. 4, **first fruits** could identify a small group of Christian (or especially Jewish Christian) martyrs living at various points in the church age or at the very end of history who are a foreshadowing of a greater ingathering of more believers later, which could then be narrated in the harvest of 14:14-20. This view is supported by the use of the **first fruits** elsewhere in the NT, where it can refer to converts who were the first of many more to come (Rom. 16:5; 1 Cor. 16:15; 2 Thess. 2:13 mg.), to the Spirit as the beginning evidence of a greater end-time inheritance (Rom. 8:23), or to Christ's resurrection as the beginning of the subsequent resurrection of all Christians (1 Cor. 15:20, 23).

However, it is better to view **first fruits** as referring here to the totality of believers throughout the ages. The presentation of saints as **first fruits** develops further the idea of Christians as sacrifices to the Lord. In the OT, the first fruits were offered to God to signify His rights of ownership, and in like manner the rest of the harvest was gathered to be used by God's people according to His sovereign plan. The word here probably refers to the totality of believers throughout the ages who finally receive their full and final redemption. This is supported by recalling that the group in 14:1-5 is the same as that in ch. 7, which represents the complete number of God's true people, true Israel. The holistic concept of first fruits is in line with Jer. 2:2-3, which calls the whole nation of Israel redeemed from Egypt "holy to the Lord, the first of His harvest." This text has relevance for Revelation 14 since chs. 8–11 and chs. 15–16 (the trumpet and bowl judgments) rely heavily on exodus themes. The passage in Jeremiah highlights Israel as set apart to God in distinction from the unbelieving nations: "Israel was holy to the Lord, the first of His harvest; all who ate of it became guilty; evil came upon them." Here Israel is pictured as the redeemed first fruits in distinction to the nations who were antagonistic toward Israel and were judged. Like Jas. 1:18 (literally "first fruits among that which is created [anew]"), Revelation 14 may also be affirming that the elect people inhabiting the new Jerusalem (= Mount Zion) in the new creation are the "first fruits" or beginning of the rest of the new creation, not an anticipation of more people to be redeemed. This is because of their identification with their first-born representative Head, Jesus (cf. 1:5; 3:14; Col. 1:18; 2 Cor. 5:17).

As with the redeemed nation in the OT, so the new Israel is an offering to be set apart for God and separated from the remainder of humanity, which has been contaminated with idolatry. Just as in the OT, the portion remaining after the first fruits was considered common or profane, so now the redeemed are specially set apart from the rest, which are unclean, common, or profane. In this respect, the idea of first fruits continues the thought behind the virgin imagery of v. 4a (see above). The use of "purchase" (or "redeem") twice in vv. 3-4 requires the conclusion that the complete number of redeemed saints is in mind. The only other use of the word with a redemptive meaning is in 5:9, which speaks of the salvation of *all* Christians, not a select group.

5 Because genuinely redeemed saints follow the Lamb, they take on the attributes of the Lamb. They have "followed" Him wherever His sacrificial example has led them. Now an allusion to Isa. 53:9 enforces further the sacrificial nature of Christian commitment: **And no lie was found in their mouth; they are blameless.** They stand in contrast to those "who say they are [true] Jews, and are not, but lie" (Rev. 3:9). The reference to not lying is not speaking merely of general truthfulness but in context focuses on the saints' integrity in witnessing to Jesus when under pressure by the beast and false prophet to compromise their faith and go along with the idolatrous lie (note references to the perseverance of the saints in 13:10; 14:12; cf. 1 John 2:22). As already briefly noted, the expression of integrity is an allusion to the character of the messianic Servant prophesied in Isa. 53:9: "nor was there any deceit in His mouth." This is striking, because it comes immediately after mention of the Servant as "a lamb that is led to slaughter" (Isa. 53:7). The saints reflect both of these messianic traits. Similar language is also found in Zeph. 3:13: "Nor will a deceitful tongue be found in their mouths." In addition to the parallel language with Revelation, Zeph. 3:11-14 speaks of God saving a remnant in the last days, those who are identified with His "holy mountain" and Zion. It appears that Zephaniah may himself be alluding to Isaiah 53, thus connecting Isaiah's Servant with the remnant. Rev. 14:1-5 depicts in part the fulfillment of the Zephaniah and Isaiah prophecy. Saints are included in the fulfillment of the Isaiah 53 prophecy because they are represented by the messianic Lamb who died for them and in whom was no lie or guilt.

Suggestions for Reflection on 14:1-5

On the rule of Christ and His protection of the redeemed. Chs. 12 and 13 have painted a picture of persecution and of the church's suffering at the hands of the devil and his agents. Yet here a counterpoint is presented in the form of a magnificent picture of Christ ruling on Mount Zion in the midst of His people. According to the commentary, the fact that this rule has already begun means that, even in the midst of suffering, Christ is protecting His people spiritually. Do we fail to understand this truth because we place too much value in external things the enemy may take from us and not enough in the saving relationship we have with Christ? How important is it, particularly for suffering believers, to understand these things in order to persevere?

On the response of praise. In vv. 2-3, the people of God, both those on earth and those in heaven, are pictured as giving heartfelt praise to God and the Lamb for the victory they have won. Is the "new song" of praise characteristic of our relationship with Christ? Do we truly focus on the greatness of what He has done for us? How important is it to observe Paul's command, "In everything give thanks; for this is God's will for you in Christ Jesus" (1 Thess. 5:18)? How does a response of praise affect us positively and draw us closer to the Lord?

On the twofold nature of discipleship. In v. 4, the Christian life is presented two ways: we turn away from the world and refuse to compromise with its values, regardless of the cost to us, and we follow the Lamb unconditionally — "wherever He goes." These are two sides of the same coin — yet do we emphasize one at the expense of the other? Why do they need to be held in balance?

On becoming like Christ. The section closes with the observation that those who follow Christ will eventually become like Him (v. 5). Why is this so? Does it equally apply in a negative sense to those who seek money, power, or position for selfish purposes? Discipleship means following Christ "wherever He goes." How characteristic is this of our Christian lives? What a tragedy it is when believers fail to follow Christ wholeheartedly and thus fail to exhibit His character to the watching world around them.

God will judge the world system and nations who give allegiance to antichristian forces, but He will give an eternal reward to the faithful who persevere through oppression (14:6-13)

6 And I saw another angel flying in midheaven, having an eternal gospel to preach
to those who live on the earth, and to every nation and tribe and tongue and
people; 7 and he said with a loud voice, "Fear God and give Him glory, because the
hour of His judgment has come; and worship Him who made the heaven and the

earth and sea and springs of waters." 8 And another angel, a second one, followed,
saying, "Fallen, fallen, is Babylon the great, she who has made all the nations drink
of the wine of the passion of her immorality." 9 And another angel, a third one,
followed them, saying with a loud voice, "If anyone worships the beast and his
image, and receives a mark on his forehead or upon his hand, 10 he also will drink
of the wine of the wrath of God, which is mixed in full strength in the cup of His
anger; and he will be tormented with fire and brimstone in the presence of the
holy angels and in the presence of the Lamb. 11 And the smoke of their torment
goes up forever and ever; and they have no rest day and night, those who worship
the beast and his image, and whoever receives the mark of his name." 12 Here is
the perseverance of the saints who keep the commandments of God and their
faith in Jesus. 13 And I heard a voice from heaven, saying, "Write, 'Blessed are the
dead who die in the Lord from now on!'" "Yes," says the Spirit, "that they may
rest from their labors, for their deeds follow with them."

A warning of judgment to the unbelieving world is announced (vv. 6-7), but it will not be heeded by the world system and its followers, which results in their final judgment at the end of history (v. 8). This final historical judgment is the precursor to the final, eternal judgment (vv. 9-11). However, the warning is intended to influence true believers to remain faithful to Christ in order to receive an eternal reward (vv. 12-13).

6 The phrase **and I saw** begins the fifth visionary segment since the commencement of the major vision section at 12:1 (the previous four sections began at 12:1; 13:1; 13:11; and 14:1). The time of this section immediately precedes that of the consummation, which is part of the focus in vv. 1-5. The focus now shifts from the redeemed to the unredeemed (vv. 6-11) in order to contrast the destiny of the two: **And I saw another angel flying in midheaven, having an eternal gospel to preach to those who live on the earth.** The angel is a messenger not primarily of grace but of judgment. His announcement emphasizes the judicial side of the gospel more than the offer of grace. The absence of the article ("the") before **gospel** is suggestive, since elsewhere in the NT the article always precedes the word, which without exception emphasizes the offer of grace in Christ. The angel does not announce a different gospel, but one that carries with it dire consequences if rejected, as Paul underscores in Rom. 1:16–3:21; 2 Cor. 2:14-16; and Acts 17:18-32 (cf. 1 Pet. 4:17). The following verses (8-11) suggest that the gospel which is announced here includes, at the least, a penal aspect; indeed, these succeeding verses emphasize the judicial side. Ch. 14 reaches its climax with two descriptions of the final judgment (vv. 14-20), which highlights the judicial tone introduced in v. 6 and further elaborated in vv. 10 and 11. The **gospel** is called **eternal** because it is immutable and permanently valid.

The wrathful nature of the heavenly being is also suggested by the similarity to the messenger of the three woes in 8:13. Each delivers his message by speaking in a loud voice while flying in midheaven and addressing unbelieving earth-dwellers. **Those who live on the earth** is a phrase synonymous with "those who dwell upon the earth" (for the latter phrase with its negative idolatrous connotation see 3:10; 6:10; 8:13; 11:10a, 10b; 13:8, 12, 14a, 14b; 17:2, 8). An additional description of the heavenly being's addressees is given at the end of the verse: **and to every nation and tribe and tongue and people**. This formula in the first part of the book refers to the saved (5:9; 7:9), but commencing in 10:11 (and again in 13:7 and 17:15) refers to the lost. There may be an allusion here to the sayings of Jesus in Matt. 24:14 concerning the preaching of the gospel to all nations, where the context speaks of the hostility of the world and apostasy within the church, even as both ideas are included in Rev. 13:1-18 and 14:9-12.

7 Whether this verse gives the only content or the further contents of the gospel preached in v. 6 is not clear. It serves well as a conclusion to the announcement of the gospel. The theme of the verse is judgment. This is "good news" (the literal meaning of "gospel") to the saints because it means the downfall of the ungodly system headed by the beast and ultimately by Satan. The preaching of the gospel (good news) in 10:7 (on which see) has the same idea, since its primary reference is to the fact that the suffering of saints, which is part of God's "mystery," will be followed by the defeat and judgment of their persecutors. Christians can be encouraged because God will defend His reputation after all.

The appropriate response to the gospel is to **fear God and give Him glory**. The expression poses the difficult question of whether the command is expected to result in genuine conversion or is a compulsory edict for antagonistic humanity, signifying that they will be forced to acknowledge the reality of God's imminent judgment (as in Phil. 2:9-11). When glory is given to God in Revelation, it is given by those who are part of God's spiritual community (so twelve times). Likewise, whenever worship of God is mentioned in the book, it is always carried out by true believers or angelic beings (so twelve times). The closest parallel verse, 15:4, bears this out. However, the next closest parallel, 11:13 ("the rest were terrified and gave glory to the God of heaven"), we have understood to be about coerced acknowledgment of God's sovereignty on the basis of the allusion to Dan.

4:34, where unbelieving Nebuchadnezzar's giving glory to God follows his punishment (see on 11:13).

In this regard, vv. 6-8 are also based on a series of expressions concerning Nebuchadnezzar from the LXX version of Daniel 4:

> An angel commands him to "give glory to the Most High" (Dan. 4:34), similar to the angelic command in Rev. 14:7.
>
> The king gives "praise" to the One who made the four-part cosmos (Dan. 4:37); cf. likewise v. 7.
>
> The angelic declaration to humanity in v. 6 through the fourfold formula of universality is based on the same formula in Daniel, of which two instances are in Dan. 3:7; 4:1.
>
> The use of "hour" as the time of the latter-day judgment (v. 7) is based on the repeated eschatological use of the same word in Daniel, which is unique to the remainder of OT usage. The approaching time of the Babylonian king's judgment is also described as an "hour" (Dan. 4:17a; for further discussion of the OT background of "hour" see on 17:12). The closest verbal parallel from Daniel for the phrase **the hour of His judgment has come** is 11:45: "the hour of his end will come," which refers to the final judgment of God's end-time opponent (cf. also Ezek. 7:7; 22:3).
>
> The last common phrase of significance is "Babylon the great" (v. 8), taken from Dan. 4:30.

Although Nebuchadnezzar responded to God, there is no evidence he became a monotheistic, God-fearing believer. The judgment which God imposed upon him left the humiliated king no choice but to acknowledge that God, not he, was the true sovereign of earth's affairs. The same will happen at the end of time for the ungodly.

The hour of His judgment has come suggests that the angelic command does not primarily apply during the whole course of the age before Christ's return, but is an edict that directly precedes and inaugurates the last judgment itself. This is supported by the use of "hour" in 17:12-18 in connection with the judgment of Babylon. Commencement of the judgment is the reason for issuing the command. It is only when **the hour of His judgment has come** that those hitherto immovable in their rebellious spirit will be made to confess that God is their sovereign judge and that He glorifies Himself by judging them.

However, the verb "worship" *(proskyneō)* refers elsewhere in the book to voluntary worship of either God or the beast, though it can have the notion of "respectfully welcome" or "prostrate oneself before," which could be consistent with the idea of a coerced acknowledgment of God. But if the notion of a coerced fearing, glorifying, and worshiping is ultimately not satisfactory, then the angel of 14:7 must be seen as issuing a final decree for genuine conversion, which the directly following context shows will go unheeded, and v. 7 would be an exhortation to unbelievers to turn from idolatrous worship of creation to worship of the Creator. God is identified as the Creator of all things as a motivation for people to worship Him instead of the creation. The verse could be analogous to Acts 14:15: we "preach the gospel in order that you should turn from these vain things to a living God, who made the heaven and the earth and the sea and all that is in them." Acts 14:18 notes that the audience continued in their idolatrous attitude, which is also the expectation in Revelation 14. The phrase "every nation" (v. 6), that is, those addressed in v. 7, is identical to the phrase "all the nations" in v. 8 and 18:3, those who are to be judged along with the Babylonian harlot because they have drunk her deceptive, intoxicating wine.

8 In the vision **another angel . . . followed** with a declaration of judgment, which draws out more explicitly the judicial nature of the prior angel's announcement in vv. 6-7. Babylon has so infected the nations as to render them incapable of heeding the first angel's declaration of the gospel. **Fallen, fallen is Babylon** is from Isa. 21:9a, where it is equivalent to the statement that the idols of Babylon are destroyed (in Isa. 21:9b). The destruction of the idolatrous system of the world is also in mind here, as the immediately following vv. 9-11 bear out.

Babylon the great is Nebuchadnezzar's prideful description (Dan. 4:30). End-time Babylon is about to fall, just as was Nebuchadnezzar. The past tenses **fallen, fallen** function like the Hebrew prophetic perfect tense, which expresses a future occurrence as though it has already occurred. The repetition expresses emphasis and anticipates the larger portrayal of Babylon's fall in 16:19 and ch. 18 (the latter passage begins its depiction with the same double expression). The ungodly social, political, and economic system dominated by the Roman Empire placed believers in the same position as Israel under Babylon. Therefore, Rome and all wicked world systems take on the symbolic name "Babylon the great." Indeed, this symbolic interpretation of Babylon is assured beyond reasonable doubt by the prophecies of God's judgment on historical Babylon, which foretold that Babylon "will be desolate forever" (Jer. 51:26) and "not rise again" (Jer. 51:64; cf. 50:39-40; 51:24-26, 62-64; so also Isa. 13:19-22). Thus, that

"Babylon the Great" is applied to the ungodly kingdom in the new covenant era shows clearly that it cannot refer to literal Babylon.

There are many who go along with the religious and idolatrous demands of the ungodly earthly order. The reason for this compliance is that Babylon **has made all the nations drink of the wine of the passion of her immorality**. The metaphor of drunkenness comes from Jer. 51:7-8: "Babylon has been a golden cup in the hand of the Lord, intoxicating all the earth. The nations have drunk of her wine; therefore, the nations are going mad. Suddenly Babylon has fallen and been broken." The literal meaning of the Greek (technically termed genitives of cause) is "the wine that causes a passion to have immoral relations with her." The Greek word for "immorality" *(porneia)* appears elsewhere in Revelation and is linked with idolatry (2:14, 20-21; 9:21; 17:2). The nations' cooperation with Babylon ensures their material security (see on 2:9, 13; 13:16-17). Without this cooperation, security would be removed. Such security is a temptation too great to resist. The phrase "made to drink" means that people must comply with society's demands in order to prosper. Once one imbibes, the intoxicating influence removes all desire to resist Babylon's destructive influence, blinds one to Babylon's own ultimate insecurity and to God as the source of real security, and numbs one from any fear of a coming judgment. This same combination of ideas finds a parallel in Hos. 4:11-12: "*harlotry, wine and new wine* take away the understanding. My people consult their wooden idol . . . for a spirit of harlotry has led them astray." Here it is unfaithful Israel who has become drunk and spiritually blind. See also Isa. 29:9: "They become drunk, but not with wine. . . . For the Lord has poured over you a spirit of deep sleep, He has shut your eyes, the prophets. . . ."

The economic interpretation of the nations' intoxicating passion for Babylon is clear from ch. 18, especially 18:3, where "the kings of the earth have committed acts of immorality (Greek *porneia*) with her" is parallel with "and the merchants of the earth have become rich by the wealth of her sensuality" (see on 18:3). The nations weep and lament about the fall of Babylon in ch. 18 because they fear that it means their own imminent demise (18:9-10, 15, 19). But a much more ultimate collapse than economic depression is at hand. Those experiencing economic tragedy in the contemporary world should be warned that it is a forerunner of a final world collapse and universal judgment by God; accordingly, they should pay heed and take stock of their own standing before God. The influence of Babylon extends to the end of history, so that people must be exhorted to the very end not to be deceived by her (note the exhortations implied in

v. 9 and expressed in v. 12, as well as in 18:3-4 and similarly elsewhere in the book).

9 Yet a third angel appears after the first two. Like them, he also announces judgment. The present tenses **worships (the beast and his image)** and **receives (a mark on his forehead or his hand)** connote continued worship of the beast and allegiance to him despite the warnings of judgment in vv. 6-8 and the penalty stated in vv. 10-11.

10 The consequences of worship of the beast are now stated. The punishment fits their crime. V. 8 has explained that the nations have allowed themselves to drink from Babylon's wine, which has made them desire to cooperate with her economic-religious system. Therefore, since the nations have willingly drunk from the wine of passion for Babylon, so they will **drink of the wine of the wrath of God**, in demonstration of the "eye for an eye" principle. The picture of pouring out wine resulting in intoxication indicates the unleashing of God's wrath, under which people are completely subjugated through judgment, resulting in extreme suffering (Pss. 60:3; 75:8; Isa. 51:17, 21-23; 63:6; Jer. 25:15-18; 51:7; cf. Job 21:20; Obad. 16). Sometimes the drunken stupor ends in physical death and destruction (Jer. 25:27-33; Obad. 16; Rev. 18:6-9). While the intoxicating effect of Babylon's wine seemed strong, it is nothing in comparison to God's wine. Babylon's wine has only temporary effects; the effects of God's wine stand forever. The divine draught is **mixed in full strength**, implying that Babylon's wine is not. The following clause **in the cup of His anger** emphasizes the definitiveness and severity of the last judgment to which all unbelievers are forced to submit.

At the last day they will be **tormented with fire and brimstone**. As throughout the book, fire is figurative for judgment (1:14; 2:18; 3:18; 4:5 [fire in conjunction with lightning and thunder]; 8:5, 7-8; 15:2; 19:12). Uppermost in thought is the suffering which results from judgment; see 9:17-18; 11:5; 16:8-9; 20:10. The idea of suffering is emphasized when "brimstone" is added to the image of "fire." The "torment" is primarily spiritual and psychological suffering, which is the meaning of the word elsewhere in the book, with reference to the nature of trials which either precede the final judgment or are part of it (9:5-6; 11:10; 18:7, 10, 15; 20:10). That their torment takes place **in the presence of the Lamb** means that those who have denied the Lamb will be forced to acknowledge Him as they are being punished in His presence (as in 6:16).

11 Together with the conclusion of v. 10, the portrait in v. 11a is drawn from Isa. 34:9-10, which describes God's judgment of Edom. Once destroyed by God's judgment, Edom would never rise again. Likewise the judgment of unbelievers at the end of time will be absolute and complete. Isaiah's prophecy is universalized to refer to the final judgment of all unbelievers throughout history who have given allegiance to the ungodly world system.

However, there is a theological debate about the nature of the final judgment. Does the portrayal mean the annihilation of unbelievers, so that their existence is abolished forever? Or, does it refer to a destruction involving not absolute annihilation but the suffering of unbelievers for eternity? The OT context could support the view that the final judgment involves annihilation of unbelievers rather than their eternal suffering. The **smoke** represents a memorial of God's annihilation of sin. On the other hand, the parallel in 20:10 refers to the devil, the beast, and the false prophet undergoing the judgment in "the lake of fire and brimstone," where "they will be tormented day and night forever and ever." There is no justification in not identifying the fate of those in 14:10-11 with that of their Satanic representatives in 19:20 and 20:10. The fact that the ungodly are thrown into the same "lake of fire" as their Satanic leaders further confirms this (so 20:15). In addition, the word **torment** (Greek *basanismos,* verb *basanizō*) in 14:10-11 is used nowhere in Revelation or biblical literature in the sense of annihilation of existence. Without exception it refers in Revelation to conscious suffering on the part of people (9:5; 11:10; 12:2; 18:7, 10, 15; 20:10; so also Matt. 4:24 ["pains" in NASB]; 8:6, 29; 18:34; Mark 5:7; 6:48 ["straining" in NASB]; Luke 8:28; 16:23, 28; 2 Pet. 2:8). The word group occurs approximately one hundred times in the LXX, always referring to conscious suffering. Therefore, the genitival phrase **the smoke of their torment** is a mixed metaphor, where **smoke** is figurative of an enduring memorial of God's punishment involving a real, ongoing, eternal, conscious torment.

The phrase **day and night** further clarifies the ceaseless nature of the suffering of the lost. The phrase is parallel with the preceding phrase **forever and ever**, so that the idea expresses a long period of uninterrupted restlessness. The same two phrases are linked in 20:10 in relation to the eternal suffering of the devil, the beast, and the false prophet. The phrase **forever and ever** occurs twelve other times in the book and always refers to eternity (i.e., God's or Christ's eternal being, God, or the saints' eternal reign; note the close verbal parallel with 19:3). In particular, the expression describing the eternal duration of the punishment ("tormented day and night forever and ever") in 20:10 appears to be balanced antithetically by the identical phrase describing the eternal duration of the saints' reign ("forever and ever") in 22:5. In 7:15, the clause "day and night" refers to the time when the whole congregation of saints will worship in God's temple in the new creation at the end of the age. Such worship and relief will continue forever; the same is true of use of the phrase "day and night" in relation to the worship of the four living creatures in 4:8.

The nature of the **torment** is explained in the second part of v. 11 not as annihilation but as lack of rest. Therefore, the smoke is metaphorical of a continued reminder of the ongoing torment of restlessness, which endures for eternity. Only two verses later in 14:13, believers find eternal "rest" when they die, which appears as the opposite of the restlessness of unbelievers. The phrase **and they have no rest day and night** describing **those who worship the beast and his image** is a verbatim repetition of the same phrase in 4:8, describing the ceaseless and eternal worship of the cherubim in heaven, which they had been doing at least since the time of Ezekiel 1.

12 Now true saints are exhorted to persevere through temporary suffering because of loyalty to Christ, in order to avoid the eternal consequences of loyalty to the beast and to receive an eternal reward (v. 13). The warning of vv. 6-11 is aimed to result in believers being motivated to persevere. Therefore, v. 12 is the main point of the segment so far (vv. 6-12). Vv. 9-13 thus follow the pattern of 13:11-18. There, mention of the worshipers of the beast and his image who bear the mark on their foreheads and hands is followed by reference to the persevering faith of believers, which enables them not to be deceived by the beast. Likewise, 14:12-13 follows vv. 9-11.

Note the parallel phrases **here is the perseverance of the saints** and "here is the perseverance and faith of the saints" (13:10), along with the further parallel "here is wisdom" (13:18). Faith involves the ability to accept the suffering entailed in refusing to compromise (13:10), and faith also provides wisdom which enables believers to avoid deception and discern the true character of the beast (13:18). Both of these definitions from ch. 13 concerning faithfulness, discernment of evil, and non-compromise are in mind with the summary statement of faith here. Included also is the idea that, if wisdom is exercised, it will prevent divine judgment, which will entail worse suffering than what Christians experience through persecution. The fact of coming judgment against their persecutors also motivates Christians to persevere. This is a motivation arising not from revenge but from a desire that judgment will show their cause to be true and will therefore vindicate the righteous name of God, which has been blasphemed by the beast and his allies.

Perseverance is explained to be keeping **the commandments of**

God and their faith in Jesus. The commandments of God is a holistic reference to the objective revelation of the old and new covenants to which the faithful remain loyal. That faith (Greek *pistis*) refers to the doctrinal content of the Christian faith (cf. Jude 3) is further evident from 2:13, where the same word occurs with the same meaning. The occurrence of **perseverance** in 13:10 and here emphasizes that what is needed in withstanding the beast's deceptions and temptations to compromise is not a temporary faith but one that endures through constant watchfulness.

13 If Christians remain loyal to the Lamb, they will suffer in the present, but afterward they will gain a reward of eternal rest: **Blessed are the dead who die in the Lord from now on.** The desire to persevere is to be motivated not only by the warning of judgment (vv. 6-11) but also by the promise of reward. Just as vv. 8 and 9-11 were interpretative elaborations of the judgment announced in vv. 6-7, so v. 13 likewise expands on the statement of persevering faith in v. 12. This is suggested by **a voice from heaven, saying**, which is similar to the elaborating phrases in vv. 8 and 9, both containing the word "saying." All believers **who die in the Lord** (the reference is to all who remain faithful to death, not just martyrs) now enter into their eternal rest and reward, **for their deeds follow with them.** The emphasis is on those "dying in the Lord," not on the precise manner of death. Like martyrs, those dying from other causes than martyrdom also will receive the blessing because they likewise in their own ways are resisting pressures to conform to idolatry (see on 6:9 and 12:11). Christ was rewarded after death for His endurance, and so will Christians, since Christ is their corporate representative (even as the angels represented the churches in 1:20).

The interjection that this blessing is pronounced by the Spirit (**"Yes," says the Spirit**) assures Christians that the blessing will be bestowed. Unlike their persecutors and compromisers, who find restful security in this life but not in the next (vv. 8, 11), Christians who endure through hard labors of oppression now will find the blessing of rest later. In 6:11 "rest" is also used (together with the bestowing of "white robes") to refer to the believers' reward after death for their enduring faith in the midst of trials. So here also not just general works of righteousness, but faithful deeds of bearing up under oppression are referred to (see further below). That the **rest** is eternal is apparent, since it is in contrast with the eternal restlessness of the wicked in v. 11. The implicit eternal duration is suggested also by the promises of comfort from life's storms made to Christians in 7:13-15 and 21:2-7, where the duration is open-ended. Though the "rest" may appear "temporary" in 6:11 ("for a little while longer"), 14:13 together with 7:13-15 and 21:2-7 show it to be the beginning of an eternal reward.

The last clause, **for their deeds follow with them**, serves as the logical basis for the preceding: people will experience rest because, despite persecution, they have persevered in keeping the commandments of God and in their faith in Jesus (v. 12). **Labors** (plural of *kopos*) in the preceding clause (**that they may rest from their labors**) does not refer to mere good works, but to faithful works which endure through distress and difficulties, which is its typical meaning throughout the NT. **Deeds** is synonymous with **labors.** People will be judged or rewarded on the basis of their **deeds,** which are a tell-tale sign of their inward faith (cf. 2:23; 22:12). The main point of vv. 6-13 is reward for the faithful, since that theme concludes the section in vv. 12-13 and represents the response by the faithful to the announcement of judgment in vv. 6-11. The record of their **deeds** identifies them before the divine court as those deserving rest (cf. 1 Cor. 15:58).

Suggestions for Reflection on 14:6-13

On the judicial aspect of the gospel message. According to the understanding of the commentary, in vv. 6-7 the gospel is presented primarily as a message of judgment. How often do we ignore this judicial aspect? Paul says the same thing: in the gospel the righteousness of God by faith is revealed (Rom. 1:16-17), but in the same gospel is also revealed the wrath of God from heaven (Rom. 1:18-32). What consequences does it have when we ignore the judicial aspect in our understanding or presentation of the gospel?

On the power of materialism and the world system. The devil and his agents use the world economic system to ensnare people through their love of money and material pleasures. V. 8 presents this in terms of being drugged or drunk, and thus becoming totally insensitive to and unaware of what is truly happening around us because of our overweening enjoyment of worldly comforts. Jesus said, "No one can serve two masters; for either he will hate the one and love the other, or he will hold to one and despise the other. You cannot serve God and mammon [money]" (Matt. 6:24). What a battle we face in this materialistic culture, yet how great the consequences of our decisions!

On the concept of everlasting conscious punishment of the lost. According to the commentary, vv. 9-11 present a picture of the everlasting conscious punishment of the unbeliever. Do you agree with the reasoning adopted by the commentary? Why is this a difficult subject for many believers? If we deny this concept, is it the beginning of a process which will end in the denial of hell's existence? For what would Jesus then have died? If Jesus suffered the penalty of sin, and if that penalty is annihilation and not eternal suffering, then would not Jesus have been annihilated and thus gone out of existence at the cross? If this logic be accepted, then it involves a Christological heresy: How could the second person of the Trinity have gone out of existence at any point?

On perseverance and reward. In vv. 12-13, the perseverance of the saints and their eternal reward are emphasized. God enables us to persevere, and He helps us in our weakness. The point of the portrayal of judgment in vv. 6-11 is to motivate believers to persevere in spite of suffering. Yet they are to rejoice not in the punishment of their enemies but in the ultimate vindication of God and His character. Perhaps we wonder if we should be motivated by the prospect of an eternal reward, yet this is how God presents it here.

Unbelievers will assuredly suffer God's thoroughgoing judgment at the very end of time (14:14-20)

14 And I looked, and behold, a white cloud, and sitting on the cloud was one like
a Son of man, having a golden crown on His head, and a sharp sickle in His hand.
15 And another angel came out of the temple, crying out with a loud voice to
Him who sat on the cloud, "Put in your sickle and reap, because the hour to reap
has come, because the harvest of the earth is ripe." 16 And He who sat on the
cloud swung His sickle over the earth; and the earth was reaped. 17 And another
angel came out of the temple which is in heaven, and he also had a sharp sickle.
18 And another angel, the one who has power over fire, came out from the altar;
and he called with a loud voice to him who had the sharp sickle, saying, "Put in
your sharp sickle, and gather the clusters from the vine of the earth, because her
grapes are ripe." 19 And the angel swung his sickle to the earth, and gathered the
clusters from the vine of the earth, and threw them into the great wine press of
the wrath of God. 20 And the wine press was trodden outside the city, and blood
came out from the wine press, up to the horses' bridles, for a distance of two
hundred miles.

14 Vv. 14-20, beginning with the visionary marker **And I looked**, form the sixth of seven sections extending from 12:1 to 15:4 (the previous such markers occurring at 12:1; 13:1, 11; 14:1, 6). Like the sixth seal, this sixth vision describes the judgment at the end of history, which is followed by a seventh section also narrating the last judgment (15:2-4; cf. 8:1, 3-5). Vv. 6-13 have announced the coming climactic judgment as a warning to professing Christians. That judgment is now depicted as actually taking place.

The judge is **one like a Son of man** who is **sitting on the cloud**, which is an allusion to Dan. 7:13 and stands in the interpretative tradition of Matt. 24:30. This tradition usually associates the Son of man's coming with both redemption and judgment. In Matthew 24, Jesus prophesies that as the Son of man He is to come on the clouds both to judge and redeem. However, the context of Rev. 14:15-20 suggests that only the judicial aspect of the Son of man's role appears to be connoted in v. 14. The heavenly figure has **a golden crown on His head**, which identifies Him as King over His people, who rule with Him and also wear "golden crowns" (4:4, 10; cf. also 2:10; 3:11; 12:1). His crown also evokes kingship over His enemies (see on 19:12). The following verses show the "sharp sickle" to be a metaphor of judgment. Seven heavenly beings are described in vv. 6-20, but the Son of man here is the only one not referred to as an angel, and 1:7, 13-20 portrays the Son of man from Dan. 7:13 as the divine Christ with precisely the same wording as here. In the OT, God alone comes from heaven or to earth in a cloud, and Dan. 7:13 is no exception to this pattern.

15-16 Another angel now appears and issues a command to the Son of man. That the angel conveys a message to the Son of man indicates the latter's functional subordination to God, not to the angel, in light of the observation that the angel (who **came out of the temple**) merely conveys a divine message from God's throne room. Christ must be informed by God about the time for judgment to begin, since "of that day or that hour no one knows, not even the angels in heaven, nor the Son, but the Father alone" (Mark 13:32; Acts 1:7). It is not clear that Christ being in heaven means that His knowledge about the timing of the final judgment changes, since even after His resurrection and ascension He is still subject to the Father's authority. Furthermore, He equates His limited knowledge to that of "the angels in heaven," so that heavenly status does not seem a sufficient condition for such a change. Angels in Revelation never announce a message which has its ultimate derivation from themselves, but are always mere conveyors of messages representing the divine will. Christ is commanded to harvest in judgment **because the harvest of the earth is ripe**. Just as God determines the time each year when the season for growing crops ends, so God has determined the time when the end of the age has been reached and when judgment must begin, because the sins of humanity have reached their full measure (cf. Gen. 15:16; Dan. 8:23-26; 1 Thess. 2:16).

17-20a The imagery of harvest in vv. 17-19 is almost identical to vv. 15-16, though there is amplification of the picture. These are not similar accounts of different judgments, though it is conceivable that the descriptions portray actions respectively of the Son of man and of the sixth angel during the time of the last judgment. However, because only in the second picture is the image of judgment explicit, many have thought that the first picture represents the ingathering of the saints, while the second represents the judgment of the wicked. If only the one judgment of the wicked is referred to, why would two parallel but somewhat different depictions be placed side by side? The presence of the Son of man in the first segment and the gory imagery of trampling grapes in the second are taken respectively as suggesting redemption and judgment. Jesus also taught a dual harvest of the saved and the lost (Matt. 3:12; 13:24-30). In fact, sometimes Jesus (and also Isaiah and Amos) referred to the harvest only as a harvest of the saved (Isa. 27:12-13; Hos. 6:11; Matt. 9:37-38; Mark 4:26-29; John 4:35-38).

On the other hand, both pictures in vv. 15-16 and in vv. 17-19 may speak of judgment only. Both feature a angel coming **out of the temple** and commanding the Son of man to put in his sickle and reap a ripe harvest, and in other places in Revelation such orders from the heavenly temple or altar bring only judgment (6:1-5; 9:13; 16:7, 17). Also, the phrase "the hour to reap has come" in v. 15 points our attention to the nine other times in Revelation where the word "hour" occurs, always in reference to a time of judgment. Finally, the vision John sees appears to be a fulfillment of Joel 3:13, "Put in the sickle, for the harvest is ripe. Come, tread, for the wine press is full; the vats overflow, for their wickedness is great. . . ." The Joel passage is the only one in the OT where both images of harvest (as in vv. 15-16) and of treading the wine press (as in vv. 17-20) occur, and there they are both images connoting judgment (for a similar OT passage, see Isa. 63:2-3). On balance, therefore, the passage probably refers to judgment only, though the alternate view is possible. But why would there be two identical accounts of the same judgment in vv. 15-20? The double narration emphasizes the severity and unqualified nature of the punishment, which reaches its climax with the extensive blood-letting of v. 20.

In any event, it is clear that vv. 17-20 portray the judgment of the wicked. The picture of the altar in conjunction with the **angel . . . who has power over fire** (v. 18) has unique correspondence with 8:3-5, where an angel by a golden altar obtains fire from the altar and throws it to the earth (twenty-three out of twenty-four occurrences of the word "fire" in the book are in scenes of judgment; see on 14:10). Since 8:3-5 depicts a judgment scene introducing the punishments of the trumpets, the same kind of scene is discernible here. This conclusion is supported further by the fact that the image of treading a wine press is without exception a metaphor of judgment in the OT. And the only other mention in Revelation of the wine press occurs in 19:15, where it refers to Christ's judgment of the evil nations. The phrase "the wine of the wrath of God" in v. 10 and **the great wine press of the wrath of God** here, together with the identical phraseology in 19:15, show that vv. 19-20 are developing only the theme of judgment from v. 10. Why "one like a Son of man" (v. 14) is introduced into one of the segments and not the other is not clear, other than that He is in some way similar to the other angelic figures (probably Christ; see on v. 14). In all, there are seven heavenly figures in vv. 6-20, reflecting the notion of completeness.

20b The concluding statement in v. 20 that the treading of the wine press was **outside the city, and the blood came out from the wine press, up to the horses' bridles** presents some difficulties. If the city refers to Babylon, the trampling could refer to the persecution of saints, the phrase being parallel to 11:2, where the phrase "they will tread under foot the holy city" alludes to Christians who are persecuted like their Lord. However, if the "city" is the true holy city (so fifteen times elsewhere in the book), then the meaning of the trampling is punishment of unbelievers, which occurs outside the eschatological holy city of righteous saints. The latter option is the better. The last clause of v. 19 (the "wine press of the wrath of God") continues the judgment language of v. 10. The first part of v. 20 is based on Joel 3:13 and Isa. 63:2-3, referring to the judgment of unbelieving nations. The context of the Isaiah text may provide additional help in identifying the city and the meaning of the trampling. In Isa. 60:12 and 63:1-6, the destruction of the nations is noted immediately after mention that the gates of the holy city will remain open for the faithful (60:11; 62:10). Therefore, though it is not stated in this way, the overthrow of the nations implicitly takes place outside the holy city and not in it. This could be what John intends to recall when he refers to the devastation of the unrighteous occurring **outside the city**. This analysis is borne out by 20:8-9, which pictures unbelieving opponents of the saints as being judged outside the "beloved city." Likewise 21:8, when taken in conjunction with 21:27 and 22:15, locates the judgment of the ungodly outside the eternal city of God. This fits with our conclusion about Mount Zion in v. 1 as a primary reference to the protection of the people of God in their new, latter-day city.

Outside Zion there will be only destruction, as predicted by the prophets. For example, Zech. 14:2-5, 12-16 affirms that the rebellious nations will be defeated in the vicinity of Jerusalem. God will stand on the Mount of Olives, in front of Jerusalem (Zech. 14:2-4), to destroy the enemy armies who have invaded the beloved city.

Perhaps uppermost in mind is Joel 3:2, 11-12, 14, which says that God will enter into judgment with the "surrounding nations" (v. 11) outside Jerusalem in the nearby "valley of Jehoshaphat" (v. 2). The presence of this thought is evident, since it is in this context that Joel 3:13, the model for Rev. 14:14-20, describes the judgment as both a grain harvest and a grape harvest in which the winepress is trodden. 19:15 will apply Isa. 63:2-6 to the scene of the defeat of the wicked living on earth at the end of time, which further confirms the presence of the same scenario here. Immediately after this, the judgment of all the wicked dead from throughout the ages will occur (14:9-11; 19:20; 20:11-15; 21:8, all describing the same set of events).

The statement about blood mounting up to **the horses' bridles** at the end of the verse is figurative battle language and functions as hyperbole to emphasize the severe and unqualified nature of the judgment. This picture of slaughter, in association with battle and horses, is a feature of the last judgment inaugurated by Christ's return, and is paralleled in 19:17-18, where destruction of the ungodly in conjunction with horses is also noted. The spreading of blood **for a distance of two hundred miles** ("1,600 stadia" or about 184 miles = 300 km.) from the city corresponds with the approximate length of Palestine measured from Tyre to the border of Egypt (1,664 stadia). This would underscore by hyperbole the extent of the nations' destruction prophesied to occur outside Jerusalem. But the number could be figurative for complete, worldwide judgment. 1,600 is the product of the squares of four and ten, both of which are figurative for completeness elsewhere in the book (the four living creatures representative of all orders of animate life, 4:6; the "four corners of the earth," 7:1; the ten horns of the dragon and the beast, 12:3; 13:1; the ten horns and kings of 17:12). The number also could well have been thought of as the square of forty, a traditional number of punishment.

In the light of the above analysis of ch. 14, the segments do not portray a strict chronology:

vv. 1-5: the beginning of eternal bliss,
vv. 6-7: a warning to repent,
v. 8: the judgment at the end of history,

vv. 9-11: the eternal consequences of judgment,
vv. 12-13: exhortation to persevere in the present,
vv. 14-20: judgment at the end of history.

Suggestions for Reflection on 14:14-20

On the terrible reality of judgment. Drawing from rich biblical imagery, these verses convey a vivid sense of the dreadful nature of the final judgment. Again, the twofold aspect of the gospel is at the forefront, for it is Jesus, the Son of man who, notwithstanding His role as Savior, executes the judgment (vv. 14-16). How seriously do we take the content of these verses in our daily lives and our consideration of the spiritual state of those around us?

The saints glorify God and the Lamb for their incomparable attributes demonstrated in achieving redemption and executing judgment (15:1-4)

1 And I saw another sign in heaven, great and marvelous, seven angels who had
seven plagues, which are the last, because in them the wrath of God is finished.
2 And I saw, as it were, a sea of glass mixed with fire, and those who had come off
victorious from the beast and from his image and from the number of his name,
standing on the sea of glass, holding harps of God. 3 And they sang the song of
Moses the bond-servant of God and the song of the Lamb, saying, "Great and
marvelous are Thy works, O Lord God, the Almighty; Righteous and true are Thy
ways, Thou King of the nations. 4 Who will not fear, O Lord, and glorify Thy name?
For Thou alone art holy; For all the nations will come and worship before Thee,
For Thy righteous acts have been revealed."

The seventh vision in the series which began in 12:1 is interrupted by the introduction in v. 1 of the seven bowl angels, who do not return until v. 5. The best explanation is that vv. 2-4 serve both as a conclusion to 12:1–14:20 and as part of the introduction to the bowls. We have observed that the literary transitions between the major segments of the book have an "interlocking" function (see comments following 8:5). These transitional segments both conclude the previous section and introduce the following section. Vv. 2-4 thus resume the idea of the last judgment, announced in 14:6-11 and depicted as occurring in 14:14-20, with a song praising God's justice expressed in the judgment. But the focus is on the saints' victory over the ungodly as well as the judgment of their opponents. The scene expands that of the saints' redemptive position in 14:1-5. These two segments together (14:1-5; 15:2-4) form a kind of parenthesis surrounding sections of judgment (14:6-11, 14-20), with the exhortation to persevere and the promise of reward in the middle (14:12-13). 8:3-5 likewise is preceded by an introductory reference to the seven angels (8:2), whose sevenfold presence is repeated again in 8:6 and whose function is narrated in 8:7ff. It temporarily interrupts the beginning of the narration of the plague series by continuing a description of the final judgment scene found in 8:1.

But how does the interlocking parenthesis of vv. 2-4 relate precisely to vv. 5ff.? As in 8:3-5, so here the interlocking indicates a thematic literary connection, which functions as a transition from one sevenfold series to the next. The seven bowls are clearly modeled on the Exodus plagues, as will be seen, and the song of 15:3-4 is an imitation of the song of Moses after the Red Sea crossing. The reference to a new, final exodus victory in vv. 2-4, which concludes the segment of 12:1–14:20, inspires a flashback in ch. 16 to the latter-day plagues leading up to the final victory. Therefore, the parenthesis in 15:2-4 primarily continues the subject of the last judgment in 14:14-20 and secondarily links the following series of bowls to the preceding segment both literarily and thematically.

1 This is the beginning of the formal introduction of the seven bowl plagues, and may serve as an introductory summary statement for 15:5–16:21. The opening clause, **And I saw another sign in heaven**, is an appropriate marker for the start of a major new section, since the nearly identical clauses inaugurate the segment beginning at 12:1-3. John sees **seven angels who had seven plagues, which are the last**, which is a further explanation of the immediately preceding great sign in heaven. A futurist perspective takes the bowls to be the last plagues which occur in history, after the woes of the seals and the trumpets have taken place. Some qualify this slightly by seeing the bowls as the content of the seventh trumpet or third woe, just as they believe that the trumpets are the content of the seventh seal.

However, **last** (Greek *eschatos*) more likely indicates the sequential order in which John saw the visions rather than the chronological order of the events depicted in the visions. This would mean that the bowls are the last formal series of sevenfold visions John saw, after he had seen the visions of seals and trumpets and those recorded in chs. 12–14. Therefore, the bowls do not have to be understood as occurring as the last events of history but are the last of the formal sevenfold visions John saw, which are expanded by further visionary scenes in the following chapters. This interpretation is supported by v. 5, which reintroduces the bowl visions with the phrase "and after these things." Throughout Revelation, the phrase "after these things" indicates the sequential order in which John saw the visions, not necessarily the order of the events they depict (so 4:1; 7:1, 9; 18:1; 19:1; see on 4:1). Therefore, v. 5 notes only that the bowls occurred last in the order of visions presented to John. Since v. 5 reintroduces the same vision that v. 1 began to introduce, it is reasonable to place "and after these things I saw" (v. 5) in synonymous parallelism with "and I saw another sign . . . seven last plagues" (v. 1).

Therefore, the introductory "and I saw . . . seven last plagues" of v. 1 is expanded in the continued introduction in v. 5 to "and after these things I saw," so that v. 1 also affirms that the bowls come last in the sequence of formal sevenfold visions seen by the seer. This means that the bowl judgments do not have to come chronologically after the series of judgments in chs. 6–14. The bowls go back in time and explain in greater detail the woes throughout the age culminating in the final judgment. One indication of this is that the final judgment has already been described as happening at the end of the seals (6:12-17; 8:1), at the end of the trumpets (11:15-19), and most recently in 14:8-11 (the final punishment of Babylon and her followers) and 14:14-20. The same judgment scene will in fact be again described at the end of the bowls (16:17-21; 19:19-21).

A second option is that "last" may be a redemptive-historical reference to the last events of history. The plagues in Revelation are "last" in the sense that they occur in the latter days (hence, "seven eschatological plagues"), in contrast to the former days when the Egyptian plagues occurred. John and the NT writers believed the latter days were inaugurated with Christ's first coming and will be culminated at His return (see on 4:1). Accordingly, the bowl plagues would extend throughout the course of the latter-day period, from Christ's first to His second coming. Ch. 16 bears out clearly that these are typological equivalents of the Egyptian plagues, as does the Red Sea imagery and context of 15:2-4 (on which see below).

A third alternative is that "last" could explain how the wrath revealed in the seals and trumpets reaches its goal. This has some merit, since the bowl judgments in contrast to the other sevenfold series have more explicit statements about the purpose of divine judgments (to punish people for worship of the beast and persecution: 16:2, 5-7, 19). The bowls are "last" in order of presentation of the visions **because in them the wrath of God is finished**. The bowls complement and round out the portrayal of divine wrath in the seals and trumpets.

A final possibility takes **finished** (Greek *teleioō*) as meaning "filled up" and thus as parallel to 15:7 and 21:9, which speak of seven bowls full of

God's wrath (though the Greek word for "full" in the latter texts is a different one). The consequent meaning of the metaphor in 15:1 is that the seven bowls are referred to as "last" because they portray the full-orbed wrath of God in a more intense manner than any of the previous woe visions.

Whichever of these options is preferred makes little difference to the overall meaning of the passage, in which the bowls refer to the judgments of God throughout the "last days" of human history, understood as the period between Christ's resurrection and His return. However, the first option might be most preferable.

2 Introduced by the visionary marker **And I saw**, this is the seventh and concluding section of the broader segment begun in 12:1. It interrupts the introduction of the bowls and resumes the theme of the final judgment from ch. 14. 14:14-20 portrayed the last judgment, and 15:2-4 builds on that scene by picturing the beast's defeat as completed and the saints enjoying the results of that victory, praising God for it.

The sight of what appeared to be, **as it were, a sea of glass mixed with fire** represents the heavenly counterpart to the Red Sea. This becomes clear in v. 3, where the saints are pictured as singing the new song of Moses, which is the latter-day counterpart of Moses' song in Exodus 15. The "sea" in Revelation generally connotes cosmic evil (see also on 4:6; 13:1; 16:3; 21:1). In the OT, the Red Sea was seen as the dwelling place of the evil sea monster (Isa. 51:9-11; Ps. 74:12-15; Ezek. 32:2). The four evil beasts of Daniel 7 are seen as arising from the sea (Dan. 7:3). In Rev. 13:1, the beast comes up out of the sea, while in the new heaven and new earth, there is no longer to be any sea (see below on 21:1). John now sees the chaotic powers of the sea as calmed by divine sovereignty. 4:6 and 5:5-6 revealed that Christ's overcoming through His death and resurrection has defeated the power of evil and so calmed the devil's watery, tumultuous abode, which has become "a sea of glass like crystal" (4:6; Jewish commentators sometimes viewed the Red Sea as becoming a sea of glass [e.g., Midrash Psalms 136.7]). Dan. 7:10-11 picture a river of fire in heaven before God's throne, in which the beast is judged and destroyed. The fact that the **sea of glass** is **mixed with fire** shows that the sea has become the place where the Lamb has judged the beast. Almost everywhere else in Revelation (see on 14:10 for references), "fire" signifies the judgment of God upon the wicked.

In fulfillment of Dan. 7:10-11, the Lamb's "overcoming" has also paved the way for the saints' "overcoming" of the beast at the sea, **those who had come off victorious from the beast and from his image and from the number of his name**. They are victorious only because the Lamb has conquered and granted them a share in the effects of His victory at the sea. They are those who have refused to compromise their faith in the midst of pressure and persecution, like the three faithful youths who refused to worship the king's image in Daniel 3 (for full explanation of the threefold reference to the beast, his image, and his number in v. 2 see on 13:15-18). Victory over **the number of his name** is included to emphasize that they have resisted alliances with the beast which would cause them to fall short of their redemption (see on 13:18 with respect to the meaning of 666). That they are **standing on the sea of glass, holding harps of God** shows that they themselves have been involved in battle against the sea-beast and have fought in the midst of the unbelieving world (see 17:15, where the "waters" are defined as ungodly masses of people in the world).

The saints now stand before God's throne in heaven (in light of where the heavenly analogue to the earthly sea of glass exists in 4:6). The reality of their resurrection is pointed to by the mention of the saints standing on the glass sea in striking similarity to the clear resurrection portrayal of the Lamb standing (5:6) by (or on) the glass sea (4:6). The conquering of both is clearly linked ("overcome" in 5:5 and "come off victorious" in 15:2 translate the same Greek verb, *nikaō*). In both passages, there are the playing of harps and singing of a redemptive song (for the same idea of "standing" in 7:9, see further in the introduction to ch. 7). The saints' weapon has been their fiery, faithful testimony (see on 11:3-7), which the beast and his allies have tried to extinguish with the waters of deception (see on 12:15-16). They are the same group as the totality of the redeemed pictured in 14:1-5, since they also hold harps in their hands. The playing of harps which they hold will form part of the praise which they render in vv. 3-4.

3a Just as the Israelites praised God by the sea after He had delivered them from Pharaoh, so the church praises God for defeating the beast on its behalf. Like God's people of old, so God's new covenant people praise Him by singing **the song of Moses the bond-servant of God**. Moses is called God's servant in Exod. 14:31, immediately before his singing in ch. 15. However, the song now is about the much greater deliverance accomplished through the work of the Lamb. The saints praise the Lamb's victory as the typological fulfillment of that to which the Red Sea victory pointed. There are references in later Judaism which affirm that the song of Exod. 15:1 implies the resurrection of the Israelite singers to sing once again in the new age (*b. Sanhedrin* 91b and *Mekilta de-Ishmael,* Shirata 1.1-10). This could be a further hint suggesting that vv. 2-3 portray a resurrection scene.

Deuteronomy 32 is also called a song of Moses (Deut. 31:19, 22, 30;

32:44), which is included together with the allusion to Exodus 15 (see on v. 3b below), since it also describes judgment (in this case against apostate Israel because of their idolatry, as also apostate Christians are warned in Revelation against being judged along with the nations). That song concludes with the thought that God will punish the enemy nations and will atone for His people (Deut. 32:43), and the same ideas are included here in vv. 2-4, where God has vindicated His people and caused them to be victorious over the power of the beast. The song is the same as the "new song" of 5:9ff. and 14:3, where the singers likewise hold harps while lauding the Lamb for His work of redemption (cf. 5:8; 14:2). That this is also a "new song" is evident since they sing not only the old **song of Moses** but also the **song of the Lamb**, which has hitherto not been sung. Therefore, the song is sung in praise not only to God but also to the Lamb, since 5:9ff. also lauds the Lamb for His redemptive work (and implicitly also the new song of 14:3).

3b The actual contents of the song itself do not come from Exodus 15 but from passages throughout the OT extolling God's character, combined here to explain the new exodus, which has happened on a grander scale than the first. Later OT interpretations of the first exodus have been selected to explain the new exodus, in order to praise God for the redemption and implicit scene of judgment pictured in v. 2. These subsequent interpretations fill out the framework of the Exodus 15 song of Moses which is in John's mind.

Great and marvelous are Thy works, O Lord God, the Almighty reflects Ps. 111:2-3, which speak of the great, splendid, and majestic work of God (see also Deut. 28:59-60 LXX, referring to the "great and marvelous plagues" to come on Israel, which are patterned after the Exodus plagues). The one praised is the **Lord God, the Almighty**, because He is absolute sovereign over the historical affairs of His chosen people. "The Lord God, the Almighty" is repeatedly found in the prophets Haggai, Zechariah, and Malachi to refer to God who sovereignly directs His people's history, and this is its meaning elsewhere in Revelation (see further on 1:8).

Just as the God of the exodus generation was praised as One whose works are perfect and all His ways just (Deut. 32:4), so likewise is He lauded again: **Righteous and true are Thy ways.** This emphasizes that God's sovereign acts are not demonstrations of raw power but moral expressions of His just character. His redemption through Christ has brought to supreme expression how He demonstrates His justice. Those trusting in Christ have the penalty of their sin paid for by His blood (so 1:5-6; 5:9; 7:14; 12:11), but those rejecting the divine provision will bear their own penalty for sin (cf.

Rom. 3:19-20). The concluding title **King of the nations** explains further that God is sovereign in His people's history because He rules all the nations with whom they come into contact. The same idea is expressed in 11:15-18, where the kingdoms of this world have become His kingdom. The title may well include Christ, since He is called "Ruler of the kings of the earth" (1:5) and "Lord of lords and King of kings" (17:14; likewise 19:16).

4 The great and true acts of the Sovereign stated in v. 3b are the reason that people should fear and glorify Him. The words the saints are singing, **Who will not fear, O Lord, and glorify Thy name?** recall Jer. 10:7: "Who would not fear Thee, O King of the nations?" Surely they will fear Him, both texts suggest, because they have witnessed His great and righteous acts. Jer. 10:1-16 contrasts God with humans and idols, affirming that God alone is due worship. The singing saints here likewise know worship is due God and the Lamb only, in contrast to the beast and his image. God is worshiped because He is holy: **For Thou alone art holy**, which again gives the basis or reason ("for" = *hoti*) for the saints' worship in v. 4a: God is worshiped *because* He is holy. The holiness of God refers not simply to a set of moral attributes but to the fact that God is completely set apart in those attributes from His creation.

The latter part of the verse, **For all the nations will come and worship before Thee, for Thy righteous acts have been revealed**, derives from Ps. 86:9-10. The sense of v. 4c, requires that *hoti* be translated this time not as "for" (as in NASB) but as "so that." The previous clause (v. 4b) gave the *basis* for the saints' worship: God is holy. This clause now gives the *result* of that truth: God is holy, *so that* all nations will worship Him. The effect of God's unique holiness is that people from all nations will recognize it and stream to worship God, which repeats the primary thought of v. 4a that God is to be feared and glorified. The phrase **all the nations** is a figure of speech called metonymy (or, more specifically, synecdoche), where the whole is substituted for the part in order to emphasize that many will worship. It does not mean that every person in every nation (the whole) will worship the Lord, but that people from every nation (the part) will do so (see also 5:9; 7:9; 13:7; 14:8; 18:3, 23 for other examples of metonymy (or more specifically synecdoche): if all without exception are referred to, some of these verses would contradictorily suggest that all are redeemed and others that all are deceived and lost).

The idea of God's incomparability from the Jeremiah and Psalm texts has not arisen in vv. 3-4 by chance, since the first formulas of divine incomparability originate from the narrative of the exodus redemption itself (Exod. 15:11; Deut. 33:26-27), which is the interpretative framework of vv.

3-4 and has been explicitly highlighted first in v. 3a by the expression "the song of Moses."

V. 4 is concluded by yet a third *hoti* clause, ***For* Thy righteous acts have been revealed** (v. 4d). V. 4d is poetically parallel with v. 4b, likewise providing a reason that people should fear and glorify God (v. 4a). God should be feared *because* He is holy and *because* His righteous acts have been revealed. V. 4 concludes suitably with another OT reminiscence of the exodus from Ps. 98:2: "The Lord . . . has revealed His righteousness in the sight of the nations." The Psalm begins with a reference to Exod. 15:1, 6, 12: "O sing to the Lord a new song. . . . His right hand and His holy arm have gained the victory for Him." It also encourages the singers of the "new song" to play harps (98:5), as in Rev. 5:8; 14:2-3; 15:2-3. The Psalm's references to the exodus form part of the basis for a final statement that God "will judge the world with righteousness, and the peoples with equity" (Ps. 98:9). The same transition of thought (the exodus leading to God's judgment of the nations) is present in Revelation 15, where the "song" of the first exodus serves as a broad model for the end-time exodus. The seven plagues of the bowl judgments will emphasize this exodus theme. God pours out His judgments on the unbelieving nations over the course of the church age, culminating in His final triumph over the beast, the latter-day Pharaoh.

The use of the OT in vv. 3-4 is not the result of random selection, but is guided by the theme of the first exodus and the development of that theme later in the OT. This is but a continuation of the latter-day Red Sea setting of v. 2. The main point of vv. 2-4 is the adoration of God and the Lamb's incomparable act of redemption and judgment.

Suggestions for Reflection on 15:1-4

On the theme of God's justice in Revelation. That the saints are pictured standing on the sea and praising God and the Lamb for their victory (vv. 2-3) gives assurance that in the very place where they suffered and were sometimes apparently defeated, God's people will be vindicated and will give praise to Him and the Lamb for deliverance. Consider how often the theme of God's justice, toward both believers and unbelievers, is visited in Revelation, and how it relates back to the portrayal of the slain Lamb in ch. 5.

On worship and the holiness of God. What does it mean for you to worship God based on the fact of His holiness alone? Why should the holiness of God inspire us to worship Him?

The seven bowl judgments: God punishes the ungodly during the inter-advent age and consummately at the last day because of their persecution and idolatry (15:5–16:21)

The resumption of the introduction to the seven bowl judgments (15:5-8)

5 After these things I looked, and the temple of the tabernacle of testimony in heaven was opened,
6 and the seven angels who had the seven plagues came out of the temple, clothed in linen, clean and bright, and girded around their breasts with golden girdles.
7 And one of the four living creatures gave to the seven angels seven golden bowls full of the wrath of God, who lives forever and ever.
8 And the temple was filled with smoke from the glory of God and from His power; and no one was able to enter the temple until the seven plagues of the seven angels were finished.

5 The introduction to the bowls begun in v. 1 and interrupted in vv. 2-4 is now resumed. **After these things I looked** marks the beginning of a new vision and, in this case, the start of a new series of visions. Just as the image of a heavenly temple being opened both concluded and introduced major visionary sections in 11:19, so again the image functions in the same way, concluding the section from 12:1–14:20; 15:2-4 and introducing the bowls. V. 5 is an expansion of the vision of the seven angels which John began to view in v. 1. He sees **the temple of the tabernacle of testimony in heaven** opened. The **temple** is called the **tabernacle of testimony** because it is the heavenly equivalent of the tabernacle of testimony, which was in Israel's presence in the wilderness and is appropriate here because of the exodus context in vv. 2-4. The "testimony" was the Ten Commandments, which Moses placed in the ark of the tabernacle (cf. Exod. 25:21; 31:18; 32:15). The law of the Lord is His testimony, which reveals His just will. The tabernacle was constructed because, in revealing His just will, God was to "dwell among them" (Exod. 25:8). It also represented the mercy of God, since it was in the tabernacle that substitutionary animal sacrifices were offered to atone for Israel's sin and to reconcile the nation to their Lord. However, now the tabernacle witnesses no longer to divine mercy but to judgment, since it is introduced in v. 5 to show that it is the source of the following bowl plagues.

The "testimony" in v. 5 includes not only the law but also the "testimony of Jesus" (see on 12:17; 19:10), who sums up the OT commandments of God in Himself. This is suggested by the fact that the "testify" (Greek *martyreō*) word group occurs seventeen times elsewhere in the book with sole reference to a testimony about or from Jesus. The point is that God will reveal His just will from His heavenly dwelling place by sending forth judgments on the earth against those who reject His testimony in Jesus Christ. The clause concerning the opening of the sanctuary is nearly identical to that in 11:19 ("and the temple of God which is in heaven was opened"). The point of the ark's appearance (as a result of the temple being opened) in 11:19 was to emphasize that God was appearing to execute final judgment. Here the same theme of judgment is present, though judgments leading up to the final judgment are included in the scheme of the bowls. Already the "temple of God" (11:1-2) was said to be on earth in the form of prophets announcing their "testimony" (11:3, 7) in God's tabernacling presence, which was a form of judgment against unbelievers (11:5-6). Now the heavenly origin of their earthly testimony and judgments is in view.

6 John sees **the seven angels** introduced in v. 1 coming **out of the temple** which has been opened. As in v. 1, they have **the seven plagues**, which must mean that they have been commissioned to execute the seven bowl judgments which follow in ch. 16, since they are not actually handed the bowls until v. 7. Four times, including this verse, the bowl punishments are called "seven plagues" (15:1, 6, 8; 21:9). The only place elsewhere in Scripture outside Revelation where the same phrase in Greek or Hebrew occurs is Lev. 26:21 (LXX): "I will further bring upon you [Israel] *seven plagues* according to your sins" (the Palestinian Targum repeats "seven plagues" four times; the Hebrew text is not dissimilar: "I will increase the plague upon you seven times"). The phrase does not appear by coincidence in Revelation 15, since the same Leviticus 26 passage has been seen as formative for the first four seal judgments (see introductory comments on ch. 6).

The Leviticus text also concerns woes which God will send on Israel if they commit idolatry. Four times it is repeated that God will judge them "seven times" if they become unfaithful. Each sevenfold figurative expression introduces a successively worse ordeal, on the condition that Israel does not repent from the preceding woe. The promise interwoven in these warnings is that if Israel repents of her idolatry (cf. Lev. 26:1, 30-31) — idolatry being the problem also in Rev. 15:5–16:21 — then God will bless them again. The warnings in Leviticus were meant to lead to repentance in true believers, while only hardening apostate Israelites. The afflictions cited there not only purge and punish, but also serve as warnings for people to repent. However, the emphasis is on successively severer ordeals because of lack of repentance from idolatry, all of which ends in final judgment. As in Leviticus and throughout Revelation, the number of seven judgments is figurative for many severe judgments and does not refer to a mere actual seven woes.

The seven angels are **clothed in linen, clean and bright, and girded around their breasts with golden girdles.** This description is almost identical to that of the Son of man in 1:13, which may imply that they are identified with Him in order to act as His representatives in carrying out judgment.

The beast was said in 13:3, 12 to have received a "fatal wound (literally 'plague')," which was inflicted by Christ's death and resurrection. The bowl punishments reveal the decisive effects set in motion by Christ's defeat of the beast, which will culminate with final judgment on him and his followers.

7 Next in the vision **one of the four living creatures** (cf. 4:6) **gave to the seven angels seven golden bowls full of the wrath of God, who lives forever and ever.** Bowls in the OT were used in conjunction with the priestly service in the tabernacle or temple. Some directly connected with the service of the temple are referred to as "golden bowls" (1 Chron. 28:17; 2 Chron. 4:8, 22). Now angelic priests minister with the bowls at the heavenly altar of the tabernacle of testimony. Though the altar is not mentioned it is implied, as is clear from 16:7, where the altar is explicitly associated with the bowl judgments. This connection with the altar shows that the bowl punishments are God's answer to the saints' prayers for vindication (see on 8:3-5). This connection is confirmed by the verbal similarity between the **golden bowls full of the wrath of God** and the "golden bowls full of incense" representing the saints' prayers in 5:8. The image of "bowls" is also derived in part from Isa. 51:17, 22. Isaiah spoke of the "bowl of the cup of reeling; the chalice of My anger," drunk first by Jerusalem but soon to be poured out on Israel's tormentors, that is, Babylon (Isa. 51:22; cf. vv. 17-23). Now the same cup will be given to spiritual Babylon, as 16:19 reveals. The bowls here symbolize the wrath of God which comes to punish sinful people.

8 The concluding statement of ch. 15 underscores the fact that the bowl afflictions do not come ultimately from the seven angels, nor from the four living beings, but only from God. The temple is **filled with smoke from the glory of God and from His power** (as in Exod. 40:34-35; 1 Kgs. 8:10-11; 2 Chron. 5:13-14; Isa. 6:4). The vision appears to allude to Ezek.

10:2-4, also an introduction to an announcement of judgment, where an angelic being clothed in linen stands close to the four cherubim in the heavenly temple, which is filled with the cloud of God's glory. Ezekiel 10 is probably combined here with Isa. 6:1, 4, which has the same theophanic language and also presents a scene of heavenly beings standing in the heavenly temple introducing an announcement of judgment. Both scenes have affinities with Ezek. 43:5 and 44:4. Isa. 6:4 is the only verse in the OT which speaks of smoke filling the temple (other texts use "glory" or "cloud"), and Isa. 6:1 and 6:4 are the only verses which use "temple" in connection with the filling.

God's presence is so awesome in expressing wrath that not even heavenly beings (the angels and four living creatures were outside the temple, according to vv. 6-7) can stand in His midst: **no one was able to enter the temple until the seven plagues of the seven angels were finished**. The unapproachability of God in both the OT and Revelation texts could be due to the awfulness of His revealed presence. The priestly nature of the seven angels is suggested, not only by their attire (see on 1:13; 15:6), but also because 1 Kgs. 8:10-11 and 2 Chron. 5:13-14 mention priests who cannot stand in the midst of the divine glory. No one, not even heavenly intercessory priests, is able to hold back the hand of God when He decides to execute judgments (cf. Dan. 4:35).

Suggestions for Reflection on 15:5-8

On the mysterious efficacy of prayer. These verses reveal the connection between the "golden bowls of incense" (5:8; cf. 8:3-5), representing the prayers of the saints (verbalized in 6:10 as a cry for God's justice), and the "golden bowls full of the wrath of God," representing God's answer to those prayers. The smoke of the incense (8:4) going up before God is met, as it were, by the smoke of God's glory (15:8) coming down from His presence. So much happens between the offering up of the prayers and the answer — much suffering, much persecution, much apparent delay in respite and relief. Yet the certain fact presented here is that God will answer. Often many years pass between the offering of a prayer and its answer. This too involves the faith and perseverance of the saints (14:12) and requires wisdom from God (13:18). How important it is as we pray to ask God for His perspective, not to mention His patience, in order that we keep on praying and never get discouraged, at all times remembering Jesus' instruction that we "ought to pray and not to lose heart" (Luke 18:1).

The trumpets and the bowls

15:1, 5-8 have introduced the seven bowl plagues. Ch. 16 explains the contents of each of these woes. Many commentators argue that the trumpets are different judgments than the bowls because the first four trumpets appear to affect only nature, whereas the first four bowls affect wicked people, and because the first six trumpets are said to be partial in their effect, whereas the bowls seem to have universal effect. But the similarities overshadow the differences. Part of the answer is that what the trumpets state in a highly figurative manner is stated more directly in the bowls. Furthermore, the second and third trumpets are said explicitly to affect humanity (8:9-11), whereas the second bowl does not say this in such a direct manner. The difference in the relative extent of their effect may merely suggest that the trumpets are part of a larger process of judgment which, according to the bowls, strikes the entire world at the same time.

Both trumpets and bowls present each of the plagues in the same order: plagues striking the earth, the sea, rivers, the sun, the realm of the wicked with darkness, the Euphrates (together with influencing the wicked by demons), and the world with the final judgment (with the same imagery of lightning, sounds, thunders, earthquake, and hail). The overwhelming likeness of the trumpets and bowls is a result of both being modeled on the Exodus plagues. Each woe in each sevenfold series (except for the sixth trumpet) is an allusion to an Exodus plague. Further, in each series seven angels execute the seven plagues. These observations point to the probability that the trumpet and bowl series refer to the same series of events. The parallelism of the two series can be set out as follows (adapted from G. R. Beasley-Murray, *The Book of Revelation* [New Century; rev. ed., Grand Rapids: Eerdmans, 1978], 238-39):

The Seven Trumpets	The Seven Bowls
Hail, fire, and blood fall on the *earth,* one third of which is burned up.	A bowl is poured on the *earth.* Malignant sores come on those who have the mark of the beast and have worshiped his image.
Seventh Exodus plague (Exod. 9:22ff.)	Sixth Exodus plague (Exod. 9:8ff.)

A blazing mountain falls into the sea. One third of the sea becomes blood, a third of sea-creatures die, and a third of ships are destroyed. First Exodus plague (Exod. 7:17ff.)	A bowl is poured on the *seas.* This becomes *blood,* and *every living thing in it dies.* First Exodus plague (Exod. 7:17ff.).
A blazing star (Wormwood) falls on a third of *rivers and fountains;* their waters are poisoned and many die. First Exodus plague (Exod. 7:17ff.)	A bowl is poured on *rivers and fountains,* and they become blood. First Exodus plague (Exod. 7:17ff.)
A third of the *sun, moon, and stars* are struck. Darkness results for a third of a night and day. Ninth Exodus plague (Exod. 10:21ff.)	A bowl is poured on the *sun,* which scorches men with fire. Seventh Exodus plague (Exod. 9:22ff.)
The shaft of the pit is opened. Sun and air are *darkened* with smoke from which locusts emerge to *torment* men without the seal of God. Eighth (Exod. 10:4ff.) and ninth Exodus plagues (Exod. 10:21ff.)	A bowl is poured on the throne of the beast. His kingdom is *darkened* and men are in *anguish.* Ninth Exodus plague (Exod. 10:21ff.)
Four angels bound at *the Euphrates* are released, with their 200 million cavalry. A third of men are killed by them.	A bowl is poured on *the Euphrates,* which dries up for kings from the east. Demonic frogs deceive kings of the world to assemble for battle at Armageddon. Second Exodus plague (Exod. 8:2ff.)
Loud voices in heaven announce the coming of the kingdom of God and of Christ. *Lightning, thunder, earthquake,* and *hail* occur. Seventh Exodus plague (Exod. 9:22ff.) + Sinai theophanic description (Exod. 19:16-19)	A bowl is poured into the air, and *a loud voice from God's throne* announces, 'It is done.' *Lightning, thunder,* and an unprecedented *earthquake* occur, and terrible *hail* falls. Seventh Exodus plague (Exod. 9:22ff.) and Sinai theophany description (Exod. 19:16-19)

The exact manner in which each parallel trumpet and bowl are related must await analysis. The bowls go back in time and explain in greater detail the woes throughout the age which culminate in the final judgment. The phrase "seven plagues, which are the last" in 15:1 was seen to refer, not to trials occurring after the seals and trumpets at the very end of history, but to the bowls coming last after the seals and trumpets in the sequence of formal sevenfold visions seen by the seer. They are "last" in that they complete the thought revealed in the preceding woe visions and portray the wrath of God in a more intense manner than in the previous visions (see further on 15:1). This means that the bowl judgments do not come chronologically after the series of judgments in chs. 6–14. The bowls go back in time and explain in greater detail the woes throughout the age and culminating in the final judgment.

The purpose of this recapitulation is to explain further the extent and application of God's latter-day exodus judgments, which began to be explained with the trumpets. The trumpet visions may be compared to incomplete snapshots and the bowls to fuller photographs. The bowls reveal more clearly that the trumpets are predominantly plagues directed against unbelieving humanity. As the Exodus plagues are both a literary and theological model for the bowls, the bowl plagues are better viewed as judgments instead of mere warnings. They demonstrate God's uniqueness and incomparable omnipotence, as well as His righteous judgment (16:5-6). These plagues reveal unbelievers' hardness of heart and the fact that they are punished because of such hardness, which is expressed by their idolatry (16:2), persistent non-repentance (16:9, 11), and persecution of the saints (16:6). Also, like the trumpets, the bowls are God's further answer to the saints' plea in 6:9-11 that their persecutors be judged. Such a link is apparent in 16:5-7 by reference to the altar and to God as "holy" and His judgments as "true." This connection with 6:9-11 also explains why the bowls are not merely warnings but ultimately punishments and are called "bowls of wrath" (16:1; cf. reference to God's wrath in 15:1). The Exodus plagues are applied typologically to the ungodly throughout the inter-advent period in the first five bowls, and to the wicked at the conclusion of history in the last two bowls. The result and goal of all seven bowl judgments is not only to demonstrate God's incomparability and the just judgment of sinners, but ultimately the glory of God (so 15:8; 16:9; cf. 11:13, 15-16; 15:4; 19:1-7). The number seven is figurative and refers not to a mere seven specific woes, but to the completeness and severity of these judgments upon the wicked.

The former chapters envision the rise of the dragon (ch. 12), followed by that of the beast (13:1-10) and the false prophet (or second beast, 13:11-18), and finally Babylon's success in deceiving the nations is noted (14:8). Ch. 16 begins a segment which reverses this order in explaining the demise of these evil protagonists: Babylon (alluded to briefly in 14:8, but expanded on in 16:17-21 and chs. 17–18), followed by the beast and the false prophet (19:17-20), and finally by the dragon himself (20:10). This reversal points further to a lack of concern for chronological sequence in the book. The elimination of the four foes in fact occurs simultaneously, as is evident from the same wording and same OT allusions being utilized in the descriptions of their defeat (note the references to their being "gathered together for war" in 16:14; 19:19; 20:8).

The command to pour out the bowls (16:1)

1 And I heard a loud voice from the temple, saying to the seven angels, "Go and pour out the seven bowls of the wrath of God into the earth."

1 A **loud voice** commands the seven angels to **go and pour out the seven bowls of the wrath of God into the earth**. That God is the speaker in v. 1 is confirmed by the fact that God has just been mentioned as being in His heavenly temple (15:5-8), and by the allusion to Isa. 66:6: "a voice from the temple, the voice of the Lord who is rendering recompense to His enemies." The phrase "pour out God's wrath" in the OT is used to indicate judgment against either covenant breakers or those who have persecuted God's people (Ezek. 14:19; Jer. 10:25; similarly Ps. 69:24; Zeph. 3:8). Sometimes the formula includes fire as the *figurative* destructive effect of the pouring, which enforces a *figurative* interpretation of the bowls (e.g., Jer. 7:20; Lam. 2:4; 4:11; Ezek. 22:21-22; 30:15-16; Zeph. 3:8). The pouring out of a bowl by each angel is certainly not literal, but is rather a metaphorical representation of the execution of a divine judgment from heaven. Further study of each bowl plague will confirm a symbolic understanding.

The first five bowls: God punishes the ungodly during the inter-advent age by depriving them of earthly security because of their persecution and idolatry (16:2-11)

2 And the first angel went and poured out his bowl into the earth; and it became
a loathsome and malignant sore upon the men who had the mark of the beast
and who worshiped his image. 3 And the second angel poured out his bowl into
the sea, and it became blood like that of a dead man; and every living thing in

the sea died. [4] And the third angel poured out his bowl into the rivers and the springs of waters; and they became blood. [5] And I heard the angel of the waters saying, "Righteous art Thou, who art and who wast, O Holy One, because Thou didst judge these things; [6] for they poured out the blood of saints and prophets, and Thou hast given them blood to drink. They deserve it." [7] And I heard the altar saying, "Yes, O Lord God, the Almighty, true and righteous are Thy judgments." [8] And the fourth angel poured out his bowl upon the sun; and it was given to it to scorch men with fire. [9] And men were scorched with fierce heat; and they blasphemed the name of God who has the power over these plagues; and they did not repent, so as to give Him glory. [10] And the fifth angel poured out his bowl upon the throne of the beast; and his kingdom became darkened; and they gnawed their tongues because of pain, [11] and they blasphemed the God of heaven because of their pains and their sores; and they did not repent of their deeds.

The first bowl: God causes suffering for the idolatrous followers of the world system (16:2)

2 The first angel sets in motion his judgment, which comes to punish people because of their idol worship (those **who had the mark of the beast and who worshiped his image**). Just as the pouring out of the bowls and the mark of the beast are figurative, so also is the reference to **a loathsome and malignant sore.** The description of the first bowl's effect is based on the literal Egyptian plague of boils (Exod. 9:9-11), which is referred to in Deut. 28:35 as "sore boils." The punishment matches the crime: those who receive an idolatrous mark will be chastised by being given a penal mark. The sore here represents some form of suffering presumably like that entailed by the spiritual and psychological "torment" of the fifth trumpet (see on 9:4-6, 10).

The second bowl: God punishes the economic facet of the world system (16:3)

3 The second bowl has striking parallelism with the second trumpet. The second trumpet strikes the sea and "a third of the sea became blood; and a third of the creatures, which were in the sea and had life, died" (8:8-9). Likewise, the second bowl strikes the sea and **it became blood like that of a dead man; and every living thing in the sea died.** Both are based on Exod. 7:17-21, where Moses turned the Nile into blood and the fish in it

died. The primary difference is that the former trumpet has partial effect and the latter corresponding bowl has total effect. The second bowl shows that what can be applied partially in the trumpets can also be applied universally at times throughout the inter-advent age. The world-kingdom of Babylon is the object of the second trumpet's woe (see on 8:8-9), and the bowls generally are linked to the judgment of Babylon. This is implied from the fact that the bowls end with Babylon drinking the cup of God's wrath (16:19; also mentioned in 14:8, 10), as well as the fact that the bowls are said to be "full of the wrath of God" (15:7) and are described as "bowls of the wrath of God" (16:1).

As with the second trumpet, the similar imagery of the second bowl may indicate famine conditions, which is inextricably linked to economic deprivation. The economic implications of the judgment are also to be seen in the light of ch. 18. In fact, the "mark of the beast," which has just been mentioned in 16:2, first appeared in 13:16-17, where it had an essentially economic connotation. The second bowl is either a symbolic parallel with or an anticipation of the dissolution of "Babylon the great" as the source of prosperous maritime commerce in ch. 18. As a result, all those who make their living on the "sea" become impoverished (18:17, 19). The phrase translated **every living thing in the sea died** can be translated "every living soul in the sea died" and is similar to the second trumpet's woe of (literally) "the dying of the creatures which were in the sea which had life [literally 'souls']" (8:9). The point of the description there was to highlight maritime disaster and famine conditions in general, in which sea life dies and humans also die and suffer. The death of sea life and humans appears to be the point here as well (every use of "soul" [Greek *psychē*] except 8:9 [!] refers exclusively to people: 6:9; 12:11 ["life"]; 18:13 ["lives"], 14 ["desire of your soul"]; 20:4). Babylon's demise is referred to as "plagues" which result in "pestilence, mourning, and famine." Therefore, the sea being turned to **blood** in 16:3 is figurative, at least in part, for the demise of the ungodly world's economic life-support system, as represented by maritime commerce, which includes human suffering and loss of life. That **blood** here (and in the second trumpet, 8:8) probably includes not only the harm of sea life but also the suffering of the ungodly is evident from the immediate context (e.g., vv. 2, 8-11) and from the use of "blood" (Greek *haima*) elsewhere in Revelation without exception for the suffering of the wicked or of Christ and the saints (for the former see 11:6; 14:20; 19:13; cf. 6:12; 8:7-8; for the latter see 1:5; 5:9; 6:10; 12:11; 17:6; 18:24; 19:2). Thus, to summarize this analysis, death need not be taken literally here but could just as well suggest scarcity of sea life and of humans who work the sea, which leads to failure of economies and the suffering caused by it.

The "sea" (Greek *thalassa*) of blood as figurative for the economic life-support system of ungodly humanity is not inconsistent with the other uses of the word in the book (twenty-four times), which are susceptible to such a symbolic interpretation (except for 18:17, 19, 21), and the "many waters" of 17:1 are a picture of unbelievers throughout the earth (17:15). Furthermore, Satan's standing "on the sand of the seashore" in 13:1 may refer to his sovereignty over the wicked nations, since in 20:8 ungodly nations are compared to "the sand of the seashore." The sea from which the beast of 13:1 emerges represents the mass of nations; for the generally negative connotation of "sea" in Revelation see also on 4:6; 13:1; 15:2; 21:1.

The third bowl: God economically punishes the persecutors of His people (16:4-7)

4 The third bowl is similar to the third trumpet (8:10-11), again with the distinction between partial and universal effect (a third of the rivers and spring as opposed to **the waters and the springs of waters**) that we saw with the second bowl and trumpet (though, in fact, **the waters** are mentioned only generally and not explicitly said to be "all the waters," so that possibly only a part could be in mind). Both the third trumpet and bowl are based on the same Exodus plague and picture water being turned into blood (see on v. 3). In both bowls, the blood is figurative, standing not only for death but for suffering in general, which may lead to literal death, though we shall see that there is a more specific focus on a particular kind of suffering. Therefore, the third bowl, like the second, is also either a figurative parallel with or an anticipation of the portrayal of the destruction of "Babylon the great" as the basis of prosperous maritime commerce in ch. 18. And just as the unbelievers constituting spiritual Babylon were the object of the third trumpet's woe (see on 8:10-11), so likewise those who persecute the saints suffer from the bowl judgment (16:6). As a result, all those who make their living on the basis of sea commerce and fishing become destitute (18:10-19). Babylon's demise is referred to as "plagues" which result in "pestilence and mourning and famine" (18:8). This again points to an economic interpretation of the nature of the saints' suffering in 16:6, and of the suffering of the ungodly envisioned in this bowl. This

is supported by the verbatim parallel between 16:6 and 18:24, which says that the ungodly world is to be judged (16:6; 18:20) because it "poured out the blood of saints and prophets" (though the wording is reversed in 18:24). Since the judgment on Babylon and her dependents in 18:8-19 clearly is partly expressed in economic terms, this parallel between 16:6 and 18:24 indicates that the cause of this aspect of economic judgment is persecution by unbelievers.

5 The phrase **angel of the waters** refers to the angel's sovereignty over the waters. The angel's declaration in vv. 5-6 provides an interpretative elaboration of the third bowl. He declares that God is righteous because **Thou didst judge these things**. The angel attributes to God the threefold name found already in 1:4, 8; 4:8; 11:17, but the third part of the formula substitutes **the Holy One** for the earlier end-time title "the One who is to come." The reason for the substitution is that **Holy One** designates God's sovereign uniqueness in beginning to execute end-time judgment (**because thou didst judge these things**) in His role as "the One who is to come." The end times or latter days, as we have seen repeatedly, have been inaugurated with Christ's death and resurrection. The context of the third bowl, however, shows it is not describing the final act of judgment, but the trials which lead up to it. The OT use of the formula especially focused on God's ability to deliver His people despite the overwhelming odds of antagonistic world kingdoms (see on 1:4, 8). The formula is used likewise in connection with the third bowl, since it is a judgment which vindicates not only God's name but also His people, who have been judged guilty by the world system. Therefore, the use of the threefold formula here implies that the act of judgment envisioned is another demonstration of God's sovereignty over history. The combined use here of **Holy One** and the verb **judge** reflects the same twofold description of God in 6:10, the appeal to God by persecuted saints that He will vindicate Himself and them by judging their persecutors. Therefore, the woe of the third bowl is part of God's answer to the saints' plea in ch. 6.

6 The introductory word **for** further elucidates the basis for the declaration of God's character in v. 5. It is based on His judgment of persecutors according to the OT principle that the punishment should fit the crime: **for they poured out the blood of saints and prophets, and Thou hast given them blood to drink. They deserve it.** The use of **poured out** for both the pouring out of blood by the wicked here and the pouring out of wrath against the wicked by angels (as in v. 4) highlights that same principle. The judgment of blood in v. 6 is the same as the woe of waters turning to blood in v. 4, especially since vv. 5-6 are an interpretative expansion of v. 4. Both occurrences of **blood** here represent not mere literal death but various degrees of suffering (see further on 6:9-10; 12:11).

This figurative interpretation is supported by Isa. 49:26, which probably stands behind the wording here: "And I will feed your oppressors with their own flesh, and they will become drunk with their own blood . . . and all flesh will know that I, the Lord, am your Savior." Those who have oppressed Israel will be dealt with in the manner that Israel has been treated, which includes various forms of suffering up to and including death. This eye-for-eye punishment is indicated by Isa 49:25, "I will contend with the one who contends with you." Drinking blood is thus not a limited reference to death, but to all kinds of suffering, including death. The precise reason people suffer under the judgment of the third bowl is that they have caused God's people to suffer. This is apparent not only from the Isaiah text but also from Ps. 79:3, 10, 12, which is echoed here (see on 16:1): "They have poured out their (Israel's) blood like water. . . . Let there be known among the nations in our sight, vengeance for the blood of Thy servants, which has been shed. . . . And return to our neighbors sevenfold into their bosom the reproach with which they have reproached Thee, O Lord."

That Babylon's punishment is linked with the judgment described here in v. 6 is apparent from the similar imagery of blood in 17:6; 18:24; and 19:2, which is part of the description of her judgment. In the same way that God (4:11), the Lamb (5:9, 12) and His followers (3:4) are "worthy" to receive blessing, the persecutors are "worthy" and deserving of being cursed.

7 Another declaration by a different angel or by Christ comes forth from the altar. The mention of the **altar** together with the declaration **true and righteous are Thy judgments** adds to the link to 6:9-10 observed in v. 5. The voice may represent the souls of the martyrs John heard crying out for justice in those verses. In the OT and elsewhere in Revelation, the name **Lord God, the Almighty** alludes to God's absolute sovereignty over the historical affairs of His people (see further 1:8 and 15:3). Just as the God of the exodus generation was praised as One whose "work is perfect" and "all His ways are just" (Deut. 32:4), so likewise is He acknowledged again in connection with the latter-day plagues. In fact, the identical phrase (**Lord God, the Almighty**) has occurred already in 15:3, where it refers to God's judgment and redemption as a part of the grand exodus at the consummation of the ages.

The fourth bowl: God punishes the ungodly because of their idolatry (16:8-9)

8 The fourth angel pours his bowl on the sun, causing it to **scorch men with fire**. God's sovereignty over the plague is expressed by the phrase **was given**, and is explicitly indicated in v. 9: "God who has the power over these plagues." It is important to recall that since the language describing the commencement of each bowl judgment is figurative (he **poured out his bowl upon**), the resulting effect of each judgment is likewise figurative (see on v. 1). Therefore, the burning of people with fire in v. 8 is also likely not literal. The pouring out of God's wrath in the OT is often figuratively expressed as accompanied by fire: "My anger and my wrath will be poured out on this place, on man and on beast . . . and it will burn and not be quenched" (Jer. 7:20); "I shall gather you and blow on you with the fire of my wrath, and you will be melted in the midst of it . . . and you will know that I, the Lord, have poured out my wrath on you" (Ezek. 22:21-22). The fourth bowl speaks figuratively, in line with OT language, of God's judgment on those who blaspheme Him (v. 8), and it cannot be assumed that literal fire is a component of this judgment. The figurative view is supported further by patterns of similar imagery in the OT and Judaism, in which interruption of the regular patterns of the heavenly light sources predominantly symbolizes covenantal judgment. The symbolism of cosmic alteration indicates that people are to be judged because they have altered God's moral laws, usually through idolatry (for references and discussion, see on 8:12).

9 The concluding effect of the fourth bowl, that the sun will scorch people with fire, is repeated in the first part of the verse. The repetition emphasizes that **men were scorched with fierce heat**. They will thus be repaid in like manner for what they have done to the redeemed, for, according to 7:16, the deceased saints will be delivered from their previous condition: "neither shall the sun beat down on them, nor any heat." That imagery is combined with language referring to economic suffering, as is also the case in Isa. 49:10, to which Rev. 7:16 alludes ("They will not hunger or thirst; neither will the scorching heat or sun strike them down"). Deut. 32:24 explains that part of the curse for covenantal disobedience is that people will be "consumed by burning heat," and this is directly linked in that verse to the woe of being "wasted by famine," which has economic connotations. This punishment of the fourth bowl, occurring prior to the return of Christ, anticipates the final judgment of Babylon, which also will be burned by fire (cf. v. 8, "scorch with fire," with 17:16 and 18:8, "burn up with fire").

This bowl plague brings about only blasphemy and non-repentance, much like the results of the sixth trumpet. The similarity suggests that the *burning* of 16:8-9 is a suffering like the three plagues of "fire and smoke and brimstone" in 9:17-18. Both there and here the plague of fire is a figurative woe comparable to the fire that the two witnesses unleash against their unbelieving opponents during the church age (11:5-7). There, the fire is a form of spiritual judgment against persecutors, which also lays the basis for their future, final punishment (see on 9:17-18; 11:5-7). The blaspheming is a defiant *slandering or defaming* of the name of the true God. God's "name" represents His attributes and character. Therefore, the reprobates utter lies about God's character as a vengeful response to the punishments which they experience under His hand. The blasphemy shows they have become like the false, beastly god which they worship, since elsewhere outside ch. 16 "blaspheming" is attributed only to the beast (13:1, 5, 6; 17:3). The beast likewise begins to engage in blasphemy only after he has been struck by a divine "plague," that is, his apparently fatal wound (13:3-8). The focus of the people's blasphemy probably includes a denial that their afflictions are sovereign punishments from God. Their blasphemy would presumably also entail a denial that God really and ultimately **has the power over these plagues**. The plural "plagues" suggests that recipients of the woe of the fourth bowl also suffer under the trials unleashed by the preceding and following bowls. **They did not repent, so as to give Him glory**, thus becoming immovable in their refusal to acknowledge God's glorious character.

The fifth bowl: God punishes hardened idolaters by causing them to suffer through revealing to them their irremediable separation from Him (16:10-11)

10 The contents of the fifth bowl are **poured out . . . upon the throne of the beast**. The **throne** represents the beast's sovereignty over his realm. Therefore, the bowl affects his ability to rule. The result of the judgment is that **his kingdom became darkened**. Like the fourth trumpet, this woe is also based on Exod. 10:21-29, where God brought darkness over Egypt (see on 8:12). The Egyptian plague was partly a polemic against the sun god Ra, of whom Pharaoh was believed to be an incarnation. The plague came against Pharaoh because of his disobedience to God's command, as well as oppression of Israel and allegiance to Egypt's idolatrous system.

The phrase **throne of the beast** is to be identified with "Satan's throne" in 2:13. There the throne refers to Pergamum as a center of Roman government and of the imperial cult, which was ultimately under Satanic control. Consequently, the similar woe in Revelation 16 is appropriately directed against world rulers who oppress the saints and foster idolatry (see on 13:1-7). This could include internal rebellion against rulers and their allies or removal of political and religious power from the state.

Exod. 10:23 explains that the darkness was so dense that the Egyptians were visually separated from one another ("they did not see one another"). Early Jewish interpreters thought, probably correctly, that the darkness of this Egyptian plague symbolized spiritual separation from the true God (Wisd. 17:2 says they were "exiled from the eternal providence"), and pictured the eternal darkness of hell which awaited them (Wisd. 17:21; likewise Midrash Rabbah Exod. 14.2 on Exod. 10:22). The darkness caused horror and fear (Wisdom 17–18). The height of their spiritual anguish was that the Egyptians' contemplation of their own wretchedness became "more burdensome than the darkness" itself (Wisd. 17:21).

Isa. 8:21-22 says that a severe famine will come on sinful Israel. The famine is linked with "darkness so that they could not see" (LXX), as well as with "distress and darkness, the gloom of anguish." Their response to the famine is to be "enraged and curse their king and their God as they face upward." Likewise in Jeremiah 13, Israel is commanded to "give glory to the Lord" (which they will not do, as in Rev. 16:9) before God "brings darkness and . . . makes it into deep darkness, and turns it into gloom" (v. 16). The darkness is interpreted as the coming captivity of the nation (vv. 19-20) which will cause "pangs" (v. 21). The darkness strikes even the kings that sit on the throne (cf. v. 13 with v. 16). This punishment comes because of idolatry (vv. 10, 13).

The darkness in Rev. 16:10 has the same general figurative significance as in the Exodus, Isaiah, and Jeremiah passages. It is metaphorical for all ordained events designed to remind the ungodly that their persecution and idolatry are in vain, and it indicates their separation from God. As with the Egyptians, this darkness induces anguish, figuratively expressed by the phrase **they gnawed their tongues because of pain**. God causes all who follow the beast to have times of anguish and horror when they realize that they are in spiritual darkness, that they are separated from God and that eternal darkness awaits them. The temporal judgment in v. 10 is a precursor of the final judgment, when unbelievers will be "cast into the outer darkness," where "there shall be weeping and gnashing of teeth" (Matt. 8:12; cf. Matt. 22:13; 25:30).

11 The suffering of v. 10 does not soften the subjects of the beast but, like Pharaoh and his subjects (cf. Exod. 10:1-2), hardens them further in their antagonism to God: **and they blasphemed the God of heaven because of their pains and their sores; and they did not repent of their deeds.** The lack of repentance here and throughout ch. 16 (vv. 9, 11, 21) is irremediable, according to the theological pattern of the hardening of Pharaoh. Though a remnant of Egyptians did repent and came out of Egypt with Israel, the vast majority refused to trust in Israel's God. The remnant from the world who repent do so only because they have been sealed by God (7:1-4; 14:1-2). The rest do not believe because they have not been so sealed but can only give allegiance to the beast, whose mark they gladly receive (13:8, 16-17). Their sinful deeds include murder, sorcery, and immorality, which is implied by the exact parallel of this verse with 9:20 ("they did not repent of the works of their hands"), which is then followed by the list of those vices in 9:21. The mention of **sores** points back to the first bowl plague and suggests that the sufferers of the fifth bowl also sustain injury from the previous bowls and vice-versa (for the same idea see on v. 9).

The sinful **deeds** from which **they did not repent** include murder and thievery, as well as idol worship, sorcery, and immorality. These vices are implied by the verbatim parallel of 16:11 with 9:20, the latter of which is followed by the above vice list:

Rev. 9:20	Rev. 16:11
They "did not repent of the works of their hands."	"They did not repent of their deeds."

Suggestions for Reflection on 16:1-11

On the bowl plagues as expressing the judgment of God. In the bowl plagues of vv. 1-11 the parallel to the plagues of Egypt come most clearly into focus, climaxing in v. 11 in the response of blasphemy rather than repentance. The commentary draws the conclusion that judgment, rather than warning, is at the heart of these plagues. Part of the reason for this conclusion is the analogy to the hardening of the heart of Pharaoh and the Egyptians, whom the plagues drove further from God rather than being an occasion for repentance, though a remnant did repent and came out of Egypt with the Israelites. How in this process are the mercy, the justice, and the judgment of God illustrated?

On God's judgment of the world's economic system. These plagues make clear how God carries out His judgment against the economic system of the world, which the enemy and his agents have used to deceive unbelievers and lure them away from worship of the true God. Collapse of the economic system eventually plunges the kingdom of the beast into darkness (v. 10). How careful are we as Christians to avoid dependence on this system or compromise with it? How closely and regularly do we examine the values governing our attitude toward money and material success? Do we depend on some aspect of the world and its physical security, which God intends to remove at the end of history? How can this become an idolatrous focus of which we may not even be conscious?

On blasphemy as blaming God. How often do we place blame on God for things that go wrong in our lives? This may take the form of suppressed bitterness rather than outright declaration, but it can nonetheless be present in our hearts. The commentary suggests that in the experience of unbelievers, the response to suffering, even suffering caused by their own sin and rebellion against God, is to blame God. Yet how often do we blame God (or others) for the consequences of our own sin? Do we realize that when we do so, we are actually perilously close to blaspheming God, insofar as blasphemy is a failure to honor God for who He truly is and for His mercy in sparing us from the judgment, punishment, and true suffering we in fact deserve?

The sixth and seventh bowls: the final judgment of the evil world system (16:12-21)

12 And the sixth angel poured out his bowl upon the great river, the Euphrates;
and its water was dried up, that the way might be prepared for the kings from the
east. 13 And I saw coming out of the mouth of the dragon and out of the mouth
of the beast and out of the mouth of the false prophet, three unclean spirits like
frogs; 14 for they are spirits of demons, performing signs, which go out to the
kings of the whole world, to gather them together for the war of the great day of
God, the Almighty. 15 ("Behold, I am coming like a thief. Blessed is the one who
stays awake and keeps his garments, lest he walk about naked and men see his
shame.") 16 And they gathered them together to the place which in Hebrew is

called Har-Magedon. [17] And the seventh angel poured out his bowl upon the air; and a loud voice came out of the temple from the throne, saying, "It is done." [18] And there were flashes of lightning and sounds and peals of thunder; and there was a great earthquake, such as there had not been since man came to be upon the earth, so great an earthquake was it, and so mighty. [19] And the great city was split into three parts, and the cities of the nations fell. And Babylon the great was remembered before God, to give her the cup of the wine of His fierce wrath. [20] And every island fled away, and the mountains were not found. [21] And huge hailstones, about one hundred pounds each, came down from heaven upon men; and men blasphemed God because of the plague of the hail, because its plague was extremely severe.

The sixth bowl: God gathers together ungodly forces in order to punish them decisively at the end of the age (16:12-16)

12 The woe of the sixth bowl (**And the sixth angel poured out his bowl upon the great river, the Euphrates; and its water was dried up**) is depicted according to the description of God's judgment of Babylon and Israel's restoration, which itself was patterned after the drying up of the Red Sea at the exodus (cf. Exod. 14:21-22 with Isa. 11:15; 44:27; 50:2; 51:10). The OT prophesied that this judgment would include the drying up of the Euphrates River (Isa. 11:15; 44:27-28; Jer. 50:38; 51:36; cf. Zech. 10:11). The prophecy was fulfilled fairly literally by Cyrus, who diverted the waters of the Euphrates (Isa. 44:27-28). This allowed his army to cross the now shallow waters of the river, enter the city unexpectedly, and defeat the Babylonians. God executed judgment against Babylon by raising up Cyrus, who was to come "from the east" (Isa. 41:2; 46:11), or "from the rising of the sun" (41:25). Jer. 50:41 and 51:11, 28 refer to "kings" whom God was preparing to bring against Babylon. The victory by Cyrus led to Israel's release from captivity (Isa. 44:26-28; 45:13). In the OT, God is always the One who dries up the water, whether for redemption or judgment.

John understands this pattern typologically and universalizes it. As noted at Rev. 14:8, the symbolic interpretation of Babylon as representing the world system is assured beyond much reasonable doubt by the prophecies of God's judgment on historical Babylon, which foretold that Babylon will be desolate forever and never again be inhabited (Jer. 50:39-40; 51:24-26, 62-64; so also Isa. 13:19-22). As at the exodus and especially at the fall of historical Babylon, the drying up of the Euphrates in Revelation 16 marks the prelude to the destruction of latter-day Babylon. This cannot be a literal geographical reference to the Euphrates River in modern Iraq, but must be figurative and universal. This is indicated by 17:1, where the Babylonian harlot "sits on many waters," which is another way of referring to the Euphrates and its water (16:12). The "many waters" of 17:1 are figuratively interpreted as "peoples and multitudes . . . and nations and tongues" in 17:15. Rev. 17:15-18 is a specific amplification of v. 12, since ch. 17 is an expansion of the sixth and seventh bowl judgments directed against Babylon (so 17:1, where one of the bowl angels introduces the judgment). A symbolic interpretation of the Euphrates River is suggested also by the figurative use of "sea," "river," or "water" elsewhere in the book *when in conjunction with the dragon, the beast, or their followers* (see on 12:15, 16; 13:1; 15:2; 17:1, 15). Therefore, *the drying up of the Euphrates' waters is a picture of how the multitudes of Babylon's religious adherents throughout the world become disloyal to it.* This is explained further in 17:16-17 (on which see).

Not only is there a figurative universalization of Babylon and the Euphrates River, but also of Cyrus and his allies: **the kings from the east** are interpretatively escalated into "the kings of the whole world" (16:14; cf. 17:18). The same phenomenon appears in 20:8. There the traditional northern enemies, Gog and Magog, which are also gathered together for the war (compare 16:14 and 19:19 with 20:8), are explained to be the nations which are "in the four corners of the earth." The common point between the OT forerunners and the latter-day fulfillment is that in each case it is God who dries the waters up; in each case a force, either good (Cyrus) or evil (Pharaoh or the kings of the east), crosses through; and in each case a battle ensues, in which God's people are delivered. The idea here is that God, as He did in the days of Cyrus, will dry up the waters of the river protecting and nurturing Babylon to allow for the kings of the earth, under immediate demonic influence but ultimately under God's sovereign control, to gather together in order for Babylon to be defeated and for His eternal kingdom and the reign of His saints to be established.

13 V. 12 is a summary statement of the sixth bowl, which shows that the judgment is commenced from heaven by angelic activity. Vv. 13-16 spell out the specific details of the bowl by explaining the secondary earthly agents who execute the woe and then asserting the purpose of the woe. The pouring out of the bowl sets in motion actions by the three great opponents of the saints and leaders of the forces of evil: **And I saw coming**

out of the mouth of the dragon and out of the mouth of the beast and out of the mouth of the false prophet, three unclean spirits like frogs. This is the first time that the phrase **false prophet** occurs in the book. It summarizes the deceptive role of the second beast of ch. 13, whose purpose is to deceive people so that they will worship the first beast. Elsewhere in the NT, the false prophets without exception speak falsehood *within the context of the covenant community of Israel or the church* in order to deceive (Matt. 7:15; 24:11, 24; Mark 13:22; Luke 6:26; Acts 13:6; 2 Pet. 2:1; 1 John 4:1). This points further to the conclusion in 13:11-17 that the second beast's activity is conducted not only outside but also within the churches, which is confirmed further here by vv. 14-16 (especially the exhortation to saints not to compromise in v. 15).

The description of the spirits as **unclean** suggests their spiritually deceptive nature. The same word is used to describe the deceptive and ungodly activities of Babylon in 17:4 and 16:2, where her uncleanness is associated with her "immorality" (Greek *porneia*). For the association of "immorality" with idolatry see on 2:14. The deceptive nature of the spirits is pointed to by the linking of the "unclean things of her [Babylon's] immorality" in 17:4 and Babylon's immoral uncleanness in 18:2-3 with Babylon's powers of ungodly deception here in vv. 13-14. In this respect, note the wording of 18:2 (Babylon is "a dwelling place of demons and a prison of every unclean spirit") in relation to the reference in vv. 13-14 to "unclean spirits like frogs . . . they are spirits of demons." These Babylonian spirits in vv. 13-14 deceive people about idol worship. See further on 14:8 for the link between Babylon's immorality and deception.

That **unclean spirits** refer to demonic beings is evident from observing that the same phrase has this meaning elsewhere in the NT (so about twenty times in the Gospels and Acts), and this is made explicit in v. 14. The only other places in biblical literature where the word "frog" appears are Exod. 8:2-13 and Pss. 78:45; 105:30, all of which describe the Exodus plague. The frogs appeared harmless, yet they "destroyed" the Egyptians (Ps. 78:45). Now they appear as wise counselors, but are spiritually corrupt. The depiction of frogs here as unclean is consistent with Lev. 11:9-12, 41-47, where frogs are counted among the "unclean" animals from which one needs cleansing. It may be that frogs are chosen to represent deceptive spirits partly because of their characteristic croaking, which is loud but meaningless. Here, in connection with the mouths of the three agents of evil, the frogs and their croaking represent the confusion brought about by deception (as suggested by Jewish commentators in interpreting the

Exodus plague of frogs: e.g., Philo, *On Dreams* 2.259-60; *On the Sacrifices of Abel and Cain* 69). Perhaps frogs are chosen as pictures of deceptive influence because they were one of the two Egyptian plagues which Pharaoh's magicians were able to reproduce through their deceptive arts (Exod. 8:7). Here also the frogs perform signs (v. 14), ultimately under the hand of God. Divine superintendence is clear from the model of the Exodus plagues; cf. also the background of Zechariah 12–14 in relation to God's sovereign gathering together of the nations for war (and see on v. 14b below). The historical plague of frogs now is applied symbolically to deceptive spirits. The allusion is one of the clearest examples in the book of a literal Exodus plague which is reapplied symbolically to a new situation and spiritualized!

14a For they are spirits of demons introduces an explanation of the unclean spirits and frogs of the previous verse. The frog plague in Egypt was partly a polemic against the goddess Heqt, who was the goddess of resurrection and was symbolized by a frog. The deceptive activity is appropriately portrayed as frog-like, since the evil triumvirate were attempting to deceive people about the purported fact of the beast's resurrection (see on 13:1-5). The rationale for demonizing the frogs from Exodus is based in part on the biblical evaluation that behind false gods and idols were demons (see on 9:20).

14b These demons are **performing signs**, which identifies them further with the work of the deceptive agents of ch. 13, especially with the activity of the second beast or false prophet, whose work is described in 13:13 and 19:20: "he performs great signs" and "[he] who performed the signs . . . by which he deceived those who had received the mark of the beast and those who worshiped his image." These demons **go out to the kings of the whole world**. Likewise, in the Exodus plagues the frogs first affected the king (Exod. 8:3-4), and Ps. 105:30 says only that "kings" in Egypt were struck by the frogs. That these are **kings of the whole world**, and not merely from one region, is shown by use of the same and like phrases elsewhere in the book and Johannine literature (3:10; 12:9; cf. 13:3 and 1 John 2:2; 5:19). In fact, "the kings from the east" (v. 12) may be synonymous with **the kings of the whole world**. The universal application is also apparent from 13:14, where idolatrous earth-dwellers are deceived, and from 19:19-20, where the "kings of the earth" are likewise deceived. The kings represent political authorities of the ungodly world system. Indeed, the phrase "kings of the earth" is used with such an earthly political sense repeatedly elsewhere in the book: cf. 1:5 and 6:15, as well as 17:2, 18 and 18:3, 9, which refer to the kings' allegiance to idolatrous Babylon.

The purpose of the deception is **to gather them together for the war of the great day of God, the Almighty**. The same phrase occurs in chs. 19 and 20, where it refers respectively to the beast and the dragon gathering kings together to fight against Christ at His final coming: "And I saw . . . the kings of the earth . . . gathered together to make war" (19:19); "[Satan] will come out to deceive the nations . . . to gather them together for the war" (20:8). Those texts and this one here refer to the confrontation between Christ and the forces of the beast at the very end of the age and are based on OT prophecy, especially from Zechariah 12–14 and possibly Zeph. 3:8-20, as well as Ezek. 38:2-9; 39:1-8, which foretold that God would gather the nations together in Israel for the final war of history. Particularly in mind behind the notion of gathering kings for battle are Zech. 14:2 ("I will gather all the nations against Jerusalem to battle"); 12:3-4 ("all the nations of the earth will be gathered together against it. 'In that day,' declares the Lord . . ."); and 14:13 ("and it will come about in that day that a great panic from the Lord will fall on them"). In Jewish literature, *4 Ezra* 13:34-35 alludes to the picture of Zech. 14:2, as does *1 Enoch* 56:5-8, in the context of the final battle of history of the nations against the Messiah. Strikingly, Zech. 13:2 (LXX) says that the activity of "false prophets and the unclean spirit" will be active in Israel contemporaneously with the gathering of the nations. The false prophets encourage idolatry (Zech. 13:2) and delude Israel about the truth (the Aramaic translation of Zech. 13:2 has "*deceitful* prophets and the unclean spirit"). Later Jewish interpreters also identified the "unclean spirit" of Zech. 13:2 as demonic (Midrash Rabbah Num. 19.8; Pesikta de Rab Kahana 4.7; Pesikta Rabbati 14.14).

All three parallel clauses in Rev. 16:14; 19:19; and 20:8 have the definite article, "*the* war," because they are referring to the well-known "war of the end" prophesied in the OT. 20:7-10 shows this war to be part of the final attack of Satan's forces against the saints. Therefore, it is the same war as in 11:7, since that battle is also one in which the beast attempts to annihilate the whole body of believers on earth (see on 11:7-10). In this light, the definite article may be an article of previous reference, not only (as noted above) to OT prophecy, but also back to the initial description of the last battle in 11:7 (which has no definite article before "war"). That the battle is called **the war of the great day of God, the Almighty** indicates that the battle is one in which God will decisively judge the unrighteous. This is the meaning of the phrase "the great day of the Lord" in Joel 2:11 and Zeph. 1:14 and of the eschatological prophecy of judgment in Joel 2:31 (also alluded to in Matt. 24:29; Mark 13:24; Acts 2:20). The nations are deceived into thinking that they are gathering to exterminate the saints, but in fact they are gathered together ultimately by God in order to meet their own judgment at the hands of Jesus (19:11-21).

15 A parenthetical exhortation is addressed to believers: **Behold, I am coming like a thief. Blessed is the one who stays awake and keeps his garments.** The voice exhorts them to be ever vigilant for Christ's final appearing, since He will come unexpectedly **like a thief**. In context, the exhortation appears abruptly and seems awkward, but upon closer study it has a similar function to the exhortations in 13:9 and 14:12: in the midst of suffering, the saints are to persevere. According to 20:8, the war is directed first against the saints, and the identical scenario is implicit in 16:14 (and in 19:19, in light of 17:14; 20:8; Zech. 14:2ff.; *4 Ezra* 13:34-35; *1 Enoch* 56:5-8; see on v. 14 above). A time will come when the beast will attempt to annihilate the entire community of faith (so 20:8-9 and 11:7). This onslaught on the "great day" of God and the Lamb (6:17) could occur at any hour, and believers must be prepared to hold firm in faith and not compromise when it does happen. The thief metaphor from the gospel tradition is used not to suggest any idea of burglary but only to convey the unexpected and sudden nature of Christ's coming. In the context of ch. 16 and Revelation in general, staying awake and keeping one's garments refers to being alert in not conceding to the idolatrous demands of beast worship (see on 3:4-5) in the face of the pressure of the final attack.

If a believer so cares for his garments, then he will not **walk about naked** and people will not **see his shame**. This develops the same imagery as 3:18, where uncovering the shame of the Laodiceans' nakedness was a metaphor drawn from God's accusations of Israel and other nations for participation in idolatry (so Ezek. 16:36; 23:29; Nah. 3:5; Isa. 20:4). Yahweh would figuratively lift up the skirts of idolaters (strip their cities bare through judgment) in order to show that they had committed fornication with false gods. John warns that such exposure due to lack of vigilance in the end-time war will identify compromising believers with the Babylonian harlot, who will be judged for her idolatry by being made "desolate and naked" (17:16). The **garments** symbolize a refusal to compromise with the world and are to be identified with the "fine linen . . . the righteous acts of the saints" (19:8-9), which are necessary for admission to the marriage supper of the Lamb, whereas nakedness, by contrast, signifies lack of righteousness.

16 After the parenthetical exhortation in v. 15, the thought of v. 14 is picked up again. The demonic spirits deceiving the kings **gathered them together to the place which in Hebrew is called Har-Magedon**, where the war is to occur. The outcome of the war is found in 17:14; 19:14-21; and 20:7-10, where the forces of the dragon and beast are portrayed as destroyed by Christ and God. Har-Magedon, or Armageddon as it is usually called, like the place names "Babylon" and "Euphrates," does not refer to a specific geographical locale, but has global application.

That Armageddon is not to be taken literally is shown by the fact that the plain of Megiddo is about a two days' walk north of Jerusalem, whereas OT prophecy generally places the last battle in the immediate vicinity of Jerusalem and Mount Zion or its surrounding mountains (Joel 2:1, 32; Mic. 4:11-12; Zech. 12:3-4; 14:2, 13-14; Ezek. 38:8 and 39:2-8 speak of the "mountains of Israel" and 38:16 of the whole land of Israel as the battleground). Zech. 12:1-14 pictures the end-time attack by the nations against Jerusalem, in which the nations are destroyed but the righteous remnant receives the Spirit of grace, as they look on the One "whom they have pierced" (v. 10) and mourn for Him. Furthermore, John himself places the location directly outside Jerusalem in 14:20 and 20:8-9, though he typologically universalizes the OT references and speaks in spiritual rather than literal geographical terms. Also, if 20:8 is a parallel referring to the same event as 16:14, as argued above (see on v. 14), then 20:9 defines Armageddon as "the beloved city" of Jerusalem, and likely as Mount Zion, both of which in John's terms refer to the worldwide church (see on 20:9). A figurative view of Armageddon is also apparent from the fact that there is no mention of a "mountain" of Megiddo in the OT or in Jewish literature. In OT times, the city of Megiddo would have sat on a "tell" or very small hill, whereas the normal meaning of the word *har* in Hebrew is a mountain.

Armageddon, literally in Hebrew the "mount of Megiddo," may have been named as the site of the last battle because Israel's battles in the plain of Megiddo became a prophetic or typological symbol of the last battle. First, the battle between Barak and Sisera took place at Megiddo (Judg. 5:19), as did the battle between Pharaoh Neco (on his way to the Euphrates!) and Josiah (2 Kgs. 23:29; 2 Chron. 35:22). Megiddo became proverbial in Judaism as the place where righteous Israelites were attacked by evil nations. In particular, the battle between Barak and Sisera served as a pattern for Israel's defeat of a foe with overwhelmingly greater power (Judg. 4:3; 5:8). God said He would draw out the commander of the army, with his chariots and many troops, to the river Kishon (Judg. 4:7), where the kings came and fought at the waters of Megiddo (Judg. 5:19). In the same way God is ultimately the One drawing the enemy kings together to do battle at Megiddo (here in vv. 12-14, 16).

But the fact that there never was any mountain of Megiddo suggests a second possibility. Not far from Megiddo is Mount Carmel, and if the mountain of Megiddo is to be identified with Mount Carmel, there may well be a symbolic reference to the site of one of the OT's greatest battles between the forces of good and evil (1 Kgs. 18:19-46), where Elijah (symbolic, along with Moses, of the church in Rev. 11:3-7) defeated the prophets of Baal. Mount Carmel thus becomes symbolically representative of the end-time church.

All of the above passages recording events occurring in the vicinity of Megiddo may stand behind the reference in Rev. 16:16, so that John's reference to this place may ring with the following typological and prophetic associations: the defeat of kings who oppress God's people (Judg. 5:19-21), the destruction of false prophets (1 Kgs. 18:40), the death of misled kings, which led to mourning (2 Kgs. 23:29; 2 Chron. 35:20-25), combined with the future expectation of a future final battle in which, in direct connection with the One "whom they have pierced" (Zech. 12:10), would occur destruction of "all the nations that come against Jerusalem" (Zech. 12:9) and mourning by all Israel's tribes (Zech. 12:10-14). That Zech. 12:1-14 is perhaps uppermost in mind is apparent from observing that Zech. 12:11 is the only instance prior to Rev. 16:16 where the name Megiddo appears in an apocalyptic context concerning God's end-time destruction of ungodly nations and the only OT text where the Hebrew spells Megiddo as *megiddon* (= English "magedon").

The seventh bowl: God punishes the ungodly world system with final judgment (16:17-21)

17 The seventh bowl describes the final destruction of the corrupt world system, which follows on the heels of the battle of Armageddon: **And the seventh angel poured out his bowl upon the air**. The presence of hailstones in v. 21 suggests a link with the Exodus plague of hail (Exod. 9:22-35). The "sun and the air" were darkened by the smoke coming out of the pit at the sound of the fifth trumpet (Rev. 9:2), which seems to associate the "air" here with demonic activity. In Eph. 2:2, Satan is referred to as the "prince of the power of the air." As in the fourth, fifth, and sixth bowls, the judgment here is also upon the unbelieving realm ruled over by the dragon and the beast. Note especially that in v. 10, the bowl is poured out "upon the throne of the beast; and his kingdom became darkened."

The utterance **and a loud voice came out of the temple from the**

throne is that of either God or Christ, since it comes from the throne itself. The announcement "**It is done**" marks the historical realization of the purpose of the seven bowls stated in 15:1: "in them (the bowls) the wrath of God *is finished.*" The declaration is the converse (using the same Greek verb) of Christ's accomplishment of redemption at the cross ("it is finished" in John 19:30). It is a part of the same event of final judgment of the wicked referred to in Rev. 21:3-6, where the same phrase, "a loud voice from the throne" (21:3), is followed by "it is done" (21:6). There the focus is on final punishment of the wicked and the destruction of the old cosmos (21:1, 8), as well as on the complete redemption of God's people in a new creation (cf. 21:1-7, 9–22:5).

18 And there were flashes of lightning and sounds and peals of thunder; and there was a great earthquake is imagery of the last judgment. It is based in large part on Exod. 19:16-18, which describes the appearance of God on Mount Sinai (see also Ps. 77:18 and Isa. 29:6, the latter of which says, "You will be punished with thunder and earthquake and loud noise"). As noted in the discussion on 8:5, Richard Bauckham has shown that 4:5; 8:5; 11:19; and 16:18-21 form a progressive sequence of allusions to Exodus 19:16, 18-19, which systematically build upon one another in expressing aspects of divine judgment, commencing with lightnings, sound, and thunders in 4:5, and at each step adding in other elements. Jesus used earthquake imagery to portray woes preliminary to the final cosmic destruction but not part of it (Matt. 24:7; Mark 13:8; Luke 21:11). These features of cosmic destruction from the OT are now applied typologically to the unqualified judgment at the end of world history. But the escalated nature of the application here is expressed by the phrase **such as there had not been since man came to be upon the earth, so great an earthquake was it, and so mighty**. And it is beyond chance that this wording is taken from Dan. 12:1: "And there will be a time of distress such as never occurred since there was a nation until that time." Daniel describes the tribulation at the end of history, when God's people will be delivered and undergo a resurrection to life, but the wicked will be raised to "disgrace and everlasting contempt" (Dan. 12:2). In the context of the plague of hail (cf. v. 21), note that Daniel's wording is itself a typological application of Exod. 9:24, where there is fire flashing in the midst of the hail so severe "such as had not been in all the land of Egypt since it became a nation."

19 The effects of the incomparable earthquake mentioned in v. 18 are elaborated: **And the great city was split into three parts, and the cities of the nations fell.** The depiction is fashioned according to the biblical expectation of a catastrophic earthquake accompanying God's latter-day appearing at the final judgment (Hag. 2:6; Zech. 14:4; Heb. 12:26-27). The object of judgment is explicitly identified: **And Babylon the great was remembered before God.** The background to the phrase **Babylon the great** is Dan. 4:30 (cf. 14:8), which is the only place in all the OT where the phrase "Babylon the great" occurs. Now the latter-day Babylon is about to face judgment, as did the proud Babylonian king who was so proud of his worldly and superficial "Babylon the great." That **the cities of the nations fell** describes the universal extent of the last judgment to take place in history. It is not just Rome or some later great capital of evil which is decimated, but all the world's cultural, political, and economic centers, because they are part of the great city and world system of Babylon. The picture here, **give her the cup of the wine of His fierce wrath**, develops the similar picture of the last judgment in 14:8, 10, where Babylon the great has fallen and her patron nations are made to "drink of the wine of the wrath of God, which is mixed in full strength in the cup of his anger" (14:10). Now we find that Babylon herself, the inducer of the nations' intoxication, will be punished in like manner, under God's judging hand, by being made to drink the wine that leads to her own destructive intoxication. On the OT background of the pouring out of wine as describing the unleashing of divine judgment see on 14:10. The judgment highlights that Babylon's punishment fits her crime, a principle already illustrated in 16:6. As she destroyed (11:18), so shall she be destroyed. V. 19, together with vv. 17-21, amplify the introductory statement of Babylon's fall (in 14:8), which is expanded in detail in 17:1–19:10.

The **great city** has been identified as Jerusalem, Rome, and the ungodly world system, which would include the former two and all other wicked people groups. The third view is preferable, as argued elsewhere in this commentary (see on 11:8 and 14:8).

20 The absolute nature of the judgment is continued by a picture of the further breakup of the cosmos: **And every island fled away, and the mountains were not found.** Virtually identical descriptions in 6:14 ("and every mountain and island were moved out of their places") and 20:11 ("earth and heaven fled away, and no place was found for them") also indicate the conclusive, universal destruction of the earth at the Judgment Day. That parts of the world **were not found** anticipates the similar portrayal of Babylon's final, definitive destruction repeated three times in ch. 18 (vv. 14, 21, 22).

21 The Exodus plague of hail (Exod. 9:22-35) is duplicated, but this time it strikes not one nation but all nations throughout the world in opposition to God: **And huge hailstones, about one hundred pounds each, came down from heaven upon men.** The hail comes down from heaven upon the unfaithful as "fire came down from heaven" upon the persecuting nations in 20:9, which also alludes to the conclusive punishment. The plague of hail, which was not the last of the original Exodus plagues, is being combined here with the cosmic phenomena surrounding the Sinai theophany of Exodus 19, alluded to in v. 18 above. Perhaps hail is easily associated with the lightning, thunder, clouds, smoke, and trumpet sounds of Sinai.

The identification of this plague with that of the plague of hail in Egypt is evident further because both v. 21 and the Exodus account emphasize the severity or large size of the hail by twice mentioning that it was "great" or "very great." V. 21 reads literally: "great hail . . . the plague of it is very great." Exod. 9:18, 24 reads literally "very great hail . . . the hail was very great" (likewise Josephus, *Antiquities* 2.304-5). The weight of the hailstones in v. 21 is said to be a "talent" (NASB "one hundred pounds"), which is variously estimated to be anywhere from forty-five to one hundred and thirty pounds (cf. Josephus, *War* 5.270).

Also echoed may be the hail that struck the Amorites in Josh. 10:11 ("the Lord threw large stones from heaven . . . hailstones"), which is seen as part of the whole redemptive program associated with the Exodus, focusing on subsequent entry into the Promised Land. Furthermore, the mention of hail in connection with the final judgment has been influenced by Ezek. 38:19-22, where hail and earthquake as well as fire and brimstone (cf. Rev. 19:20; 20:9, 10) mark the final stage of judgment on the end-time enemy. Note the formative influence of Ezekiel 38–39 on v. 14, as well as on 19:19 and 20:8.

The people suffering the judgment **blasphemed God because of the plague of the hail, because its plague was extremely severe.** This does not necessarily mean that some were left after the judgment of the hail, but that they were blaspheming during the onslaught of the woe, just as in 6:15-17 people undergoing the commencement of the final judgment try to hide during its execution (note also the parallel between 6:14 and 16:20 noted above). In contrast to vv. 9 and 11 above, which also refer to people blaspheming, there is no mention of people refusing to repent, which also suggests that the end has come, so that no room is now left for repentance.

Vv. 17-21 could be viewed as the beginning of the last judgment in history, with chs. 17–19 giving subsequent chronological developments of that judgment. However, it is best to view the following chapters as supplemental perspectives on the same events concerning the last judgment pictured in 16:17-21, as well as in the sixth and seventh seals, the seventh trumpet, and the final judgment scene in 14:14-20.

Suggestions for Reflection on 16:12-21

On the importance of reading the Bible contextually. These verses again show how important it is to the read the Bible carefully and in context. The commentary has argued that John's vision takes the account of the historical fall of Babylon, relates it backward to the defeat of Pharaoh at the Red Sea, and uses it typologically to predict the fall of the latter-day Babylonian world system. At the same time, all the original elements of Babylon's destruction (the city itself, its king, the river on which it sits, and the manner of its fall) are universalized. Failure to understand this leads many contemporary commentators to isolate particular people and places as the site of the last-day warfare, even to the point of predicting a rebuilding of Babylon, which would in fact nullify OT prophetic declarations affirming that Babylon would be decimated by the Persians, never to rise as a world power again (e.g., see Isa. 13:17-22; Jer. 50:13, 39; 51:62-64). The same is true of the mention of Armageddon in v. 16. We have tried to set forth in the commentary the richness of biblical allusions, which points to a universal reference, yet how many have tried to locate Armageddon as a particular place, focusing on the involvement of ethnic Israel, and thereby missed the main point regarding the nature of the battle as of worldwide extent, and fought between the forces of the enemy and the church?

On the reality of demonic activity and our lack of readiness to fight it. Vv. 13-14 highlight the activity of unclean spirits coming forth from the devil and his agents, performing signs which influence the kings of the earth and draw them together for war. Because they are identified as frogs, they may be linked with the Egyptian goddess of resurrection, who was symbolized as a frog. The NT is full of accounts of the reality of the kingdom of darkness. Our rationalistic age makes it difficult for us to see with the same eyes as the biblical writers, yet these same age-old forces are still very much at work (on which see, e.g., Eph. 6:10-17). Does part of their deception convey the notion that they do not exist? Do we really understand how to fight this activity of such forces? Do we sometimes fight only attitudes or actions they produce, rather than confronting the underlying reality? Our battle is not only against the world's influence and the influence of our own indwelling sin and the detrimental influence of our old nature on us, but our "struggle is . . . against the powers, against the world forces of this darkness, against the spiritual forces of wickedness in the heavenly places" (Eph. 6:12).

On the cry from the cross and the cry from the throne. The commentary points out that the cry from the throne "It is done" echoes the cry of Jesus from the cross (John 19:30), using the same Greek verb. This can hardly be an accident. Using the analogy of the inauguration of the kingdom through the cross and resurrection, consider how Jesus' cry set in motion the breaking in of God's kingdom, yet in such a way that it would only reach fulfillment at the time of the second cry, when there would be not only the final redemption of God's people (Rev. 21:1–22:5), but the decisive and final judgment of God's enemies. Could the loud voice uttering the cry belong to Christ Himself? How is this an encouragement to us as we live in the time in between the two cries?

The final judgment of Babylon and the beast (17:1–19:21)

The influence of the world's economic-religious system and the state, their alliance, and the downfall of both (17:1-18)

Rev. 17:1–19:10 is a large interpretative snapshot of the sixth and seventh bowls, which have foretold the judgment of Babylon (which was first explicitly prophesied in 14:8). This is followed in 19:11-21 by an expanded description of the last battle, in which Christ triumphs over the forces of evil. Although only one verse in ch. 17 describes Babylon's judgment (v. 16), the larger literary unit commencing at 17:1 is dominated by it. Much space is taken up with the beast in ch. 17 because the woman's significance and power cannot be fully understood except in her relationship to the beast. Ch. 17 (in development of 16:12-13) emphasizes what leads up to the demise of Babylon, which becomes the full-blown focus in ch. 18.

The introduction to the vision: the angel announces to John that he is to witness a vision about the judgment of the world's idolatrous economic-religious system (17:1-3a)

[1] And one of the seven angels who had the seven bowls came and spoke with me, saying, "Come here, I shall show you the judgment of the great harlot who sits on many waters, [2] with whom the kings of the earth committed acts of immorality, and those who dwell on the earth were made drunk with the wine of her immorality." [3] And he carried me away in the Spirit into a wilderness.

1 The angel who reveals the vision of ch. 17 and who interprets it (vv. 7-18) is referred to as **one of the seven angels who had the seven bowls.** This is the first indication that ch. 17 amplifies the sixth and seventh bowls. The main point of the vision is **the judgment of the great harlot who sits on many waters.** This judgment is another mention of God's answer to the prayers of the saints' plea in 6:10. Symbolizing Babylon as a harlot connotes her alluring and seductive nature in attempting to draw people away from Christ. The angel speaks to John in words taken from God's judgment on historical Babylon in Jer. 51:13, "O you who dwell by many waters, abundant in treasures, your end has come." Babylon's "sitting" on many waters speaks of her sovereignty over the nations, for "sitting" in Revelation (3:21; 4:2, 4; 5:1; 14:14; 18:7, etc.) indicates sovereignty, whether used of God, Christ, the angels, or evil beings. 18:7 confirms this, since there Babylon

says "I sit as a queen." At the least, the sitting implies the woman's alliance with the world and the beast.

2 Part of the basis of Babylon's judgment is the fact that **the kings of the earth committed acts of immorality** with her **and those who dwell on the earth were made drunk with the wine of her immorality**. The kings' and the nations' acquiescence to immorality refers not to literal immorality, but figuratively to acceptance of the religious and idolatrous demands of the ungodly earthly order. As in 14:8, **her immorality** is a Greek genitive of association (= "have intercourse with her"), as evident from the parallelism of **committed acts of immorality** with her (cf. also 18:9) with **the wine of her immorality**. The same synonymous parallelism occurs in 18:3, though with slight variation in wording. The nations' cooperation with Babylon ensures their material security (see on 2:9; 13:16-17). The intoxicating effect of Babylon's wine removes all desire to resist Babylon's destructive influence, blinds them to Babylon's own ultimate insecurity and to God as the source of real security and numbs them against fear of a coming judgment. For the OT roots, see Hos. 4:11-12: "Harlotry, wine and new wine take away the understanding. My people consult their wooden idol . . . for a spirit of harlotry has led them astray." Elsewhere in Revelation idolatry and immorality (Greek *porneia*) are closely linked (2:14, 20-21; 9:21; 14:8). The economic interpretation of the nations' intoxicating passion and the kings' immoral passion for Babylon is clear from 18:3, 9-19, where the same phrases for immorality and intoxication of 17:2 are equated with terms for economic prosperity, and the nations' loyalty to Babylon lies in her ability to provide economic prosperity for them (see also on 14:8). An economic interpretation of the verse is confirmed by the allusion to Isa. 23:17, where Tyre "will play the harlot with all the kingdoms on the face of the earth." Tyre is called a harlot because she caused destruction and induced uncleanness among the nations by economically dominating them and influencing them by her idolatry. That idolatry is included together with an economic emphasis is clear from Isa. 23:18, where Tyre's illicit wages "will be set apart to the Lord" in the future instead of to any other false object of dedication as formerly. That Tyre is in mind at least as an analogy to Babylon is clear from the repeated reference in Revelation 18 to the Ezekiel 26–28 pronouncement of Tyre's judgment and the specific allusion in v. 23 to Isa. 23:8 (see on 18:23).

Therefore, Babylon is the prevailing economic-religious system in alliance with the state and its related authorities, as it exists in various forms throughout the ages. Of course, the generally known fact that harlots in the ancient world (as today) offered their bodies and sexual services for payment only enhances the economic nature of the Babylonian prostitute.

3a The angel carried John **away in the Spirit into a wilderness.** "In the Spirit" is a formula of prophetic commissioning, based on the similar formulas expressing Ezekiel's repeated prophetic commissions, e.g., Ezek. 2:2: "the Spirit entered me and set me on my feet"; Ezek. 3:12: "The Spirit lifted me up" (likewise Ezek. 3:14, 24; 11:1; 43:5). Ezekiel is commissioned with prophetic authority to announce judgment to sinful Israel. Similarly, John's transport into the realm of the Spirit underscores his prophetic commission and authority (see 1:10; 4:2 and especially 21:10, where allusion to the Ezekiel commissions also occurs in the same manner). And as with Ezekiel, John's inspired message in 17:3ff. is an announcement of judgment.

The seer's transport **into a wilderness** alludes to Isa. 21:1-2, where a vision from God (so Isa. 21:10) is revealed to the prophet Isaiah and is described as coming "from the wilderness, from a terrifying land" (21:1). This allusion is confirmed by the fact that Isa. 21:1-10 is a vision of judgment *against Babylon* and by the fact that the phrase "fallen, fallen is Babylon" of Isa. 21:9 appears in Rev. 18:2 as well as in 14:8, which itself looks ahead to chs. 17–18. In both Isaiah and Revelation, the desert is central to the vision, though in the former the vision has its source in the desert, whereas in the latter the prophet is taken to the desert to see the vision. Is there significance in the fact that John is taken into the wilderness? After all, he has visionary experiences in various places — earth (1:9-10), sea and earth (10:8ff.), heaven (4:1), on the seashore (13:1), and on a mountain-top (21:9-10). But the allusion to Isaiah 21 is clear. The desert is at the same time a place of protection for God's people (both following the exodus and in the end time), but also the habitation of fierce animals like serpents and of evil spirits. It is the place of sin, judgment, and persecution of the saints (see on 12:6 for further elaboration of how God protects His people in the desert). It is a "terrifying land" (Isa. 21:1) in which Babylon's fall is predicted (Isa. 21:9).

This verse affirms that the whole vision of ch. 17 appears in the spiritual dimension of a wilderness or desert. There the harlot dwells, **sitting on a scarlet beast . . . having seven heads and ten horns** (v. 3b). The only other occurrence of **wilderness** (Greek *erēmos*) in the book outside 17:3 is in 12:6, 14. There also in a wilderness a "red dragon having seven heads and ten horns" (cf. 12:3 with 17:3) persecutes the people of God (12:13-17). Part of Babylon's judgment in ch. 18 for persecuting the saints in the desert is that she herself is made into a desert-like place (similarly Isa. 13:20-22; Jer.

50:12-13; 51:26, 29, 43) where only demonic spirits dwell (cf. 18:2, which is introduced by the Isa. 21:9 allusion). The harlot of ch. 17 persecutes the saints (v. 6) in the desert and deceives the earth-dwellers (v. 8). The desert is also where John witnesses the judgment both of Babylon (vv. 15-17) and of the beast and his allies (vv. 13-14). Therefore, on the biblical principle of an eye for an eye, the judgment of Babylon is decreed in the very place where she persecuted the saints.

In addition, Isa. 21:1, which undoubtedly lies behind this text, uniquely combines references to the desert and the sea: "The oracle, concerning the wilderness of the sea." It is not coincidental that vv. 1, 3 here picture Babylon apparently being in a wilderness and *at the same time* sitting on many waters. This seems geographically contradictory. However, this is symbolic geography. Already in 12:15-16, an overflowing river appears in the desert. There and here, persecutors of the church are associated with water, because water is metaphorical for evil and deception (for the same significance of "sea" see on 4:6; 13:1; 15:2; 16:3; 21:1).

An alternative interpretation of the desert's significance here is that John is taken there not simply because it is an appropriate setting for Babylon's sin to be revealed, but also because it is a place of spiritual security and detachment from the world's dangers. There he can truly see the evils of Babylon and avoid her deception.

Yet perhaps even there, he "wonders" or "marvels" (vv. 6-7, Greek *thaumazō*) at her appearance, a word used of unbelievers' worshipful adoration of the beast (13:3; 17:8). Following this line of thought, though he comes close to admiration for the beast and the woman (see on vv. 6-7 below), he is protected from actually worshiping the beast because of his secure place in the desert. On either interpretation, what is undoubtedly true is that, as in 12:6 and 12:13-17, the desert here has both positive and negative connotations. It is in the desert that John both declares God's judgment on Babylon and understands her true evil from a place of spiritual security. If John could come close to being attracted to the woman and beast, how easy it must be for his readers to be seduced. Conceivably, he had to paint these characters of evil in such horrid form so that saints would not be too easily attracted (see further on v. 7 below).

Suggestions for Reflection on 17:1-3a

On the significance of the desert in these verses. These verses present us with a nuanced understanding of the significance of the desert. Revelation consistently presents the desert as the place where, in spite of ever-present danger, God provides security for His people. It is in this place of attack upon God's people that God now declares His judgment of the attackers. John needed to be taken into the desert (understood as the place of God's security) in order to avoid being mesmerized by the harlot. How easily is it possible for God's people to be seduced by her attractive appearance and the economic and social advantages she offers to those who cooperate with her? If this is the most materialistic and wealthy society in human history, are these temptations even greater for us today? What would it involve for us to compromise our faith in order to gain material or social advantage from our own Babylon?

The vision and the seer's response: John is frightened and perplexed by the magnificent appearance of the hostile economic-religious system in its alliance with the state (17:3b-7)

And I saw a woman sitting on a scarlet beast, full of blasphemous names, having
seven heads and ten horns. 4 And the woman was clothed in purple and scarlet,
and adorned with gold and precious stones and pearls, having in her hand a
gold cup full of abominations and of the unclean things of her immorality, 5 and
upon her forehead a name was written, a mystery: "BABYLON THE GREAT, THE
MOTHER OF HARLOTS AND OF THE ABOMINATIONS OF THE EARTH." 6 And I saw
the woman drunk with the blood of the saints, and with the blood of the witnesses of Jesus. And when I saw her, I wondered greatly. 7 And the angel said to
me, "Why do you wonder? I shall tell you the mystery of the woman and of the
beast that carries her, which has the seven heads and the ten horns."

3b We have begun to understand the evil and seductive identity of the woman in the opening verses of ch. 17. Her wicked character continues to be seen in the present section, especially her close identification with the beast, who, we have already seen (e.g., in ch. 13), is a deceiver and persecutor of God's people. However, enigmatically part of the woman's appearance in vv. 3b-7 also reflects something apparently good about her (see on vv. 4 and 7 below). What is this apparent benign aspect of her appearance and why is such a wicked character described in this manner?

John now sees **a woman sitting on a scarlet beast full of blasphemous names, having seven heads and ten horns** (for full discussion of this description see on 12:3; cf. 13:1-2). The portrayal of the beast is almost identical to that in 13:1, so the same beast is pictured here again. There and here the wording alludes to Dan. 7:3-7, 20, 24. The heads and horns represent the fullness of power held by evil kingdoms who persecute God's people, since this is their figurative meaning in Daniel 7 (e.g., the fourth beast's ten horns in Dan. 7:7 are explicitly identified as "ten kings" in Dan. 7:24). The beast's red color associates him with the red dragon of 12:3. The color indicates royal attire and hence kingship, but more particularly the persecuting nature of the dragon in 12:3 and the beast here, who spill the red blood of the saints. The **blasphemous names**, as in 13:1, refer to the beast's false claims of universal sovereignty. Though closely associated with the beast, the woman is not to be equated with the beast. That the woman rides the beast connotes her alliance with it. She represents the ungodly world as it works with the state socially, culturally, and economically to persecute Christians (17:6; 18:24; 19:2). They are also mutually involved in deception of ungodly multitudes throughout the earth (e.g., 14:8; 17:2, 8).

4 The description of the woman confirms that she represents worldly economic forces which are in collusion with the state in persecuting Christians (for the economic focus see also on 14:8; 17:2): **And the woman was clothed in purple and scarlet, and adorned with gold and precious stones and pearls**. The description of her clothing is repeated in 18:16, where she is described as the "great city" or Babylon. The parts of her attire are listed as products of trade in 18:12. Therefore the woman, draped with these products, is identified with a prosperous trading system. Her clothing is **scarlet**, representing her persecution of the saints. Both Isaiah and Jeremiah speak of harlots with red attire symbolizing their spilling of the blood of the righteous (Isa. 1:15-23; Jer. 2:34). The woman holds **in her hand a gold cup full of abominations and of the unclean things of her immorality**, much like Jeremiah's description of historical Babylon as a golden cup intoxicating the nations and driving them mad (Jer. 51:7). These unclean things also include idolatrous practices, for in 16:13-14 and 18:2 demons are referred to as unclean spirits, and demons stand behind idols (1 Cor. 10:19-20). The **abominations** in the woman's cup are also references to idolatry, for that word is used frequently in the OT to refer to idolatry (Deut. 29:17; 2 Kgs. 23:24; 2 Chron. 34:33; Jer. 16:18, etc.). The unclean things are associated with **her immorality**. "Immorality" (Greek *porneia*) and the related verb elsewhere in the book are figurative expressions for idolatry (so 2:14, 20-21; cf. 9:21; see on 14:8; 17:2), as they are here. As we saw in the letters, there is a clear connection in Revelation between illicit forms of economic activity (including simply the worship of money) and idolatrous practices, and the woman represents both. That economic factors can incite idolatry is well attested in first-century Asia Minor (e.g.,

see on 2:14, 20-22). Customarily, each trade guild had patron gods to which members paid homage in a pagan temple, where worship was directed to a bust of Caesar. Christians who abstained from such idolatry risked economic ostracism and loss of their trading privileges. The harlot of ch. 17 represents these and other like religio-economic aspects of society that lure Christians to compromise and trust in the world's security instead of security in Christ.

5 The nature of the woman is revealed by the fact that **upon her forehead a name was written, a mystery: "BABYLON THE GREAT, THE MOTHER OF HARLOTS AND OF THE ABOMINATIONS OF THE EARTH."** In Revelation, a name on a forehead reveals the individual's character and relationship either to God (7:3; 14:1) or to Satan (13:16; 14:9). The woman's name reveals clearly her alliance with the beast. The first part of the name, **Babylon the great**, comes directly from Dan. 4:30, where it expresses the extent of Nebuchadnezzar's power, about which he boasts. His proud independence from God led to his downfall. The mystery of the name refers to the "mystery" (Dan. 4:9) of the dream Nebuchadnezzar had which warned him of the disaster ahead should he continue in his pride. Revelation connects this mystery with the mystery of the last-days fall of spiritual Babylon (cf. Rev. 1:20; 10:7), which will fall because of pride and evil ("mystery" in the OT occurs with an eschatological sense only in Dan. 2:28-29, which is partly in the background here). This was a mystery prophesied and (in the days of the seventh trumpet, according to 10:7) shortly to be fulfilled. The **mystery** refers to what is contained in the hidden counsel of God and now being revealed to His servants. In 1:20 and 10:7, the "mystery" involved the unexpected (though not contradictory) way in which Daniel's prophecy about the establishment of Israel's latter-day kingdom and the defeat of evil empires was beginning to be fulfilled. The notion of "mystery" in both those chapters is that the kingdom begins ironically through the suffering of Christ and His people (e.g., cf. 1:5-6, 13-14 with 1:20; see on 1:20). Similarly here, but now in application to the kingdom of evil, it refers to the ironic, mysterious way in which God will fulfill His prophetic words concerning Babylon's destruction — that kingdom will turn against itself (as the next verses will reveal) and begin to self-destruct even before the return of Christ, who will finally demolish Babylon. This was indeed a mystery not as clearly seen by Isaiah, Jeremiah, and Daniel, but is now made clearer to John. Fulfillment of prophecy always fleshes out details that were not contained in broadly-given OT prophecies.

The woman is given the additional titles, **Mother of harlots and of the abominations of the earth**, thus indicating her central role in directing idolatrous practices and false religion. Babylon is portrayed as a woman in the desert and also as a city (18:10), thus bringing her into contrast both with the mother of 12:1, who also lives in the desert, and with the bride of 19:7-8; 21:2, 10, who is also described as a city (21:2). That such a contrast is intended is evident from the strikingly identical introductory vision formulas for the harlot and the church in 17:1 and 21:9-10. Such contrasts with the church throughout the ages, both on earth and glorified, make clear that Babylon is not a geographical locality but a demonically-directed economic and spiritual reality present throughout the church age. The woman in ch. 12 gave birth to the church, while the harlot of ch. 17 attempts to destroy the church.

6 Those who do not submit to the economic and religious practices of Babylon will be persecuted and even killed: **And I saw the woman drunk with the blood of the saints, and with the blood of the witnesses of Jesus.** The "and" is explanatory, yielding the meaning that true saints are those who are **witnesses of** (or to) **Jesus**, which is why they are persecuted, in that their witness sparks antagonism from the world (cf. 6:9). This persecution could take the form of ostracism from one's trade. Revelation gives us actual examples of punishment by exile (1:9), imprisonment (2:10), and death (2:10, 13), so this activity of Babylon and the beast was already beginning to unfold as John wrote. The **blood of the saints** thus encompasses not just martyrdom (see also on 6:9) but all forms of suffering endured by believers. John's response to the vision of the woman is great amazement: **And when I saw her, I wondered greatly** (literally, "I wondered with great wonder"), which we will shortly see (in v. 7) includes both fright and perplexity.

7 John's great **wonder** or amazement is repeated three times in vv. 6-7, the last of which is in a question from the angel: **"Why do you wonder?"** This is not merely a question about the seer's amazement at the unusual vision. Rather, several ideas are evoked by the question. The angel is really asking why John should be afraid and troubled by the vision, as he was by earlier visions (e.g., cf. 1:17). It is best taken as a rhetorical question whose implied answer is a rebuke: John should not be fearful and perplexed.

The same language of being amazed or "appalled" in Dan. 4:19 expresses Daniel's fearful and shocked reaction to the vision of the judgment of the Babylonian king. Likewise, John expresses fear about the nightmarish vision he has just seen concerning the horrible nature of the beast and the Babylonian woman and their persecution. Likely, part of what contributed to his troubled spirit was shock and fear over the blasphemous claims of the beast and the severe persecution envisioned.

Also contributing to the seer's shock may have been the parabolic portrayal of Babylon in the guise of a religiously faithful figure. She is attired (17:4) almost identically to the bride-city of Christ, who is "adorned with every kind of precious stone," pearls and gold (21:18-21), and clothed in linen (cf. 18:16 and 19:8). The linen is defined as the "righteous acts of the saints" in 19:8, which may have momentarily led John to think that the Babylonian woman was not all bad but had some attractive spiritual features. Enhancing such an impression may have been the fact that the high priest in the OT is described also as adorned with gold, purple, scarlet, linen, and precious stones (Exod. 25:7; 28:5-9, 15-20; 35:9). Such an appearance may have caused John temporarily to "admire" this aspect of the woman. That "admiration" may be part of how John's "amazement" is to be understood is pointed to by the same use of the word "wonder" (Greek *thaumazō*) in 17:8 and 13:3, where people "wonder" or are "amazed" at the beast, which leads them to worship him. This makes it more understandable that the angel's question contains a rebuke for admiring the woman. This could be apparent also from 19:10 and 22:9, where an angel rebukes the seer ("do not do that") and redirects actions of worship from a wrong object of reverence to God.

Consequently, John may have been temporarily captivated by what appeared, in part, to be a spiritually attractive figure, and was blinded (at least temporarily) to the full, true ungodly nature of the harlot. The apparent spiritual attractiveness may have been enhanced by the fact that elsewhere in Revelation believers, indeed so-called Christian prophets led by Jezebel (see 2:20-24), were contending that some identification with the world was good. In particular, they were contending that worship of other gods (associated with economic well-being) was not incompatible with being a faithful Christian. John now realizes that these are not merely misguided Christians, but that Jezebel and her followers are none other than Babylon herself in the midst of the church, who eventually will be judged along with persecutors outside the church. This identification of Babylon with Jezebel in Rev. 2:20-24 is enhanced from recognizing that later in ch. 17 John describes the Babylonian harlot by appealing to allusions to the OT figure of Jezebel (on which see below).

That John's lack of clarity about the vision explains a significant basis for his amazement is evident from the angel's assertion that he will explain the hidden meaning (**the mystery**) of the vision of the beast and woman seen in vv. 3-6. Dan. 7:16 (part of the passage in Daniel 7 which lies behind the portrayal of the beast in ch. 17; see on v. 3b above) also emphasizes the need for clarity. The angel, however, questions John's fear, perplexity, and astonishment and brings reassurance by saying he will unfold **the mystery of the woman and of the beast.** That is, he will unfold the judgment about to come upon them in spite of the woman's apparent magnificence and triumph, enabling John to have divine insight that pierces through the ambiguous appearance of the woman. Thus, one should beware of being attracted and confused by this woman draped in such dazzling, bejeweled attire and clothed in linen (so 18:16), since all her embrace can offer is a full strength draught of abominations and unclean things. Even temporary attraction or confusion about her will cause the believer to be unable to perceive clearly her truly evil and deceptive nature and, thus, to be taken in to some degree by her and to compromise.

Suggestions for Reflection on 17:3b-7

On the relevance of the Babylonian whore for all ages. If the woman represents cultural, economic, and idolatrous religious power united in institutional form throughout the ages, how would that institution be identified or express itself in that particular part of the contemporary world where we live today (government, church, business, school, etc.)?

On temptations to compromise. In what ways can modern-day institutions of the world that are evil appear good and admirable in the eyes of Christians? In what ways are believers tempted to compromise with these institutions?

On the anesthetic effect of Babylon's influence. The intoxicating effect of Babylon's wine removes all desire to resist Babylon's destructive influence, blinds people to Babylon's own ultimate insecurity and to God as the source of real security, and numbs them from fear of a coming judgment. Reflect on those aspects of the ungodly world's influence on us that blinds us to the ultimate insecurity of the world and to the reality that true security can be found only in Christ and God. Likewise, what aspects of the ungodly world's influence on us have the potential of numbing us from reflecting on the reality of God's coming judgment?

On the sources of persecution. What institutions carry out persecution against Christians today in those countries where believers suffer for their faith? Are there religious institutions that cooperate with political and/or economic institutions in persecuting Christians? If so, which ones? Is anything like this beginning to take shape on the horizon in western Europe or North America?

On discerning what is evil. How can Christians increase their awareness of what institutions around them are evil and so protect themselves from being deceived and consequently compromising in some way? If v. 7 provides the answer for John, how could it provide an answer for Christians today?

The interpretation of the vision of the woman (17:8-18)

The interpretation of the beast: the deceptive career of the Satanic state and its allies will be revealed as a sham when they are judged by Christ at the end of time (17:8-14)

8 "The beast that you saw was and is not, and is about to come up out of the
abyss and to go to destruction. And those who dwell on the earth will wonder,
whose name has not been written in the book of life from the foundation of the
world, when they see the beast, that he was and is not and will come. 9 Here is
the mind which has wisdom. The seven heads are seven mountains on which
the woman sits, 10 and they are seven kings; five have fallen, one is, the other is
yet to come; and when he comes, he must remain a little while. 11 And the beast
which was and is not, is himself also an eighth, and is one of the seven, and he
goes to destruction. 12 And the ten horns which you saw are ten kings, who have
not yet received a kingdom, but they receive authority as kings with the beast for
one hour. 13 These have one purpose and they give their power and authority to
the beast. 14 These will wage war against the Lamb, and the Lamb will overcome
them, because He is Lord of lords and King of kings, and those who are with Him
are the called and chosen and faithful."

8a The threefold description of God found already in 1:4, 8; 4:8; 11:17; and 16:5 is altered and applied to the beast: **The beast that you saw was and is not, and is about to come up out of the abyss and to go to destruction.** This is also a parody of Christ's death and resurrection (1:18; 2:8). That the beast **is not** refers to the continuing effects of his defeat by Christ at the cross and resurrection (see on 13:3, where "death" is equivalent to "is not"). The conclusion of the third member of the formula (he goes **to**

destruction) is an ironic contrast with the altered form of the third part of the divine formula in 11:17 ("Thou hast taken thy great power and hast begun to reign"). The application of the threefold formula for divine eternity to the beast is intended to ridicule the beast's vain efforts to defeat the *true* eternal Being and His forces. The application also suggests that the beast's existence extends from the beginning of history to its end, but the close of the formula shows a clear contrast with God's existence: the beast's former, apparently sovereign form of existence throughout history will cease (though on his everlasting destruction see on 19:19-20; 20:10).

The language of the angel mirrors what Daniel saw in his vision: the beasts came up from the sea (Dan. 7:3 — and are likened to kings who come up out of the earth in v. 17) and then went to destruction (7:11, 17-26). The Daniel allusion emphasizes the beast's demise and the irony of it, since already implicit in Daniel 7 itself is the same kind of ironic parody of the beast in relation to the Son of man (see the concluding comments on ch. 13). The third member of the formula in 17:8a (**is about to come up out of the abyss and to go to destruction**) is a development of the use of Dan. 7:21 in Rev. 11:7. In 11:7, "the beast that comes up out of the abyss will make war with them, and overcome them and kill them." That the beast's origin is from the abyss here and in 11:7 suggests the demonic roots and powers of the beast (as in 9:1-2, 11; cf. 20:1-3, 7). Though the beast appears temporarily to defeat the entire church community in the end time, his victory will be short-lived. He will soon thereafter **go to destruction**. The threefold formula corresponds to the career of Satan in 20:1-10, so that both refer to the same events from the vantage point respectively of the beast and of Satan. There Satan will be said to have existed in the past (20:1 = "he was," in that he existed prior to the action of the angel in vv. 2-3). He is locked up in an "abyss" (20:2-3 = "is not"). But then, "after these things he must be released for a short time" (20:3, 7-9 = "is about to come up out of the abyss"; cf. v. 10 below). And finally, he will also go to destruction (20:9-10).

After defeating the saints, the beast and his allies will then "wage war against the Lamb, and the Lamb will overcome them" (v. 14), and all those formerly defeated by the beast will accompany the Lamb in finally defeating the beast for all time. Though during the church age the beast's continued persecution of the saints (13:3ff.) makes it appear that he was "healed" from his death wound, the persecution he conducts at the last stage of history will be more severe. He will attempt to stamp out the entire church. The beast's imitation of Christ will be shown as a sham in the end. Whereas Christ's resurrection results in Him living for evermore (1:18), the beast's resurrection results in his destruction. It takes divine wisdom to discern the difference in the destinies of the Lamb and the beast (so v. 9a).

8b Multitudes will marvel at the beast's resurgence: **And those who dwell on the earth will wonder, whose name has not been written in the book of life from the foundation of the world, when they see the beast, that he was and is not and will come.** "Wonder" has the idea of admiring in a worshipful sense, as is apparent from 13:3ff., where also marveling (the same Greek word *thaumazō*) after the beast is developed in the following verses by words denoting worship of the beast. As in 13:8, 14, the earth-dwellers (unbelieving idolaters, as in 6:10; 13:8, 14, etc.) are deceived into worshiping the beast. What precisely will deceive them about the beast will be that though he was defeated (**is not**) at the end of his former existence (**he was**), he will be able to appear to recover from the defeat ("he is about to come up out of the abyss," v. 8a). This is also how the beast deceives the multitudes in 13:3, where the world is amazed at his recovery from the apparently fatal wound inflicted by the cross and resurrection. The beast's apparent health will lead many to follow him. This situation will continue until Christ's return, when He will demonstrate the reality of His spiritual victory at the cross by achieving physical victory over Satan's forces.

The earth-dwellers will not be able to withstand deception by the beast because their **name has not been written in the book of life from the foundation of the world** (see on 3:5 and 13:8 for the background and relevance of the allusions to Dan. 7:10; 12:1-2). To be **written in the book of life** refers metaphorically elsewhere to believers whose salvation has been secured, so (negatively) names **not written in the book** refers to unbelievers who do not benefit from having such security (see on 3:5; 13:8; 20:12; 21:27). As in 13:8, this security began before historical time began, **from the foundation of the world.** The protection for those written in the book comes from the Lamb (13:8; 21:27). Here the stress is on those who will not receive the salvific protection of the book.

9a Those who are written in the book are protected spiritually by the Lamb and are not deceived by the enemy and his agents: **Here is the mind which has wisdom.** This verse develops further Daniel's prophecy that in the end-time tribulation true saints will need spiritual "understanding" and "insight" to avoid being deceived by an evil king who exalts his sovereignty over God and persecutes God's people who do not acknowledge him (so Dan. 11:33; 12:10; see further on 13:18). Those with wisdom and understanding will also be able to understand the angel's explanation of the vision outlined in vv. 9b-18, which develops Daniel's prophecy in order to underscore it in the minds of the "called and chosen and faithful" (v. 14). Part of God's plan is to save His chosen ones through exhortations to have wisdom, to which they respond positively on the basis of divine protective grace.

The beast John has seen in the vision in v. 3 is none other than the wicked state force prophesied in Daniel. John and his churches are reminded of the OT prophetic warning from Daniel about temptations to compromise with this evil power. Continued recollection of the prophecy will keep believers alert to the danger so that they will not be deceived like many others in the church, who will remain ignorant of the Scriptures, consequently be taken off guard and led astray by the beast, and thus compromise with the state's ungodly demands.

9b The angel states the interpretation of the beast's seven heads: **The seven heads are seven mountains on which the woman sits**. These have sometimes been identified with Rome's seven hills and therefore with the Roman Empire. The other seven occurrences of the word "mountain" (Greek *oros*) in Revelation, however, carry the figurative meaning of "strength." This usage points beyond a literal reference to Rome's hills to the figurative meaning of kingdoms, especially in the light of 8:8 and 14:1, where mountains figuratively refer to kingdoms. The identification with kings is confirmed by the next phrase (v. 10) which explicitly equates the mountains with "seven kings." In the OT, mountains symbolize human or divine kingdoms (Isa. 2:2; Jer. 51:25; Ezek. 35:3; Dan. 2:35, 45; Zech. 4:7), so the reference is not to a specific location featuring seven mountains. The identification is also confirmed by Dan. 7:4-7, where seven is the total number of heads of the four beasts (= kingdoms), which also is the source of the seven heads in 13:1 (on which see; note that Daniel's beast had four heads). For the interchangeableness of "kings" and "kingdoms," see Dan. 7:17 ("These great beasts . . . are four kings") and 7:23 ("The fourth beast will be a fourth kingdom"). In light of all this, it is no surprise that the angel identifies the heads or mountains as seven kings (or kingdoms). There is a metaphorical shift from the beast with seven heads in 13:1 and 17:3. The beast is now pictured not as possessing heads but as being heads. This is evident from the implicit picture of the woman now sitting on the seven heads instead of on the beast, as in v. 3. This identification is made explicit in v. 11. The equivalence of heads with the beast (vv. 3, 9b) suggests that "heads" connotes authority, and here oppressive authority (cf. the blasphemous names on the heads in 13:1).

The number **seven** is not a literal number designating the quantity of kings in one period of time, but is figurative for the quality of fullness or completeness, as in the OT, Daniel 7:4-7 (see above), and throughout Revelation (e.g., 1:4, 20; 4:5; 5:6; 12:3; 13:1). "Seven" or "seventh" occurs about forty-five times in the book outside 17:3-11, and all are within figurative expressions. As in 12:3 and 13:1-2, fullness of oppressive power is the emphasis. The seven mountains and kings represent the oppressive power of world government throughout the ages which arrogates to itself divine prerogatives and persecutes God's people when they do not submit to the evil state's false claims.

The broader identification of the **seven heads** is confirmed by Dan. 7:3-7, where the total of seven heads of the four beasts identifies distinct empires which span centuries. This is evident from the following considerations:

Just as the kingdoms with seven heads in Dan. 7:4-7 spanned the time from Babylon all the way at least to Rome (whose dominance lasted several centuries after Christ), so the seven-headed beast in Revelation 17 likewise spans many centuries and likely all of history, especially since the features of the four Daniel empires are applied in Revelation not to four different animals but to one beastly figure.

The sea-beast image throughout the OT symbolizes different wicked kingdoms which span centuries (Pss. 74:13-14; 89:10; Isa. 27:1; 30:7; 51:9; Ezek. 29:3; 32:2-3; Hab. 3:13-14; see above on 12:3).

The kind of authority the beast has is the direct antithesis of that which the Lamb exercises (17:14), so that the beast exercises not mere earthly sovereignty in any one epoch but the ages-long sovereignty of "the great dragon . . . the serpent of old" (cf. 12:3, 9 with 13:1-3).

That the NT elsewhere held the same conception is apparent from the Johannine epistles, where the figure of the end-time opponent prophesied in Daniel is a present reality, not only someone to come at the conclusion of history but one who has already manifested himself corporately in the form of false teachers within the church (1 John 2:18, 22; 4:1-4; 2 John 7; so also 2 Thess. 2:3-10).

Thus, the beast is a trans-temporal figure.

In John's time, the contemporary embodiment of the beast was Rome. Rome's seven hills may have been part of what influenced John to use the figurative number "seven."

10 **And they are seven kings; five have fallen, one is, the other is yet to come; and when he comes, he must remain a little while** confirms the trans-temporal nature of the beast and the figurative understanding of his seven heads argued for above. **Fallen** likely refers to death, the manner of death being unspecified. The three-part description reflects the ironic threefold expression applied to the beast in v. 8 (and so also in v. 11), which has been seen as a parody of the divine name. Since the threefold name for God refers to His existence throughout history, so the application of the formula to the beast's heads mirrors and connotes the same trans-temporal existence. Therefore, the seven kings are figurative for kings throughout history through whom the beast acts. Five heads of the age-old beast have been slain. In this sense, the beast "is not" (vv. 8, 11). However, though he is defeated, he lives on (he "is"), because the sixth head is presently alive (v. 10). And a seventh is yet to appear. The latter two heads remain only to be slain as well, the last (representing the end-time manifestation of beastly power in the state: see on 13:1-3 and 17:8a) at the end of history.

As elsewhere in the book, John tells the churches that the end is not far off or could come quickly: **the other** (= the seventh) **is yet to come**. John's primary intent in 17:10 is not to count kings (such as Roman emperors, since if John did begin a count, we cannot even be sure with what emperor he would have begun). **Five** simply shows many human governments have come and gone. Six is the number of man and serves well to indicate the present activity of the beast in any generation. John's goal here is mainly to inform his readers how far they stand from the conclusion of the full sequence of seven oppressive rulers. He is telling them that only one more, seventh, short reign will elapse until the end of the oppressive dominance of (what for them was) Rome, which represents all ungodly oppressive powers. This expectation is to be understood, as elsewhere in Revelation, to express an idea of imminence, yet there is an indeterminate distance between the present and the future culmination (as likewise in 6:11, on which see; see also on 12:12; 22:6-7, 12).

Besides the current manifestation of the ancient beast in Rome, another manifestation will come in the future. It has not yet come but, when it does, it will **remain a little while**, which phrase refers to the final stage of history. This means that the first six "heads" (= figurative kingdoms) are reigns that, collectively, last a long time, likely throughout history, in contrast to the seventh "head." When the final earthly incarnation of evil comes, it will be unable to establish an enduring reign. It will remain only a short time. This is the same coming noted in 20:3b, where at the end of the age the dragon "must be released for a short time." This parallel shows again the solidarity of the dragon with the beast. The many wicked kingdoms of the world can be referred to as "the [one] kingdom of the world" (11:15) because of the one all-pervasive Satanic spirit ruling through all these kingdoms. This has precedent in Dan. 2:44-45, where God's decisive defeat of the fourth and last evil world kingdom also entails the judgment of the preceding three world kingdoms, so that these three kingdoms are corporately identified as one with the fourth.

Some have argued that seven Roman emperors are referred to here. This ignores the symbolic nature of numbers in Revelation, but also presents us with a further problem, for the sixth Roman emperor was Nero, who died in 68, over twenty years prior to John's vision. John wrote in the reign of Domitian, who was the twelfth emperor. Others identify the five kings with five literal empires, Egypt, Assyria, Babylon, Persia, and Greece, the sixth being Rome (which would fit historically) and the seventh a kingdom yet to come. However, this does not fit with the historical identification of the empires in Daniel 7 which this vision fulfills (comparing Dan. 7:6; 8:8, 21 yields an identification of the third kingdom as Greece). Further, the sixth and seventh empires are pictured in 18:9 as mourning the downfall of the harlot, prompting the question how Rome, purportedly the sixth empire, could be understood to have survived to see that day. How also could the eighth empire be one of the seven? And how are we to account for the various world empires which have arisen since the days of John? If, however, we keep in mind the figurative nature of numbers in Revelation, we will avoid all such pitfalls.

11 The final stage of the beast's manifestation will not last long, because he will be destroyed before he can carry out his purposes in deceiving and destroying the church: **And the beast which was and is not, is himself also an eighth, and is one of the seven, and he goes to destruction.** Repetition of the threefold formula emphasizes again the ironic parody in v. 8, but with a further change: the beast **is himself also an eighth, and is one of the seven, and he goes to destruction.** This change identifies the beast even more clearly with the seven heads. As in v. 9 (on which see), the metaphor changes again slightly; the beast is not pictured as having heads or being heads, but is said to be one of the seven heads, and is equated with the eighth head, which may then represent a ruler even more completely identified with the beast himself. The point is that the manifestation of the dragon and beast through one of their authoritative heads or earthly kings at any particular historical epoch is tantamount to the full presence of the dragon or beast himself.

Eighth has a figurative meaning, as with other numbers in Revelation. "Eight" likely had such significance in earliest Christianity. After six days of creative activity, God rested on the seventh day. The day of rest completed the creative process and may have been seen as initiating an eighth day, in which the regular operation of the new creation began. Likewise, Christ died on the sixth day of the week, rested in the tomb on the Sabbath day, and rose from the dead on the eighth day. Therefore, calling the beast an "eighth" may be a way of referring to his future attempted mimicry of Christ's resurrection (see on 13:3 for the healing of the fatal wound and the beast's mimicry of Christ's resurrection in 5:6). On the other hand, the number of the beast, 666, indicates that such mimicry falls short of its intended goal (see on 13:18). In the immediate context of v. 11, eight occurs in parallel with the preceding "he is about to come up out of the abyss" and "he will come" (v. 8), both of which express the Satanic counterpart to the third member of the threefold phrase reflecting the three-part formula for God in His eternal existence (the One "who is to come," 1:4; see further on v. 8a above). That **eighth**, with its implication of resurrection, is part of this threefold formula and confirms that it is best taken as some form of mimicry of Christ.

Eighth may in addition refer to succession or descent. In this sense, that he is **one of the seven** can easily be translated he is "one *from* the seven," which means he is "descended from the seven" (a genitive of relationship). If this is the case, then the expression means that he is of the same evil nature as the preceding kings. As offspring are of the same nature as their progenitors, so the eighth is of the same evil nature as the prior seven. Understanding the phrase as an idiom of descent helps us see that the translation "he is *one* of the seven" (NASB, NEB) is incorrect, which is a further argument against an exclusively held "return of Nero" theory in which, according to some scholars, the beast is regarded as a reincarnation or resurrected form of the dead emperor Nero. Rather, he is **one of the seven** with respect to his nature, not his prior individual existence. Therefore, the phraseology cannot support the idea that the eighth has actually already existed as one of the former heads.

Though the eighth head has the same wicked nature as the others, he is different from them in that he is an even fuller embodiment of Satanic power, and is unlike the rest in that his reign concludes history. Though the eighth king will be a new, escalated manifestation of Satanic might, he will still be part of the beast which has been decisively slain through Christ's redemptive work. Believers can be comforted that the future career of the beast is not some new outbreak of invincible demonic power. The apparently contradictory "is not" in vv. 8a, 8b, and 11, which stands in contrast to the "is" in v. 10 (understanding that the kings are only instruments through whom the beast works), also emphasizes his defeat and inability to mount any decisive opposition to the already established kingdom of Christ. Nonetheless, he is allowed to continue to exist in the present, as though he were in good health, and to deceive and persecute, which has a very real effect on unbelievers (this is the significance of the "is" of v. 10; see on 17:8).

Though in the future the beast will rise again (vv. 8a, 8b, 11) and appear to be able to conduct insurmountable opposition against the kingdom of the church on an unprecedented scale (11:7; 20:7-9), the fact of his past invisible defeat at the cross ensures that he will go to destruction, an event which all eyes will see. In 13:3ff., the beast's parody of Christ's resurrection focuses on his apparent restoration to power, whereas in 17:8-11 the parody focuses on the beast's final appearance in history, which ultimately leads to his destruction. In this sense, 13:3ff. and 17:8-11, though portraying similar mimicries of Christ, picture different events in the career of the beast.

To enforce the figurative nature of the number of kings in v. 11, Richard Bauckham (*The Climax of Prophecy: Studies in the Book of Revelation* [Edinburgh: Clark, 1993], 405) rightly suggests the relevance of the Hebrew idiom known as the "graded numerical saying," which uses two consecutive numbers in parallel to indicate something that is illustrative and representative rather than literally exhaustive. For instance, Prov. 6:16 ("There are six things which the Lord hates, yes, seven which are an abomination to Him") lists some representative examples of sin, which represent all sins in general and serve as specific illustrations of such sins (cf. also Prov. 30:15, 18, 21, 29). In fact, "seven" followed by "eight" also occurs in the OT as part of this idiom (Eccl. 11:2). Of special notice is Mic. 5:5, which says that "seven shepherds and eight leaders of men" will be raised up in the time of Israel's prophesied victory over the nations. Likewise, John's similar enumeration is not a literal counting of how many emperors there will be before Christ's final coming, but is illustratively representative, symbolizing all the evil, antagonistic rulers of Rome, and probably those preceding Rome, which will exist before their own extreme sin brings on the final climactic destruction of all evil kingdoms at the end of time.

12 Having interpreted the beast's heads, the angel turns to an interpretation of the horns: **And the ten horns which you saw are ten kings, who have not yet received a kingdom**. As Dan. 7:4-7 was the source of the seven heads, so Dan. 7:7-8, 20, 24 is the source of the **ten horns.** Both Daniel and this verse identify the horns as kings. That the prophecy is as yet unfulfilled is clear from the phrase **who have not yet received a kingdom**. The number ten does not likely refer to ten literal kings, but is figurative for the great power of these kings who will arise in the future (for the figurative sense of the **ten horns** see on 12:3; 13:1). The fact that the Lamb's seven horns are clearly figurative for fullness of power and are also a partial allusion to Dan. 7:7-8, 20 further confirms the figurative interpretation here (see on 5:6). Just as the beast is a trans-temporal force opposing the eternal Lamb, so the ten kings span the ages, since they are the direct opposite of the "called and chosen and faithful" (v. 14). This figurative idea of universal plenitude of power suggests that the **ten horns** are identical to "the kings of the earth" in 17:18 (and in 16:14, 16; 17:2; 18:3, 9; 19:19). This equivalence is demonstrated by the parallel use of "kings of the earth" in 16:14 (cf. 16:16) and 19:19 and the "ten horns . . . ten kings" in 17:12-14, all of which refer to allies of the beast in fighting against the Lamb and God in the final battle of history. Furthermore, the OT background of the image of the kings of the earth committing acts of immorality with the harlot (cf. 17:2; 18:3, 9) also has them turning against her and destroying her (cf. Ezekiel 16 and 23, where Jerusalem represents the harlot; see below on v. 16).

The horns are earthly agents through whom the spiritual forces of evil work, which is confirmed by 12:3, which portrays the dragon as having the ten horns (signifying universal power) throughout the centuries of his existence. Yet in ch. 17, the ten horns seem to be located on the seventh head, since both are yet to come. Dan. 7:7-8, 19-20, 23-24 could confirm this, since the ten horns there are located only on the head of the beast who was to come at the end of history. Perhaps this signifies a concentration of universal power in the very last days when the beast and his agents temporarily appear to conquer the church. Thus, in light of the discussion so far on v. 12, the "ten horns" and "ten kings" represent the final phase of the universal plenitude of ungodly kingly power that has spanned the entire interadvent age.

The fulfillment of the prophecy will be marked by the fact that **they receive authority as kings with the beast for one hour**. The authority is likely given by God, in light of v. 17, and the fact that God is the subject of so many authorization clauses elsewhere in the book (e.g., 6:2, 4, 8; 7:2; 9:1, 3, 5; 13:5, 7; 16:8). The duration of this reign will be **one hour**. The time reference is taken from Dan. 4:17a in the Greek OT (Old Greek, though not in the Hebrew text), where it refers to the beginning of the period during which God caused King Nebuchadnezzar, the Babylonian king, to become like a beast. Here also God is sovereign, even over the authority of ungodly kings who ally with the beast in order to defeat end-time Babylon and to prepare to oppose the Messiah (cf. vv. 13-14).

The phrase **one hour** is repeated in 18:10, 17, 19 with reference to the time when Babylon is judged by God. Their "hour" of reigning likely focuses on the final "hour" of Babylon's destruction in earlier verses of ch. 18, since destroying Babylon in v. 16 is the climactic expression of their time of rule. "Hour" (Greek *hōra*) is also used in Daniel 8–12, uniquely in all of the OT, to refer to the final eschatological hour of history when the saints are persecuted, the forces of evil are destroyed, and the saints are rewarded (see the OG of Dan. 8:17, 19; 11:35, 40, 45; 12:1; the Hebrew generally refers to the "end time" or "time of the end," rather than "hour," though the meaning is the same). Here not only Dan. 4:17 (see above) is in mind, but also the later uses of "hour," especially that which focuses on the final activities of the end-time opponent and his defeat (Dan. 11:40-45; an "hour" was apparently the shortest period of time that could be named).

13 The ten kings are united in one goal: **These have one purpose and they give their power and authority to the beast**. That **they give their power** shows that they do not simply reign along with the beast but rather submit to his authority. But why do they form an alliance to be led by the beast?

14 Their purpose is now revealed: **These will wage war against the Lamb** (though we will see in v. 16 that part of their purpose is to destroy Babylon before mounting an attack on the Lamb). However, they will not triumph, for **the Lamb will overcome them.** The language of the first clause comes from Dan. 7:21: "that horn was waging war with the saints and overpowering them." There, as in Rev. 17:12, the kings are portrayed as horns. But there is a change in that the last part of Daniel's wording is reversed: now it is the Lamb who conquers the agents of the enemy. The prediction of the beast's victory over the saints in Dan. 7:21 and its fulfillment in Revelation (e.g., 11:7) become an ironic type or analogy of his own final defeat. The language by which the beast was described in Dan. 7:21 and Rev. 11:7; 13:7a as defeating the saints is now applied to the portrayal of the Lamb overcoming the forces of the beast and his horned allies. His defeat must fittingly occur according to the same war-

like method by which he attempted to oppress. The reversed portrayal shows that he must be punished by means of his own sin, indicating again the application of the OT principle of "an eye for an eye." This verse is the true answer to the cry of the beast's followers, "who is able to wage war with him [the beast]?" (13:4).

The basis for the Lamb's victory lies in the fact that **He is Lord of lords and King of kings**. The title is taken from the OG of Dan. 4:37. Just as the Babylonian king was addressed by virtually the same title, so the king of latter-day Babylon (Rome) in John's day was similarly addressed. The title in Daniel 4 refers to God as the One who demonstrated His true, divine sovereignty and revealed Nebuchadnezzar's claims to the title as empty by judging the (literally) beastly king of "Babylon the great." Now the title is applied typologically to the Lamb. The Lamb demonstrates His deity on the Last Day by judging the beast which carries "Babylon the great." And He exposes as false the divine claims of the emperor and all others like him.

The saints fight and conquer along with the Lamb: **And those who are with Him are the called and chosen and faithful**. They represent the vindication of the persecuted saints of Dan. 7:21 and Rev. 6:9-11; 12:11; and 13:10, 15-17. Strikingly, Dan. 7:22 promises that after the horned beast attempts to conquer the saints, God will give the judgment to "the saints of the Highest One." This became the basis for the expectation that the saints will judge the wicked in the end time (so 1 Cor. 6:2).

Suggestions for Reflection on 17:8-14

On finding wisdom in the Word. "Here is the mind which has wisdom" (v. 9) is a critical phrase at the heart of this section. God has provided wisdom to those who study and heed His Word. The phrase directs us back to Dan. 11:33 and 12:10, which clearly state that only those with wisdom and insight will have a true understanding of God's actions in history, especially in the latter days (which have been inaugurated at Christ's first coming). The commentary sets forth the proposition that careful examination of Scripture yields an accurate interpretation of the career of the beast and the various kings and kingdoms referred to in these verses, some of which are in existence during the church age. Here, as often elsewhere in Revelation, is particularly demonstrated the truth that the meaning of the various visions must be sought first and primarily from Scripture, rather than only from current events. How should this alert us to the paramount importance of finding wisdom first in the Word of God rather than in the world around us? Many, among even sincere believers, have seriously misunderstood passages like this because they have strayed from this important principle.

The interpretation of the woman in relation to the waters and to the beast: at the end of history God will inspire the state and its allies to turn against the economic-religious system in order to remove its security and to destroy it (17:15-18)

15 And he said to me, "The waters which you saw where the harlot sits are peoples and multitudes and nations and tongues. 16 And the ten horns which you
saw, and the beast, these will hate the harlot and will make her desolate and
naked, and will eat her flesh and will burn her up with fire. 17 For God has put it in
their hearts to execute His purpose by having a common purpose, and by giving
their kingdom to the beast, until the words of God should be fulfilled. 18 And the
woman whom you saw is the great city, which reigns over the kings of the earth."

15 The angel now interprets **the waters which you saw where the harlot sits** (see 17:1) as **peoples and multitudes and nations and tongues**. The same formula of universality coined from Daniel (Dan. 3:4, 7; 4:1; 5:19; 6:25; 7:14) occurs throughout Revelation (also see on 7:9; 10:11; 11:9; 13:7; 14:6). In both books, the formula refers to subjects under Babylon's domination. Isa. 17:13 also uses the metaphor of "many waters" for "many nations" (for "waters" linked with or representing nations cf. likewise Isa. 8:7; 23:10; Jer. 46:7-8; 47:2). The "many waters" have already been seen to be an allusion to Jer. 51:13, where they refer to the waters of the Euphrates and the channels and canals which surrounded Babylon (see on v. 1). These waters helped the city to flourish economically and provided security against outside attack. The multitudes of fallen humanity which the waters now represent are the basis for Babylon's economic trade and economic security.

16 The coalition of **the ten horns . . . and the beast** forms first to destroy the harlot, before attempting to do the same to the Lamb: **And the ten horns which you saw, and the beast, these will hate the harlot and will make her desolate and naked, and will eat her flesh and will burn her up with fire.** The images of the harlot's destruction are borrowed from the pictures of God's judgment against another harlot — unfaithful Israel. The portrayal of the harlot's desolation is sketched according to the outlines of the prophesied judgment of apostate Jerusalem by God in

Ezek. 23:25-29, 47: "your survivors will be *consumed by the fire*" (v. 25); "they will also *strip you of your clothes*" (v. 26); "and they will deal with you in *hatred* . . . and leave you *naked and bare.* And the nakedness of your harlotries shall be uncovered" (v. 29); "they will . . . *burn* their houses *with fire*" (v. 47). Likewise, Ezek. 16:37-41 prophesies against faithless Israel: "I shall gather together all your lovers with whom you took pleasure . . . they will *tear down* your shrines . . . and will leave you *naked and bare* . . . they will . . . *burn* your houses *with fire.*" Ezekiel even saw the harlot Israel drinking from a cup (23:31-34), as does the harlot Babylon in v. 4 above. This prophecy was historically fulfilled when Babylon conquered Jerusalem (for other OT references to Israel as a harlot see 2 Chron. 21:11; Ezek. 16:15, 17, 28, 35, 41; 23:1-21, 44; Isa. 1:21; 57:3; Jer. 2:20; 3:1; 13:27; Hos. 2:2-5; 4:12, 15, 18; 5:4; 9:1; Mic. 1:7).

The same imagery is now reapplied to the desolation of the Babylonian harlot. What Babylon did to Israel in the OT epoch is now turned around and applied to the Babylonian world system in the new covenant age. The kings of the earth (cf. v. 2, or "kings from the east," 16:12) gather together for war and turn against Babylon. Her waters are dried up (16:12), and she is destroyed. These kings represent the political arm of the world system, which turns against the economic-religious arm in a kind of worldwide civil war. The drying up of the Euphrates in 16:12 is a picture of how the multitudes of Babylon's religious and economic adherents throughout the world (also pictured as "waters" in v. 15) become disloyal to it (see on 16:12). Later (18:9-11), it appears that these kings, along with the merchants (representing Babylon's economic component), have occasion to weep over her destruction, perhaps suggesting the kings were duped by the beast to do his will and then regretted the loss of their own security, thus illustrating the fact that Satan causes people to destroy even that which is precious to them.

The Babylonian harlot is also modeled on Jezebel, who represents the spirit of idolatry, a spirit still active in the churches (2:20-24). The object of this destruction includes the apostate church, which has "committed acts of immorality" by cooperating with the idolatrous economic system (see on 2:14, 20-22). Their leader has even been referred to under the image of a harlot (2:20-22). Her followers will have the shame of their nakedness revealed (16:15; the reference to "the shame of your nakedness" in 3:17-18 may indicate the presence of Jezebelic activity in Laodicea). Strikingly, the phrase (they) **will eat her flesh** is reminiscent of Jezebel's destiny: "the dogs shall eat the flesh of Jezebel" (2 Kgs. 9:36). Jezebel's destruction, according to the same verse, likewise happened according to the word of the Lord, just as is the case here.

Note the many other parallels between the OT Jezebel and the Babylonian harlot, which further link the latter to the false prophetess Jezebel active in at least one of the seven churches:

Both were heavily adorned or made up (2 Kgs. 9:30; Rev. 17:4).
Both were queens (1 Kgs. 16:31; Rev. 17:18; 18:7).
Both controlled seductively (1 Kgs. 21:25; Rev. 17:2).
Both were guilty of spiritual fornication or immorality (2 Kgs. 9:22; Rev. 17:1-2).
Both engaged in witchcraft (2 Kgs. 9:22; Rev. 18:23).
Both were greedy for wealth (1 Kgs. 21:7; Rev. 18:11-19).
Both persecuted the saints (1 Kgs. 18:4; Rev. 17:6).
In both cases a righteous remnant opposed her sinful ways (1 Kgs. 19:18; Rev. 17:14).
God avenged on both the blood of His servants (2 Kgs. 9:7; Rev. 19:2).
The destruction of both occurs quickly (2 Kgs. 9:33-37; Rev. 18:10, 17, 19).
God judges the followers of both (1 Kgs. 18:40; 2 Kgs. 10:19; Rev. 2:23; 18:9-10; 20:15).

Thus the false teacher Jezebel in Rev. 2:20-22 is in fact part of "Babylon the great," which is raising its head within the church itself through the figure of a purported Christian teacher, who is really a false teacher. The content of her false teachings within the church of Thyatira was probably an expression of the Babylonian system's worldly ideas communicated with a veneer of Christian-sounding language. The overlap between the apostate segment of the church and the wider, antagonistic pagan system is presupposed in 18:4ff., where those on the verge of compromise are exhorted to "come out of her." This is an allusion to Isa. 48:20; 52:11; Jer. 50:8; 51:6, where Israel is exhorted to come out of impure Babylon when the time for restoration to Jerusalem comes.

Some commentators have limited the reference of the harlot only to the apostate church, especially because Ezekiel 23 and the other abovementioned OT references pertain only to apostate Israel's judgment. Furthermore, apostate Israel is often referred to as a harlot in the OT (e.g., 2 Chron. 21:11; Ezek. 16:15, 17, 28, 35, 41; 23:1-21, 44; Isa. 1:21; 57:3; Jer.

2:20; 3:1; 13:27; Hos. 2:2-5; 4:11-12, 15, 18; 5:4; 9:1; Mic. 1:7). Indeed, the portrait of the harlot throughout Revelation 17 draws also from the similar depiction in Jer. 2:20–4:31: there Judah is a harlot (2:20) who "had a harlot's forehead" (3:3), who causes sin in others (2:33), on whose "skirts is found the lifeblood of the innocent" (2:34), whose "dress (is) in scarlet," who decorates herself "with ornaments of gold" (4:30), and whose lovers will despise her and try to kill her (4:30). Israel is called a harlot because, though she is married by faith to Yahweh, she has spiritual intercourse with idols.

However, in the prophets "harlot" can also refer to other ungodly nations: in Nah. 3:4-5 and especially Isa. 23:15-18, Nineveh and Tyre are called harlots because they cause ruin and uncleanness among the nations by economically dominating them and influencing them by their idolatry. Furthermore, the harlot in Revelation 17 is called "Babylon the great," which is an allusion to the proud, pagan Babylonian city in Dan. 4:30.

Apostate national Israel of the first and following centuries also composes Babylon, but does not exhaust it by itself (against some writers, who see only apostate Israel here). Nevertheless, unbelieving Israel's partial inclusion in Babylon also accounts for some of the allusions from the OT about Israel as a harlot and her impending judgment. Furthermore, apostate Israel performed her share of persecution together with past and present pagan oppressors of the faithful remnant (Matt. 21:33-42; 23:29-35; Acts 7:51-52; 13:45; 14:2; 1 Thess. 2:14-16; see above on 2:9-10; 3:9).

Therefore, though most past commentators have tended to identify Babylon with only ungodly Roman culture, only the apostate church, or only apostate Israel, it is better to see these identifications as not mutually exclusive. The wicked religious-economic culture of the evil Roman world system (which is trans-temporal) is the focus, and the apostate church and unbelieving Israel are included with it inasmuch as they have become part of the sinful world system.

Consequently, Babylon refers to apostate national Israel, to the pagan world system, and to the apostate church which cooperates with it. That "Babylon the great" is the entire corrupt economic-religious system and not merely the apostate church is apparent from the references to Babylon in chs. 14, 16, and 18 (see 14:8; 16:18-21; 17:4-6, 18; ch. 18). Nevertheless, John's overriding concern is to *warn the churches about compromise with this system* so that they will not be judged with it. John wants to warn them that the false teaching of Jezebel is none other than the ideology of the world.

17 The beast and his allies will overthrow Babylon, **for God has put**

it in their hearts to execute His purpose by having a common purpose, and by giving their kingdom to the beast, until the words of God should be fulfilled. Even though the beast and the kings join together in a common cause, God Himself is the ultimate author of the events. He brought about the devilish alliance, unbeknownst to the kings or to the beast, in order to fulfill (**until the words of God should be fulfilled**) His deeper purposes, the purposes prophesied concerning the fourth beast and the ten horns in Dan. 7:19-28, which are unfolded in greater and clearer detail in Revelation 17. Likewise, the declaration in 10:7 (on which see) that "the mystery of God is finished" refers to an unexpected form of OT prophetic fulfillment, especially from Daniel (see also on 17:5, 7 for the use of "mystery" in connection with unexpected fulfillment). Here, the unexpected fulfillment is the apparently victorious kingdom of evil unknowingly beginning to self-destruct by battling against itself and destroying its own economic-religious infrastructure (see also on v. 16). Only an initiative from God could cause them to commit such a nearsighted and foolish act. At the end of history God will cause Satan to be divided and fight against himself, so that he will be brought to his final defeat (cf. Mark 3:26).

Civil war occurs throughout the ages and is an anticipation of the final civil war. The OT also predicts that it will happen among the forces of evil at the close of the age (Ezek. 38:21; Hag. 2:22; Zech. 14:13). Vv. 16-17 view the final civil war as happening on an escalated scale, since Babylon represents the universal economic-religious system throughout the earth. Contributing to the picture of war among former allies are the prophecies from Ezek. 16:37-41 and 23:22-29, 47 that harlot Israel's illicit lovers (the idolatrous nations) will turn against her and destroy her. According to the pattern of vv. 14-16, the Jewish work *4 Ezra* 13:30-38 predicts that there will be civil war among wicked nations, and then they will unite to "fight against" God's Son when he comes. It could be argued on the basis of Ezek. 38:21; Hag. 2:22; and Zech. 14:13 that eschatological civil war was clearly revealed in the OT as part of the demise of evil and therefore should not be considered an unexpected development in Revelation 17. However, these prophecies refer simply to God's enemies raising their sword (or hand) against one another. The details of the civil war are vague, and this is what ch. 17 elaborates in more clarity. Indeed, the evil kingdom's destruction of its own economic-religious power bloc is ironic and unforeseen in the OT. This unexpected fulfillment of civil war was perhaps dimly seen already in the OT itself, but is now given more clarity.

18 The **woman** is interpreted as the **great city, which reigns over**

the kings of the earth. She includes the entire evil economic-religious system of the world throughout history. That she has sovereignty over the world demonstrates that she must be identified more broadly than simply with unbelieving Israel or the apostate church. Likewise, 18:23 reveals her universal nature by describing her as one who has deceived all the nations. Note the parallels between the two women of Revelation, the bride of Christ and the Babylonian harlot, representing contrasting trans-temporal realities existing during the period between Christ's first and second comings:

One is a pure bride (21:9) and the other an impure harlot (17:1).
The language introducing each is almost identical (17:1 and 21:9-10).
Both are adorned with costly jewels and linen; the harlot's outward attire hides her inner corruption (17:4; 18:16), but the bride's reveals the glory of God (21:2, 9-23).
One woman relies on heaven (12:1), the other on the kings of the earth (17:15).
Each is seen in a desert and referred to as a city (12:14 and 21:2; 17:3 and 17:18).

Suggestions for Reflection on 17:15-18

On the presence of the harlot within the church. The commentary presents a series of detailed parallels between the OT Jezebel and the Babylonian harlot. Rev. 2:20-24 suggests that a spirit of Jezebel is active in at least one of the seven churches. The figure of the harlot here also draws on other OT passages alluding either to unfaithful Israel or to pagan nations. We expect to find false ideology in the world (= the pagan nations), or even in dead or ungodly religious systems (= unfaithful Israel), but it is hard to contemplate such false teaching operating within what professes to be the body of Christ. How are we to identify such idolatrous, Jezebelic activity and false teaching in the church today? How important is it to realize that even in the church we may be confronting supernatural spiritual dynamics of an evil nature? Remember that Jezebel's teaching in Revelation 2 is called "the deep things of Satan" (2:24). Satan still masquerades an as angel of light. What strategies can we employ to discern false teaching and to defeat the attacks of the enemy in the form of false teaching in the church? How can we discern when the world (that is, the Babylonian world system) exercises influence within our own churches?

Saints who do not compromise with the idolatrous world are to rejoice over God's judgment of it because this demonstrates the integrity of their faith and of God's justice and glory and leads to God's consummate reign and union with His people (18:1–19:10)

The promise of the angel in 17:1 that he would show John the harlot's judgment is fulfilled in detail throughout ch. 18. Ch. 17 focuses on the beast and his allies (and thus what precipitates the woman's fall in ch. 18). 18:1–19:6 (or 19:8) pictures Babylon's demise as a continuation of the vision begun in 17:3 (which itself elaborates on 16:14-21). Note the verbal repetition of 17:2 in 18:3. Both ch. 17 and ch. 18 are developments of the initial announcement of Babylon's fall in 14:8. The events depicted in ch. 18 are not set out in a pure chronological sequence, but are laid out in this way:

1. The fall of Babylon is predicted (vv. 1-3).
2. God's people are exhorted to separate from Babylon *before* her judgment, lest they suffer with her (vv. 4-8).
3. Those cooperating with Babylon will lament *after* her judgment (vv. 9-19).
4. The faithful will rejoice over her judgment once it is accomplished (vv. 20-24).
5. Conclusion to Babylon's fall (19:1-6, perhaps including vv. 7-8).

The logic moves progressively. The declaration of Babylon's coming punishment is the basis for the following four things:

exhortation of saints to escape Babylon lest they be judged with her (vv. 1-8),
Babylon's allies lamenting because they perceive their own demise (vv. 9-19),
the saints rejoicing (vv. 20-24), and
the climactic purpose of glorifying God as just (19:1-6 [or -8]).

An angel announces Babylon's judgment and its severe effects, which will come because of her idolatrous seduction of people (18:1-3).

[1] After these things I saw another angel coming down from heaven, having great authority, and the earth was illumined with his glory. [2] And he cried out with a mighty voice, saying, "Fallen, fallen is Babylon the great! And she has become a

dwelling place of demons and a prison of every unclean spirit, and a prison of every unclean and hateful bird. [3] For all the nations have drunk of the wine of the passion of her immorality, and the kings of the earth have committed acts of immorality with her, and the merchants of the earth have become rich by the wealth of her sensuality."

1 As throughout the book (4:1; 7:1, 9; 15:5; 19:1), the phrase **after these things** refers to the order of the visions, not to the order of events portrayed in the visions (see on 4:1). The **great authority** of the angel and the fact that **the earth was illumined with his glory** confirm the validity of his message of judgment. Ezekiel's vision of the restoration of Israel (Ezek. 43:2) is accompanied by a "voice . . . like the sound of many waters" (cf. Rev. 18:2) and the observation that "the earth shone with His glory." This is an appropriate background text, as one of the major themes of this chapter is an exhortation to God's true people to separate from the world and be restored to the Lord (see on v. 4). The portrayal is similar to that of the luminous angelic appearance in 10:1, which is likely a christophany (an appearance of Christ). That the angel is Christ is confirmed by the fact that every ascription of "glory" to a heavenly figure in the book refers to either God or Christ (to God: 4:9, 11; 5:13; 7:12; 11:13; 14:7; 15:8; 16:9; 19:1; 21:11, 23; to Christ: 1:6; 5:12-13). The allusion to Ezekiel anticipates the vision of 21:10ff., which is based on Ezekiel 40–48. That is, the desolation of Babylon prepares the way for God's dwelling in the new creation. The allusion to the divine glory prophesied to be in the new temple of Ezekiel anticipates the full revelation of the eternal temple in Revelation 21.

2 That the angel **cried out with a mighty voice** further highlights the authority of this pronouncement (for similar angelic pronouncements see 7:2, 10; 10:3; 14:7, 9, 15; 19:17). The angel is more glorious than Babylon (v. 1) and has an authority more compelling than Babylon's. Therefore, together with the glorious appearance of the angel, the loud voice is meant to get the attention of any who are in danger of falling under Babylon's spell. The certainty of the judgment is underlined further by narrating the consequences of the destruction in the past tense, as if it has already happened. The prophecy and fulfillment of historical Babylon's past fall is viewed as a historical pattern pointing forward to the fall of a much larger Babylon.

This verse explains Babylon's desolate condition resulting from her judgment: **Fallen, fallen is Babylon the great! And she has become a**

dwelling place of demons and a prison of every unclean spirit, and a prison of every unclean and hateful bird. This description of desolation most closely approximates the similar portrayal of Babylon's and Edom's judgment in Isa. 13:21 and 34:11, 14. These judgments are viewed as typological anticipations of universal Babylon's judgment at the end of history. The demonic nature of Babylon is revealed where, contrary to the outward appearance of beauty and glory she projects (17:4; 18:16), she is said to have become a dwelling place for demons and unclean spirits. As her outward glory is stripped away, all that is left are the skeletal remains, surrounded by foul spirits. Isaiah prophesied that, following earthly Babylon's destruction, she would be left as the dwelling place of various unclean and strange animals, including howling hyenas, jackals, and shaggy goats (literally "goat demons"; see Isa. 13:20-22; 34:11). This revelation shows that the demonic realm has been Babylon's guiding force.

3 The cause of Babylon's judgment lies in her idolatrous seduction of nations and rulers: **For all the nations have drunk of the wine of the passion of her immorality, and the kings of the earth have committed acts of immorality with her, and the merchants of the earth have become rich by the wealth of her sensuality.** The reference is not to literal immorality (Greek *porneia;* see on 2:14, 20; 14:8; 17:2; 18:9), but to acceptance of Babylon's religious and idolatrous demands in return for economic security (cf. 2:9; 13:16-17). The OT allusion is to Isa. 23:17, where Tyre is said to "play the harlot with all the kingdoms on the face of the earth." That Tyre is in mind is clear from the repeated reference to the Ezekiel 26–28 pronouncement of Tyre's judgment in vv. 9-22 and the specific allusion to Isa. 23:8 in v. 23. The merchants who cooperated with Babylon became wealthy, but economic security would be removed from the faithful who lived in Babylon but were not "of Babylon," those who refused to cooperate with her idolatry. To **drink** here refers to one's willingness to commit to idolatry in order to maintain economic security. Once one imbibes, the intoxicating influence removes all desire to resist Babylon's destructive influence, blinds one to Babylon's own ultimate insecurity and to God as the source of real security, and numbs one against any fear of a coming judgment (for these metaphorical meanings of "drink" see above on 14:8).

Babylon will be judged for this seductive activity. As the chapter will reveal, coercing the nations to trust in her purported economic resources, as she herself does, is an expression of pride and a form of idolatry for which also condemnation occurs (see on vv. 7, 23).

Suggestions for Reflection on 18:1-3

On the perils of falling under Babylon's spell. The loud voice of the angel is meant to gain the attention of those who might be in danger of falling under Babylon's spell. How are we in similar danger today? The power of Babylon's allure is surely at least as powerful as in John's day. Do we really understand that behind the facade of incredible wealth and luxury lie insecurity and, ultimately, the dwelling place of demons?

An angel exhorts God's people to separate from cooperating with the Babylonian system lest they also suffer its just punishment (18:4-8)

[4] And I heard another voice from heaven, saying, "Come out of her, my people,
that you may not participate in her sins, and that you may not receive of her
plagues; [5] for her sins have piled up as high as heaven, and God has remembered
her iniquities. [6] Pay her back even as she has paid, and give back to her double
according to her deeds; in the cup which she has mixed, mix twice as much for
her. [7] To the degree that she glorified herself and lived sensuously, to the same
degree give her torment and mourning; for she says in her heart, 'I sit as a queen
and I am not a widow, and will never see mourning.' [8] For this reason in one day
her plagues will come, pestilence and mourning and famine, and she will be
burned up with fire; for the Lord God who judges her is strong."

4 The unidentified voice of v. 4 may be that of God (note **my people**), of Christ (in continuation of v. 1), or of an angel representing God (much as Jeremiah was the divine spokesman conveying the exhortation to "come forth"). The report of Babylon's coming judgment in the preceding verses is the basis for exhorting wavering believers not to participate in the compromising idolatrous system and encouraging those not compromising to keep maintaining their faithful course: **And I heard another voice from heaven, saying, "Come out of her, my people, that you may not participate in her sins, and that you may not receive of her plagues."** The exhortation to separate from Babylon's ways because of God's coming judgment is patterned after the repeated exhortations of Isaiah and Jeremiah, especially Jer. 51:45: "Come forth from her midst, My people" (see also Isa. 48:20; 52:11; Jer. 50:8; 51:6). Strikingly, the judgment which elicits the exhortation in Jeremiah 51 is portrayed with similar metaphors of desolation as in Rev. 18:2, for Jer. 51:37 reads, "Babylon will become . . . a haunt of jackals, an object of horror and hissing, without inhabitants."

That the exhortation of Rev. 18:4 also strongly echoes that in Isa. 52:11 ("Depart, depart, go out from there") is evident from the immediately following clause in the Isaiah text ("touch nothing *unclean*"), which refers to the idols of Babylon. The purpose of separating is to escape the coming judgment; cf. Jer. 51:45 ("And each of you save yourselves from the fierce anger of the Lord"). There may also be echoes of the angels' exhortation to Lot and his family to go out from the apparent security of Sodom in order not to suffer the judgment of that city (Gen. 19:12-22). Christians are not being called to withdraw from economic life or from the world in which they live, but they may be ostracized because of their refusal to compromise. They are to remain *in* the world to witness (11:3-7) and to suffer for their testimony (6:9; 11:7-10; 12:11, 17; 16:6; 17:6; 18:24), but they are not to be *of* the world (14:12-13; 16:15). V. 4 is not an exhortation to unbelievers who have always been outside the church, but is addressed rather to those within the confessing community of faith who can already be referred to by God as "My people." This is an exhortation to persevere in the true faith.

5 Babylon will be punished with such plagues because **her sins have piled up as high as heaven, and God has remembered her iniquities**. Spiritual Babylon mirrors the old earthly Babylon, whose judgment "reached to heaven and towers up to the very skies" (Jer. 51:9). The sins that have mounted up before God remind Him to punish the sinners. The image of sin mounting up to heaven is metaphorical of the great amount of sin committed, which God recognizes. Babylon has so multiplied her sin that God must multiply His judgments against her in order to maintain His justice.

6 The nature of God's judgment, implicitly mentioned in v. 5, is now elucidated. Babylon's punishment is commensurate with her crime: **Pay her back even as she has paid, and give back to her double according to her deeds; in the cup which she has mixed, mix twice as much for her**. The imperative **pay her back** could be directed to God's human (20:4) or angelic (16:7ff.; 18:21) agents of retribution, or could be an entreaty addressed to God by the angelic figure speaking here. The wording evokes Psalm 137: "O daughter of Babylon . . . how blessed will be the one who repays you with the recompense with which you have repaid us" (Ps. 137:8; cf. likewise Jer. 50:29; 51:24). The punishment of historical Babylon is typological of that of the end-time Babylonian system. The principle of the "punishment fitting the crime" appears to be contradicted by the concluding clauses of v. 6, which refer to punishing Babylon "double" for her sin. But the Greek here represents a Hebrew expression meaning "give back the equivalent" (cf. Isa. 40:2; Jer. 16:18; Matt. 23:15; 1 Tim. 5:17). This resolves the contradiction between the immediately preceding and following statements about commensurate punishment and also alleviates the metaphorical difficulty of putting twice as much into Babylon's cup, which has already been described as "full" (17:4).

7 The principle is again made clear: **To the degree that she glorified herself and lived sensuously, to the same degree give her torment and mourning.** She will be punished to the same degree that she sinned in obtaining glory and luxury. Self-glorification is sinful, since glory can be rightfully given only to God (e.g., 15:4; 19:1). The angel of v. 1 reflects the true glory of God, in contrast to the bogus glory of Babylon. Her sin is pride and self-sufficiency, which must inevitably lead to her fall (2 Sam. 22:28; Prov. 16:18). Isaiah (47:7) said of earthly Babylon, "Yet you said, 'I shall be a queen forever,'" and spiritual Babylon here speaks the same words: **for she says in her heart, "I sit as a queen and I am not a widow, and will never see mourning."** Even as earthly Babylon relied on her many subject nations to uphold her, so also does spiritual Babylon, but the latter will fall as did the former, when her subjects turn against her. Her proud confidence will be revealed as a delusion. The church must beware of trusting in economic security, lest she be judged along with the world (as with the potential judgment of the Laodiceans, who said "I am rich, and have become wealthy, and have need of nothing," 3:17).

8 The political and economic arrogance noted in v. 7b is emphasized as the cause for her sudden destruction: **For this reason in one day her plagues will come, pestilence and mourning and famine, and she will be burned up with fire; for the Lord God who judges her is strong.** Even as disaster came upon earthly Babylon in one day (Isa. 47:9), even as she was burned by fire (Isa. 47:14), so also will it be with spiritual Babylon. The clause **she will be burned up with fire** is virtually identical to 17:16 and therefore develops the prophecy about the beast and his allies turning against the economic-religious system and destroying it. Not only does God put it into their hearts to annihilate Babylon, but they are the very agents of **the Lord God who judges her.**

Suggestions for Reflection on 18:4-8

On being in the world but not of it. The commentary suggests that one of the lessons of these verses is that Christians should be in the world but not of it. To be "of" the world means that we have compromised our values to share in the world's present wealth and advantages, but at the cost of also inheriting a share in its coming judgment. The worldliness both outside and inside our churches is always making godly standards appear odd and sinful values seem normal, so that we are tempted to adopt what the world considers to be "normal." How do we practically avoid such contamination while we are holding down jobs, buying houses and cars, making prudent financial plans for retirement, and so on? Is the tithe a good place to start, as it signifies giving the first of all we have to God? Yet the rest of our finances must also be managed according to God's ways. Is this kind of teaching and discipleship available in our local churches? Are we continuously grappling with stewardship issues? Jesus talked a great deal about money, and for good reason. Are we examining what He said and putting it into practice?

Those who cooperate with the Babylonian system will lament her judgment because it means their own demise (18:9-19)

9 "And the kings of the earth, who committed acts of immorality and lived sensuously with her, will weep and lament over her when they see the smoke of her burning, 10 standing at a distance because of the fear of her torment, saying, 'Woe, woe, the great city, Babylon, the strong city! For in one hour your judgment has come.' 11 And the merchants of the earth weep and mourn over her, because no one buys their cargoes any more; 12 cargoes of gold and silver and precious stones and pearls and fine linen and purple and silk and scarlet, and every kind of citron wood and every article of ivory and every article made from very costly wood and bronze and iron and marble, 13 and cinnamon and spice and incense and perfume and frankincense and wine and olive oil and fine flour and wheat and cattle and sheep, and cargoes of horses and chariots and slaves and human lives. 14 And the fruit you long for has gone from you, and all things that were luxurious and splendid have passed away from you and men will no longer find them. 15 The merchants of these things, who became rich from her, will stand at a distance because of the fear of her torment, weeping and mourning, 16 saying, 'Woe, woe, the great city, she who was clothed in fine linen and purple and scarlet, and adorned with gold and precious stones and pearls; 17 for in one hour such great wealth has been laid waste!' And every shipmaster and every passenger and sailor, and as many as make their living by the sea, stood at a distance, 18 and were crying out as they saw the smoke of her burning, saying, 'What city is like the great city?' 19 And they threw dust on their heads and were crying out, weeping and mourning, saying, 'Woe, woe, the great city, in which all who had ships at sea became rich by her wealth, for in one hour she has been laid waste!'"

The first and last sections of vv. 9-19 (vv. 9-11 and 15-19) emphasize that the mourning of those who prosper from cooperation with the idolatrous economic system occurs because they see in its downfall their own economic downfall. The middle section (vv. 12-14) amplifies the cause for their mourning by highlighting a representative sampling of aspects of the economic prosperity which will be lost. The main point of the entire segment is the despair because of economic loss, which is a response to Babylon's judgment narrated in vv. 1-8. The despair functions also implicitly to predict judgment, which leads up to the command to the saints to rejoice in v. 20, which begins the next section. The prediction of Tyre's judgment in Ezekiel 26–28 forms the model for the prophecy of that part of Babylon's judgment recorded in vv. 9-19, though the model extends through to v. 22. The past downfall of Tyre and those who mourn over it is a prophetic foreshadowing of the fall of the last great economic system. *Thematically,* the section also can be divided into the lament of the kings of the earth (vv. 9-10), the lament of the merchants of the earth (vv. 11-17a), and the lament of the mariners (vv. 17b-19). In Ezek. 27:29-30, 35-36 the same three groups express sadness over Tyre's demise.

9 The angelic figure who spoke in vv. 4-8 appears to continue speaking in vv. 9-20. In response to Babylon's demise, **the kings of the earth . . . weep and lament** over Babylon and **the smoke of her burning** because they have lost their lover, with whom they **committed acts of immorality** (Greek *porneia;* see on 2:14, 20; 14:8; 17:2; 18:3). This idolatrous involvement allowed them to live **sensuously** or luxuriously, as in Ezek. 27:33, where Tyre "enriched the kings of earth." The close connection between idolatry and economic prosperity was a fact of life in Asia Minor, where allegiance to both Caesar and the patron gods of the trade guilds was essential for people to maintain good standing in their trades (see especially on 2:9-10, 12-21). Local and regional political leaders had to support this system in order to maintain their own political stability and to benefit economically from their high positions.

Smoke and **burning** have already been part of the description of the final judgment of the followers of the beast who sell their soul to economic well-being (cf. 14:9-11 with 13:15-17; note the allusions to Gen. 19:24, 28 and the punishment of Sodom here and in 14:10-11). They may not yet perceive that their loss involves much more than material security. The kings referred to here appear to be representative of all earthly rulers, whereas the kings of 17:16 who attack the harlot may be a more limited group.

10 The response of the kings to Babylon's destruction continues. The kings weep and lament, standing at a distance, **because of the fear of her torment**. Babylon's economic demise means suffering and loss for them. That the focus is economic is shown by the fact that the same phrase ("because of the fear of her torment") occurs in v. 15, followed by an expression of alarm that such a great economic system could be dismantled so quickly (v. 17, "in one hour such great wealth has been laid waste"; so also v. 19). What they say as they lament is **"Woe, woe, the great city, Babylon, the strong city! For in one hour your judgment has come."** They are in awe not only because of the judgment itself, but because of its suddenness (**in one hour**). **Judgment** shows that the unbelieving kings perceive in Babylon's doom the judicial hand of God. This could be an underlying reason for their lament, since they may fear the same judgment for their complicity in Babylon's crimes. Calling her **great** and **strong** reveals further the idolatrous nature of Babylon, since these are words appropriately applied only to God, especially in describing His judgment of Babylon (18:8) and her allies (6:17; 16:14; 19:17).

The time designation **one hour** refers in 17:12 to the brief time when Babylon's former allies turn against her and destroy her. It is emphasized by its repetition in 18:17, 19. The time reference is taken from Dan. 4:17a in the OG (but not in the Hebrew text), where it refers to the beginning of Nebuchadnezzar's period of punishment on account of his refusal to acknowledge God's sovereignty and his lack of mercy to the poor (Dan. 4:25-27, Hebrew text). That the time reference is from Daniel 4 is confirmed by the fact that **the great city, Babylon** is a paraphrase of "Babylon the great" from Rev. 14:8; 16:19; and 17:5, which allude to Dan. 4:30. The reference, as in 17:12, is to the time in which the worldly system is to be judged by God, resulting in the removal of its prosperity. As in Dan. 4:25-27, the sin is refusal to acknowledge God's sovereignty and contributing to the economic destitution and even death of faithful saints (17:6; 18:20, 24; 19:2; references to martyrdom throughout Revelation generally encompass all forms of suffering up to and including death: see on 2:10; 6:9; 7:14).

Vv. 9-10 follow the pattern of Ezek. 26:16-18 where, in response to the fall of prosperous Tyre, the princes fear, tremble, and take up a lament. Ezek. 27:28-32, which speaks of the lament of the merchants and mariners, is partly formative for vv. 11-19, confirming the strong influence of Ezekiel here. The Ezekiel background (see especially 27:33-36) confirms the suggestion that the kings' lament over Babylon's desolation is grounded in the fear of their own imminent economic loss. The contrast of unbelievers lamenting about Babylon's fall (vv. 9-19) with believers rejoicing and praising God (18:20–19:6) over the same event suggests further that the response of mourning is an ungodly reaction to Babylon's demise, which is a characteristic reaction of those deserving final judgment (see further on vv. 17-19).

11 In addition to the kings' mourning, **the merchants of the earth weep and mourn over her, because no one buys their cargoes any more.** This continues the allusion to Ezekiel 27:28-32. Her destruction and removal means that there are no longer any buyers for the merchants' goods (cf. Ezek. 27:33-36). Therefore, the merchants do not lament altruistically over Babylon's destruction, but do so because her loss means their own imminent economic loss.

12-13 A representative list of trade products shows what cargo will no longer be purchased by the Babylonian economic system. The items at the beginning of the list (**gold . . . precious stones and pearls and fine linen and purple . . . and scarlet**) personify the Babylonian economic system because they form the symbolic clothing of the harlot in both 17:4 and 18:16. The list of products is based partly on Ezek. 27:12-24, where approximately half of the items here are listed together along with the repetitive use of "traders" (= "merchants," as in vv. 11a, 15). The items in common with Ezekiel are not the result of a mere literary construct but an actual part of the trade system. The trade goods in the list are selected because they represent the kind of luxury products in which Rome overindulged in an extravagantly sinful and idolatrous manner. More description is given of the land merchants' (vv. 11-17a) and sea merchants' (vv. 17b-19) loss than of the kings' loss (vv. 9-10) to get the attention of the churches who are in danger of compromising economically.

14 The theme of Babylon's judgment from the preceding verses is repeated for emphasis. **And the fruit you long for has gone from you** expresses the fact that the core of Babylon's being is committed to satisfying herself with economic wealth instead of desiring God's glory. That **all things that were luxurious and splendid** (literally "bright") **have passed away from you and men will no longer find them** suggests that the pseudo-glitter and glory of Babylon's wealth will be replaced by the genuine divine glory and brightness reflected in God's end-time people and city and God's Son. "Bright" (Greek *lampros*) is used in the latter manner in 15:6; 19:8; 22:1, 16; cf. likewise, 21:11, 23-24, where God's "glory" is linked to "brightness."

15 Now the **merchants** respond to Babylon's destruction. The statement **The merchants of these things, who became rich from her, will**

stand at a distance because of the fear of her torment, weeping and mourning repeats from vv. 9-11 the themes of the loss of the merchants' wealth, the distant stance of Babylon's followers due to fear, and their mourning. The repetition emphasizes further the devastating judgment of the economic system and the loss it brings to those dependent on it.

16 The merchants' mourning is now continued through their verbal lament. The cry of v. 10, "**Woe, woe, the great city,**" is repeated, highlighting the calamity of the judgment. The second refrain of v. 10, concerning Babylon's strength, is now defined as her wealth, figuratively pictured as clothing: **she who was clothed in fine linen and purple and scarlet, and adorned with gold and precious stones and pearls**. This follows the same pattern of Ezekiel 27, where a full list of goods is found (27:12-24), and part of the list is metaphorically applied to the clothing worn by Tyre, pictured as a person (cf. Ezek. 27:7: fine linen and purple). The picture of an ungodly economic system as a person dressed in luxurious clothing made of trade products is also influenced by the figurative portrayal of Tyre's king in Ezek. 28:13.

The religious facet of the economic system is highlighted by the OT's description of the high priest's garments and parts of the sanctuary as adorned with gold, purple, scarlet, fine linen, and precious stones (Exod. 28:5-9, 15-20). All the same items appear in the words used to describe the harlot's attire in 17:4 and here. In this light, it appears likely that the repeated OT portrayal of the priestly attire has influenced the selection of items from vv. 12-13 which are applied to the harlot. An additional influence on the description of the harlot comes from Ezekiel's condemnation of unfaithful Israel as one adorned with gold, silver, linen, and silk who trusted in her beauty and played the harlot (Ezek. 16:13-16). The prophet also cried, "Woe, woe" to Israel (Ezek. 16:23) even as the angel does here to Babylon. The presence of this imagery suggests further that the harlot, though primarily reflecting the pagan system, includes also unfaithful Israel and even those from the Christian community who have compromised and effectively become part of the pagan culture. The point is to picture a system in which apostate religion has merged with the ungodly world.

V. 16 is intended to contrast the impure urban harlot (see on 17:4, 16) and the pure urban bride of Christ in 21:2, 9-23. Indeed, the Lamb's bride is also adorned with every kind of precious stone including gold, and the list of twelve stones there is based on the list in Exod. 28:17-20, which describes the high priest's garment (see on 21:18-21).

17a The third refrain from the woe of v. 10 ("for in one hour your judgment has come") is also interpreted economically: **for in one hour such great wealth has been laid waste!** On the suddenness of Babylon's demise (**one hour**) see on v. 10. The merchants' perception of their own imminent and swift fall is the real cause for their woe, which has begun in v. 16. Therefore, the woe is selfishly motivated.

17b-19 This section lays even further emphasis on the detrimental effects of Babylon's fall on her dependents. The emphasis is strengthened further through repetition of the weeping and lamenting language of 18:9: they **were crying out as they saw the smoke of her burning**, and **they threw dust on their heads and were crying out, weeping and mourning.** These cries of lamentation are not a token of true repentance, but are expressions of sorrow for their own demise. The pattern of Ezekiel 27 continues to be followed, since there also (vv. 28-33) those who conduct the business of sea trade lament, weep, cry bitterly, mourn, and throw dust on their heads because Tyre's demise means the demise of their sea commerce. The twofold woe from v. 10 is repeated as in v. 16: **woe, woe, the great city.** This interprets "Babylon, the strong city" of v. 10 in an economic manner: **in which all who had ships at sea became rich by her wealth.** The final clause of the woe (**for in one hour she has been laid waste**) emphasizes once again that the suddenness of Babylon's desolation is the cause of the lament, yet as with the prior laments in vv. 10, 16-17 this one is also selfishly inspired by concern for the sailors' and merchants' own economic loss. Such selfishness and self-centeredness points further to the ultimate identification of the mourners in vv. 17b-19 with Babylon and, therefore, also with Babylon's ultimate, final judgment. If the merchants have nothing to trade and sell because of Babylon's fall, then all maritime commerce will cease, and the need to carry goods by water will cease. All who make money from such sea commerce will be out of a job and face economic collapse.

The verbal repetitions from vv. 9-11 in vv. 15-19 underscrore that these two sections carry the main point of vv. 9-19: despair over economic loss in response to Babylon's judgment.

Suggestions for Reflection on 18:9-19

On the destructive power of human self-interest. The commentary suggests that the mourning and weeping of the kings, merchants, and mariners over the destruction of Babylon reflects their own self-interest rather than genuine repentance and recognition of the righteousness of God and of His judgment. Entanglement in the things of this world, and particularly pursuit of material wealth, focuses us inward on ourselves, blinds us to the interests of others, and numbs us to the approaching judgment of God, such that we do not even recognize it when it comes. The people represented in these verses are about to lose something of far greater value than their material wealth, yet their obsession with that wealth leaves them apparently oblivious to their impending and eternal judgment. How often do we tragically see this played out in the lives of people around us? Even if we are not witnessing the events of the very end of history, is it not true that the same principles operate regardless? How can we guard ourselves against this kind of poison entering our lives? We need to "come out" of Babylon increasingly so that we "will not participate in her sins and . . . receive of her plagues" (18:4).

Those who separated from Babylon should rejoice over her judgment because it vindicates their faith and God's just character (18:20-24)

20 "Rejoice over her, O heaven, and you saints and apostles and prophets, because God has pronounced judgment for you against her." 21 And a strong angel took up
a stone like a great millstone and threw it into the sea, saying, "Thus will Babylon,
the great city, be thrown down with violence, and will not be found any longer.
22 And the sound of harpists and musicians and flute-players and trumpeters
will not be heard in you any longer; and no craftsman of any craft will be found
in you any longer; and the sound of a mill will not be heard in you any longer;
23 and the light of a lamp will not shine in you any longer; and the voice of the
bridegroom and bride will not be heard in you any longer; for your merchants
were the great men of the earth, because all the nations were deceived by your
sorcery. 24 And in her was found the blood of the prophets and of saints and of
all who have been slain on the earth."

The segment begins (v. 20) with an allusion to Jer. 51:48, which announces the response of those allied with God to Babylon's destruction: heaven and earth will shout for joy over Babylon's destruction narrated in vv. 9-19. The segment ends (v. 24) with an allusion to Jer. 51:49, which states that persecution was one of the reasons for the judgment. These two outer boundaries of the section emphasize persecution as a cause of Babylon's judgment. The main point is the "rejoicing" in v. 20a, which occurs because of God's judgment (vv. 20b-24).

20 An address in response to Babylon's terrible fall is given: **"Rejoice over her, O heaven, and you saints and apostles and prophets, because God has pronounced judgment for you against her."** The addressees of the exhortation are both in heaven and on earth, which represents all believers, though angelic beings are probably included, as in 12:12. Just as there saints were commanded to rejoice because of the inaugurated victory over Satan, so now they are commanded to rejoice because of the consummated victory over the Satanic system. Instead of Jeremiah's "heaven and earth" rejoicing (Jer. 51:48), where "earth" likely represents Israel, the angel speaks of heaven and the **saints and apostles and prophets** rejoicing, thus showing again how the church is now the continuation of true Israel.

The reason for rejoicing is that God has given judgment against Babylon (v. 20b). It is best to see the suffering saints who cried for vengeance in 6:9-11 at the center of the heavenly throng who are exhorted to rejoice in 18:20. This is confirmed by the continuation of the ch. 18 narrative in 19:1-2, where the basis for the "Hallelujah" ("because His judgments are true and righteous; for . . . He has avenged the blood of His bond-servants on her") is formulated in explicit allusion to 6:10 ("How long, O Lord, holy and true, wilt Thou refrain from judging and avenging our blood on those who dwell on the earth?"). Together with 19:5, 18:20 is the climax of the saints' cry for vindication from 6:10, though anticipated in various ways also in 11:18; 14:18; 15:4; and 16:5-6. The focus is not on delight in Babylon's suffering but on the successful outcome of God's execution of justice, which demonstrates the integrity of Christians' faith and God's just character (see further on 6:10). God will judge Babylon just as severely as she persecuted others in order to make the punishment fit her crime. The presence of this "eye for eye" judgment is apparent from noticing that those commanded to rejoice over her judgment are the very same people who suffered from her persecution.

As stated above, v. 20 is the climax of the saints' cry for vindication from 6:10. Here for the first time we find clearly expressed the rejoicing of the saints at these events. The rejoicing does not arise out of a selfish spirit of revenge, but out of a fulfilled hope that God has defended the honor of His just name by not leaving sin unpunished and by showing His people to have been in the right all along and the verdict rendered by the ungodly world against the saints to be wrong (6:10). This is in keeping with the OT law of malicious witness: if "he has accused his brother falsely, then you shall do to him just as he had intended to do to his brother" (Deut. 19:18-19). Even the saints' rejoicing corresponds to the sin of the wicked system, which had previously rejoiced over the unjust death of the two witnesses (11:10).

21 The judgment of Babylon, and its devastating effects, are repeated again in different ways in vv. 21-23, which, together with v. 20b, serve as the basis of the rejoicing in v. 20a. The judgment of Babylon is expressed parabolically through the vision of an angel who **took up a stone like a great millstone and threw it into the sea**. The picture is based on Jer. 51:63, where Jeremiah commands his servant Seraiah to "tie a stone" to a scroll (literally "book") containing the prophecy of Babylon's judgment, and to "throw it into the middle of the Euphrates," declaring in the process that in this same way will Babylon sink down and never again rise. Likewise the angel here interprets his symbolic action to mean **Thus will Babylon, the great city, be thrown down with violence, and will not be found any longer**. The Ezekiel 26–28 background to ch. 18 has not been forgotten, for Ezek. 26:12 and 21 state that the stones of Tyre will be thrown into the water and that Tyre will never be found again. Both Babylon and Tyre are thus used as prophetic typological forerunners of spiritual Babylon. And both may have been modeled after God's punishment of Egypt in Neh. 9:11, "their pursuers Thou didst hurl into the depths, like a stone into raging waters" (cf. Exod. 15:4-5). But why the change from a stone to a millstone? The angel likely is using Jesus' warning that whoever causes His little ones to stumble would be better off having a millstone hung around his neck and be drowned in the sea (Matt. 18:6; note the parallel to the dual woe [the throwing down of the stone and its being cast into the sea] of v. 21). And like the angel here, Jesus warned against the arrogant who deceive (cf. Matt. 18:6-7 with Rev. 18:3, 23). Those in the church who are guilty of such deception (2:14, 20) should take warning lest they suffer Babylon's fate.

22-23a Vv. 5-7 and 20 have asserted that Babylon's judgment is suited to its crime, and vv. 22-23 reveal how the punishment fits the crime, which continues to depict the effects of Babylon's destruction, especially most immediately from the millstone portrayal in v. 21. The point of vv. 21b-23 is to show that the persecutor will be punished by means of her own sin. Babylon's economic system persecuted Christian communities by ostracizing people from the various trade guilds if they did not conform to worship of the patron deities of the guilds. This usually resulted in loss of economic standing and poverty (so 2:9). Christian craftsmen were removed from the marketplace, and the common pleasures of life enjoyed in normal economic times were taken away from them. In answer, God will remove Babylon's loyal tradesmen: **and no craftsman of any craft will be found in you any longer; and the sound of a mill will not be heard in you any longer, and the light of a lamp will not shine in you any longer**. Even as the blood of the saints "was found" in her (v. 24), Babylon's economic basis will no longer **be found**, and in fact Babylon herself will "not be found" (v. 21). The daily pleasures taken from Christians through economic, social, or political persecution (2:9-10; 6:10; 13:16-17; 16:6; 17:6) will be taken from the world system: **and the sound of harpists and musicians and flute-players and trumpeters will not be heard in you any longer . . . and the voice of the bridegroom and bride will not be heard in you any longer.**

Passages from Jeremiah 25 (judgment on unfaithful Israel) and Ezekiel 26 (judgment on Tyre) continue to be pieced together to depict this judicial principle (cf. Ezek. 26:13: "and the sound of your harps will be heard no more"; Jer. 25:10: "I will take from them . . . the voice of the bridegroom and the voice of the bride, the sounds of the millstones and the light of the lamp"). The statement in v. 14, "and all things that were luxurious and splendid have passed away from you and men will no longer find them," is elaborated in more detail in vv. 21-23a. Babylon's persecution was selective in John's day, but he foresaw a time in which she would attempt to exterminate completely the Christian community (so 11:7-10; 20:7-9; cf. also 13:16-17). God will likewise punish her for her persecution and attempted annihilation of the church by overthrowing her completely.

23b The angel's pronouncement of devastation begun in v. 21 continues. He gives three reasons for Babylon's destruction in vv. 23b-24. The first is that her **merchants were the great men of the earth**. The reference is to God's judgment of Tyre in Isa. 23:1-18, where Tyre's merchants were "princes, whose traders were the honored of the earth" (Isa. 23:8). Tyre here is used again as a prophetic forerunner of spiritual Babylon. These merchants were concerned only for their own glory instead of acting as stewards responsible for what had been entrusted to them by God. God judged Tyre for the proud flaunting of her economic wealth, and He destroyed it. Ezekiel likewise sees God condemning Tyre for believing that her wealth made her divine rather than human: "your heart is lifted up and you have said, 'I am a god'" (Ezek. 28:2). Babylon's judgment because of self-glory has already been announced in v. 7. One expression of that was the overwhelming pride of her **merchants**, the **great men**, who will be laid low. The point is that the chief purpose of humanity according to Revelation is to glorify God and to enjoy Him, not to glorify oneself and enjoy one's own achievements (e.g., 4:11; 5:12-13; 7:12; 15:3-4; 16:9; 19:1, 7). Self-glorification necessitates judgment in which a forced humbling occurs. It is idolatrous for Babylon and her allies to see themselves as "great" (11:8; 14:8; 16:19; 17:5, 18; 18:2, 10, 16, 19, 21, 23; even though it is angels or men who use the word with reference to Babylon, they do so with reference to Babylon's self-understanding). In truth, only God is truly great (see on v. 10). This title is reserved only for the true God (cf. "the great God" in manuscripts 051 and א of 19:17, as well as "great" in descriptions of various attributes of God in 6:17; 11:17; 15:3; 16:14). To focus on humanity as the center of everything and to forget God is the greatest sin — it is idol worship.

The second reason for Babylon's judgment is that **all the nations were deceived by your sorcery**. By magic Babylon deceived the nations into worshiping idols instead of the true God. Sorcery, immorality, and idolatry are very closely related. In Rev. 9:20-21, idolatry, sorcery, and immorality (Greek *porneia*) are linked together (as also in Gal. 5:19-21). Immorality (Greek *porneia*), as we have seen, is a common term for idolatry in Revelation (2:14, 20-21; 14:8; 17:1-2, 4-5; 18:3, 9). Sorcery and idolatry are also linked in the OT (2 Chron. 33:5-7; Mic. 5:12-14; sorcery, idolatry, and immorality in Isa. 57:3-7). The OT Jezebel was judged for immorality and sorcery (2 Kgs. 9:22). Jezebel's similar operation in Rev. 2:20-21 is why she is associated with Babylon and why her punishment is described as "death" (2:22-23), as is Babylon's in 18:8. Earthly Babylon was judged for her sorcery and immorality (Isa. 47:9-15), where sorcery is linked with seeking guidance from astrologers, rather than the Lord. In Rev. 21:8 and 22:15, sorcery is placed in close conjunction with immorality and idolatry.

24 The third reason for Babylon's judgment is now given: **And in her was found the blood of the prophets and of saints and of all who have been slain on the earth.** In earthly Babylon, declared Jeremiah, "the slain of all the earth have fallen" (Jer. 51:49). Nineveh, another prophetic forerunner of the end-time Babylon, was judged not only for her immorality and sorcery, but also because she was a city of blood (Nah. 3:1-4). Babylon and Nineveh of old were sinful world empires that are set forth as models for the annihilation of the last corrupt world system. The fact that Babylon, Tyre, and Nineveh, as well as unfaithful Israel and Sodom, are all used in ch. 18, as well as chs. 16 and 17, as prophetic forerunners of the Babylonian world system shows again that spiritual Babylon is not one specific nation at a given point of time, but rather represents all forms of evil government from the resurrection of Christ until His return. In John's day, the Roman Empire represented this wicked system, for by his time Christians had been persecuted not only in Israel, but throughout the Roman Empire. Yet the concluding clause **all who have been slain on the earth** points to a universal reference well beyond the Roman Empire and its time. This description of **all who have been slain** may be literal and allude to Christian martyrs, but it is best taken figuratively for all kinds of persecution, including death (see on 6:9; 13:15).

SUGGESTIONS FOR REFLECTION ON 18:20-24

On the fundamental division between the kingdom of God and the kingdom of darkness. These verses set forth an intriguing contrast between the lamentation of the lost in vv. 9-19 and the rejoicing of the saints in vv. 20-24. The lost grieve over Babylon's destruction only insofar as it affects their personal material security. The saints rejoice over that destruction not merely because it vindicates them or is advantageous to them, but especially because it demonstrates the righteousness of God and the justice of His judgment, and God's ultimate just dealing with evil. As the commentary states on v. 20: "God has defended the honor of His just name by not leaving sin unpunished and by showing His people to have been in the right and the verdict rendered by the ungodly world against the saints to be wrong." The events by which God secures justice for His people do not set them up to express their own personal revenge. The saints weep (or *should* weep) over the loss of every soul. They do not rejoice because they have "won" at the expense of others, but because God has been vindicated. The lost, on the other hand, cannot see past their own self-interest. The suffering of others, even the destruction of an entire world system, concerns them only because of the negative effect on their own fortunes. Here in a paragraph is the difference between the kingdom of darkness and the kingdom of light. What ultimately divides the two is the willingness (or lack thereof) to recognize who God is and to give Him the honor and worship He alone is due. Particularly in the West, we live in a profoundly anthropocentric culture which utterly fails to place God and His glory at the center, and if we do not resist this, we will find ourselves slipping all too easily into the hold of the kingdom of darkness.

The declaration of Babylon's coming judgment is also the basis for the saints' glorifying God's kingship (19:1-6)

1 After these things I heard, as it were, a loud voice of a great multitude in heaven,
saying, "Hallelujah! Salvation and glory and power belong to our God; 2 because
His judgments are true and righteous; for He has judged the great harlot who
was corrupting the earth with her immorality, and He has avenged the blood
of His bond-servants on her." 3 And a second time they said, "Hallelujah! Her
smoke rises up forever and ever." 4 And the twenty-four elders and the four living
creatures fell down and worshiped God who sits on the throne saying, "Amen.
Hallelujah!" 5 And a voice came from the throne, saying, "Give praise to our God,
all you His bond-servants, you who fear Him, the small and the great." 6 And I

heard, as it were, the voice of a great multitude and as the sound of many waters and as the sound of mighty peals of thunder, saying, "Hallelujah! For the Lord our God, the Almighty, reigns."

The dual theme of reward to the saints and destruction of their enemies announced by the seventh trumpet (11:15-19) is picked up again in ch. 19, as is evident from the verbal similarities, especially in 19:5-6:

> the threefold description of believers (11:18),
> the declaration of the commencement of God's reign (11:15-16), and
> the roar of thunder (11:19).

The new section of Rev. 19:1-6 (perhaps extending to 19:8) actually continues the last literary segment of ch. 18 (18:20-24) and may be seen as the conclusion of that segment by emphasizing Babylon's fall.

1 The phrase **after these things** refers primarily to the vision of Babylon's demise, especially as portrayed in 18:20-24. After the preceding vision and extended audition (18:1-3 and 4-24 respectively), John hears something like **a loud voice of a great multitude in heaven**, proclaiming **Hallelujah!** This is the Greek transliteration of a Hebrew phrase meaning "Praise the Lord!" God is to be praised because **salvation and glory and power** belong to Him alone. The entire assembly of the saints praise God at the consummation of history (vv. 1-3, 5b-8) for His judgment of Babylon and His accomplishment of salvation for His people by His mighty power.

2 Here it becomes explicit that God's judgment of Babylon in ch. 18 is the reason for the outburst of praise in v. 1. The praise occurs **because His judgments are true and righteous** (cf. Ps. 19:9). The second clause **for He has judged the great harlot who was corrupting the earth with her immorality** expands the meaning of the first. The description reiterates themes from the previous chapters (17:1-5; 18:3, 7-9). To "corrupt" (Greek *phtheirō*) can also mean to "destroy" (note the mention of persecution in the following phrase). Inclusion of this meaning is evident from 11:18, where the enemy undergoing final judgment is described with the same language as here ("those who destroy the earth"). Both 11:18 and 19:2 are dependent on Jer. 51:25, containing God's judgment on Babylon ("Behold, I am against you, O destroying mountain, who destroy the whole earth").

The third clause, **and He has avenged the blood of His bond-servants on her** (literally **from her hand**), interprets God's judgment as His vengeance. The literal meaning is awkward. If it is interpreted as equivalent to "at her hand," it could be translated "on her" (thus NASB, NIV, ESV). But the Greek here likely reflects the typical OT use of the phrase "from the hand of" in larger expressions like "God delivered you *from the hand of* your enemy," where "hand" is figurative for oppressive power (so at least forty-five times). Though the larger idea of vengeance on Babylon is still in view, the literal meaning of the phrase would be that God has avenged the blood of His servants shed by the hand of Babylon. This is the meaning of the closest OT parallel, 2 Kgs. 9:7, where God says that He will "avenge the blood of My servants the prophets, and the blood of all the servants of the Lord, at [literally 'from' = 'shed by'] the hand of Jezebel." The allusion to this text based on the closeness of the wording is confirmed by the reference to Jezebel, for the spirit of Jezebel has resurfaced at Thyatira (2:20), and the Babylonian harlot has been compared to Jezebel in 17:16 (on which see).

This verse represents a further answer to the cry of the saints in 6:10: "How long, O Lord . . . wilt Thou refrain from . . . avenging our blood on those who dwell on the earth?" Both verses allude to Ps. 79:10: "Why should the nations say, 'Where is their God?' Let there be known among the nations in our sight, vengeance for the blood of Thy servants, which has been shed," so that the church is included in the Israelite "servants" who cry for vengeance.

3 As in v. 1, the repetition of **Hallelujah!** and its following explanation again provides the further basis for the first **Hallelujah!** and shows that what is precisely underscored is the finality of Babylon's judgment: **her smoke rises up forever and ever**. This is a reference originally to God's judgment on Edom ("its smoke shall go up forever," Isa. 34:10). Here the fall of Edom is taken as an anticipatory typological pattern of that of the world system, which will never rise again after God's judgment. The same verse has been alluded to in 14:11 to refer to the smoke of the torment of individual unbelievers. Babylon is spoken of corporately, but its members are also referred to individually, in the same way that the bride of Christ is alluded to both corporately and as a group of individuals (see on vv. 7-9). The fates of the corporate and the individual are inextricably linked, as 18:4 demonstrates: those wishing to be saved must leave Babylon or suffer her fate.

4 **The twenty-four elders and the four living creatures** now join in the exclamation of the saints; they **fell down and worshiped God who sits on the throne saying, "Amen. Hallelujah!"** "Amen," a Hebrew word expressing trust, is part of their declaration of praise. The phrase echoes

Ps. 106:48, where the wording ("Amen. Hallelujah"), as in Rev. 19:4, functions as part of Israel's thanksgiving to God for gathering them to Himself after delivering the nation from their enemies who oppressed them (cf. Ps. 106:42-48 with Rev. 19:1-2, 7-9). Now the consummate **Amen. Hallelujah!** is expressed because God's end-time covenant community have been decisively delivered at the end of history.

5 A **voice came from the throne**, possibly that of Christ (in line with the similar expressions in 6:6; 16:1, 17). The voice declares **Give praise to our God, all you His bond-servants, you who fear Him, the small and the great**. If this is the voice of Jesus, He stands as the great representative of the saints confirming and assenting to their prior rejoicing. But on the analogy of John 20:17 ("I ascend to My Father and your Father, and My God and Your God"), might Jesus not rather have said "*My* God," to distinguish Himself from His earthly followers? If **from the throne** is understood as "from the area around the throne," the voice could also be that of another heavenly creature. Those exhorted to praise are first called **all** you His bond-servants (Pss. 134:1; 135:1). They are the ones whose blood was shed by Babylon (note "the blood of His bond-servants," v. 2). All believers are included in this number, for all believers bear the name "bond-servant" (2:20; 7:3; 19:2; 22:3; and see on 11:18). In this respect, the following phrase **you who fear Him, the small and the great** is a further identification of the servants, the first phrase again linking this verse to 11:18 ("Thy bond-servants the prophets and . . . those who fear Thy Name").

6 This segment ends here as it began in v. 1. The same innumerable multitudes shout even louder: **And I heard, as it were, the voice of a great multitude and as the sound of many waters and as the sound of mighty peals of thunder, saying, "Hallelujah! For the Lord our God, the Almighty, reigns.** The phrase "the sound of abundant waters" is used of the noise made by the four cherubim in Ezek. 1:24 (in the Hebrew text), but in Ezek. 43:2 (LXX) the same phrase in Hebrew is interpreted as "a voice of a *camp* [*parembolē*], as the voice of many redoubling their cries," which likely refers to angels, but would have been easily susceptible to application to heavenly saints by later readers, which is the reference here.

The expression **the Lord . . . reigns** may be a sweeping allusion to a series of Psalms and other OT passages that use the same expression to refer in context to God establishing His kingship after judging Israel's enemies, especially in Canaan and culminating in David's occupation of Jerusalem (Pss. 93:1; 96:10; 97:1; 1 Chron. 16:31; plausibly also Pss. 47:3, 7-8; 99:1). Isa. 52:7 (using "God" instead of "the Lord"); Zech. 14:9; and

Rev. 19:6 use the expression to speak of the eschatological future, when God would again establish His kingship universally on earth after defeating His enemies, of which the Psalm accounts were anticipatory models. The Isaiah and Zechariah passages are uppermost in mind, since Rev. 19:6 indicates the future fulfillment of those two end-time prophecies.

In light of this OT background, the Greek verb may best be translated "begun to reign" (with an ingressive sense), since, in view of Babylon's defeat (ch. 18), it is the establishment of God's rule that appears to be in mind. Although in one sense God's reign is timeless (**the Lord . . . reigns**, as the NASB translates), in another sense it is truly fulfilled in the created universe only as a result of His final judgment of Babylon and can thus be said to have "begun." This is supported by the parallel in 11:17: "We give Thee thanks, O Lord God, the Almighty . . . because Thou . . . hast begun to reign." In fact, the verse is also a development of 11:15: "The kingdom of the world has become the kingdom of our Lord, and of His Christ; and He will reign forever and ever."

Suggestions for Reflection on 19:1-6

On the nature of our praise of God. Often our praise of God is focused on what He has done for us — whether our salvation or things related to our daily lives. Yet here the praise of the saints is centered on who God is and what He has done entirely apart from the circumstances of our individual lives — the fact that His judgments are righteous and true, the fact that He has judged the harlot, and the fact that He reigns over all. While there is nothing wrong with our praising God for what He has done in our lives — it is always a good thing to acknowledge His faithfulness and providential mercies toward us — how often do we step back and thank Him simply for who He is and what He has done in the wider context of His creation, and what He has done simply for the glory of His name?

Babylon's coming judgment and the consequent establishment of God's reign is the basis for and leads to the righteous vindication and consummate union of Christ with His righteous people at the very end of history, for which they glorify God (19:7-10)

7 "Let us rejoice and be glad and give the glory to Him, for the marriage of the
Lamb has come and His bride has made herself ready." 8 And it was given to her
to clothe herself in fine linen, bright and clean; for the fine linen is the righteous

acts of the saints. 9 And he said to me, "Write, 'Blessed are those who are invited
to the marriage supper of the Lamb.'" And he said to me, "These are true words of
God." 10 And I fell at his feet to worship him. And he said to me, "Do not do that; I
am a fellow servant of yours and your brethren who hold the testimony of Jesus;
worship God. For the testimony of Jesus is the spirit of prophecy."

7-8 Vv. 7-8 form the conclusion of the section beginning with 18:1, but at the same time, together with vv. 9-10, form a transitional segment between that and the following section. The innumerable crowd of v. 6 lift their voices to glorify God once again: **"Let us rejoice and be glad and give the glory to Him, for the marriage of the Lamb has come and His bride has made herself ready."** The opening words of the verse, **Let us rejoice and be glad**, allude to Ps. 118:22-24, where the rejoicing comes about because God has caused the stone the builders rejected to become the chief cornerstone. It also alludes to Jesus' words, "Rejoice, and be glad, for your reward in heaven is great, for so they persecuted the prophets who were before you" (Matt. 5:12). God has vindicated both His Son and those who follow Him. This section shows us that the existence of Babylon served as a necessary preparation for the bride's marriage to the Lamb. The oppression and temptation of Babylon were the fire God used to refine the faith of the saints in order that they be prepared to enter the heavenly city (for a similar notion see on 2:10-11; cf. also 6:11; Rom. 8:28ff.; 1 Pet. 4:12, 19; Phil. 1:28-30).

In v. 7, the bride is said to have prepared herself for the marriage, which places the emphasis on the bride's responsibility in making herself ready. The clothing is defined in v. 8 as **fine linen, bright and clean; for the fine linen is the righteous acts of the saints.** The righteous acts seem to be defined in context as holding to the testimony of Jesus (v. 10). The word "testimony" occurs seven other times in Revelation, usually as part of the expression "testimony of Jesus" and usually with the idea of bearing witness to Him in word and deed (1:2, 9; 6:9; 11:7; 12:11, 17; 20:4). Therefore, a possible meaning of the passage is that saints must persevere in their faith before the marriage can take place. A classic theological tension is thus expressed in these two verses. On the one hand, the bride prepares herself (v. 7), while on the other hand she is given her garments (v. 8). One way of resolving the tension is by suggesting that a transformed life is the proper response by those God has justified. However, it would be even better to view vv. 7-8 as suggesting that a transformed life is not only the proper response but in fact a *necessary* response.

White clothes in Revelation, when worn by the saints, always signify *a gift from God given* to those with tested and purified faith (3:5-6, 18; 6:11; 7:13-14; in 3:18, the idea of buying the clothes from Christ is used to encourage believers to identify with Christ's clothes in 1:13-14, which means to identify with Him and not with the compromising world). Therefore, the white clothes are not merely the saints' righteous acts but the *reward for* or *result of* such acts. This emphasizes God's justifying or vindicating action. The final clause of v. 8 could thus be paraphrased: "the fine linen is the reward for or result of the saints' righteous deeds." The white robes would then represent two inextricably related consummative end-time realities: (1) human faithfulness and good works as a necessary evidence of a right standing with God and (2) vindication or acquittal accomplished by God's final judgments against the enemy on behalf of His people.

The only other occurrence of **the righteous acts** (Greek *ta dikaiōmata*) in the book is in 15:4, where it refers to God's end-time judgments against the saints' oppressors. Six of the seven other uses in Revelation of related words (deriving from Greek *dikaioō,* "declare righteous") refer to God's just judgments (15:3, 4; 16:5, 7; 19:2, 11). Reference to the righteous judgments of God has just been made in v. 2. The angels are dressed in fine linen, in their role of vindicating the saints in pouring out bowls of wrath (15:6–16:1). Christ judges the enemy "in righteousness" (v. 11), accompanied by those clothed in fine linen (v. 14). The oppressed saints who accompany Christ as He vindicates them are wearing the symbolic clothing of their vindication, which is performed by Christ as they stand by and watch.

Nevertheless, in the process of emphasizing God's final latter-day vindication and gift of righteous standing, the importance of the righteous acts *by the saints* must not be lost sight of. Indeed, elsewhere in the book the plural genitive "of the saints," when modifying nouns and referring to Christians, always alludes to something either possessed by (16:6; 17:6; 18:24; 20:9) or performed by believers (5:8; 8:3-4; 13:10; 14:12). A contrast is probably intended between the bride clothed in bright linen and her righteous acts and the Babylonian harlot who is "clothed in fine linen" (18:16), holds a cup "full of abominations and of the unclean things of her immorality" (17:4), and has committed "iniquities" (18:5, literally "unrighteous acts").

Therefore, the phrase "righteous deeds of the saints" is probably intentionally ambiguous, expressing two ideas: (1) righteous acts performed by the saints (subjective genitive) and (2) righteous acts for the saints (God's final just, acquitting or vindicating judgments, objective genitive).

The OT background to the passage is Isa. 61:10, where the Lord clothes His people with "garments of salvation" and "a robe of righteousness, as a bridegroom decks himself... And as a bride adorns herself...." Isaiah's phrases underscore the activity of God in providing these clothes. This righteousness comes ultimately from God, as the next verse reveals: "The Lord God will cause righteousness and praise to spring up" (61:11). Rev. 21:2 follows suit by developing vv. 7-8 with a passive sense, "I saw the holy city ... made ready as a bride adorned for her husband." This is in line with the passive sense of receiving white garments elsewhere in the book (see above).

Therefore, the clauses in vv. 7b-8, **His bride has made herself ready** and **it was given to her to clothe herself in fine linen, bright and clean** continue the meaning of the marriage metaphor from v. 7a. As in the initial clause of v. 7 and in Isaiah, the primary point is not that the saints' effort contributes to the acquisition of righteousness (though the concept of the necessary response of righteous acts by the saints is vital) but that God's people are finally entering into the intimate relationship with Him which has been initiated by Himself. Throughout Revelation, the verb "prepare" or "make ready" (Greek *hetoimazō*) refers to an event which occurs ultimately as a result of God's decree, the most striking of which is 21:2: "I saw the holy city, new Jerusalem, coming down out of heaven from God, made ready as a bride adorned for her husband" (so also 9:7, 15; 12:6; 16:12).

Believers may be depicted here as priests, since the high priest was clothed in linen (Exodus 28 and 39), as are the priests of the end-time temple in Ezekiel (Ezek. 44:17). The linen worn by the harlot Babylon (18:16), along with her adornment with various precious stones, suggests an attempt by her to seize the place of priesthood for herself, again contrasting Babylon with the true bride of Christ, clothed with the genuine linen from above. In 6:11 (the fifth seal, occurring during the church age), believers who died were given white robes and told to rest until the full number of their fellow servants was completed. The clothes of the corporate church, however, cannot be considered white until all believers have entered the kingdom. In 7:9-17, believers have received their white garments, and so this scene is temporally parallel to v. 8, which is somewhat vague since in it the saints are clothed throughout the church age and also at the very end of the age. In v. 8, the garments are mentioned within the context of the marriage of the Lamb. In 7:15, although the marriage is not explicitly mentioned, it is implied in the phrase: "He who sits on the throne shall spread His tabernacle over them." "Tabernacling" speaks of intimate communion with the presence of God, and part of the background to that verse is in Ezek. 16:8-10, where God spreads His skirt over Israel and enters into covenant with her.

Consequently, the saints are clothed with pure linen as a symbol of God's righteous final, end-time vindication of them because, in spite of persecution, they persevered in righteousness on earth. The full-orbed meaning of the pure garments is that God's righteous vindication involves judging the enemy at the very end of time, which shows that the saints' faith and works have been in the right all along. This dual sense of **fine linen** here suits admirably the rhetorical purpose of the entire book, which includes exhortations to believers to stop soiling their garments (3:4-5) and not to be found naked (3:18; 16:15). This underscores the aspect of human accountability highlighted by v. 7b: "His bride has made herself ready." Yet the readers can be encouraged to obey the exhortation with the knowledge that God has provided grace for them to clothe themselves now by the power of the Spirit.

9 The angel commands John to **Write: "Blessed are those who are invited to the marriage supper of the Lamb."** The same idea is expressed by the picture of Christ dining with His people in 3:20. Use of the word **invited** (literally "called," Greek *kaleō*) underlines God's sovereign role in salvation: the word is used at least twenty-five times by Paul in this way. The "called" are "chosen ones" (Rev. 17:14). Here the picture changes a little, for whereas in vv. 7-8 the corporate church is pictured as the bride, now individual believers are portrayed as invited to the marriage supper. The same thought is present in 12:17, where the woman is the church and the seed her individual members. The concluding clause, **And he said to me, "These are true words of God"** formally affirms the truth of vv. 7-9a. V. 9 functions much like 21:5b, "and He said, 'Write, for these words are faithful and true,'" which confirms the truth of 21:2, which contains the same marriage metaphors as vv. 7-8 here, even as v. 9 confirms the truth of the marriage metaphors of the previous two verses. In ch. 21 also, the wedding clothing is interpreted as intimate communion with God (21:2-3), along with the added idea of protection (21:4).

10 This verse is both a conclusion to the broad "judgment of Babylon" section beginning at 17:1, and especially that part of it starting at 18:1, and at the same time an introduction to the section describing the last battle, which commences at v. 11. In response to the angel's declaration in v. 9b, John worships him: **And I fell at his feet to worship him**. He is immediately rebuked: **And he said to me, "Do not do that; I am a fellow**

servant of yours and your brethren who hold the testimony of Jesus; worship God." It is appropriate to revere God's words, but not the messenger who brings them. The angel is but a mere **fellow servant** of John's and of **your brethren who hold the testimony of Jesus**. Perhaps John mistook the angel for the divine figure from heaven in 1:13-16 and 10:1-3, who is worthy of worship. The passage is an example of how easy it is to fall into idolatry (a problem among some in John's readership; see on 2:14-15, 20-21; 9:20) for which the judgment described throughout ch. 19 comes into play. The difficulty of this mistaken identification is reinforced in 22:8-9, where John astonishingly repeats the very same offense.

The last phrase of the verse, **For the testimony of Jesus is the spirit of prophecy**, shows how both believers and angels can be fellow-servants who testify to Jesus. The **testimony of Jesus** (see also 6:9; 12:17) can be either the testimony *from* Jesus (Greek subjective genitive) given to the church and now transmitted as witness by believers, or the testimony *to* or *about* Jesus (Greek objective genitive). The end result is similar. Our testimony is about Christ. We are not to bring attention to ourselves or to any other created being. That **the testimony of Jesus is the spirit of prophecy** could mean that the testimony is a prophetic utterance inspired by the Spirit. Alternatively, it could mean that testifying to Jesus is the work of a prophetic spirit, that is, of prophets. This is supported by the parallel passage in 22:8-9, where (similarly) the angel refers to "your brethren the prophets," though without any reference to the divine Spirit. The meaning of the phrase would thus be: "those giving testimony to Jesus are prophetic people." Therefore, angels in heaven and believers on earth are fellow-servants in that they both have prophetic roles. Prophets here are not (as in some other parts of the NT) those who hold an exclusive office but the same group mentioned as prophets elsewhere in the book, where the prophetic role of the entire church is in mind (so 11:3, 6, 10).

Suggestions for Reflection on 19:7-10

On the refining of believers. The commentary states that Babylon's existence was necessary in that it provided the occasion for the refining of believers necessary for them to enter the eternal kingdom. How often do we view those who cause us pain as undesirable obstacles to be removed, rather than seeing the possibility that God has placed them in our lives to bring forth His character in the face of suffering? What is more important — our earthly comfort, or the forming of Christ within us? The fact that God detests the wickedness of Babylon and will certainly judge it does not prevent Him from using it to accomplish His purposes in our lives.

On the white clothes as both gift and reward. The commentary presents the view that the white clothes are both a gift from God and a recognition of our righteous conduct in this life. All righteousness comes from God, yet those who receive His gift of righteousness and walk in it will be rewarded. This helps us to understand the refining process better. No matter what the suffering, there is a heavenly reward — and what greater reward could there be than being finally identified with Christ through resurrection and having a permanent place in the new eternal creation in God's intimate presence (on which see 21:1–22:4)?

Christ will reveal His sovereignty and faithfulness to His promises by judging Babylon's former allies in order to vindicate His people (19:11-21)

Now, by way of ultimate conclusion to the section on Babylon's fall commencing at 17:1, the most expanded description of Christ's defeat and judgment of the ungodly forces at the end of history is prophetically portrayed. First, the description of Christ with His heavenly armies in anticipation of defeating their enemy is given (vv. 11-16), then the declaration of the imminent destruction of the enemy (vv. 17-18), and lastly the scene is climaxed by the defeat of the beast and false prophet along with their followers (vv. 19-21). The destruction of Babylon recounted in 17:1–19:6 (or 19:8) was not a complete defeat of all the forces of wickedness. In fact, 17:12-18 reveals that God's agent in defeating Babylon was the beast and his forces. Therefore, for the victory to be complete, these forces must also be destroyed. Above all, the "testimony of Jesus," emphatically mentioned twice in v. 10, must be seen as true. The judgment of Babylon, followed by that of the beast, the false prophet, and their followers, demonstrates that those who rendered this testimony were in the right after all and that the testimony is true. That the actual weapon of judgment is Christ's word of truth suggests further that the purpose of this section, together with that of vv. 1-6, is to serve as a basis for the statements concerning the marriage supper of the Lamb in vv. 7-10, in order to emphasize the foundation of the saints' vindication and to provide a demonstration of the truth they proclaim (cf. the "true words of God," v. 9). This truth to be demonstrated will lie hidden to unbelievers until the final, full revelation of Christ at His final coming.

Christ will reveal His sovereignty and faithfulness in fulfilling His promise to judge evil by defeating the forces of wickedness at the end of history (19:11-16)

11 And I saw heaven opened; and behold, a white horse, and He who sat upon it
is called Faithful and True; and in righteousness He judges and wages war. 12 And
His eyes are a flame of fire, and upon His head are many diadems; and He has a
name written upon Him which no one knows except Himself. 13 And He is clothed
with a robe dipped in blood; and His name is called The Word of God. 14 And the
armies which are in heaven, clothed in fine linen, white and clean, were following
Him on white horses. 15 And from His mouth comes a sharp sword, so that with it
He may smite the nations; and He will rule them with a rod of iron; and He treads
the wine press of the fierce wrath of God, the Almighty. 16 And on His robe and
on His thigh He has a name written, "KING OF KINGS, AND LORD OF LORDS."

11 The introductory phrase, **And I saw heaven opened**, indicates the beginning of another vision. The vision of heaven opened introduces a scene of judgment, as elsewhere in Revelation (so 4:1; 11:19; 15:5). Next John saw **a white horse, and He who sat upon it is called Faithful and True**. "White" in Revelation speaks of purity or the reward for purity (e.g., 3:4-5). In 19:7-8, white garments represent not only righteousness but the final, eschatological vindicating reward for those who have persevered through persecution. The idea of vindication is likely included in most earlier uses of "white" in the book (1:14; 2:17; 3:4-5; 4:4; 6:11; 7:9, 13; 14:14). In particular, in 14:14 and 20:11 the color conveys ideas not only of divine holiness and purity but also of juridical vindication of truth through final judgment.

The rider on the horse **is called Faithful and True**. Christ will be faithful and true to fulfill His promise to judge the wicked, and to vindicate His name and His followers. This is confirmed by the use of the same phrase in the plural in 21:5 and 22:6, which refer to the sure fulfillment of the prophecy of the new creation and the new Jerusalem. The rider is further described thus: **and in righteousness He judges and wages war**. The phrase **in righteousness** alludes to similar descriptions in the Psalms of God's vindication of His afflicted people and judgment of their oppressors (Pss. 9:8; 72:2; 96:13; 98:9). This judicial action is now carried out by Christ on behalf of His people. Acts 17:31 also alludes to the same Psalm texts in affirming the future day of judgment to be executed by Christ. The allusion to "waging war" appears to refer not to literal battlefield conflict but to a legal battle and judgment, as does the heavenly combat between the angelic armies in ch. 12 (see on 12:7-9).

12a The metaphor **and His eyes are a flame of fire** evokes Christ's role as divine judge, which is clear from vv. 14-21. The same phrase is used in 1:14, where Christ stands in the midst of the churches, and in 2:18-23, where He knows and judges the spiritual condition of the ungodly who claim to be members of the covenant community. The link with these earlier uses suggests that apostates are among those judged in the present scene. This is confirmed further by the "sharp sword" proceeding from the mouth of Christ in v. 15, which also pertains to Christ's judicial relationship to the disobedient in the church communities (1:16; 2:12). The following context shows that unbelievers outside the covenant community are also judged (see on vv. 16-21). A similar phrase in Dan. 10:6 ("his eyes were like flaming torches") lies behind 1:14 and 2:18 in their description of the Son of man. The primary purpose of this heavenly being resembling a man (Dan. 10:16) is to reveal the decree that in the "latter days" (Dan. 10:14) Israel's persecutors will be judged (see Dan. 10:21–12:13) and Israel delivered.

The description of the horseman continues: **and upon His head are many diadems.** The only others wearing diadems are the dragon (12:3) and the beast (13:1). The diadems represent the devil's and the beast's false claims of sovereign, universal authority, which is in opposition to the true "King of kings, and Lord of lords" (v. 16). Comparing these texts makes clear the conscious antithesis. The dragon has seven diadems and the beast ten, but there is an undefined multiplicity on Christ's head. His kingship is eternal, while theirs is limited. The crown of the Satanic horseman of 6:2 is removed and given to the heavenly horseman before the former is overthrown. Christians also wear crowns as a reward for their faith (2:10; 3:11; 4:4) to show that they have been identified with their crowned Savior, just as Jesus promises in 3:21: "He who overcomes, I will grant to him to sit down with Me on My throne" (so also 2:26-28).

12b Now we have a further pictorial explanation of Christ, who in the previous verse has been described as a warrior who executes judgment by defeating the enemy. If there is an OT background for the diadems on the horseman's head and His secret name (**and He has a name written upon Him which no one knows except Himself**), it is Isa. 62:2-3, which is supported by the allusions to Isa. 63:1-3 in vv. 13 and 15. According to Isaiah, latter-day Jerusalem will receive a new name, a diadem, and a crown. The "new name" of Isa. 62:2 will show Israel's new, intimate "married" relationship with God, as described in Isa. 62:4-5. The latter verses also refer to

Israel as a "bride" and God as the "bridegroom," connecting with the wedding metaphor of Rev. 19:7-8. The new name ("another name") promised to Israel in Isa. 65:15 may also be in mind. Christ, the bearer of the diadem, fulfils this prophecy by giving His saints this new name of His (Rev. 2:17), which is also the name of the city of God, the new Jerusalem (3:12). There is an explicit link between 19:12 and 2:17. Both allude to Isa. 62:2-3 and 65:15, both speak of a name which is in some sense confidential, and both speak of a new name having been written which no one knows about except the one who receives it (2:17) or Christ Himself (v. 12). Therefore, that no one knows the name in v. 12 except Christ refers to the fact that the prophecy of Isaiah 62 and 65 has not yet been consummately fulfilled. Christ's "new name" in 3:12 is there so closely linked to (if not explicitly equated with) "the name of My God" that it also has divine overtones.

The names assigned to Christ in vv. 11, 13, and 16 are all divine, and the new name undoubtedly is also. It could refer to Yahweh ("LORD" in most English translations of the OT), the Hebrew name by which God revealed Himself to Moses (Exod. 3:14). The name "Yahweh" in the OT typically expresses God's covenantal relationship with Israel, especially in fulfilling the promises given to the patriarchs. So latter-day Israel will "know" the name Yahweh in an escalated manner when God fulfills prophecy through Christ by restoring Israel and revealing His character in a greater way (cf. Exod. 6:3, 7 with Isa. 49:23; 52:6; Ezek. 37:6, 13). This is supported by the observation that the name may be written on Christ's head or diadems (which have just been mentioned), just as the name Yahweh was written on a gold plate on the high-priest's forehead. There is probably an intended contrast with the diadems on the beast's head, on which there were also "blasphemous names" (13:1; likewise, the name on the harlot's forehead, 17:5; cf. 17:3). If Christ's name is written on the foreheads of believers (14:1; ch. 22), God's name is probably written on Christ's diadems. That no one yet knows the name refers to the fact that the full revelation of Christ's identity, particularly in relation to judgment, will only be given on His return and His judgment of the world.

Commentators have observed that the assertion that no one knows the name except Christ is formally contradicted by the revelation of His name in vv. 11, 13, and 16. But the contradiction stands only when the expression of v. 12 is understood as a literal statement rather than as symbolic in nature. The written name of the harlot in 17:5 is stated first as a mystery, then immediately identified as "Babylon the great." The "mystery" does not refer to keeping the name "Babylon" secret, but to *discovering the proper meaning of the known name* in the light of its historical significance. In 1:20 and 10:7, the "mystery" involves the unexpected way in which Daniel's prophecy about the deliverance of Israel and the defeat of its evil opponents will be fulfilled: in the cross and in those who follow the way of the cross. These mysteries will be no more when the fulfillment of OT prophecy is consummated, yet the point in Revelation is that believers can understand their significance now, even if they are hidden to the world. This is parallel to 14:3, where "no one . . . except" true believers can learn the "new song" of salvation; so likewise, they alone can now know and experience Christ's name, as a result of His revelatory initiative.

In the OT, to "know" a name means to have control over the one who carries that name and to know or share in the character of that one. Therefore, the confidential nature of the name has nothing to do with concealing a name on the cognitive level, but alludes to Christ being absolutely sovereign over humanity's experiential access to a true understanding of His character. To some He reveals His name (= character) by bringing them into a saving relationship with Him (as in 2:17; 3:12; 22:3-4; Luke 10:22; Matt. 16:16-17), though this knowledge is not yet complete, but to others He reveals His name only through an experience of judgment, and to them the true significance of His name remains a mystery and unknown until that judgment occurs. The content of vv. 11-12 concerns experiencing the true character or identity of Christ though judgment, and so the significance of the fact that no one knows His name is that unbelievers will only understand His name (already known to believers, as made clear, for instance, in vv. 11, 13, 16) at the time of their judgment. If the name is symbolic in nature, it is not a problem that it could even be revealed by a plurality of names (Savior, Lord, Redeemer, etc.). Therefore, the symbolic meaning of the "unknown name" is to affirm that Christ has not yet consummately fulfilled the promises of salvation and judgment, but will reveal His character (= name) of grace and justice when He comes to carry out those promises in vindication of His followers.

13 This verse elaborates further on the depiction of Christ's appearance as a messianic warrior in vv. 11-12. The rider is portrayed as **clothed with a robe dipped in blood**, an allusion to the description of God judging the nations in Isa. 63:1-3: "With garments of crimson colors . . . garments like the one who treads in the wine press . . . their lifeblood is sprinkled on My garments." Christ is here identified as that divine warrior. In Isa. 63:4, the warrior seeks "vengeance" and "redemption" on behalf of His people, and the same goal is implicit here. In addition to the name of "Faithful and

True" (v. 11), the rider's confidential written name of v. 12 is also revealed as **the Word of God.** The word **called** is also used to reveal the spiritual interpretation of names of people and places in 11:8; 12:9; and 16:16. Furthermore, like the name in v. 11, **the Word of God** expresses a judicial role, since the rider will judge by means of God's word (so vv. 15, 21). The four other appearances of the phrase "the Word of God" in Revelation occur in conjunction with either the "testimony" (6:9) or the "testimony of Jesus" (1:2, 9; 20:4). This shows that the Word of God is revealed most fully in the life, acts, and teachings of Jesus Christ, and it shows how appropriate it is for Christ Himself to bear the name **the Word of God.** In the OT, "word" can also take on the idea of promise or "prophetic word" (1 Kgs. 8:56), and the same meaning is evident in Rev. 17:17 ("until the words of God should be fulfilled"), so the title in v. 13 may allude to Christ's execution of final judgment on the remaining enemies of God, in fulfillment of OT and NT prophecy.

14 The heavenly armies follow the rider: **And the armies which are in heaven, clothed in fine linen, white and clean, were following Him on white horses.** Elsewhere in the NT, angelic armies accompany Christ from heaven in executing the final judgment (Matt. 13:40-42; 16:27; 24:30-31; 25:31-32; Mark 8:38; Luke 9:26; 2 Thess. 1:7; Jude 14-15). These armies, however, probably consist of the saints rather than angelic forces, as is suggested by the parallel reference in 17:14, "The Lamb will overcome them . . . and those who are with Him are the called and chosen and faithful." Furthermore, in Revelation, with one exception (15:6), only saints wear white garments (3:4-5, 18; 4:4; 6:11; 7:9, 13-14). The saints here and in 17:14 take part in the final judgment only in that their testimony is the legal evidence condemning their oppressors (for such an understanding of a witness which judges see Matt. 12:41-42 and parallels; Rom. 2:27). The saints' garments here and throughout the book should also be understood as priestly garments, since the same garments worn by the heavenly beings are also likely conceived as priestly in Rev. 15:6; Dan. 10:5; 12:6; and Ezek. 9:2, as well as the similar garments worn by Christ in Rev. 1:13. The saints with white robes in 7:9, 14-15 also have a priestly function. Likewise, the "fine linen, bright and clean" of v. 8 has priestly connotations (on which see). Christ's followers reflect their representative's priestly character as they accompany Him when He executes judgment.

15 In the wording **And from His mouth comes a sharp sword, so that with it He may smite the nations; and He will rule them with a rod of iron; and He treads the wine press of the fierce wrath of God, the Almighty** are found four OT allusions, which continue to expand the picture of Christ's warlike appearance in vv. 11-13 and show that in executing final judgment Christ will fulfill the prophecies in these OT texts:

The **sharp sword** in the rider's mouth comes from Isa. 49:2, where Isaiah says of God's servant, "He has made my mouth like a sharp sword." Here Isaiah's prophecy is reaffirmed and Jesus is identified implicitly as the servant Israel (as in Luke 2:32; Acts 26:23, both allusions to Isa. 49:6).

With this sword, the rider will **smite the nations**, which alludes to another of Isaiah's references to Christ, "He will strike the earth with the rod of His mouth" (Isa. 11:4). The same verse in Isaiah states that God's servant will judge in righteousness, a thought echoed here in v. 11b.

The rider will rule the nations with a **rod of iron**, thus alluding to Ps. 2:9, where the Messiah "breaks" the nations with a "rod of iron." The "rod" of v. 15, like the sword coming from Christ's mouth, connotes God's word of accusation, which will condemn the ungodly and consign them to perdition.

Finally, the rider **treads the wine press of the fierce wrath of God, the Almighty**. The wording is a continued allusion to the OT prediction of God's last great act of judgment (Isa. 63:2-6) begun in v. 11, again applied to Christ.

The meaning of the phrase **the wine press of the fierce wrath of God** is that the wine press is or represents the wrath of God. The destruction of the lost will be as thoroughgoing as the grapes being crushed in the winepress (for fuller OT background of the picture see on 14:8, 10).

16 Yet another name is adduced to explain further the undisclosed name of v. 12: **And on His robe and on His thigh He has a name written, "KING OF KINGS, AND LORD OF LORDS."** The name is written on the rider's robe and thigh. The thigh (translated "side" in NIV) was the typical location of the warrior's sword (e.g., Exod. 32:27; Judg. 3:16, 21; Ps. 45:3) and the symbolic place under which the hand was placed to swear oaths (e.g., Gen. 24:2, 9; 47:29). The title is taken from the OG of Dan. 4:37, where it is a title for God. It was applied to Christ earlier in 17:14. Just as the Babylonian king wrongly took this title to himself (as reflected in his thinking that he himself was responsible for the glory of all that lay around him, Dan. 4:30), so the king of latter-day Babylon was similarly addressed. Even as God demonstrated His sovereignty to Nebuchadnezzar, so will

Jesus deal with latter-day Babylon. The application of this title to Jesus underscores His deity, since it was used of God in Daniel 4.

Suggestions for Reflection on 19:11-16

On the consummate end-time revelation of Jesus Christ. This passage offers a picture of Christ far different from, yet complementary to (and hinted at by) the portrait of His earthly life presented in the Gospels. He is represented as a divine warrior executing judgment and ruling sovereignly over all. His true identity cannot be known or controlled by others. He will crush His enemies in the winepress of the wrath of God. Not only that, His saints will assist Him in the execution of this judgment. How often do we consider the full biblical picture of Jesus? The mystery is of One who hung defenseless on the cross, taking the punishment for our sins and calling us to serve Him in weakness, yet who one day will ride forth to execute vengeance, with us alongside Him. A true understanding of Christ can only come as we consider all these elements of who He is. He has given everything, as must His followers, to reach those still outside His grasp, yet by virtue of His holiness must bring God's righteous rule to creation by judging those who choose to bring destruction on the earth (Rev. 11:18).

An angel announces the imminent destruction of the last enemy (19:17-18)

17 And I saw an angel standing in the sun; and he cried out with a loud voice, saying to all the birds which fly in midheaven, "Come, assemble for the great supper of God; 18 in order that you may eat the flesh of kings and the flesh of commanders and the flesh of mighty men and the flesh of horses and of those who sit on them and the flesh of all men, both free men and slaves, and small and great."

17-18 John sees **an angel standing in the sun; and he cried out with a loud voice.** We now have portrayed before our eyes the results of Christ's defeat of the forces opposed to God, which has begun to be depicted in vv. 11-16. This angel has an appearance similar to that of the angel in 18:1, who came down from heaven, illumining the earth with his glory. Both angels bring judgments associated with birds: **saying to all the birds which fly in midheaven, "Come, assemble for the great supper of God"** (cf. 18:2). The first angel announced the fall of Babylon, and this second angel announces the fall of the beast and false prophet, Babylon's former allies, the latter completing the process begun in the former.

The invitation to the birds to **assemble for the great supper of God** is a macabre parody of the invitation to the saints to gather for the marriage supper of the Lamb (v. 9). The angel announces the coming defeat of the beast and his allies with the same language used by Ezekiel to refer to the end-time destruction of God and Magog, "Speak to every kind of bird. . . . Assemble and come . . . to my sacrifice . . . that you may eat flesh and drink blood. You shall eat the flesh of mighty men, and drink the blood of the princes of the earth . . . and you will be glutted at My table with horses and charioteers, with mighty men and all the men of war" (Ezek. 39:17-20). That the birds are flying **in midheaven** is added to the Ezekiel imagery and confirms a non-literal view, since the very same phrase describes the speaking eagle of 8:13, who announces coming judgment. Such a link may show that the third of the "woes" announced by the eagle (= the seventh trumpet) is being further developed here. The prophecy of God's triumph over His enemies in Ezekiel 39 still awaits fulfillment, but now the angel updates it by identifying Christ as the agent of defeat and by identifying Gog and Magog as the beast, the false prophet, and their armies.

But why allude to Ezekiel at this point, especially since other OT prophetic passages concerning the end-time defeat of evil forces could have been drawn from (e.g., Daniel 2, 7–12, Zechariah 14)? The portrayal of Ezekiel 39 has been included because its main point is that God will make His holy name known both to Israel and to Israel's oppressors during captivity by means of defeating Gog and Magog. The goal of revelation of the divine name introduces (Ezek. 39:7) and concludes (39:21-29) the description of the slaughter (39:8-20). God will save Israel and judge His enemies. The same dual theme with respect to the revelation of Christ's name has been the overriding concern in Rev. 19:11-16. The allusion to Ezekiel 39 confirms the presence of this concern and underscores the defeat narrated in 19:19-21 as the means by which Christ will reveal His name in deliverance to His people and in judgment to their oppressors.

Suggestions for Reflection on 19:17-18

On God's upholding His name. Throughout the OT, God was concerned for the upholding of His name. Facing defeat, Joshua asked God what He would do for the sake of His name (Josh. 7:9; cf. Lev. 18:21; 24:16; Deut. 28:58; Pss. 66:2; 115:1; Isa. 42:8; Jer. 16:21; Ezek. 36:21-23). The allusion in these verses to Ezekiel 39, with its theme of the vindicating of God's name in the latter-day battle (39:7, 25), reinforces the similar theme of vv. 11-16. The focus on God's name helps us remember that it is not primarily our name or interests God is concerned about, but rather the vindication of *His* name and the revelation to the universe that He alone is righteous. All those who follow Him will likewise be vindicated solely because of their identification with His name. Sometimes we have to leave the defense of our name or reputation in God's hands, secure in the knowledge that what the world thinks of us now is of no consequence, but that in the light of eternity what God thinks of us is paramount and that it is our faithful identification with Him that is crucial.

Christ will defeat the beast, the false prophet, and their followers at the end of history (19:19-21)

19 And I saw the beast and the kings of the earth and their armies, assembled to
make war against Him who sat upon the horse, and against His army. 20 And the
beast was seized, and with him the false prophet who performed the signs in his presence, by which he deceived those who had received the mark of the beast and those who worshiped his image; these two were thrown alive into the lake
of fire which burns with brimstone. 21 And the rest were killed with the sword
which came from the mouth of Him who sat upon the horse, and all the birds were filled with their flesh.

19 After the announcement of coming judgment, John sees a vision of the judgment itself, so that this section is at least temporally parallel with vv. 17-18 and likely comes earlier since vv. 17-18 portray what happens directly after the battle (as v. 21 will clarify). He sees **the beast and the kings of the earth and their armies, assembled to make war** (literally "gathered together to make the war") **against Him who sat upon the horse, and against His army**. This is essentially the identical wording ("gathering together for war") used in 16:14 and 20:8 to describe the prelude to the last battle of history. Satan and his agents are the immediate powers behind this gathering of the kings (16:14; 20:8), which accounts partly (see below) for the passive form of the verb here (**assembled** = "gathered together"). That the allusion to God's battle against Gog and Magog in vv. 17-18 (Ezek. 38:2-9; 39:1-8) is not accidental is clear from seeing that the kings are figuratively identified as Gog and Magog in 20:8. Ultimately, of course, the passive verb indicates that God is directing and controlling these events, as Ezekiel affirms (e.g., 38:4; 39:2). A further allusion in all three verses (16:14; 19:19; 20:8) is to Zech. 14:2, "I will gather all the nations against Jerusalem to battle. . . ." Zechariah goes on to speak of the unique day of the Lord (14:7), the day when living waters will flow out of Jerusalem (14:8), the same living waters Ezekiel (47:1-12) refers to as flowing from the eschatological temple.

Rev. 16:14; 19:19; and 20:8 all have an article before the word "war," which carries the meaning of *the* war rather than simply *a* war. *The* war is the same great final battle between the Lamb and the forces of evil portrayed in these parallel verses and prophesied in the OT. Therefore, it is the same war as in 11:7, since that battle also is one in which the beast "will make war with them [the saints]" and will attempt to destroy the whole body of believers on earth (see on 11:7-10). Ps. 2:2 also rings in the background, "The kings of the earth take their stand, and the rulers take counsel together against the Lord and against His Anointed"; note the undoubted reference to Ps. 2:9 in v. 15.

20 The actual judgment pictured in v. 19 and earlier occurs in two parts. First, the beast and the false prophet are judged: **And the beast was seized, and with him the false prophet.** This is followed by their being thrown into the lake of fire, and then by the execution of their followers (v. 21). The description of the beast and the false prophet here reminds us of the reason for their judgment: the beast made divine claims (see on 13:3, 7-8), and the false prophet deceived people into recognizing these claims: **who performed the signs in his presence, by which he deceived those who had received the mark of the beast and those who worshiped his image** (for an explanation of the latter phrase see on 13:14-15).

The fact that they are said to have been cast into the lake of fire while alive (**these two were thrown alive into the lake of fire which burns with brimstone**) suggests not absolute annihilation but an everlasting, conscious punishment. That is, they will continue to live in the lake of fire. This interpretation is confirmed by the further statement concerning them in 20:10: "They will be tormented day and night forever and ever" (see also 14:10-11 on the final end of one who worships the beast: "He will be tormented with fire and brimstone in the presence of the holy angels and in the presence of the Lamb. And the smoke of their torment goes up forever and ever; and they have no rest day and night."). Note that fire and brimstone are part of God's judgment on Gog and Magog in Ezek. 38:22. Allusion is also made to Dan. 7:11: "I kept looking until the beast was slain, and its body was destroyed and given to the burning fire." In Daniel, the fiery place of the beast's punishment is mentioned immediately after the "river of fire" flowing from before God's throne (Dan. 7:10). It can hardly be coincidence that the *lake of fire* in Rev. 20:10 is mentioned immediately before the description of the *great white throne* and the judgment of God in 20:11-15. The apparent temporal nature of the punishment in Dan. 7:11 (the beast slain and its body destroyed) is interpreted in the wider perspective of an eternal punishment in the light of 20:10 and 14:10-11, which may have already been hinted at by Dan. 12:2 ("many . . . who sleep . . . will awake, these to everlasting life, but the others to disgrace and everlasting contempt"). The description of judgment does not suggest that two literal individuals were cast bodily into the fire, but only that all who function in the corporate role of beast and false prophet at the end of history will be punished thus (see on ch. 13 for definition of these two roles).

21 The armies following the beast and false prophet were **killed with the sword which came from the mouth of Him who sat upon the horse, and all the birds were filled with their flesh**. The sword coming out of Christ's mouth is an allusion to Isa. 49:2 and Isa. 11:4, which is repeated from v. 15 (on which see). The sword is likely figurative, connoting the accusatory word of God, and representing a decree of death (see on v. 15). This could be supported by the "courtroom" scene in 20:11-12, where unbelievers are accused of evil deeds. After the indictment follows the execution of their punishment in 20:15, which mirrors that of the beast and false prophet in both 19:20 and 20:10 (where they are thrown into the lake of fire). This is in line with Matt. 25:41, where the final judgment is executed by the mere pronouncement of Christ's words, "Depart from me, accursed ones, into the eternal fire which has been prepared for the devil and his angels."

Suggestions for Reflection on 19:19-21

On the reality of spiritual warfare. These verses make clear that history will end in a time of war. The devil and his forces have always actively opposed God, but their rebellion will culminate in one last ferocious battle. Although Christians are people of peace, they are also called to conduct inaugurated warfare before the final battle consummated by Christ. That is, the battle has begun now — not against flesh and blood, but against the powers of darkness, as Paul reminds us (Eph. 6:10-17). Refusal to be aware of the present battle and not participating in it will mean dreadful loss, as the enemy will never cease attacking the church. What does spiritual warfare mean for us in our time? How do we properly conduct it? How do we oppose powers of darkness without attacking people? Is the role of prayer, which may be the most effective weapon, largely forgotten in our fast-paced and busy way of life? We pray and trust that our Savior, who began this battle at His first coming, will finish it for our own final victory, vindication, and above all His own glory.

The millennium is inaugurated during the church age as God limits Satan's deceptive powers and as deceased Christians are vindicated by reigning in heaven. The millennium is concluded by a resurgence of Satan's deceptive assault against the church and the final judgment (20:1-15)

This chapter, though we have treated it as a separate section, is closely related literarily to the previous major segment extending from 17:1 to 19:21. That section dealt with the announcement of the fall of Babylon at the end of time (ch. 17), the elaboration of Babylon's fall, especially the responses drawn forth both from unredeemed and redeemed multitudes (18:1–19:10), and Christ's judgment of the ungodly world forces at the end of history (19:11-21). Our comments will argue that 20:1-6 refers to the course of the church age, which temporally *precedes* the narration of final judgment in chs. 17–19, while, on the other hand, 20:7-15 recapitulates the description of final judgment in 19:11-21 (as well as 16:14-21, on which see). The only hope of obtaining any clarity about ch. 20 is to interpret it primarily first in the light of its immediate context, then in the light of the closest parallels elsewhere in the book, and finally in the light of other parallels in the NT and OT.

The millennium is inaugurated during the church age by God's curtailment of Satan's ability to deceive the nations and to annihilate the church and by the resurrection of believers' souls to heaven to reign there with Christ (20:1-6)

There are three predominant views of the millennium, though within each perspective there are wide variations of interpretation which cannot be catalogued here. Some believe that the millennium will occur after the second coming of Christ. This view is traditionally known as premillennialism. Postmillennialism, by contrast, has held that the millennium occurs toward the end of the church age and that Christ's climactic coming will occur at the close of the millennium ("postmillennial" means "after the millennium"). Others believe that the millennium started at Christ's resurrection and will be concluded directly before His final coming. This view has been called amillennialism. It is better to refer to this third view as "inaugurated millennialism," since "amillennial" literally means "no millennium." Postmillennialism and amillennialism, and some premillennial interpreters, have approached Rev. 20:1-6 according to a symbolic interpretation. Traditionally, many premillennial commentators have approached the text with a so-called "literal" approach.

Starting with its very first verse, Revelation conveys information in symbolic form (see 1:1, where the whole book is said to be a predominantly symbolic communication). "I looked," "I saw," or similar expressions, used repeatedly by John to introduce symbolic visions (4:1ff.; 12:1-3, "appeared"; 13:1-3; 14:1; 17:1-3) appear in 20:1 and 20:4, likely indicating that these visions are to be interpreted symbolically. What John sees and hears (for instance, people resurrected and living for one thousand years) constitute the vision he has seen, which must then be interpreted *first* symbolically. This vision, with words like dragon, chain, abyss, serpent, locked, sealed, and beast, is no exception to the rule. Therefore, the words "resurrection" and "life," for example, do not by themselves give a clue about whether the visionary, symbolic portrayal has a one-to-one (physical) correspondence to a historical referent (people with physical resurrection bodies) together with its initial figurative meaning, or whether the symbolic portrayal has a figurative reference which does not have a one-to-one (physical) correspondence to a historical referent (e.g., people who experience a spiritual resurrection). Thorough exegesis must decide in each case.

The *visionary* level of interpretation (what John actually saw) and the *symbolic* level (what the items in the vision connote biblically above and beyond any specific historical reference) must not be confused with the third, *historical level* (the particular historical identification of the resurrected people and the other objects seen in the vision). Literal interpreters of the book (those seeing a one-to-one correspondence between the book's images and only a physical reality) acknowledge these distinctions, but at critical points, including 20:1-6, they too often neglect the visionary and symbolic levels of communication by collapsing them into the referential, historical level.

A simple and fairly undebatable example of these three hermeneutical levels is the vision in 1:12, 20. This is clearly a vision ("I saw") in which John sees "seven golden lampstands" (the *visionary level*). The "lampstands" are identified with the seven churches on the *historical level,* but there is no one-to-one physical correspondence between the lampstands and the churches (the churches are not physical lampstands!). The *symbolic level* of the vision is that the churches are pictured as lampstands. But why? One must try to determine why the churches are figuratively likened to lampstands to discover the symbolic meaning (at least part of the symbolic meaning is that, since lampstands were part of the old temple and light-giving in the OT, so the church is part of a new temple and gives the light of God's revelation to others). Something similar is going on in 20:1-8.

The following considerations demonstrate that the events of 20:1-6 (the millennium) refer to events *prior in time* to the last battle of 19:11-21, thus indicating that the millennium itself is to be identified with the church age. Further support for this view will be introduced in the following exegesis of the text.

1. *Use of the conjunction "and."* Premillennial interpreters view 20:1-6 as following 19:11-21 in historical sequence: the millennium follows the battle and the throwing of the beast and false prophet into the lake of fire. The significant argument for this is based on use of the word "and" (Greek *kai*), which is said to indicate historical sequence in both chapters. Hence, "and" in 20:1 introduces events subsequent to those of ch. 19. However, often in Revelation "and" functions as a transitional word simply indicating a new vision and not necessarily chronological sequence. In fact, only three out of thirty-five occurrences of "and" in 19:11-21 clearly indicate sequence in historical time (the initial *kai* in vv. 20a, 21a, 21b, and perhaps also v. 14a), while the remainder serve as visionary linking devices.

Even the repeated phrase "and I saw" in 19:11, 17, and 19 introduce not sections in chronological sequence but concurrent sections having to do with the same time of the last war; they do not even introduce different subsequent stages of that war. On the other hand, the majority (though by no means all) of the "and"s in ch. 20 do refer to historical sequence (though "and I saw" in v. 4 introduces the events of vv. 4-6 as occurring at the same time as the events of binding in vv. 1-3). Which of the two categories does the critical "and" in v. 1 ("*and* I saw an angel coming down from heaven") fall into? Where "and I saw" occurs in Revelation, *followed by reference to* "an angel coming down / out of heaven" (10:1; 18:1) or "ascending from the rising of the sun" (i.e., from heaven, 7:2) and "having" some kind of power (10:1; 18:2), it always introduces a vision either reverting to a time *before the preceding section* (as in 7:2 and 18:1, where NASB fails to include the "and") or occurring *at the same time as the preceding section* (as in 10:1). 20:1 fits into this pattern, since there is also an "and I saw formula" followed by "an angel coming down from heaven" and "having" power (a "key"). And as we observed above, the three phrases "and I saw" in 19:11, 17, and 19 introduced sections temporally parallel with each other. We should not be surprised, then, that, contrary to the premillennial view, "and I saw" in 20:1 does not introduce events occurring *after* those of 19:1-21. However, this time, as elsewhere in the book (7:2; 18:1), it is not synchronous with 19:11-12 but takes us back to a time preceding that previous section.

2. *Allusions to Ezekiel 38–39 in both 19:17-21 and 20:8-10.* Both passages contain repeated allusions to the battle of Ezekiel 38–39, suggesting that both refer to the same battle. Indeed, both 19:17-21 and 20:8-10 recount the same battle as 16:12-16, which is highlighted by the repetition of "gather them together for the war," though 19:19 varies insignificantly.

16:14: *tous basileis tēs oikoumenēs holēs synagagein autous eis ton polemon*
"the kings of the whole inhabited earth to gather them together for the war" (it is the "spirits of demons" who do the "gathering" here)

19:19: *tous basileis tēs gēs . . . synēgmena poiēsai ton polemon*
"the kings of the earth . . . gathered together to make [the] war"

20:8: *ta ethnē . . . tēs gēs ton Gōg kai Magōg synagagein autous eis ton polemon*
"the nations . . . of the earth, Gog and Magog, to gather them together for the war"

The phrase in 16:14 probably refers to the same confrontation between the forces of the beast and Christ at the very end of the age which is mentioned in chs. 19 and 20. The three synonymous phrases in 16:14; 19:19; and 20:8 are based on OT prophecy, especially from Zechariah 12–14 (and possibly Zeph. 3:8 LXX). The specific allusion is to Zech. 14:2, where the article is also missing: *episynaxō panta ta ethnē epi Ierousalēm eis polemon* ("I will gather together all the nations against Jerusalem for war"). The verse foretold that God would gather the nations together in Israel for the final war of history.

All three parallel clauses in 16:14; 19:19; and 20:8 have the article *(ton polemon)* because they are referring to "the [well-known] 'War of the End'" prophesied in the Zechariah passage. Therefore, 19:19 and 20:8 are recapitulated prophetic narratives of the same future battle described in 16:14! Rev. 20:7-10 shows this "war" to be part of the final attack of Satan's forces against the saints. Therefore, it is the same "war" also as in 11:7, since that battle also is one in which the "beast" attempts to annihilate the whole body of believers on earth at the very end of time (see on 11:7-10). In this light, the definite article in 16:14 and its following parallels may be an article of previous reference, not only to the OT prophecy but also back to the initial description of the last battle in 11:7, where the article is missing.

If 20:1-6 (the millennium) precedes the time of 20:7-10, and if 19:17-21 is temporally parallel to the battle of 20:7-10, then 20:1-6 is temporally prior to the battle of 19:17-21. Most commentators of all millennial persuasions agree that in 19:17-21 John views the Ezekiel 39 prophecy as being specifically fulfilled in the future, and the same perspective must obviously be in place in 20:8-10, for he would likely not change his view in the space of a few verses. This distinguishes the battle against Gog and Magog from the more general struggle against Babylon throughout the church age. That John has in mind a specific prophecy-fulfillment connection with Ezekiel 38–39 is borne out by the broader context of Revelation 20–21, where a fourfold ending of the book reflects the end of Ezekiel 37–48: resurrection of God's people (Rev. 20:4a; Ezek. 37:1-14), messianic kingdom/millennium (Rev. 20:4b-6; Ezek. 37:15-28), final battle against Gog and Magog (Rev. 20:7-10; Ezekiel 38–39), and final vision of the new temple and new Jerusalem, described as a restored Eden and as sitting on an exceedingly high mountain (21:1–22:5; Ezekiel 40–48). Some have argued that Revelation 19 and 20 refer to two different battles, being thus multiple fulfillments of the same Ezekiel prophecy. Yet if this were the case, one would expect to find the portrayal in Rev. 20:7-10 to appear as a continuation of the battle in 19:17-21. Not only, however, does it *not* appear that 20:7-10 picks up where 19:21 left off, but the battle in 20:7-10 has a beginning just like that of 19:17-21, where the armies are gathered against God's people: note the similarity between 19:19 and 20:8. Furthermore, this language is based on the same allusion to Ezek. 38:2-8 and 39:2, together with Zechariah 12–14 (especially 14:2), which also stands behind the parallel phrases in Rev. 16:14 and 19:19 (see further on 16:14; 19:19; 20:8 and below on the relationship of those three passages).

Others have tried to distinguish the battle in Ezekiel 38–39 from that in Revelation 20 by noting that in Ezek. 39:4 the enemy invaders are destroyed as they "fall on the mountains of Israel" (likewise 39:17) and in Rev. 20:9 they are destroyed by fire. However, this observation serves not to distinguish the two portrayals but in fact to identify them as referring to the same battle, since Ezek. 38:21 (cf. 39:17-21) states that God slays the enemy with a sword "on all my mountains" (likewise 39:17, "sacrifice on the mountains of Israel"), and Ezek. 38:22 and 39:6 say that God defeats the same enemy by fire. The two depictions in Ezekiel are different metaphorical ways of underscoring the same defeat of the enemy by God. In fact, these two metaphorical versions of the same battle in Ezekiel are reflected in the two battles of Rev. 19:17-21 and 20:7-9: in the former the enemy is destroyed by a sword, and in the latter the foe is defeated by fire.

Neither is there sufficient basis for distinguishing the Ezekiel prophecy from Revelation 20 because Gog and Magog come from the north in Ezekiel 38–39, and allegedly also in Revelation 19, whereas in Revelation 20 Gog and Magog are identified with all nations of the earth. However, Rev. 19:15-21 refers to "the nations" in general (19:15) and "the kings of the earth" (19:19) as the antagonists of Christ, not nations from the north, so that they are not necessarily different from the nations in 20:8 (see further below on v. 8). Indeed, 19:15 refers to "the nations" as part of an allusion to Isa. 11:4 and Ps. 2:8, which have a universal perspective; in the former, John's "nations" appear to be equivalent to Isaiah's "earth," and in the latter the "nations" are explained further as "the nations" even to "the very ends of the earth." Therefore, if Revelation 19 is alluding to the Ezekiel battle, there is no reason to distinguish it from Revelation 20 on the basis of a different geographical perspective on Ezekiel's enemy. Both Revelation accounts are probably universalizing the enemy of Ezekiel, but this should not lead to the conclusion that John is developing Ezekiel contrary to its original contextual intention (see further on v. 8 for the rationale).

3. *The connection between recapitulation in Ezekiel 38–39 itself and Rev. 19:17–20:10.* As alluded to briefly above, Ezekiel 39 recapitulates the same battle narrated in Ezekiel 38. This would suggest that if John is following any model in 19:17-21 and 20:7-10, he would be following the generally acknowledged pattern of recapitulation in Ezekiel 38–39 (see further on 20:5-6 [and 4. below] for the broader similarity between 20:4–22:5 and Ezekiel 37–48). Indeed, recapitulation is typical elsewhere in Ezekiel, as well as in the other prophetic books of the OT.

4. *The relationship of 16:12-16 and 19:19 to 20:8.* Not only do Rev. 16:12-16; 19:19-20; and 20:8 have in common the same language describing the "gathering together" of forces for the war (noted above), but they also share the notion that the forces gathered have been *deceived* into participating. This reinforces the impression that Satan's *deception* of the nations in 20:8 "to gather them together for the war" is the same event as the *deception* of the nations in 16:12-16 and 19:19-20, where respectively demons "gather them together for the war" of Armageddon (16:14) and "the kings

of the earth and their armies" are "gathered together to make war" (19:19) and where deception of all who are antagonistic to Christ is mentioned (19:20). And just as the war of Armageddon in ch. 16 is followed by the destruction of the cosmos (16:17-21), so likewise does a vision of the dissolution of the world follow the final battle of 20:7-10.

5. *The relationship of the "nations" in 19:13-20 to the "nations" in 20:3.* If 20:1-3 chronologically follows 19:17-21, then there is an incongruity, since there is no sense in protecting the nations from deception by Satan in 20:1-3 after they have just been both deceived by Satan (16:13-16; cf. 19:19-20) and destroyed by Christ at his return (19:11-21; cf. 16:15a, 19). Some suggest that survivors were left among the rebellious nations of 19:11-21 following Christ's absolute victory over them, yet 19:18 states clearly that "all men" who were unbelieving and on the side of the beast were killed: birds will "eat the flesh of kings and the flesh of commanders and the flesh of mighty men and the flesh of horses and of those who sit on them and *the flesh of all men, both free men and slaves, and small and great.*" Others suggest that included among the rebellious nations were saints who did not participate in the battle, and it is their descendants who become deceived and fight against Christ at the end of the millennium. Yet, apart from the inherent improbability of such a theory and lack of any evidence in the text for it, the fact is that, outside 20:3, in nineteen out of twenty-three occurrences of "the nations," the nations are explicitly differentiated from the redeemed.

6. *The curtailing of the deception of 20:3 refers back to the events of 12:9, not those of 19:20.* Some suggest that the statement of 20:3 that Satan was thrown into the abyss in order that "he should not deceive the nations any longer" refers to the fact that the demise of the beast and false prophet in 19:20 curtailed his activity in the millennium, which chronologically followed. However, the title for Satan in 20:2 ("the dragon, the serpent of old, who is the devil and Satan") is borrowed directly from 12:9 ("the great dragon . . . the serpent of old who is called the devil and Satan"). Furthermore, even as 20:3 speaks of Satan as one who deceives the nations, so also 12:9 describes him as the one who "deceives the whole world." In light of the close verbal connections, it is more natural to suppose that the curtailing of Satan's deception through his being thrown into the abyss in 20:3 refers to the same events as his being thrown out of heaven and down to earth in 12:8-9 (see further on 12:8-10). This suggests that the events of 20:1-3 are synchronous to (occurring at the same time as) the events of ch. 12, that is, as encompassing the church age.

The millennium is inaugurated during the church age by God's curtailment of Satan's ability to deceive the nations and to annihilate the church (20:1-3)

[1] And I saw an angel coming down from heaven, having the key of the abyss and a
great chain in his hand. [2] And he laid hold of the dragon, the serpent of old, who
is the devil and Satan, and bound him for a thousand years, [3] and threw him into
the abyss, and shut it and sealed it over him, so that he should not deceive the
nations any longer, until the thousand years were completed; after these things
he must be released for a short time.

1-3 In the light of the preceding, the descending angel in v. 1 introduces a vision in vv. 1-6 going back before the time of the final judgment of history just narrated in 19:11-21. The time-span of the vision will be seen to extend from Christ's resurrection until His return. The angel appearing in v. 1 has **the key of the abyss and a great chain in his hand.** This key is the same as the "keys of death and of Hades" (1:18) held by Christ as a result of His resurrection. These keys function now to place Satan under restraint during the church age, which commences with the resurrection. The key is also to be identified with the "key of David" (3:7), which Christ uses to protect the faithful church in the present age from Satan's devices (3:8-9). Christ's sovereignty over the sphere of the dead is also amplified in ch. 6, where His opening of the fourth seal pictures His ultimate authority during the church age over the subordinate Satanic powers of "Death and Hades" (6:8). The key is also to be identified with the "key of the bottomless pit" (9:1), which represents God's authority over the demonic realm, including His protection of those He has sealed from demonic deception (9:4). In striking similarity to 20:1, both 6:8 and 9:1-2 portray good angels (the fourth living creature and the fifth trumpet angel) as Christ's intermediaries executing His authority over demonic beings in the realm of the dead. The **key of the abyss,** therefore, is similar to the keys in chs. 1, 3, 6, and 9, but particularly in chs. 6 and 9.

The **abyss** (cf. also 9:1-2) is not a geographical place, but the spiritual realm in which the powers of darkness operate. It is the opposite of heaven, the spiritual place where God and His angels function. It is true that the angel in 9:1-2 opens the abyss (equivalent to "unsealing"), while the angel in vv. 1-3 locks it, but the opening signifies only a limited exercise of demonic authority by divine permission during the church age, thereby implying a larger prohibition or restriction, which is the focus of 20:1 (the opening of the demonic realm during the church age has been alluded to previously in the unleashing of the four horsemen, especially the fourth, and it is apparent that Satan himself is operating among the churches on earth in 2:13). If so, this means that the ch. 9 unlocking qualifies the locking of ch. 20, suggesting that the latter is not an absolute incarceration of Satan in every way. Note also that the keys are for both opening and closing in 3:7-9, depending on the nature of God's purposes in the situation. The keys in ch. 3 show that Christ's sovereignty includes His authority not only to raise the dead at the end of the age but also to impart spiritual life in the present age. This imparting of life includes, should Christ so will, making the devil unable to deceive any longer the members of "the synagogue of Satan" in Philadelphia, so that they can come to the truth and receive spiritual life (see on 3:7-9). Therefore, control of the keys in ch. 3 and in 20:1 indicates the ability to curtail Satan's activities to a degree, but not completely, according to Christ's sovereign will.

Could the opening of the pit in 9:2-3 assume that, prior to the release of the demonic beings there, they were absolutely confined to the abyss without any effect on the earth and that this is related to the binding of 20:2-3, so that accordingly, an absolute binding of Satan is also in mind in the latter passage? This view is possible but we think ours is more viable. One should also ask whether a limited binding in 20:2-3 qualifies the former confinement in 9:2-3 or what could be construed as an absolute confinement in 9:2-3 (which we doubt) explains the confinement in 20:2-3. The crucial question is whether each context qualifies the binding or sealing in the other. We believe the context of 20:1-8 does qualify the binding.

The angel **laid hold of the dragon, the serpent of old, who is the devil and Satan, and bound him for a thousand years**. If the above analysis is correct in placing the events portrayed in 20:1-6 before the last battle in 19:11-21 and in generally identifying 20:1 with the earlier "key" passages, then the binding and the millennium are best understood as Christ's authority which restrains the devil in some manner during the church age. This would mean that the restraint of Satan is a direct result of Christ's resurrection. The binding, expulsion, and fall from heaven of Satan portrayed in chs. 12 and 20 are to be seen in conjunction with other NT passages using similar terminology. Jesus speaks of binding the "strong man" to plunder his goods (Matt. 12:29; Mark 3:27), implying that He has come to bind the enemy. Jesus sees Satan falling from heaven even as He gives the disciples authority to trample on his powers (Luke 10:18-19; see also John 12:31). Paul states that Christ "disarmed" the demonic rulers through the cross (Col. 2:15), and Heb. 2:14 speaks of Christ rendering the devil powerless. According to Rev. 20:7-9, the end point of the binding occurs immediately before Christ's final coming.

What does Satan's binding mean? Satan no longer has authority over the realm of the dead in the way he did before Christ's resurrection, for Christ has triumphed over death (1:18). 20:3 specifies in more detail how the devil is under Christ's authority: the angel **threw him into the abyss, and shut it and sealed it over him, so that he should not deceive the nations any longer, until the thousand years were completed.** This binding of Satan does not refer to a complete cessation of his activities, but is rather to be seen in line with what Jesus taught on the binding of Satan in Matt. 12:29 and Mark 3:27: Satan is still active, but now must operate subject to Christ's authority. His destructive powers mysteriously serve to further the deeper and wider purposes of God, as in Rev. 9:1-2, where plagues are released to harden further the hearts of those opposed to Him. The fact that the "ruler of this world" is "cast out" (John 12:31) means that henceforth Jesus can draw "all men" (the saved from every nation) to Himself (John 12:32). Satan is no longer able to **deceive the nations** concerning the plan of God's salvation, which is the point of the limiting purpose clause of 20:3 (**so that he should not . . .** , which gives the main point of the first three verses).

Sealing (which has the general meaning of "having authority over") does not mean absolute confinement. The sealing of Christians (7:3; 9:4) does not protect them in every way but protects them only from spiritual harm even while they may yet suffer physical persecution, and so the sealing of Satan here prevents him from inflicting spiritual harm on the saints, while not implying an absolute end to his evil activities. The sealing of Satan is to be understood particularly in connection with the curtailment of his powers of deception. The opening of the abyss in 9:1-2 results in the oppression of unbelievers without the seal of God, whereas the closing of the abyss in vv. 1-3 here results in the protection of those with the seal. These two passages portray the same time period (the church age). The first passage focuses on those whom Satan is permitted to deceive (i.e., unbelievers). The second passage deals with a restraint on his ability to deceive believers, but also (as we will see directly) a limitation on his deception of unbelievers. At the end of the church age, this binding will be loosened: **after these things he must be released for a short time**. Vv. 7-10 make clear what kind of deceiving activities have been restrained, for precisely where v. 3 leaves off (**until the thousand years were completed . . . he must be released for a short time**), v. 7 resumes, "And when the thousand years are completed, Satan will be released from his prison." At that time, he will be allowed to deceive the nations into gathering together for the final battle (v. 8).

So what does the binding precisely mean? Satan's deceptive powers are restricted in two ways. First, during the church age he is unable to deceive the elect among the peoples of the world and prevent them from being saved and God's church from being built. Second (and this is the primary focus of the "binding"), until God's appointed hour, he is unable *to deceive the pagan nations into gathering together for a final assault on the church* (see further on v. 7 below). Yet, in truth he is never released from his subservience to Christ, for his very deception at the end of the age is a part of Christ's sovereign plan; the "must" at the end of v. 3 expresses the will of God and the certainty of the divine plan (so also 1:1; 4:1; 11:5; 17:10; 22:6). The devil fails in this final attempt to exterminate the church and meets his own final defeat and punishment. This final onslaught by Satan occurs in the very **short time** at the end of the millennium and directly before the final judgment.

In this light, it may be helpful to fill out from the broader context of Revelation and from the wider biblical framework what is not explicitly said in ch. 20, though it is implied to one degree or another there. During the period from the resurrection to Christ's return (the three and a half years of 11:3), the church, protected spiritually even though it will suffer physically (see on 11:1-2), holds the "keys of the kingdom of heaven" against which hell will not prevail (Matt. 16:19), which must surely be identified with the "keys of death and of Hades" (Rev. 1:18), the "key of David" (3:7), and the "key of the abyss" (20:1; = the "key of the bottomless pit" of 9:1). These keys symbolize sovereignty over the realm of "death and Hades," which includes control over opening the door to eternal life and closing the door to the enemy's deceiving powers. But at the **short time** at the end of the age (the three and a half days of 11:9), both the beast (11:7) and Satan himself (20:3, 7) will, in the sovereign purposes of God, be released from the abyss to gather the nations. Persecution by deceived multitudes will break out against the worldwide church (the continuation of true Israel), such that it would vanish were it not for God's intervention on its behalf. The beast coming up out of the abyss to make war on the witnessing community (11:7, which describes the same reality as the release of Satan in vv. 3, 7) is the devil's earthly agent in leading the final deception and onslaught, as 16:12-16 and 19:19-21 also attest (on which see). Just as the beast represents Satan's authority throughout history in 13:1-2 (cf. 12:3), so the beast's ascent at the end of history can be spoken of in 20:3, 7 as the dragon's ascent because the former again represents the latter.

The abyss thus represents a spiritual sphere in which Satan still operates (albeit in a restrained manner) throughout the church age. Rev. 6:8 pictures the region of Death and Hades (= the abyss) riding throughout the earth to cause destruction. It is wrong to picture the devil as "cast out" in some spatial sense so that he is no longer present on earth. This would be to take "abyss" in an overly literalistic manner. Rather, the abyss represents (as does "heaven" throughout the book) a spiritual dimension which exists alongside and in the midst of the earthly sphere, not above it or below (similarly, the heavenly sphere in 2 Kgs. 6:15-17 and the Satanic sphere in Eph. 6:10-17; cf. 2 Cor. 10:3-5). In this sense, Satan is never removed entirely from the earth, and at the end of the age he will be released, but only in order ultimately to meet his final destruction.

That Satan's binding is not complete in every respect is consistent with the name **the serpent of old** which, in connection with the thought of deception in v. 3, is an allusion to Gen. 3:1, 14 (as argued above on 12:9; see on vv. 4-6 for the parallels between 12:7-12 and 20:1-6). There also, he exercises his deceiving powers by destroying God's first covenant community by leading Adam and Eve to believe that God's command to them in Gen. 2:16-17 was not true (Gen. 3:1, 4) and that God Himself had deceptive motives in forbidding them to eat of the tree (Gen. 3:4-5). This prevented humanity from carrying out its commission to subdue the ends of the earth for the Lord. The last Adam has come to enable the covenant community now to fulfill this mission. The binding restrains the serpent so that he cannot accomplish what he formerly did in the garden.

In the OT age, Satan was able to delude the majority in Israel so that they were not able to fulfill their commission to be a saving light to the nations (as in Isa. 49:6). As a result, the good news of God's kingdom was not heralded to the pagan nations and they remained in spiritual darkness (e.g., Acts 14:16; 17:30). Also, because of her sin, the nation remained subdued under Satanic oppression from foreign nations which attempted to exterminate her. This attempted extermination was climaxed by Satan's attack on Christ, who summed up true Israel in Himself. Satan finally appeared successful when his agents put Christ to death, but the resurrection demonstrated that Satan had failed.

Rev. 12:2-5 telescopes this process of Satanic oppression against the covenant community, climaxing with Christ's death and resurrection. All who subsequently identify with Jesus as true Israel begin to fulfill the commission to be a light to the nations, so that Satan's veil of deception over the nations is lifted (cf. Isa. 49:6; Luke 2:32; Acts 13:47; 26:18, 23; Gal. 3:26, 29; 6:15). This means that the devil will not be able to stop the preaching of the gospel or its expanding reception (= the church) during most of the age preceding Christ's return. So Christ commands His followers to "make disciples of all the nations" (Matt. 28:19). The gospel will "be preached in the whole world for a witness to all the nations, and then the end shall come" (Matt. 24:14). But at the end of the age, directly preceding Christ's return, Satan will be allowed for a **short time** to stop the preaching of the gospel and to draw the curtain of delusion over the nations, especially with the goal of mounting a devastating attack against the people of God as he did before in Eden and against Israel (destroying northern and then southern Israel and casting them into exile) and at the cross against Jesus, the true Israel (see Isa. 49:3 for the messianic Servant as true Israel). The same truth is stated by Paul when he speaks of the restraining of the lawless one which will be removed at the end of the age, but will result in the enemy's destruction by the appearance of Christ's coming (2 Thess. 2:6-12).

Suggestions for Reflection on 20:1-3

On the nature of the limits placed on Satan. In these verses we are afforded a glimpse into the age-long battle between God and the devil. The commentary suggests that the binding of Satan at the resurrection is similar to the sealing of believers in that it speaks of a genuine limitation of the devil's power extending to the very latter stages of the church age. This limitation particularly relates to his ability to deceive the elect. How do you reconcile this with the presence in general of evil in the world? Do we exaggerate the power of the devil because we place too much importance on the worldly areas where he is freer to work his wicked plans?

On the puzzle of the continuing reality of deception. According to the commentary, the devil deceived Adam and then the majority of Israel, but now is restrained from deceiving the elect in Christ. Why is it that sometimes Christians appear to be deceived anyway? The restraint placed on the devil by God does not provide license to His people to fail to study His Word or to submit to spiritual authority. Do some believers take God's protection and mercy for granted? How do we humbly acknowledge our need for God's protection while at the same time aggressively taking up our responsibilities as those who are under His rule?

The millennium is inaugurated for deceased saints during the church age by the resurrection of their souls, placing them in the heavenly condition of having authority, as priests and kings with Christ, over spiritual death (20:4-6)

4 And I saw thrones, and they sat upon them, and judgment was given to them.
And I saw the souls of those who had been beheaded because of the testimony
of Jesus and because of the word of God, and those who had not worshiped
the beast or his image, and had not received the mark upon their forehead and
upon their hand; and they came to life and reigned with Christ for a thousand
years. 5 The rest of the dead did not come to life until the thousand years were
completed. This is the first resurrection. 6 Blessed and holy is the one who has a
part in the first resurrection; over these the second death has no power, but they
will be priests of God and of Christ and will reign with Him for a thousand years.

These verses reveal that the primary point of the millennium is to demonstrate the victory of God's people, who throughout the church age will suffer Satan's attacks but who will also, in return for their faithfulness, receive an eternal crown of glory. This is just as Paul says: "For if we died with Him, we shall also live with Him; if we endure, we shall also reign with Him" (2 Tim. 2:11-12). Rev. 12:7-11, like 20:1-6, presents a vision that shifts from heaven to earth. There also, as here, the initial scene portrays an angel casting Satan out (vv. 7-9), followed by the effects of Satan's fall, which are stated to be the inaugurated kingship of Christ (v. 10) and of His people (v. 11). The parallels between chs. 12 and 20, though they are not identical at every point, suggest that the scenes depict the same events and mutually interpret one another. Both commence with a heavenly scene (12:7 = 20:1). Both portray a recorded or presupposed angelic battle with Satan (12:7-8 = 20:2). Both record Satan's fall to earth or the abyss (12:9 = 20:3). In both, the devil is given the same description (12:9 = 20:2-3). Both refer to a little or short time yet to be allocated to Satan (12:12 = 20:3). In both, the fall of Satan results in the kingdom of Christ and His saints (12:10-11 = 20:4). In both, the saints' kingship is based not only on Satan's fall but on their faithfulness in holding to their testimony or the testimony of Jesus (12:11 = 20:4).

Thus, the difference between Satan's being "thrown down to the earth" in 12:9 (and similarly in 12:10, 12) and being bound and cast "into the abyss" in 20:2-3 indicates in the ch. 12 vision a curtailment of the influence of Satan (see on 12:9-12), as a result of Christ's death and especially His resurrection. The corresponding mention of "binding" and "throwing" the devil "into the abyss" in vv. 2-3 expresses another aspect of the curtailment of the devil's influence as a result of Christ's redemptive work. The devil has lost his power to deceive in 12:9-12, and in being "thrown down to the earth" he tries to exercise it all the more, but is ineffective with regard to genuine believers. That he is thrown into the abyss and sealed in it (vv. 2-3) also indicates loss of his ability to deceive the world into mounting a universal attack on the church to annihilate it. In this way, the passages in chs. 12 and 20 generally correspond and are complementary.

Likewise, in both 12:7-11 and 20:1-6, resurrection is directly linked to the casting down of Satan. The resurrection of Christ in 12:5 results in Michael, Christ's heavenly representative, casting Satan out of heaven, and the angel of vv. 1-3 doing likewise. The mention of the saints' resurrection in 20:4-5 is probably a reference to their share in Christ's own resurrection, which results in their power to rule spiritually over the devil. If the fall of Satan in ch. 20 is generally equivalent to that in ch. 12, then his confinement in the abyss indicates not only his inability to deceive as formerly but also his inability to overturn God's saving verdict on behalf of the saints in the heavenly court (see on 12:9-11). This is borne out by the heavenly court imagery of 20:4 (on which see).

The **short time** of 20:3 (Greek *mikros chronos*) and the "short time" of 12:12 (so NASB, literally "little time" = Greek *oligos chronos*), though somewhat different, may also overlap to some degree. The "little time" in ch. 12 indicates the believers' imminent expectation throughout the church age of the consummation of the kingdom and the final defeat of Satan. Even the "little while longer" of 6:11 *(mikros chronos)* refers to imminent expectation, in this case by exalted believers in heaven, since only God knows the day and hour of the end. 20:3b and 7-8 further clarify the meaning of the "little time" in 12:12 in at least two ways. First, they explain the basis for the devil's "great wrath" (12:12) directed against both the lost and the saved. As Satan is restrained in the abyss (v. 3), his anger intensifies. Second, the short time he is allotted to attack the saints (20:3b, 7-8) may infuriate him further. As in 12:12, from Satan's perspective, the time is still short, as it has been throughout the church age; from the divine perspective, at this point, the time really is literally short. In that sense, vv. 3 and 7-8 clarify that the "short time" of v. 3 is the final stage of the "little time" of 12:12.

4 The focus on what has taken place in the abyss in vv. 1-3 shifts to what has happened at the same time in heaven as a result of the binding of Satan. The events of both vv. 1-3 and vv. 4-6 occur during the same period,

which is referred to as **a thousand years.** That this is not a literal chronological number is apparent from:

> the figurative use of numbers (including multiples of one thousand: 5:11; 7:4-9; 9:16; 14:1; 21:16) consistently elsewhere in the book,
> the figurative nature of much of the immediate context ("chain," "abyss," "dragon," "serpent," "locked," "sealed," "beast"),
> the predominantly figurative tone of the entire book (so 1:1),
> the figurative use of the number one thousand in the OT (figurative non-temporal uses: Deut. 1:10-11; 32:30; Josh. 23:10; Job 9:3; 33:23; Pss. 50:10; 68:17; Song Sol. 4:4; Isa. 7:23; Isa. 30:17; figurative temporal uses: Deut. 7:9; Ps. 84:10; Eccl. 6:6; especially 1 Chron. 16:15-17 = Ps. 105: 8-10, where God's "covenant forever" and "everlasting covenant" are equated with "the word which He commanded to a thousand generations"), and
> the use in Jewish writings and early Christianity of "a thousand years" as a figure for the eternal blessing of the redeemed (2 Pet. 3:8; *Jubilees* 13:27-30; *2 Enoch* 25–33; *Barnabas* 15; *Testament of Isaac* 6–8). In light of these examples, the millennium should probably be taken figuratively (possibly as a reference to a long period of time), as in Ps. 90:4: "For a thousand years in Thy sight are like yesterday when it passes by."

Perhaps the figurative notion is that if the suffering saints endure their brief trials of "ten days" (2:10), they will receive the reward of a millennial reign. The intensifying of ten to a thousand (one thousand being ten to the third power), together with the lengthening of days to years, might suggest that present momentary affliction results in greater glory even in the intermediate state prior to eternal glory. See further on vv. 5-6 below.

The first effect of the devil's fall into the abyss is that Christians are enabled to sit on thrones: **And I saw thrones, and they sat upon them.** This represents the angelic court of Daniel 7, which declares final judgment against the Satanic fiend, thus vindicating the saints he has oppressed ("thrones were set up . . . the court sat . . . the beast was slain," Dan. 7:9-11). John is not speaking of people sitting on literal thrones, but is conveying figuratively the idea (expressed at the end of v. 4) of the saints reigning with Christ as a result of their coming to life. The third phrase of the verse, **judgment** [Greek *krima*] **was passed for them** (not **judgment was given to them**, as in NASB) is an allusion to Dan. 7:22 ("judgment was passed in favor of the saints"). In Daniel 7 this judicial vindication is a necessary condition for the saints to assume kingship together with the Son of man (7:11-14, 18, 27).

Judgment was passed for them carries the same meaning as "God has pronounced judgment [*krima*] for you against her" (18:20). **Them** thus refers to the saints and, as it is directly linked to the preceding phrase **they sat upon them**, it clearly identifies those sitting on the thrones as deceased saints. Elsewhere in Revelation, elders (angelic beings who represent the saints) are identified as sitting on thrones (4:4; 11:16), and it is possible that they also may be included here with the believers that they represent.

These deceased saints are now part of God's heavenly court, in partial fulfillment of the promises that the saints who overcome will exercise authority with Christ over the nations and will sit with Him on His throne (2:26-27; 3:21; see also Matt. 19:28; Luke 22:30 for the same thought). They carry out their reign with Him probably by their agreement with and praise of His judicial decisions. As in v. 4 and in Dan. 7:22, the judgment is followed by the mention of the saints possessing the kingdom. The reality portrayed here can be seen as an answer to the cry of the suffering saints in 6:10 for vindication and the avenging of their blood. V. 4 is not a first answer to that initial petition but a further expansion of the answer already implicit in 6:11, where the white robes and the rest are the beginning of the answer (as also is the "rest" in 14:13). The consummation of their rule and of the answer to their prayer does not come until Christ's return.

These saints are pictured here as **the souls of those who had been beheaded because of the testimony of Jesus and because of the word of God, and those who had not worshiped the beast or his image, and had not received the mark upon their forehead and upon their hand**. This is the same group as pictured in 6:9, "the souls of those who had been slain because of the word of God." They are saints who died while holding to their faith despite suffering and persecution of various sorts. The parallel with 6:9 suggests strongly that the scene here is also picturing deceased saints reigning in heaven, not on earth (so likewise 7:14-17). They remained faithful to death, whether through martyrdom or by natural means. Believers are referred to as **souls** to distinguish their deceased human bodies from their present heavenly existence, in which they yet await the final resurrection of their glorified bodies. If such a distinction of soul and body is not held, an awkward picture emerges: "bodies of beheaded people." The scene takes place in heaven, and the saints are deceased, for the forty-six occurrences of "throne(s)" (Greek *thronos*) in Revelation refer entirely to the heavenly dimension (forty-two times, though the throne in 22:1, 3 is located in the new heavens and earth) or to the demonic realm (2:13). Not once out of all these many uses does "throne" refer to an earthly throne.

As "slain" in 6:9 refers not only to physical martyrdom but to persecution of all sorts, so **beheaded** here could be a figurative way of expressing the same thing. Even if martyrdom is referred to, Christians died in many other ways than by beheading. That all forms of suffering are *generally* referred to by John (as opposed to an emphasis on literal martyrdom) is substantiated by 1:9 and 12:11, where "because of the word of God and the testimony of Jesus" and "because of the word of their testimony" respectively occur and where all forms of suffering are referred to (see also on 2:10 for degrees of persecution up to and including death). However, there is legitimate debate over whether the subsequent phrases (**those who had not worshiped the beast or his image, and had not received the mark upon their forehead and upon their hand**) refer to the same group as **the souls of those who have been beheaded** or to a different group of saints. The structure of the Greek could suggest that a second group is referred to. This second, wider group would be all faithful believers, as in 13:15-17, whether this refers to those killed for their faith (in other ways than being literally "beheaded") or those who suffer other forms of persecution. It could mean that the first group does refer only to literal martyrs, who are then joined on their thrones by the rest of the deceased saints (those sitting on the thrones comprising both groups). If **those who had not worshiped the beast or his image, and had not received the mark** simply amplifies **the souls of those who had been beheaded**, which is possible though less likely, then it would refer only to martyrs throughout v. 4 (though the martyrs would be representative of all deceased saints).

One way or another, all deceased saints, those who participate in the first resurrection (v. 5) and reign for a thousand years, are likely pictured in v. 4. The reason for this is that, according to v. 6, only those who take part in the first resurrection (= "they came to life" in v. 4) will overcome the second death and reign with Christ. Yet according to vv. 14-15, all saints whose names are written in the book of life will overcome the second death, which is the judgment of God on the lost. In fact, the promise given to the faithful saints of the first resurrection that they will be priests and reign with Christ (v. 6) is based on Exod. 19:6, which Rev. 1:6 and 5:9-10 clearly apply to the whole community of saints. This means that "the rest of the dead" (v. 5), those who do not share in the first resurrection, must be unbelievers on their way to eternal judgment. Those who are saved become priests serving eternally in God's presence, while the lost are forever separated from Him.

The conclusion of v. 4 affirms that the deceased saints **came to life and reigned with Christ for a thousand years.** The verb is best taken as a Greek ingressive aorist, similar to uses of the same verb in 2:8 and 13:14 and carrying the meaning of a life beginning at a certain point. Just as the verse began with images of kingship, so it ends on the same note. The saints' vindication as a result of the judgment of Satan consists in the resurrection life and kingship which they have received. This is the primary point of v. 4. Vv. 5-6 explain the meaning of this resurrection life in relation to priesthood and kingship.

5-6 V. 4 has affirmed that the saints' exercise of judgment, coming to life, and reigning with Christ are effects of the binding of Satan in vv. 1-3. Now these effects are interpreted further as **the first resurrection** and its attendant blessing of being **priests of God and of Christ**, protected from the **second death**, and of reigning as kings. The resurrection existence of the saints is the basis on which the second death has no authority over them: **Blessed and holy is the one who has a part in the first resurrection; over these the second death has no power.** This authority over the second death is expressed in the phrase **they will be priests of God and of Christ and will reign with Him for a thousand years.**

The rest of the dead who **did not come to life until the thousand years were completed** are the lost, who have no share in the thousand-year reign of the saints and no protection against the punishment in the lake of fire. This statement is parenthetical, and the thought of v. 4 is directly continued in v. 5b ("This is the first resurrection"). The statement in 22:5 that the saints "shall reign forever and ever" in eternity is a continuation of the reign begun during the millennial period, and is not to be superimposed on 20:4-6, as if the two reigns were identical in time. Just as the devil's captivity is limited to a thousand years, the saints' *intermediate* reign is likewise limited, but is followed by a *consummate* stage of reigning in eternity (see the introductory comments on vv. 1-6 concerning the identification of the thousand years with the church age).

The background for the dual office of priesthood and kingship is based not only on Exod. 19:6 (see on 1:6; 5:10), but also on Isa. 61:6, which refers to the end-time restoration of God's people when the entire nation "will be called the priests of the Lord" and will exercise kingly rule over the nations. Interestingly, Zech. 6:13 refers to a messianic-like figure who will "rule on His throne" and "will be a priest on His throne," which may stand behind Christ's dual role at points throughout Revelation, with which the saints are corporately identified. The additional mention that believers will also be priests serving Christ suggests that Christ is on a par with God, which is underscored elsewhere in the book (e.g., 5:13-14; 7:9-17; cf. 22:3-4).

The futurist view suggests that the thousand-year period (whether interpreted literally or figuratively as an extended period) commences with Christ's return and views the coming to life (Greek *zaō*) of the righteous in v. 4 (during the millennium) and of the ungodly in v. 5a (at the end of the millennium) as literal physical resurrections. Historic amillennialism, on the other hand, has understood the first resurrection as spiritual and the second as physical. It is argued that the words "coming to life" used in one passage (virtually all commentators understand the "coming to life" [resurrection] of v. 5a as physical in nature) must carry the same meaning in the other (vv. 4b-5b), and hence that if the physical resurrection of the wicked in v. 5a is described as a coming to life, the same phrase in v. 4b must refer to a physical resurrection of the saints. Further, it is argued that a physical resurrection is likely in mind in v. 4b, since a study of the word "resurrection" (vv. 5b-6, Greek *anastasis*) elsewhere in the NT shows it to refer to a physical resurrection thirty-nine out of forty-one times.

A response to the premillennial interpretation of these verses is based on the following considerations:

1. *The meaning of "resurrection" and "life" as used here.* It is important to recognize that *anastasis* is found in Revelation only here in 20:5-6. In addition, "first" (Greek *prōtos*) appears with "resurrection" *(anastasis)* nowhere else in the Bible. Nor does "second" appear in connection with "death" anywhere else in biblical literature (other than the related use in 21:8). Studies of words expressing the idea of "first" and "second" must therefore be conducted to determine better the meaning (on which see below) and to determine what "resurrection" means here. In addition, the verb *zaō* ("live") has a range of meanings in Revelation and elsewhere in the NT and can be used with reference to both physical and spiritual resurrection in the same context. In 1:18 and 2:8, it refers to a physical resurrection, and in 16:3 and 19:20 it refers to some form of physical life. In 3:1; 7:17; and 13:14, however, it refers to a form of spiritual existence, as also in six other places where it refers to God's attribute of timeless spiritual existence, so that the predominant meaning in Revelation is spiritual life or a spiritual coming to life.

However, most striking is the observation that elsewhere in the NT *anastasis* and *zaō* (or the noun *zōē*, "life"), together with other synonyms, are used interchangeably to refer to both spiritual and physical resurrection *within the same immediate context.* For instance, in Rom. 6:4-11, Paul says (according to the following paraphrase) that we have been buried with Christ *spiritually* so that, even as Christ was raised *(egeirō) physically* from the grave, we might receive a new life *(zōē) spiritually* (6:4); that if we have become conformed *spiritually* (in our conversion) to His *physical* death, so shall we be conformed *spiritually* to His *physical* resurrection (*anastasis,* that His resurrection life will begin to become real in our present spiritual existence, v. 5). We have died with Christ *spiritually* that we should live with Him *(syzaō) spiritually* (6:8, another reference to our present spiritual resurrection life). Therefore, Paul concludes, we should consider ourselves *spiritually* dead to sin but *spiritually* alive to God in Christ Jesus. Then Paul says, "the life that He [Jesus] lives [*zaō*], He lives [*zaō*] to God" (v. 10); ". . . even so consider yourselves . . . to be alive [*zaō*] to God in Christ Jesus" (v. 11). Paul takes words like "death," "life" *(zōē, syzaō)* and "resurrection" *(anastasis)* (the latter two words found in Rev. 20:4-6) and mixes two different senses of them in one passage: spiritual (pertaining to our present spiritual resurrection life in Christ), and physical, referring to Christ's resurrection (though *anastasis* is not explicitly used in a spiritual sense, it is clearly synonymous with *syzaō* and *zōē*). Note also how Paul states that we have already experienced a resurrection in our coming to Christ (Eph. 2:6; Col. 3:1).

The same is true in John 5:24-29. There, Jesus teaches that one who hears His word already ("now") has life *(zaō) spiritually* and has already passed from death to life *(zōē) spiritually* (v. 24). But an hour is coming, Jesus continues, when those who are dead *physically* will rise *physically,* and those who have heard His voice will experience a physical and eternal "resurrection of life" *(anastasin zōēs),* but others will experience a physical "resurrection [*anastasis*] of judgment." Here again, the spiritual and physical senses of the words "life," "death," and "resurrection" are used interchangeably in one passage (though again *anastasis* is not explicitly used in a spiritual sense, it is clearly synonymous with *zōē,* as a genitive of apposition "resurrection which is life"; but *zōe* is used spiritually in v. 24). Furthermore, v. 25 and vv. 28-29 refer to the same resurrection prophecy from Dan. 12:1-2, which means that the prophesied resurrection of Dan. 12:2 is interpreted by Jesus to be both spiritual (v. 25) and physical (vv. 28-29).

Must then the verb *zaō,* "live," have the same (i.e., physical) meaning throughout Rev. 20:4-5? The immediate and broader context of Revelation must determine the meaning. Consider that the "second death" in v. 6 clearly refers to a spiritual death of the unrighteous involving conscious, eternal suffering (see on vv. 10, 14-15). On the other hand, the death of the righteous mentioned in v. 4 ("the souls of those who had been beheaded") refers to a literal, physical death. Therefore, in vv. 4-5 there is a first death of believers, which is physical and is different in nature from the second death of unbelievers, which is spiritual. *If there are two different kinds of deaths, it is plausible to infer that the two different resurrections would reflect the same dual nature of the deaths.* That is, the resurrection of believers is spiritual, whereas the resurrection of unbelievers is physical. The first, physical death of saints translates them into the first, spiritual resurrection in heaven, whereas the second, physical resurrection of the ungodly translates them into the second, spiritual death. This interpretation suits the thought of v. 6, since a first, eternal, spiritual resurrection is the minimal condition needed to prevent one from suffering a second, eternal, spiritual death. As the bodily resurrection of the wicked shows, bodily resurrection by itself does not provide protection against the second death. There is a second, final, physical resurrection (of both believer and unbeliever), as there is a first, physical death (of both believer and unbeliever). But the first resurrection is experienced only by believers, whereas the second death is experienced only by unbelievers.

2. *The significance of first-second and old-new antitheses elsewhere in Revelation and the Bible.* This contrast between physical or corruptible realities and incorruptible, eternal realities runs through chs. 20 and 21. The qualitative distinction between the two resurrections is also suggested by the qualitative antithesis between the "first" (old) creation and second ("new") creation in 21:1, where the former was pre-consummate or temporary, while the latter is consummate and eternal. Strikingly, in 21:4-8 there is a formal antithesis between "[the first physical] death" and "the second [spiritual] death." In 21:4, physical "death" is the focus of the clause "the *first things* have passed away," which is contrasted with "the second [spiritual] death" (21:8), which is part of the "new" things of the eternal new creation (21:5). 21:1, 4 are a clear allusion to Isa. 65:16-17, where the same qualitative contrasts occur between the first or "former" earth or "troubles," and the "new heavens and a new earth." In Isa. 43:18-19 and 65:16-17, the first or "former" things, referring to the present, old creation, stand in contrast to the "new," everlasting creation (cf. Isa. 65:19-22 and 66:22) which will replace it. Isa. 66:22 affirms that one of the qualitative differences is that the new heaven and new earth will remain forever, in

contrast to the former, which passed away. Thus, the distinction between "first" and "second" and "old" and "new" throughout Revelation focuses not so much on *temporal succession* (as argued by premillennialists with respect to the two resurrections) as on the *qualitative difference* between that which is transient and that which is eternally enduring.

This understanding is consistent with similar "first-second" and "old-new" contrasts elsewhere, such as with the "first Adam" and "last Adam" in 1 Cor. 15:22, 42-49 and the "old (first) covenant" and "new (second) covenant" in Heb. 8:6–10:9. The first Adam had a perishable, inglorious body, and he brought death, whereas the last Adam had an imperishable and glorious body, and He brought eternal life. The first covenant was temporary and led to death (e.g., Heb. 8:13), while the second was eternal and led to life. Neither in Revelation, 1 Corinthians, or Hebrews does "first" function as an ordinal in a process of counting things which are *identical in kind;* rather, it functions to identify things which are *opposite to and different in quality from one another.*

Consequently, here in vv. 4-6 *there are two different kinds of death — one corruptibly physical and one incorruptibly spiritual, and, correspondingly, there are two different resurrections — one eternally spiritual and one physical.* Some clarification is still needed. Could the idea that the "second death" is not literally physical but spiritual restrict the nature of that death too much? Does it not also include the physical existence of the reprobates who have been resurrected? The answer is yes, but remember that unbelievers suffer not temporarily in hell, but suffer eternally both spiritually and physically, though this physical suffering does not include physical destruction. The key is that it is an eternal spiritual suffering in the midst of some kind of ongoing eternal physical suffering. Likewise, believers who experience the first resurrection will later experience a fully consummated spiritual and physical resurrection in the new creation. So the first resurrection, though incomplete, launches an eternal spiritual resurrection, which will be consummated later in an eternally greater spiritual yet fully physical form. The first-second antithesis carries over in that the second resurrection represents the eternal consummation of the first.

3. *Biblical evidence for the intermediate state.* On our understanding, the "first resurrection" describes an intermediate, beginning eternal state between physical death and physical resurrection. Some contend that there is no example in the Bible of the eternal state being a state of resurrection existence, but that is not the case. In Rev. 2:10-11, believers are promised that if they remain faithful until physical death, they will receive

"the crown of life," which in turn will prevent them from being harmed by the second, spiritual death. It could reasonably be assumed that the "life" referred to here is the heavenly existence of the saints between physical death and physical resurrection and is consummated in physical resurrection. The same truth is presented in 6:9-11, where deceased saints appear as living souls without bodies, waiting for the physical resurrection. Jesus taught the same when He said to the Sadducees that God "is not the God of the dead, but of the living; for all live to Him" (Luke 20:38). Therefore, said Jesus, God is still the God of Abraham, Isaac and Jacob, who are "sons of the resurrection" (Luke 20:36) and thus presently alive to Him, even before their final physical resurrection. The Sadducees denied not only the physical resurrection but also that there was any conscious existence after death, and in this passage Jesus rejects both false beliefs. The metaphorical picture is that of a soul leaving an earthly body and ascending to heaven, where a more intense condition of blessedness is experienced. This is similar to Phil. 1:21, 23: "to die is gain . . . to depart and be with Christ . . . is very much better" (cf. also 2 Cor. 5:8: "we . . . prefer rather to be absent from the body and at home with the Lord"). Paul states in Rom. 6:4-5 that our life in Christ can be referred to as a spiritual resurrection, and that life in Christ continues on into the intermediate state, after physical death. 1 Pet. 4:6 refers to people who, "though they are judged in the flesh as men" [= physical death], "may live [*zaō* = living in the intermediate state] in the Spirit according to the will of God."

In the light of this and other Scriptures, it is reasonable to interpret the ascent of the soul at the time of death into the Lord's presence as a form of spiritual resurrection, in anticipation of the physical resurrection and consummation of eternal life, which will occur at the Lord's return. That such a translation can be termed a "resurrection" is appropriate, because the souls of the saints are entering a higher state of blessedness and resurrection existence than they had before on account of their regeneration (for a similar thought in early Christian literature, see Ignatius, *Romans* 2.2; 4.3; *1 Clement* 5.4, 7; *Acts of Paul*), and because they experience the immediate presence of God and Christ (Rev. 6:9-11; 7:14-17). Consequently their role as kings and priests becomes intensified. Their labor of perseverance on earth is successfully accomplished so that they can rest (6:11; 14:13). They have greater assurance of vindication (see on 6:11; cf. 19:8) and of protection from the second death, because of their intermediate existence of escalated spiritual life.

4. *The basis of the fourfold ending of Revelation in the fourfold ending*

of Ezekiel 37–48. As noted earlier, the parallels are striking: the resurrection of the saints (Rev. 20:4a; Ezek. 37:1-14), the messianic kingdom (Rev. 20:4b-6; Ezek. 37:15-28), the final battle against Gog and Magog (Rev. 20:7-10; Ezekiel 38–39), and the new temple and new Jerusalem (Rev. 21:1–22:5; Ezekiel 40–48). The same Greek verb and verb form, translated "they came to life" is used in Rev. 20:4 and Ezek. 37:10 LXX (likewise 37:6, 14, where *zaō* occurs) in the prophecy of the dry bones (God's people) being raised to life. That "they came to life" in Rev. 20:4 alludes to Ezek. 37:10 is apparent from the fact that the third person plural aorist active indicative of *zaō* occurs in the Greek OT elsewhere only in Num. 14:38, which is a mundane reference and has no reference to any concept of resurrection. This makes Ezek. 37:10 uniquely parallel in all of the OT to the same verb form in Rev. 20:4. The resurrection in Ezekiel is symbolic or spiritual in nature, and focuses on the spiritual renewal of Israel when it is restored from captivity, a point on which both premillennial (at least most) and amillennial OT interpreters of Ezekiel agree. Ezek. 37:10 is now universalized in Revelation and applied to the church.

The meaning of "coming to life" in terms of spiritual (as opposed to physical) resurrection in Ezek. 37:10, 14 is clarified by 36:26-28, since it develops the latter text: "I will give you a new heart and put a new spirit within you. . . . I will put My Spirit within you . . . and you *will live* in the land." Rev. 20:4 likely follows the same symbolic or spiritual view of "coming to life," since it alludes to Ezek. 37:10, 14. Indeed, as is clearly the case in Ezekiel 37, it is possible that the vision of Rev. 20:4-6 is a *picture* of deceased saints being bodily resurrected, but that this picture *is to be interpreted symbolically* as a spiritual resurrection. This approach would be a partial answer to the literalist objection that a bodily resurrection must be envisioned. This understanding of 20:4 is supported by the fact that the language of "priests," "kingdom," and "reigning" in vv. 4-6 is taken from descriptions of Israel in Exod 19:6 and Dan. 7:27 and applied here and in Rev. 1:6, 9 ("kingdom") and 5:9-10 to the church. In addition, Ezek. 37:10 has already been applied in 11:11 (the breath of life coming back into the witnesses) to connote figuratively and spiritually the church's continued existence, vindication, and release from the world's captivity into the immediate presence of God (see on 11:11-12). Rev. 20:4 takes Paul's concept of spiritual resurrection at conversion (Rom. 6:4-11; Eph. 2:6; Col. 3:1) and uses the terminology of Ezekiel to apply it to the intensified form of spiritual resurrection which occurs upon the believer's death.

5. *The premillennial problem of a judgment after the final definitive*

judgment. In 15:1, John states that with the seven plagues or bowl judgments the wrath of God is finished. In 16:12-16, the sixth bowl judgment concludes with the nations gathered at Armageddon, following which the seventh bowl judgment represents the end of history. It is clear that 19:17-21 picks up the narrative where 16:16 leaves off and concludes it. This means that 19:17-21 covers the same timeframe as the sixth and seventh bowl judgments, thus bringing to a definitive end the wrath of God against unbelievers. How then could there be a further, much later judgment related in 20:7-10? Thus, 20:7-10 is likely referring to the same final judgment narrated in the last bowl (16:17-21) and in 19:17-21. If this is so, then 20:1-6 precedes the final judgment at Christ's final second coming.

6. *The affirmation of the Bible concerning one physical resurrection.* The Bible states consistently that there is only one physical resurrection at the end of history (Isa. 26:19-21; Dan. 12:2; John 5:28-29; Acts 24:15; 2 Thess. 1:7-10). This final resurrection is mentioned again in Rev. 20:12-15, which includes the physical resurrection of the saints along with that of the unrighteous. V. 5a mentions only the physical resurrection of the wicked in order to stress that they do not share in the first spiritual resurrection. If, as on a premillennial understanding, we take v. 4 to refer to a first physical resurrection at the beginning of a millennial period, followed by a further resurrection at its end, the reference would stand in serious tension with the consistent and universal teaching of the rest of the Scriptures that there is only one final resurrection. Some say there is precedent for several resurrections, since Christ was raised first, and then those who believe in him will be raised later, thus suggesting two resurrections. Even if it is true, however, that the final resurrection was inaugurated in Christ's resurrection thousands of years before the final resurrection of the saints, this does not count as a separate resurrection followed by a completely different resurrection, since Christ's resurrection is viewed as part of the later resurrection of His people and not separate from it (1 Cor. 15:20-23). It would be possible but very strange to apply this corporate solidarity in Christ's resurrection to many subsequent resurrections, so the burden of proof rests on such a position.

7. *The problem of a "mixed population" during a literal earthly millennium.* A theological problem with the premillennial view is that it means that resurrected believers with glorified, newly created bodies would be living in the old creation with people with corruptible bodies, many of whom will become unbelievers at the end of the millennium. The response that the incorruptible Christ dwelled with people having corruptible bodies for forty days after His resurrection is interesting but not fully satisfying.

8. *The figurative meaning of the number "one thousand."* There is good biblical reason to believe that the number "one thousand" as used here is figurative rather than literal. We have already seen that the numbers in Revelation are symbolic in nature. The use of "signify" (NASB mg.; Greek *sēmainō*) in 1:1 with reference to the whole book encourages the reader to expect a predominance of symbolic over literal language, including references to numbers (see on 1:1).

The Bible also uses this particular number figuratively: "He has remembered His covenant forever, the word which He commanded to a thousand generations" (Ps. 105:8; see 1 Chron. 16:15). Ps. 90:4 should probably be taken figuratively (as a reference to a long period of time), "For a thousand years in Thy sight are like yesterday when it passes by." The same is true in 2 Pet. 3:8, "With the Lord one day is as a thousand years, and a thousand years as one day" (for further references see on v. 4 above). It may be used as a contrast with the brief period of conflict immediately before the Lord's return, which is "three and a half days" in 11:11 and "one hour" in 17:12. "One thousand" also signifies the idea of completeness in Revelation, as in the measurements of the eternal city in 21:16, where "twelve thousand stadia" represents the number of God's people (twelve) multiplied by one thousand, in order to express the completeness of that people. "One thousand years" would thus signify the complete duration of the church age. Multiples of one thousand have previously been used figuratively in Revelation (see on 7:4-9; 9:16; 14:1; cf. 5:11) to express either a large number, a complete number, or both. It does not necessarily signify a very long period of time (however we might construe that), but points more to the idea of a fullness of time allowed by God's sovereignty at the end of which will surely come the ultimate victory of Christians who have suffered. We have already suggested that if the suffering saints persevere through their short trials of "ten days" (2:10), they will be given the reward of a millennial reign. The intensifying of ten to a thousand (one thousand being ten to the third power), together with the lengthening of days to years, might suggest that momentary affliction in the present results in a far greater glory even in the intermediate state prior to eternal glory.

9. *Problematic OT passages that are considered by some to support premillennialism.* Some premillennialists have proposed that at least three OT passages offer significant support for a premillennial view of Rev. 20:1-6. Because of lack of space, the following interpretative perspectives can only be presented in the form of very brief sketches that require further elaboration, especially with respect to the amillennial views proposed.

First, Isa. 24:21-22:

21a So it will happen in that day,
21b that the LORD will punish the host of heaven on high, and the kings of the earth on earth.
22a They will be gathered together *like* prisoners in the dungeon,
22b and will be confined in prison;
22c and after many days they *will be* punished.
23 Then the moon will be abashed and the sun ashamed, for the LORD of hosts will reign on Mount Zion and in Jerusalem, and *His* glory will be before His elders.

Many premillennialists regard this passage as predicting an absolute binding of Satan (in v. 22a-b), which is also described in Rev. 20:1-3. However, the amillennial view can affirm any of the following three interpretations of the passage, none of which demand an absolute binding of the devil in Rev. 20:1-3. First, the "confinement" predicted by Isa. 24:21-22 is qualified in Rev. 20:1-8 as a binding with respect to only Satan's ability to deceive all the nations to gather against the church universal and to try to extinguish it. Or, second, v. 22c ("and after many days they will be punished") is a recapitulation of v. 21a ("So it will happen in that day") and thus also of vv. 21b-22b. This would reflect a typical use of recapitulation with such time designations among the prophets (e.g., Jer. 31:31, "days are coming," and 31:33, "after those days," which refer to the same time). These verses are then about the final judgment at the very end of earth history. Thus v. 23 is about the eternal new heavens and earth. Or, third, v. 21 was inaugurated at Christ's first coming and then v. 22a-b occurs during the church age and v. 22c at the consummation, as does v. 23.

Second, Isa. 65:20:

> No longer will there be in it an infant *who lives but a few* days, or an old man who does not live out his days; for the youth will die at the age of one hundred and the one who does not reach the age of one hundred will be *thought* accursed.

The premillennial view takes this verse literally and describes death as a reality during the millennium, but not the arrival of the eternal new heavens and earth, though some might want to argue that the millennium is a second inaugurated fulfillment of new creation (the first being when one is regenerated as a Christian, e.g., 2 Cor. 5:17), which is then consummated in the eternal new creation, after the so-called millennium. However, there is no other evidence in the NT for a second stage of inauguration of the new creation. In contrast to the premillennial perspective, the amillennial view can affirm two interpretations of this passage:

Isa. 65:20 is a figurative way of referring to a long, indeed, eternal life, since all of 65:17-25 is clearly about the eternal new heavens and earth, as 66:22 also bears out. If this is true, then the broader context of eternal new creation surrounding 65:20 makes it likely that this verse is to be taken figuratively. It is extremely difficult to say that 65:17-25 is about the millennium and that 66:21-24 is about the eternal new creation. If a premillennialist were to affirm that both 65:17-25 and 66:21-24 are about the millennium, it would contradict Rev. 21:1, which applies Isa. 65:17 and 66:22 to the destruction of the old cosmos and the replacement of it with an eternal new creation (likewise Isa. 65:17 is applied to the passing away of the old earth in Rev. 21:4). In the same way, 2 Pet. 3:13 applies Isa. 65:17 and 66:22 not to a millennium, but to the eternal "new heavens and new earth." Furthermore, Isa. 66:24 appears to refer to the beginning of eternal punishment, which would correspond antithetically with an eternal new creation in vv. 22-23 (where references to eternal blessings are started). Also, the second part of Isa 65:17 says, "the former things [of the old creation] shall not be remembered or come to mind." But if this refers merely to a millennium on an old (but renewed) earth, then the fact that death will occur during the millennium (according to the premillennial view of 65:20) and again when Christ's human enemies are defeated at the end of the millennium appears to contradict the promise in 65:17b that "the former things" of the old creation "shall not be remembered or come to mind." Indeed, the worst feature of the old creation — death — will "come to mind" during the millennium.

Or, as an alternative possibility that is also consistent with an amillennial view, Isa. 65:20 is about the inaugurated stage of the new creation (the fulfillment of which is noted in 2 Cor. 5:17) and refers to the idea that physical life is not eternal in the inaugurated phase of the new creation.

Third, Zech. 14:16-19: According to the premillennial view, after the decisive end-time victory of God narrated in vv. 1-3 and supposedly recapitulated in vv. 12-15, the nations will go up from year to year to worship God at Jerusalem during the millennium, but those nations who do not go up will be punished with a plague of judgment (described in vv. 16-19), much like the majority of the nations who were defeated by God directly before the beginning of the millennium.

Yet there are problems with such a proposal. For instance, Zech 14:11 says that after the decisive triumph of God which introduces the purported millennial period, "there will be no more curse." This statement is directly alluded to in Rev. 22:3. Both Zech. 14:11 and Rev. 22:3 clearly allude to the fact that the curse of Gen. 3:14-19 will be forever done away with, and Rev. 22:3 places this statement clearly during the time of the new eternal creation. This means that Zech. 14:11 refers to the eternal consummated kingdom and not to a preceding purported millennial kingdom, as premillennialists contend. Yet according to the premillennial view, more nations will be cursed during this same period, since (on this view) Zech. 14:12-15 recapitulates the battle of Zech. 14:1-3, and Zech. 14:16-19 portrays the nations being "cursed" and "punished" for their millennial disobedience. This is a seemingly unsolvable problem for the premillennialist. How can there be a "curse" during this millennial period when Zech. 14:11 says that this curse will be done away with during the same period? The premillennialist could try to say that Zech 14:11 is about the eternal new creation after the millennium, but v. 11 is a continuation of a narrative of the period directly following God's defeat of the unbelieving nations in vv. 1-3, which then introduces the purported millennial period (vv. 4-10), of which v. 11 is clearly a further description. Thus, it is difficult to see how a premillennialist could place v. 11 as part of the eternal new creation when vv. 4-10 are about the purported millennial period.

A viable amillennial proposal understands Zech. 14:1-3 to refer to the decisive victory of Christ described in Rev. 16:17-21; 19:19-21; and 20:7-8 *following the millennium, which we have argued is the church age* (see further on those verses for justification of this position). After the millennium or church age comes the final defeat of the enemy, followed by the eternal new creation, in which there is no longer any curse (Zech. 14:4-11). In this case, Zech. 14:12-15, which apparently introduces a new thought or visionary segment, would not be a recapitulation of vv. 1-3, but would rather focus on the defeat of the nations at Christ's first coming. As was the case with John, Zechariah's visions are not necessarily to be understood in strict chronological order. The punishment of the unbelieving nations described in Zech. 14:16-19 occurs during the church age, directly following Christ's inaugurated defeat of the nations, and is thus recognizably synchronous to Rev. 11:4-6, where the two witnesses execute "plagues" on unbelievers.

The basis of such an interpretation would initially derive from a number of OT texts cited in the NT that describe Christ's defeat of the nations as occurring at His first coming and culminating at His return. For example, see Gen. 49:8-12 and Isa. 11:1, 10 and its inaugurated fulfillment in Rev. 5:5, as well as Rom. 1:5 and 16:26, where the positive "obedience of the nations" is stated, but Christ's victory over even the unbelieving nations is implied in the light of the Genesis 49 prophecy, which is alluded to in the Romans passage. Also note that the prophecy of the victory of the nations in Num. 24:14-19 begins to see fulfillment in Christ's first coming (see Rev. 2:28; 22:16, where the prophecy of Isa. 11:1 is inaugurated).

In addition, the prophecy of the nations gathering to defeat "the Lord and . . . His Messiah" from Ps. 2:1-2 begins to be fulfilled at the cross (Acts 4:25-26), and the Messiah's victory over the nations in Ps. 2:8-9 commences in Christ's first coming (especially His resurrection) in Rev 2:26-27 and then is consummated at His return in Rev. 19:15. Thus understood, Zech 14:16-19 could well be referring to unbelievers feigning to profess faith in Christ during the church age but who do not worship in the true Holy Spirit or in the truth during that age (cf. John 4:21-24), and who will consequently be judged. Those among the nations who profess to trust in Christ yet do not worship him in truth and sincerity will fall under His condemnation. Other OT texts referenced in the NT could easily be adduced to support this view to one degree or another.

Some premillennialists might well fault this view in that they would doubt that there was a significant victory over the nations at Christ's first coming, yet in so doing they would fail to notice the ironic nature of His victory through the cross, which is then replicated in the obedient church. In fact, one of the repeated NT affirmations is that the great victory over Satan, who rules over the sons of disobedience among the nations (see, e.g., Eph. 2:1-3), began at the cross (like "D-Day") and will be consummated at Christ's final coming (like "V-Day").

Premillennialists might also attempt to fault this view because the battle of Zech. 14:1-3 and the battle of vv. 12-15 appear to be the same. We do not radically disagree that the two battles are very similar, and indeed are organically related. But this does not mean they are completely identical in their timing. In fact, note again from above that the prophecy of Ps. 2:8-9, which seems there to be a final consummative battle, commences in Christ's first coming (and especially His resurrection) in Rev. 2:26-27 and then is consummated at His return in Rev. 19:15 (the same thing happens with the Isa. 49:2 description of the messianic Servant's mouth being like a sword, which is inaugurated at Christ's first coming [Rev. 1:16; 2:12, 16] and consummated at His last coming [Rev. 19:15]). The very same wording about the eschatological defeat of the nations from the Psalm describes the initial defeat and the consummation of the defeat. We believe that something like this is going on in the relation of the similar batttle descriptions of Zech. 14:1-3 and Zech. 14:12-15, the former portraying the consummative battle, which was commenced in the church age in the latter.

Suggestions for Reflection on 20:4-6

On the saints' heavenly rule. The saints are pictured here as participating in the rule of Christ in His heavenly court prior to the last judgment and physical resurrection. What is the nature of this rule, and in what sense is it an answer to the prayers for vindication recorded in 6:9-11?

On the significance in Revelation of Exod. 19:6. How can you trace the promise of Exod. 19:6, "And you shall be to Me a kingdom of priests and a holy nation" through Revelation from Israel to the church on earth to the church in its heavenly existence as pictured in these verses? Why is a proper understanding of the application of this verse so important to our understanding of Revelation as well as of the church's role on earth and in heaven?

Satan will be released from his prior restraint to deceive the nations again so that they will attempt to annihilate the church (20:7-10)

[7] And when the thousand years are completed, Satan will be released from his
prison, [8] and will come out to deceive the nations which are in the four corners
of the earth, Gog and Magog, to gather them together for the war; the number
of them is like the sand of the seashore. [9] And they came up on the broad plain
of the earth and surrounded the camp of the saints and the beloved city, and
fire came down from heaven and devoured them. [10] And the devil who deceived
them was thrown into the lake of fire and brimstone, where the beast and the
false prophet are also; and they will be tormented day and night forever and ever.

7 After emphasizing that the initial judgment of Satan (vv. 1-3) resulted in the blessing of life for God's people (vv. 4-6), John now underscores in vv. 7-15 the final judgment of the second death for Satan and all who are allied with him. At the conclusion of v. 3 it was forecast that Satan would be "released" from the abyss at the conclusion of the thousand years. The assurance that this will be fulfilled is now given: **And when the thousand years are completed, Satan will be released from his prison**. The "abyss"

of vv. 1-3 is called a **prison** to highlight the fact that where the devil resides during the thousand years he is restrained in some significant manner, though not in every way (see above on vv. 1-3).

8 The particular manner in which the devil has been restrained is reiterated from v. 3. He has been restricted specifically in his ability to deceive the nations into joining forces to attack and completely annihilate the church, but this restraint, in God's own purpose, is now removed, and he will lead an army drawn from the **four corners of the earth**, a Hebrew expression for the whole earth (Isa. 11:12; cf. "four winds" in Ezek. 37:9; Dan. 7:2): he **will come out to deceive the nations which are in the four corners of the earth, Gog and Magog, to gather them together for the war; the number of them is like the sand of the seashore.** The assembling of these antagonistic forces against God's people is seen as a fulfillment of the prophecy in Ezekiel 38–39 that "Gog and Magog" and "many peoples" would gather together for war against Israel. In particular, the language of "gathering together" the nations derives from Ezek. 38:2-7 and 39:2, together with passages from Zechariah 12–14 and Zephaniah 3, which also stand behind the parallel phrases in Rev. 16:14 and 19:19. All of these OT texts foretell that *God* will gather the nations together in Israel for the final war of history (see further on 16:14 and 19:19). Against this background, the definite article before "war" ("*the* war") in 16:14; 19:19 and here may be an article of previous reference, referring not only to the OT prophecy of the final battle but also back to the initial (anarthrous) description of the last battle in 11:7. Thus, all these references refer to the *same final battle,* not different battles.

Thus John has already recorded the fulfillment of the very same Ezekiel and Zech. 14:2 prophecies in 19:17-21 and the fulfillment of Zech. 14:2 in 16:14-16. The repeated occurrences of the Ezekiel and Zechariah references ("the war" of Zech. 14:2 is repeated three times) do not designate three separate fulfillments or different analogical uses but the same fulfillment narrated in three contexts (see on 16:14 and 19:19 for textual comparisons and use of Ezekiel and Zech. 14:2 and other possible OT backgrounds). As noted, this is strong evidence of recapitulation between 16:14; 19:19; and 20:8.

Ezekiel distinguishes Gog and Magog from the other nations of the earth who are allied with them (38:2-7, 15, 22; 39:4). But in Rev. 20:8 "Gog and Magog" are not distinguished from the other nations but are figuratively equated with all the nations. In addition, whereas "Gog and Magog" and their allies come out of "the remote parts of the north" in Ezekiel (38:6,

15), now they come from throughout the whole earth, **the four corners of the earth** (though Ethiopia and Put, from the south, were also among the allies in Ezek. 38:5). This is a universalization of the Ezekiel prophecy, suggesting a universalization of oppressed Israel, which becomes equivalent in v. 9 to "the camp of the saints and the beloved city" and is to be understood as the church throughout the earth. The same universalization occurs in 16:12, 14, where "the kings from the east" appear to be interpreted as "the kings of the whole world," which further identifies the two passages as referring to the same events (see on 16:12-16). It is also possible that all the invading nations mentioned as well as implied in Ezekiel 38–39 are now referred to as "Gog and Magog" because John may have understood that this nation headed up and represented the others, including Put and Ethiopia, who were not from the north. Such a viewpoint may be supported by Ezek. 38:14, 16, 18 and 39:1, 6, 11, which refer to Gog or Magog as the main invader who would attack and suffer defeat (note also Ezek. 38:7: "prepare yourself [Gog], you and all your companies"). Even so, there would still appear to be some greater degree of universalization in Rev. 20:8, since the nations in Ezekiel 38–39 appear to come only from, at most, two major directions, while here they proceed from all four points of the compass.

These multitudes refer not to demonic forces, as some think, but to antagonistic peoples throughout the earth. The primary reason for this is that they are identified as "nations," which elsewhere in the book always means human peoples (e.g., 19:15). The demonic beings of ch. 16 are not synonymous with the nations, but are the instrumentality through which the devil gathers together the nations for the final assault against God and his people.

Ezek. 38:2-3 describes Gog as "prince of Rosh, Meshech, and Tubal." Some premillennial interpreters suggest that this means "Gog is the prince (leader) of Russia, Moscow, and Tobolsk," who will lead an army invading latter-day Israel. However, Meshech and Tubal are Hebrew names for peoples from East Anatolia (part of present-day Turkey). These names have nothing to do with any contemporary city. The names probably became proverbial in Judaism, though not necessarily in isolation from the original Ezekiel context, and applicable to any terrifying force threatening God's people (much like we may today call an evil despot "another Hitler"). Neither does Rosh refer to "Russia" on the basis of sound or etymology, but is best translated as "chief" or "prince" (of Meshech and Tubal), as it is hundreds of times elsewhere in the OT.

Many dispensationalists identify Gog and Magog as Russia, supposing that nation to be the foe at the second coming of Christ and before the millennium, but Revelation mentions Gog and Magog as the foe only at the *end* of the millennium. This would seem to require a dispensationalist belief in the revival of the Russian menace after the thousand years! Indeed, in v. 8, Gog and Magog do not refer to an individual nation from the north distinguished from other nations and consisting of countable troops, but they are now equated with all the nations from every point of the compass coming with uncountable hosts. Therefore, Gog and Magog cannot be identified with any specific nation of the twenty-first century such as Russia. That the **number** of the nations assembled are, as mentioned, **like the sand of the seashore**, underscores their innumerability and the apparent overwhelming odds in their favor against the saints. Josh. 11:4; Judg. 7:12; and 1 Sam. 13:5 use the same metaphor for the multitudinous forces of the nations arrayed to fight against Israel at various times.

9 The allusion to Ezekiel continues here: **And they came up on the broad plain** [literally "breadth"] **of the earth and surrounded the camp of the saints and the beloved city, and fire came down from heaven and devoured them.** In Ezekiel, the multitudinous end-time enemy (Ezek. 38:15, 22; cf. v. 8 above) "goes up" against God's people (Ezek. 38:11, 16). Likewise here: **and they came up . . . and surrounded the camp of the saints and the beloved city.** They then undergo a fiery judgment (Ezek. 38:22). Again, likewise here: **fire came down from heaven and devoured them.** Habakkuk portrays in similar words Babylon's invasion of Judah as marching forth on "the breadth of the earth [literally and NASB mg.; LXX 'the plain of the earth'] to seize dwelling places which are not theirs" (Hab. 1:6). Since in Dan. 12:2 (LXX) "breadth of the earth" refers to the area throughout the earth (where the dead lie), it is plausible that the same worldwide meaning attaches to the nearly identical phrase here in v. 9, especially in the light of the description of the same event in 11:7-10 (on which see) and the following identification of the **camp of the saints** and **the beloved city** as the church scattered throughout the earth. **The camp of the saints** is an allusion to the camp of the Israelites in the desert. The church has been located in the desert in 12:6, 14, understood as the place of God's protection during the church age, so the reference is appropriate. **The saints**, a term used to describe the Israelites in the OT, is used thirteen times in Revelation, always with reference to the church (see especially 5:8-9; 13:7-10; 14:12).

The camp of the saints is equated with **the beloved city**, which further underlines the reference to the church for, according to 3:12, all believers in Christ will have the name of this new city written upon them. There are twelve references to the eternal city in chs. 21–22. The phrase "the holy city, Jerusalem, coming down out of heaven from God" in 21:10 (cf. 21:2) is a clear verbatim parallel to 3:12 ("the new Jerusalem, which comes down out of heaven from My God"), identifying the cities in both contexts as the same. Its walls and foundations have written on them (respectively) the names of the twelve tribes of Israel and the twelve apostles, thus portraying the universal people of God. The church, composed of people from every nation (21:24-26; 22:2), will enter this eternal city. The phrase **the beloved city** may have its origins in Ps. 87:2-3: "The Lord loves the gates of Zion more than all the other dwelling places of Jacob. Glorious things are spoken of you, O city of God" (cf. also Psalm 122; Isa. 66:10; Zeph. 3:14-17). According to the Psalm, the Lord loves His city, composed of people from the nations of the world, who are now being enrolled as true Israelites (see the list in Ps. 87:4; vv. 5-6 go on to say that these nations will be considered "born" as Israelites).

The "city" of persecuted saints in v. 9 is the inauguration of the new creation, composed of the community of faith, which finds its consummation in 21:2ff. This city, though an eternal reality, can be spoken of as present now in an inaugurated or incomplete way, as in Gal. 4:26 ("the Jerusalem above," pictured as the church) and Heb. 12:22-23 ("you have come to Mount Zion and to the city of the living God, the heavenly Jerusalem, and to myriads of angels, to the general assembly and church of the first-born who are enrolled in heaven").

The nations attack the church, but before they can destroy it, **fire came down from heaven and devoured them.** The actual language of fire coming down and consuming is drawn directly from the story of Elijah and the soldiers sent against him in 2 Kgs. 1:10-14, language quoted also in Rev. 11:5 with reference to the fate of those who attack the two witnesses (the church) during the church age. There, the fire was figurative for a preconsummative judgment, whereas here in 20:9 it refers figuratively to the final judgment. The fire is probably not to be taken literally, but, regardless, the point is that God will deliver His people by judging their enemies.

10 The devil is again highlighted as the one who deceived the nations into attacking the saints. The reason for reiterating this deception is to set forth his judgment: **And the devil who deceived them was thrown into the lake of fire and brimstone, where the beast and false prophet are also; and they will be tormented day and night forever and ever.** Vv. 7-10 are probably a recapitulation of 19:17-21, which makes unlikely the supposition that the devil is cast into the fire many ages after his Satanic cohorts at the end of ch. 19. The Satanic trinity will suffer everlasting conscious punishment, as is affirmed in the case of all unbelievers in 14:10-11, which is a parallel description of the lake of fire and the last judgment with its reference to the eternal torment of fire and brimstone (so likewise v. 15). Some have questioned how suffering could apply to an entity such as the beast or the false prophet, if they represent the persecuting power of the state or of false religion. However, these entities (like the holy city of 21:2-4, which is composed of the saints) are representative of the people who compose them, who themselves suffer the eternal consequences of their actions. Further, there is no doubt that evil demonic powers lie behind both the beast and the false prophet, powerful spirits subject to Satan (see on 13:2, 11-17). If that is the case, the reference here would be to the eternal torment of these demonic spirits, who will suffer alongside their master in the lake of fire. Matt. 25:41 corroborates this: "Depart from me, accursed ones [i.e. the lost], into the eternal fire which has been prepared for the devil and his angels" (the angels are also personal beings). The devil as an individual is eternally punished, according to this verse, as are the individual followers of the beast in 14:10-11.

The suffering is conscious, because the word "torment" in Revelation always refers to conscious suffering (see further on 14:10-11). It is eternal, because the phrase "forever and ever" refers in Revelation to an endless period, as in God's eternal reign (11:15), the duration of His eternal glory and power (1:6; 5:13; 7:12), His eternal life (4:9-10; 10:6; 15:7), and the eternal life of Christ (1:18). In particular, the use of the same expression for the explicitly unending reign of the saints in 22:5 must mean that the same temporal phrase in 20:10, hardly more than a chapter earlier, refers to a similar unending period. The "lake of fire" is not literal in nature, as Satan and his angels are spiritual beings. "Fire" in Revelation speaks of divine judgment, and that judgment, whatever form it takes, is certain to be terrible.

There is no verb in Greek with the clause **where the beast and the false prophet *are* also**. The NASB adds the "are." Premillennialists typically see the beast and the false prophet in the lake of fire for a thousand years *before* the devil was cast there. This issue is confused in the NIV, which refers to the devil being thrown into the lake of fire "where the beast and false prophet *had been thrown.*" But the beast and the false prophet can be seen as thrown into the fire *at the same time as* the devil, if the (omitted but understood) verb is taken most naturally in the same tense as the verb in the preceding clause, "the devil . . . was thrown": "the devil . . . was thrown . . . where the beast and the false prophet were also thrown." The overall perspective of the passage definitively determines whether the episodes are simultaneous or separated by an interval of time and the context favors a simultaneous notion.

That the episodes are simultaneous or directly following one another is borne out by our overall analysis of ch. 20 so far, which has suggested that the events of 19:11-21 and 20:7-10 are contemporaneous. This is further supported by the fact that in 19:20 the beast and the false prophet are thrown into "the lake of fire," the same phrase occurring here with respect to the devil. In 20:14-15 and 21:8, the "lake of fire" is called "the second death," which is the final, eternal punishment and begins for all the ungodly (unbelievers, the beast, the false prhophet, and the devil) at the same time, at the destruction and re-creation of the cosmos (so vv. 10-15; 21:1-8). The strong verbal parallels between v. 10 and 14:10-11 (eternal torment with fire and brimstone) suggest that the same reality is referred to there.

The first death (= physical death) occurs until the present cosmos is destroyed. Unbelievers who die are thereafter held in the realm of "death and Hades" (v. 13), prior to the last judgment and second death, which is the lake of fire (v. 15). God cast the fallen angels into Hades, there to be reserved until the final judgment (2 Pet. 2:4; Jude 6). Christ came to unlock the keys of death and Hades (Rev. 1:18) and to ensure that deceased believers would immediately enter the presence of the Lord, there to be kept until Christ's return. The "second death" cannot begin until all have died the first physical death. On any millennial view, the first death will cease at the annihilation and renovation of the creation. That is why the casting of the beast and false prophet into the lake of fire in 19:20 *cannot occur before the period of the millennium,* as premillennialism suggests. The reason for this is that the second death, which *initiates* the punishment of the lake of fire, does not, on any millennial view, *occur until after* the great white throne judgment in vv. 11-15. It is at that judgment, *following the millennium,* that death and Hades give up the dead in them, who are then judged and thrown into the lake of fire (v. 15).

Consequently, the description of the last battle and the casting of the beast and the false prophet into the lake of fire in 19:17-21 must describe the same set of events as the battle in 20:7-10, and the millennium must, therefore, refer to the events *preceding* that battle, that is, the church age. If the punishment of the beast and the false prophet in 19:20 did occur long before the events portrayed in 14:10-11 and v. 10, it would have spoken of them as having been *thrown into death and Hades* rather than *thrown into the lake of fire.*

Suggestions for Reflection on 20:7-10

On the preoccupation with name- and date-setting. This passage, with its mention of Gog and Magog and its roots in Ezekiel 38–39, has provided a rich vein of material for those trying to link references in the Bible to present-day nations and localities and thus to predict events of the "last days" and propose elaborate eschatological timetables. The commentary has explained why these references are best taken figuratively. Why is it that people are so drawn to the name- and date-setting which has so confounded the understanding of Revelation, particularly in modern times? In what ways could such approaches take away from the God- and Christ-centered focus of Revelation?

On God's love and justice. These verses present the lake of fire as a place of everlasting conscious punishment. Why do we have difficulty reconciling this truth with the loving character of God as also presented by the Bible? How do we reconcile the love and the justice of God? How do they meet at the cross?

The final judgment will occur at the end of world history, at which time all people will be resurrected and judged according to their works and the guilty will be consigned to eternal punishment (20:11-15)

[11] And I saw a great white throne and Him who sat upon it, from whose presence earth and heaven fled away, and no place was found for them. [12] And I saw
the dead, the great and the small, standing before the throne, and books were
opened; and another book was opened, which is the book of life; and the dead
were judged from the things which were written in the books, according to their
deeds. [13] And the sea gave up the dead which were in it, and death and Hades
gave up the dead which were in them; and they were judged, every one of them
according to their deeds. [14] And death and Hades were thrown into the lake of
fire. This is the second death, the lake of fire. [15] And if anyone's name was not
found written in the book of life, he was thrown into the lake of fire.

11 The vision in v. 11 of God sitting on the great white throne (**And I saw a great white throne and Him who sat upon it, from whose presence earth and heaven fled away, and no place was found for them**) takes us back to similar visions in 4:2 and 5:7 of God on His throne, which allude primarily to Dan. 7:9 and Ezek. 1:26-28. The white color of the throne denotes the holiness of God. The judgment about to proceed from the throne is from the holy God, who judges not only to punish sin but also to vindicate His persecuted people. The One seated on the throne throughout Revelation is God (e.g., chs. 4–5; 19:4; 21:5; cf. Rom. 14:10). But it would not be problematic if it were Jesus seated on the throne here in 20:11 (in light of such texts as 5:12-13; 7:17; 22:1-3; Matt. 25:31ff.; John 5:22-27; Acts 17:31; 2 Cor. 5:10; 2 Tim. 4:1). Therefore, regardless of who is sitting on the throne, both God and Christ execute the last judgment. The visions in chs. 4, 5, and 20 are all rooted in Daniel 7, which features God sitting on the throne and books being opened. Whereas the vision in chs. 4–5 refers to the present reign and judgment of God and Christ, which began with Jesus' resurrection, the scene in ch. 20 is about the culmination of that judicial rule in the final judgment at the end of history.

Earth and heaven have **fled away**, as in the very similar descriptions of the final judgment in 6:14 and 16:20. That this signifies the end-time cosmic destruction is apparent further from 21:1, which affirms that "a new heaven and a new earth" replaced the vanishing first heaven and first earth. The phrase **no place was found for them** is from Dan. 2:35 (the Greek text of Theodotion; the Hebrew is similar: "not a trace of them was found"), where it describes the destruction of the wicked kingdoms at the end time. Rev. 12:8 makes the same allusion to underscore the inaugurated defeat of the devil and his forces by the death and resurrection of Christ (on which see). Now the same wording from Daniel is applied to the complete destruction of the entire evil world system, which likely includes its material aspects (so also Ps. 102:25-27; Isa. 51:6; 2 Pet. 3:7, 10, 12).

12 That John sees **the dead, the great and the small, standing before the throne** assumes (in light of vv. 4-5; Dan. 12:2; John 5:28-29; Acts 24:15) that the last, great resurrection of the unrighteous and the righteous has finally taken place. The clauses **books were opened; and another book was opened, which is the book of life** combine allusion to Dan. 7:10 ("the books were opened") and Dan. 12:1-2 ("everyone who is found written in the book, will be rescued . . . these to everlasting life"). The "books" in Daniel 7 focus on judgment, but the book of Daniel 12 is an image of redemption for true saints (which excludes the lost). Therefore, John's vision gives assurance that the prophecy of final judgment and redemption will occur. The judgment at the end is what is highlighted here in v. 12, though final salvation is secondarily included (see on 3:5; 13:8; 17:8 for the "book of life" and especially for the OT background). As in 13:8 and 17:8, the "book of life" is introduced to bring attention to those excluded from it. The phrase **and the dead were judged from the things which were written in the books, according to their deeds** reveals the preoccupation with judgment, and shows vv. 11-15 to be an expansion of the earlier brief account of final punishment in 11:18 ("the time came for the dead to be judged"). In both places, however, the reward of the righteous is mentioned or implied (so here, in the reference to the book of life). Strikingly, the same phrase "the small and the great" refers to all classes of believers in 11:18 and to all classes of unbelievers in 19:18, so the similar wording here may be an all-inclusive reference to both (as in 2 Chron. 15:13; Ps. 115:13; Jer. 16:6). The records **written in the books** refer figuratively to God's own memory, which never fails.

13 The future judgment is reiterated: **And the sea gave up the dead which were in it, and death and Hades gave up the dead which were in them; and they were judged, every one of them according to their deeds.** It is possible that the **sea** symbolizes the realm of evil (as elsewhere in Revelation; see on 13:1; 15:2), within which Satanic forces operate and which imprisons all unbelievers. If so, God now forces the authorities over this demonic realm to release their captives for judgment. **Sea** is placed in parallelism with **death and Hades**, which in 6:8 are probably images linked to demonic powers. As such, it prepares the way for the reference to the evil connotation of the sea in 21:1, which is to be "no longer" in the new creation. If deceased believers are included in the picture here, it is only because, until the final resurrection, though their spirits are with the Lord, their physical bodies still lie under the power of death and Satan (cf. 1 Cor. 15:50-57). The resurrected saints find refuge from judgment in the **book of life** (as implied in v. 15, on which see).

14 That **death and Hades were thrown into the lake of fire** probably means that, as the forces which held sway following the first, physical death, they are now ended and replaced by the eternal punishment in the lake of fire. It expresses the fact that unbelievers formerly held in the *temporary* bonds of **death and Hades** will be handed over to the *permanent* bonds of **the lake of fire**. Alternately, but less likely, is the view that the statement may reflect the fact that death and Hades can be seen not simply as spiritual locations but as actual demonic powers operating behind the physical realities of death (much as the beast and the false prophet can be seen as powers operating behind the physical realities of human government and religion). Death and Hades appeared together in 6:8 to identify the fourth rider (and his associate), who appears to be a personal, Satanic agent. If this view is correct, then 20:14 refers to the eternal punishment of Satan's demonic forces, which have previously held sway.

The lake of fire has already been defined as unending, conscious punishment for all who are consigned to it (see on v. 10; 14:10-11). Now it is also termed **the second death**. This shows that torment in the lake of fire is not physical death in the sense of annihilation but suffering that is primarily spiritual in nature (though including some kind of physical suffering), since Satan and his angels are exclusively spiritual beings. Corporeal suffering is likely included for unbelieving humans, at least in part because they suffer spiritually while possessing resurrected bodies, which never die physically. A figurative understanding of the second death is supported, not only by the incompatibility of a literal physical death with eternal suffering, as well as the obviously non-literal "lake of fire," but also by the analysis of vv. 4-6 above, where there was found to be a physical and spiritual resurrection, as well as a physical and spiritual death (see on vv. 4-6). According to 21:4, 8, physical death (the first death) will have "passed away," whereas the lake of fire, the second death, will last forever (cf. 14:10-11; 20:10). Part of the reality of suffering the second death is eternal separation from the presence of God in His city. The same categories of wicked people who will suffer this death are also said to dwell outside the heavenly city, while the righteous enjoy the blessings of participation in it (cf. 21:8 with 22:15; so also 21:27; 22:14-15, 19). Elsewhere the NT can also speak of a spiritual death which separates people from God (e.g., Luke 15:24, 32; Eph. 2:1; Col. 2:13).

15 The note of final judgment is rung once more for emphasis: **And if anyone's name was not found written in the book of life, he was thrown into the lake of fire**. This implies that all who are found written in the book of life are spared from the judgment, which 3:5 and 21:27 make explicit (cf. Dan. 12:1: "and at that time your people, everyone who is found written in the book, will be rescued"). What is it about the book of life which spares them? The fuller title for the book is "the book of life of the Lamb who has been slain" (13:8; and 21:27 has "the Lamb's book of life"). The life granted them in association with the book comes from their identification with the Lamb's righteous deeds and especially with His death, which implies likewise that they are identified with His resurrection *life* (cf. 5:5-13). They do not suffer judgment for their evil deeds because the Lamb has already suffered it for them: He was slain on their behalf (so especially 1:5 and 5:9; see on 13:8). The Lamb acknowledges before God all who are written in the book (3:5) and who are identified with His righteousness and His death.

Suggestions for Reflection on 20:11-15

On God's character and His judgment. How do the holiness and justice of God compel Him to judgment? What is the meaning of the statement in the commentary that God judges both to punish the rebellious and to vindicate His people? Does a lack of understanding of God's holiness and justice lie behind our modern tendency to downplay the reality of the everlasting conscious punishment set in motion by the great white throne judgment?

The new creation and the church perfected in glory: in the new world to come, the community of the redeemed will be completed, perfected, inviolable, and glorious because God's consummated, glorious presence will reside among them forever, whereas the unfaithful will be excluded from such blessing (21:1–22:5)

This section could be divided into two parts, 21:1-8 and 21:9–22:5, though it is preferable to discern at least three sub-units within the larger segment, on the basis of introductory vision phraseology: 21:9-21; 21:22-27; and 22:1-5, given also that there are shifts of theme at just the points where the introductory vision formulas occur. 21:1 follows on the heels of 20:11, where "earth and heaven fled away" from the presence of God, and "no place was found for them." Whereas in 20:12-15 judgment follows the cosmic destruction, in 21:1-8 a new creation follows the prior cosmic dissolution and replaces the old order. The theme of the new creation dominates ch. 21, though the preceding idea of judgment is not altogether forgotten (21:8, 27). 21:9–22:5 primarily recapitulates 21:1-8. The purpose of this last major segment is to highlight the contrast between the church imperfect (chs. 1–3) and the church perfected. Whereas chs. 1–3 focus on the churches' weaknesses throughout the old age, one intention of 21:9–22:5, in contrast, is to foresee primarily the church in her perfected state for all eternity. The purpose of the contrasts with the sins of the church and those of Babylon, and the ultimate purpose of the entire segment, is to exhort believers in the present to persevere through temptations to compromise so that they may participate in the consummated glory of the perfected church.

The new creation will be where the faithful will experience the salvation blessing of intimate communion with God, but the unfaithful will be excluded from this blessing (21:1-8)

1 And I saw a new heaven and a new earth; for the first heaven and the first earth
passed away, and there is no longer any sea. 2 And I saw the holy city, new Jerusalem, coming down out of heaven from God, made ready as a bride adorned
for her husband. 3 And I heard a loud voice from the throne, saying, "Behold, the
tabernacle of God is among men, and He shall dwell among them, and they shall
be His people, and God Himself shall be among them, 4 and He shall wipe away
every tear from their eyes; and there shall no longer be any death; there shall no

longer be any mourning, or crying, or pain; the first things have passed away."
5 And He who sits on the throne said, "Behold, I am making all things new." And
He said, "Write, for these words are faithful and true." 6 And He said to me, "It is
done. I am the Alpha and the Omega, the beginning and the end. I will give to
the one who thirsts from the spring of the water of life without cost. 7 He who
overcomes shall inherit these things, and I will be his God and he will be My son.
8 But for the cowardly and unbelieving and abominable and murderers and immoral persons and sorcerers and idolaters and all liars, their part will be in the
lake that burns with fire and brimstone, which is the second death."

1 The first thing John sees is **a new heaven and a new earth**. The reason he sees a new cosmos is that **the first heaven and the first earth passed away**. The Greek word translated "new" is *kainos,* which usually indicates a newness in quality or essence rather than time (in which case *neos* is normally used; see further below). The first creation was impermanent, but the second will last forever (on the first-second and old-new distinction elsewhere in Revelation and the Bible see on 20:6). This points to the transformation of the fundamental physical structure of the creation. That "there shall no longer be any night" (22:5; cf. 21:25) indicates another difference, especially in contrast to Gen. 8:22: "While the earth remains . . . day and night shall not cease." Despite the discontinuities, the new cosmos will be an identifiable counterpart to the old cosmos and a renewal of it, just as the body will be raised without losing its former identity.

The allusions to Isaiah behind the phrases in 21:1, 4-5 (see below) are also best understood as prophecies of the transformation of the old creation instead of an outright new creation *ex nihilo.* It should not be assumed, however, that a renewal means that there will be no literal destruction of the old cosmos, just as the renewed resurrection body does not necessitate the analogous notion with regard to the physical body. That new creation follows the pattern of Christ's resurrection is demonstrated by the exegetical link between new creation and resurrection (also alluding, as in 21:1, to Isa. 65:17-18) in Paul (2 Cor. 5:14-17; Col. 1:15-18; cf. Eph. 1:20 with 2:6-15) and in Revelation itself (see on 1:5 and 3:14). Strikingly, Paul likewise sees in Rom. 8:18-23 the renovation of the corrupted creation inextricably linked to the resurrection of the children of God.

John focuses on the role of the redeemed saints in the new creation. This is apparent in that the vision of 21:1–22:5 is primarily dominated by various figurative portrayals of the glorified community of believers. Whereas 3:14 has pointed to the beginning of fulfillment of the new creation prophecy of Isa. 43:18-19 and 65:17 in Christ's resurrection, the same Isaiah allusions here and in vv. 4-5 are applied to the church, most probably in its glorified state, though including more than that, as the references to a new heaven and earth indicate.

John describes what he is seeing in the words of Isa. 65:17 and 66:22 (which is a virtual repetition of 65:17). Isa. 65:16-18 prophesies a restoration of Israel in a new earth and heaven where joy and gladness will prevail, in contrast to the old earth characterized by weeping and crying. Isa. 66:22 speaks of the permanence of the new heaven and earth, as opposed to the temporary nature of the old. Israel's return from Babylon fulfilled this prophecy only in an extremely limited and incomplete sense, leaving its final fulfillment long in the future. Through His death and resurrection, Christ began the establishment of the new Jerusalem (see on 3:14, where He is described as "the Beginning of the creation of God"), and this prophecy has been inaugurated throughout the church age, as people believe in Christ and become part of a "new creation" (2 Cor. 5:17; similarly Gal. 6:15).

21:1 asserts that the inaugurated Isaiah prophecy will be fulfilled consummately at some future time. The vision does not describe features of the church age *prior* to the end, since the conditions portrayed emphasize the absence of every form of visible and invisible threat to the *entire* redeemed community, in both its spiritual and physical aspects (e.g., 21:1, 4, 8, 27; 22:3, 5).

The passing away of the old world is described additionally by the phrase **and there is no longer any sea**. Elsewhere in Revelation, the **sea** represents

> the origin of cosmic evil (especially in the light of OT background; see 4:6; 13:1; 15:2; 16:3),
> the unbelieving, rebellious nations who cause tribulation for God's people (13:1; Isa. 57:20; cf. Rev. 17:1-2, 6),
> the place of the dead (20:13),
> the main arena in which the world's idolatrous trade takes place (18:11-19), and
> a literal body of water, part of the old creation (5:13; 7:1-3; 8:8-9; 10:2, 5-6, 8; 14:7).

The use here is likely a summarizing statement about how the various nuances of the sea throughout the book relate to the new creation. Therefore, it encompasses all of the above five meanings. That is, when the new creation comes, there will no longer be any threat from Satan, threat from rebellious nations, or death ever again in the new world, so that there is no room for the sea as the place of the dead. There also will be no more idolatrous trade practice using the sea as its main avenue. Even the perception of the literal sea as a murky, unruly part of God's creation is no longer appropriate in the new cosmos, since the new cosmos is to be characterized by peace. However, there will be a lake of fiery punishment (20:10, 14-15), but it will be located enigmatically outside the geographical perimeters of the new heavens and earth (21:27; 22:15). Just as there must be an eternally consummated form of the new creation in which God's people dwell, so must there be an eternally consummated form of a realm of punishment in another dimension where unbelievers dwell.

While all the above meanings of "sea" are in mind, the allusion to Isaiah 65 and the immediate context suggest a focus on the sea as representing figuratively the threat of evil and tribulation for God's people, a threat which no longer exists in the eternal state. The assertion that **there is no longer any sea** is further explained in v. 4, "and there shall no longer be any death." The close parallels show that the latter develops the former. The evil nuance of the sea (included in the above five aspects) metaphorically represents the entire range of afflictions which formerly threatened God's people in the old world. The allusion to Isa. 65:17 in vv. 1 and 4b and to Isa. 65:19 in v. 4b confirms the preceding explanation. In Isa. 65:16-19 and 51:10-11 the emphasis is not on the passing away of the material elements of the old world but on God's doing away with the "former troubles" (65:16) due to oppression during captivity, so that "there will no longer be . . . the voice of weeping and the sound of crying" (65:19).

This conclusion is supported by recognizing particularly the echo from Isa. 51:10-11 noted briefly above. This passage metaphorically equates the removal of the waters at the Red Sea deliverance to the removal of sorrows at the consummation of the ages (see further on v. 4). The absence of the sea may represent an element of escalation in the new creation, in contrast even to the pre-fall cosmos, which contained seas within it. This is true regardless of whether "sea" is understood literally or figuratively, though the above discussion shows that in all likelihood it is figurative for old world threats. This means that the presence of a literal sea in the new creation would not be inconsistent with the figurative "no sea" in 21:1.

2 The new world that v. 1 portrays as replacing the old is now called

the holy city, new Jerusalem. John uses the words of Isa. 52:1b ("Jerusalem, the holy city") to describe what he sees. This holy city, Isaiah prophesied, will be restored through the coming of the One who announces the gospel (52:7) in a latter-day deliverance from captivity and restoration to God's presence (52:11-12). The command to Zion "to clothe yourself in your beautiful garments" (52:1a) forms the basis for the picture of the bride adorning herself with jewels in Isa. 61:10, which in turn forms the basis for this verse, which describes the new Jerusalem as **made ready as a bride adorned for her husband.** The fact that this Jerusalem is called **new** alludes to Isa. 62:1-2, which states that Jerusalem "will be called by a new name" at the time of its end-time glorification. Already in 3:12, identification with Christ's new name has been seen as essentially the same as identification with God's name and the name of the new Jerusalem. All three names refer to the intimate, latter-day presence of God and Christ with their people, as expressed in vv. 3-4 (see also 14:1-4). Although for John the new creation has already been inaugurated (see on 3:14), and elsewhere the NT sees the new, invisible, heavenly Jerusalem as beginning to replace the old (Gal. 4:26-31; Heb. 12:22), the visionary words **I saw the holy city, new Jerusalem, coming down out of heaven from God** expresses the consummation of that reality.

Thus, the city is **made ready as a bride adorned for her husband**, fulfilling Isaiah's prophecy (62:1-5) that Jerusalem will be like a bride married to God. Isaiah foresaw rejoicing by those the Lord would clothe at the time of Israel's final restoration. The similar allusion in Rev. 19:7-8 about God's intimacy with His redeemed people clarifies further that the bride is a metaphor for the saints. Throughout Revelation, the verb "make ready" or "prepare" (Greek *hetoimazō*) refers to God's actions, not human actions (so 9:7, 15; 12:6; 16:12). So also here the intimate union of God and His people, and possibly His vindication of them, is a prophetic decree which v. 2 pictures as being fulfilled in the future. To be **made ready as a bride adorned for her husband** conveys the thought of God's preparation of His people for Himself. Throughout history, God is forming His people to be His bride, so that they will reflect His glory in the ages to come (so Eph. 5:25-27), which the following context of Revelation 21 develops (cf. 2 Cor. 11:2).

Isaiah's prophecy finds its fulfillment not in physical Israel but in the church as the continuation of true Israel, for Rev. 3:12 shows that both Jewish and Gentile believers (in the Philadelphia church) are included in the new Jerusalem, and 21:10-14 will reveal that the names of the apostles appear alongside those of the tribes of Israel in the new city's structure. The woman of 12:1 (representing the community of faith in its suffering existence on earth) is an anticipation of the completed bride of v. 2, now finally secure from any dangers and residing in the midst of God's perfect, full presence. Isaiah 61–62 serves as the background to both portrayals.

The image of the city, therefore, is likely figurative, representing the fellowship of God with His people in an actual new creation.

3 The introductory phrase **and I heard a loud voice from the throne, saying** has appeared earlier in almost identical form at 16:17 and 19:5. The announcement could come from the cherubim (as the following phrase refers to God in the third person), or possibly from God. The voice in v. 3 provides elaboration of the city and marriage metaphors of v. 2. These pictures are explained to describe the intimate communion which God and His people will have with one another: **Behold, the tabernacle of God is among men, and He shall dwell among them, and they shall be His people, and God Himself shall be among them**. The image of God's tabernacling over Israel at Sinai and in the wilderness as connoting a marriage relationship has already been observed as part of the background for the marriage of the Lamb and His bride in 19:7-8 (on which see for the background in Ezek. 16:8-10). This reflects the prophetic promise of Ezekiel 43:7 that in the days of the new temple God "will tabernacle (or dwell) among the sons of Israel forever."

An even more specific allusion is to Ezek. 37:27, which picks up the promise of Lev. 26:11-12 that a final time of restoration will come when God Himself will tabernacle or make His dwelling in the midst of Israel, who will be His people and He will be their God. Already Rev. 7:15 has understood the prophecy of Israel's restoration in Ezek. 37:27 as fulfilled by Gentile as well as Jewish Christians (see on 7:15). Paul, quoting Lev. 26:12, teaches that the tabernacle is already present in preliminary form in the church (2 Cor. 6:16), but John here sees its completed fulfillment in the new creation. The OT prophecies without exception speak of a singular "people" (Greek *laos*) among whom God will dwell. Rev. 21:3 (contrary to NASB) changes the prophetic singular to plural "peoples" *(laoi)* in order to make obvious that the prophecies originally focusing on Israel have been fulfilled in "every tribe and tongue and people and nation" (so 5:9; 7:9), though the latter are seen as an expanded continuation of true Israel. Zech. 2:10-11 anticipates this verse in foreseeing an ethnic expansion of the boundaries of true Israel by identifying "many nations" as "My people," an identification always used elsewhere in the OT for Israel.

God promised to Abraham that the nations were to be blessed only through the blessing of His Israelite seed (Gen. 12:1-3; 17:2-8; 26:24; Gal. 3:16). Ezek. 47:14 also bases Israel's eternal inheritance of the land and temple on the Abrahamic promise, and Ezek. 47:22-23 affirms that the only way Gentiles will be able to share in the promised inheritance of the new temple and land will be to become part of Israel: Gentile "aliens . . . shall be to you [Israel] as the native-born among the sons of Israel; they shall be allotted an inheritance with you among the tribes of Israel." It is certainly clear NT doctrine that Gentiles do not partake of Israel's OT promises by becoming a part of old ethnic Israel's theocratic society. Revelation, like Paul (Gal. 3:16, 29), reveals that the nations are able to share in true Israel's redemptive blessing by means of trusting in Jesus, the true seed of Abraham and the only authentic Israelite, who died and rose for Jew as well as Gentile. All those represented by Jesus, the ideal king and Israelite, are themselves considered part of true Israel and share in the blessings He receives (see, for instance, on 2:17; 3:7, 9; 7:4-8; 12:1-2, 5, 17).

Only Jews were allowed to enter the old tabernacle, and among them only the priests. However, now in v. 3 the divine presence is not limited by the physical boundaries of an Israelite sanctuary, since not only all believing Israelites, but all peoples experience God's intimate tabernacling presence. Jew and Gentile have not only been united in Christ but have also gained the status of priests serving before God's presence (20:6; 22:3-4). This is therefore the first hint that there is no literal temple in the new Jerusalem, a fact which is explicitly stated in 21:22, where the ultimate redemptive-historical reason for the absence of a physical temple building is that God and Christ are the final, enduring form of the temple, to which the physical OT temple always pointed.

4 In this new creation, God's people will no longer experience any of the forms of suffering characteristic of the old creation: **and He shall wipe away every tear from their eyes; and there shall no longer be any death; there shall no longer be any mourning, or crying, or pain**. When this occurs in the future, it will be a fulfillment of prophecy from Isa. 25:8: "the Lord God will wipe tears away from all faces" (see also on Rev. 7:17). Both Isa. 35:10 and 51:11 predict that at the time of Israel's full restoration to God the people will experience "everlasting joy" and "gladness" because they will be protected from their former sufferings of "sorrow and sighing," which will have fled away. It is more than coincidental that only one verse earlier in Isaiah 51 the prophet reflects on the first exodus, when God caused the sea to dry up (Isa. 51:10), comparing

the first deliverance to the latter-day deliverance of God's people, even as the eradication of the sea in Rev. 21:1 removes all barriers to the final fulfillment of God's fellowship with His people in vv. 2-4. The subsequent similar sayings that "there shall no longer be any curse" (22:3) and that "there shall no longer be any night" (22:5) also indicate that none of the evils and threats of the old world can hinder the saints from fully enjoying the consummate presence of God. The "curse" (see 22:3) of death and its associated sufferings, which were introduced in the first Eden, will be removed in the last Eden. The conclusion of v. 4 that **the first things have passed away** again fulfills Isaiah's prophetic utterances, "Do not call to mind the former things. . . . Behold, I will do something new" (Isa. 43:18-19), "For behold, I create new heavens and a new earth; and the former things shall not be remembered or come to mind" (Isa. 65:17). V. 1 has introduced the theme of the first heaven and earth passing away, which is reiterated in its parallel expression in v. 4.

5 The theme of the new creation coming in its finality is continued in vv. 5-8. The speaker here (**And He who sits on the throne said**) is undoubtedly God. The first divine statement, **Behold, I am making all things new**, draws again from Isaiah (as did vv. 1, 4, alluding to chs. 43, 65, and 66): "Behold, I will do something new" (Isa. 43:19; cf. Isa. 66:22). In 2 Cor. 5:17, Paul sees the same Isaiah prophecy (Isa. 43:18-19 and 65:17) beginning to be fulfilled through Christ's death and resurrection. John adds the word **all** to highlight the consummate fulfillment of the prophecies. This does not suggest salvific universalism, but rather that all the people of God, along with the heavens and the earth, will be transformed into a new creation. The present tense (**I am making**) does not refer to the present time of the church age, but enforces the certainty that the future new creation will occur.

God commands John: **Write, for these words are faithful and true**, which is rooted in Isa. 65:16 (for a similar description of Christ rooted in the same verse, see 3:14). In Isaiah the Hebrew text refers to God as the God of truth (Hebrew *amen*), whose blessing in 65:17 is to be that of the new creation which He will bring about. The promise is **faithful and true** because, as Isaiah prophesied, God Himself is the One who, without doubt, will carry it out. The statement of v. 5b, **these words are faithful and true**, will be repeated verbatim in 22:6, which functions as a conclusion to the new creation promises of 21:1–22:5 and has therefore probably been formed from the same Isaiah 65 wording.

6 The next word John hears is the Greek word *gegonan,* literally

they, that is, the prophetic promises, **are done** (NASB "It is done"). This underscores the climactic nature of the fulfillment of the prophecies woven throughout vv. 1-5, though uppermost in mind is the "new things" of v. 5. Similarly, 16:17 uses almost the same expression (*gegonen,* "It is done") to indicate final fulfillment. However, there it stresses the fulfillment of God's promises to judge the ungodly. Here, it designates the accomplishment of the new creation, which was set in motion at the cross when Jesus cried, "It is finished!"

The divine speaker identifies Himself as **the Alpha and the Omega, the beginning and the end**. Along with the similar expressions, "the first and the last, the beginning and the end" (22:13), these titles describe God's control over history, especially as He brings it to an end in salvation and judgment. Use of the first and last letters of the alphabet was an ancient figure of speech for the totality of everything in between. Vv. 5-6 are only the second time in the entire book where God is explicitly quoted. The first is in 1:8. Both there and here the title **the Alpha and the Omega** occurs. That this title appears at the beginning of the book and at the end is fitting and cannot be coincidental. That is to say, the totality of all the events narrated and portrayed between 1:8 and 21:6 lie under God's absolute sovereignty, as does all history prior to the writing of Revelation. Therefore, the two titles in 21:6 refer to God's absolute sovereignty over all events in history. On this basis, the readers are assured that just as God brought the first creation into being, just as certainly He will bring it to conclusion.

The remainder of v. 6 shows that the two titles provide assurance that God in His absolute sovereignty is able to give blessings to His redeemed people: **I will give to the one who thirsts from the spring of the water of life without cost**. The same pattern appears in 22:12-13, where similar divine titles provide assurance that Christ will "render to every man according to what he has done" climactically at the end of history. This includes both blessing (21:6; 22:17) and judgment (21:8; 22:15). The allusion here is first to Isa. 49:10, "They will not hunger or thirst. . . . For He who has compassion on them . . . will guide them to springs of water." The living waters, which portray eternal life, have their origin in God and the Lamb (so 22:1, 17 and similarly Jer. 2:13; Ps. 36:8-9; Joel 3:18; John 4:10; 7:38). This is the life of eternal fellowship with God and Christ reserved for those who have maintained their faith in the Lamb's atoning death and their testimony to His redemptive work. The allusion is also to Isa. 55:1 (which itself develops the thought of Isa. 49:10): "Ho! Every one who thirsts, come to the waters;

and you who have no money come, buy and eat. Come, buy wine and milk without money and without cost." In line with the preceding context of vv. 1-5, the church fulfills the restoration prophecy of Isa. 49:10 and 55:1, whereas Jewish tradition interpreted Isa. 49:10-13, 21 to be fulfilled only by Jewish exiles (e.g., *Pesikta Rabbati* 31).

7 V. 7 defines God's people, the recipients of the new creation promises, as overcomers. Overcomers conquer through refusal to compromise their faith, even though it may cost them their lives (see further on 2:28-29). V. 7 summarizes the reception of the multiple promises in vv. 1-6 by saying **He who overcomes shall inherit these things**. The purpose of this verse, and of the whole of 21:1–22:5, is to encourage the true Christian to persevere through hardship in order to inherit the fullness of God's blessings. All the promises made to the overcomers in the letters section (chs. 2 and 3) are fulfilled in this closing section, which describes the new Jerusalem and the eternal reward of the believer:

"the tree of life, which is in the Paradise of God" (2:7 and 22:2),
inclusion in the new temple (3:12 and 21:22ff.),
participation in "the new Jerusalem, which comes down out of heaven from my God" (3:12 and 21:2, 10),
God's name written on one's person (3:12 and 22:4),
one's name written in the book of life (3:5 and 21:27),
bright garments as a reward (3:5 and 21:2, 9ff.; cf. 19:7-8),
a bright stone and a luminary, whether star or lamp (2:17, 28 and 21:11, 18-21, 23; 22:5, 16),
consummate reigning with Christ (2:26-27; 3:21 and 22:5), and
exclusion from the second death (2:11; 21:7-8).

These blessings are summed up in the one promise of v. 7, **I will be his God and he will be My son**. This fulfills a prophetic promise given to David for the One who would come from his house, "I will be a father to him and he will be a son to Me" (2 Sam. 7:14); "He will cry to me, 'Thou art my Father.' . . . I also shall make him My first-born, the highest of the kings of the earth" (Ps. 89:26). The promise is applied according to the concept of corporate representation by which Christ represents His people. This is in line with the individual and corporate fulfillment of Ps. 2:8-9 already mentioned in Rev. 2:26-27. Since saints are in Christ (cf. 1:9), they will inherit fully what Christ inherits (note the eternal reign of Christ in 5:12-13 and 11:15 and that of the saints in 22:5).

8 On the other hand, those who are not included among God's people will be excluded from His presence, which is itself judgment. The list of vices is a summary of typical sins which the author has been warning the churches not to commit. The **cowardly and unbelieving** are not just unbelievers in general but more precisely those who have claimed to belong to the covenantal church community but who, driven by fear of humans rather than of God, have compromised in the face of persecution. The **cowardly** are those in the visible community of faith who have "turned back" in the holy war with the world and have not been courageously faithful in the battle against the beast. **Cowardly** (Greek *deilos*) suggests an empty faith, since it is followed by **unbelieving** (cf. Matt. 8:26 and Mark 4:40, where the same word is followed by references to those having little or no faith).

Also included in the list are the **abominable and murderers and immoral persons and sorcerers and idolaters and all liars**. These sins have reference to pagan unbelievers, as well as some within the visible covenant community. Indeed, forms of fornication and idolatry common in the pagan world were threats testing the faith of some in the churches (see on 2:14, 20-21 for this in general and for the meaning of "immorality," Greek *porneia*). These vices are associated with a context of idol worship in both the OT and the NT (see on 9:21 for references), as well as in Revelation. For **abominable** as a reference to idolatry, see on 17:4-5. Such sins either form part of the activities involved in idolatry, or, as abominations, they actually become acts of idolatry themselves (for idolatry involving murder [child-sacrifice] see also Ps. 106:36-38). **Murderers** include those agents of the beast and the harlot who have persecuted the saints who refuse to cooperate with the economic system of idolatry (13:15; 17:6). **Immoral persons** (or "fornicators," Greek *pornoi*) may be linked to cult prostitution, which was also associated with pagan temples and worship as far back as ancient Canaanite culture. Likewise, sorcery and magic were often practiced in connection with idolatry (**sorcerers and idolators**) long before NT times (see Lev. 19:26-29; Deut. 18:9-11, the latter of which associates child sacrifice and sorcery). Interestingly, 2 Kgs. 9:22 links "harlotries" and "witchcrafts" with Jezebel (for further on Jezebel see on 2:20-24).

The catalog of sins concludes with **all liars**. The phrase likely points to a focus on those whose Christian profession is betrayed either by compromising behavior or false doctrine. The word refers to false apostles in 2:2 and to ethnic Jews falsely claiming to be God's true people in 3:9. John uses the phrase elsewhere to refer to those within the church whose behavior or doctrine contradicts their purported profession of faith in Jesus (1 John 2:4, 22; 4:20; 5:10).

An almost identical list of sinners as in v. 8 occurs in 22:15, and a similar but abbreviated catalog concludes ch. 21 (v. 27). Both these subsequent lists end with "lying," which emphasizes the judgment on those whose apparent Christian profession is contradicted by their lifestyle or false doctrine. Tit. 1:16 expresses a similar thought: "they profess to know God, but by their deeds they deny Him, being detestable and disobedient, and worthless for any good deed." Possibly also in mind are those who promote the lie about the beast (13:12-15). In 3:9, lying is associated with being a devotee of Satan (likewise in 2:9), the original liar (John 8:44) and deceiver (Rev. 12:9; 20:2-3). Rev. 14:5 says the genuine people of God persist in not lying, which refers to perseverance in professing the truth about the gospel and in not compromising. The absence of liars in the new world shows that the coming order will exist on a higher moral level than even the pre-fall cosmos, where the Satanic liar was allowed entrance.

The wicked have their part **in the lake that burns with fire and brimstone, which is the second death**. This figurative portrayal of punishment indicates that there is additional suffering beside the anguish of separation from God (for discussion of **fire and brimstone** and the eternal nature of **the second death** see on 14:10-11; 19:20; 20:10). As observed already, the antitheses of old vs. new and first vs. second contrast the partial and temporal with the consummate and eternal (see on 20:5-6). So here **second death** refers to a perfected and eternal punishment. It is noteworthy that the new creation is what the righteous alone "inherit" (v. 7). The unrighteous, whether pseudo-Christians or the non-Christian world in general, will not inherit the coming new world and therefore will not reside within the borders of the new cosmos. 21:1–22:5 shows that the blessing of God's presence permeates the entire new creation, whereas 21:8 and 27 indicate that God's judgment is revealed outside the confines of the new world (see also 22:15). Even though the second death is a perfected punishment, those who suffer it do so outside the geography of the new universe, since we have already been told that "there shall no longer be any death . . . or pain" in the new order of things (v. 4).

Suggestions for Reflection on 21:1-8

On the nature of the new creation. How many people think about the afterlife as an ethereal eternal existence, some even picturing saints floating forever on clouds? Unfortunately, this is not only the perspective of nominal believers; even many true Christians sometimes have such a view. But the new creation is described in these verses as a fundamental physical transformation of the old creation and its renewal. At this time, the body will be raised from the dead and be gloriously transformed. This bodily transformation is pictured in our passage as the church becoming a perfected bride. The saints to whom John is writing now see their future in the plan of God. The new creation is a place of righteousness and holiness (2 Pet. 3:13). The making of all things new refers primarily to the inhabitants of the new creation as well as its physical topography, in which they will live. Thus, the destiny of God's people is to live with resurrected physical bodies in the newly transformed physical environment of the eternal new earth and heavens. This a quite a different picture of the eternal afterlife than many of God's people have.

On identification and intimacy with God. Various images used here speak of the closest possible relationship between God and His people. The church is prepared as a bride. Christians are given a new name, which identifies them with the character of God and as being in a marriage relationship with Him. God tabernacles or dwells intimately with His people. If this is our destiny, how should we be preparing ourselves for it? How often is the subject of intimacy with God addressed among Christians? How often do we dwell on Paul's teaching in Eph. 5:22-33, which uses marriage as the closest human analogy to our relationship with Christ? How can we cultivate intimacy with God in a society so devoted to pleasure, superficiality, and over-activity? God wants our true desire and joy to be in Him, and His promise of intimately tabernacling with us is the way we will enjoy and desire Him forever. What are we doing now to cultivate our desire for Him? Ps. 119:111 is one way that we can grow in our joy and desire for God: "I have inherited Thy testimonies [God's word] forever, for they are the joy of my heart." Reading and meditating on God's word leads to thinking God's thoughts after Him, which increases our joy in Him.

On the promises of God. The commentary notes how all the promises of God made to the earthly saints in the letters are fulfilled in this section. How important it is to reflect on the fact that God is faithful to His promises and that it is not unspiritual or selfish to suppose He rewards those who seek and serve Him, since that is His will for us. God does want our best. How often do we list the promises He has already fulfilled for us and use that as an encouragement for the fulfillment of all that is yet to come?

In the world to come the community of the redeemed will be inviolable, completed, perfected, and glorious because of the consummated, glorious, and eternal presence of God (21:9–22:5)

The remainder of the vision can be divided in the following thematic manner: initial view and appearance of the city (21:9-14), the measurements of the city (21:15-17), the material of the city (21:18-21), the internal features of the city (21:22-27), and the symbols of the presence of God in the city (22:1-5).

Broadly speaking, the structure of the city is based on the vision in Ezekiel 40–48, which prophesies the pattern of the latter-day temple (chs. 40–44) and the arrangement of the city and the land around it (chs. 45–48). This section further interprets the yet-future fulfillment of Ezekiel by collapsing temple, city, Garden of Eden, and new creation into one end-time picture portraying the one reality of God's communion with His people. Ezekiel does identify temple, city, and land as representing the same entity, while not merging them in quite the same way. He understands both the land and the temple (37:25-28), as well as the city (48:35), as signifying God's everlasting dwelling place. The fact that here the bride is equated with the city (vv. 2, 10) shows that a literal city is not being described.

Rev. 21:9–22:5 recapitulates 21:1-8 and amplifies the picture there of God's consummate communion with His people and their consummate safety in the new creation. The bride of v. 2 is developed in vv. 9-11; the tabernacle of v. 3 is developed in vv. 22-24; the water of v. 6 is developed in 22:1; and the fate of the sinners of v. 8 is developed in v. 27. The reference to the "beloved city" under attack (20:9) suggests that the city portrayed in 21:9–22:5 is revealed in hidden, partial form throughout the church age as a result of Christ's redemptive work (see on 20:9). The segment here reveals the perfected form of the city. The extensive parallels noted between vv. 1-8 and 21:9–22:5 argue against the contention of some that the second section portrays an earlier earthly millennium, while the first section describes the eternal state.

The initial view and appearance of the city: the glorious presence of God establishes the inviolable and completed community of the redeemed (21:9-14)

9 And one of the seven angels who had the seven bowls full of the seven last plagues, came and spoke with me, saying, "Come here, I shall show you the bride,

the wife of the Lamb." [10] And he carried me away in the Spirit to a great and high
mountain, and showed me the holy city, Jerusalem, coming down out of heaven
from God, [11] having the glory of God. Her brilliance was like a very costly stone,
as a stone of crystal-clear jasper. [12] It had a great and high wall, with twelve gates,
and at the gates twelve angels; and names were written on them, which are those
of the twelve tribes of the sons of Israel. [13] There were three gates on the east
and three gates on the north and three gates on the south and three gates on
the west. [14] And the wall of the city had twelve foundation stones; and on them
were the twelve names of the twelve apostles of the Lamb.

9-10 The recapitulation begins in vv. 9-10, where John is shown **the bride, the wife of the Lamb . . . the holy city, Jerusalem, coming down out of heaven from God.** These are almost identical phrases to those in v. 2. Here the hearing and then seeing pattern observed elsewhere in Revelation recurs (see, e.g., on 5:5, where he hears about a "lion" and in 5:6 sees a "lamb"). In v. 9, he hears that he will see the bride; in v. 10, he sees the holy city, which interprets what he heard. Just as vv. 3-8 explain the meaning of the bride and city of vv. 1-2, so similarly does 21:11–22:5 expand the significance of the bride and city in 21:9-10.

The wording in vv. 9-10 is almost identical to that in 17:1, 3, which introduced Babylon. This underlines the contrast between the two women, the harlot Babylon and the bride of the Lamb. The immoral and unfaithful conduct of Babylon is contrasted with the faithfulness of the bride. Both cities (Babylon and the new Jerusalem) are adorned with gold, precious stones, and pearls (17:4; 21:18-21). The harlot's adornment (17:4) represents worldly economic forces which, in collusion with the state, are persecuting Christians and seducing them to compromise their faith (for the economic focus see also 14:8; 17:2; 18:16). The adornment of the bride, however, represents her faithful works or her vindicated condition as a result of those acts (see further on 19:7-8; 21:2). Her adornment with precious foundation stones of the temple (vv. 18-21) shows that God Himself has provided her redemption, which reflects the glory of the new creation (see similarly 1 Cor. 3:5-15 and 1 Pet. 2:4-7). The parallelism of the two portrayals suggests that the portrait of the bride in this section is symbolic rather than literal, as was that of Babylon (e.g. 17:9, 12, 15, 18). Both pictures are introduced by the word "show" (Greek *deiknymi*), which in 17:1 clearly refers to a symbolic vision. The harlot represents human culture in opposition to God, while the bride represents not a literal place or city but the redeemed community faithful to God (see above on v. 3). There is a literal new cosmos, but the point of the vision is to focus on exalted saints as the central feature of the new order (see further on v. 1 above).

John is **carried . . . away in the Spirit**, as was Ezekiel (3:12, 14; 11:1; 43:5). As in Ezekiel's case, John's repeated rapture into the realm of the Spirit further underscores his prophetic commission and authority (see on 1:10; 4:2; and especially 17:3, where allusions to the Ezekiel commissions occur in the same manner). It is significant that this verse combines Ezek. 43:5 ("And the Spirit lifted me up") with Ezek. 40:2 ("In the visions of God He brought me into the land of Israel, and set me on a very high mountain; and on it . . . there was a structure like a city"). This combination indicates beyond doubt that the vision in Rev. 21:11ff. is to be identified with the blissful vision of the future temple in Ezekiel 40–48. The angel transports John to a **great and high mountain** where also the new city-temple is likely located. OT prophecy, as in Ezekiel, understood the coming Jerusalem to be situated on a high mountain (see also Isa. 2:2-3; 4:1-5; 25:6–26:2; Mic. 4:1-2).

What Ezekiel saw was to happen in the future is still seen by John as set for the future. Both visions prophesy the same reality of the final, permanent establishment of God's presence with His people. However, the different pictorial details in John's vision serve to interpret the Ezekiel vision.

11 The theme of God's presence with His people, briefly developed in vv. 1-8, is introduced here and runs throughout 21:11–22:5. The city of v. 10 is further described as **having the glory of God**. In the new creation, God's presence will not be limited to a temple structure with the people outside the structure, but the people themselves will be both the city and the temple in which God's presence resides (so vv. 2-3, 12-14). In the light of the clear allusions to Isaiah 40–66 in 21:1–22:5, the reference to **the glory of God** must derive from Isa. 58:8 and 60:1-2, 19, where there is the prophetic portrayal of "the glory of the Lord" residing in the latter-day Jerusalem (for allusions to Isaiah 40–66 in ch. 21, see for instance the references to Isa. 65:17-19 in vv. 1-2, 4, Isa. 54:11-12 in v. 19, and Isa. 60:19-20 in v. 23). Note particularly Isa. 60:1-3: "Arise, shine; for your light has come, and the glory of the Lord has risen upon you. . . . The Lord will rise upon you. . . . And nations will come to your light, and kings to the brightness of your rising." Whereas v. 2 speaks of the bride adorned for her husband, this verse clarifies that the clothing is in fact God's glory, which is none other than His awesome, tabernacling presence with His people. This confirms our conclusion above that v. 3 interprets the city and marriage pictures of v. 2 as referring to the intimate communion which God will have with His people.

The city's **brilliance was like a very costly stone, as a stone of crystal-clear jasper**. This continues the Ezek. 43:5 allusion from the previous verse. Ezekiel saw the glory of God coming into the new temple, and the earth shone with His glory (43:2; cf. also 43:4-5). This glory is compared to a **brilliance** or "star" (Greek *phōstēr*), the same word used in the Greek OT (LXX) in Dan. 12:3, where God's latter-days people "shine brightly like the brightness of the expanse of heaven." It is also used by Paul when he speaks of God's people shining like stars as they hold forth the word of life to an unbelieving world (Phil. 2:15). Zechariah prophesied that God would be a wall of fire around the latter-day Jerusalem and would cause His glory to dwell in her midst (Zech. 2:5). Note how Christ is referred to metaphorically as "the bright morning star" (22:16; cf. 2:28). As in 4:3, when John attempts to describe God's glory, the closest he can come is to refer to it as radiant precious stones. This partly accounts likewise for the similar descriptions of the city in vv. 18-21.

12-13 The city is now described as having **a great and high wall, with twelve gates, and at the gates twelve angels; and names were written on them, which are those of the twelve tribes of the sons of Israel**. The wall represents the inviolable nature of the city's (= the renewed covenant community's) fellowship with God, as implied by v. 27 and 22:14-15. This alludes to Isa. 26:1-2: "In that day this song will be sung in the land of Judah: 'We have a strong city; He sets up walls and ramparts for security. Open the gates, that the righteous nation may enter . . .'" (LXX: "He will make salvation a wall and a surrounding wall").

That the first part of the city structure which John sees is a wall and gates continues the allusion to Ezekiel 40–48 begun in vv. 9-11. The multiple gates of the Ezekiel temple in ch. 40 and the twelve gates of the city in Ezek. 48:31-34 are merged into one group of twelve gates arranged around the one city-temple of John's vision (and note the repeated reference to temple walls in Ezekiel 40–43, e.g., 40:5). One angel is stationed at each gate, a feature not found in Ezekiel. In this respect, they are comparable to the angels of the churches and the twenty-four elders, who represent the true people of God, the true Israel (e.g., see on 4:4). Both this vision and that of Ezekiel feature four groups of three gates facing north, east, south, and west, and in both each gate has one of the names of the twelve tribes of the sons of Israel written on them.

14 In addition to the twelve gates in the wall, **the wall of the city had twelve foundation stones, and on them were the twelve names of the twelve apostles of the Lamb**. The number twenty-four (the sum of the twelve tribes and the twelve apostles) has also occurred in the scene of the twenty-four elders in 4:3-4. In both scenes, the glory of God shines like jasper (4:3; 21:11), suggesting that the twenty-four elders of ch. 4 are angelic beings representing the sum of all God's people of both covenants (see on 4:4). The number twenty-four may also be based collectively on David's organization of the cult of temple servants into twenty-four orders of priests (1 Chron. 24:3-19), twenty-four Levitical gatekeepers (1 Chron. 26:17-19), and twenty-four orders of Levites who were commissioned (1 Chron. 25:1-31) to prophesy "in giving thanks and praising the Lord" (25:3). Jewish tradition (the Qumran pesher on Isaiah 54) explained the precious stones of Isa. 54:11-12 as symbols of the twelve priests and the heads of the twelve tribes who represented Israel before God. The Chronicles background is enhanced here because of the temple context throughout ch. 21 and the Jewish "priestly" interpretation of Isa. 54:11-12 in association with the number twenty-four. The integration of the apostles together with the tribes of Israel as part of the city-temple's structure (the structure prophesied in Ezekiel 40–48) confirms further our assessment in 7:15; 11:1-2; and 21:2-3 that the multiracial Christian church will be the redeemed group who, together with Christ, will fulfill the Ezekiel prophecy about the future temple and city. This is in line with other NT passages where the whole covenant community forms a spiritual temple in which God's presence dwells (1 Cor. 3:16-17; 6:19; 2 Cor. 6:16; Eph. 2:21-22; 1 Pet. 2:5).

It is noteworthy that in v. 14 the apostles are part of the foundation, whereas the tribes are part of the gates in the wall built on the foundation. One might have expected the opposite, since Israel preceded the church in redemptive history. However, the reversal figuratively highlights the fact that fulfillment of Israel's promises has finally come in Christ who, together with the apostolic witness to His fulfilling work, forms the foundation of the new temple, the church, which is the new Israel (so also Eph. 2:20-22).

In 3:12 Christ promised that the one overcoming, whether Jewish or Gentile Christian, will become "a pillar in the temple of My God . . . and I will write on him the name of My God and the name of the city of My God, the new Jerusalem, which comes down out of heaven from My God, and My new name." That was the first substantial hint in the book that later, in ch. 21, the concepts of city and temple would be collapsed into the one concept of the presence of Christ and God with His people (see further on 3:12 and 22:4). The present argument that the city and the temple of ch. 21 are one and the same is in line with our prior identification of temple, altar, outer court, and holy city as the Christian community in 11:1-2 (on which see), and is consistent with our previous identifications of the church with Israelite prophecies, names, and institutions (see on 1:6-7, 12; 2:9, 17; 3:9, 12; 5:10; 7:2-8, 14-15).

Suggestions for Reflection on 21:9-14

On the church as God's temple. The city in these verses is introduced in conscious contrast to the harlot Babylon of ch. 17. It is presented, by means of very clear allusions to the prophet, as the fulfillment of Ezekiel's vision of the new temple. The primary characteristic of the city-temple is the presence of God's glory, which is an escalation of God's glorious presence in Israel's old temple. The very same OT prophecies of the end-time temple alluded to in Rev. 21:3 are also appealed to by Paul in 2 Cor. 6:16 (Lev. 26:12 and Ezek. 37:27) in supporting the notion that the church is the temple of God. The practical conclusion that Paul draws from the church being the beginning form of the temple is found in 2 Cor. 7:1: "Therefore, having these promises [the temple promises being uppermost in mind], beloved, let us cleanse ourselves from all defilement of flesh and spirit, perfecting holiness in the fear of God." Priests in the OT were to keep temples clean from defilement. Now that believers are part of the temple in this age, they are to keep the temple from sinful defilement. To the degree that we do this, God's glorious tabernacling presence will shine increasingly through us. There is likely some hint of this notion here, though ch. 21 does picture the consummated form of the purified and glorious temple in the final, eternal new creation. When sin infects believers now, they (being part of the temple) should see the tension between their present lives and this vision of the pure, consummated, and glorious temple. What implications does the contrast to the harlot have for the present conduct of the church in its albeit imperfect inaugurated manifestation of God's temple on earth? Have we lost an emphasis on holiness previous Christian generations may have had? To what extent does the world see the glory and character of God in us now? We are His image, a people placed in the end-time temple to reflect His glory.

The measurements of the city: God's permanent presence secures and guarantees the perfected inviolability of the redeemed community (21:15-17)

15 And the one who spoke with me had a gold measuring rod to measure the
city, and its gates and its wall. 16 And the city is laid out as a square, and its length

is as great as the width; and he measured the city with the rod, fifteen hundred miles; its length and width and height are equal. [17] And he measured its wall, seventy-two yards, according to human measurements, which are also angelic measurements.

15 Vv. 15-17 continue to present an amplified version of vv. 1-8. The image of an angelic figure measuring parts of the city-temple with a measuring rod is a further allusion to Ezek. 40:3-5. Throughout Ezekiel 40–48, an angel measures parts of the temple complex. In the LXX, the verb "measure" (Greek *diametreō*) and the noun "measure" (Greek *metron*) appear about thirty times each. The angel **had a gold measuring rod to measure the city, and its gates and its wall.** The measuring portrays the security of the inhabitants (Jew and Gentile alike, as is evident from 3:9-12 [on which see]; 21:12-14, 24-26; 22:2) against the harm and contamination of unclean and deceptive people (so 21:27; 22:14-15). This measuring of the city-temple here figuratively represents the placing of God's boundaries around the city by which it is protected from harm and from the entrance of any form of evil. The measuring is thus the same as the sealing of believers pictured in 7:3 (on which see). In 11:1-2, the angel also measures the temple, which there represents the church as the place of God's dwelling on earth. In that case, however, only the inner court (representing the security of the believers' place with God) is measured, whereas the outer court (presenting the vulnerability of the church to attack and persecution) is left unmeasured. Now, however, the entire temple is measured, for in the consummated form of the temple God's people are protected in every way, spiritually as well as physically (cf. v. 4).

16 John next sees that **the city is laid out as a square** and sees an angel who **measured the city with the rod, fifteen hundred miles**, literally "twelve thousand stadia." The city is actually cubic, since **its length and width and height are equal**. Ezek. 45:2 likewise asserts that the temple complex the prophet is to measure will be a square. The Holy of Holies in Solomon's temple was also cubic (1 Kgs. 6:20, which is probably alluded to here). The altars in the tabernacle of Moses were square (Exod. 27:1; 30:2), as was the priest's breastpiece (Exod. 28:16). The repeated mention of measuring in this verse underlines the main point that God is promising that His presence will be with His people. This is highlighted by the allusion to Zech. 2:2, where the angel goes "to measure Jerusalem, to see how wide it is and how long it is." This in turn is connected with the assurance that God will be a wall of fire around the city and the glory in her midst (Zech.

2:5). God's return to Jerusalem is also connected with His measuring of the temple itself as a part of measuring the city (Zech. 1:16), so that the ideas of the end-time temple and the end-time Jerusalem overlap. The idea is likely that God's glorious and fiery presence in the temple will spread and cover the entire city, thus sanctifying the city as a big sacred temple space.

The equal measurement of twelve thousand stadia of each of the city's dimensions reinforces the figurative idea of the completeness of God's people found earlier in the twelve tribes and apostles; it is twelve multiplied by one thousand, a number of completeness. The figurative nature of the number is indicated by the height of the wall, recorded as "one hundred and forty-four cubits" (= approximately two hundred and sixteen feet) in v. 17, which is not in proportion with the height of the city if the "twelve thousand stadia" in v. 16 is taken literally. It is possible that the calculation is of the wall's thickness instead of height, but two hundred and sixteen feet is only a fraction of the width needed for the base of a wall which is fifteen hundred miles high. The enormous size of the city (the perimeter being approximately five and a half thousand miles, taking one Greek stadion to be two hundred yards) makes it about the same size as the then-known Hellenistic world, thus further suggesting that the temple-city represents the redeemed of all nations.

If John is indicating that the measurements of vv. 15-17 include all redeemed humanity (not just Jewish believers in a restored Jerusalem), this might provide the key to understanding John's simplifying and abbreviating use of details from the Ezekiel 40–48 vision, together with his universalization of some of the elements from that vision. The city's measurements are not physically literal or architectural, nor are they nationalistic symbols of a restored temple and Jerusalem, as appears to be the case in Ezekiel 40–48, but rather symbolize the inclusion of the Gentiles as part of the true temple and Jerusalem. Some commentators have noticed that the portrayal in vv. 16-17 has striking similarity to ancient descriptions of the city of Babylon. If the similarity is drawn intentionally, then the purpose would be to contrast the true, everlasting city with the false, impermanent city of Babylon. The latter tries to ascend to heaven by its own ungodly, human effort (Gen. 11:4; Rev. 18:5), while the other will be established by descending from heaven from God. Such a direct contrast with the Babylonian system is likely because of the explicit link in vv. 9-10 to the introduction to the vision of Babylon's destruction in 17:1, 3. As seen above, the purpose of the link was to contrast various features of Babylon with the new Jerusalem (see on vv. 9-10).

17 The angel now measures the wall to be one hundred and forty-four cubits. The only other occurrences of the number appear in 7:4-9 and 14:1, 3, where the 144,000 are not a remnant of ethnic Jews at the very end of the age, but represent the totality of God's people throughout the ages, who are viewed as true Israelites (see on 7:4-8 and 14:1). The wall and its dimensions here represent the same reality, since vv. 12-14 have equated the essential parts of the "great and high wall" (v. 12) with the representatives of the entire people of God. Some have observed that the number in 7:4-8 and 14:1, 3 is the result of the square of the twelve tribes of Israel (= one hundred and forty-four) multiplied by one thousand (another number of completeness) to equal 144,000. This figurative reckoning is confirmed from v. 16, where each of the four sides of the cubic new Jerusalem equals twelve thousand stadia, the sum of which equals 144,000, which have just been seen in v. 16 to represent the completeness of God's people. Now the immediately following statement in v. 17 that the wall equals one hundred and forty-four cubits echoes the 144,000 as the complete number of God's people. This results in a nice figurative proportional relationship between the numbers of vv. 16 and 17, whereas a literal reckoning results in a bizarre and unnatural picture (see above on v. 16). The figurative nature of the number is indicated by the fact that one hundred forty-four cubits would be hopelssly out of proportion to a city fifteen hundred feet high. Literalists have suggested that the measurement is only of the wall's thickness, not height, but if the wall were measured in the same way the city was, then its height, width, and length would have been measured (as also in Ezek. 40:5 and 42:20). Furthermore, the wall's height is likely in mind since in the OT height was a characteristic feature noted about walls in order to emphasize the security they provided for cities (e.g., Deut. 3:5; 28:52). Here and in v. 16, the dimensions of cubits and stadia should not be given contemporary equivalents in imperial or metric measurements, since the figurative nature and intention of the original numbers become distorted.

Understanding the verse this way explains the following phrase **according to human measurements, which are also angelic measurements**. One might assume that a human standard of measurement would be different than an angelic standard. But John's visions come with two levels of meaning. On one level, he sees visions composed of earthly pictures which he can understand, whether it be lions, human figures, books, or someone measuring a wall in an ordinary manner. However, the purpose of the visionary images is to reveal to John the deeper meaning or heavenly truths which the earthly images symbolize (1:20; 4:5; 5:6, 8; 7:13-14;

11:4, 8; 14:4; 16:13-14; 17:9, 12, 15, 18; 19:8; 20:2, 14; 21:8, 22). In 1:20, we are told that the (literally seen) stars are to be symbolically understood as angels and the (literally seen) lampstands as churches. Here likewise we are given a literal picture or vision (the human measurements) followed by its interpretation (**which are also angelic measurements**). John sees in a vision someone measuring the dimensions of a city wall according to the standard of human measurement with which he would be familiar from everyday life, though the literal calculation would have probably left the readers confused, since the size of the walls would be nonsensically out of proportion to the rest of the city's measurements. But, in order to alleviate the confusion over the literal disproportion, John then adds that this vision of "human measurement" is to be understood more deeply according to its symbolic, heavenly, or "angelic" meaning. This reminds the readers that if their comprehension of his vision is limited only to a surface level (the physically literal meaning), they will misunderstand it.

Suggestions for Reflection on 21:15-17

On the significance of the measurements of the temple. The commentary presents evidence that the measurements of the city wall (based on Ezekiel 40–48) emphasize the security of the city, that is, the security of God's glorified covenant community in the eternal new creation. Nothing can harm them any more, nor can any evil threaten them. This is already true of the church's spiritual relationship to God, as we have seen from the significance of the "measuring" (also based on Ezekiel 40–48) of the church as the invisible temple in 11:1. But remember that the physical side of the church's temple — our physical existence — is not protected in this age, since we must witness by sacrificing our bodies in various ways (see on 11:2). In what ways are we willing to sacrifice ourselves to witness to Christ in order that others may come into a secure relationship with God? When the time of witness is over in the final new cosmos, both our spirits and our bodies will be finally protected forever, which is pictured in this passage and is our hope.

The material of the city: God's permanent presence guarantees the perfected security of the redeemed community and causes it to reflect His glory (21:18-21)

18 And the material of the wall was jasper; and the city was pure gold, like clear
glass. 19 The foundation stones of the city wall were adorned with every kind of

precious stone. The first foundation stone was jasper; the second, sapphire; the third, chalcedony; the fourth, emerald; [20] the fifth, sardonyx; the sixth, sardius; the seventh, chrysolite; the eighth, beryl; the ninth, topaz; the tenth, chrysoprase; the eleventh, jacinth; the twelfth, amethyst. [21] And the twelve gates were twelve pearls; each one of the gates was a single pearl. And the street of the city was pure gold, like transparent glass.

18-20 Now follows a description of the material which composes the city wall and its foundations and gates, as well as a parenthetical comment about the material of the entire city itself. The figurative description continues to emphasize the truth presented in vv. 12-17: the entire people of God redeemed throughout the ages will experience complete security in the new creation because of God's perfect and consummate presence there. The city represents the fellowship of God's people with His everlasting presence (see on 3:12; 11:1-2; 21:2-7, 9-17; note Isa. 52:1ff.; 62:1-5; Ezek. 48:35; Zech. 1:16; 2:2-5), and the wall (see on v. 12) represents the secure boundaries He has placed around this fellowship. The statement that **the city was pure gold, like clear glass** points back to the description in v. 11 of the city as shining like crystal with God's glory. The city is made of pure gold (v. 18), like Solomon's temple, which was overlaid with gold (1 Kgs. 6:20-22). Use of precious stones in 4:3 (especially jasper; cf. v. 11) to portray the divine glory points to the same use here. The material of the wall thus reflects the glory of God's holiness.

The wall's foundation stones **were adorned with every kind of precious stone**. This develops the theme of the bride's adornment introduced in v. 2. The list of the twelve jewels is based on the twelve stones in the high priest's breastpiece of judgment (Exod. 28:17-20; 39:8-14). Eight of the stones in the Exodus lists are repeated here, and the others are rough equivalents. Written on each stone of the breastpiece was the name of one of the twelve tribes (Exod. 28:21; 39:14), so that when the priest entered the temple to perform his duties, he represented all the tribes of Israel. The vision of Rev. 21:19-20 thus applies to the foundation stones of the new city-temple the jewels representing the tribes of Israel in Exodus. This means that the tribes of Israel, God's preeminent people in the OT, are being equated with the apostles as the foundation of the new city-temple, since the names of the twelve apostles are written on those foundations (v. 14). The apostles are thus the paramount representatives of true, end-time Israel, the church (see on v. 14).

The jewels of Aaron's breastpiece are transferred to the foundation stones of the new Jerusalem because the breastpiece was meant to be a miniature version or replica of the Holy of Holies, being made of the same colored material and in the same square shape. The Holy of Holies was itself constructed on the pattern of the heavenly Holy of Holies (Exod. 25:40; Heb. 8:5). Strikingly, 1 Pet. 2:5 also affirms that believers, even in this age, are simultaneously building stones, a temple, and priests: "you also, as living stones, are being built up as a spiritual house for a holy priesthood." It is not coincidental that already in v. 16 there has been an echo of the Holy of Holies described in 1 Kgs. 6:20, where the length, width, and height of the Holy of Holies are equal in measurement (the arrangement of the jewels along a quadrangle in connection with the four points of the compass suggests that they symbolized n a foreshadowing manner the glory of the entire new creation). A similar logic based on the description of the precious stones of the breastpiece in Exod. 28:17-20 likely lies behind the establishing of the foundations of Solomon's temple complex with large precious stones, a depiction which, together with Exodus 28 and Ezekiel 40–48, also forms part of the model for Rev. 21:18-20 (see 1 Kgs. 5:17; 7:9-10). In this respect, it is relevant to note that the precious stones of the upper part of the temple in 1 Kings 7 form four rows together with the sculptured cedar, which is similar to the four rows of stones in Exodus 28. The latter temple of the new world will be eternally secure and even more glorious than the former temple of the old world, which did not last.

The precious stones appear in fact to compose the foundations (**The first foundation stone was jasper; the second, sapphire** . . .), which fits nicely with the parallel in v. 21 that "each one of the gates was a single pearl." This is supported by the parallel in Isa. 54:11-12, "Your foundations I will lay in sapphires. . . . I will make your battlements of rubies . . . and your entire wall of precious stones." The precious stones of Isaiah's city are metaphorical for the presence of God yielding permanent peace, which the people inhabiting the latter-day Jerusalem will experience, as the context in Isa. 54:11-17 indicates. Isa. 54:4-8 refers to Israel as a wife who in the end times will be restored to the Lord as her husband, just as Rev. 19:7-9 and 21:2 picture the church as an end-time bride. In the light of Isaiah 54, the precious stones, together with the foundation, wall, and gates of the city in Revelation 21, are best seen as symbolizing the permanent safety of God's people together with God's glorious presence (e.g., vv. 2-4, 10-11, 18-23).

Both Exodus and Isaiah link God's glory with the precious stones, so that it may be deduced that one of the purposes of the variously colored precious stones in this section (e.g., vv. 11, 23; 22:5) is to reflect the luminous divine glory. 4:3, 9-11 confirms this, where three of the precious stones are mentioned and their significance is directly linked with emphasizing God's glory. The meaning of such metaphors in ch. 21 is that the saints are qualified to be in God's glorious presence, which protects them forever because God is incorruptible. The stones also indicate that 21:1–22:5 portrays the institution of a new creation like the first creation preceding the sin of humanity, since some of the same stones were found in the garden of that first creation.

Also relevant to the imagery of vv. 18-21 is the similar portrayal in Ezek. 28:13 of Adam (figuratively compared to the king of Tyre) as a beautiful, perfect being:

> You were in Eden, the garden of God;
> Every precious stone was your covering:
> The ruby, the topaz and the diamond;
> The beryl, the onyx and the jasper;
> The lapis lazuli, the turquoise and the emerald;
> And the gold, the workmanship of your settings and sockets,
> Was in you.

Ezekiel 28 more directly inspired the picture of the harlot Babylon in 18:16, which is contrasted with the holy bride here (see on 18:16). The idea is that though what was fallen in Adam remains (in the person of the harlot), God has by contrast restored a people for Himself to complete the mandate Adam failed to fulfill. The new Jerusalem is thus a restoration of God's original creation. If the king of Tyre's former privileged position and subsequent fall is described with the imagery of Adam's blessed state and subsequent fall, it is unlikely to be coincidental that the bride in ch. 21 is described as a building adorned with precious stones. In Ezek. 28:12-16, the stones are inextricably linked with perfect righteousness, a likely connotation also of the stones in ch. 21, which is confirmed from the fact that v. 27 highlights that no uncleanness and sin will be allowed into the new Jerusalem, in fulfillment of OT prophecy (Isa. 52:1; 60:20-21; Ezek. 44:9; Zech. 14:21).

21 Each one of the gates was a single pearl. The twelve gates, like the twelve foundation stones, are drawn from the OT language of the twelve tribes of Israel and here represent the latter-day people of God, the church. The language is again figurative, for it is hard to conceive of a pearl big enough to be a gate proportional to a wall approximately two hundred and sixteen feet high. Just as the "city was pure gold, like clear glass" (v. 18), so also **the street of the city was pure gold, like transparent glass.** This emphasizes further the similar feature in v. 18; the words **pure** (Greek *katharos*) and **transparent** (Greek *diaugēs*) underscore the city's ability to reflect the luminous glory of God. The phrase **the street of the city** occurs elsewhere in the book only in 11:8 ("the street of the great city"), where it is the place the bodies of the witnesses lay. The point of repeating it here is to underscore that the street where the witnessing community was portrayed as slain is replaced by the street where they are to be glorified (so likewise "street" in 22:2). The addition of **pure gold, like transparent glass** probably highlights further that the apparently inglorious path they trod in the old city has been transformed into a dazzlingly glorious one in the new city.

Suggestions for Reflection on 21:18-21

On the significance of the materials of the city. The presentation of the city as composed of precious stones reveals it to be the fulfillment of Aaron's breastpiece and, in turn, of the end-time symbolism of the Holy of Holies (which the breastpiece represented). The Holy of Holies was the very place of God's dwelling in the OT, a place which pointed to His cosmic dwelling in the final new creation. Whereas under the old covenant the presence of God was purely localized, it now extends throughout the new creation. In addition, allusion is also made to the portrayal by Ezekiel of Adam as the original bearer of the precious stones. Now Christ, the new Adam, through the church, fulfills the mandate of God to extend Eden where the first Adam failed. It is important to understand the significance of the material of the city in order to understand its nature and purpose.

The internal features of the city and its inhabitants: the glorious presence of God and the Lamb will elicit the response of praise by true believers in contrast to pseudo-believers, who will be excluded forever from God's presence (21:22-27)

22 And I saw no temple in it, for the Lord God, the Almighty, and the Lamb, are its
temple. 23 And the city has no need of the sun or of the moon to shine upon it, for
the glory of God has illumined it, and its lamp is the Lamb. 24 And the nations shall

walk by its light, and the kings of the earth shall bring their glory into it. [25] And
in the daytime (for there shall be no night there) its gates shall never be closed;
[26] and they shall bring the glory and honor of the nations into it; [27] and nothing
unclean, and no one who practices abomination and lying, shall ever come into
it, but only those whose names are written in the Lamb's book of life.

22 As with vv. 9-21, so vv. 22-27 amplify the initial vision of the new Jerusalem in vv. 1-8 and thus explain it further. The OT prophesied that a temple would be rebuilt along with the renovation of Jerusalem. However, John says **I saw no temple in it**. It is not that John saw no temple but only that he saw no physical or architectural temple. Rather, **the Lord God, the Almighty, and the Lamb, are its temple**. The end-time temple described by Ezekiel in four chapters (40–43) is now summarized and interpreted in this one phrase. Jeremiah prophesied that "they shall say no more, 'The ark of the covenant of the Lord.' And it shall not come to mind, nor shall they remember it, nor shall they miss it, nor shall it be made again. At that time they shall call Jerusalem 'The Throne of the Lord,' and all the nations will be gathered to it" (Jer. 3:16-17). Haggai (2:9) prophesied that the latter glory of God's house would be greater than the former, and Isaiah (65:17-25) spoke of God restoring Jerusalem within the setting of a new heavens and a new earth.

In light of this verse, John would probably have understood these OT prophecies as fulfilled in the future by God and Christ replacing the former physical temple and ark with their glorious habitation, which will make the glory of the former temple fade in comparison. This replacement was inaugurated with Christ's first coming, when He referred to His own resurrection as the rebuilding of the temple (John 2:19-22; Mark 14:58; 15:29). Analogously Matt. 21:42; Mark 12:10-11; Luke 20:17-18; and Acts 4:11 ("very corner stone") picture Christ as the "chief corner stone" of the temple (cf. also Rom. 9:32-33), and Eph. 2:20 portrays Christ as the "corner stone" of the temple, which there represents the church. The inauguration is also hinted at in Rev. 1:12-20, where the resurrected Christ is the central feature of the heavenly temple scene (walking in the midst of the temple-church lampstands). It is clear that this verse does not refer to a *literal* temple, whether the OT temple or a supposedly rebuilt end-time temple. In fact, the same is true elsewhere in Revelation. "Temple" (Greek *naos*) generally refers to the *heavenly* temple of the present: 7:15 (though there including the consummation); 14:15, 17; 15:5-6, 8; 16:1, 17. In 11:1-2, the "sanctuary" identifies the people of God who are already members of God's temple in heaven even though still living on earth, yet still identified as "the temple of God." "Temple" also refers to the temple of God's presence which dominates the new age of the future (3:12; 7:15; 11:19). Indeed, the only other use of the actual phrase "temple of God" outside 11:1 appears in 11:19, with reference to the end-time *heavenly* temple, which is the same reality that protected believers during their sojourn on earth. Believers dwelling in the final form of God's temple, as depicted here in 21:10-22, will be protected forever from every kind of danger. In this light, Christ's earlier promise to each overcomer in 3:12 that He will make him "a pillar in the temple of My God" might better be translated "a pillar in the temple *that is* My God" (appositional genitive).

The equation of God and the Lamb with the temple correlates well with our earlier figurative equation of redeemed saints with the new Jerusalem and its foundations, gates, and wall. Throughout 21:9–22:5 John excludes most of the detailed descriptions of the Ezekiel 40–48 temple and its ordinances because he understands it as fulfilled in God's and Christ's presence rather than in the form of a physical and localized structure. This expectation of a non-architectural temple is, for the most part, a break with Judaism, which consistently affirmed the hope of a final, material temple structure on a scale greater than any before.

23 And the city has no need of the sun or of the moon to shine upon it. John continues to speak figuratively. There may or may not be a literal sun and moon in the new cosmos, but the point here is that God's glory is incomparable in relation to any light-giving sources, whether in the old or new creation. God's glory is sufficient to make the city (= the saints) resplendent. The wording of the entire verse is based directly on Isa. 60:19: "No longer will you have the sun for light by day, nor for brightness will the moon give you light; but you will have the Lord for an everlasting light, and your God for your glory." The reason (**for**) the city of John's vision did not need the luminaries is that **the glory of God has illumined it, and** that **its lamp is the Lamb.** John substitutes for Isaiah's last phrase about the glory of God **its lamp is the Lamb**, thus underlining the deity of the Lamb alongside that of God. In the new creation, God's presence alone is what beautifies God's people and satisfies their every need. This is also a fulfillment of Ezek. 43:2, 5, where the prophet sees from the vantage point of the future that "the earth shone with his glory" and that "the glory of the Lord filled the house" (= the temple).

24-26 The allusions to Isaiah 60 continue in these verses:

"And nations will come to your light, and kings to the brightness of your rising. . . . The wealth of the nations will come to you" (Isa. 60:3, 5).	**And the nations shall walk by its light, and the kings of the earth shall bring their glory into it** (v. 24).
"And your gates will be open continually; they will not be closed day or night, so that men may bring to you the wealth of the nations, with their kings led in procession" (Isa. 60:11).	**And in the daytime (for there shall be no night there) its gates shall never be closed; and they shall bring the glory and the honor of the nations into it** (vv. 25-26).

Isaiah 60 develops further Isa. 2:2, 5 (which also stands in the background of v. 24): "all the nations will stream" to Zion and devout Israelites will "walk in the light of the Lord." John sees that the pilgrimage of the nations to latter-day Jerusalem, which Isaiah foresaw, will in fact take place in the future new Jerusalem, which lies in view before his own eyes. The phrase **the kings of the earth shall bring their glory into it** must be interpreted from the Isaiah background. Isa. 60:5-14 and 61:4-6 speak of the kings bringing their literal physical power and wealth to Israel. However, Isaiah 60 and its context portray the nations not merely bringing literal treasures to Israel, but also bringing themselves as worshipers of God. Isa. 60:6b says the nations will not only "bring gold and frankincense," but also "will bear good news of the praises of the Lord," as opposed to other rebellious nations which will perish (60:12). Similarly, Isa. 49:6 speaks of Israel as God's light to the nations and of His salvation, which will reach to the ends of the earth. Isa. 66:12 speaks of the glory of the nations coming to Israel as an overflowing stream, as God extends peace to her like a river. The glory spoken of in Rev. 21:24-26 focuses not on the literal wealth of nations, but is grounded in Isaiah's picture of glory in the form of praise arising to God from the nations, which then results in Israel's peace with them. Presumably, this refers to those formerly antagonistic but subsequently redeemed from among the nations who will submit to God, praise Him, and so become unified with redeemed Israel (see for instance Isa. 11:6-12).

Therefore, the reason that vv. 24-26 refer to the nations bringing glory and honor into the city is to highlight the fact that they are bringing not literal riches, but themselves as worshipers before God's end-time presence (so vv. 3-5). The **glory and honor of the nations** is grammatically a Greek genitive of source, meaning the glory and honor *arising from the nations,* and directed as praise toward God and the Lamb. This interpretation is supported by the observation that the phrase "glory and honor" (or "honor and glory") appears elsewhere in the book only in 4:9, 11 and 5:12, 13, where it refers without exception to praise of God and the Lamb. All the redeemed can bring into the new creation is their righteous acts (14:13; 19:8), which they continue to perform by praising God. It is these very righteous acts which reflect the divine glory, as a comparison of 19:7-8 with 21:2-8 and 21:9-27 reveals; only that which is clean and holy and thus reflects the glory of God will be admitted to the new Jerusalem. In support of this interpretation is Isa. 49:17-18 (a chapter already alluded to in v. 6), where those who enter Jerusalem are compared to "jewels" adorning a "bride"; the Septuagint identifies some of these people who will enter as Gentiles. Jewels, like the precious stones of the preceding verses, both reflect and represent the glory of God. Therefore, the nations no longer claim glory for themselves independently from God, as they formerly did in idolatrous allegiance to the beast, but acknowledge that all honor and glory belong only to God. There is a subtle contrast here with the kings of the old earth who brought their wealth into Babylon (ch. 18). The portrayal here is metaphorical; the depiction is that of nations now bringing everything they possess to God. The picture of riches signifies the absolute, wholehearted subservience of the nations to God.

The fact that the gates **shall never be closed** is underlined by the phrase **for there shall be no night there**, where "for" (Greek *gar*) is better rendered more emphatically as "indeed." The absence of night emphasizes the fact that the redeemed will be unhindered in having access to God's glorious presence. God's presence does not fully dwell in the fallen creation because evil resides there. The divine glory is now completely manifested, because there will be no more darkness or evil in the new world (cf. 22:5 for a fuller statement of the same truth). The statement is identical in meaning to the introductory expressions in vv. 1, 4 ("there is no longer any sea . . . there shall no longer be any death . . . any mourning, or crying, or pain") and to the concluding statements in 22:3 ("there shall no longer be any curse") and 22:5 ("there shall no longer be any night").

The nations and **the kings of the earth** likely include some who had persecuted God's people (for the former cf. 11:2; 18:3, 23; 19:15; for the latter cf. 1:5; 17:2, 18; 18:3). If so, they subsequently repented and will be allowed entrance to the city. The "nations" are twice seen in the book as composing the company of the redeemed (5:9; 7:9), and those mentioned here are presumably the same group. They are best identified with those in 5:9-10 who were purchased "from every tribe and tongue and people and nation," were made a kingdom, and reigned as kings throughout the church age (see on 5:9-10; 7:9 as well as on 1:5-6 and 20:4-6 for the concept of reigning in the church age). Converted kings are the subject, since the phrase "kings of the earth" is an expansion of "kings" from Isa. 60:3, 11 (see above).

Therefore, the perpetually open gates and the apparent ceaseless pilgrimage of Gentiles into the city throughout eternity are not intended to be understood literally, since it would not take a finite number of Gentiles an infinite eternity to enter the new Jerusalem. Likewise, there is no basis for seeing the entrance of the nations and kings into the city as suggesting a kind of universalism wherein non-elect peoples whose names are not written in the book of the Lamb will enter the new Jerusalem. Only the elect will come into the city, which is indicated by v. 27b, where the phrase "those whose names are written in the Lamb's book of life" clearly has its antecedent in the nations and kings who enter the city in vv. 24-26. Neither can the portrayal refer to some kind of deliverance from the lake of fire, since Revelation elsewhere views followers of the beast as suffering that punishment for eternity and not temporarily (cf. 14:10-11 and 20:10 with 21:8, 27; 22:14-15). This is supported by 22:11, which also contrasts ungodly people with godly people and views each as essentially permanently set in their respective ways. Furthermore, 22:18-19 speaks of the judgment of the impious in definitive and absolute terms.

In the light of the above analysis, it would be wrong to think that vv. 24-26 contains a literal depiction of nations residing outside the newly created city (or a millennial city on the first earth), in which redeemed Israelites already dwell, and then streaming in to join the Israelites. Though Isaiah 60 could be read this way, it is better to see John's use of the OT as emphasizing the consummated redemption of those from among the nations, which will happen simultaneously with the final redemption of Jewish Christians. Prophecy portrays the future with language which is understandable to the prophet and his contemporary readership. The prophetic language of Isaiah employs imagery corresponding to the social and cultural realities of his own day, which he could understand, to describe realities of the new creation that were to be fulfilled in ways he probably could not have fully imagined.

Bringing glory into the city in vv. 24 and 26 is spatial language, but it conveys a non-spatial notion. This is supported by recalling that the dimensions of the city in vv. 15-17 are spatial, but the meaning conveyed is non-spatial. Consequently, it would be incorrect to infer that the picture of people making a pilgrimage into the new Jerusalem means that there is a literal pilgrimage from outer spaces into the city's inner space. The point of the figurative picture is that the believing Gentiles will never be separated from open, eternal access to God's presence and that nothing evil can threaten such access. Whereas in the old world the gates of Jerusalem, and of all ancient cities, had to be closed at night to protect the inhabitants from unexpected intruders, the new city faces no such danger. Though direct entrance by humans to the tree of life was blocked by angelic beings throughout history (Gen. 3:24), at the end of history angels stand guard to ensure that people retain free access (22:14).

Finally, those who walk in the city's light are not separate in identification from the city itself, just as the woman and her children of ch. 12 were but different metaphorical ways of referring to the same reality of God's people. Likewise, the saints are pictured as the bride at the marriage feast, but also as invited guests (19:7-9). The cartoon poster of Uncle Sam portrayed him inviting Americans to enlist during the two world wars, yet he himself was America. Symbolism allows for such overlaps of identification.

27 Those not submissive to God will never enter the city of His presence: **nothing unclean and no one who practices abomination and lying, shall ever come into it**. This is the same group referred to in v. 8; the word **unclean** is added to stress the sin of idolatry and unfaithfulness to God (for the identification of abomination and uncleanness with idolatry see on 17:4-5). Included among these are people who may never have had association with the church, but the focus is on those who made profession of faith but contradicted it by their sinful lifestyles, which was the telltale sign that they were pseudo-believers and "liars" (see on v. 8). Those allowed to enter are those whose names are written in the Lamb's book of life. The phrase "book of life" appears five times outside v. 27 (3:5; 13:8; 17:8; 20:12, 15). In each case, as here, it is a metaphor referring to the elect saints, whose salvation has been determined and secured. Their names have been entered into the census book of the eternal new Jerusalem before history began. This alludes partly to Isa. 4:3: "he who is left . . . in Jerusalem will be called holy — everyone who is recorded for life in Jerusalem."

The **book** then is a picture of security in God's eternal city, and the phrase **of life** clarifies what kind of security is provided. Their names were **written in the Lamb's book of life** before the creation, which means that they were identified at that time as ones who would benefit from the Lamb's redemptive death. Therefore, they have been given the protection of eternal **life**, which comes as a result of the Lamb's death and His resurrection life. This prehistorical identification with the Lamb has protected them from the deceptions of the world which threaten to suppress their trust in the Lamb, and has enabled them to be ready to enter the gates of the city to enjoy the life for which they were destined (see on 13:8b for discussion of the phrase there, "written from the foundation of the world in the book of life of the Lamb"; see further also on 3:5).

The rhetorical situation must be kept in mind. John's intent in v. 27 is not merely to give information about future destinies, but to warn people in the churches at the time (and thus subsequently) by describing the final outcome of their choices and actions.

Suggestions for Reflection on 21:22-27

On the development in Scripture of the concept of the temple and its implications for us as believers living in the presence of God. The commentary presents the development of the biblical concept of the temple. In the OT, the temple was a physical reality. Christ refers to His body as a new temple. Believers are then referred to as a new temple, with Christ as the chief cornerstone. Finally, in these verses, the final form of the eternal temple is constituted by the presence of God in the midst of His people gathered from every nation. What links all this together is the presence of God. If that is the case, what are the implications for us as believers living in an inaugurated, but not fulfilled, spiritual temple? Are we aware of the presence of God in our midst? What does this mean for our understanding of the need for personal and corporate holiness? Do we truly conduct our daily lives as if we were living in His presence? How can this encourage us in the practice of prayer?

The garden, the river, and the inhabitants and luminary of the city: the consummate, glorious presence of God with His people ensures the eternal absence of any curse and establishes their everlasting roles of priests and kings in praising and reflecting His glory (22:1-5)

1 And he showed me a river of the water of life, clear as crystal, coming from the
throne of God and of the Lamb, 2 in the middle of its street. And on either side of
the river was the tree of life, bearing twelve kinds of fruit, yielding its fruit every
month; and the leaves of the tree were for the healing of the nations. 3 And there
shall no longer be any curse; and the throne of God and of the Lamb shall be in it,
and His bondservants shall serve Him; 4 and they shall see His face, and His name

shall be on their foreheads. [5] And there shall no longer be any night; and they shall not have need of the light of a lamp nor the light of the sun, because the Lord God shall illumine them; and they shall reign forever and ever.

1-2a Rev. 22:1-5 is the conclusion to all of ch. 21, and it continues the photographic blowup of the new Jerusalem in 21:9-27 with a last expanded view of the new Jerusalem, which was introduced in 21:1-7. The opening verse of ch. 22, **And he showed me a river of the water of life, clear as crystal, coming from the throne of God and of the Lamb** combines the prophetic picture of a spring or river of living water flowing out of latter-day Jerusalem and its temple, which appears respectively in Zech. 14:8 and Ezek. 47:1-9; see likewise Joel 3:18 ("a spring will go out from the house of the Lord"). Ezek. 47:9 even speaks of the life-giving property of the water: "so everything will live where the river goes." But these verses reach even further back to the description of the primeval garden in Gen. 2:10: "a river flowed out of Eden." In association with the first Eden's river, the "gold . . . the bdellium and the onyx stone" (Gen. 2:12) were features around one of the river's tributaries, which compares to the precious stones (cf. 21:18-20) surrounding the river of v. 1 (the **river of the water of life**). The **water of life** (which could also be translated "waters which are life" or "living waters") pictures eternal life (so v. 17) and has its origin in God and the Lamb, as the concluding clause (v. 1b) bears out.

As in Ezekiel 47, the living water flows from the temple, though now God and the Lamb are the temple (21:22). Though the Holy Spirit may be in mind (cf. John 7:37-39; see also Ezek. 36:25-27 and John 4:10-24), the water metaphor primarily represents the life of eternal fellowship with God and Christ, which is borne out by the way vv. 3-5 develop vv. 1-2. That the river is pure and the water **clear as crystal** indicates the purifying nature of the water. The water purifies people's sins, so that they may enter into the intimate presence of God, as portrayed in vv. 3-5 (so similarly vv. 14, 17). That the river flows down **the middle of its street** shows that the imparting of eternal fellowship with God is at the heart of the city's significance. The tree(s) of v. 2b (on which see below) then follow the pattern of Ezek. 47:12: "And by the river on its bank, on one side and on the other, will grow all kinds of trees for food." There is also a similarity to the prophecy of latter-day Zion in Isa. 35:6-10: "For waters will break forth in the wilderness . . . the scorched land will become like a pool, and the thirsty ground springs of water . . . and a highway will be there . . . and it will be called the Highway of Holiness . . . the unclean will not travel on it . . . but the redeemed will walk there, and the ransomed of the Lord will return, and come with joyful shouting to Zion . . . and sorrow and sighing will flee away." In addition to the unusual combination of the water metaphor with urban road portrayals, note the references to the unclean (cf. Rev. 21:27) and the return of the ransomed to Zion (cf. 21:3), where there will be no more sorrow (cf. 21:4; 22:3). The picture of the nations advancing on the city's main street may imply that they wade in the life-giving waters as they walk, just as Ezekiel did in his prophetic vision of the end-time temple (Ezek. 47:3-4).

2b And on either side of the river was the tree of life, bearing twelve kinds of fruit, yielding its fruit every month; and the leaves of the tree were for the healing of the nations. The scene is based on Ezek. 47:12 (see above), which itself is modeled partly on the garden and river of Gen. 2:9-10, so that both Ezekiel and Revelation envision an escalated reestablishment of the Garden of the first creation, in which God's presence openly dwelled. Even the decorative palm trees and cherubim portrayed as part of Ezekiel's temple (41:18-26) allude to the garden setting of Eden. The depiction in Ezekiel's temple was anticipated earlier in the Solomonic temple, which also included carvings of flowers (e.g., 1 Kgs. 6:18, 29, 32, 35; 7:18ff.). The allusion to Ezek. 47:12 supports a picture of trees growing on either side of the river, so that the singular "tree" of v. 2 is likely a collective reference to trees. And in any event, how could one tree grow on either side of the river? The absence of the article "the" (which would underline that a singular particular tree was being referred to) may point further to a collective meaning. The one tree of life in the first garden has become many trees of life in the escalated paradisal state of the second garden. But since these trees are all of the same kind as the original tree, they can be referred to from the perspective of their corporate unity as "*the* tree of life" (so Rev. 2:7), just as we might refer to a grove full of oaks as an oak grove. Interestingly, some passages in Jewish literature maintained a tension between an expectation of a singular tree of life and the plural trees of Ezekiel 47 (cf. *Tanhuma* Genesis, Parashah 1.18; *Tanna de-be Eliyyahu Rabbah* 93). Another feature of escalation is that, whereas the original paradise was only a small geographical part of the earthly creation, now the paradisal temple encompasses the entire geography of the new creation.

The living waters impart life because they come from God's presence, drawing His people into intimate communion with Him. The river of Ezek. 47:8-9, 12 heals and brings life to the world around it. The imagery of the river in Ezekiel 47 appears to fit into such a figurative portrayal, since similar OT imagery of restored Zion clearly employs water figuratively to signify the renewed life of the saints in their final reunion with God; cf. Isa. 35:6-9 (see above on vv. 1-2a) and Joel 3:18: "all the brooks of Judah will flow with water; and a spring will go out from the house of the Lord" (so likewise Isa. 41:17-20; 43:18-21).

The reference to the **tree of life** also shows that John understood the foreseen flourishing of the new cosmos in Ezek. 47:12 as the reestablishment of an eternal Eden (an escalated form of the original Eden, since it will be eternally incorruptible). Gen. 3:22, 24 refers to the tree of life: if Adam had been able to eat from it, he would have been able to live forever. Presumably, the tree there represented the presence of God, which could impart eternal life to all who would be able to enter into it.

The medicinal effects of the water and of the leaves of the tree that it nourishes here are not limited to the natural realm, nor even to privileged ethnic Israel, but are for all peoples throughout the world who have believed the gospel: **the leaves of the tree were for the healing of the nations.** Outside chs. 21–22, the only clear references to the "nations" as God's people occur in 5:9 and 7:9 (see also on 21:24-26 above). 5:9 explains best the meaning of the nations' "healing." The figurative picture of being healed by the leaves of the tree of life means that Christ was slain on behalf of the believing nations, so that they were released from the penal curse of their sins by His blood (cf. 5:9 with 1:5). Christ suffered death on their behalf in the present age, so that they would not have to suffer it in the age to come. Does the tree's fruit continue to heal throughout eternity even as it continues to produce fruit? The answer must be negative, since there will be no more death or pain to be healed from in the new creation (21:4). Just as the tears which God will wipe away do not refer to pains being endured throughout eternity, but rather describe a once for all relief from such pains (see 21:4; 7:16-17), so it is here. This shows another aspect of this escalation of Eden. John uses the imagery of Ezek. 47:12 to describe eternal realities beyond his comprehension. The tree could not literally yield fruit **every month**, for the very timing depends on a calendar based on solar days and lunar months, whereas there is no sun or moon in the new creation (21:23; 22:5). A total of twelve months of fruit-bearing, together with **twelve kinds of fruit**, reinforces the repeated multiples of twelve already used in the vision to highlight the fullness of redemptive provision and to link it with the number representing the fullness of God's people who benefit from it.

The worldwide extent of the paradisal city-temple

The city-temple revealed in chs. 21–22 encompasses the entirety of the newly created earth. Three reasons can be given:

Isa. 54:2-3 suggest the notion of an escalated new Jerusalem or end-time temple spreading out to the nations.

Uncleanness was to be kept out of the OT temple precincts, and 21:27 and 22:15 make it clear that uncleanness is to be kept out of the entire new creation.

John says in 21:1 that he saw "a new heaven and a new earth," and then in 21:2 and 21:9–22:5, he sees only a paradisal city-temple.

The new heaven and earth and the garden-city-temple probably interpret one another and refer to the same reality of the entire new heavens and earth. Isa. 65:17-18 (v. 17 is alluded to in Rev. 21:1) seem to equate the new heavens and earth with the renewed city of Jerusalem.

The basis for the world-encompassing nature of the new city-temple lies in the OT concept that the temple was a microcosmic model for the entire heaven and earth; cf. Ps. 78:69: "And He built His sanctuary like the heights, like the earth which He has founded forever." The jewels on the high priest's breastpiece, which were a small replica of the Holy of Holies, also symbolized the earthly or heavenly cosmos by pointing back to the stones of the original creation. The same jewels are now part of the new city-temple in ch. 21 (see on 21:18-20). The OT temple was the localized dwelling of God's presence on earth. In that it was meant to be a symbolic reflection of the creation as a whole, it pointed to the end-time goal of God's tabernacling throughout the whole creation, a theme that Rev. 21:1–22:5 seems to be developing.

At the same time, the idea of the new city-temple is related not only to the old temple, but (as is indicated by the presence of the precious stones) can be traced back to the Garden. There are indeed hints that the Garden of Eden was the archetypal temple in which the first man worshiped God:

Eden was where Adam walked and talked with God, as did the priests in the temple.

In Gen. 2:15 God places Adam in the Garden to "cultivate" it and "keep" it. These two verbs (Hebrew *ʿabad* and *šamar*) and their cognate nouns are also used of priests keeping the service of the tabernacle (Num. 3:7-8; 8:25-26; 18:5-6; 1 Chron. 23:32; Ezek. 44:14). Adam is thus presented as the archetypal priest who serves in and guards God's first temple.

When Adam failed in his duty and was expelled from the Garden, two cherubim took over his priestly role: they "guarded" the way to the tree of life (Gen. 3:24). The same cherubim reappear guarding the ark of the covenant in the Holy of Holies.

The tree of life was probably the model for the lampstand placed directly outside the Holy of Holies.

That the Garden was the first temple is also suggested by the wood and stone carvings that gave the temple a garden-like appearance (1 Kgs. 6:18, 29, 32, 35; 7:18-20).

The entrance to Eden was from the east, which was also the direction from which one entered the tabernacle and the later temples of Israel.

Not only was Adam to guard the temple, he was to subdue and fill the earth (Gen. 1:28). It is plausible to suggest he was to extend the boundaries of the Garden until it extended throughout the whole earth. What he failed to do, Revelation presents Christ as having finally done. The Edenic imagery beginning in 22:1 reflects an intention to show that the building of the temple, which began in Genesis 2, will be completed in Christ and His people and will encompass the whole new creation.

3 V. 3 further explains the statement in v. 2 concerning the "healing of the nations." First, **there shall no longer be any curse**. The phrase is taken from Zech. 14:11. The "curse" (Hebrew *ḥerem*) referred to people being put under a ban for complete destruction because of their sin. In the time of Zechariah, Jerusalem had suffered such destruction, though not completely. There will yet be, according to Zechariah, a final onslaught of the nations against Jerusalem to purify her from a segment of impure inhabitants (Zech. 14:2-3). But after that attack, a future time will come when purified Jerusalem will never again be threatened by the curse of destruction for her sin: "people will live in it, and there will be no more curse, for Jerusalem will dwell in security" (14:11). The curse instead will come on the attackers (14:12-15). While those inhabiting the new Jerusalem will be immune from the curse, those kept outside will suffer it, part of the effect of which is eternal separation from the benefits of God's presence (so Rev.

21:8; also 21:27; 22:15). The inhabitants of the eternal city are able to dwell there because they have been delivered and definitively "healed" from the final curse because the Lamb suffered that punishment on their behalf (see on 21:27b; 22:2). The curse of physical and spiritual death set on the human race by Adam in the first garden is permanently removed by the Lamb in the last garden at the time of the new creation. In primeval time, humanity was expelled from the garden sanctuary, and its entrance thereafter closed to sinful humanity. At the end time, the redeemed will be ushered into the opened gates of that sanctuary again as a result of the Lamb's work.

The various physical sufferings and sorrows associated with the fallen condition of humanity, to which even the redeemed are susceptible, will be entirely removed and no longer pose a threat in the new order. This means that the saints will not only be free from the danger of being separated from God, but they will be secure from the *entire range* of persecutions and afflictions threatening them in the former world (note the phrase **any**, literally "all" or "every," **curse**). Therefore, the removal of the curse includes elimination of both physical and spiritual evils.

There will be no form of curse in the new Jerusalem because God's consummate ruling presence will fill it: **the throne of God and of the Lamb shall be in it.** There is only one throne, as is clear from 3:21: "I also overcame and sat down with my Father on His throne" (similarly 5:11-13; 7:17). All who enter the city have access to the presence of God and the Lamb. They respond to His blessing in service: **and His bondservants shall serve Him.** The observation that in 7:15 the saints "serve" (Greek *latreuō*) God as priests in His heavenly temple shows that here also they are performing priestly service in the temple of the end-time city. This echoes the prophecy of Isa. 61:6 ("you will be called the priests of the Lord . . . ministers of our God"), which will be fulfilled in the new cosmic temple. That Isa. 61:6 is in mind is evident if we recall that allusions to Isaiah have been woven throughout Rev. 21:1–22:5 (especially note Isa. 61:10 in 21:2 and allusions to Isaiah 60 in 21:23-26 and 22:5). The saints' service is to God and the Lamb. That both are sitting on only one throne and together form one temple (21:22) enhances their perceived unity. This unity is also highlighted in that both carry the title "Alpha and Omega" (1:8; 21:6; 22:13). Such statements as these in 21:22 and 22:3 were among those which gave rise to later Trinitarian formulas.

4 In the old creation, God's presence was primarily located in Israel's temple, as well as, of course, in heaven. Christians had access to the Spirit's presence, but the fullness of the special revelatory presence of the

Trinity was not yet revealed. Now the divine presence fully permeates the new Jerusalem, the eternal temple and dwelling place of the saints, since **they shall see His face**, a hope expressed by OT saints (Pss. 11:4-7; 27:4; cf. Ps. 42:1-2). The whole community are priests privileged to see God's face in the new Holy of Holies, which encompasses the entire paradisal city-temple, that is, the entire new creation.

The assertion that **His name shall be on their foreheads** intensifies the notion of intimate fellowship with God. It is beyond coincidence that God's name was written on the high priest's forehead in the OT ("Holy to the Lord": Exod. 28:36-38). The high priest represented Israel and was consecrated to God so that he could enter into God's presence in the Holy of Holies to offer propitiatory sacrifices on Israel's behalf, in order to make the people acceptable before God and so that they would not incur His wrath. As was the case with the high priest's jewels in Exod. 28:17-21 (see on 21:18-20), so in v. 4 the privilege of being consecrated to be acceptable in the immediate presence of God, formerly reserved only for the high priest, is now granted to all of God's people. This expresses further the priestly nature of God's new people.

For further OT background of the idea of the **name** here, we can note that the idea of a new name in Isaiah 62 is repeatedly associated with latter-day Zion and that the various new names attributed to the end-time city there all have "God" included in them. The name of God here and elsewhere in Revelation (see on 2:17 and 3:12; cf. also 14:1) indicates the security of the believer and his or her place in God's eternal city. In 3:12, Christ emphasizes the nuance of security by saying that He will write on the overcomer "the name of My God, and the name of the city of My God . . . and My new name," and metaphorically equates this with making the one "who overcomes" an immovable "pillar in the temple of My God." The theme of security associated with the figurative use of God's name elsewhere in the book fits neatly into the theme of the eternal security of the saints in the new Jerusalem narrated so far. We have also seen that the name written on believers refers to the character of God, which they reflect (see on 2:17). Therefore, at the end of time the righteous "shall be like Him, because we shall see Him just as He is" (1 John 3:2; cf. Job 19:25-27; Ps. 17:15; Matt. 5:8; 1 Cor. 13:12), a process which has already begun (2 Cor. 3:18).

5 The vision ends with an expression, **there shall no longer be**, similar to those with which it began in 21:1, 4. This highlights one final time the overall point of the vision, that the saints will not only be free from the danger of being separated from God, but will be secure from the entire range of sufferings threatening them in the old world, which had to be removed before the end-time revelatory fullness of God could be manifested. The affirmation that **they shall not have need of the light of a lamp nor the light of the sun, because the Lord God shall illumine them** fulfills the prophecy of Isa. 60:19-20: "No longer will you have the sun for light by day, nor for brightness will the moon give you light; but you will have the Lord for an everlasting light, and your God for your glory. Your sun will set no more . . . and the days of your mourning will be finished." This continues the thought of 21:23, which also alluded to Isa. 60:19. There, the city had "no need of the sun or of the moon to shine upon it," for the glory of God and the Lamb illumined it.

The language in v. 5 is figurative, and the main point is that nothing from the old world will be able to hinder God's glorious presence from completely filling the new cosmos or the saints from unceasing access to that divine presence. Thus is answered consummately the prayer of the OT saints (Num. 6:25-26; Pss. 4:6; 31:16; 67:1) that the Lord would shine the light of His countenance upon them. Uppermost in thought is the blessing of Num. 6:25-27, since there the shining of God's face is to result in preservation and peace for the saints, which is equated with the Aaronic blessing of invoking God's name "on the sons of Israel" in connection to the temple (Num. 6:27).

The role of God's people as "lampstands" bearing the light of the divine lamp will finally be perfected (cf. 1:20 with 1:4 and 4:5, as well as with 21:11-26 and 22:5). The clouds, the night, and the dark shadows of the old world will no longer be able to diminish Christ's light through the "lampstands," but He will shine as the "lamp" of the new world in an unlimited manner (so 21:23).

It is not coincidental that v. 4 has also referred to the divine name on Aaron's forehead and applied it to all of God's people as His priests. The "age-long benediction" of Numbers 6 reaches its fullest possible application in the new world. In the old covenant, such a revelation of God's face would have brought death (Exod. 33:20), but now it is the means of eternal life and kingship. The role of kingship is appended to priestly functions, because Adam had such a dual role and failed and because the Messiah Himself was finally to fulfill this dual role. The saints are so identified with the throne of the Messiah that they are identified with both His priestly and kingly roles (see further on 20:5-6). The saints exercise sovereignty over the new creation in a way similar to how Adam was to rule "over every living thing that moves on the earth" (Gen. 1:28; see Psalm 8). Part of the purpose of Christ fulfilling the role of the last Adam is, in corporate solidarity with His people, to rule over the eternal new creation, which includes the holy angels (Heb. 2:5-16), who are designed merely to be servants of the redeemed (Heb. 1:14; also perhaps indicated by the position of angels as gatekeepers in Rev. 21:12). However, exalted believers *are* different from the first Adam in that, whereas God only commissioned Adam to rule (a commission he failed to fulfill), now God *promises* that His people *will certainly* reign without end.

Suggestions for Reflection on 22:1-5

On the development of the worldwide paradisal city-temple and our role as priests in it. The commentary traces the development of the extent of the temple from the Garden to the new Jerusalem. How helpful is this in developing your understanding of one of the main "story lines" of the Bible? Would you concur with the way the commentary links the precious stones of the Garden, the high priest, and the eternal city? Would you agree with its portrayal of the idea of priesthood throughout the Bible? What does it mean to be admitted as a priest today to God's temple, as it exists in the form of the church? If Adam was a priest who failed in his duty, and Christ was the Priest who succeeded, how do we, as Christ's servants, function as priests in the inaugurated temple of the church? Adam and Eve failed as priests because they did not sufficiently recall God's word when challenged by the serpent. Compare God's word in Gen. 2:16-17 with Eve's quotation of it in Gen. 3:2-3. How did Eve get it wrong? Adam and Eve also failed because they let uncleanness (the serpent) come into their sanctuary. What uncleanness is in our lives, or threatens to come and defile us? What is our role in extending the boundaries of the temple in this age? What does it mean to extend those boundaries and how does this relate to Christian witness? How far will the boundaries reach in the age before Christ returns?

The purpose of the 21:1–22:5 vision

This vision sets the two cities of Revelation — earthly Babylon and the eternal Jerusalem — in sharp opposition to one another. The same phrase is used to introduce both cities (17:1 and 21:9). Both have a street (11:8 and 21:21). Babylon is impure (17:4), but Jerusalem is pure (21:21). Both are adorned with gold and precious stones (17:4; 18:16; 21:18-21). The superficial similarities between the two are not surprising, for throughout Revelation the forces of evil imitate those of good: there are false apostles (2:2), a false synagogue (2:9; 3:9), a false prophet (16:13; 19:20; 20:10), and a Satanic figure with horns like a lamb (13:11), as opposed to Christ, a Lamb with horns (5:6). There is a threefold name for the beast (17:8, 10-11) and a threefold name for God (1:4, 8, etc.).

Some of the other contrasts observable in 21:1–22:5 between the harlot and the new Jerusalem have been discussed above (see on 21:9-10). In addition, note the following:

> One is a pure bride (21:2, 9), the other a harlot (17:1-2; 18:9).
>
> One does business with unrighteous kings and is attacked by them (17:16, 18), but the other receives the loyalty of righteous kings (21:24).
>
> One receives extorted wealth (18:11-17), while the other receives the glory and honor of the nations (21:24-26).
>
> Those inhabiting one are full of impurities (17:4-5; 18:2-3), while all such people are barred from the other (21:8, 27).
>
> The one is full of slaughter and blood (17:6; 18:24), while the other is full of healing and life (22:1-2).
>
> The saints are exhorted to flee one (18:4) but enter the other (22:14).
>
> The sins of one are piled up to heaven (18:5), as she sought to link earth to heaven with self-glorifying pride (cf. Gen. 11:1-9), while the other comes down from heaven to link heaven with earth (21:2) and glorify God.
>
> The one will be split into three parts and destroyed (16:17-19), whereas the other will remain forever (21:6-7), both events being introduced by "It is done."
>
> The two have contrasting names written on their foreheads (17:5; 22:4).
>
> The names of their respective inhabitants are or are not written in the book of life (17:8; 21:27).
>
> One glorifies herself (18:7), and the other reflects the glory of God (21:11, 23).
>
> One becomes the dwelling place for demons (18:2), while the other becomes a dwelling place for God (21:3, 22).

The contrast is linked to the warning of 21:8, which is addressed to churches where the harlot has had her foothold. Furthermore, the depiction of the new city is replete with antitheses to the sinful churches of chs. 2–3; the perfections of the city are set over against the imperfections of the churches in the letters.

The primary point of contrasting the harlot with the bride is to exhort the faltering churches, plagued by compromise with the harlot, to stop compromising, and increasingly to reflect facets of their coming consummated perfection, in anticipation of it. The portrayal of the new covenant, the new temple, the new Israel, and the new Jerusalem affirms the future fulfillment of the main prophetic themes of the OT and NT, all of which find their ultimate climax in the new creation. The kingdom of the new creation itself is the most overarching of biblical promises, of which the above four new things — covenant, temple, Israel, and Jerusalem — are but facets.

The prophetic vision in 21:1–22:5 of the perfected people of God in unending fellowship with Him is intended to comfort and motivate believers to persevere through temptations to compromise. John exhorts God's people to remain faithful, which is his ultimate goal in writing. This is why the book concludes in 22:6-21 with an epilogue of repeated exhortations, promises, affirmations of Christ's imminent coming, and warnings to the saints. The prospect of their final victory should motivate them to shun any thought of earthly compromise which would threaten possession of their eternal inheritance. The contrast between the present imperfections of the church, as stated in chs. 2 and 3, and its final glory, as described here, should cause them to cry out for a greater manifestation of God's glory in their lives.

While the main *pastoral* goal of the book's argument is to exhort God's people to remain faithful so that they will inherit final salvation, this is not the most important *theological* idea in the book. The major theological theme of the book is that God should receive worship and glory as a result of accomplishing consummate salvation and final judgment (see on 4:11; 5:11-13; 19:1, 5, 7; cf. 1:6; 11:16-17). This notion of divine glory is central to 21:1–22:5 since, as we have seen, the new Jerusalem (or God's people) can only be defined in relation to its luminescent reflection of God's glory. Indeed, the central feature of the city is God and the Lamb, who shine as a lamp upon the city (21:22-23; 22:5), so that the more complete definition of the new Jerusalem includes God's people in full fellowship with God and Christ, reflecting the glory of God and Christ.

Epilogue (22:6-21)

This section is the formal conclusion to the whole book. It is closely related to the introduction (1:1-3) in that both identify the book as a communication from God (using the language of Dan. 2:28-29, 45), both highlight John as a "witness" to the revelation which he received, and both underscore the revelation as a "prophecy" communicated to "hearers," though the introduction pronounces a blessing on all who obey it, whereas the conclusion issues an emphatic curse on all who disobey it. The epilogue shows clearly that the purpose of the book is to induce holy obedience among God's people in order that they receive the reward of salvation. No less than eight of the final sixteen verses underscore this intention either through exhortations to obedience, through promised blessings for holy living, or through warnings of judgment for unholy living (vv. 7, 9, 11-12, 14-15, 18-19). This is in keeping with 1:1-3, where the main point was blessing for obedience. Such blessing is one of the main goals of the revelation (1:1) and of John's witness to it (1:2).

For both introduction and epilogue, promises and warnings alike are based on events which are yet to unfold (cf. 1:3b with 22:7a-b, 11b-12, 18-20). On the basis of the repeated conclusions containing references to Christ's coming or the nearness of the end, the epilogue can perhaps be broken down into five sections containing exhortations: vv. 6-7, 8-10, 11-12, 13-17, and 18-20. The five repeated exhortations to holiness are the main point of the epilogue, since they are supported by the exclamations about Christ's coming. V. 21 is a typical epistolary closing, not only for vv. 6-20 but for the entire book.

The first exhortation to holiness (22:6-7)

6 And he said to me, "These words are faithful and true"; and the Lord, the God of
the spirits of the prophets, sent His angel to show to His bond-servants the things
which must shortly take place. 7 "And behold, I am coming quickly. Blessed is he
who heeds the words of the prophecy of this book."

6 This verse serves as a concluding statement for both the vision of 21:1–22:5 and the whole book. As such, it also introduces vv. 7-21, the formal conclusion to the entire book. The voice John hears (Jesus or an angel speaking on His behalf) declares that **these words are faithful and true**.

The phrase, a verbal repetition of the phrase in 21:5, is based on Isa. 65:16, which expresses confidence in God's forthcoming act of new creation (see further on 21:5). The verbal repetition shows that v. 6 summarizes the preceding vision of the new Jerusalem.

This echoes Dan. 2:45, "the dream is true, and its interpretation is trustworthy," which is the conclusion to a prophetic vision about the victorious establishment of God's kingdom. It inspires certainty that the prophetic vision has divine authority and hence that its contents are true and reliable. The allusion has the same meaning here. Whereas Dan. 2:45 (OG; and Dan. 2:28 MT, OG, Theod.; 2:29 OG) prophesied that the kingdom would come "in the latter days," the heavenly voice now says that **the Lord . . . God . . . sent His angel to show to His bond-servants the things which must shortly** (literally "quickly") **take place**. The language of God revealing what must happen in the last days introduces and concludes the vision in both Daniel 2 and the entire book of Revelation. This Daniel 2 allusion, or part of it, is used four times in Revelation to introduce and conclude major sections, so that it forms the broad outline of the entire book (see on 1:1, 19; 4:1). In particular, 22:6 reproduces the exact wording of 1:1, so that it should be viewed as the formal conclusion to the whole book, and as showing the reader that Revelation, like Daniel 2, is primarily about the establishment of God's kingdom throughout the earth and the judgment of evil world kingdoms. The Danielic formula refers not only to prophesied future events, but includes inaugurated fulfillment of the latter-day prophecy of Daniel 2. As in Rev. 1:1, so here in 22:6 the change from Daniel's "after these things" to **shortly** (or "quickly") hints not merely at imminence, but also at inauguration.

The phrase **the Lord, the God of the spirits of the prophets** uses what is probably a Greek objective genitive and so means "the God who rules over or inspires the spirits of the prophets." As in 10:7, the reference may be to a special class of prophets, probably the OT and NT prophets, through whom God left an inscripturated record inspired by the Holy Spirit, as He rules over the spirits of these prophets. **Of the prophets** may be a second objective genitive (the Spirit inspires the prophets), or it might also be a simple genitive of possession. The prophets possess a spirit which receives inspiration from God. The mention of John's "brothers" as "prophets" in v. 9, without mention of the divine Spirit, lends weight to this option, as does the similar phrase in 19:10, "the spirit of prophecy," which is best understood as an adjectival genitive ("the prophetic spirit"). Furthermore, it seems strange to refer to the Holy Spirit in the plural, though the plural does occur for the Holy Spirit three times earlier in the book (see "the seven Spirits" in 1:4; 4:5; 5:6).

Mention of John's "brothers" as "prophets" in v. 9, combined with the similar mention of John's brothers, for whom "the testimony of Jesus is the spirit of prophecy" in 19:10 could suggest that the phrase refers to the *human* spirits of *all Christians* as prophetic people. However, since the phrase **the Lord, the God of the spirits of the prophets** is bracketed in this verse by allusions to Daniel 2, it is probable that the word "prophets" here is restricted to the OT and NT prophets. In support of **the spirits of the prophets** referring to those holding special prophetic office may be the echo of Num. 27:16 ("the Lord, the God of the spirits of all flesh"), where it refers to God replacing Moses with Joshua as the prophetic spokesman for God's people (cf. Num. 27:12-21). There, an apparent distinction exists between God's prophetic leaders and the rest of humanity (in this case all Israel).

The chain of the book's revelatory communication is from God to Jesus to an angel to John and finally to Christians (so 1:1; cf. 22:8), which implies that John held a specific prophetic office, which is confirmed by the Dan. 2:28-29, 45 allusion here and in 1:1, 19 and 4:1 (on which see for evidence of John's prophetic office; see also on 4:2; 10:9-11).

In 1:1 and here, Christians are called **His bond-servants.** This refers here and throughout the book (except probably in 10:7, on which see) to Christians in general. The meaning of **bond-servants** as all saints means that the visions of the book were shown not only to John but in some sense to all believers, who were considered **bond-servants** along with him (see on 1:1). The wording does not mean that the churches saw the visions in the same manner as John, but that they experienced (and continue to experience) the visions vicariously through John's record of them.

7 Included in the things "which must shortly take place" is Christ's own coming: **And behold, I am coming quickly**. This refers to His final appearance, but includes His earlier comings throughout the church's existence, all of which are imminent for every generation of the church. The repeated declarations of Christ's comings in chs. 1–3 points to this conclusion (see on 1:7; 2:5; 3:3, 11), as does our analysis of the inaugurated use of the Dan. 2:28-29, 45 allusion in 1:1, 19 and 4:1. He who **heeds the words of the prophecy of this book** will be **blessed**, a repetition of the similar statement in 1:3, so that "blessing" roughly brackets the book. This suggests that the goal of the book is that God's true people obey its revelation and be blessed with salvation. **The words** referred to in vv. 6 and 7b form a bracket around **blessed** to underscore it as the book's goal. The blessing

is the bestowal of salvation itself, as is evident from the use of "blessed" (Greek *makarios*) in 14:13; 16:15; 19:9; 20:6; and 22:14.

The second exhortation to holiness (22:8-10)

8 And I, John, am the one who heard and saw these things. And when I heard and
saw, I fell down to worship at the feet of the angel who showed me these things.
9 And he said to me, "Do not do that; I am a fellow servant of yours and of your
brethren the prophets and of those who heed the words of this book; worship
God." 10 And he said to me, "Do not seal up the words of the prophecy of this
book, for the time is near."

8 John implicitly identifies himself as a witness to the book's revelation, and thus is a crucial instrument for the "blessing" of v. 7 to be received: **And I, John, am the one who heard and saw these things.** He makes explicit his identification as a prophetic witness in v. 18 ("I testify . . ."). He is in a long line of prophets who witnessed to Israel about God's covenantal stipulations, her disobedience to them, and the consequent impending judgment, especially for idolatry (e.g., 2 Kgs. 17:7-23; 2 Chron. 24:18-19; Neh. 9:26-27a). The notion of "seeing and hearing" is the basis for a legal witness, as in 1 John 1:1-2: "what we have heard, what we have seen with our eyes . . . we . . . bear witness." As with the OT prophets, so John's witness is also directed to the covenant community. The believing remnant will be blessed for their obedience, but the rest will be judged for their disobedience. The repeated use of "he who has an ear, let him hear" in the letters to the seven churches (see on 2:7) shows that John follows Jesus and the OT prophets in bringing to the faithful not only the promise of blessing, but also the warning of judgment.

As in 19:10, so again John begins to worship the angel who communicated Christ's revelation to him.

9 And again the angel responds by forbidding John to worship him, since he also is merely a divine servant like John, the prophets, and the rest of those who obey God: **And he said to me, Do not do that; I am a fellow servant of yours and of your brethren the prophets and of those who heed the words of this book.** The angel's words could be taken to identify two distinct groups, prophets and other believers, or the second phrase could be a description of the prophets. On the other hand, elsewhere in Revelation (1:1; 22:6), "servants" are understood as all Christians, which might suggest that the **prophets** here are all believers, understood as a prophetic people who also heed the words of this book. On this question, see further on v. 6 above.

Instead, the angel exhorts John to **worship God**. John may have mistaken the angel for the divine, heavenly Christ of 1:13ff. and 10:1ff., who deserves worship. Since this is the second time that John substitutes a false object of worship for the true, v. 10 underscores the subtle problem even for faithful Christians. What this shows is how easy it can be to worship and wrongly revere a human messenger of God when he powerfully preaches the word of Christ (1 Cor. 3:4-7; cf. also Acts 14:7-18). The angel's command reminds us that the reward of blessing mentioned in v. 7 is secondary. The ultimate goal of the book's revelation is to inspire worship of God.

10 The angel commands John: **Do not seal up the words of the prophecy of this book, for the time is near**. If the revelation is sealed, the churches cannot know its contents or respond in worship. The command **do not seal up** implies that writing down the vision is just as much under the aegis of divine authority as the revelation of the vision was. Elsewhere, the writing down of the vision or its parts is explicitly commanded, which suggests that divine authority extends to the writing (1:10-11, 19; 2:1ff.; 19:9; 21:5; cf. 22:6 with 22:10). Vv. 18-19 bears this out. John's prophetic commission is on a par with the commissions of the OT prophets (in this respect, see on 1:10-11; 4:1-2; 17:3a; 21:9-10).

The prohibition against sealing is directly related to the opposite command given to Daniel: "But as for you, Daniel, conceal these words and seal up the book until the end of time" (Dan. 12:4; see also Dan. 8:26; 12:9). Daniel prophesied about the rise and fall of evil earthly kingdoms and the final victory of the kingdom of God, but he did not understand how or when all this would unfold, though he knew it was not for his own day (Dan. 12:13). Therefore, the "sealing" of Daniel's book meant that its prophecies would be neither fully understood nor fulfilled until the end.

What Daniel prophesied can now be understood (the unsealing), because the prophecies have begun to be fulfilled, and the latter days have begun. Therefore, the language of unsealing what is written indicates also the revelation of greater insight into the prophecies, a greater insight kept from OT saints (so likewise Eph. 3:4-5, where insight is now given "which in other generations was not made known . . . as it has now been revealed to His holy apostles and prophets in the Spirit"; cf. also 1 Pet. 1:12). In particular, Christ's death, resurrection, and reign over history and the saints' tribulation are the inaugurated fulfillment of OT prophecies. Similarly,

Christ unsealed the book in ch. 5 (on which see 5:1-2). Even if these two books are not identical, generally they both contain to a significant degree revelatory material pertaining to OT prophecies, some of which have been fulfilled and some of which await fulfillment.

The prophecy is not to be sealed, **for the time is near**. The same clause occurs in 1:3, where it explains an allusion to Dan. 2:28-29, 45 found in 1:1. There it indicated not merely a reference to imminent future events but also the very beginning of fulfillment of OT prophecy. The prophecies sealed up by Daniel have begun to be fulfilled, continue to be fulfilled in the present, and will do so until their consummation in the future.

The main point in vv. 8-10 is to "worship God" (v. 9), a worship motivated by His gracious revelation to John of the prophetic meaning of Christ's death and resurrection for believers' present lives and for the future.

The third exhortation to holiness (22:11-12)

11 Let the one who does wrong, still do wrong; and let the one who is filthy, still
be filthy; and let the one who is righteous, still practice righteousness; and let
the one who is holy, still keep himself holy. 12 Behold, I am coming quickly, and
My reward is with Me, to render to every man according to what he has done.

11 Again the angel appeals to the conclusion of Daniel's prophecy:

Many will be purged, purified and refined, but the wicked will act wickedly, and none of the wicked will understand, but those who have insight will understand. (Dan. 12:10)	**Let the one who does wrong, still do wrong; and let the one who is filthy, still be filthy; and let the one who is righteous, still practice righteousness; and let the one who is holy, still keep himself holy.** (Rev. 22:11)

Both passages make two declarations about the destiny of the unrighteous and two about the destiny of the righteous and then state that both groups will remain in their present condition. The difference is that the passage from Daniel is a prophetic statement of fact whereas that of Revelation seems to constitute a command. But how could an angel order unbelievers to remain in their sin? Several responses have been suggested by commentators:

Some suggest that the expressions are not deterministic because humans have free will and because there is always opportunity to repent. But such an analysis does not correspond well with the Daniel 12:10 allusion in 22:11, which speaks of events to occur based on God's prophetic decress and not on human volition.

Some have suggested that v. 11a simply means that the wicked are no longer to be exhorted to obey God, yet this again avoids the issue of the imperative that is addressed to the wicked.

Others hold that for John the end was so close that there was no longer time to alter character or habits. Yet this would imply that John was incorrect, for there has been abundant time since. If John was only referring to the last stage of history, however, this view would be more plausible.

And some say that John means that human character is unalterable, but, however true this may be, this again avoids John's use of the Dan. 12:9-10 prophecy as signaling the beginning of fulfillment (see below).

Both of the commands in v. 11 are better understood in view of the context of the whole book, especially against the OT background of the "hearing" formula in the letters (and 13:9) and of the "hardening" theme from the Exodus plague narratives behind the trumpets and bowls. The situation which the exhortations of v. 11 address is not unique to a last stage of history, but is one which has already occurred repeatedly in the OT, in the ministry of Jesus, and again at the time of writing in the Asia Minor churches. The repeated exhortation in the letters, "he who has an ear, let him hear," is based on Isaiah's exhortation to idolatrous Israel (Isa. 6:9-10). Unbelievers are not exhorted to "hear," but believers are called on to "hear" and obey God's word. The same exhortation from Isaiah is applied by Jesus (Matt. 13:9-17) to the unfaithful Israel of His day. When people failed to listen to ordinary teaching, Isaiah and Jesus resorted to prophetic declarations and actions, as well as the use of parables, which served to bring the judgment of God on the unrighteous by further hardening their hearts, while shocking wandering believers into repentance.

The visions of Revelation, with their unusual and even bizarre features, serve as prophetic statements through which the same process occurs. John, like Jesus and Isaiah before him, was addressing a diluted church and a rebellious world, as well as the community of faithful believers. Many in the covenant community had become apostate and insensitive to the prophetic word. To such communities God sent prophets whose words functioned to increase the blindness of the apostate to confirm their judged status, but served to shock the elect remnant out of the spiritual torpor characteristic of the majority. The impious were even exhorted not to understand, which was a punishment for their apostasy and idol worship (accordingly, idolatrous Israel is commanded to keep worshiping idols in Jer. 44:25 and Ezek. 20:39). The church, the present "Israel of God" (cf. Gal. 6:16), has become as spiritually lethargic as ethnic Israel of old, and God likewise reveals His double-edged word to them (1 John 2:4, 22; 4:20; 5:10). Of course, there is always a remnant of unbelievers who are given "ears to hear," so that they are not ultimately intractably wicked and unrepentant. Accordingly, they are shocked into the faith by the visionary parables for the first time and thus join the covenant community. For full discussion of the Isaiah background to this theme, see on 2:7.

The question remains: How does the Dan. 12:9-10 allusion contribute to the theological background of dual exhortations here in v. 11? The Daniel text predicts that during the latter days pseudo-members of the covenant community will not understand the dawning fulfillment of prophecy (alluded to in Rev. 22:10) and consequently will continue to disobey God's laws, whereas the godly will have insight and discern the beginning of fulfillment of prophecy occurring around them. They will respond by obeying God's word. The change from prediction in Dan. 12:10 to imperatives here in Revelation expresses awareness that the fulfillment of Daniel's prophecy is commencing in John's own time and that genuine believers should discern this revelation and respond positively to it. Consequently, the revelation about OT fulfillment in v. 10 is the basis of and inspires the dual response of v. 11, following the prophetic pattern of Dan. 12:9-10. These events are determined or "predestined" to occur, since they are prophetic, and are not descriptions of mere future possibilities. Though this conclusion is theologically difficult, it correlates admirably with the prophetic nature of Daniel and with the notion that peoples' identification with Christ or the beast has been determined by whether their name has been written in the Lamb's book of life (see on 13:8; 17:8; 20:12, 15; 21:27; as well as on 3:5).

12a A further basis for the exhortations of v. 11 is found in v. 12: **Behold, I am coming quickly**. In chs. 1–3, Christ's comings, as noted above, refer to His appearances throughout the church age as well as at its end (see on 1:7; 2:5; 3:3, 11; 22:7). The use of "quickly" or "soon" as part of the Dan. 2:28-29, 45 formula has been found already to indicate fulfillment in the near future, or indeed fulfillment as already beginning (see on 1:1).

Here, however, the emphasis is on Christ's future final return, as is shown by the promise, **My reward is with Me, to render to every man according to what he has done**. The only other use of "reward" (Greek *misthos*), in 11:18, refers clearly to the recompense at the end of time. Does this mean, then, that John thought mistakenly that Christ would return imminently? A better possible solution is that "quickly" here (perhaps also in v. 7) suggests the *suddenness* of Christ's return, whenever it does occur. This is supported from 16:15 ("I am coming like a thief. Blessed is the one who stays awake"). In fact, the Ethiopic version of 22:7 has "I come quickly *as a thief*," which shows a possibly early identification of this passage with the thief metaphor of 16:15. The theme of unexpected, quick execution of judgment in the end time occurs already in the OT (see Isa. 47:11 and Mal. 3:1-5: "And the Lord, whom you seek, will suddenly come to His temple. . . . But who can endure the day of His coming? . . . And He will sit as a smelter and purifier of silver. . . . Then I will draw near to you for judgment"; cf. Jer. 6:26).

Another way of resolving the difficulty is to accept that the phrase does refer to temporal nearness (rather than suddenness), but to place the focus on "nearness" with respect to the *next major event* to occur in God's redemptive-historical program. After Christ's death and resurrection and Pentecost, the next significant event in God's salvation scheme is the final coming of Christ, when reward and punishment are meted out. Whether this occurs in one year or five thousand, it could still be referred to as "near," since it is the next *major* event in the decretive order of God's redemptive plan.

Nevertheless, it is more probably a reference to a swift "unexpected" appearance, the latter with respect to the possibility that Jesus could come at any time, as in Matt. 24:36–25:13 (cf. Acts 1:7; 1 Thess. 1:9-10; 2 Tim. 4:8; Tit. 2:13). Matt. 24:36 and Acts 1:7 affirm the impossibility of knowing the time of Christ's coming, yet express the need for alertness about it (cf. Matt. 24:36, 42, 44; 25:13; Luke 12:35-40). 2 Pet. 3:8-13 holds the following themes in tension with one another:

No matter how long the duration of time until the end, it is not long to God, since "one day is as a thousand years."

Though the time may seem long in human terms, "the Lord is not slow about His promise . . . the day of the Lord will come like a thief."

Christian expectation of the end, and Christian obedience may even

> have a mysterious way of "hastening the coming of the day of God" (e.g., cf. Matt. 24:14 and Mark 13:10 with 2 Pet. 3:11-12? Cf. Matt. 6:10?).

The same notions are likely inherent in Rev. 22:12.

12b Jesus's second assertion in v. 12, **My reward is with Me, to render to every man according to what he has done**, is an allusion to Isa. 40:10, "Behold, the Lord God will come with might, with His arm ruling for Him. Behold, His reward is with Him, and His recompense before Him" (cf. similar language in Isa. 62:11). This refers to God's work of bestowing blessings of salvation on His faithful people, though judgment of the unfaithful is likely implicit. That the "reward" and "recompense" focus on salvation is apparent in that Isa. 40:10 is the content of the good news of Isa. 40:9 and a result of God's forgiveness of "iniquity" (40:2). In Revelation, however, the wording of Isaiah has been interpreted to refer to the works of righteous and unrighteous, for which they are either blessed or judged, which may also be implied in Isaiah.

The same promise in Isa. 62:11, like that in Rev. 22:12, is supplemented with the image of "going through gates" of a city (cf. Isa. 62:10 with Rev. 22:14). This verse does not mean that it is on the basis of good works that a person will be justified, for such works apart from Christ can save no one, since perfection is required for acceptance before God (Matt. 5:48; 1 Pet. 1:16; cf. Lev. 19:2). This is supported by Rev. 5:9-10, which says that Christ is the only One worthy to be accepted before God and that He was slain and redeemed by His blood people from their sins so that they also could be considered worthy. Indeed, this idea is not far away here since the idea connoted by "those who wash their robes" in 22:14 goes back to 7:14, "they have washed their robes and made them white in the blood of the Lamb." On the other hand, "works" are considered a necessary condition for salvation at the final judgment. But how? Works are a sign demonstrating that a person has *already met* the ultimate, causal, necessary condition for salvation, which is redemptive justification from sin by Christ's death and resurrection (cf. also Eph. 2:6-10).

The main point of vv. 11-12 is the exhortation in v. 11, which is grounded in and inspired by the revelatory information in vv. 10 and 12. The unexpected time of Christ's coming should motivate His genuine people to live godly lives in expectation of that event (cf. 2 Pet. 3:11-14). On the other hand, the ungodly are not spurred to repentance but only to further obduracy in the face of such revelation about Christ's coming.

The fourth exhortation to holiness (22:13-17)

13 "I am the Alpha and the Omega, the first and the last, the beginning and the
end." 14 Blessed are those who wash their robes, that they may have the right to
the tree of life, and may enter by the gates into the city. 15 Outside are the dogs
and the sorcerers and the immoral persons and the murderers and the idolaters,
and everyone who loves and practices lying. 16 "I, Jesus, have sent My angel to
testify to you these things for the churches. I am the root and the offspring of
David, the bright morning star." 17 And the Spirit and the bride say, "Come." And
let the one who hears say, "Come." And let the one who is thirsty come; let the
one who wishes take the water of life without cost.

13 At various points in the book, God has been referred to as "the Alpha and the Omega" (1:8; 21:6) and "the Beginning and the End" (21:6), and Christ has been called "the First and the Last" (1:17; 2:8). Now all these titles are combined and applied to Christ to highlight His deity. The ascriptions figuratively connote the totality of polarity: the fact that Christ is present at and sovereign over the beginning and end of creation is boldly stated to indicate that He is also present at and sovereign over all events in between.

14 Reminding the reader about Christ's omnipresence and omnipotence throughout history inspires confidence in Him as a faithful rewarder and just judge and provides motivation for Christians' continued perseverance in the midst of earthly trials. In light of this, the declaration in v. 14, **Blessed are those who wash their robes**, serves also as an exhortation for the saints to persevere through trial and suffering to receive their final reward, as spoken of in v. 12. The metaphor is a development of the similar thought in 7:14. The washing of robes speaks not of any righteousness the saints have earned themselves but of the standing of righteousness God has given them because of the blood (see 7:14) that Christ shed on the cross. This is clear from 19:7-8: "His bride has made herself ready" on the basis of the divine ability "given to her to clothe herself in fine linen, bright and clean; for the fine linen is *the righteous acts of* the saints" (recall that this last phrase refers to the saints' vindicated standing before God *and* their consequent righteous deeds, on which see 19:7-8).

The reward for such enduring faith is that the believers are **blessed**, which is then explained as their receiving of authority: **that they may have the right to the tree of life, and may enter by the gates into the city**. This is essentially the same blessing as that received by those washing their garments in 7:14-17, as the expansion of this blessing with the metaphor of water in v. 17 below shows. The image connotes the blessing of salvation, especially as it has been pictured in the vision of the new Jerusalem. The language of a **tree of life** and open **gates** picks up on the Isaiah 60 and Genesis 3 imagery of 21:24–22:3, where the worshiping nations file through the open gates of the holy city and have access to the **tree of life**, in contrast to the unholy, who are not able to enter (see on 21:24–22:3). Allusion is made here to Isa. 62:10, "Go through, go through the gates," which action occurs in order for believers to receive the salvation promised in 62:11, "Behold, His reward is with Him, and His recompense before Him," which has just been alluded to in Rev. 22:12. This reward is for all believers, not just a special class of martyrs, for v. 15 will make it clear that the division of groups in this context is that between *all* the wicked apostates and *all* the righteous of the redeemed community.

15 The image of unbelievers barricaded outside the city in 21:27 is paraphrased here. As in 21:8, 27, the kind of people excluded from the city is described. All three lists conclude with liars, which highlights the counterfeit nature of these people as pseudo-Christians (so that pagan liars are not the main focus). They say they are believers, but their sinful actions betray their confession. They may even deny their faith verbally when confronted with persecution (see further on 21:8). Such a person is not just a liar, but one **who loves and practices lying**. This is not duplicity in general but a desire to benefit both from the spiritual advantages of being a part of the church and from the economic security of being a part of the ungodly world. John uses the phrase elsewhere to refer to people whose claim to membership in the covenant community is contradicted either by their ungodly lifestyle or false doctrine (1 John 2:4, 22; 4:20; 5:10).

A new item in v. 15 not found in the "sin lists" of 21:8, 27 is **dogs**. Dogs are despised creatures throughout Scripture (so Matt. 7:6), concerned only about their physical well-being. Likewise, those referred to here have an insatiable craving to preserve their earthly security, which is a mark of the beast (13:15-18). "Dogs" in the OT can refer to covenant-violators (Ps. 59:6, 14) and unrighteous watchmen and shepherds whose focus (as with the liars) is economic gain (Isa. 56:10-11). It is also used of male cult prostitutes, whose wages are an "abomination" (cf. Rev. 21:27) that cannot be brought into the temple (Deut. 23:17-18). John's use of "dog," along with the description of those excluded from the temple-city in 21:27 as those who practice "abomination," suggests that the Deuteronomy passage is echoed here, especially when it is recalled that the lists in ch. 21 and here catalog sins associated with idolatry. Paul applies the same canine metaphor to Jewish Christians who profess to be part of the Christian church in Philippi but whose idolatrous actions and beliefs show otherwise (Phil. 3:2-3, 18-19). Also likened to dogs are professing Christians in the readership of 2 Peter who apostatize (2:20-22) by all kinds of corruption, including engaging in false teaching (2:1-3, 13-14, 16).

As in 21:8, 27, the reference is to those being excluded from the final inheritance and consummate form of the city. That these reprobates are outside the city indicates that they will have no place in the new creation, since new creation and the city are probably synonymous concepts (see on 21:1–22:5). This "outside" location is the lake of fire, since the godless people listed in 21:8 are in the lake of fire. The punishment of being cast outside the garden, which was commenced in Gen. 3:23-24, continues for the reprobate into eternity on an escalated scale.

16 The statement **I, Jesus, have sent My angel to testify to you these things for the churches** reiterates the first verse of the book (1:1-2), though here the angel testifies, whereas earlier John was the subject. As in 1:1-2, the object of the testimony is not merely part of the book, but its entirety. The forensic sense of **testify** is brought out clearly in vv. 18-19, where the penalty for disobeying the testimony is stated (for the legal sense of "testify" see also on 1:9; 11:3; 22:20). The threefold repetition of "testify" in vv. 16, 18, and 20 emphasizes this legal nuance.

There are a number of ways to identify the **you** and **the churches**:

You may refer to the individual members of the seven churches, and **the churches** may refer to the churches generally, or even the church universal. If the seven churches are taken as representative of the church universal (as we have argued; see on 1:4, 11), the same meaning is arrived at.

You may, as in the letters, refer to a group within a church or to a church itself, followed by a wider reference in each letter to all the **churches**.

The following variations all involve the idea that the testimony from Jesus to His angel to John is also mediated to the prophets in the local churches, who in turn deliver it to the churches. Taking the Greek preposition *epi* as "over" rather than "for," the translation may be "I . . . testify these things to you [who are] *over* the churches," that is, the prophets in the churches through whom John's own prophetic message is mediated. A similar idea would be in mind taking *epi* as "to," with the translation being, "I . . . testify these things to you to the churches," where John is testifying to the prophets who in turn testify to the churches. Or *epi* could be taken as "against": "I . . . testify these things to you *against* the churches" (the prophets bringing God's legal judgment on account of disobedience). Or, finally, *epi* could be taken as "for": "I testify these things to you *for* the churches" (the prophets bringing the message for the benefit of the churches).

The preposition could be taken as "in" or "among," the translation being, "I . . . testify these things to you in (or among) the churches," thus identifying where the testimony will occur, **you** and **the churches** being identified as the same group. A striking parallel in favor of this is in 1:4, where John begins to speak "to the seven churches," which he immediately further defines as "you": "Grace to you." In fact, 1:4 is the only place in the entire book where the same combination of words occurs. In addition, virtually all commentators agree that the epilogue in vv. 6-21 is an epistolary closing which forms a literary closure with the epistolary introduction in 1:4ff., so that one might expect some affinity between them. Finally, there are several phrases and themes from the introduction of ch. 1 alluded to and developed here (e.g., vv. 6-7, 18).

This last option, where **you** and **the churches** are identified as the same group, is, on balance, the most viable, and it is not greatly different in substance from the first and second options. It is possible, however, that a separate group of prophets (as in the third option) could be in view in the **you**.

For the second time in the conclusion, Jesus identifies Himself. And, as in v. 13, the self-ascription combines names attributed to Jesus earlier in the book: **I am the root and offspring of David** (5:5), **the bright morning star** (2:28). The title combines two OT prophecies concerning the messianic King's triumph over His enemies at the end of time, Num. 24:17 and Isa. 11:1, 10. That Jesus applies these names to Himself *in the present* shows that He has already begun to fulfill these prophecies. This is confirmed by the earlier application of both prophetic names to Jesus' resurrection (see on 5:5 and 2:28). The point here is that the messianic victory has begun and will be consummated by Jesus. In 5:5, the title was only "root of David," but now **offspring** is combined with the previous name. It is conceivable that, whereas the Isaiah 11 passage views the Messiah as descending from the Davidic line, Jesus could be seen here as the "root of David" in that He is Himself the source or origin of David, as well as His descendant. It is more likely, however, that **root** is explained by **offspring**, so that it is a metaphorical term for "descendant." The metaphor is the same as in Isa. 11:10 ("the nations will resort to the root [= descendant] of Jesse"); a similar Hebrew use of "root" appears in Sirach 47:22. Furthermore, "root" also has the idea of "sprout" or "growth from" in Isa. 53:2, where, significantly, it refers to the Messiah. The main point of the title is to identify Jesus as the One who fulfills the prophecy that one of David's descendants would be the Messiah. Therefore, the phrase in v. 16b should be rendered "the root and the offspring *from* David."

That both inaugurated and future fulfillments are intended is apparent because the *dawn* of a new day or age was a metaphorical association of the **bright morning star**. Christ has begun a new redemptive day, which He will culminate at His final return. This is also pointed to by 2 Pet. 1:17-19, where "the morning star arises" is synonymous with "the day dawns," both of which may be metaphors for the inauguration of the OT "prophetic word" in Christ's first coming. Allusion may also be made to Isa. 60:1-3: "Arise, shine, for your light has come . . . and nations will come to your light, and kings to the brightness of your rising." This would again suggest that the star is already beginning to shed its light. This initial fulfillment suggests further that Jesus' final "coming" as Messiah, referred to in 22:7, 12, 17, and 20, has in fact been inaugurated in the past through His many "comings" to the church (see on 1:7; 2:5; 3:3, 11 and on vv. 7, 12 above).

17 **And the Spirit and the bride say, "Come."** The Spirit is the Holy Spirit. The bride represents the true people of God (see on 19:7-8; 21:2, 9ff.), who says through the power of the Holy Spirit, "Come." The symbol of "bride" has only been used previously for the church's future, consummated marriage to Christ at His final return (19:7-9; 21:2ff., 9ff.). The application of it to the church in the present suggests that what has been prophesied in earlier chapters to be fulfilled in God's people at the very end has begun already in their midst (as in 2 Cor. 11:2; Eph. 5:25-27). Not all in the visible church can say "come," but only those who have ears to hear the exhortation of the Spirit: **And let the one who hears say, "Come."** This command is a paraphrase of the repeated exhortations in the seven letters: "He who has an ear, let him hear what the Spirit says to the churches" (2:7, 17, etc.; likewise 13:9). The Spirit's admonitions do not penetrate the spiritual ears of pseudo-members of the church, but such admonitions

serve to shock genuine members out of the stupor from which a number in the visible church suffers (for full discussion of the formula see on 2:7). Recall, however, that even a remnant of pseudo-believers may be shocked into the true faith for the first time, if they have already been "written in the Lamb's book of life" (cf. 21:27). Of course, this is true also of a remnant of unbelievers outside the church who hear and respond positively to the gospel. Whereas the true corporate church says "come" in the first line of v. 17, now the focus shifts to individual saints.

The **"Come"** spoken by **the bride** and by **the one who hears** could be addressed to Christ as an entreaty to return. That is, the church, first corporately and then individually, entreats Christ through the power of the Holy Spirit. **And let the one who is thirsty come. And let the one who is thirsty take the water of life without cost** is then directed to people as exhortations to believe. But it is also possible, if not preferable, to take the three imperatives of "come" and the imperative "drink" as addressed to individuals. This is supported by the fact the latter part of the verse develops 21:6, "I will give to the one who thirsts from the spring of the water of life without cost." 21:6 (on which see for its OT background) draws on Isa. 55:1, but 22:17 draws even more explicitly on the Isaiah text: "Ho! Everyone who thirsts, come to the waters; and you who have no money come, buy and eat. Come, buy wine and milk without money and without cost" (cf. also John 7:37-38). The three repeated imperatives of "come" to people in Isaiah are likely the model for the three "come"s of Rev. 22:17. If so, they are not addressed to Christ. But how can the corporate church or individual believers command themselves to come? The awkwardness is resolved if the first command is viewed as issued by prophetic leaders through whom the Spirit speaks (cf. 19:10) and the second as issued by individual believers "who hear" to other believers who still are dull of hearing.

In contrast to 21:6, the focus of the water metaphor is now on the one who receives the water. Before Jesus can give the water, the thirsty one must "come" to Jesus. This "coming" must be an entire life of faith, by which one has "overcome" temptations to compromise (see 21:6-7). Therefore, the focus of the exhortations is not an open-ended "invitation" to the world in general, but rather commands to the people of God to persevere throughout the age and up until the final coming of Christ. Of course, the function of the true church is to issue this invitation, not only to its own community, but also to the world (cf. 11:3-13).

The section ends as it began. There is a reward for those "who wash their robes" in v. 14, as there is for those who "come" and desire the water in v. 17. Vv. 13 and 15-16 support v. 14, and vv. 15-16 also support v. 17: if believers are not like the sinners of v. 15, and if they listen to the testimony about Jesus as the sovereign God (v. 13) and the one who fulfills messianic prophecy (v. 16), then they will inherit the blessing with which they are exhorted in v. 14. And if saints are not like the wicked (v. 15) and they listen to the testimony about Jesus who fulfills messianic prophecy (v. 16), then they likewise will inherit the blessing of v. 17. Therefore, the main point of v. 14-17 lies with the two rewards promised in vv. 14 and 17.

The fifth exhortation to holiness (22:18-20)

18 I testify to everyone who hears the words of the prophecy of this book: if anyone adds to them, God shall add to him the plagues which are written in this
book; 19 and if anyone takes away from the words of the book of this prophecy,
God shall take away his part from the tree of life and from the holy city, which are
written in this book. 20 He who testifies to these things says, "Yes, I am coming
quickly." Amen. Come, Lord Jesus.

18-19 Though vv. 18-19 could be viewed generally as an exhortation, they are better seen as a warning. These verses summarize the Apocalypse, viewing it as a new law code for a new Israel, modeled on the old law code to the nation of Israel in a series of passages throughout Deuteronomy:

> Listen to the statutes . . . you shall not add to the word . . . nor take away from it. (Deut. 4:1-2; see also 12:32)
>
> And it shall be when he hears the words . . . every curse which is written in this book will rest on him, and the Lord will blot out his name from under heaven. (Deut. 29:19-20)
>
> **I testify to everyone who hears the words . . . if anyone adds to them, God will add to him the plagues that have been written in this book, and if anyone takes away from the words of the book . . . God will take away his part from the tree of life and from the holy city . . .** (Rev. 22:18-19)

Further similarities enhancing the link between Deuteronomy and Rev. 22:18-19 are:

In the light of the directly preceding and following contexts of each of the three Deuteronomy passages, it is clear that all three are specific warnings against idolatry, as is the case here (see also 21:8, 27; 22:15).

A positive response to both the OT and NT warnings results in the reward of life in the new land (Deut 4:1; 12:28-29; Rev. 22:14, 17-19).

Both also use the terminology of "plagues" to describe the punishment for unfaithfulness (Deut. 29:21-22 and Rev. 22:18).

To add to or take away from the words of God's revelation, according to Deut. 4:2-4; 12:29-32, means to accept the false teaching that idolatry is compatible with worship of the one true God. From the incident of the golden calf (Exodus 32) to that of Baal of Peor (Num. 25:1-9, 14-18, referenced in Deut. 4:3), Israel faced the temptation to engage in idolatry, the worship of other gods. Such false teaching amounts to "adding to" God's law. Furthermore, it is tantamount to "taking away from" God's law, since it violates the positive laws against idolatry, consequently nullifying their validity. This is not mere general disobedience but false teaching about the inscripturated word and following such deceptive teaching. Belief in the abiding truth of God's word is the presupposition for positive obedience to it. The ancient Near Eastern treaty documents, after which Deuteronomy 4 is modeled, were also protected against intentional alteration by means of inscriptional sanctions and curses. This Deuteronomic background is remarkably suitable to Rev. 22:18-19, since the descriptions in the three vice lists of 21:8, 27; 22:15 all conclude by emphasizing the deceptiveness of the ungodly in connection with idolatry.

This analysis also fits well with the situation of the churches portrayed in chs. 2–3, which depicts all the churches facing idolatry to one degree or another, and often not successful in their response. Strikingly, in the light of the above Deuteronomy background, some of the false teachers and their followers encouraging idolatry in the church of Pergamum are identified as those "who hold the teaching of Balaam, who kept teaching Balak to put a stumbling block before the sons of Israel, to eat things sacrificed to idols, and to commit acts of immorality" (2:14). The same deceptive teaching was also prevalent in the church of Thyatira (see on 2:20-23). Such false prophets who distort the truth are either adding false theology or taking away from the revealed truth.

The rewards named in 22:12-19 are best understood against the background of the letters, since they correspond to the promises to the "overcomers" in chs. 2–3: rendering to each as his work deserves (2:23; 22:12), eating of or sharing in the tree of life (2:7; 22:14, 19), and identification with the city of God (3:12; 22:14, 19). Those who overcome the threat of idolatry will inherit these promises. Indeed, in this context, the "washing of the robes" in v. 14 must refer to keeping oneself undefiled by the pollution of idol worship, resulting in the same twofold reward being withheld from the transgressors according to v. 19 (see on 3:4-5 and 7:14 for the full meaning of the "washing" imagery). Consequently, the warnings of vv. 18-19 are directed, not primarily to pagans outside the church, but to all in the church community, as the warnings of Deuteronomy were addressed to all Israelites (pagans, of course, are not excluded from the warnings). The "plagues" referred to in v. 18 include not just punishment in the lake of fire but all inflictions incurred by the ungodly prior to that judgment (on which, e.g., see on 8:6-12; 9:18-20; 11:6; cf. also 16:9, 21). Therefore, the whole range of plagues recorded in the book will come on the apostate, which is supported by the Deut. 29:20 allusion: "every curse which is written in this book will rest on him" (likewise Deut. 29:21; 28:58-61; Jer. 25:13).

The punishment in 22:18-19 is formulated in ironic terms: those *adding* to the *book* will have *added* to them the plagues of the *book;* those *taking away from the words of the book* will have *taken away* from them the eternal blessings *which are written in this book.* The purpose of the ironic statement is to express figuratively the "eye for eye" nature of biblical judgment, where people are punished in proportion to their sin, and sometimes by the very means of their own sin (see on 11:5 for a similar ironic formulation). It is most likely that v. 19 refers not to loss of salvation but to denial of it for those who have claimed outwardly to be Christians but never had true faith. The characteristic highlighted repeatedly in the closing portion of the book is not that of genuine believers losing their redeemed status, but the counterfeit, double-dealing nature of people in the Christian community who will not receive the final reward (see above on 21:8, 27; 22:15). The earlier discussion of the promise in 3:5 ("I will not erase his name from the book of life") confirms this conclusion, as does the prior study of the converse statements in 13:8 and 17:8. From the foundation of the world, the worshipers of the beast, some of whom are in the church, were destined to have no inheritance in the eternal city (13:8; 17:8). Nevertheless, for a time it may have seemed that some of these people were heading for such a reward. The phrase in v. 18a (**to everyone who hears the words of the prophecy**) is an almost exact repetition of 1:3a ("those who hear the words of the prophecy"), which confirms that it is those within the visible, professing community of faith who are being warned and who are in danger of judgment.

The punishment for disobedience is severe since, like the author of Deut. 4:2-4, John is writing not his own words but the very words of God. Of course, John's words are not merely from the Father, but also from the Spirit and the Son (so 1:1; the conclusions of each letter in chs. 2–3; 19:9; 21:5; 22:6). Uppermost in John's mind is that the book represents the words of Christ Himself, who has just been mentioned in v. 16.

20 Vv. 16 and 18 have said that the angel and John have testified by respectively revealing and writing down the vision as a whole. The Spirit should also be viewed as a third witness (cf. possibly 19:10, as well as the concluding verse of each of the seven letters; cf. also 22:17a). Now Jesus is affirmed as a fourth witness: **He who testifies to these things says**. The mounting up of witnesses emphasizes the legal nature of the book, for which people who hear it read are accountable. For the legal sense of "testify" in Revelation and Johannine literature see on 1:9; 11:3; 22:16. **These things** probably refer to the entire vision, since the same phrase is used three times in the preceding verses with that meaning (22:8, 16). Further, the warning in vv. 18-19 is against tampering with any part of the book. But the theme of Christ's coming, reiterated three times in vv. 7-17 and an important part of the vision as a whole, is also included in the things testified to by Jesus.

Jesus' reaffirmation throughout the Apocalypse about His "coming" is reaffirmed emphatically: **Yes, I am coming quickly**, though the focus here is on His final coming. This statement serves to confirm the validity of His testimony. That is, Jesus assures the churches about the truth of the complete vision by guaranteeing that His final advent, which He promised at His first coming, will soon occur and thus bring to completion what He has revealed throughout the book. It is conceivable that also in mind are Jesus' future prior comings which culminate in the last coming (see on 1:7; 2:5; 3:3, 11; 22:7, 12). Within vv. 18-20, v. 20 serves as the basis of the dual warning about adding and taking away from the book. Jesus' last coming is the reason for heeding the warning, because at that time He Himself will enforce the penalties for disobeying John's warning.

John responds to Jesus' reaffirmation with an **Amen**, an utterance of trust. On the basis of his faith in Jesus' declaration, he declares his desire and hope that Jesus **come** (an imperative with the sense of "polite entreaty").

The conclusion of 22:6-20 and of the whole book (22:21)

21 The grace of the Lord Jesus be with all. Amen.

21 The closing benediction **The grace of the Lord Jesus be with all** is a typical conclusion to NT letters (almost universally so in Paul). The point here, as in the other NT letters, is that the writer expresses his desire that God's grace enable the addressees to understand and obey the contents of the letter. We are reminded here again, as in 1:1-4, that the writing is broadly conceived of as a letter, the contents of which are apocalyptic and prophetic in genre (see on 1:1-3). As in the introduction at 1:4, so at the end here, **grace** from Christ is pronounced over all the churches. The main purpose of NT letters is to address problems which have arisen in the various churches. The various writers appeal to the readers' present and future participation in the blessings of Christ as the basis for their appeals to obedience. If the epistolary form of Revelation functions like that of the rest of the NT letters, then its purpose is to address contemporary problems among the seven churches by appealing to this reality of the hearers' present and future share in Christ's blessings.

That such an "already and not-yet" scope functions throughout the book is apparent also because the function of every other NT epistolary introduction is to set out the major themes of the letter, which deal with both present and future concerns. The precise boundaries of the formal introduction in ch. 1 are difficult to pinpoint. It could end at vv. 3, 6, 8, or 20. But, whichever is the case, each section of the introduction contains themes pertaining to beginning and future fulfillment of OT prophecy. Therefore, it is reasonable to assume that the entire book is likely permeated with the same dual "already and not yet" themes.

The call to obedience has been emphasized repeatedly here in each of the five concluding portions in vv. 6-20. Perseverance in obedience will result in God's blessing now and in the consummative form of the end-time rewards mentioned in the conclusions of the letters. These rewards are also summarized in ch. 21 and repeated partially again in 22:12, 14, and 17b (and implied by contrast in 22:19). As noted in the introduction to vv. 6-21, the main pastoral point of the book is that faithful endurance to the end will result in eternal blessing. The primary theological point of the book, however, is that such faithful obedience leading to reward should have the ultimate result of worshiping and glorifying God and Christ (for the latter point see 1:6; 4:9-11; 5:12-14; 21:1–22:5).

Suggestions for Reflection on 22:6-21

On the significance of being a faithful witness. These verses portray John in his role of prophetic witness to the revelation he has received. It is his responsibility to pass it on faithfully. In fact, as v. 18 makes clear, through his testimony he acts as a legal witness for or against those who hear his words. How can we today assume the role of faithful witness to the truth of God's word as we have received it? Do we realize that our words bring others into account, even though we do not speak as the direct bearers of revelation in the way John did? How important is it that our witness be worked out in deeds as well as words? Do we reflect on how serious it is when God's people fail to bear witness? Across the world today, more are suffering for bearing faithful witness to Christ than ever before in history. Why is it that when others are giving their lives for the sake of Christ, many of us are reluctant even to risk mild embarrassment?

On the continuing threat of idolatry to the covenant community. The book ends with reminders that a significant part of its message deals with pseudo-believers in the visible covenant community. If such pseudo-belief is outwardly expressed in idolatrous practices, as the commentary suggests, what do those kind of practices look like in our social context? Do we understand that idolatry is a continuous threat through which the devil still seeks to undermine the church? We become like that to which we are most committed. Accordingly, we are reflecting either the character of the unspiritual world or the character of God. Why is it so serious when we who claim Christ's name do not reflect His character but the world's unspiritual character? The reason is that if Christians are to shine the light of God's glorious presence throughout the earth, as this commentary has discussed, they must be reflectors of His character (i.e., images of Him in the temple of His presence) and not a part of the world's darkness. If the bent of a professing Christian's life is no different than those in the world, then that person must ask "do I really know the Lord?"

On the goal of the book and the goal of our lives. The commentary states that while the main pastoral point of the book is that faithful endurance to the end will result in eternal blessing, the primary theological point of the book is that such faithful obedience leading to reward should have the ultimate result of glorifying God and Christ. How often is this the measuring stick for our personal faith and for the way in which our church life is conducted? How seriously has the self-centered, self-fulfillment focus of our culture affected our ability to see our mission as a people created primarily to glorify their God?

Index of Scripture and Other Ancient Writings

Lamentations

Ezekiel